Päivi Juvonen and Maria Koptjevskaja-Tamm (Eds.)
The Lexical Typology of Semantic Shifts

Cognitive Linguistics Research

Editors
Dirk Geeraerts
John R. Taylor

Honorary editors
René Dirven
Ronald W. Langacker

Volume 58

The Lexical Typology of Semantic Shifts

Edited by
Päivi Juvonen
Maria Koptjevskaja-Tamm

DE GRUYTER
MOUTON

ISBN 978-3-11-061067-3
e-ISBN (PDF) 978-3-11-037767-5
e-ISBN (EPUB) 978-3-11-039306-4
ISSN 1861-4132

Library of Congress Cataloging-in-Publication Data
A CIP catalog record for this book has been applied for at the Library of Congress.

Bibliographic information published by the Deutsche Nationalbibliothek
The Deutsche Nationalbibliothek lists this publication in the Deutsche Nationalbibliografie; detailed bibliographic data are available on the Internet at http://dnb.dnb.de.

© 2018 Walter de Gruyter GmbH, Berlin/Boston
This volume is text- and page-identical with the hardback published in 2016.
Typesetting: fidus Publikations-Service GmbH, Nördlingen
Printing and binding: CPI books GmbH, Leck

♾ Printed on acid-free paper
Printed in Germany

www.degruyter.com

In memory of Peter Koch

Table of contents

Maria Koptjevskaja-Tamm
1. "The lexical typology of semantic shifts": An introduction —— 1

Peter Koch †
2. Meaning change and semantic shifts —— 21

Alexei Shmelev
3. Semantic shifts as sources of enantiosemy —— 67

Ekaterina Rakhilina and Tatiana Reznikova
4. A Frame-based methodology for lexical typology —— 95

Carita Paradis
5. Corpus methods for the investigation of antonyms across languages —— 131

Robert Östling
6. Studying colexification through massively parallell corpora —— 157

Åke Viberg
7. Polysemy in action: The Swedish verb *slå* 'hit, strike, beat' in a crosslinguistic perspective —— 177

Päivi Juvonen
8. Making do with minimal lexica. Light verb constructions with MAKE/DO in pidgin lexica —— 223

Susanne Vejdemo and Sigi Vandewinkel
9. Extended uses of body-related temperature expressions —— 249

Michael Fortescue
10. The semantic domain of emotion in Eskimo and neighbouring languages —— 285

Galina Yavorska and Galyna Zymovets
11. Motivational scenarios and semantic frames for social relations in Slavic, Romance and Germanic languages – friends, enemies, and others —— 335

Antoinette Schapper, Lila San Roque and Rachel Hendery
12. *Tree*, *firewood* and *fire* in the languages of Sahul —— 355

Daniela Marzo and Birgit Umbreit
13. **Investigating lexical motivation in French and Italian** —— 423

Wiltrud Mihatsch
14. **Types of motivation in folk plant taxonomies** —— 457

Maksim Russo
15. **Differences and interactions between scientific and folk biological taxonomy** —— 493

Markus Ising
16. **Holistic motivation: Systematization and application to the COOKING domain** —— 533

Matthias Urban
17. **Motivation by formally analyzable terms in a typological perspective: An assessment of the variation and steps towards explanation** —— 555

Subject index —— 577
Language index —— 581
Author index —— 591

Maria Koptjevskaja-Tamm
1. "The lexical typology of semantic shifts": An introduction

1.1 Introducing the key notions: Semantic shift, motivation, semantic association, semantic parallel

Pervasiveness of polysemy and the fact that lexical meanings are subject to semantic change belong to linguists' basic knowledge about the lexicon as a complex dynamic system. There is also a standard assumption that the two phenomena are interrelated in that a semantic change from one meaning to another usually involves a transitional stage where the two co-exist within one and the same polysemous lexeme (e.g. Sweetser 1990: 9; Blank 1999: 131; Evans and Wilkins 2000: 549; Traugott and Dasher 2002: 11). This, in turn, reflects speakers' perception of the two concepts as closely related and, often, that one of them comes from, or is motivated by the other. The cover notion of *semantic shift*, as it is used here, refers to a pair of meanings A and B which are linked by some genetic relation, either diachronically (cf. Latin *caput* 'head' and French *chef* 'chief') or synchronically, e.g. as two meanings of a polysemous lexeme (cf. English *head*, as in *I've hit my head*, i.e. 'top part of body', and as in *I've met my department head*, i.e. 'leader of others') (cf. Zalizniak et al. 2012 and Newman 2015 for discussions of the notion of semantic shift). It is worth emphasizing that the term *semantic shift* (often used interchangeably with *(semantic) extension*) is understood panchronically, in spite of the possible dynamic connotations of its name. Another useful term in this connection is *heterosemy*, which refers to "cases (within a single language) where two or more meanings or functions that are historically related, in the sense of deriving from the same ultimate source, are borne by reflexes of the common source element that belong in different morphosyntactic categories" (Lichtenberk 1991: 476). To continue with the HEAD example, the pair *head* (like *my head*) and *ahead* (*ahead of me*) is an example of heterosemy.

Seen from another perspective, the same phenomena can be considered as examples of *motivation*: if we take a given word of a given language as a reference point and its meaning M_1 as derived from another meaning, M_2, the meaning M_1 may be described as being motivated by the meaning M_2, be it diachronic semantic evolution or synchronic polysemy. Motivation is understood here as a certain parallelism between a cognitively relevant conceptual relation between two lexical units, on the one hand, and a perceptible formal relation between the two, on the other hand (Koch 2001: 1156), i.e., a particular *meaning-form correlation*. In Koch's terminology, the conceptual relation between 'top part of body' and 'leader of others' in our examples above is metaphorical similarity, which, on the formal side, is paralleled by formal identity between the two exponents in each of the two cases (apart from the more or less trivial diachronic differences between Latin and French). Motivation may of course involve other cognitive and formal relations between lexical units. To continue with Koch's (2001) examples and terminology, the cognitive relation of contiguity between a tree and its fruit is expressed by the formal relation of compounding in the case of English *pear-tree* vs. *pear*, by formal identity (polysemy) in Russian (*gruša* for both), by gender alternation in Italian (*pero* M vs. *pera* F), by suffixation in French (*poirier* vs. *poire*), and by a lexicalized phrase in Sardinian (*arbore di pira* vs. *pira*, alongside *pira* for both). As the Sardinian example shows, motivation by polysemy and motivation by word-formation devices (including phrase formation) are not strictly opposed to each other in that one and the same language may combine both. The common denominator in all these cases is the form-meaning link between the words for PEAR TREE and PEAR FRUIT, which is often referred to by the cover term *semantic association* (e.g., Matisoff 2004; Vanhove [ed.] 2008; Urban 2012).

Different patterns of polysemy/heterosemy, semantic shifts and lexical motivation in general result from a complex interplay of universal cognitive processes and cultural/historical/linguistic variables. Some patterns are cross-linguistically frequent, i.e., have cross-linguistically frequent *semantic parallels*, e.g., the extension of 'see' and 'hear' verbs to 'smell' and 'taste' (Viberg 2001); others show a genetically and/or areally restricted distribution, e.g., the conflation of 'eat' and 'drink' in many Papuan and Australian Aboriginal languages (Aikhenvald 2009), but also in a few other languages of the world (Vanhove [ed.] 2008). Still others are very local or even language-specific, as 'beef' expressed as 'big meat' in some of the languages of Hindukush – the mountainous region comprising northern Pakistan, north-eastern Afghanistan and the northern-most part of Indian Kashmir, e.g. *yaṭa ɣwaxa* in Pashto, *uyúm čhap* in Burushaski, *ghav masii* in Indus Kohistani (Koptjevskaja-Tamm and Liljegren forthc.). It also seems that languages in general can differ both in the extent to which their lexicon is motivated as well as in the particular ways in which it is motivated (Kibrik 2012 ; Urban 2012).

1.2 The main research traditions behind the volume: Cognitive semantics, lexical typology, historical and areal linguistics

This volume focuses on semantic shifts and motivation patterns in the lexicon seen cross-linguistically. It builds therefore on several research traditions – cognitive linguistics, lexical typology, historical and areal linguistics – and contributes to all of these.

Questions of polysemy and semantic shifts, and in particular universal metaphoric and metonymic processes, are, of course, a central concern of cognitive semantics, and the relevant knowledge accumulated within this theoretical framework is impressive (the literature too extensive to be listed here). The recent years have also seen a number of excellent cognitively oriented cross-linguistic publications concerned with semantic shifts (e.g., Ibarretxe-Antuñano 2006, 2008; Sharifian et al. [eds.] 2008; Maalej and Yu [eds.] 2011; Idström and Piirainen [eds.] 2012). However, cognitive semantics has on the whole operated with a relatively limited number of languages and has relatively modestly empirically-founded insights with regard to large-scale cross-linguistic semantic comparison (cf. e.g. van der Auwera and Nuyts 2007). A part of the reason for this has to do with methodological complications inherent in systematic cross-linguistic research on polysemy, metaphor and metonymy. To start with, the notion of polysemy and what counts as different senses is, of course, an extremely complicated matter. This is especially true for cognitive semantics, for which linguistic meanings always imply a certain construal of a particular situation (cf. Langacker 2015) and are laden with particular associations, intimately related to the speakers' 'world' knowledge. In line with the general usage-based view within cognitive linguistics, the meanings of linguistic expressions are consequences of their uses, and word meanings are always associated with certain constructions. Conversely, conventional meanings associated with linguistic expressions only partially sanction the senses evoked in particular contexts. As a consequence, there are different opinions on what counts as polysemy both within cognitive linguistics and also among different semantic theories, practices (such as dictionary entries) and language users (see Riemer 2005 and Gries 2015). Turning to metaphor and metonymy, there are on-going intensive debates within cognitive semantics about the level of generalisations in proposed metaphorical and metonymical shifts (e.g., A THEORY IS A BUILDING vs. ORGANIZATION IS PHYSICAL STRUCTURE) and debates about semantic shifts seen as possible transformations on the underlying image schema. In addition, Conceptual Metaphor Theory emphasizes conceptual association that does not boil down to individual metaphorical uses or to linguistic convention. But to quote Gibbs (2015: 183),

> cognitive linguists, and others, should articulate criteria for identifying metaphoric patterns in language and inferring specific conceptual metaphors from discourse. These procedures should be specified with sufficient detail so that other researchers can possibly replicate the analysis and emerge with similar conclusions.

Translated into the methodology of systematic cross-linguistic research, this means that we can only test the extent to which some concrete manifestations of suggested metaphors hold (e.g., whether verbs for seeing are systematically extended to perception, or whether words for 'warm' are systematically extended to emotions), rather than whether the conceptual metaphors KNOWING IS SEEING or AFFECTION IS WARMTH as a whole are universal.

Questions of universality vs. specificity of linguistic phenomena (specificity to particular languages, to areally and/or to genetically related languages) are central to modern typological research. Systematic study of cross-linguistic variation in words and vocabularies, i.e. typological research on lexicon (lexical typology) has until recently been relatively modest, as opposed to grammatical and phonetic typology with their impressive progress in the recent decades (Koch 2001; Koptjevskaja-Tamm 2008; Koptjevskaja-Tamm, Vanhove, and Koch 2007). Fortunately, interest in lexical-typological issues has been on the rise during recent years, as witnessed by an impressive flow of new publications. A large portion of this research can be characterized as "onomasiological lexical typology", or domain-categorization lexical typology, dealing with how languages cut up a particular cognitive domain among their (lexical) expressions – e.g., BODY (Majid, Enfield, and van Staden [eds.] 2006), CUT and BREAK (Majid and Bowerman 2007), LOCATION (Ameka and Levinson [eds.] 2007), PUT and TAKE (Narasimhan and Kopecka [eds.] 2012) etc. The main themes of the present volume, i.e. what different meanings can be expressed by one and the same lexeme or by lexemes that are related to them synchronically and/or diachronically, belong within "semasiological lexical typology". Some of the important recent publications here (often combining the onomasiological and semasiological perspectives) concern GIVING; SITTING, STANDING and LYING; and EATING and DRINKING (Newman [ed.] 1997, 2002, 2009), PAIN (Reznikova, Rakhilina, and Bonch-Osmolovskaya 2012), BODY (Mihatsch and Dvořák 2004; Koch 2008; Steinberg 2015), PERCEPTION (Vanhove 2008), AQUA-MOTION (Maisak and Rakhilina [eds.] 2007), and TEMPERATURE (Koptjevskaja-Tamm [ed.] 2015). The probably most significant large-scale investigations of cross-linguistically recurrent semantic associations are reported in Urban (2012, also 2009 and 2010; see also Blust 2011 for a reply to Urban 2010).

It is important to emphasize that systematic cross-linguistic comparison is dependent on comparable data coming from (many) different languages. Cross-linguistic identification of studied phenomena presupposes a procedure which ensures that we compare like with like. However, another key concern for cross-linguistic and typological research is to find a reasonable level of abstraction, at which the language-specific details can be reduced to manageable patterns. The two concerns interact in various ways, and what counts as "like and like" is often dependent on the research object and goal. Crucially, cross-linguistic identification of phenomena should involve theory-neutral or framework-neutral definitions and concern "observable phenomena that pattern interestingly in the world's languages" (Nichols 2007: 231). Translated into the phenomena studied in this volume, this means, among other things, a fairly pragmatic stance on what counts as meaning/sense and/or semantic shift. A useful notion in this connection is François' (2008: 180) *colexification*, i.e., association of two or more functionally distinct senses with the same lexical form, whereby "functionally distinct senses" are identified as senses that are expressed by different lexemes in other languages. The notion of colexification allows the researcher to ignore issues of polysemy, vagueness of meanings etc.

Diachronic change and synchronic polysemy/heterosemy/motivational patterns of linguistic units have long been thought by linguists to represent two sides of one and the same phenomenon. Many important studies discuss particular universal vs. genetically and/or areally restricted motivational patterns and stress their relevance for reconstructing semantic shifts – e.g., Matisoff (1978) for Tibeto-Burman languages, Yavorska (1992) for Slavic and Germanic, Evans (1992) and Evans and Wilkins (2000) for Australian languages, Enfield (2003) for SE Asian languages, Epps (2013) for the Amazonian languages, François (2010) for the Oceanic languages, Vanhove (ed.) (2008) for many different languages, and Wilkins (1996) and Koch (2008) in general (cf. also Heine and Kuteva 2002 on semantic shifts involved in grammaticalization). For at least two linguistic areas, lexico-semantic parallels have been systematically used as areality indicators, i.e., pointing to the network of prolonged linguistic contacts – the Meso-American (Smith-Stark 1994; Brown 2011) and the Ethio-Eritrean (Hayward 1991, 2000) languages. The works by Urban (2012, also 2009 and 2010) mentioned above are extremely important in this connection. The following two enterprises directed at unveiling cross-linguistically recurrent patterns of semantic associations deserve special mention (see Koptjevskaja-Tamm and Liljegren forthc. for an overview and discussion of lexico-semantic parallels in areal studies):

1) *The Catalogue of Semantic Shifts in the Languages of the World* (http://semshifts.iling-ran.ru/) at the Institute of Linguistics, Russian Academy of Sciences in Moscow is a searchable computer database (not yet fully implemented online) that currently contains more than 3000 semantic shifts found in 319 languages (Zalizniak 2008, Zalizniak et al. 2012).
2) *CLICS: Database of Cross-Linguistic Colexifications* (List et al. 2014, http://clics.lingpy.org/main.php) is an online database of colexifications in 221 languages. It is based on four different freely available online resources and contains 16 239 different links among the 1280 concepts it operates with (all in all 45 667 cases of colexification).

1.3 Introducing the volume

In spite of all the laudable publications and resources listed above, our broader knowledge of semantic shifts and motivational patterns cross-linguistically is very restricted. And even the general state-of-the-art with respect to the conceptual, taxonomic and terminological foundations for identifying, describing and discussing recurrent semantic shifts is at present far from satisfactory.

The present volume is intended as a contribution to this fascinating research field. Its key feature is its *lexico-typological orientation*, i.e., a heavy emphasis on systematic cross-linguistic comparison (Koptjevskaja-Tamm 2008, Koptjevskaja-Tamm, Vanhove, and Koch 2007). It presents therefore current theoretical and methodological trends in the study of semantic shifts and motivational patterns based on an abundance of empirical findings across genetically, areally and typologically diverse languages. The chapters in this volume suggest and test different general methodologies for identifying and describing semantic shifts and form/meaning correlations within the lexicon and provide a detailed semantic analysis of semantic shifts relevant for several cognitive domains across a number of languages. Some of the papers focus on the relationship between synchronic and diachronic lexical semantics, while all discuss the complex interaction among the various factors relevant for cross-linguistic similarities or differences in semantic shifts and form/meaning correlations, such as universal cognitive parameters, genetic and/or contact relations, and culturally specific stereotypes and discourse practices. The volume brings together linguists from Sweden, Denmark, Germany, the Netherlands, Russia, Ukraine and Australia and combines expertise in cognitive semantics and in the Moscow school of semantics, in typology, and in computational, historical and areal linguistics.

In what follows I will introduce and briefly describe the general composition of the volume and its individual chapters.

PART 1 of the volume is concerned with foundational, i.e. theoretical and methodological issues in lexical typology, such as classification and identification of semantic shifts, representation of semantic information and generalizations, cognitive processes behind semantic shifts, data collection, etc. It opens with an encyclopaedic chapter by the late Peter Koch focusing on semantic shift from a diachronic perspective. The chapter starts with the roots of research on meaning change, but is mainly devoted to recent developments in this research, concerning categories, mechanisms and pathways of meaning change. The following chapter by Shmelev is closely related to it in its diachronic orientation. It focuses on the types of semantic shifts that may lead to enantiosemy, which is here understood in a broad and diachronically oriented sense as the opposition of two linguistic items that go back to, or originate from the same item. This sense is contrasted with the narrow synchronic sense of "enantiosemy" (or "auto-antonymy"), covering a particular – and very rare – case of polysemy, when one and the same lexeme has two opposite meanings, e.g. the Russian word *proslušat' (lekciju)* that may mean either 'to hear' or 'to fail to hear, to miss'. Shmelev understands likewise "linguistic items" broadly in that they may include words (not necessarily belonging to the same word class), phrases, morphemes and morphemic complexes, as Russian *isxod* 'end' and *isxod-n-aja* (*isxod*-ADJ-F.SG.NOM) *točka* 'starting point'. When such linguistic items belong to the same language, they manifest polysemy or heterosemy. They may also belong to different languages, as for instance, *čerstvyj* 'stale' in Russian and *čerstvý* 'fresh' in Czech. Shmelev finally choses a broad understanding of "opposition", that includes not only different kinds of antonymy (like contradictory, such as *dead – alive*, or contrary, such as *big – small*), but also various kinds of converse pairs, which are related to opposite perspectives on or opposite participants in the same situation, such as *to sell – to buy*, or *host – guest*. He therefore casts a wide net in studying phenomena that are often treated separately (cf. Koch this volume for the discussion of auto-antonymous change as opposed to metonymical auto-converse change), primarily across Slavic. He claims that enantiosemy in the broader sense is a regular phenomenon, rooted in general principles of cognition and communication, with several recurrent groups that may be reduced to well-known semantic shifts, such as conventionalization of pragmatic effects (irony, evaluation, conversational implicatures), metonymy (including polarization of a given situation) and metaphors.

Rakhilina and Reznikova advocate an ambitious and general approach to lexical-typological studies, the "frame method", that has been developed by the Moscow Lexico-Typological Group (led by Rakhilina) and tested on several lexical domains (e.g., AQUA-MOTION, ROTATION, PAIN, VARIOUS QUALITIES, SOUNDS) across a large number of genetically and areally different languages. They contrast the "frame method" with two other prominent approaches to lexical typology – the "Nijmegen" method of semantic typology, developed and applied in numerous publications led from the Max-Planck Institute of Psycholinguistics in Nijmegen (e.g., Ameka and Levinson [eds.] 2007; Majid, Enfield, and van Staden [eds.] 2006; Majid and Bowerman [eds.] 2007; Narasimhan and Kopecka [eds.] 2012), and the Natural Semantic Metalanguage school, initially launched by Anna Wierzbicka (e.g., Wierzbicka 1987, 1999, 2005, 2007; Goddard 2012). The main principle behind the "frame method", taken from the Moscow semantic school with Apresjan as the portal figure (e.g., Apresjan 2000), but also prominent in other approaches (e.g., in the corpus techniques going back to Firth 1957), is that lexical meanings can be studied and reconstructed by observing the word's "surroundings", primarily collocation. Reznikova and Rakhilina propose that semantic cross-linguistic comparisons, both onomasiological and semasiological, should depart from a set of conceptual frames that underlie the domains under examination and that can be revealed through the analysis of word combinability in natural texts (corpora, spontaneous speech, etc.). The term "frame", as used here, refers to the full set of a predicate's arguments present in a prototypical situation and is therefore somewhat different from "frame" in its classical Fillmorian understanding (see Fillmore and Baker 2010, framenet.icsi.berkeley.edu). For example, 'oldness' consists of four main frames that can roughly be described as 'worn' (*old shoes, rags...*), 'aged' (*old people, horses, trees...*), 'former' (*old address, government, procedure...*) and 'ancient' (*old myths, music, grammatical construction...*) (Taylor 1992; Rakhilina 1999). The results obtained by this approach can be visualized as semantic maps, in which nodes are associated with frames. A lexeme of a given language may either correspond to an individual frame or to a cluster of conceptually similar frames, which seem to be formed in a predictable way across languages, even though a particular language may choose its own pattern. Such a frame-based approach allows us to investigate and represent both the cross-linguistic patterns in how languages carve up semantic domains, as well as to compare, in a systematic way, the cross-linguistic variation in the semantic shifts relevant for them. It is also well suited for typological research on semantic change. Particularly interesting in the present context are the various interrelations between the onomasiological and semasiological sides of the frame-based lexico-typological studies (e.g., patterns of polysemy across languages involve "frames" rather than vaguely defined meanings; metaphors may diagnose frame clusters, since cognitively similar frames produce similar semantic shifts, etc).

The combination of opposite meanings and semantic shifts, found in Shmelev's chapter, is also prominent in the chapter by Paradis, who discusses the issues of semantic shifts (this time in a synchronic perspective) and polysemy in relation to antonymy. However, in spirit, Paradis' chapter is closer to the one by Rakhilina and Reznikova in that its methodology is both onomasiologically and semasiologically oriented and heavily relies on co-occurrence patterns of words in drawing conclusions about their meanings. Paradis' starting assumption is that all languages have a set of particularly appropriate word pairs that express opposite properties along salient meaning dimensions such as SIZE (*large – small*), LUMINOSITY (*light – dark*), STRENGTH (*strong – weak*), or MERIT (*good – bad*). It is also known that one and the same word may have different antonym partners when used in different "frames", to use Rakhilina and Reznikova's teminology – i.e., in different senses, or along different dimensions, e.g. *light – dark* (LUMINOSITY) vs. *light – heavy* (WEIGHT) or when applied to different entities, e.g. *old – young* (about people) vs. *old – new* (about artefacts). Particularly interesting in the present context is the issue of how oppositions and antonymy (do not) "translate" in metaphorical shifts, as for instance, *a sharp/dull knife*, but *a sharp/? contrast*. The existence of such contextually motivated lexical variation in the choice of antonyms both across and within domains may therefore be seen as a symptom of polysemy. However, as Paradis mentions, there have only been a few attempts to describe variation and polysemy across opposable meanings along different dimensions cross-linguistically. She therefore proposes corpus based and corpus driven techniques for the identification of antonyms cross-linguistically and for the subsequent description of their usage patterns in different semantic frames and in different linguistic constructions. The techniques capture the co-occurrence patterns of antonymic partners within sentences, as well as antonym use in continuous constructions, or contrastive frames, such as *young and old alike*, *neither long nor short*. This methodology allows us to draw semantic maps of lexicalization patterns using onomasiological dimensions (e.g., SIZE, HEIGHT, WEIGHT, LUMINOSITY) as the point of departure from which contextually motivated lexical semantic variation emerges both across and within domains. These techniques have so far been tested for a limited set of languages (Swedish, Dutch, English, Japanese, Russian), but may hopefully be applied to a larger number of languages for which there are reasonably big machine readable corpora.

The use of machine readable corpora for the purposes of lexical typology is also advocated by Östling, but this time it is massive parallel corpora that are at stake, more precisely 1,142 translations of the New Testament in 1001 languages. The use of massive parallel corpora as a source of comparable data in different languages is on the rise in linguistic typology, but their applications for the purposes of lexical comparison have so far been limited – most prominently to various aspects of motion verbs, e.g. how these carve up the motion domain among themselves (cf. Wälchli and Zúñiga 2006, Wälchli and Cysouw 2012). Östling suggests that massive parallel texts can also be used for automatically extracting preliminary data on colexification patterns, i.e. on whether and how languages associate two or more functionally distinct senses with the same lexical form (see François 2008: 180). He tests three different colexification patterns that occur in a sufficient number of languages and for which there is information in other resources – 'stone/mountain', 'hand/arm' and 'tree/fire'. The conclusion is that although the automatically extracted word lists contain errors, their quality can be sufficiently good to find real areal patterns, such as the 'tree'/'fire' colexification that is widespread among the Australian and Papuan languages (see Schapper, San Roque, and Hendery, this volume). In other words, this is a quick and dirty method which provides a preliminary answer to the question "where, if at all, does tree-fire colexification occur" in a few seconds, which may open up interesting and fruitful directions for more careful and time-consuming lexico-typological work.

PART 2 of the volume encompasses cross-linguistic studies of several central semantic domains/concepts as sources and targets of semantic shifts. These include semantic shifts from HITTING, TEMPERATURE and BODY, MAKE/DO, semantic shifts leading to (motivational patterns for) SOCIAL RELATIONS and EMOTIONS, as well as colexification patterns among the concepts 'tree', 'fire' and 'firewood' (where the issue of sources vs. targets of semantic shifts is for the most part irrelevant). An important leitmotif running through all the chapters is the nature of the discovered and described cross-linguistically recurrent semantic shifts and motivational scenarios. To what extent are they universal (and may be explained by universal cognitive parameters and processes) or restricted? In the latter case, are they genetically limited, have arisen due to language contacts and/or are rooted in culturally specific stereotypes and discourse practices and may therefore serve as windows onto folk models of various phenomena? This overarching issue is approached in many different ways and from many different angles.

Viberg focuses on the polysemy of a single verb in a single language, namely the Swedish verb slå 'hit, strike, beat', but his chapter is truly cross-linguistic in at least two different senses. First of all, the analysis is based on a parallel corpus (not a massive one as in Östling's case, but also much richer and more diverse in terms of content), which makes it possible to see how the meanings of the Swedish verb are reflected in translations. Secondly, the results of the semantic analysis is compared to the earlier studies of hitting verbs in other languages (e.g., Riemer 2005 on Warlpiri, Schultze-Berndt 2000 on Jaminjung, Hook, Pardeshi, and Liang 2012 on Asian languages, Family 2011 on Persian and Gao 2001 on Mandarin), i.e. put in typological perspective. Viberg's major hypothesis is that a large proportion of the many meanings of this verb are best understood as semantic shifts from a prototype representing *slå* as a hand action, i.e. a goal-directed physical action sequence. The meaning of the verb interacts with the meaning of nouns serving as arguments to produce new meanings in context, many of which become lexicalized and serve as the source for further meaning shifts. Viberg shows how meanings are related in networks and adds examples of diachronic processes that may break some of these interconnections.

Juvonen's chapter is dedicated to the fascinating issue of how pidgin languages (or rather their speakers) manage to communicate with the extremely limited lexica typical of such languages, often ranging somewhere between 150 and 500 common lexical items. A simple answer is – by the "recycling of meaning", i.e., by the multiple uses of the few lexical items there are in various constructions and contexts, which therefore undergo diverse semantic shifts. To understand how this occurs Juvonen focuses on the uses of the verbs MAKE/DO across 32 documented pidgin varieties from different parts of the world. In doing this, she addresses the issues of polysemy and heterosemy in pidgin lexica, the question of syntactic frames (in terms of light verb constructions) and the question of semantic shifts in terms of the kind of polysemantic patterns found across different pidgin languages. Most significantly, although the kinds of semantic shifts that affect MAKE/DO expressions in pidgins are also attested elsewhere, the proportions among them (with metonymical extensions constituting the overwhelming majority) seem to make some of the pidgins stand out against many of the other languages.

Vejdemo and Vandewinkel's chapter is devoted to the extended uses of temperature terms in combination with particular body-related expressions (cf. "warm heart" or "cold eyes") across seven languages – English, Ibibio, Japanese, Kannada, Mandarin Chinese, Ojibwe, and Swedish. It is, thus, at the intersection of three areas – TEMPERATURE, BODY and EMOTIONS – that are fundamental to the human experience of the world and have been the focus of attention for many studies, including a number of cognitively oriented studies dealing with metaphor and metonymy: TEMPERATURE and BODY are known to serve as the source domains for many metaphors in different languages, including EMOTIONS (Geeraerts and Grondelaers 1995; Kövecses 1995; Lakoff and Johnson 1999; Koptjevskaja-Tamm [ed.] 2015; Enfield and Wierzbicka [eds.] 2002; Sharifian et al. [eds.] 2008; Maalej and Yu [eds.] 2011). The chapter's primary contribution is methodological, i.e., to empirically test conceptual metaphors suggested in the literature by systematically checking acceptability and/or meaning of various combinations of (basic) temperature terms with a body-related name. It turns out that all the studied languages have such expressions and that certain body-related names tend to re-occur in them (mostly 'heart', 'head', 'voice', 'smile' and 'eyes'). The authors found support for two conceptual metaphors: CONTROL IS COLD/LACK OF CONTROL IS HOT and CARING IS WARM/UNCARING IS COLD, and for the transfer of temperature scales to scalar target domains, mostly emotions.

The domain of EMOTIONS as the target domain for semantic shifts is likewise studied in Fortescue's chapter, this time across Eskimo and neighbouring languages (primarily Chukotko-Kamchatkan in the Far East of Eurasia). What makes Fortescue's study a particularly valuable addition to linguistic studies of emotions is the fact that Eskimo languages may be rather unique in delimiting the extent of this domain by displaying a rich array of emotional "roots" (bound stems) that constitute a distinct morphological category. Fortescue approaches the question of polysemy and semantic shift over time by reconstructing a set of proto-Eskimo roots and concludes that the diachronic and comparative data promise to contribute to the debate as to what constitutes a 'basic' emotion in linguistic terms, and how these relate to the five or six 'primary' emotions described by psychologists. He further suggests that there has been a general metonymic shift from predominantly physical/visceral correlates of emotion to more general and abstract, and further to culturally determined meanings by means of contextual modulation.

Etymological reconstruction, coupled with extensive synchronic cross-linguistic comparison, is also applied by Yavorska and Zymovets, this time to the domain of SOCIAL RELATIONS (such as FRIEND, ENEMY, POWER, GOVERNMENT etc.) in Slavic, Romance and Germanic. The paper focuses on the synchronic patterns of polysemy manifested by such words in genetically related languages and interprets them in diachronic terms, i.e., in terms of 'source – target' models of semantic shifts. Some of them turn out to be restricted to one language or to a limited group of languages (e.g., 'enemy' => 'devil' for *vrag* in East Slavic), where others appear to be good candidates for cross-linguistically recurrent motivational patterns (e.g., 'enemy' = 'NEG-friend').

The distinction between language-specific/genetic/areal vs. universally recurrent patterns is brought to the fore in Schapper, San Roque, and Hendery's chapter. The main issue here is to what extent colexification (polysemy) patterns can serve as indicators of areality, in this case the genetic and areal connections among the languages of Australia, New Guinea and surrounding islands, i.e., across the area known as "Sahul". To this end the authors provide a first in-depth survey of lexical expressions for 'tree', 'firewood' and 'fire' in 300 Australian and Papuan languages, inspired by sporadic suggestions in earlier literature that colexification of these three concepts may be widespread across the Sahul languages. Schapper, San Roque, and Hendery plot the frequency and geographical distribution of colexification patterns for the three concepts in individual languages and include analysis of the relationships between simple and complex terms for these concepts, which further clarifies geographic and genetic patterns of colexification and differentiation. It is found that the most common pattern in the region is to colexify 'firewood' and 'fire', but not 'tree', contra earlier claims. Nevertheless, patterns present in Sahul are rare worldwide, indicating that Sahul is a large diffusion area worthy of further investigation in linguistic studies by Papuanists and Australianists collectively – the conclusion that is also drawn in Östling's chapter (see above). In general, the chapter supports the idea that the study of colexification patterns provides a resource for studies of language contact and typology in general that has so far scarcely been exploited.

The final part of the volume, PART 3, considers cross-linguistic variation in motivational strategies, as pertaining to particular cognitive domains, to the organization of whole lexica or to that of their subparts (nominal or verbal).

The chapters by Marzo and Umbreit and by Mihatsch deal with variation in motivation (which includes both polysemy and word-formation devices) within the Romance languages, while at the same time drawing much more general methodological and theoretical conclusions. Marzo and Umbreit, in contrast to the other authors, approach a particular aspect of motivation, *motivatability*, via judgements of ordinary native speakers rather than via the linguists' introspection. These, in turn, are assumed to depend on several factors, such as frequency of the stimulus, the salience of its meaning and the conceptual relation between the stimulus and other lexical units. The chapter reports on a comparative study of French and Italian based on a new two-step questionnaire method for eliciting such opinions, the results of which speak in favour of the initial assumptions.

Both Mihatsch and Russo focus on motivational patterns in the biological taxonomies and their theoretical implications. Mihatsch's primary concern is the difference between the motivation patterns (i.e., polysemy and word formation) above and below the basic level, whereas Russo's main interest lies in various recurrent cases of semantic shifts whereby animals belonging to different taxa in the scientific biological classification receive identical or similar names. This may in turn be interpreted as pointing to a discrepancy between the scientific and the folk categorization of the corresponding living beings. Mihatsch provides a wealth of illustrations from Romance taxonomies of plant names (often complemented by further cross-linguistic parallels). Russo's chapter has an even wider cross-linguistic foundation. It is based on the author's work within the "Catalogue of semantic shifts in the languages of the world" at the Institute of Linguistics, Russian Academy of Sciences, Moscow (cf. Zalizniak 2008, Zalizniak et al. 2012), and contains examples from a large number of genetically, areally and structurally diverse languages that are documented in this catalogue.

The last two chapters are likewise systematically cross-linguistic. Ising introduces the term *holistic motivation* in order to account for expressions such as English *lady's slipper*, where a target concept (a specific PLANT) is associated with a source concept (the plant's flower looks like a SHOE FOR WOMEN) and is therefore expressed with the term literally denoting this source concept. The chapter shows how this widespread phenomenon can be integrated into the traditional theory of linguistic motivation and reports on a typological case study that systematically searched 75 languages for holistic motivation in the target domain of COOKING.

In the final chapter of the volume, Urban focuses on motivation by word-formation devices to the exclusion of motivation by polysemy and addresses a question raised by one of the founding figures of lexical typology, Stephen Ullmann (1962, 1966): to what degree do languages differ in the extent to which they resort to morphologically analyzable lexical items? In tackling this question, Urban follows the classical typological methodology in a way and at a scale that is basically unprecedented in lexical typology, by investigating translational equivalents for a standard set of 160 mostly nominal meanings in a representative global sample of 73 languages. It turns out that languages manifest profound variability in this area and that the relative prevalence of analyzable items in a language shows correlations with the size of its consonant inventory, the complexity of its syllable structure and the length of its nominal roots. This suggests that, typologically, languages with a simple phonological structure are those in which analyzability in the lexicon is most profound. Urban concludes by discussing possible functional explanations for this observation: the shorter the nominal roots, the smaller the number of distinct roots that can be generated and the higher the danger of inflation of homophonous roots. Creation and conventionalization of morphologically complex, motivated lexical items can therefore be seen as the long-term outcome of speakers' strategies to counter such lexical ambiguities.

1.4 Final words

The presentation in the preceding sections has hopefully demonstrated that the volume is an important contribution to research on semantic shifts and motivational patterns across languages in several ways:

descriptively – by bringing in a wealth of data on (often previously unknown) semantic shifts in several (often previously undescribed) cognitive domains and on motivational patterns across a considerable number of languages

methodologically – by suggesting and testing different general methodologies for carrying out lexical typological studies, and for identifying and analyzing semantic shifts and motivational patterns, both synchronically and diachronically *theoretically* – by providing new insights into the interaction among universal cognitive parameters, genetic, socio-cultural and/or contact relations in the shaping of lexicon and on the relationship between synchronic and diachronic lexical semantics and thus contributing to the current discussions within cognitive linguistics and cognitive theory of language in general, typology and historical linguistics.

The volume has a long prehistory. The idea was born in the joint international research project "Core vocabulary in a typological perspective: semantic shifts and form–meaning correlations" running in the period of 2006–2009 and funded by INTAS (International Association for the promotion of co-operation with scientists from the New Independent States of the former Soviet Union). The project, with Maria Koptjevskaja-Tamm as Principal Investigator and Päivi Juvonen as Project Manager, involved about 20 scientists from Stockholm (Sweden), Kyiv (Ukraine), Moscow (Russia), Paris (France) and Tübingen (Germany), many of whom are represented in the volume. These were later joined by other colleagues with similar research interests.

The first chapter in the volume has a special history and status. It was written by Peter Koch, one of the leading figures in the INTAS-project, an outstanding researcher, a highly estimated teacher and a generous and warm person. The chapter was originally intended for another volume, "The Routledge Handbook of Semantics", edited by Nick Riemer (2015), but could not be completed because of Peter's tragic and unexpected death in July 2014. The existing – and very extensive – draft was in German, and it was not feasible to accommodate it to the handbook in any reasonable way. We are very happy to have this excellent chapter in the volume, skillfully translated by Dr. Tessa Say and edited by Maria Koptjevskaja-Tamm, Daniela Marzo and Nick Riemer. This has been possible thanks to Peter Koch's family, who granted us the permission to publish the chapter, and thanks to the welcoming and enthusiastic support from Birgit Sievert and Dirk Geeraerts at de Gruyter and to the financial support from the Universities of Bochum, Stockholm and Tübingen. Most of the contributions in the volume are written by Peter Koch's students, friends and close colleagues, and it is an honour to dedicate this book to him.

1.5 References

Aikhenvald, Aleksandra. 2009. 'Eating', 'drinking' and 'smoking': A generic verb and its semantics in Manambu. In John Newman (ed.), *The linguistics of eating and drinking*, 91–108. Amsterdam & Philadelphia: John Benjamins.

Ameka, Felix K. and Stephen C. Levinson (eds.). 2007. The typology and semantics of locative predication: Posturals, positionals and other beasts. *Linguistics,* 45(5).
Apresjan, Jurij. 2000. *Systematic lexicography.* Translated from Russian by K. Windle. Oxford: Oxford University Press.
Auwera, Johan van der and Jan Nuyts. 2007. Cognitive linguistics and linguistic typology. In Dirk Geeraerts and Hubert Cuyckens (eds.), *The Oxford handbook of cognitive linguistics*, 1075–1091. Oxford: Oxford University Press.
Blank, Andreas. 1999. Kognitive Linguistik und Bedeutungswandel. In Inge Pohl (ed.), *Interdisziplinarität und Methodenpluralismus in der Semantikforschung* (Sprache – System und Tätigkeit, 29), 125–147. Frankfurt: Peter Lang.
Blust, Robert. 2011. 'Eye of the Day': A response to Urban (2010). *Oceanic Linguistics* 50 (2). 524–535.
Brown, Cecil. 2011. The role of Nahuatl in the formation of Mesoamerica as a linguistic area. *Language. Dynamics and Change* 1. 171–204.
Enfield, Nicholas J. 2003. *Linguistic epidemiology. Semantics and grammar of language contact in mainland Southeast Asia.* London & New York: RoutledgeCurzon.
Enfield, Nicholas J. and Anna Wierzbicka (eds.). 2002. The body in description of emotion. *Pragmatics and cognition*, special issue 10 (1–2).
Epps, Patience. 2013. Inheritance, calquing or independent innovation? Reconstructing morphological complexity in Amazonian numerals. *Journal of Language Contact*, 6. 329–357.
Evans, Nicholas. 1992. Multiple semiotic systems, hyperpolysemy and the reconstruction of semantic change in Australian languages. In Günter Kellerman and Michael Morrisey (eds.), *Diachrony within synchrony: Language, history and cognition*, 457–508. Berlin: Peter Lang.
Evans, Nicholas and David P. Wilkins, 2000. In the mind's ear: The semantic extensions of perception verbs in Australian languages. *Language* 76. 546–592.
Family, Neiloufar. 2011. Verbal islands in Persian. *Folia Linguistica* 45 (1). 1–30.
Fillmore, Charles J. and Colin Baker. 2010. A frames approach to semantic analysis. In Bernd Heine and Heiko Narrog (eds.), *The Oxford handbook of linguistic analysis*, 313–349. Oxford: OUP.
Firth, J. Roderick. 1957. *Studies in linguistic analysis.* Oxford: Blackwell.
François, Alexandre. 2008. Semantic maps and the typology of colexification: intertwining polysemous networks across languages. In Martine Vanhove (ed.), *From polysemy to semantic change*, 163–215. Amsterdam & Philadelphia: John Benjamins.
François, Alexandre. 2010. Des valeurs en héritage: Les isomorphismes sémantiques et la reconstruction des langues. In Injoo Choi-Jonin, Marc Duval, and Olivier Soutet (eds.), *Typologie et comparatisme*. Orbis-Supplementa 29, 129–145. Louvain: Peeters.
Gao, Hong. 2001. *The physical foundation of the patterning of physical action verbs. A study of Chinese verbs.* [Travaux de l'institut de linguistique de Lund, XLI]. Lund: Lund University PhD dissertation.
Geeraerts, Dirk and Stefan Grondelaers. 1995. Looking back at anger: Cultural traditions and metaphorical patterns. In John Taylor and Robert E. MacLaury (eds.), *Language and the cognitive construal of the world*, 153–179. Berlin & New York: Mouton de Gruyter.
Gibbs, Raymond. 2015. Metaphor. In Ewa Dąbrowska and Dagmar Divjak (eds.), *Handbook of cognitive linguistics*, 167–189. Berlin & New York: de Gruyter Mouton.

Goddard, Cliff. 2012. Semantic primes, semantic molecules, semantic templates: Key concepts in the NSM approach to lexical typology. In Maria Koptjevskaja-Tamm and Martine Vanhove (eds.), *New directions in lexical typology*. [Special issue]. *Linguistics*, 50 (3). 711–743.

Gries, Stefan. 2015. Polysemy. In Ewa Dąbrowska and Dagmar Divjak (eds.), *Handbock of cognitive linguistics*, 472–489. Berlin & New York: de Gruyter Mouton.

Hayward, Richard J. 1991. A propos patterns of lexicalization in the Ethiopian Language Area. In Daniela Mendel and Ulrike Claudi (eds.), *Ägypten im afroorientalischen Kontext. Special issue of Afrikanistische Arbeitspapiere*, 139–156. Cologne: Institute of African Studies.

Hayward, Richard J. 2000. Is there a metric for convergence. In Colin Renfrew, April McMahon, and Larry Trask (eds.), *Time depth in historical linguistics* (Papers in the Prehistory of Languages), vol. 2, 621–640. Cambrdige: The McDonald Institute for Archaeological Research.

Heine, Bernd and Tania Kuteva. 2002. *World lexicon of grammaticalization*. Cambridge: Cambridge University Press.

Hook, Peter, Prashant Pardeshi, and Hsin-Hsin Liang. 2012. Semantic neutrality in complex predicates: Evidence from East and South Asia. In Maria Koptjevskaja-Tamm and Martine Vanhove (eds.), *New directions in lexical typology*. [Special issue]. *Linguistics*, 50 (3). 605–632.

Ibarretxe-Antuñano, Iraide. 2006. Cross-linguistic polysemy in tactile verbs. In June Luchenbroers (ed.), *Cognitive linguistics investigations across languages, fields, and philosophical boundaries* (Human cognitive processing 15), 235–253. Amsterdam & Philadelphia: John Benjamins.

Ibarretxe-Antuñano, Iraide. 2008. Vision metaphors for the intellect: Are they really cross-linguistic? *Atlantis* 30 (1). 15–33.

Idström, Anna and Elisabeth Piirainen (eds.). 2006. *Endangered metaphors*. Amsterdam & Philadephia: John Benjamins.

Kibrik, Andrej. 2012. Toward a typology of verb lexical systems: A case study in Northern Athabaskan. In Maria Koptjevskaja-Tamm and Martine Vanhove (eds.), *New directions in lexical typology*. [Special issue]. *Linguistics*, 50 (3). 495–532.

Koch, Peter. 2001. Lexical typology from a cognitive and linguistic point of view. In Martin Haspelmath, Eckehard König, Wulf Oesterreicher, and Wolfgang Raible (eds.), *Language typology and language universals. An international handbook*, vol. 2, 1142–1178. Berlin & New York: De Gruyter.

Koch, Peter. 2008. Cognitive onomasiology and lexical change: Around the eye. In Martine Vanhove (ed.), *From polysemy to semantic change*, 107–137. Amsterdam & Philadelphia: John Benjamins.

Koptjevskaja-Tamm, Maria. 2008. Approaching lexical typology. In Martine Vanhove (ed.), *From polysemy to semantic change*, 3–52. Amsterdam & Philadelphia: John Benjamins.

Koptjevskaja-Tamm, Maria. (ed.). 2015. *The linguistics of temperature*. Amsterdam & Philadelphia: John Benjamins.

Koptjevskaja-Tamm, Maria, Martine Vanhove, and Peter Koch. 2007. Typological approaches to lexical semantics. *Linguistic Typology* 11 (1). 159–186.

Koptjevskaja-Tamm, Maria, and Henrik Liljegren. (forthc.). Lexical semantics and areal linguistics. In Raymond Hickey (ed.), *The Cambridge Handbook of areal linguistics*. Cambridge: Cambridge University Press.

Kövecses, Zoltan. 1995. Anger: Its language, conceptualization, and physiology in the light of cross-cultural evidence. In John Taylor and Robert E. MacLaury (eds.), *Language and the cognitive construal of the world*, 181–196. Berlin & New York: Mouton de Gruyter.
Lakoff, George, and Mark Johnson. 1999. *Philosophy in the flesh*. New York: Basic books.
Langacker, Ronald. 2015. Construal. In Ewa Dąbrowska and Dagmar Divjak (eds.), *Handbook of cognitive linguistics*, 120–142. Berlin & New York: de Gruyter Mouton.
List, Johann-Mattis, Thomas Mayer, Anselm Terhalle, and Matthias Urban. 2014. CLICS: Database of cross-linguistic colexifications. Marburg: Forschungszentrum Deutscher Sprachatlas (Version 1.0, online available at http://CLICS.lingpy.org, accessed on 2014-12-29).
Maalej, Zouheir A. and Ning Yu (eds.). 2011. *Embodiment via body parts. Studies from various languages and cultures*. Amsterdam & Philadelphia: John Benjamins.
Maisak, Timur and Ekaterina Rakhilina. 2007. Glagoly dviženija i naxoždenija v vode: leksičeskie sistemy i semantičeskie parametry. [Verbs of motion and location in water: lexical systems and semantic parameters.] In Timur Maisak and Ekaterina Rakhilina (eds.), *Glagoly dviženija v vode: leksičeskaja tipologija* [Verbs of motion and location in water: lexical typology.], 664–693. Moscow: Indrik.
Majid, Asifa and Melissa Bowerman (eds.). 2007. Cutting and breaking events: A cross-linguistic perspective. |Special issue]. *Cognitive Linguistics* 18 (2).
Majid, Asifa, Nicholas J. Enfield, and Miriam van Staden (eds.). 2006. Parts of the body: Cross-linguistic categorisation. [Special issue]. *Language Sciences*, 28(2–3).
Matisoff, James. 1978. Variational semantics in Tibeto-Burman: the "organic" approach to linguistic comparison. *Occasional Papers of the Wolfenden Society on Tibeto-Burman Linguistics*, Volume VI. Publication of the Institute for the Study of Human Issues (ISHI), Philadelphia.
Matisoff, James. 2004. Areal semantics – Is there such a thing?". In Anju Saxena (ed.), *Himalayan languages: past and present* (Trends in Linguistics 149), 347–393. Berlin & New York: Mouton de Gruyter.
Mihatsch, Wiltrud and Boštjan Dvořák. 2004. The concept FACE: paths of lexical change. In Wiltrud Mihatsch and Reinhild Steinberg (eds.), *Lexical data and universals of semantic change* (Stauffenburg Linguistik 35), 231–254. Tübingen: Stauffenburg.
Narasimhan, Bhuvana and Anetta Kopecka (eds.). 2012. *Events of 'putting' and 'taking': A crosslinguistic perspective*. Amsterdam & Philadelphia: John Benjamins.
Newman, John. 2015. Semantic shift. In Nick Riemer, Nick. (ed.), *The Routledge Handbook of Semantics*, 266–280. London: Routledge.
Newman, John (ed.). 1997. *The linguistics of giving*. Amsterdam & Philadelphia: John Benjamins.
Newman, John (ed.). 2005. *The linguistics of standing, sitting and lying*. Amsterdam & Philadelphia: John Benjamins.
Newman, John (ed.). 2009. *The linguistics of eating and drinking*. Amsterdam & Philadelphia: John Benjamins.
Nichols, Johanna. 2007. What, if anything, is typology? *Linguistic Typology* 11 (1). 231–239.
Rakhilina, Ekaterina. 1999. Aspectual classification of nouns: A case study of Russian. In Abraham Werner and Leonid Kulikov (eds.), *Tense-aspect, transitivity and causativity*, 341–350. Amsterdam & Philadelphia: John Benjamins.

Reznikova, Tatiana, Ekaterina Rakhilina, and Anastasia Bonch-Osmolovskaya. 2012. Towards a typology of pain predicates. In Maria Koptjevskaja-Tamm and Martine Vanhove (eds.), *New directions in lexical typology*. [Special issue]. *Linguistics*, 50 (3). 421–466.
Riemer, Nick. 2005. *The semantics of polysemy*. Berlin & New York: Mouton de Gruyter.
Schultze-Berndt, Eva Friederike. 2000. *Simple and complex verbs in Jaminjung. A study of event categorisation in an Australian language.* MPI Series in Psycholinguistics 14. Nijmegen: University of Nijmegen PhD dissertation.
Sharifian, Farzad, René Dirven, Ning Yu, and Susanne Niemeier (eds.). 2008. *Culture, body and language. Conceptualizations of internal body organs across cultures and languages.* Berlin & New York: Mouton de Gruyter.
Smith-Stark, Thomas. 1994. Mesoamerican calques. In Carolyn J. MacKay and Verón ca Vásques (eds.), *Investigaciones Lingüísticas en Mesoamérica*, 15–50. México, D.F.: Universidad Nacional Autónoma de México.
Steinberg, Reinhild. 2015. *Lexikalische Polygenese im Konzeptbereich KOPF*. Tübingen: Stauffenburg Verlag.
Sweetser, Eve. 1990. *From etymology to pragmatics: Metaphorical and cultural aspects.* Cambridge: Cambridge University Press.
Taylor, John R. 1992. Old problems: adjectives in Cognitive Grammar. *Cognitive Linguistics* 3 (1). 1–35.
Traugott, Elizabeth. C. and Richard B. Dasher. 2002. *Regularities in semantic change.* Cambridge: Cambridge University Press.
Ullmann, Stephen. 1962. *Semantics. An introduction to the science of meaning.* Oxford: Blackwell.
Ullmann, Stephen. 1966. Semantic universals. In Joseph H. Greenberg (ed.), *Universals of language. Report of a conference held at Dobbs Ferry, New York, April 13–15, 1961*, 217–262. Cambridge, Mass. & London: MIT Press.
Urban, Matthias. 2009. 'Sun' and 'moon' in the Circum-Pacific language area. *Anthropological Linguistics*, 51 (3/4). 328–346.
Urban, Matthias. 2010. 'Sun' = 'Eye of the day': A linguistic pattern of Southeast Asia and Oceania. *Oceanic linguistics*, 49 (2). 568–579.
Urban, Matthias. 2012. *Analyzibility and semantic associations in referring expressions. A study in comparative lexicology.* Leiden: Leiden University PhD dissertation.
Vanhove, Martine. 2008. Semantic associations between sensory modalities, prehension and mental perceptions: A crosslinguistic perspective. In Martine Vanhove (ed.), *From polysemy to semantic change*, 342–370. Amsterdam & Philadelphia: John Benjamins.
Vanhove, Martine (ed.). 2008. *From polysemy to semantic change*. Amsterdam & Philadelphia: John Benjamins.
Viberg, Åke. 2001. Verbs of perception. In Martin Haspelmath, Eckehard König, Wulf Oesterreicher, and Wolfgang Raible (eds.), *Language typology and language universals. An International Handbook*, vol. 2, 1294–1309. Berlin & New York: De Gruyter.
Wälchli, Bernhard, and Michael Cysouw. 2012. Lexical typology through similarity semantics: Toward a semantic map of motion verbs. In Maria Koptjevskaja-Tamm and Martine Vanhove (eds.), *New directions in lexical typology*. [Special issue]. *Linguistics*, 50 (3). 671–710.
Wälchli, Bernhard, and Fernando Zúñiga. 2006. The feature of systematic source-goal distinction and a typology of motion events in the clause. In Giannoula Giannoulopoulou and Torsten Leuschner (eds.), The lexicon: typological and contrastive perspectives. [Special issue]. *Sprachtypologie und Universalienforschung (STUF)* 59 (3). 284–303.

Wierzbicka, Anna. 1987. Kinship Semantics: Lexical universals as a key to psychological reality. *Anthropological Linguistics*, 29(2). 131–156.
Wierzbicka, Anna. 1999. *Emotions across languages and cultures: Diversity and universals.* Cambridge: Cambridge University Press.
Wierzbicka, Anna. 2005. There are no "color universals". But there are universals of visual semantics. *Anthropological Linguistics*, 47 (2). 217–244.
Wierzbicka, Anna. 2007. Bodies and their parts: An NSM approach to semantic typology. *Language Sciences*, 29. 14–65.
Wilkins, David P. 1996. Natural tendencies of semantic change and the search for cognates. In Mark Durie and Malcolm Ross (eds.), *The comparative method reviewed. Regularity and irregularity in language change,* 264–304. New York & Oxford: Oxford University Press.
Yavorska, Galyna M. 1992. *Leksiko-semantičeskaja tipologija v sinxronii i diaxronii* [Lexical semantic typology in synchrony and diachrony]. Kiev: Naukova dumka.
Zalizniak, Anna. 2008. A catalogue of semantic shifts: towards a typology of semantic derivation. In Martine Vanhove (ed.), *From polysemy to semantic change,* 217–238. Amsterdam & Philadelphia: John Benjamins.
Zalizniak, Anna, Maria Bulakh, Dmitry Ganenkov, Ilya Gruntov, Timur Maisak, and Maxim Russo. 2012. The catalogue of semantic shifts as a database for lexical semantic typology. In Maria Koptjevskaja-Tamm & Martine Vanhove (eds.), *New directions in lexical typology.* [Special issue]. *Linguistics*, 50 (3). 633–669.

Peter Koch †
2. Meaning change and semantic shifts

Abstract: This chapter focuses on semantic shift from a diachronic perspective. It starts with the roots of research on meaning change. The bulk of the chapter is devoted to the recent developments, primarily in the context of cognitive semantics, and is concerned with categories, mechanisms and pathways of meaning change. Two of the important distinctions here involve meaning innovation vs. meaning change (through propagation of an innovation in a speech community), as well as the speaker- vs. the hearer-induced meaning change (reanalysis), which build on two completely different pragmatic scenarios. Much attention is paid to the different semantic types of lexical meaning change, such as generalization vs. specialization, co-hyponymous transfer, metonymic change, metaphorical change, meaning change based on contrast, etc. The other issues dealt with in the chapter include lexical meaning change and parts of speech, and relations between lexical meaning change and other processes of lexical diachrony (word formation and borrowing). It concludes with the discussion of causes, nature and consequences of meaning change, and with suggestions for possible future research.

2.1 Introduction/definitions/historical perspective[1]

Meaning change is a constantly present phenomenon in human language. In everyday language it is so massively and permanently entrenched that, unlike other forms of change, it is even – at least occasionally – noticed by speakers:

---

[1] The chapter was originally intended for *The Routledge Handbook of Semantics*, edited by Nick Riemer (2015, Routledge), but could not be completed because of Peter Koch's tragic and unexpected death in July 2014. The existing – and very extensive – draft was in German, and it was not feasible to accommodate it to the handbook in any reasonable way. It is a great privilege to have this excellent chapter in the volume, skillfully translated by Dr. Tessa Say and edited by Maria Koptjevskaja-Tamm, Daniela Marzo and Nick Riemer, who together also agreed on several changes. These include a few minor inconsistencies in the original, such as a couple of wrong examples, insufficient explanations to a couple of figures, etc., as well as a few cases of inadequate translation. A two pages long section on grammaticalization has been deleted, as less relevant for the present volume, and some of the headings have been adjusted to reflect the general

For generations, a 'friend' was simply an ally. A supporter. Someone to regard with affection and trust. Then Facebook comes along, and suddenly the meaning of 'friend' is called into question [...]
(https://www.americanexpress.com/us/small-business/openforum/articles/11-ordinary-words-that-have-new-meaning-in-social-media-1/?intlink=us-openforum-related-editorial-7&modal=invite; last access on 24.6.2014).

2.1.1 Historical perspective[2]

While traditional rhetoric was primarily concerned with rules for the construction of discourse and not with reflection on the linguistic system, it did not overlook the problem of meaning change in its theory of tropes (metaphor, metonymy, etc.) (cf. Neumann 1998; Gévaudan 2008; Winter-Froemel 2011). This is particularly so with catachresis, that is, cases where there is a need for a term and the lexical gap is filled by applying a trope to an already existing word, such as in the metaphorical sense of Engl. *wing* in (1).

(1) Engl. *wing* 'organ of flight of an animal' → 'subordinate part of a building' (cf. OED: s.v. *wing*, n., I.1.a. and II.9.a.).

A linguistic classification of meaning change was first developed in the context of 19th century diachronic linguistics, largely taking up, but also going beyond, rhetorical categories. We are thinking here in particular of figures such as Reisig, Bréal, Paul, Nyrop and – in a class of his own – Wundt. A subsequent classification, more highly suffused with semiotics and association theory, was elaborated in the first half of the 20th century (Roudet 1921; also Zoltán Gombocz) and took on its canonical form with Ullmann (1957: 213–244; 1964: 211–227). Since there was little interest in a truly structuralist theory of meaning change (Coseriu 1964), for decades Ullmann remained the standard reference. It was only in the context of cognitive semantics that a breath of fresh air wafted into the theory of meaning change (the respective approaches are dealt with extensively in section 2.3).

---

orientation of the volume. The editors would like to thank Peter Koch's family, who granted us the permission to publish the chapter, Birgit Sievert and Dirk Geeraerts at de Gruyter Mouton for their enthusiasim, and the Universities of Bochum, Stockholm and Tübingen for their financial support.

2 Cf. Nerlich 1992; Blank 1997: 7–46; Geeraerts 2010: 1–46.

2.1.2 Definition of meaning change

The term *meaning change* (or *semantic change*) is not only widely used in the English language, it also prevails in international terminology, although on closer inspection it proves to be an imprecise one. With respect to the the lexicon, we can also talk about a broader notion of *lexical change*. A complete picture of lexical change can only be obtained if the semasiological and onomasiological perspectives are combined, as the English example shown in Figure 1 demonstrates (cf. Koch 2014: 74 f.; see, for example, (43) and section 2.3.3.7.).

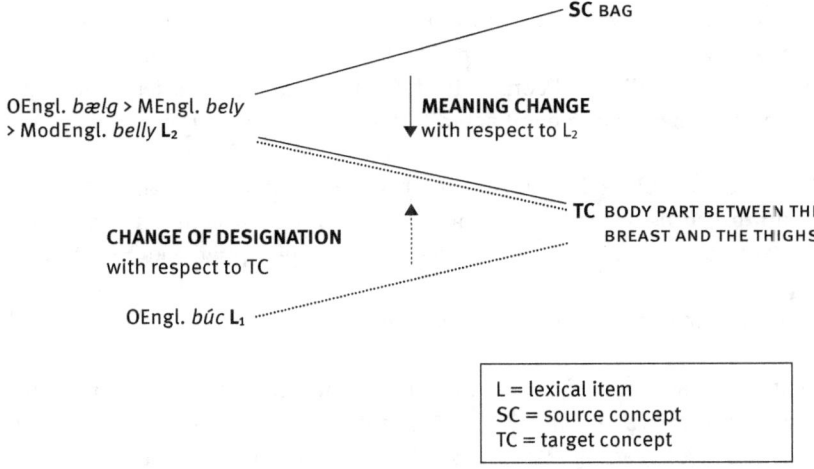

Figure 1: Meaning change and change of designation

The solid lines represent the fact that the lexical item OEngl. *bælg* > ModEngl. *belly* (= L_2), which meant BAG (= SC), acquired the new sense BODY PART BETWEEN BREAST AND THIGHS (= TC). This is the semasiological description of a lexical change focusing on the semantic change of a given lexical item. However, this semantic change went hand in hand with another kind of change (represented by the dotted lines in Figure 1) that only the onomasiological perspective reveals: The concept BODY PART... THIGHS (TC) was expressed by *búc* (L_1) in Old English and is expressed by *belly* (L_2) in Modern English. This describes a change of designation with respect to the TC. The specific subject of this semasiologically-oriented chapter is the meaning change SC → TC with respect to L_2; change of designation at best serves as the onomasiological background to certain considerations.

2.2 Critical issues and topics

2.2.1 Innovative meaning change

The term *meaning change* seems at first sight to suggest an interpretation whereby the meaning M of a word is so pliable that it can be transformed *as a whole* into a new meaning M' (cf. Werth 1974). This would not be out of place in the context of a conception of semantics that privileges monosemy (cf. Ruhl 1989). However, the phenomenon of meaning change is – seen from the reverse perspective – a strong argument *against* a monosemy-privileging conception of semantics in synchrony as well as diachrony. The tortuous path of meaning change followed by an extreme case such as (2), raises a doubt as to what the continuity in *a single* meaning M > ... > M'''' could consist in. It is questionable whether at any synchronic point in its development it actually had only *one* meaning.

(2) CLat. *bustum* 'place for burning corpses' → 'tomb' → VulgLat. *bustum 'sculpture of the deceased on a tomb' → 'sculpture of the upper body of the deceased on a tomb' → It. *busto* 'sculpture of the upper body' → 'human upper body'
(cf. Cortelazzo and Paolo 1999: s.v. *busto*).

A more plausible scenario of meaning change is one where the existing meaning M1 of a word acquires a new meaning M2, so that the word becomes polysemous with the two senses/readings M1 and M2. Figure 2 represents an attempt to show the continuous nature of lexicalization/conventionalization. Firstly, there is only one meaning in the language system (M1); then a new meaning surfaces (M1 (M2)), which gains in strength (M1 > M2) and finally settles in a polysemy having equal status to the original meaning (M1 = M2) (see also 2.3.1 below). Polysemy is therefore the synchronic result of meaning change (initially Bréal 1921: 143 f.; cf. Wilkins 1996: 267–270; Durkin 2009: 225 f.). Blank (1997: 112 f., 406–424) referred to this diachronic construction of polysemy in more precise terms as innovative meaning change.

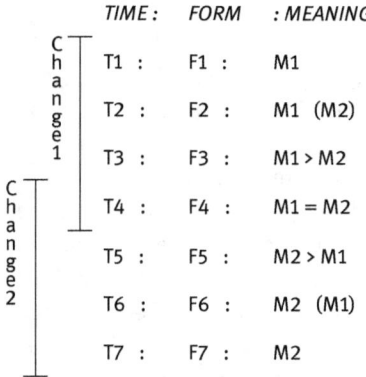

Figure 2: Cycle of genesis and disappearance of lexical polysemy in semantic change (simplified after Wilkins 1996: 269 f.)

Examples (3) and (4) are two – otherwise semantically comparable – examples of this process. Firstly, the OE word *witnes* (3a) and CLat. *tēstimōnium* (4a) only had the meaning 'testimony' (with *witnes* this is not apparent from the chronology of the textual evidence, but rather from the abstract derivational suffix *-nes*). Once the new sense of 'person giving testimony' has been acquired we have in Old English and Old French the polysemy shown in (3b) and (4b). Step (a) → (b) corresponds to Change 1 in Figure 2 and is thus a step in innovative meaning change (for further development see 2.2.2. below).

(3) (a) OEngl. *witnes* 'testimony'
    (b) OEngl. *witnes* 'testimony'; 'person giving testimony'
    (c) ModEngl. *witness* 'testimony'; 'person giving testimony'
        (cf. OED, s.v. *witness*, n., 2.a. and 4.a.).

(4) (a) CLat. *tēstimōnium* 'testimony'
    (b) OFr. *tesmoin* 'testimony'; 'person giving testimony'
    (c) ModFr. *témoin* 'person giving testimony'
        (cf. Rey 1992, s.v. *témoin*).

The sequence F1–F2–F3–F4 in Figure 2 refers to the fact that over time the signifier also changes on account of the progression of the change (cf. e.g. L_2 in Figure 1). This is, however, irrelevant for our purposes, so that we can conceive of the signifier as essentially continuous while the meanings change.

2.2.2 Reductive meaning change

The resulting polysemy of *witnes* (3b) in Old English has survived in contemporary English (3c), even though the 'testimony' sense is now marked and archaic. However this is not so in French, where *témoin* no longer has the sense 'testimony' (4c). Here, then, a Change 2 in the sense of Figure 2 has taken place: Of the two senses M1 and M2 the former has died out (for the gradation from T4 to T7 see 3.1. below). Blank (1997: 113, 121, 424 f.) speaks here of reductive meaning change.

Occasionally, it is only the entire sequence from T1 to T7 that is referred to as *a* meaning change in the literature, because only at time T7 is the meaning of the word in question completely different. However, there are good reasons for considering innovative meaning change (= Change 1 in Figure 2) and reductive meaning change (= Change 2) as two mutually independent processes. Firstly, Change 2 need not necessarily take place, because, as example 3 shows, the state of polysemy can persevere for a very long time. Secondly, the scenario M1 → M1 = M2 → M2 shown in Figure 2 is very widespread, but not inevitable; M1 → M1 = M2 → M1 is also possible. Where there is no distinction between Change 1 and Change 2, the counterintuitive conclusion must, in such cases, be drawn that – at the end of the day – there has in fact been no meaning change.

In what follows, the focus will be on innovative meaning change, as it is here that interesting new results emerge, while loss through reductive meaning change merely leads to loss.

2.2.3 Semantic shift/extension

The terms (semantic) shift/extension are very commonly used in the English language literature on meaning change. The new sense in (1) would therefore be widely referred to as metaphorical shift/extension of the old sense, the new sense in (3) and (4) as metonymic shift/extension of the old. But a meaning change of type (5) is often also simply labeled extension (as in Ullmann 1964: 229–231; see section 2.3.7.2.):

(5)   CLat. *passer* 'sparrow' → Rum. *pasăre* 'bird' (cf. 2.3.3.1.).

Crucial to this type of change is the fact that the logical extension of the term widens in passing from the old to the new meaning (also: generalization; in more detail 2.3.3.1.). This is not the case in (1), (3) or (4), where very different mechanisms, not purely logical, are at work (this is dealt with in greater depth in 2.3.3.3 and 2.3.3.4.). Extension should therefore not be equated with generalization (cf.

Blank 1997: 193–197). Basically, in its commonly accepted usage, the term extension, as well as semantic shift, describes nothing other than innovative meaning change with the emergence of polysemy (2.1.). Example (5) should logically be referred to as semantic shift/extension by generalization.

2.3 Current contributions and research

2.3.1 Meaning innovation and meaning change

Like any kind of language change, meaning change is an invisible-hand process (cf. Keller 1994). Speakers/hearers normally have no intention of changing the meaning of linguistic signs, all they do is communicate as effectively as possible. It often happens that in the current discourse they use a sign in an ad hoc way in something other than its usual sense, for example, by using a rhetorical trope (metonymy, metaphor, etc.) or another kind of semantic extension. This, then, is meaning innovation at the discourse level (which, incidentally, according to Figure 1, from an onomasiological perspective goes hand in hand with innovation of designation). Nonce innovations, which go unheeded, occur constantly in discourse, but this is not language change. Only when an innovation is propagated in a speech community through being repeatedly adopted in the individual discourses of different individuals can a change be said to have taken place (cf. Coseriu 1988; Croft 2000: 4 f.; Winter-Froemel 2008: 239–244).

The term *propagation* focuses on the social aspect of this process, the term *entrenchment* on the psycholinguistic aspect (cf. Langacker 1987; Croft 2000: 231–236; Schmid 2007) while the term *conventionalization* highlights the semiotic tension between discourse and system.

Alongside conventionalization, reference is also made, for example, to usualization (Blank 1997: 122 f.; 2001:1603) or institutionalization (cf. Brinton and Traugott 2005: 45–47). Of course, processes of usualization etc. are observed not only in lexical meaning change but also in other forms of semantically relevant change in the lexicon and the grammar. Lexicalization can be spoken of only in relation to the lexicon (cf. Brinton and Traugott 2005: 20–23; also on the different uses and aspects of this term). See Figure 2 in 2.1. for an attempt to show the continuous nature of lexicalization/conventionalization.

Such processes can be described in finer detail from the point of view of propagation (cf. Koch 1994: 203–207; Blank 1997: 119–130). A first step from meaning innovation to conventionalization often occurs only in part of a community's linguistic activities, e.g. initially in one specific variety of the historical language, and only later does the innovation then spread throughout the entire speech community. Thus, *schiao* 'servant' was commonly used as a greetings formula (40) initially only in the Venetian dialect of Italian before spreading throughout the entire Italian language community in the form *ciao*. However, it may also happen that a meaning innovation becomes conventionalized in a specific variety, and – at least for the time being – remains blocked there. Meaning (b) from French *rentrer* (6), for example, was common in the colloquial language probably from the end of the 17th century, but is to this day absent from the standard language.

(6) (a) Fr. *rentrer* 'to re-enter'
    (b) Fr. (colloquial) *rentrer* 'to enter'
        (cf. Rey 1992: s.v. *entrer*, p. 752; TLFi: s.v. *rentrer*, I.A.6).

Discourse traditions talk of another intermediate stage from which meaning innovations can gradually spread (cf. on this concept Koch 1997; Wilhelm 2001). For instance, meaning (b) from French *organiser* (7) initially established itself in the political discourse traditions of the French Revolution before being adopted into the general French vocabulary.

(7) (a) Fr. *organiser* 'to give the structure and interdependence of parts which subserve vital processes, to form into a living being'
    (b) Fr. *organiser* 'to give a definite and orderly structure'
        (cf. Rey 1992: s.v. *organe*).

As we have seen, meaning innovation in current discourse is not meaning change, but the latter presupposes the former. It is therefore essential to understand the reason for the meaning change from a speaker-hearer interaction perspective, which is the view typically adopted in usage-based approaches (cf. e.g. Bybee 2006; Barlow and Kemmer 2000; Winter-Froemel 2014). Where inferences, implicatures and relevance play a significant role at the level of current discourse, this gives us an important interface between diachronic semantics and pragmatic approaches (for example, Grice 1975; Sperber and Wilson 1995; Levinson 2000). For instance, according to the invited inferencing theory of semantic change (cf. Traugott and Dasher 2002), which is of central importance in certain forms of metonymy and specifically the phenomenon of subjectification (see 2.3.3.3.), the process of conventionalization presented above corresponds to the development from pragmatically colored utterance-token meanings through utterance-type meanings to coded meanings in the semantics of the language system.

A classic question, which arises in a usage-based understanding of meaning change, is that of the role of speaker vs. hearer in innovation meaning (2.3.2.).

So far, the focus in this section has been on innovative meaning change. Reductive meaning change (2.2.) can in many respects be thought of as its mirror image, as Figure 2 also shows (= Change 2). Firstly, there is polysemy in the language system (M1 = M2), then in the course of diachrony M1 is increasingly less used (first M2 > M1, then M2 (M1)) and finally dies out completely (only M2; of course, M2 may die out instead of M1: see 2.2.). This process of reduction (the counterpart to propagation) can also be described in finer detail, if differentiations are made in varieties or discourse traditions. For instance, Fr. *chenu* (8) acquired meaning (b) in addition to the older meaning (a) ((b), however, is found only in the popular register). Meaning (a) initially had no particular variety marker, and has today retreated into the literary register.

(8) (a) Fr. *chenu* 'hoary' (now literary)
    (b) Fr. (popular) *chenu* 'good'
       (cf. TLFi: s.v. *chenu*, I.A.1. and II.).

2.3.2 Speaker-induced vs. hearer-induced meaning change

Traditional rhetoric is explicitly defined as an *ars bene dicendi*, i.e. a body of production-oriented instructions. Tropes are presented as expression-oriented, speaker-induced rhetorical devices that the hearer has to keep up with. No doubt, this model applies to many cases of meaning innovation, and, thus, indirectly to the many types of meaning change discussed in section 2.3.3. In generating these *speaker-induced* changes, the first ad hoc step had to be taken by a given speaker S_1 who chose a given lexical (or grammatical) item denoting a given SC in order to express a new TC (cf. Figure 3). The hearer H_1 would have picked up this ad hoc innovation, and, acting as speaker S_2 in a subsequent communicative act, would have passed it on to a hearer H_2 who, as speaker S_3 would have circulated it further, and so on (cf. Koch 2001a: 225–228; 2012: 283):

Figure 3: Innovation by the speaker

The meaning change OEngl. *bælg* 'bag, purse'→ MEngl. *bely* 'body part between breast and thighs' (Figure 1 and (43)) can, for example, be seen as having come about according to this schema. It is clear in this case that S_1 has chosen an expressive metaphor to refer to the body part in question. But this schema is by no means restricted to metaphorical innovation/change. Aside from the model shown in Figure 3, meaning changes may involve a totally different type of pragmatic punctuation (Figure 4). Speaker S_1 uses a given lexical (or grammatical) item to express its conventional meaning. This time the speaker S_1 does not intend any innovation at all, but it is the hearer H_1 who "invents" something new. Acting in turn as speaker S_2 in a subsequent communicative act, H_1 may pass this innovation on to a hearer H_2 who, as speaker S_3 may circulate it further, and so on. This would be the beginning of a *hearer-induced* change (cf. Koch 2001a: 226–229; 2012: 283–287):

Figure 4: Innovation by the hearer

This is the scenario of reanalysis. As Detges and Waltereit (2002) have shown, reanalysis of a given sound string is mainly a semantically motivated process (that *may* be accompanied by formal changes such as grammatical rebracketing). It presupposes, among other things, a principle of reference, whereby the hearer H_1 assumes that a conventional meaning of the sound string s/he hears corresponds to what seems to be meant in the situation in which the sound string is uttered. If the (competent) hearer deviates from the actual conventional sense, his/her personal interpretation must nevertheless be cognitively linked to the conventional sense and compatible with the context and with H_1's overall pragmatic interpretation of the utterance. Our example (4) Latin *tēstimōnium* is open to such an interpretation. The speaker S_1, say a judge, wants to express the concept TESTIMONY (SC) in accordance with the linguistic tradition (4a), and produces an utterance like the one in (9), probably in the context of a trial.

(9) CLat. *Audiāmus tēstimōnium proximum!* 'Testimony!' (lit. 'Let us listen to the next testimony!')

However, one of the hearers H_1 in the audience, switches to PERSON GIVING TESTIMONY (4b), second meaning = TC), because this interpretation, too, is compatible with the context and with H_1's overall pragmatic interpretation of the utterance. Exactly the same reasoning applies of course to the ad hoc innovation underlying (3) OEngl. *witness*.

Speaker-induced meaning change and hearer-induced meaning change (reanalysis) are thus two completely different pragmatic scenarios.

2.3.3 Semantic types of lexical meaning change

The schema in Figure 1 raises the question as to the nature of the conceptual relation between SC and TC, i.e. the semantic route the speaker or the listener takes with their meaning innovation. The relevant distinction between types of lexical meaning change can be found, albeit with some differences, in any text book on diachronic linguistics (particularly comprehensive, for example, are Campbell 2013: 211–246; Hock and Joseph 1996: 215–252; Lehmann 1995: 254–273; Luraghi and Bubenik 2011: 286–310; Sihler 2000: 94–134). In what follows, we will seek an essentially cognitive-semantic definition of each type.

2.3.3.1 Generalization vs. specialization

Generalization (also broadening or widening of meaning) and specialization (also narrowing of meaning) are two – complementary – taxonomic types of meaning change where the source concept and target concept are to be found on different levels of the hierarchy of concepts. For instance, in example (10) a taxonomic sub-/super-ordination relation holds between the two concepts involved, MOVE (= TC) and MOVE ON ONE'S FEET (SC), where SC ⊂ TC. A change from a concrete to an abstract meaning takes place, i.e. the word becomes, as it were, a hyperonym of itself: It gains in extension and loses in intension (generalization). In terms of traditional rhetorical categories, we have here lexicalization of a species-for-genus synecdoche.

(10) OEngl. *gán* 'to move on one's feet' → 'to move, pass along (irrespective of the mode of progression)'
(cf. OED: s.v. *go*, v., B.1.a. and B.2.a.).

The converse of this is shown in example (11), where a taxonomic sub-/super-ordination relation holds between the two concepts involved, DOG (= SC) and DOG USED FOR THE CHASE (TC), where TC ⊂ SC. A change from an abstract to a concrete meaning takes place, i.e. the word becomes, as it were, a hyponym of itself: It loses in extension and gains in intension (specialization). In terms of traditional rhetorical categories, we have here lexicalization of a genus-for-species synecdoche (cf. Nerlich and Clarke 1999).

(11) OEngl *hund* 'quadruped of the genus *Canis*' → MEngl. *hund* 'quadruped of the genus *Canis* kept or used for the chase'
(cf. OED: s.v. *hound*, n.[1], 1. and 2.)

As a theory that confined itself to taxonomic relations in the lexicon, it was obvious for structural semantics to apply its entire apparatus of componential analysis to generalization and specialization to show that not only did the 'meaning' of the word in some vague sense change, but the whole meaning *structure* did too (Coseriu 1964). Thus, the lexical opposition CLat. *avunculus* (12a) vs. *patruus* (12b), which resided in the features [maternal line] vs. [paternal line], was lost in the transition from classical Latin to French. *Patruus* died out, and with the disappearance of the aforementioned oppositional features *avunculus* > Fr. *oncle* (12a) took on the less specific meaning (generalization).

(12) (a) CLat. *avunculus* 'mother's brother' → Fr. *oncle* 'mother's or father's brother'
 (cf. Rey 1992, s.v. *oncle*).
 (b) CLat. *patruus* 'father's brother'

Conversely, the change from CLat. *avis* to Sp. *ave* (13a) is a case of specialization, where Spanish *ave* acquired the feature [non-little] in addition to the features of the original Latin word, so that it now stands in opposition to *pájaro* (with the feature [little]) (13b).

(13) (a) CLat. *avis* 'bird' → Sp. *ave* 'non-little bird'
 (cf. Corominas and Pascual 1980–91, s.v. *ave*).
 (b) Sp. *ave* 'non-little bird' vs. Sp. *pájaro* 'little bird' (< CLat. *passer* 'sparrow'; cf. (5))

While generalization and specialization have up to this point been modeled as processes operating on intra-linguistic hence language-specific signifiers in the sense of Saussure (1916) and Hjelmslev (1970), cognitive semantics, and in particular prototype theory (e.g. Rosch 1973, Taylor 1995: 38–80) sees encyclopedic knowledge as playing a role in these two types of meaning change, which also entails pronounced asymmetries in the structure of our (folk-)taxonomic hierarchies. Data from the diachrony of the Latin-Romance lexicon empirically substantiate an emblematic example of prototype theory rather neatly: As can be clearly understood from the centrality of the concept SPARROW within the taxonomic category BIRD, the classical Latin term *passer* for this prototype has, through generalization, come to be the term used in Romanian (*pasăre*) for the whole category (cf. ex. (5) in 2.2.3).

Conversely, from a feminist linguistic point of view, it is interesting to note that the existence of an androcentric world view, in which the male human being is the prototype for human beings, explains why in certain languages (not all, there appear to be many provisos!) the classical Latin term *homo* for the entire category has, through specialization, come to denote the prototype in French (*homme*), as in (14) below:

(14) CLat. *homo* 'human being' → Fr. *homme* 'human being'; 'male human being' [similarly – with the same Etymon – Sp. *hombre*, It. *uomo* etc.; cf. also Engl. *man*]

Prototypicality-based differences in salience seem to be responsible for a whole series of processes of generalization and specialization (Koch 1995: 30–34; Blank 1997: 204 f., 384–388; Geeraerts 1997: 77 f.). However, it should be noted that these types of salience are by no means universal (in North America, for example, the concept ROBIN is central to the category BIRD) and in some cases they are legitimate only in very specific frames of human practice. Thus the example of generalization in (15) could only have originated in a nautical context, where the usual form of arrival is precisely to-get-to-the-shore.

(15) Lat. *ad-ripare* 'to get to the shore' → Fr. *arriver*, It. *arrivare* 'to arrive'

According to Blank (1997: 200f) the more or less pronounced similarity between category members and the prototype allows generalization in the sense of expansion from the center of the relevant category to peripheral – but still relatively similar – members to take place. There is no denying that even the most peripheral members of the category BIRD have a certain similarity with the prototype SPARROW (as in (5)). Similarity with the prototype is not, however, of much help when it comes to specialization, as in the case of (14), where the category indicated by Latin *homo*, has indeed shrunk, *despite* the obvious similarities between its prototype and the more peripheral members.

Nevertheless, it is by no means possible to explain all cases of generalization and specialization as the effect of prototypicality (cf. Blank 1997: 386 f.; more vigorously affirmed by Koch 2005: 177). The problem that arises in generalizations to a superordinate level within the taxonomic hierarchy, is that the cue validity is very low at levels above the basic level, so that prototypicality hardly plays a role: What, for example, should the prototype of the category ANIMAL or the category PLANT be? In the case of the generalization in (16) it is clear that prototypicality does not play a role.

(16) CLat. *planta* 'seedling, bedding plant' → MedLat. 'plant' (thence Fr. *plante*, Engl. *plant*, etc.)
(cf., also on the historical scientific background in particular, Rey 1992: s.v. ② *plante*).

Cases of specialization need not necessarily be associated with prototypicality either. Regarding, for example, the two parallel processes of specialization in (17a–b) (which are connected not etymologically, but possibly through language contact), in the 13th–14th centuries, when the change must have occurred, meat was certainly not prototypical for the mass of the population but rather a rare and thus highly desirable food.

(17) (a) OEngl. *mete* 'food' → MEngl. *mete* 'flesh of animals used for food' (cf. OED: s.v. *meat*, n., 1.a.; 3.a.).
(b) OFr. *viande* 'food' → MFr. *viande* 'flesh of animals used for food' (cf. Rey 1992: s.v. *viande*).

From a prototypicality perspective, it is completely puzzling why the general concept TO PLACE in CLat. *collocare* specialized in various Romance languages to the horizontal position (18a) in one case and to hanging (18b) in another:

(18) (a) CLat. *collocāre* 'to place' → Fr. *coucher* 'to lie down' (cf. Rey 1992, s.v. *coucher*).
(b) CLat. *collocāre* 'to place' → Sp. *colgar* 'to hang (up)' (cf. Corominas and Pascual 1980–1991).

To thoroughly understand generalization and specialization, it is essential to clarify the cognitive relations operating within taxonomies (cf. Koch 2005: 177–183). On the one hand, a similarity exists between all concepts on the same taxonomic level (co-taxonomic similarity; see also 2.3.3.2.). As we saw above, the similarity can be more or less pronounced depending on proximity to the prototype. On the other hand, concepts on a taxonomically lower level differ from those on the next higher level due to the fact that additional contiguities emerge at the lower level (typical frames, in which the concept in question appears as an element, or typical elements in the frame, which the concept itself constructs: see 2.3.3.3. below). This becomes perfectly clear in the different forms of lexical change. The semantic-taxonomic relation between the source concept and the target concept is, for instance, the same in (11) and (19): The concept CANIS is taxonomically superordinate to the concept CANIS USED FOR THE CHASE. In (19), a case of composition in diachrony (not meaning change!), the constituent *hunting* in the lexical target unit means that at least *one* typical contiguity relation (within the frame HUNT) has now become completely explicit.

(19) ModEngl. *dog* 'quadruped of the genus *Canis* [primarily domesticated, the editors' note]' → *hunting(-)dog* 'quadruped of the genus *Canis* kept or used for the chase'
(cf. OED: s.v. *hunting dog*, 1.; first mention in 1863).

In (11), the target lexical unit is expanded as a consequence of the same typical contiguity relation (within the frame HUNT), even though this is not explicitly realized in the morphology (formal identity between the lexical source unit and the lexical target unit). The explicit (19) or implicit (11) typical contiguity relation, which the now taxonomically subordinate word adds to its meaning, determines the dissimilarity-in-similarity of the other words on the lower level of the hierarchy (in terms of feature semantics this would be a distinctive feature).

Overall, we can say that specialization involves the transition to a concept on a taxonomically lower level, where one (or more) implicitly present typical contiguity relations highlight the dissimilarities in the remaining (co-taxonomically) similar concepts on the lower level.

The relevant scenario is likely that of reanalysis (see 2.3.2.), which in this case is realized as follows: A word, that belongs semantically to a not too low taxonomic level is frequently used in a context or co-text, on which a particular frame is imposed. Hearers will now increasingly infer a contiguity relation related to this frame, which is eventually added to the meaning of the word, so that it permanently shifts to a lower taxonomic level. In the case of OEngl/MEngl *hund* (cf. (11)), this can be illustrated with the help of corpus evidence such as (20) or (21) (without committing ourselves as to how far the process in question has already advanced here). OEngl/MEngl *hund* 'quadruped of the genus *Canis*' is in both cases used in a co-text, which clearly evokes the frame HUNT: (20) *huntes* 'hunters', also *hors* 'horses'; (21) *hauekes* 'hawks', *hors* 'horses' and *wepnes* 'weapons'.

(20) (Late) OEngl. *Đa huntes wæron swarte...& here hundes ealle swarte...& hi ridone on swarte hors.*
'the hunters were black..., and their hounds all black... and they rode on black horses'
(*c*1131; *O.Engl. Chron.* an. 1127, cit. OED: s.v. *hunt.* n.[1]).

(21) MEngl. *Hundes and hauekes and hors and wepnes.*
 'hounds and hawks and horses and weapons'
 *(c*1200; *Trin. Coll. Hom.* 179, cit. OED: s.v. *hawk.* n.¹*)*.

The meaning of *hund* (later *hound*) is eventually augmented with this contiguity relation in such a way that it, i.e. the meaning, shifts to a lower taxonomic level: 'quadruped of the genus *Canis* kept or used for the chase', thereby differentiating itself from the meanings of the remaining (co-taxonomically) similar words on the lower level denoting the other breeds of dogs (according to the OED, s.v. *hound*, n.¹, 2., first recorded use circa 1200).

Generalization behaves in exactly the opposite way: transition to a concept on a taxonomically higher level takes place, whereby typical contiguity relations get "stripped" and co-taxonomic similarities at the lower level come to the fore while the distinction remains in the background.

We can, of course, where it makes sense, build upon this understanding of generalization and specialization through the concept of prototypicality ((5), cf. the discussion in connection to (10), (14) and probably also (12), with the aforementioned reservations also (15)), although this concept is not indispensable ((11), (13a), (16) – (18)). In each case, co-taxonomic similarities and typical contiguity relations operate on the next lower level and give rise to differentiation at this level, too. The relevant contiguity relations arise from socially, culturally, economically, etc. relevant, in part probably also universally valid frames.

2.3.3.2 Co-hyponymous transfer

In 2.3.3.1. meaning change takes place in the vertical dimension of taxonomies, so now the question arises whether a change can also occur in the horizontal dimension. This does indeed happen, a fact so far only adequately recognized by Blank (1997: 207–216). In example (22), SHREW (= SC) and MOUSE (= TC) are each ordered by (co-taxonomic) similarity on the same level (SC ⊄ TC and TC ⊄ SC), and both are subsumed under one and the same concept C°, let's say: RODENT ANIMAL (SC ⊂ C° and TC ⊂ C°). This is also the case in (23), where LION and PUMA are in relation to each other and in relation to the superordinate concept (let's say: BEAST OF PREY). In (24) we have synchronic evidence that the meaning of the polysemous English word *fir* corresponds to Latin *pinus* and Latin *abies*. While it is true there is no diachronic evidence of a clear succession in these meanings, the current polysemy can only have arisen by the word having "migrated" between concepts on the same taxonomic level (subordinate to the concept CONIFER).

(22) CLat. *sōrex* 'shrew' → Fr. *souris* 'mouse'
(cf. Rey 1992, s.v. *souris*).

(23) Sp. *león* 'lion' → Sp. (South-American) 'puma'
(cf. Moliner 2008, s.v. *león*; Blank 1997: 208).

(24) Engl. *fir* = Lat. 'pinus' / = Lat. 'abies'
(cf. OED, s.v. *fir*).

This type of meaning change therefore occurs between concepts on the same taxonomic level, which share co-taxonomic similarity with each other: in diachrony a word becomes, as it were, its own co-hyponym, hence Blank speaks of co-hyponymous transfer.

Overall, this type of vocabulary change happens relatively seldom and it is easy to see why: in the context of an initial polysemy (cf. 2.1) the word in question, at least in a transitional phase, unites two co-hyponymously related meanings, which from the point of view of lexical distinction is actually dysfunctional (cf. (24)). Nonetheless, co-hyponymous transfer occurs, typically in zoological and botanical (folk-)taxonomies. Speakers are not always certain in their knowledge, with the result that the particularly narrow (co-taxonomic) similarity between the two concepts involved leads to confusion or that the speaker blurs the category boundaries between the two concepts (as in (22) and (24). However, it seems even here to be somewhat untypical for the polysemic phase between the innovative and the reductive meaning change (cf. 2.3.1.) to hold in the long run, as in the case of (24). For instance, in the case of (22), French restored lexical distinctiveness in the 15th century with the help of a borrowing from Latin (*musaraigne* < MedLat. *musaraneus*), which clearly refers to the concept SHREW.

A particular type of case is represented by those processes of hyponymous transfer where people come into contact with the fauna and flora of a completely foreign country (typically European colonizers in the New World or in other parts of the world). If they encounter a hitherto unknown animal or plant, they can of course adopt the name the local inhabitants use in their own language (which would then be borrowing); but they can also assign to the new animal the name of a similar animal known to them, as happened in the case of (23). Lexical distinctiveness is not threatened here to the same extent as in the cases discussed above, since the known and the new animal do not occur in the same frame.

2.3.3.3 Metonymic change

Ancient rhetoric summed up the principle of metonymy as a rhetorical trope by stating that this trope takes its expression from near and close things ("ab rebus propinquis et finitimis trahit orationem": *Rhetorica ad Herennium* 4, 32, 43). Traditional rhetoric also provided for metonymic catachresis (see 1.1.), whereby the metonymic principle was also recognized as a form of meaning change. The following are typical examples of metonymic change:

(25) CLat. *coxa* 'hip' → Fr. *cuisse*, It. *coscia* 'thigh'
(cf. Rey 1992, s.v. *cuisse*; Cortelazzo and Paolo 1999, s.v. *coscia*).

(26) MedLat. *collātio* 'reading from the *Collationes* (lives of the Fathers) before compline in Benedictine monasteries' → 'light refection taken by the monks after the reading of the *collatio*'
[hence – in both types of meaning – Fr. *collation* and Engl. *collation*, later through generalization both become 'light meal']
(cf. Rey 1992, s.v. *collation*; OED, s.v. *collation*, n., 7.–9.).

(27) Engl. *happy* 'involving good fortune, favorable' → 'feeling great pleasure due to one's circumstances'
(cf. OED, s.v. *happy*, a., 3. and 4.)

(28) CLat. *tēstimōnium* (> OFr. *tesmoin*) 'testimony' → OFr. *tesmoin* 'person giving testimony'
(cf. (4).)

The proximity which exists here between the source concept and target concept, can of course be spatial (25), or temporal (26) in nature, but it can also refer among other things to a CAUSE-EFFECT relation (27), or a CONTAINER-CONTAINED relation (28). Structural semantics had no tools with which to adequately capture metonymy as, firstly, it was purely taxonomically oriented (cf. 2.3.3.1.), and, secondly, it confined itself to describing intra-linguistic signifiers, while encyclopedic knowledge clearly has a great bearing on metonymy. Roudet (1921) and subsequently Ullmann (1957: 231–234; 1964: 218–220) overcame the former limitation through an association psychology interpretation of metonymy in terms of a contiguity relation, as did Jakobson (1971) in his structuralism open to phenomenology (cf. also Holenstein 1972: 41–43, 317 f.). Cognitive semantics, which to a certain extent rediscovered metonymy and hence metonymic change, was then – unsurprisingly – able to overcome the latter restriction.

An approach to explaining metonymy, which has now become the classic one within cognitive semantics, draws on the notion of domain or the Idealized Cognitive Model (ICM). On this view, metonymy is where a linguistic element referring to a source concept SC, is used to denote a target concept TC, where SC and TC belong to the same domain or the same ICM (cf. Lakoff and Johnson 1980: 36; Lakoff 1987; Radden and Kövecses 1999: 21; Barcelona 2002). This – the argument goes – distinguishes metonymy from metaphor, which involves two domains (cf. 2.3.3.4.). A problem arises here from the fact that the terms domain and in particular ICM are ultimately rather unclear. It can, of course, be readily agreed that in the case of (25) SC = HIP and TC = THIGH belong to the same domain (namely HUMAN BODY). In a case like (26), it is already doubtful whether one would want to consider SC = READING FROM *Collationes* and TC = LIGHT REFECTION AFTER READING as belonging to a common domain MONASTIC LIFE or whether to assign them to two completely different domains, READINGS and MEALS. In (28), we probably have two completely different domains, ACT OF COMMUNICATION for SC = TESTIMONY and PERSON for TC = PERSON GIVING TESTIMONY, while TRIAL serves as one and the same domain for both.

Croft (1993) modifies this approach, in that he no longer assigns a given concept to a domain but assigns it instead to a so-called domain matrix, a combination of different domains, relative to which the concept is profiled. In the case of (27), for instance, one could postulate a concept HAPPY, whose domain matrix would include, among others, the domains QUALITY OF THINGS OR SITUATIONS and FEELINGS. Metonymy would be brought about by highlighting the FEELINGS domain instead of the QUALITY domain. The metonymic process thus takes place not so much within a domain (25) as within a domain matrix.

Nonetheless, modifications to the domain approach cannot solve all the problems associated with metonymy (cf. Geeraerts 2010: 215–217, who also looks at problems – of little interest to us here – regarding the delimitation of purely synchronic metonymic effects). The domain matrix approach is, first of all, overgenerative, as in the first step it covers the phenomenon of facets (here additional demarcation criteria would be required, see below). The question also arises as to the nature of the relationship connecting the various domains with the matrix for a given concept. Furthermore, the aforementioned criticism, that the domain-concept itself (and equally the ICM-concept) is not clear and is in danger of being over-used, still holds (cf. Koch 1999: 152 f.; 2005: 167 no. 13; Feyaerts 2000: 62 f.; Riemer 2001; Panther and Thornburg 2007; and even Croft and Cruse 2004: 261 no. 1). As revealed by its application to various examples, the term also encompasses taxonomies, areas of life and frames, if we define frame in the following sense:

> A semantic frame [...] is a coherent structure of related concepts where the relations have to do with the way the concepts co-occur in real world situations (Geeraerts 2006: 16).

It is therefore preferable to base our understanding of metonymy on the latter frame concept, which also implies recourse to the aforementioned concept of contiguity relation, which plays a somewhat marginal role in cognitive semantics (cf. Taylor 1995: 122; Croft 1993: 347; Ungerer and Schmid 1996: 115 f.; Radden and Kövecses 1999: 19; more explicitly Dirven 1993: 14; Feyaerts 2000: 63–65). Geeraerts defined metonymic effects in synchrony (hence in polysemy) accordingly:

> Metonymy is a semantic link between two readings of a lexical item that is based on a relationship of contiguity between the referents of the expression in each of those readings (Geeraerts 1997: 96).

The possible charge that the notion of contiguity, and thus the frame concept under consideration here, is unclear may be countered with the assertion that the relation of contiguity is – outwardly – unequivocally distinct from other relations. It cannot be ascribed to any form of similarity, be it of a taxonomic (2.3.3.2.: SC ⊄ C° and TC ⊄ C°), or metaphorical type (2.3.3.4.). It also bears little resemblance to taxonomic super- or subordination: SC ⊄ TC and TC ⊄ SC. Consequently, where the contiguity-motivated frame concept is concerned, there is no danger of confusion with taxonomies or with metaphorical schemata, let alone with areas of life in a very vague sense. On the other hand, the concept of contiguity is broad enough to allow internal diversity (on this see below).

To understand the diachronic process of metonymic change, it is now important to also consider the above-mentioned concepts of highlighting and perspectivization (cf. also Taylor 1995: 90, 107 f., 125 f.; Ungerer and Schmid 1996: 128 f.; Panther and Thornburg 2007: 242). From a Gestalt theoretical perspective, we are dealing here with a conceptual figure-ground effect (Rubin 1921: 3–101; Köhler 1947: 171 f., 181–187, 202–205, 253). Metonymic change can thus be characterized as a change in the meaning of a linguistic unit, which is set in motion as follows:

(I) an element E_1 of a given frame (= source concept SC) shifts from figure to ground, while a contiguous element E_2 (= target concept TC) shifts from ground to figure (see Figures 5a vs. 5b), or

(II) an element E_2 (= source concept SC) within a given frame shifts from figure to ground, while the frame as a whole (= target concept TC) shifts from ground to figure (see Figures 6a vs. 6b), or

(III) the shift occurs in reverse from the frame to the element.

(Cf. Koch 1995: 40 f.; 1999: 151–153; 2012: 267 f.; Blank 1997: 242 f.).

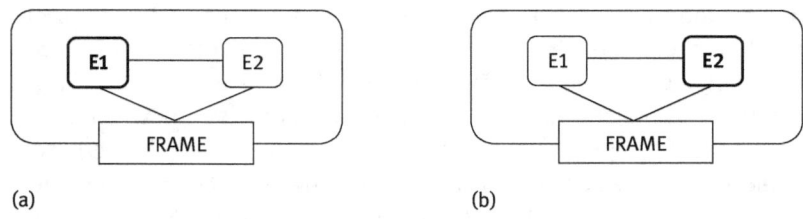

Figure 5: Figure-ground effects between two elements of a frame

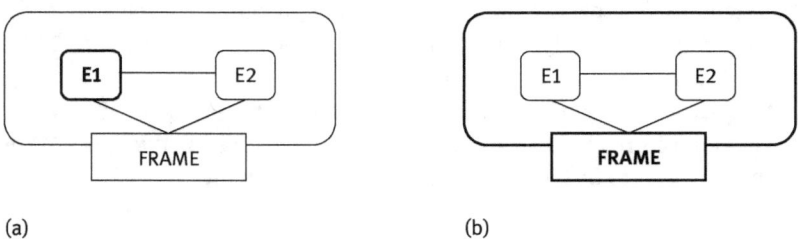

Figure 6: Figure-ground effects between an element of frame (a) and frame as a whole (b)

Metonymic change takes place according to schema (I) in the examples cited at the beginning of this section: (25) HIP = E_1 = SC → THIGH = E_2 = TC in the frame HUMAN BODY; (26) READING FROM *Collationes* = E_1 = SC → LIGHT REFECTION AFTER READING = E_2 = TC in the frame EVENING IN BENEDICTINE MONASTIC LIFE; (27) INVOLVING GOOD FORTUNE = E_1 = SC → FEELING GREAT PLEASURE = E_2 = TC in the frame LUCK; (28) TESTIMONY = E_1 = SC → PERSON GIVING TESTIMONY = E_2 = TC in the frame TRIAL.

Metonymic change takes place according to schema (II) in example (29): COUNTER = E_1 = SC → PUBLIC HOUSE = frame as a whole = TC; and according to schema (III) in (30): FIREPLACE = frame as a whole = SC → FIRE = E_1 = TC.

(29) Engl. *bar* 'counter in a public house' → 'public house'
(cf. OED, s.v. *bar*, n.¹, III.28.a.).

(30) CLat. *focus* 'fireplace' → Fr. *feu*, Sp. *fuego*, It. *fuoco*, etc. 'fire'
(cf. Rey 1992, s.v. *feu*; Corominas and Pascual 1980–1991, s.v. *fuego*; Cortelazzo and Paolo 1999, s.v. *fuoco*).

Notwithstanding the sharp external distinction from the other conceptual organizing principles and relations dealt with above, the terms *frame* and *contiguity* are – internally – still broad enough to encompass a wide variety of relation types.

Traditional rhetoric had already recognized the distinctions between various types of semantic relations within metonymy hinted at earlier (cf. on this in cognitive semantics, e.g. Radden and Kövecses 1999: 29–44; Geeraerts 2010: 31–33): OBJECT–LOCALLY ADJACENT OBJECT (25); EVENT–TEMPORALLY ADJACENT EVENT (26); CAUSE–EFFECT (27); ACTION–AGENT (28); CONTENT–CONTAINER (29); CONTAINER–CONTENT (30); etc. A very abstract, purely binary categorization is that of co-presence (e.g. (25), (28), (29), (30)) and succession (e.g. (26), (27); according to Ullmann 1957: 232 f. previously in Gombocz's work; cf. now in particular Blank 1999b). A compromise between unity and diversity is represented by the attempt made to not simply list the subtypes of metonymy, but to classify them in a three-dimensional prototypical structure (cf. Peirsman and Geeraerts 2006; Geeraerts 2010: 217–220).

Traditional rhetoric had also already recognized the problem of whether cognitive relations corresponding to the meronomic schema PART-WHOLE (31) or WHOLE-PART (32) were to be considered the basis of metonymy.

(31) Rum. *picior* 'foot' → 'leg'
(cf. Tiktin and Lüder 2003, s.v. *picior*).

(32) OEngl. *weddung* 'action of marrying' → MEngl. *wedding* 'performance of the marriage-rite'
(OED, s.v. *wedding*, vbl. n., 1. and 2.a.).

If these meronomic case types of metonymy are separated out, they should – according to *one* rhetorical tradition – be assigned to synecdoche, where they stand in opposition to the taxonomic subtype of synecdoche (species-for-genus and genus-for-species: cf. 2.3.3.1.). If one is prepared to abandon the rather controversial entity synecdoche (cf. Seto 1999; further literature in Koch and Winter-Froemel 2009), it would make sense to assign meronomic case types to metonymy (the other solution in the rhetorical tradition; cf. among others Ullmann 1957: 89, 203, 204, 222, 232, 234; 1964: 212; Lakoff and Johnson 1980: 36; Croft 1993: 350; Blank 1997: 253–255; Radden and Kövecses 1999: 30–36; Koch 1999: 153 f.; Panther and Thornburg 2007: 238). Ruiz de Mendoza Ibáñez (2000: 115 f.) sees things differently, in that he ascribes all metonymies to the meronomic schema. Peirsman and Geeraerts (2006: 278 f.) do not go to such extremes, although they do consider (spatial bounded) PART-WHOLE relations to be the prototypical core of contiguities underlying metonymies. Without wanting to go that far, it can still be affirmed with good conscience that the meronomic type of metonymy is only a special case of element-frame- or frame-element-based metonymy (Figures 6a and 6b and case types II and III): FOOT = E_1 = SC → LEG = frame as a whole =

TC (31); (32): ACTION OF MARRYING = frame as a whole = SC → PERFORMANCE OF THE MARRIAGE-RITE = E_1 = TC (cf. Koch 2012: 274 f.). What additionally speaks for inclusion of meronymy in metonymic change is the fact that in the individual case there is often a smooth transition between meronymic change and other element-frame- or frame-element-based types. We therefore analyzed (29) as a case of CONTENT-CONTAINER, although it could also be LOCATED-LOCATION or even PART-WHOLE. Likewise, in (30) in addition to CONTAINER-CONTENT, LOCATED-LOCATION or even WHOLE-PART may be considered. In each case, the contiguity relation within a frame should be understood as a common designation.

An attempt was also made to revive in some degree the old rhetorical device of synecdoche, by even incorporating generalization (= species-for-genus) and specialization (= genus-for-species) into metonymy (cf. e.g. Lakoff 1987: 77–90, 287; Radden and Kövecses 1999: 34 f.; with provisos Peirsman and Geeraerts 2006: 307 f.). This is incompatible, however, with a strict separation between contiguity relations within frames on the one hand, and with relations of taxonomic sub- and super-ordination on the other, as was done above.

The fundamental distinction between taxonomies and frames does not mean that interrelations between the two cognitive principles of organization – each also relevant to meaning change – cannot be observed. There is widespread recognition that the metonymic effect is accompanied by a shift of reference (cf. Nunberg 1995; Croft 1993). In fact, in many cases of metonymic change – but, as we shall see, in no way all – the taxonomic categories of source concept SC and target concept TC are referentially disjoint (C_P and C_Q stand for the referent classes corresponding to the concepts P and Q):

(33) (a) P and Q are contiguous concepts.
     (b) $C_P \cap C_Q = \emptyset$.

This is true for all cases of metonymic change cited so far in this article ((25)–(32)). We can speak here of referent-sensitive metonymy. A further interesting observation from a taxonomic perspective, consists in the fact that in many cases the contiguity relation between P and Q is, strictly speaking, valid only for a prototypical subset of C_P and/or C_Q (cf. Geeraerts 1997: 68–75; Koch 1995: 40 f.; 1999: 149–151). This is particularly evident in examples (27), (29) and (30). During the lexicalization process these restrictions on the prototypical subsets are, as a rule, abandoned, so that finally the metonymic relations apply to referent classes C_P and C_Q as a whole apply (inductive generalization according to Dik 1977).

While the prototypical bridge is important for metonymy, it does not necessarily presuppose that, as formulated in (33b), the referent classes C_P and C_Q must be disjoint. Thus in the case of (34), the output-contiguity YOUNG PERSON – OFF-

SPRING applies only to the prototypical subset, in which C_P and C_Q overlap referentially (very often we discuss a person's lineage while s/he is young; but one can of course also speak of young people independently of their lineage and also of daughters or sons who have left childhood far behind them).

(34) OEngl. *child* 'young person below the age of puberty' → MEngl. *child* 'offspring'
(OED, s.v. *child*, n., B.I. 2.a. and B.II.8.a.).

Since contiguity here plays a central role in change, and since C_P und C_Q are far from having referential identity, it seems reasonable to assign such cases to metonymy (another example can be found in (38)). In contrast to the cases in (25) – (32) and to the description in (33), we would be speaking here of non-referent-sensitive metonymy, which would be rendered as follows (cf. Koch 2001a: 218–225; 2012: 272 f.):

(35) (a) P and Q are contiguous concepts.
 (b) $C_P \cap C_Q \neq \emptyset$.

Note, however, that contiguity in the range $C_P \cap C_Q$ is non-referent-sensitive only at the moment of innovation. In the course of lexicalization, the reading Q = TC is transferred via inductive generalization also to referents for which P = SC does not hold.

The transition from (33) to (35) – in the context of a contiguity relation between P and Q – involves greater referential interweaving of C_P and C_Q. If we go one step further, we arrive at complete referential identity of the two categories with a simultaneous contiguity relation between P and Q:

(36) (a) P and Q are contiguous concepts.
 (b) $C_P = C_Q$.

This is the constellation which is referred to in the literature as that of facets (cf. Cruse 2000: 114–117; Croft and Cruse 2004: 116–125; Kleiber 1999: 87–101). For example, in a word such as English *book*, whose facets TOME (37a) and TEXT (37b) are in contiguity with each other, but where the test of referent identity shows that $C_P = C_Q$, the typical figure-ground effect for metonymy may fail to materialize (37c). Since this constellation – of potential interest in synchronic-lexicological terms – appears not to be relevant to lexical change, we will not consider it further (cf. Cruse 1993: 349 f.; Koch 2012: 273 f.).

(37) (a) Engl. This **book** weighs ten pounds. [TOME]
    (b) Engl. This **book** is a history of Great Britain. [TEXT]
    (c) Engl. This **book** which is a history of Great Britain weighs ten pounds. [TOME + TEXT]

In addition to internal referential differentiation, internal communicative differentiation in metonymy is also of interest (cf. Koch 2001a: 225–228; 2012: 283–287). If, from a rhetorical perspective, one understands metonymy as a trope, then it necessarily follows that here we are dealing with – on the level of innovation – speaker choice. For some cases of metonymic change this can, in fact, be safely assumed; see (25), (27), (31) and (32). Very often, however, metonymic change starts with reanalysis by the hearer (cf. 2.3.2.). Contiguity relations within frames represent axes along which the semantic analysis of an expression in a given situation can move relatively easily without the overall (often pragmatic) interpretation of the expression being affected by it. Ex. (28) above can serve as an illustration of this too. Where the Latin expression *Audiamus testimonium proximum!* 'Let's hear the next *testimonium*!' is used in the context of a trial, the – conventionally correct – analysis of *testimonium* as TESTIMONY is just as good as the innovative analysis PERSON GIVING TESTIMONY. Similarly, re-analysis can be assumed to underlie the cases of metonymic change in (26), (29), (30) and (32).

Finally, three particularly interesting subtypes of metonymic change are discussed here. Firstly, much attention has been paid to the notion of subjectification (De Smet and Verstraete 2006), a term not always used consistently. According to Langacker (e.g. 1999) subjectification is, as his example (38) shows, a perspectivization process, which starts with the objective construal of an onstage object of conception (here: PEASANT), but with an additional subjective construal by the conceptualizer in the background – (here: RUDE FELLOW); the objective construal then completely fades away with subsequent reduction to the element of subjective construal.

(38) Engl. *boor* 'peasant' → 'rude fellow'
    (OED, s.v. *boor*, n., 1. and 3.a./b).

Subjectification in the sense of Traugott (e.g. 1999, Traugott and Dasher 2002) includes an additional feature in that, as (39) exemplifies, perspectivization moves from (an element of) a conceptualized described event in the extralinguistic world towards (an element of) a conceptualized speech event.

(39) Engl. *observe* 'to notice, remark, perceive' → 'to say by way of remark, state'
    (OED, s.v. *observe*, v., 8. and 10.).

Subjectification – in either of the two senses – is a case of metonymy, but not every metonymy is subjectification.

Secondly, a special case of subjectification in Traugott's sense in light of the concept of delocutivity introduced by Benveniste can be analyzed as metonymy (cf. Benveniste 1966; Anscombre, Létoublon, and Pierrot 1987; Koch 2012: 281–283). Accordingly, the now internationally well-known Italian greeting *ciao* goes back to Venetian *schiao* 'servant' (40a), which among other things was used as a greetings formula (in the sense of 'I am your humble servant'). A typical frame in which the word form *schiao*, the concept SERVANT and the speech act GREETING were linked by strong contiguity relations, prompted listeners to reanalyze the word *schiao* so that it took on *per se* the (speech act-)meaning GREETING (40b).

(40) (a) Venet. *schiao* 'servant' [commonly used in the greetings formula "Schiao!"]
 (b) Venet. *schiao* 'greeting' → It. *ciao* 'greeting'
 (cf. Cortelazzo and Paolo 1999, s.v. *ciao*).

Thirdly, a type of metonymic change should be mentioned here, which concerns not only words, but words in whole structures (see 4.). Verbs surrounded by their arguments are an almost ideal example of the linguistic expression of frames (cf. the well-known analysis of converse verbs such as English *buy* and *sell* in terms of frame-semantics, e.g. in Fillmore 1977).

One type of metonymic change can be designated *auto-conversion*, where one and the same lexical verb (like English *rent* in (41)) can express two opposing perspectivizations within the associated frame, which then manifests itself in a rearrangement of the syntactic form of the arguments relative to their semantic roles ((a)→(b)).

Auto-converse change also occurs with nouns, such as CLat. *hospes* (42) where the relation HOSPITALITY can be seen in both of the two opposing perspectives HOST and GUEST (cf. also 2.3.3.5.).

(41) (a) Engl. *The tourists **rent**ed a boat from the fisherman.*
 (b) Engl. (Am.) *The fisherman **rent**ed a boat to the tourists.*

(42) CLat. *hospes* (> e.g. It. *ospite*, Sp. *huesped*, etc.) 'host' (in It.) → 'guest' (in It. und Sp.)
 (Ernout and Meillet 1994, s.v. *hospes*; Walde and Hofmann 1938, s.v. *hospes*).

2.3.3.4 Metaphorical change

In the rhetorical tradition, the term *metaphor* is, firstly, commonly used in the broad sense of trope (especially in Aristotle, *Poetica* 21, 7 p. 1457 b), and secondly – and this is of special interest to us here – as a specific trope, which, as a reduced comparison, is based on similarity ("similitudinis est ad verbum unum contracta brevitas": Cicero, *De oratore* 3, 39, 157). As for metaphorical catachresis (see 1.1.), the metaphorical principle was already recognized as a form of meaning change in rhetoric. The following are typical examples of metaphorical change:

(43) OEngl. *bælg* 'bag, purse'→ MEngl. *bely* 'body part between the breast and the thighs'
(OED, s.v. *belly*, n., I.1. and II.3.a.; cf. also Figure 1 in section 1.2.).

(44) OFr. *chevalet* 'little horse'→ MFr. *chevalet* 'trestle'
(Rey 1992, s.v. *cheval*).

(45) ModEngl. *shark* 'fish of the sub-order *Squali*'→ MEngl. 'ruthless, greedy person'
(OED, s.v. *shark*, n.[1], 1.a. and 2.a.).

(46) OEngl. *scearp* (> ModEngl. *sharp*) 'well adapted for cutting or piercing'→ 'acute (of sight)'
(OED, s.v. *sharp*, a. and n.[1], A.1.a. and A.3.c.).

(47) Sp. *largo* 'long (spatial)'→ 'long (of time)'
(Corominas and Pascual 1980–1991, s.v. *largo*).

(48) MEngl. *spenden* 'to pay out'→ 'to employ, pass (time)'
(OED, s.v. *spend*, v.[1], 1.a. and 4.a.).

(49) OFr. *monter* 'to go up'→ 'to rise, increase'
(Rey 1992, s.v. *monter*).

Here we can see some typical patterns of similarity relations between target concept and source concept, that have already been identified in the traditional understanding of metaphor: the similarity between body parts and distinctively shaped objects (43), between everyday objects and animals (44), between humans and animals (45), between time and space (47), between the abstract and concrete (47)–(49), as well as synesthetic similarity (46). As with metonymy (2.3.3.3.), the purely taxonomic orientation of structural semantics (cf. 2.3.3.1.) and its restriction to intra-linguistic signifiers meant it had no devices for adequately capturing metaphor. As the examples show, the relevance of encyclopedic knowledge is also evident in metaphor. Here, too, the association psychology interpretation of metaphor overcame the former limitation by returning to the similarity relation in the works of Roudet (1921) and subsequently Ullmann (1957: 231–234, 1964: 218–220) as well as Jakobson's (1971) structuralism open to phenomenology. Cognitive semantics was able to overcome the latter restriction – again unsurprisingly – making metonymy, metaphor, and hence metaphorical change one of its central research areas.

Lakoff and Johnson's (1980) Conceptual Metaphor Theory, in which the domain concept is key, has been one of the classical components of cognitive semantics for over thirty years. Unlike metonymy (2.3.3.3.), source concept and target concept here belong by definition to two different domains (cf. Croft 1993). The metaphorical effect consists in the mapping from a source domain to a target domain. The blurring of the domain concept, which we objected to in 2.3.3.3., turns out to be less serious here. Indeed, the conceptual leap that is typical of metaphor takes place sometimes between the very general forms of perception SPACE and TIME in Kant's sense (e.g. (47)) or between different forms of perception (synesthesia; e.g. (46)), sometimes between different frames in the sense of 2.3.3.3. (e.g. (43), (48) and (49)), and in some cases also between different taxonomies (e.g. (44), (45); it remains open to investigation whether this is true for both the frame criterion and the taxonomic criterion). All this may be summarized, at least from a metaphor-theoretical perspective, under the key word domain, but without the important differentiation of subtypes that we have sketched out.

A crucial factor in mapping across frames, taxonomies, etc., is without doubt a relation of analogy or similarity. It should be clarified here that metaphorical similarities – no different, incidentally, to contiguities (see 2.3.3.3.) – are not to be understood as relations pre-existing in the world between pre-existing concepts, but that metaphorizing consists in detecting similarities (cf. Lakoff and Johnson 1980: 112–114, 147–155, 210–222).

As a *similarity* effect *across frames, taxonomies*, etc., metaphor (and the resulting change though lexicalization) is very clearly differentiated from other semantic effects (and the resulting forms of change): in the case of co-hyponymous transfer (2.3.3.2.), there is a similarity effect within taxonomies, in the case of metonymy (2.3.3.3.) a contiguity effect within frames.

An interesting observation from a taxonomic perspective, is that in many cases the similarity relation between the source concept and the target concept only holds, strictly speaking, for a prototypical subset of the source referent class (cf. Geeraerts 1997: 75 f.; Koch 1995: 39, 1999: 149–151). A particularly clear example of this can be found in (45). To understand this metaphor, it is essential to conceive of the shark as a rapacious man-eating beast, to see the blue, gray and man-eating sharks as prototypes rather than, for example, the harmless whale sharks or basking sharks. During the lexicalization process such restrictions on the prototypical subsets are usually abandoned (for a similar effect in metonymy see. 2.3.3.3.).

Already Weinrich (1967) was key in going beyond traditional metaphor theory by highlighting that not only are individual source and target pairs related to each other, but so too are all image fields present in human languages. Continuing in this vein, but with a greater emphasis on the conceptual level, Lakoff and Johnson's Conceptual Metaphor Theory, which has already been mentioned, sees a link between entire source concept networks and entire target concept networks. The individual metaphor therefore appears to be merely the application of a general metaphorical pattern, which is apparent in a greater number of meaning changes and/or non-lexicalized metaphors.

This approach explains the mapping between entire frames particularly well. Underlying the example in (48) is the pattern TIME IS MONEY (Lakoff and Johnson 1980: 7–9), which is also apparent in other expressions such as English *amount of time*, *lose time*, *waste one's time*, etc. Within the source frame MONEY, the concepts MONEY, AMOUNT, LOSE, WASTE etc. have similar contiguity relationships to each other as the concepts TIME, PERIOD, BE UNABLE TO CONTROL, PASS NEEDLESSLY, etc. The very common orientational pattern MORE IS UP; LESS IS DOWN (Lakoff and Johnson 1980: 15 f.) underlies the example in (49) and is also found, for example, in French *hausse des prix* 'rise of the prices', *prix élevés* 'high prices', *baisse des prix* 'fall of prices', etc. In view of cases like (47), we can, continuing Lakoff and Johnson's line of thought, include among our forms of perception a fundamental metaphorical pattern TIME IS SPACE, for which research has already provided overwhelming evidence (cf. e.g. Haspelmath 1997).

In cases like (43), a fundamental target frame BODY can be identified, although it is not possible to assign it to a specific typical source frame. Also, when mapping between taxonomies ((44), (45)), metaphorical patterns can be identified that are, at best, of such generality that they inevitably become overgenerating: ARTEFACTS ARE ANIMALS (44) or HUMANS ARE ANIMALS (45). With synesthetic metaphors like (46), the potential idiosyncrasy of the metaphor becomes even more pronounced.

Lakoff and Johnson's Conceptual Metaphor Theory is finally pushed to its limits with expressive metaphors. The expressive-negative value of *butcher* in the metaphor *in praesentia* in the discourse in (50) cannot be understood in terms of a simple binary mapping model BUTCHER → SURGEON, since a butcher carries out his work as conscientiously as a surgeon does.

(50) Engl. *That surgeon is a butcher.*

(51) Fr. *boucher* 'butcher'→ 'unskillful surgeon or doctor'
 (TLFi, s.v. *boucher*, I.A.; ÉTYMOL. ET HIST., 3.b).

These are theories undoubtedly better suited to creating something completely new from the interaction between concepts in the center, such as Black's (1962) interaction theory of metaphor or, more recently, – admittedly going well beyond the question of metaphor – blending theory (cf. Fauconnier 1997: especially 18–25, 168–171; Fauconnier and Turner 2002; Geeraerts 2010: 201–213). The latter proposes a ternary model with, initially, two mutually interacting mental spaces (an input space 1 SURGEON and an input space 2 BUTCHER), and thirdly – as emergent structure – a blended space SURGEON AS BUTCHER, which reveals the opposition between GOAL: HEALING (space 1) and MEANS: BUTCHERY (space 2) and with it the emerging element BUNGLE, UNSKILLFULNESS (blended space) (cf. Evans and Green 2006: 401–406). This may now be relevant not only for metaphors in the discourse such as (50), but also for metaphorical change of meaning, such as (51), where the same semantic effect as in (50) has been lexicalized in French. Here, it seems that the lexicalized target concept does not corresponds to the input space 1, but to the blended space UNSKILLFUL SURGEON/DOCTOR. Example (45) English *shark* could certainly be similarly analyzed, while Lakoff and Johnson's binary mapping model seems sufficient for (47) Spanish *largo*. It is possible to classify corresponding metaphors (including cases of metaphorical meaning change) in this way, whether purely catachrestic in nature in the sense of classical rhetoric (see 2.1.1), so that the binary mapping-model suffices to describe them (as in (44), (46) – (49)), or whether they contain an expressive surplus, which cannot be captured without the ternary blending model (as in (45), (51), originally also (43)).

All in all, the principal difference between metaphorical and metonymic meaning change should be clear. This does not, however, contradict the fact that they can also be connected with each other (metaphtonymy; cf. Goossens 1990; Geeraerts 2002; 2010: 220–222). In the detail, they concern very different scenarios:

(52) (a) Engl. *giggle* 'to laugh in a nervous way' → 'to say while giggling'
 (b) Engl. *giggle* 'to say while giggling' → 'to say as if giggling'

(53) Engl. *catch s. o.'s ear* 'ensure s. o.'s attention'

(54) Engl. *beat one's breast* 'to beat one's breast' → 'to express guilt'

(55) CLat. *altus* 'high' → It. *alto* 'of great amount'
(Georges and Georges 1913, s.v. 1. *altus*; Pfister [1984 ff.], s.v. *alto*, col. 379, 25 ff.; col. 386, 9–21).

Firstly, in the course of diachronic filiation, a metonymic step in meaning change (e.g. (52a)) can be simply followed by a metaphorical step (in this case (52b)): metaphor from metonymy. Secondly, both types of change can be interrelated – typically in idioms – as in (53), where the constituent *catch s.th.* metaphorically takes on the meaning 'ensure s.th.', while the constituent *ear* metonymically takes on the meaning 'attention': metaphor within metonymy. Thirdly, a metonymic step may in retrospect be interpreted as metaphorical – this could be called metonymy into metaphor. Leaving aside contentious examples like (54) (Riemer 2001: 386–390 prefers the term hypermetonymy because the metaphorical interpretation does not seem to have been proven), and focusing instead on cases like (55), what is originally a metonymy (a great amount of things forms a HIGH pile) is reinterpreted as a metaphor (high in the vertical spatial dimension is seen as similar to a great amount; cf. Taylor 1995: 138; Radden 2002). Since (55), viewed from the end state, is a case of the concrete orientational metaphorical pattern MORE IS UP; LESS IS DOWN (see above, also (49)), manifest in many languages, the metaphorical interpretation is ensured (which is why an Italian example was chosen here, because the Latin etymon did not have the meaning 'of great amount', since this is a historically authenticated case of meaning change).

2.3.3.5 Meaning change based on contrast

Contrast-based meaning change is a relatively rare occurrence. A comparatively widespread form is antiphrastic change (cf. Blank 1997: 220–225). As the well-known example in (56) illustrates, the contrast relation here is not a direct one between the source concept and the target concept, but rather occurs at the level of connotation: in earlier agrarian societies the weasel was seen as MALICIOUS, because it rampaged in chicken coops; it seemed therefore to be the opposite of NICE.

(56) OFr. *belete* 'nicey' → 'weasel' (> ModFr. *belette*)

The antiphrasis here must have been a euphemistic change of designation (see 2.1.2., Figure 1) with the purpose of avoiding the taboo (cf. Allan and Burridge 1991), with the result that the traditional Old French word *mostoile* was replaced by *belete*. In other cases of antiphrastic change the innovation was likely due to irony in the discourse (on the rhetorical background, see Knox 1989).

Auto-antonymous change [or "enantiosemy", editors' comment], in which a word actually takes on the meaning of its exact antonym (cf. Blank 1997: 225–229), is extremely rare. Cases such as CLat. *hospes* (42) and CLat. *altus* (57) only apparently belong here, but are in reality auto-converse; the latter does not, as Abel (1884) thought, demonstrate the inherent contrariety of the words, especially in old languages, but can express – metonymically – the perspective from both the bottom and the top of the vertical dimension (cf. Blank 1997: 279). A real auto-antonymous example is *bad* in English slang (58), from which it is clear that permanent auto-antonymy can generally arise only under very special expressive conditions, otherwise it would lead to communication problems.

(57) CLat. *altus* 'high' → 'deep'
(Ernout and Meillet 1994, s.v. *altus*; Walde and Hofmann 1938, s.v. *alō*).

(58) Engl. *bad* 'not good' → Engl. (slang) 'possessing an abundance of favorable qualities'
(OED, s.v. *bad*, a., A.1.4.b).

2.3.3.6 Pejorization and meliorization of meaning

Two axiological types of meaning change are occasionally recognized: pejorization and meliorization of meaning (cf. the literature cited at the beginning of 2.3.3.) As, however, Blank (1997: 333–339) has convincingly shown, we are here dealing with a fundamental misconception. There may, indeed, in many cases of meaning change be a pejorative or ameliorative effect, individually specified in each instance, but in all cases one of the common types of meaning change as discussed in 2.3.3.1. – 2.3.3.5 is present. Thus metonymy underlies the 'pejorization' in English *boor* (38), metaphor in Fr. *boucher* (51) and antiphrastic change in Fr. *belette* (56); metonymy underlies the meliorization in Venet. *schiao* > It. *ciao* (40) and auto-antonymous change in English *bad* (58). Ullmann (1964: 231–235) very rightly saw in this case that pejorization and meliorization belong not to nature but only to the consequences of semantic change.

2.3.3.7 Intensification and weakening of meaning

Also the cases of intensification and weakening of meaning variously listed in the text books (cf. the literature cited at the beginning of 2.3.3.) do not constitute meaning changes in their own right, but are rather a consequence of certain common types of meaning change as discussed in 2.3.3.1.–2.3.3.5. (cf. Blank 1997: 326–333 on what follows).

Various types of semantic change (especially metonymy, metaphor, specialization, antiphrastic change) can have the function of euphemistic changes of designation (see 2.1.2.), for example, OFr. *belete* (56) instead of *mostoile* for the target concept WEASEL. From an onomasiological perspective, the euphemistic substitute has a weaker meaning than the original normal word because it acts as a disguise. We know from experience, however, that the new euphemistic designation becomes the normal word in the course of diachrony (as in the case just cited: ModFr. *belette*). The transformation from euphemism to normal word can then unequivocally be described as 'intensification of meaning'.

Conversely, various types of semantic change (especially metonymy, metaphor, generalization, auto-antonymous change) can function as expressive changes of designation. OEngl. *bælg* (43) instead of *búc* (cf. OED, s.v. *bouk*, 1.; see Figure 1 in section 2.1.2.) for the target concept BODY PART BETWEEN BREAST AND THIGHS may originally have been expressive in nature (more in the sense of PAUNCH – something like an emergent structure according to blending theory: 2.3.3.4). From an onomasiological perspective, the expressive substitute has a more intense meaning than the original normal word because it is more severe, often somewhat dysphemistic. We know from experience, however, that the new expressive designation becomes the normal word in the course of diachrony (as in the case just cited: MEngl. *bely* > ModEngl. *belly*; in this case the blended space PAUNCH fades out leaving only the input space 1 BODY PART BETWEEN BREAST AND THIGHS remaining in the long term). The transformation from the new expressive term to normal word can then unequivocally be described as weakening of meaning.

2.3.4 Lexical meaning change and parts of speech

In principle, the different types of meaning change occur in all word types. The examples cited so far have been mainly nouns as well as a series of verbs ((10), (15), (18), (39), (41), (48), (49), (52)), idioms ((53), (54)), and a few adjectives ((27), (46), (47), (55), (57), (58)). Since, because of their argument structure (valency), in semantic terms verbs express frames corresponding to all situation structures, and in syntactic terms create whole sentence patterns, the panorama of meaning change in verbs turns out on closer inspection to be considerably more complex than in other word types (cf. Blank 1997: 188–190, 205 f., 260–264, 272–278; Koch 2004). This can be illustrated with just a few examples. Meaning change may, for example, affect the argument-independent core of the verb's meaning, as is the case with the generalization of OEngl. *gān* (10) or the specializations from CLat. *collocāre* (18). The argument level can also be affected in varying ways in verbal meaning change. On the one hand, an (essentially metonymic) auto-conversion can take place (cf. 2.3.3.3. with the example English *rent* (41)), on the other hand, there can be a change in the semantic class of the verb and hence the argument roles. For instance, the subject and the direct object of English *observe* (39) in the original meaning are realized respectively as EXPERIENCER and an EXPERIENCED, which metonymically become (SPEECH) AGENT and THEME. Finally, a slot with an AGENT-role can be added to the argument structure in a causative metonymy, so that the PATIENT role no longer appears as a direct object, but as a subject ((59), although the reverse pattern also occurs with omission of the causative AGENT).

(59) Fr. *sortir* 'to go out' → 'to take out'
(Rey (1992), s.v. *sortir*).

As the examples we have cited suggest, adjectives do not generally exhibit such complex forms of meaning change, although metonymies, for example, can also be found, that recall changes of perspective within argument structures. Thus in English *happy* (27) the entity role characterized by this adjective (expressed as a head noun or subject of the copula), is metonymically transformed from EXPERIENCED to EXPERIENCER.

2.3.5 Relations between lexical meaning change and other processes of lexical diachrony

Meaning change, word formation and borrowing are traditionally cited as the main types of lexical change (and with it the creation of neologisms). However, in lexical diachrony various forms of relations arise between these types of processes.

Ullmann (1957: 238–240; 1964: 222f) considered ellipsis to be a separate type of meaning change based on contiguity of names (i.e. signifiers). On this view, Engl. *station* 'stopping place' (60a) acquires through syntagmatic contiguity with *railway* (b) the meaning of 'stopping place for railway trains' (c). On closer inspection, however, it becomes clear that this sort of ellipsis with semantic relevance in the lexicon is to be understood as a complex process that can be viewed from different perspectives (cf. Blank 1997: 281–297; Gévaudan 2007: 130–132, 166 f., 173). Step (60a) → (60b) is, semasiologically speaking, a case of word formation (composition); however, step (b) → (c) is, from an onomasiological perspective and hence with regard to the same concept STOPPING PLACE FOR RAILWAY TRAINS, a case of change of designation that takes place through ellipsis of a constituent (in this case the modifier). If we consider the word *station* in isolation, however, the relationship between (a) and (c) is, from a semasiological perspective, one of meaning change, in this case, specialization.

(60) (a) Engl. *station* 'stopping place'
    (b) Engl. *railway station* 'stopping place for railway trains'
    (c) Engl. *station* 'stopping place for railway trains'

Folk-etymology (cf. Durkin 2009: 202–206) does not have to go hand in hand with meaning change (cf. e.g. English [U.S. dialects] *sparrow-grass* for *asparagus*, where a previously unmotivated word gets a motivation without the meaning really changing). Sometimes, however, this is the case, and then Ullmann (1957: 234–238; 1964: 220–222) speaks of folk-etymology as a type of meaning change in its own right based on similarity of names (i.e. of signifiers). On this view, OFr. *ouvrable* 'intended for working' (61b) acquires the meaning 'with open shops' (61d) due to the similarity between the root and the signifier of the root of Fr. *ouvrir* (61c). Although here, too, things are more complex (cf. Blank 1997: 303–317). Step (61a) → (61b) is, from a diachronic perspective, a case of word formation (derivation). In the synchrony of Old French, *ouvrable* (61b) was motivated from *ouvrer* (61a). The latter verb died out on the way to modern French removing the motivation for *ouvrable*. A new motivation was now found in the verb *ouvrir* ((61c) → (61d)), with the consequence that the meaning of *ouvrable* altered accordingly. Comparison of (61b) with (61d) shows that the signifiers of the roots are not only formally similar, identical even, (see (61a) and (61c)) but also semantically contiguous, and that, therefore, in the bridging context *jour* ..., metonymic reanalysis (cf. 2.3.3.3.) has taken place, which according to Blank, can be observed if not in all then in nearly all cases of folk-etymology with meaning change.

(61) (a) OFr. *ouvrer* 'to work'
    (b) OFr. *ouvrable* 'intended for working' (in *jour ouvrable* 'working day')
    (c) Fr. *ouvrir* 'to open'
    (d) ModFr. *ouvrable* 'with open shops' (in *jour ouvrable* 'working day')

While in borrowings the signifier of the word in question – depending on the degree of integration – is adapted in varying degrees to the phonology of the target language, it is generally assumed that the word is borrowed with its source-language meaning (that is, with respect to the polysemy of the word in the source language, only with the sense relevant to the language contact situation). However, meaning change can arise *during* the borrowing process itself. There is, typically, reanalysis in the contact situation, whereby certain elements from the context characteristic of the source culture and/or the relevant extra-linguistic reality are read into the word meaning, the outcome being either specialization (e.g. (62)) or metonymic change (e.g. (63); cf. Winter-Froemel 2014):

(62) Sp. *sombrero* 'hat' → Engl. *sombrero* 'Mexican hat'

(63) Engl. *flipper* 'lever in a pinball machine' → Germ. *Flipper* 'pinball machine'

2.3.6 Causes, nature, and consequences of meaning change

As a first approximation, we can, after Ullmann (1964), distinguish between the causes, nature, and consequences of meaning change.

2.3.6.1 Causes/motivations of meaning change/innovation

As far as causes are concerned (cf. Ullmann 1964: 197–210), it should first be made clear that we are not actually dealing with the causes of the completed change, but at best the causes of the underlying innovation (cf. also Blank 1997: 370 f.; see 2.3.1.). Thus Blank (1999a; cf. also 1997: 345–405) speaks rather of the 'motivations' for lexical semantic change and, revising Ullmann's proposals, in particular from a pragmatic and cognitive-semantic point of view, mentions the following factors: (i) new concepts; (ii) abstractness of concepts/low accessibility of referents; (iii) sociocultural change; (iv) close conceptual/factual relations (frames, prototypicality, blurred boundaries); (v) inherent problems in the lexicon (complexity of words, lack of motivation, lexical gap); (vi) emotionally marked concepts (expressivity, taboo).

A clear distinction should be made between onomasiological and semasiological perspectives (section 2.1.2.): are we dealing with motivation for an innovation of designation or motivation for a meaning innovation? The distinction between innovations by the speaker and innovations by the hearer is now important (see 2.3.2.). In addition, a distinction should be made between motivation for the *fact* of meaning innovation as such and motivation for a particular *type* of innovation meaning (generalization, metonymy, metaphor, etc.).

From the speaker's perspective, there is a very general ultimate motivation for the *fact* of meaning innovation: the desire or need, should the occasion arise, for an innovation of designation (dependent only on the intention of the speaker: see 2.3.1.). In this sense, all of the above factors (i)–(vi) represent motivations for innovations of designation, which then in turn can be completed through meaning innovation (or other lexical means). Motivations for choosing specific *types* of meaning innovation arise only in some cases. It is well known that abstract concepts (ii) are preferably realized in concrete terms through metonymies or metaphors (2.3.3.4.: (47), (49), (55)). Sociocultural change (iii) can, through the reorganization of taxonomies (2.3.3.1.: (12)) or frames, lead to meaning innovations and then to changes. Word length (v) may suggest ellipses (2.3.5.: (60)). Metaphor (2.3.3.4.: (43), (45)), metonymy (2.3.3.3.) and auto-antonymy (2.3.3.5.: (58)) are particularly suited to expressive purposes.

From the hearer's perspective, the *fact* of the meaning innovation is only conceivable under conditions of reanalysis (2.3.2.). The only *types* of meaning innovation that are possible here are, as we have seen, specialization (2.3.3.1.: (19)) and metonymy (2.3.3.3.: (28)); and in the lexicon, also due to lack of motivation (v), in the form of folk-etymologies (2.3.5.: (61)).

The above factors (i)–(vi) may, accordingly reversed, also be seen as motivations for reductive meaning change (where (i) becomes an 'obsolete concept'). Here, in all cases we are now dealing with the *fact* of the reductive meaning change (in which there are no varying semantic types) and therefore solely motivation at the level of designation: Elimination of the need for a designation, especially in (i), or designation by another word for reasons (ii) – (vi).

2.3.6.2 The nature of meaning change

The nature of meaning change concerns the relation between innovation and change (2.3.1.), the roles of speaker and hearer in innovation (2.3.2.), and the types of lexical (2.3.3.) and grammatical meaning change. Types of meaning change concerns the different conceptual relations between SC and TC in Figure 1. If this criterion is strictly adhered to, a revision is needed of Ullmann's classification (1964: 211–235), according to which the types metaphor, metonymy, folk-etymology and ellipsis determine the nature of semantic change while generalization (Ullmann's extension), specialization (restriction), pejorization and meliorization belong to the consequences (for a review: Blank 1997: 43f, 193–197). The ambiguity of the term extension already noted in 2.3. is evident here. If it is taken in the sense of generalization, then it concerns, along with specialization, metonymy and metaphor, the conceptual relations SC-TC and is therefore central to the nature of meaning change. (The complex nature of folk-etymology and ellipsis was discussed in 2.3.5., the issue of pejorization and meliorization in 2.3.3.6.).

2.3.6.3 The consequences of meaning change

Taking the term extension as presented in 2.2.3. in the sense of 'increasing the number of senses' (which perfectly resonates with Ullmann), we arrive at the only actual remaining consequence of innovative meaning change, the emergence of polysemy, just as the consequence of reductive meaning change is the disappearance of a polysemy (cf. Blank 1997: 406–438; and 2.1 and 2.2. above).

2.4 Future directions

The various questions that remain open and the numerous theoretical and methodological ties with other areas open up a wealth of interesting new research perspectives in the field of meaning change, of which only a few are mentioned here.

With the huge upsurge in Corpus Linguistics in the last 25 years, it is possible to empirically and accurately investigate the issue of propagation (see 3.1.) with the help of extensive diachronic corpora, although this requires not only technical know-how but also more profound methodological reflection (cf. the various contributions in Allan and Robinson 2012).

The effectiveness of a usage-based approach to the study of meaning change has already been noted (2.3.1.). It became clear that certain pragmatic innovation scenarios and certain semantic types of meaning innovation fit particularly well together (cf. on reanalysis: 2.3.3.1., 2.3.3.3.). This should be examined in greater depth. Since, as we saw, the perspective of the innovating speaker is primarily centered not on meaning innovation but on innovation of designation, the onomasiological perspective should give greater consideration to the usage-based view (see Fig. 1.) or at least be coupled with the semasiological perspective (cf. e.g. – with a different orientation in the detail – Koch 2008 [typology: see below]; Geeraerts, Gevaert, and Speelman 2012 [Corpus Linguistics: see above]; Winter-Froemel 2014).

We have seen that meaning change within the diachrony of the lexicon does not stand in isolation but interacts with other lexical processes (see 2.3.5.). It can even be shown that the different conceptual relations SC-TC, illustrated here in

2.3.3., as *one* dimension of lexical diachrony can be coupled in a variety of ways with the *second* dimension word formation and the *third* dimension borrowing (cf. Lipka 2002: 136 f.; Koch 1999: 157–159; 2001a: 231–233; 2012: 296–300; Blank 2003; Gévaudan 2007; cf. here also the parallels between meaning change in (11) and word formation in (19)).

Since Construction Grammar has in the meantime also opened up linguistic diachrony (cf. Traugott 2003; Bergs and Diewald 2008; Fried 2013), it seems reasonable to contemplate something like a meaning change of constructions, as constructions are indeed here conceived as linguistic signs with a list of contents. When Dancygier and Sweetser (2014: 127–161) speak of the figurative meaning of grammatical constructions, phenomena with a clear diachronic basis also come into view. But even in the lexicon, where word formations can be described in the framework of 'construction morphology' (Booij 2010), the above-mentioned three-dimensional approach offers the possibility of modeling lexical change, including meaning change, essentially as construction change (cf. Koch 2014).

It has become clear, sometimes implicitly, sometimes explicitly, that the individual semantic types of meaning change (2.3.3.) occur with varying frequency. In the perspective of the above three-dimensional lexical model, the problem is conceivable in the abstract: how often do the individual conceptual relations SC–TC identified for meaning change in 2.3.3. occur in processes of lexical change (including word formation and borrowing)? It would be worthwhile investigating why contiguity relations appear to be the most common (cf. Koch 2012: 300 f.).

If linguistic typology had until recently concentrated on grammar and phonology, something like a lexical/semantic typology has in the meantime emerged (cf. Luque Durán 2001; Koch 2001b; Koptjevskaja-Tamm 2008; Evans 2011). It is not only synchronic inventories that are relevant here, but also crosslinguistic observations on the polygenic SC → TC paths of meaning change and – from an onomasiological perspective – of change of designation, which gives us an insight into fundamental cognitive schemata (cf. in the area of grammar e.g. Bybee, Perkins, and Pagliuca 1994; in the area of the lexicon e.g. the various contributions in Vanhove 2008; Steinberg 2014; on a crosslinguistic examination of metaphorical schemas: Dancygier and Sweetser 2014).

2.5 References

Abel, Carl. 1884. *Über den Gegensinn der Urworte*, Leipzig: Wilhelm Friedrich.
Allan, Kathryn and Justyna A. Robinson (eds.). 2012. *Current methods in historical semantics*, Berlin & Boston: de Gruyter Mouton.

Allan, Keith and Kate Burridge. 1991. *Euphemism and dysphemism. Language use as shield and weapon*. New York etc.: Oxford University Press.
Anscombre, Jean-Claude, Françoise Létoublon, and Alain Pierrot. 1987. Speech act verbs, linguistic action verbs, and delocutivity. In Jef Verschueren (ed.) *Linguistic action. Empirical-conceptual studies*, 45–67. Norwood, N.J.: Ablex.
Aristotle. Aristotelis de poetica liber, textu Gulstoniano; cum prælectione, versione, et notis editoris, Gulielmi Cooke, A. M. Coll. Regal. Socii; ET In Academia Cantabrigiensi Graecae Linguae Praelectoris. Accedit Elegia Grayiana græce. Cantabrigiæ, MDCCLXXXV. [1785]. Eighteenth Century Collections Online. Gale, CW3316869475.
Barcelona, Antonio. 2002. Clarifying and applying the notions of metaphor and metonymy in cognitive linguistics: An update. In René Dirven and Ralf Pörings (eds.) [Cognitive Linguistics Research 20] *Metaphor and Metonymy in Comparison and Contrast*, 207–277. Berlin & New York: De Gruyter Mouton.
Barlow, Michael and Suzanne Kemmer (eds.). 2000. *Usage-based models of language*. Stanford: Stanford University Press.
Benveniste, Émile. 1966. Les verbes délocutifs. In Émile Benveniste, *Problèmes de linguistique générale (I)*, 277–285. Paris: Gallimard.
Bergs, Alexander and Gabriele Diewald (eds.). 2008. *Constructions and language change*. Berlin & New York: Mouton de Gruyter.
Black, Max. 1962. Metaphor. In Max Black *Models and metaphors*, 22–47. Ithaca, N.Y.: Cornell University Press.
Blank, Andreas. 1997. *Prinzipien des lexikalischen Bedeutungswandels am Beispiel der romanischen Sprachen*. Tübingen: Niemeyer.
Blank, Andreas. 1999a. Why do new meanings occur? A cognitive typology of the motivation for lexical semantic change. In Andreas Blank and Peter Koch (eds.) *Historical semantics and cognition*, 61–89. Berlin & New York: Mouton de Gruyter.
Blank, Andreas. 1999b. Co-presence and succession. A cognitive typology of metonymy. In Panther, Klaus-Uwe and Günter Radden (eds.) *Metonymy in language and thought*, 169–191. Amsterdam & Philadelphia: Benjamins.
Blank, Andreas. 2001. Pathways of lexicalization. In Haspelmath, Martin, Ekkehard König, Wulf Oesterreicher, and Wolgang Raible (eds.) *Language typology and language universals. An international handbook*, 2 vol, 1596–1608. Berlin & New York: Walter de Gruyter.
Blank, Andreas. 2003. Words and concepts in time: towards diachronic cognitive onomasiology. In Eckardt, Regine, Klaus von Heusinger, and Christoph Schwarze (eds.) *Words in time. Diachronic semantics from different points of view*, 37–65. Berlin & New York: Walter de Gruyter.
Booij, Geert. 2010. *Construction morphology*. Oxford: Oxford University Press.
Bréal, Michel. 1921. *Essai de sémantique (Science des significations)*, 5th edn. Paris: Hachette.
Brinton, Laurel J. and Traugott, Elizabeth C. 2005. *Lexicalization and language change*. Cambridge: Cambridge University Press.
Bybee, Joan L. 2006. From usage to grammar. The mind's response to repetition. *Language*, vol. 82, no. 2, pp. 711–733.
Bybee, Joan L., Revere Perkins, and William Pagliuca. 1994. *The evolution of grammar. Tense, aspect and modality in the languages of the world*. Chicago: University of Chicago Press.
Campbell, Lyle. 2013. *Historical linguistics. An introduction*, 3rd edn. Edinburgh: Edinburgh University Press.

Cicero, Marcus Tullius. 1942. *De oratore*. With an English translation by E.W.Sutton, completed by H. Rackham. London: Heinemann.
Corominas, Joan and José A. Pascual. 1980–1991. *Diccionario crítico etimológico castellano e hispánico*, 6 vol. Madrid: Gredos.
Cortelazzo, Manlio and Zolli Paolo. 1999. *Il nuovo etimologico: DELI – Dizionario etimologico della lingua italiana*, 2nd edn. Bologna: Zanichelli.
Coseriu, Eugenio. 1964. Pour une sémantique diachronique structurale. *Travaux de Linguistique et de Littérature*, vol. 2, no. 2, pp. 139–186.
Coseriu, Eugenio. 1988. Linguistic change does not exist. In Albrecht, Jörn, Jens Lüdtke and Harald Thun (eds.) *Energeia und Ergon. Sprachliche Variation – Sprachgeschichte – Sprachtypologie. Studia in honorem Eugenio Coseriu*, 3 vol., 147–157. Tübingen: Narr.
Croft, William. 1993. The role of domains in the interpretation of metaphors and metonymies. *Cognitive Linguistics*, 4: 335–370. [also in René Dirven and Ralf Pörings (eds.) [Cognitive Linguistics Research 20] *Metaphor and metonymy in comparison and contrast*, 161–206. Berlin & New York: De Gruyter Mouton]
Croft, William. 2000. *Explaining language change. An evolutionary approach*. Harlow etc.: Longman.
Croft, William and D. Alan Cruse. 2004. *Cognitive linguistics*. Cambridge etc.: Cambridge University Press.
Cruse, D. Alan. 2000. *Meaning in language. An introduction to semantics and pragmatics*. Oxford: Oxford University Press.
Dancygier, Barbara and Eve Sweetser. 2014. *Figurative language*. Cambridge: Cambridge University Press.
De Smet, Hendrik and Jean-Christophe Verstraete. 2006. Coming to terms with subjectivity. *Cognitive Linguistics*, 17: 365–392.
Detges, Ulrich and Richard Waltereit. 2002. Grammaticalization vs. reanalysis: a semantic-pragmatic account of functional change in grammar. *Zeitschrift für Sprachwissenschaft*, 21: 151–195.
Dik, Simon C.. 1977. Inductive generalizations in semantic change. In Paul J. Hopper (ed.) *Studies in descriptive and historical linguistics: Festschrift for Winfred P. Lehmann*, 283–300. Amsterdam & Philadelphia: John Benjamins.
Dirven, René. 1993. Metonymy and metaphor. Different mental strategies of conceptualisation. *Leuvense Bijdragen*, 82: 1–28.
Durkin, Philip. 2009. *The Oxford guide to etymology*. Oxford: Oxford University Press.
Ernout, Alfred and Alfred Meillet. 1994. *Dictionnaire étymologique de la langue latine*, 4th edn. Paris: Klincksieck.
Evans, Nicholas. 2011. Semantic typology. In Jae Jung Song (ed.), *The Oxford handbook of linguistic typology*, 504–533. Oxford & New York: Oxford University Press.
Evans, Vyvyan and Melanie Green. 2006. *Cognitive linguistics. An introduction*. Edinburgh: Edinburgh University Press.
Fauconnier, Giles. 1997. *Mappings in thought and language*. Cambridge, etc.: Cambridge University Press.
Fauconnier, Giles and Mark Turner. 2002. *The way we think. Conceptual blending and the mind's hidden complexities*. New York: Basic Books.
Feyaerts, Kurt. 2000. Refining the inheritance hypothesis. Interaction between metaphoric and metonymic hierarchies. In Antonio Barcelona (ed.) *Metaphor and metonymy at the crossroads. A cognitive perspective*, 59–78. Berlin & New York: Mouton de Gruyter.

Fillmore, Charles J. 1977. Scenes-and-frames-semantics. In Antonio Zampolli (ed.) *Linguistic structures processing*, 55–81. Amsterdam: Benjamins.
Fried, Mirjam. 2013. Principles of constructional change. In Thomas Hoffmann and Graeme Trousdale (eds.) *The Oxford handbook of construction grammar*, 419–437. Oxford: Oxford University Press.
Geeraerts, Dirk. 1997. *Diachronic prototype semantics. A contribution to historical lexicology*. Oxford: Clarendon.
Geeraerts, Dirk. 2002. The interaction of metaphor and metonymy in composite expressions. In René Dirven and Ralf Pøring (eds.) *Metaphor and metonymy in comparison and contrast*, 435–465. Berlin & New York: Mouton de Gruyter.
Geeraerts, Dirk. 2006. A rough guide to cognitive linguistics. In Dirk Geeraerts (ed.) *Cognitive linguistics. Basic readings*, 1–28. Berlin & New York: Mouton de Gruyter.
Geeraerts, Dirk. 2010. *Theories of lexical semantics*. Oxford: Oxford University Press.
Geeraerts, Dirk, Caroline Gevaert and Dirk Speelman. 2012. How *anger* rose: Hypothesis testing in diachronic semantics. In Kathryn Allan and Justyna A. Robinson (eds.) (2012) *Current methods in historical semantics*, 109–131. Berlin & Boston: de Gruyter Mouton.
Georges, Karl Ernst and Heinrich Georges. 1913. *Ausführliches lateinisch-deutsches Handwörterbuch*, 8th edn. Hannover: Hahnsche Buchhandlung.
Gévaudan, Paul. 2007. *Typologie des lexikalischen Wandels. Bedeutungswandel, Wortbildung und Entlehnung am Beispiel der romanischen Sprachen*. Tübingen: Stauffenburg.
Gévaudan, Paul. 2008. Tropen und Figuren. In Ulla Fix, Andreas Gardt and Joachim Knape (eds.) *Rhetorik und Stilistik / Rhetoric and stylistics*, 728–742. Berlin & New York: Mouton de Gruyter.
Goossens, Louis. 1990. Metaphtonymy: The interaction of metaphor and metonymy in expressions for linguistic action. *Cognitive Linguistics* 1, 3223–3240.
Grice, H. Paul. 1975. Logic and conversation. In Peter Cole and Jerry L. Morgan (eds.), *Speech acts*, 41–58. New York: Academic Press.
Haspelmath, Martin. 1997. *From space to time. Temporal adverbials in the word's languages*. München: LINCOM EUROPA.
Hjelmslev, Louis. 1970. Pour une sémantique structurale. In Louis Hjelmslev, *Essais linguistiques*, 2nd edn, 96–112. København: Nordisk Sprog-og Kulturforlag.
Hock, Hans Heinrich and Brian D. Joseph. 1996. *Language history, language change, and language relationship. An introduction to historical and comparative linguistics*. Berlin & New York: Mouton de Gruyter.
Holenstein, Elmar. 1972. *Phänomenologie der Assoziation. Zur Struktur und Funktion eines Grundprinzips der passiven Genesis bei E. Husserl*. Den Haag: Nijhoff.
Jakobson, Roman. 1971. Two aspects of language and two types of aphasic disturbances. In Roman Jakobson and Morris Halle. *Fundamentals of language*, 43–67. Den Haag & Paris: Mouton.
Keller, Rudi. 1994. *On language change. The invisible hand in language*. New York: Routledge.
Kleiber, Georges. 1999. *Problèmes de sémantique. La polysémie en questions*. Villeneuve d'Ascq: Presses Universitaires du Septentrion.
Knox, Dilwyn. 1989. *Ironia. Medieval and renaissance ideas on irony*. Leiden etc.: Brill.
Koch, Peter. 1994. Gedanken zur Metapher – und zu ihrer Alltäglichkeit. In Annette Sabban and Christina Schmitt (eds.) *Sprachlicher Alltag. Linguistik – Rhetorik – Literaturwissenschaft. Festschrift für Wolf-Dieter Stempel 7. Juli 1994*, 201–225. Tübingen: Niemeyer.

Koch, Peter. 1995. Der Beitrag der Prototypentheorie zur Historischen Semantik. Eine kritische Bestandsaufnahme. *Romanistisches Jahrbuch*, 46: 27–46.
Koch, Peter. 1997. Diskurstraditionen: zu ihrem sprachtheoretischen Status und ihrer Dynamik. In Barbara Frank, Thomas Haye and Doris Tophinke (eds.) *Gattungen mittelalterlicher Schriftlichkeit*, 43–79. Tübingen: Narr.
Koch, Peter. 1999. Frame and contiguity: On the cognitive bases of metonymy and certain types of word formation. In Klaus-Uwe Panther and Günter Radden (eds.), *Metonymy in language and thought*, 139–167. Amsterdam & Philadelphia: Benjamins.
Koch, Peter. 2001a. Metonymy: unity in diversity. *Journal of Historical Pragmatics*, 2: 201–244.
Koch, Peter. 2001b. Lexical typology from a cognitive and linguistic point of view. In Martin Haspelmath, Ekkehard König, Wulf Oesterreicher and Wolfgang Raible (eds.). *Language typology and language universals. An international handbook*, vol 2: 1142–1178. Berlin & New York: de Gruyter.
Koch, Peter. 2004. Rollensemantik – diachronische Aspekte. In Rolf Kailuweit and Martin Hummel (eds.). *Semantische Rollen*, 421–434. Tübingen: Narr.
Koch, Peter. 2005. Taxinomie et relations associatives. In Adolfo Murguía (ed.) *Sens et Références/Sinn und Referenz. Mélanges Georges Kleiber/Festschrift für Georges Kleiber*, 159–191. Tübingen: Narr.
Koch, Peter. 2008. Cognitive onomasiology and lexical change: Around the eye. In Martine Vanhove (ed.). *From polysemy to semantic change*, 107–137. Amsterdam & Philadelphia: Benjamins.
Koch, Peter. 2012. The pervasiveness of contiguity and metonymy in semantic change. In Kathryn Allan and Justyna A. Robinson (eds.). *Current methods in historical semantics*, 259–311. Berlin & Boston: de Gruyter Mouton.
Koch, Peter. 2014. Between word formation and meaning change. In Franz Rainer, Wolfgang U. Dressler, Francesco Gardani and Hans Christian Luschützky (eds.). *Morphology and Meaning*, 71–96. Amsterdam & Philadelphia: Benjamins.
Koch, Peter and Esme Winter-Froemel. 2009. Synekdoche. In Gerd Ueding (ed.). *Historisches Wörterbuch der Rhetorik*. 1992–2012, vol. 9, columns 356–366. Berlin & New York: de Gruyter.
Köhler, Wolfgang. 1947. *Gestalt psychology. An introduction to new concepts in modern psychology*. New York: Liveright.
Koptjevskaja-Tamm, Maria. 2008. Approaching lexical typology. In Martine Vanhove (ed.). *From polysemy to semantic change*, 3–52. Amsterdam & Philadelphia: Benjamins.
Lakoff, George. 1987. *Women, fire, and dangerous things. What categories reveal about the mind*. Chicago: University of Chicago Press.
Lakoff, George and Mark Johnson. 1980. *Metaphors we live by*. Chicago: University of Chicago Press.
Langacker, Ronald W.. 1987. *Foundations of cognitive grammar*, vol. 1: Theoretical prerequisites. Stanford: Stanford University Press.
Langacker, Ronald. 1999. Losing control: grammaticization, subjectification, and transparency. In Andreas Blank and Peter Koch (eds.) *Historical semantics and cognition*, 147–175. Berlin & New York: Mouton de Gruyter.
Lehmann, Christian. 1995. *Thoughts on grammaticalization*, 2nd edn. München: LINCOM.
Lehmann, Winfred P.. 1995. *Historical linguistics. An introduction*, 3rd edn. London: Routledge.
Levinson, Stephen C.. 2000. *Presumptive meanings. The theory of generalized conversational implicature*. Cambridge (Mass.): MIT Press.

Lipka, Leonhard. 2002. *English lexicology. Lexical structure, word semantics & word-formation*, 3rd edn. Tübingen: Narr.
Luque Durán, Juan de Dios. 2001. *Aspectos universales y particulares del léxico de las lenguas del mundo*. Granada: Granada Lingvistica.
Luraghi, Silvia and Vit Bubenik. 2011. *The continuum companion to historical linguistics*. London: Continuum.
Moliner, María. 2008. *Diccionario de uso del español. Edición electrónica 3.0*, Madrid: Gredos.
Nerlich, Brigitte. 1992. *Semantic Theories in Europe 1830–1930. From Etymology to Contextuality*. Amsterdam & Philadelphia: Benjamins.
Nerlich, Brigitte and David D. Clarke. 1999. Synecdoche as a cognitive and communicative strategy. In Andres Blank and Peter Koch (eds.) *Historical semantics and cognition*, 196–213. Berlin & New York: Mouton de Gruyter.
Neumann, Uwe. 1998. Katachrese. In Gerd Ueding (ed.). Historisches Wörterbuch der Rhetorik. 1992–2012, vol. 4, columns 911–915. Berlin & New York: de Gruyter.
Nunberg, Geoffrey. 1999. Transfers of meaning. *Journal of Semantics*, 17: 109–132.
OED = *Oxford English dictionary. CD-ROM version 3.00*. 2002. Oxford: Oxford University Press.
Panther, Klaus-Uwe and Linda L. Thornburg. 2007. Metonymy. In Dirk Geeraerts and Hubert Cuyckens (eds.). *The Oxford handbook of cognitive linguistics*, 236–263. Oxford: Oxford University Press.
Peirsman, Yves and Dirk Geeraerts. 2006.. Metonymy as a prototypical category. *Cognitive Linguistics*, 17: 269–316.
Pfister, Max. 1984 ff. *Lessico etimologico italiano*, vol. 1. Wiesbaden: Reichert.
Radden, Günter. 2002.. How metonymic are metaphors? In René Dirven and Ralf Pörings (eds.) [Cognitive Linguistics Research 20] *Metaphor and Metonymy in Comparison and Contrast*, 407–434. Berlin & New York: De Gruyter Mouton.
Radden, Günter and Zoltan Kövecses. 1999. Towards a theory of metonymy. In Klaus-Uwe Panther and Günter Radden (eds.). *Metonymy in language and thought*, 17–59. Amsterdam & Philadelphia: Benjamins.
Rey, Alain. 1992. *Dictionnaire historique de la langue française*, 2 vol., Paris: Dictionnaires le Robert.
Rhetorica ad Herennium. 2011. Theodor Nüßlein (ed.). Berlin: de Gruyter.
Riemer, Nicholas. 2001. Remetonymizing metaphor: hypercategories in semantic extension. *Cognitive Linguistics*, 12: 379–401.
Rosch, Eleanor. 1973. On the internal structure of perceptual and semantic categories. In Timothy E. Moore (ed.) *Cognitive development and the acquisition of language*, 111–144. New York: Academic Press.
Roudet, Léonce. 1921. Sur la classification psychologique des changements sémantiques. *Journal de psychologie*, 18: 676–692.
Rubin, Edgar. 1921. *Visuell wahrgenommene Figuren. Studien in psychologischer Analyse*. København etc.: Gyldendalske Boghandel.
Ruhl, Charles. 1989. *On monosemy. A study in linguistic semantics*. Albany: State University of New York Press.
Ruiz de Mendoza Ibáñez, Francisco José. 2000. The role of mapping and domains in understanding metonymy. In Antonio Barcelona (ed.) *Metaphor and metonymy at the crossroads. A cognitive perspective*, 109–132. Berlin & New York: Mouton de Gruyter.
Saussure, Ferdinand de. 1916. *Cours de linguistique générale*. Paris: Payot.

Schmid, Hans-Jörg. 2007. Entrenchment, salience, and basic levels. In Dirk Geeraerts and Hubert Cuyckens (eds.) *The Oxford handbook of cognitive linguistics*, 117–138. Oxford: Oxford University Press.
Seto, Ken-ichi. 1999. Distinguishing metonymy from synecdoche. In Klaus-Uwe Panther and Günter Radden (eds.) *Metonymy in language and thought*, 91–120. Amsterdam & Philadelphia: Benjamins.
Sihler, Andrew L. 2000.: *Language history: An introduction*. Amsterdam & Philadelphia: Benjamins.
Sperber, Dan and Deirdre Wilson. 1995. *Relevance. Communication and cognition*, 2rd edn. Oxford & Cambridge (Mass.): Blackwell.
Steinberg, Reinhild. 2014. *Lexikalische Polygenese im Konzeptbereich KOPF*. Tübingen: Stauffenburg.
Taylor, John R. 1995. *Linguistic categorization. Prototypes in linguistic theory*, 2nd edn. Oxford: Clarendon.
Tiktin, Hariton and Elsa Lüder. 2003. *Rumänisch-Deutsche Wörterbuch*, 2nd edn., vol. 3. Wiesbaden: Harrassowitz.
TLFi = *Trésor de la Langue Française Informatisée*, 2004. Nancy: ATILF.
Traugott, Elizabeth Closs. 1999. The rhetoric of counter-expectation in semantic change: a study in subjectification. In Blank, Andreas and Peter Koch (eds.) (1999) *Historical semantics and cognition*, 177–196. Berlin & New York: Mouton de Gruyter.
Traugott, Elizabeth Closs. 2003. Constructions in grammaticalization. In Brian D. Joseph and Richard D. Janda, (eds.) *The handbook of historical linguistics*, 624–647. Oxford: Blackwell.
Traugott, Elizabeth Closs and Richard B. Dasher. 2002. *Regularity in Semantic Change*. Cambridge: Cambridge University Press.
Ullmann, Stephen. 1957. *The principles of semantics. A linguistic approach to meaning*, 2nd edn. Oxford: Blackwell.
Ullmann, Stephen. 1964. *Semantics. An introduction to the science of meaning. The principles of semantics. A linguistic approach to meaning*, 2nd edn. Oxford: Blackwell.
Ungerer, Friedrich and Hans-Jörg Schmid. 1996. *An introduction to cognitive linguistics*. London & New York: Longman.
Vanhove, Martine (ed.). 2008. *From polysemy to semantic change*. Amsterdam & Philadelphia: Benjamins.
Walde, Alois and Hofmann, J.B. 1938. *Lateinisches etymologisches Wörterbuch*, 3rd edition, Heidelberg: Winter.
Weinrich, Harald. 1967. 'Semantik der Metapher, *Folia linguistica*, vol. 1, pp. 2–17.
Werth, Paul. 1974. Accounting for semantic change in current linguistic theory. In John M. Anderson, and Charles Jones (eds.) *Historical linguistics I*, 377–415. Amsterdam: North Holland.
Wilhelm, Raymund. 2001. Diskurstraditionen. In Martin Haspelmath, Ekkehard König, Wulf Oesterreicher, and Wolgang Raible (eds.) *Language typology and language universals. An international handbook*, vol I, 467–478. Berlin & New York: Walter de Gruyter.
Wilkins, David P.. 1996. Natural tendencies of semantic change and the search for cognates. In Mark Durie and Malcolm Ross (eds.) *The comparative method reviewed*, 264–304. Oxford: Oxford University Press.
Winter-Froemel, Esme. 2008. Towards a comprehensive view of language change. Three recent evolutionary approaches. In Ulrich Detges and Richard Waltereit (eds.) *The paradox of*

grammatical change. Perspectives from Romance, 215–250. Amsterdam/Philadelphia: Benjamins.
Winter-Froemel, Esme. 2011. Les tropes et le changement linguistique – points de contact entre la rhétorique et la linguistique. In Sarah Dessì Schmid, Ulrich Detges, Paul Gévaudan, Wiltrud Mihatsch, and Richard Waltereit (eds.). *Rahmen des Sprechens. Beiträge zur Valenztheorie, Varietätenlinguistik, Kreolistik, Kognitiver und Historischer Semantik. Peter Koch zum 60. Geburtstag*, 227–239. Tübingen: Narr.
Winter-Froemel, Esme. 2014. Formal variance and semantic changes in borrowing: Integrating semasiology and onomasiology. In Eline Zenner and Gitte Kristiansen (eds.) *New perspectives on lexical borrowing*, 65–100. Berlin: Mouton de Gruyter.

Alexei Shmelev
3. Semantic shifts as sources of enantiosemy

Abstract: Enantiosemy arises from semantic shifts when the meaning of a linguistic item takes two different paths with the resulting formation of two opposite meanings. It is a regular phenomenon probably depending on general principles of cognition and communication. A phenomenon close to enantiosemy is "void" negation (a linguistic unit has the same meaning with and without negation). The paper focuses on the most common sources of enantiosemy and "void" negation with the data mostly coming from Slavic languages, such as the following ones: shifts within a semantic frame (polarization of actants, other components of situation and ways to look at it); temporal metonymy; conventionalization of pragmatic inferences; conventionalization of irony; conventionalization of evaluation; reevaluation of a term of abuse; opposite results of similar actions; opposite ways of achieving similar results; interaction between surface negation and implied negation. In addition, enantiosemy may arise from various combinations of different mechanisms. The paper explicates the mechanisms involved and suggest a coherent theoretical analysis of the data. The overall conclusion is: in most cases, the phenomena of "void" negation and enantiosemy have regular sources and cross-linguistic parallels.

Very little research has been done on enantiosemy, and many instances of enantiosemy in Slavic languages remain unnoticed. The main purpose of the chapter is to introduce the types of enantiosemy and to reveal its sources.

The term *enantiosemy* in its narrow sense refers to the occurrence of two opposite meanings for one and the same lexical unit. For example, the Russian word *proslušat' (lekciju)* may mean either 'to hear' (a lecture) or 'to fail to hear, to miss' (a lecture) (so, enantiosemy in its narrow sense is a very particular case of polysemy). Hence another term is often used for enantiosemy, namely, auto-antonymy.

Enantiosemy in this narrow sense is a rare phenomenon. Indeed, the majority of theories of antonymy single out as obligatory the coincidence of combinatorial properties, or the possibility of substitutions in the same context. However, if the same word form regularly has two opposite meanings in the same context, how

---

Alexej Shmelev (Moscow Pedagogical University)

can the addressee know which of the two opposite meanings is intended? Examples of enantiosemy that one can find in the linguistic literature are unsystematic and may seem anecdotal, and the opposition of two meanings of the same lexical unit is generally not a genuine antonymy as it is understood in most theories of lexical semantics.[1]

In a broader sense, "enantiosemy" is a diachronic phenomenon; the term may be understood as referring to the opposition of two linguistic items (not only words but also phrases, morphemes and morphemic complexes; consider the Russian *isxod* 'end' and *isxodnaja točka* 'starting point') that go back to the same item; if we deal with words, they may belong to different parts of speech. Enantiosemy in the broader sense is not restricted to linguistic expressions whose explications only differ by negation or "more – less" or "good – bad" components; other distinctions may appear. In addition, the opposing meanings may be related to opposite perspectives or opposite participants of the same situation (as in the pairs *to sell* vs. *to buy*, *host* vs. *guest*). The opposite items may belong to the same language or to different languages (a phenomenon called "interlanguage enantiosemy"). For example, the Russian adjective *čerstvyj* 'stale' has the same origin as the Czech word *čerstvý* 'fresh'. In the present chapter, I will use the term "enantiosemy" in the broader sense.

Enantiosemy arises from semantic shifts when the meaning of a linguistic item takes two different paths with the resulting formation of two opposite meanings. My claim is that enantiosemy in the broader sense is a regular phenomenon probably depending on general principles of cognition and communication. My aim is to show that although instances of enantiosemy might seem to be of great variety, their sources may be reduced to quite regular and well-known semantic shifts. The most common sources of enantiosemy are the following: conventionalization of pragmatic effects (irony, evaluation, conversational implicatures), metonymy (including polarization of a given situation) and metaphors.

A phenomenon close to enantiosemy is "void negation". The term suggests that a linguistic unit has the same meaning with and without negation. The Russian word *pogoda* means 'weather' in standard Russian while *nepogoda* (literally, 'not-weather') means 'foul weather'; however, the word *pogoda* means 'foul weather' in some Russian dialects. In other words, *nepogoda* in standard language has the same meaning as *pogoda* in some dialects.

---

[1] Thus, in accordance with the approach developed within the framework of Moscow Semantic School, an antonymous relation is formed by lexical units whose explications when reduced to the level of semantic primitives differ by negation or "more-less" or "good-bad" components; the difference is reduced to these components alone (Apresjan 1995: 104).

Semantic shifts that can result in enantiosemy (and "void negation" as well) will be discussed in greater detail below (most examples are taken from Slavic languages, mainly Russian). It should be said that it is not important for the purposes of the present study whether the phenomena under consideration have been conventionalized and become part of the linguistic arsenal or occur only occasionally in speech. I am primarily interested in typology of semantic shifts that may lead to enantiosemy. From the standpoint of typology, regular occurrences in speech stand a good chance of being conventionalized in some languages and therefore are just as typologically significant as conventionalized phenomena. In other words, I will deal with occasional enantiosemic use, which may be regarded as "enantiosemy *in potential*", or "rudimentary" enantiosemy.

3.1 Conventionalization of pragmatic effects

3.1.1 Conventionalization of irony and reevaluation

Irony is the most common source of enantiosemy. It is usually understood as the use of a linguistic expression to denote something opposite to its literal meaning. In other words, irony may be described as an occasional enantiosemy. If the ironic use of an expression is conventionalized in a language, genuine enantiosemy occurs.

For instance, expressions referring to a need are often used ironically in the Russian language (with implied negation). The general rule is that such expressions in their literal meaning require the perfective aspect of the dependent verb, while the ironic use of the same expressions occurs in combination with the imperfective verb. For example, *Mne nužno tuda pojti* (perfective infinitive) means 'I need to go there' while *Nužno mne tuda xodit'* (imperfective infinitive) is understood as 'I do not need to go there' (although its literal meaning is 'I need to go there').[2] The ironic reading is conventionalized for some expressions; e.g., Russian dictionaries define the idiomatic meaning of the phrase *očen' nužno*

---

2 One may also note the difference in word order: the literal reading suggests the subject (in dative) followed by the word *nužno* (word-for-word translation is 'to-me it-is-necessary there to-go') while the ironic reading arises if the word *nužno* is followed by the subject (word-for-word translation is 'it-is-necessary to-me there to-go'); the sentence is pronounced with a specific "ironic" intonation in the latter case.

(literally, 'there is a great need') as 'there is no need' (the latter reading usually requires a dependent imperfective infinitive).

More often than not, enantiosemy resulting from irony involves evaluation, which may lead to the "good – bad" opposition. The most typical situation consists in a shift from "good" to "bad". Thus, the Russian adjective *xorošij* 'good' most often has an ironic reading when used in the shorter form *xoroš* (this reading is usually mentioned in Russian dictionaries as a separate lexical meaning). For example, the sentence *But then, I'm at fault too* (from *Gone with the Wind* by Margaret Mitchell) reads in the published Russian translation as *No ja tože, konečno, xoroš* (literally, 'But of course, I am good too'). One should add that the derivative *xorošen'kij* (with a diminutive suffix) is understood ironically in the collocation *xorošen'koe del'ce* (roughly, 'what a nice affair').

Enantiosemy involving evaluation does not necessarily result from irony. Its source may consist in adding two opposite evaluations to the originally neutral term (which is most typical of terms for 'odor', 'weather', 'appearance', and so on). The conventionalization of evaluative connotations can occur in a situation when a word is typically employed with evaluative elements. Enantiosemy arises when the evaluation differs in different types of usage. Evaluative connotations often arise for words with the meaning 'smell': when such connotations are conventionalized, they acquire the meaning 'pleasant smell, aroma, fragrance' or, in contrast, 'bad smell'. This leads to the opposite meanings (interlanguage enantiosemy) of the Russian word *von'* 'stink' and the etymologically identical Church Slavonic *vonja* 'aroma, fragrance' (the Russian word *obonjanie* 'sense of smell' with the same root is evaluatively neutral), the enantiosemy of the English word *odor*, which has the somewhat outdated meaning 'aroma, fragrance' and the common meaning in contemporary speech (for example, in deodorant ads) of 'bad smell'. The aforementioned Russian word *pogoda* 'weather' means 'fine weather' in some Russian dialects (namely, southern and western dialects) and 'bad weather, foul weather' in most other dialects. Consider also the Polish word *uroda* 'beauty' and the Russian word *urod* 'ugly person' (both words from *rod-* 'birth').[3]

Let us also consider the Russian adjective *zaslužennyj* (from the verb *zaslužit'* 'to deserve, to merit'). The *Small Academic Dictionary* (Evgen'eva 1981: 572) identifies the following shades of meaning for this adjective: 'attained through work or merits' (*zaslužennaja nagrada* 'merited award'; *zaslužennaja blagodarnost'* 'merited gratitude') and 'received in accordance with behavior or actions; just'

---

[3] Etymologically, the Russian word *urod* was formed with the negative prefix *u-*. Consider, however, the Russian word *roža* 'ugly face' derived from the same root *rod-* with no negative prefix.

(the actions are assumed to be bad: cf. *zaslužennoe nakazanie* 'merited punishment'; *zaslužennye upreki* 'merited blame'). Nevertheless, one can surmise that the meaning is the same in both cases and that the noun with which the adjective *zaslužennyj* is paired contributes the evaluative element. Even if we recognize that we are truly dealing with different "shades of meaning", these shades can hardly be called "opposite" in the strict sense of the word. In contrast, the noun *zasluga* 'merit' shows aspects of enantiosemy. In its principal and free meaning, it signifies 'someone's actions that deserve a positive evaluation' (*boevye zaslugi* 'distinguished military service'; *Èto ego zasluga* 'This is his work'; *U nego mnogo zaslug* 'He has a lot of achievements'). In the set expression *polučit' po zaslugam* 'to get what one deserves', it is more often used to refer to something that merits a negative evaluation (e.g., the standard headline of an article in a "Courtroom Reports" newspaper column is *Prestupnik polučil po zaslugam* 'The criminal got what he deserved'). Thus, the enantiosemy of the word *zasluga* exists only potentially today, and it would not apparently be justified to call it a fact of the contemporary Russian language. Nevertheless, in keeping with the approach of the present chapter, such cases can be viewed as "enantiosemy *in potential*": if the usage pointing to something that merits a negative evaluation is totally conventionalized and becomes the only possible case in Russian, we would deal with the enantiosemy of the word *zasluga* as such.

One can also mention the Russian word *angel* 'angel' (borrowed from Greek), which can denote both a holy angel (this is the free meaning) and an evil spirit (as a rule, this meaning appears only in fixed contexts: cf. *angel t'my* 'angel of darkness', *angel satany* 'angel of Satan'). In the latter case, the word is often pronounced (and spelled) *aggel* in usage oriented at Church Slavonic pronunciation; nevertheless, the pronunciation (and spelling) *angel* is also widespread, regardless of whether one is speaking about an "angel of light" or an "angel of darkness". This form is used, for example, in the Synodic translation of the Holy Scripture even when it indicates "evil angels". Here one can, once again, surmise two different lexical meanings: 'good spirit' and 'evil spirit' (and thus enantiosemy arises). At the same time, one can consider that the meaning is the same in both cases ('spiritual being endowed with reason and willpower' [Dal' 1978: 16]) and that the opposite evaluations derive from the context of usage (and then there is no enantiosemy, of course). We should note that counterparts of this word are marked by the same two types of use in most languages and, in particular, the English word *angel*. Thus the definition 'good spirit' proposed by Wierzbicka (1972: 13) clearly does not characterize all of its usages; cf. the following examples from the Bible (the Psalms are numbered in accordance with the Eastern tradition): *sending evil angels* (Psalms 77, 49); *everlasting fire, prepared for the devil and his angels* (Matthew 25, 41); *the angel of the bottomless pit* (Revelation 9, 11).

The question of whether a special lexical meaning should be postulated for them remains open; different solutions are proposed by different English dictionaries. Anyway, it is another example of "rudimentary" enantiosemy.

The opposite meaning often arises for words that express a strong emotional evaluation. For example, one often uses words whose original meaning involves the negative evaluation of an object to express admiration. Enantiosemy arises when such use becomes conventionalized, and it is often set down in dictionaries. For example, the *Small Academic Dictionary* ascribes to the word *šel'ma* 'rogue' a special shade of meaning that it interprets in the following way "...used as an expression of approval or admiration for something" (Evgen'eva 1984b: 709). Something similar occurs in the case of certain English swear words that can be used to express a friendly attitude towards the addressee. Cf. the examples in Larina (2003: 187), who notes that, for a number of swear words, "dictionaries set down a similar enantiosemy, in which opposite meanings are combined in a single lexeme": *You're a right, little bastard* (said tenderly by a girl to a youth); *Come here, you little bollocks* (said lovingly by a mother to her three-year son); *You are a silly bugger* (a friendly exclamation after a joke is uttered). In the same way, in the Canadian and U.S. slang *bad* means 'good; excellent, great, wonderful'; the English *terrific*, according to dictionaries, can mean both 'awful' (*terrific spectacle* 'awful sight') and 'stunning, marvelous' (the latter meaning is more widespread in modern speech).[4]

Opposite evaluations may be located not only on the "good – bad" axis but also on a scale of intensity: something can be characterized as being more or less significant, in which case we deal with "more-less" opposition. Let us consider several examples of the development of opposite evaluations on the scale "significant – insignificant" for certain pronominal expressions. As Pen'kovskii (1995; 2004: 50–60) has remarked, the Russian word *tak* 'so, just' serves as a universal marker of insignificance, i.e., of something that can be disregarded (*tak, pustjaki* 'just trifles'). In this way, the word *tak* can be used for intentionally decreasing significance: *Eto ne prestuplenie, a tak, melkij prostupok* 'This is no crime but just a small fault'; *On ne ženix, a tak, prosto znakomyj* 'He's no suitor but just an acquaintance'. At the same time, the word *tak* can be used as an intensifier (i.e., for increasing significance) – cf. *tak xorošo/ploxo* ≈ 'very good/bad'; *Ja tak ustal* ≈ 'I'm very tired'. Dictionaries also note the enantiosemy of the word *tak*. The *Small Academic Dictionary* gives the meaning of 'nothing, nothing special that would be worth speaking about' with the specification "used for evaluating someone's

---

4 It is worth noting that the English word *awful* was originally used as a term to mean full of awe, even better than awesome.

qualities (usually middling, not lofty) or actions (trifling, unsubstantial)" and, on the other hand, a meaning described as follows: "Denotes a high level or strong degree of manifestation of some quality, action or state" (Evgen'eva 1984b: 332).

A similar enantiosemy exists in the totality of uses of the word *ničego* 'nothing'. On the one hand, it has a meaning that is defined by the *Small Academic Dictionary* as 'insignificant, unimportant, without meaning' (Evgen'eva 1984b: 501). Pen'kovskii notes in the aforementioned article (1995: 38), "*ničego* is a frequent companion of *tak: – Èto tak, ničego* 'It's a trifle, nothing at all'; *Ničego, eto tak...* 'It's nothing, just a trifle'". On the other hand, it is used in the cliché *ničego sebe* 'holy cow! holy mackerel!', which indicates that something deserves special attention on account of its exceptional qualities.

The combination in one word of opposite evaluations on a scale of intensity does not just occur in pronominal expressions. For example, the Russian word *bescennyj* (literally, 'of no price') has an outdated meaning that is defined by the *Small Academic Dictionary* as 'not valuable, of little value' (Evgen'eva 1981: 87) and the modern "opposite" meaning 'invaluable, precious'.[5] Whereas the Russian expression *sumasšedšie ceny* (literally 'crazy prices') normally refers to extremely high prices, its counterparts in certain Western European languages (French *les prix fous*, English *crazy prices*) can refer both to extremely high and to extremely low prices (it is no coincidence that they are used in ads for unprecedented sales).[6]

3.1.2 Conventionalization of pragmatic inferences

A whole series of units acquires meanings that are opposite to their original meanings through the conventionalization of pragmatic inferences. Their appearance is governed by a general rule that Iakovleva (1994: 263) has formulated as follows: "the modalization of a word leads to the development of a meaning that is antonymic to its original prototypic meaning".[7] For example, the word *bukval'no*

---

[5] It is worth noting that the English *priceless*, which usually refers to something so valuable that no price can be set, can also mean 'worthless'; so, the same kind of enantiosemy exists in English.
[6] In Russian, the expression *smešnye ceny* 'funny prices' is most often used in ads about sales or discounts. However, the collocation *sumasšedšie ceny* 'crazy prices' has begun to appear in ads (especially translated ads) in recent years. Thus this expression is beginning to be enantiosemic in Russian, too.
[7] When Iakovleva (1994) uses such words as "modal", "modalization" etc., she means that the speaker emphasizes his/her statement rather than just describes reality.

'literally' in its "modal" meaning is an indicator of hyperbole (cf. *Ty bukval'no oglušil menja ètoj novost'ju* 'You literally stunned me with this news') and therefore sends a signal of sorts to the addressee: "Don't take me literally!" (in other words, negation is implied). One may note that when the word *bukval'no* in the "literal" meaning is stressed while if it has the "modal" meaning, the stress is on the collocating expression.[8]

The source of this kind of enantiosemy may be presented as follows. Using the word *bukval'no* in its "literal" sense, the speaker states, "I mean what I am saying". In fact, this follows from the principle of cooperativeness; there is no need to insist on it. If the speaker emphasizes that s/he actually means what s/he is saying (stressing the word *bukval'no*), this would suggest that the collocating expression might be understood figuratively (and the figurative interpretation might seem even more plausible) and the speaker commits him/herself to the "literal" interpretation. In contrast, if the collocating expression is stressed, the emphasis is on the choice of words: the word *bukval'no* indicates that the collocating figurative expression is perfectly suitable for the described situation. However, it goes without saying that any relevant description should suit the situation (again, from the principle of cooperativeness); so, the use of *bukval'no* implies that the speaker means that the expression is not only suitable but constitutes the most adequate way of describing the situation.

The conventionalization of pragmatic inferences is tied to the enantiosemy of such prefixal verbs as *pereizbrat'* <X> 'to reelect X, to elect X another time' and 'to elect another person instead of X';[9] *obojti* 'to circumvent' (*obojti lužu* 'to circumvent the puddle') and 'to walk all over' (*obojti sad* 'to walk all over the garden'); *projti (mimo)* 'to pass by' and *projti (naskvoz')* 'to pass through'. Here the very meaning of the prefixes is such that it directly permits the appearance of totally opposite inferences. For example, verbs with the prefix *pere-* with the meaning of a repeated performance of an action can mean 'to do the same thing again' or 'to do it differently': *perepisat'* can mean 'to copy or reproduce a text' or 'to write a text anew or differently'. The source of the two opposite inferences is quite clear. One may want to do something again for two opposite reasons: (i) if the actor does not like the result of his/her action, s/he may want to do it again to achieve

---

[8] The same is true for such words as *nastojaščij* 'real', *podlinnyj* 'genuine', etc.: if stressed, they convey their "literal" meanings, but if the stress is on the collocating expression, they convey their "modal" meanings.

[9] Consider also the English verb *to replace*: it can mean 'to put back; to restore or return to the original or proper place' (as in *she replaced the old bath mat after washing it*) or 'to put something new in the place of' (as in *she replaced the old bath mat with a new one*).

a better result; (ii) if the actor likes the result of his/her action, s/he may want to do it again to achieve the same result. The enantiosemy of the prefixes *pro-* and *ob-* is connected with a certain general rule of the linguistic conceptualization of "moving past". Speaking about the "remarkable at first sight" opposition of meanings that the Russian word *mimo* 'past' can express, Anna Zalizniak (1994: 261) noted that it, "describing the trajectory of movement of one object (X) with regard to another (Y), can denote both that they 'met' and that they 'passed by each other without meeting'". In the same way, verbs of motion with the prefix *pro-* (which are largely similar to collocations with the word *mimo*) can imply both a motion through a certain point and motion that passes the point by.[10] This duality is preserved in many verbs that are not verbs of motion: *prosmotret'* 'to look through and get acquainted with' and 'to miss or not notice while looking'; *proslušat'* (*doklad*) 'to hear (a talk) through' and 'not to hear, to miss'.[11] Similarly, motion that is indicated by verbs with the prefix *ob-* can involve successive contact (*ob"exat' vse goroda* 'to drive through all the towns') as well as the lack of contact (*ob"exat' gorod storonoj* 'to pass a town by'). As a result, many verbs with this prefix are enantiosemic: cf. *obnesti* 'to go around and offer to everyone' (*obnesti gostej vinom* 'to go around and offer wine to the guests') and 'not to offer <to someone> when going around' (*vsex ugostil, a menja obnes* 'he treated everyone yet passed me by'). Let us note that this type of enantiosemy arises not just for prefixal verbs: in the collocation *krizis minoval* 'the crisis passed', the verb *minovat'* means that the crisis has occurred (and ended), while the collocation *beda minovala* 'the misfortune passed by' means that the misfortune did not take place although it could have (Zalizniak 1994: 276).

Opposite inferences also arise for expressions with the meaning that something is conspicuous. Such an expression can imply both that something is clear beyond all doubt and that, on the contrary, it only seems so, while things are totally different in reality. This is the origin of the enantiosemy of the English word *apparent*. According to dictionaries, it means 'clear, patent' (*apparent error* 'patent mistake') and, on the contrary, 'seeming, false' (*apparent cause* 'seeming cause, i.e., not the real cause').

The conventionalization of pragmatic inferences also explains why the expression *dolgo rešalsja <sdelat' čto-to>* 'hesitated a long time <to do something>' means almost the same thing as its negation *dolgo ne rešalsja* 'hesitated a

---

[10] The English adverb *by* has the same duality: it may mean 'close at hand, near' (as in *to stand by*) and 'away; aside' (as in *to put the money by*).
[11] The English verb *overlook* and the noun *oversight* have the same property: they can mean 'to look at something carefully' as well as 'to miss something'.

long time not <to do something>': both indicate a long state of indecision. Indeed, when someone hesitates *(rešaetsja)* about doing something, it means that s/he still has not decided whether to do it or not. Thus if a person hesitates *(rešaetsja)* to do something for a long time, this implies that s/he cannot decide to do it for a long time, i.e., that s/he hesitates not to do it *(ne rešaetsja)*.

People may not want to deal with a person because they consider him/her to be a lot lower than them or a lot higher than them. This leads to two opposite inferences and, respectively, two opposite notions of the word *neprikasaemyj* 'untouchable'. On the one hand, this is a member of the lowest caste in India; on the other, this word is often used in contemporary texts to denote particularly important individuals that are *neprikosnovennyj* 'immune' and that cannot be persecuted. Compare, on the one hand, *Ja nizšaja sekta, neprikasaemyj* 'I'm a member of the lowest caste, an untouchable' (Vasily Grossman) and, on the other, the following example from the *Russian National Corpus*: *Daže esli svidetel'skie pokazanija i prjamye uliki privodjat k bossam, dejstvitel'nym vladel'cam "tovara", oni ostajutsja neprikasaemymi* 'Even if witness testimony and direct evidence point to the bosses or true owners of the "goods", they remain untouchable'. The following example (also from the *Russian National Corpus*) is particularly amusing, as it combines the expression *svjaščennaja korova* 'sacred cow' deriving from Indian culture and the word *neprikasaemye* 'untouchables' that is used in the opposite sense than in India: *Est' li v krae "svjaščennye korovy", neprikasaemye dlja vas?* 'Are there "sacred cows" in the territory that are untouchable for you?' (we deal with the "more – less" opposition here).

Since pragmatic inferences are based on the universal principles of communication, most of the examples discussed in this section may have cross-linguistic parallels.

3.2 Metonymy as a source of enantiosemy

3.2.1 Polarization of actants ("conversive enantiosemy")

The polarization of actants takes place when two participants in a situation (actants) begin to be perceived as "opposite," while the description of the situation from the standpoint of one of these participants is perceived as "opposite" to the description of the same situation from the standpoint of the other. Clearly, such "opposite" descriptions of a situation are metonymically connected since they presuppose contiguity, that is, contact or proximity in time or space. Examples include the situation of buying and selling (the roles of buyer and seller are polarized), visiting (the roles of guest and host are polarized), borrowing, and leasing. As the situation is one and the same, its descriptions from "opposite" points of view can make use of the same lexical unit (with a change of diathesis), which can begin to be perceived as enantiosemic (for example, the Russian verb *odolžit'* 'to lend' with the constructions *komu* 'to whom' and *u kogo* 'from whom' means 'to grant a loan' and 'to contract a debt', respectively). Another example cited by Bally (1950: 191) is the French verb *louer* that means 'to lease/rent out' and 'to lease/rent' – cf. *louer un appartement* 'to lease out/lease an apartment', *louer une voiture* 'to rent out/rent a car', etc. Moreover, a unit denoting a certain situation may serve to denote the "opposite" participants in the situation. If the respective participants in a situation are seen as "opposite," "actant enantiosemy" arises. The word *dolžnik* (derived from the word *dolg* 'debt') denotes in modern Russian the person who takes out a debt. However, in early 19th-century Russian, it could also denote the "opposite" participant in the situation: the creditor, i.e., the person who lent the money out. "Actant enantiosemy" is not necessarily linked to the use of word formation. For example, the French *hôte* describes "opposite" participants in a situation where one person visits another: this word may have the meaning of 'host' (*remercier ses hôtes de leur hospitalité* 'to thank one's hosts for their hospitality') as well as 'guest' (*bienvenu, vous êtes notre hôte* 'welcome, be our guest').

Let us cite a few more examples of words having "opposite" meanings due to the polarization of actants. The Russian verb *torgovat'* is used to denote the same situation of buying and selling yet from different standpoints: its principal contemporary meaning is 'to engage in selling, to sell goods to buyers' (for example, *torgovat' xlebom, lesom; torgovat' v lavke* 'to sell bread, timber; to sell in a shop'). At the same time, the *Small Academic Dictionary* also cites the obsolete or colloquial meaning of 'to enquire about the price or bargain with a view to buying something' and illustrates it with an example from Ostrovsky's play *Crazy Money*: *Ja vspomnila, čto videla odnu kupčixu v magazine, kotoraja torgovala kusok materii; ej žal' i mnogo deneg-to otdat', i kusok-to iz ruk vypustit'* 'I recalled seeing a merchant's wife in a shop who bargained over a piece of cloth. She neither wanted to spend a lot of money nor to let go of the cloth' (Evgen'eva 1984b: 385). Thus this verb can describe the activities both of the buyer and of the seller, i.e., of "opposite" participants of the situation of buying and selling. The noun *kupec* (derived from the verb *kupit'* 'to buy') denotes someone who engages in commerce or sells; however, the *Small Academic Dictionary* also cites the obsolete meaning 'buyer' for the word. Another case in point would apparently be the "opposite" meanings of the English adjective *arguable*, which, depending on the context, can mean 'debatable' (i.e., something against which one can find arguments) and 'supportable by argument' (i.e., something in whose defense one can find arguments).

The English verb *to confess* means both 'to make confession; to tell one's sins to the spiritual father in the sacrament of penance' and 'to hear confession'; accordingly, the corresponding noun *confessor* may refer both to a person who makes confession and to a priest who is authorized to hear confessions. It is worth noting that the Russian verb *ispovedovat'* can have the same readings, namely, 'to make confession' and 'to hear confession'; the first reading appears with the object referring to sins while the second reading presupposes the object referring to a person. However, the corresponding noun *ispovednik* 'a person who confesses' can only refer to a person who makes confession; he who hears confession is called *duxovnik* (from *dux* 'spirit'), and the pair *ispovednik – duxovnik* is usually regarded as a pair of antonyms.

3.2.2 Temporal metonymy

Words with temporal semantics are highly prone to enantiosemy. One of the sources of enantiosemy in this domain is the fact that metonymy is actively used for denoting time. Metonymy is transfer by "contiguity," and periods of time that are conceptualized as being "opposite" are often considered contiguous. For example, the word *mjasopust* is defined as follows in the *Dictionary of the Russian Language of the 11th-17th Centuries* (Filin 1982): '1. Permission to eat dairy and meat products in the Church statute', '2. Sunday before *Maslenitsa* [Shrovetide], during which one can eat meat for the last time by the statute of the Orthodox Church', and '3. The forty-day period of Lent before Easter or a fast in general' (Bulygina and Shmelev 1997). As 'a fast in general' and Lent in particular involves the prohibition of eating dairy and meat products, we see that the first and third meanings of the word *mjasopust* are directly opposite (their explications differ in absence/presence of negation). The solution of the paradox lies in the fact that the word *mjasopust* is connected with the "terminological" collocation *mjasopustnaja nedelja*, which denotes the Sunday before *Maslenitsa* or the last day when the Church permits eating meat (this collocation is equivalent to the second of the aforementioned meanings of the word *mjasopust*). However, it can be metonymically transferred to the period that directly precedes this day (i.e., the period when it is permitted to eat meat) and the period that follows this day (i.e., the period when it is forbidden to eat meat: *Maslenitsa* and Lent). The enantiosemicity of the word *mjasopust* is enhanced by the possibility of understanding its inner form in different ways: the second element can be associated both with the verb *pustit'* 'to allow' and with the word *pustoj* 'empty', which denotes a lack or prohibition.¹²

The "void negation" in such expressions as *podoždat', poka on (ne) pridet* 'to wait until he comes' is apparently also linked to temporal metonymy. During the period of waiting, "he" does not come. The end of this period is the moment when "he" comes.

Metonymic shifts in denoting time also explain the fact that certain linguistic units can denote both weekends or holidays and working days. For example, the Italian word *feria* (from the outdated verb *feriare* 'not to work, to rest') has the meaning 'holiday, day of rest' (the plural form *ferie* can denote a vacation or leave) as well as the colloquial meaning 'workdays' (for the derived adjective *feriale*, 'everyday' is the principal meaning – cf. the expression *giorno feriale* 'working day'¹³). Similar paradoxes exist in Russian. For example, in many Slavic languages, Sunday is denoted by a word deriving from the collocation *ne delat'* 'not to do' (cf., for example, Ukrainian *nedilja*, Belorussian *njadzelja*, Bulgarian *nedelja*, Polish *niedzela*, etc.). In Russian, this meaning has been preserved in expressions deriving from Church Slavonic calendric terms (e.g., the aforementioned collocation *mjasopustnaja nedelja*). At the same time, the word *nedelja* was transposed in the Russian language to the seven-day period including Sunday. In contemporary Russian, it predominantly refers to the week's working section or workdays, i.e., it has acquired the opposite meaning than it had initially.¹⁴

3.2.3 "Mixed feelings"

An interesting source of enantiosemy is linked to "mixed feelings," i.e., to a situation in which the subject is a certain emotional state that combines the characteristic traits of two opposite emotional states ("good" and "bad"), somewhat like

---

12 Here the problem of interpreting the word *mjasopust* is described in general terms. For a more detailed discussion, see the aforementioned article (Bulygina and Shmelev 1997).
13 Consider the French *jour ferié* 'holiday', which is etymologically identical to the Italian expression but means the opposite.
14 See examples in Shmelev (2002: 327): *Prixodite na nedele* 'Come during the week' (most likely not on Saturday or Sunday) or even *Malo vam nedeli, tak vy ešče i v vyxodnye zvonite* 'A week is too short for you so that you must also call me on weekends'. The semantic transition here is typologically close to the emergence of the meaning 'workweek' for the English word *week*, which can be illustrated by such examples as *40-hour week* and *She spends the week in town but is at home on Sundays*. We should note, by the way, that the word *weekday* (literally 'day of the week') has the exclusive meaning 'workday' in contemporary English.

the lyrical hero of Catullus' well-known poem *Odi et amo*. Generally speaking, depictions of emotional states easily shift to contiguous emotions, leading to the appearance of semantic chains whose links can correspond to emotional states that are considered to be "opposite". This explains the enantiosemy of "emotional terms".

For example, *žalost'* 'pity' can be associated both with love (in certain Russian dialects, *žalet'* means 'to love') and with contempt.[15] In itself, contempt probably would not be considered to be the opposite of love. However, contempt is often accompanied by hatred (as Pen'kovskij [2004: 59–60] noted, this association seems "quite natural for us"), and hatred is clearly the opposite of love. At the same time, given that the meaning 'hatred' has not factually emerged for Russian words with the root *žal*, it would be unfounded for the time being to speak about enantiosemy in the strict sense of the term, although such a cognitive source of enantiosemy clearly exists.

Note that words with the meaning 'pity' provide material that is directly connected with enantiosemy. For example, the Polish word *litość* 'compassion, empathy, pity' is etymologically identical to the Russian word *ljutost'* 'ferocity'. The "missing link" can be seen in the Czech word *lítost* that denotes a special emotion that has been described in detail by M. Kundera in his novel *The Book of Laughter and Forgetting* and interpreted by Zalizniak (2000: 101) with a reference to Wierzbicka (1992: 166–169) as "a feeling of acute pity for oneself that arises as a reaction to humiliation and evokes a feeling of aggression in return".

3.3 Metaphors

A common source of enantiosemy is the presence of two opposite spatial metaphors of time in the metaphorical systems of many languages. One of them is based on a notion that the world is stable and motionless, while time "goes by". In such a case, the past is seen as being ahead and the future as lying behind. The other metaphor is based on a notion that time is constant and motionless, while the "observer" moves through time from the past to the future. In such a view, the future lies ahead, and the past is behind.

As a result, the same linguistic expressions with the same initial spatial meaning can signify directly opposite things with respect to time (the "more –

---

[15] Levontina (1997: 110) notes that the adjective *žalkij* 'pitiful' "includes this evaluation directly in its meaning".

less" opposition). Both the past and the future can be seen as lying ahead. This leads to the enantiosemy of the Russian prefix *pred-* 'fore-' when used in a temporal sense (it points to an earlier moment of time in the adjective *predyduščij* 'foregoing; previous, preceding' from *idti* 'to go' and to a later moment of time in the adjective *predstojaščij* 'lying ahead; forthcoming; [literally] standing ahead' from *stojat'* 'to stand'). Similarly, the Russian adverb *vpered* can mean both 'before' (*vpered podumaj, potom sdelaj* 'think before you act') and 'after, from now on' (*vpered ne serdi menja* 'don't anger me from now on'). In a similar way, the English morpheme *fore* indicates anteriority in such words as *forerunner* and *before* and posteriority in such words as *forward* (e.g., in the sentence *I am looking forward to seeing you soon*).[16]

Certain language units that indicate "being behind" can also be enantiosemic (insofar as they can relate to both "earlier" and "later" periods of time). For example, the expression *zadnim čislom* (literally, 'with a rear date') can mean, according to the *Small Academic Dictionary* (Evgen'eva 1981: 516), both 'later, after a certain period of time' (cf. the expression *utverdit' dokument zadnim čislom* 'to approve the document later') and 'earlier, at an earlier date' (cf. the expression *pometit' dokument zadnim čislom* 'to mark the document with an earlier date; to antedate'[17]). The prefix *za-*, which is apparently etymologically connected with the root *zad* 'rear', can relate both to the beginning and to the end of a process. Let us cite examples of two enantiosemic words with this prefix. The adverb *zatemno* has two meanings according to the *Small Academic Dictionary* (Evgen'eva 1981: 582): 'before dawn, while dark' and 'after darkness'. The opposite nature of these meanings can be clearly seen in that the word *zatemno* in the former meaning is naturally collocated with the word *ešče* 'still' (as in both of the examples illustrating this meaning in the *Small Academic Dictionary*: ... *uexal ešče zatemno* 'he left before dawn'; ...*po staroj šaxterskoj privyčke prosypalsja ešče zatemno*...'by the old miners' custom, he used to wake up before dawn') and, in the latter meaning, with the word *uže* 'already' (as in the example from the *Small Academic Dictionary*: *Astaxov vernulsja k vzvodu uže zatemno* 'Astakhov returned to the platoon when it was already dark'). The noun *zavjazka* in the literary language has the meaning, among others, 'beginning, starting point <of some activities>' (Evgen'eva 1981: 506), while it is used in contemporary jargon with the "opposite" meaning 'end of something; a state where something is finished once and for all' (Elistratov 1994: 146): *Vse, zavjazka, bol'še ni gramma ne p'ju!* 'That does it! I won't drink a drop from now on!'

---

16 Consider also Lakoff and Johnson (1980: 41–45).
17 Consider also the English verb to backdate 'to date before the actual date; predate'.

3.4 "Insidious" negation

3.4.1 Pressure of surface negation

Situations when a speaker "gets tangled up" in negations, e.g., inserts an extra negation or, in contrast, does not insert a negation where the meaning of the phrase requires it, may seem to be accidental at first sight yet are a fairly frequent occurrence typologically. This can occur when another (explicit or implicit) negation already exists in the phrase. Of particular interest are cases when errors of this sort become so common that it is no longer clear whether they are still errors or become linguistic conventions of a special type. Let us consider two examples in some detail.

The English verb *to unpack* is formed by adding the reversative prefix *un-* to the verb *to pack*; the corresponding participle being *unpacked*. In addition, *unpacked* may be understood as derived from the participle form *packed* by adding the negative prefix *un-*; in the latter case it would mean 'not packed'. However, as a result of the presence of a negative prefix, when the speaker wants to express the meaning 'not unpacked', s/he frequently uses the same word *unpacked*, which can therefore signify both 'unpacked' (literal meaning) and 'not unpacked' (this was brought to my attention by Barbara Hall Partee). Although purists sometimes assess such usage as being erroneous, it occurs fairly often in the speech of native speakers who strictly follow the rules of literary usage. Let me cite a discussion about this expression.

Geoffrey Nunberg, a well-known linguist from Stanford University, posted on May 16, 2005, a story on the site *Language Log*[18] that recounted how Dan Menaker, who worked as a proofreader in *The New Yorker* magazine, discovered in one of the short stories a sentence that had been missed by three other editors. The sentence reads: *They had only just moved in; their boxes lay on the kitchen floor, still unpacked.* Nunberg commented this in the following way: "What the writer meant to say, of course, was "not yet unpacked", or more accurately if less grammatically, "still ununpacked". But most people take a moment to realize that the sentence doesn't actually mean that". He went on to exclaim: "And indeed, if Menaker hadn't spotted the mistake, it would have made it into the pages of the *New Yorker*". Mark Liberman called such usage "insidious overnegation". At the same time, he noted that such usage is fairly common (in a message posted on the

---

[18] http://itre.cis.upenn.edu/~myl/languagelog/archives/002164.html

same site the next day,[19] he noted that a Google search yielded 785 examples of the use of the expression *still unpacked* and, moreover, that there are numerous examples of the word *unpacked* (without the word *still*) meaning 'not unpacked', such as:

> Amid the clutter and **unpacked** [emphasis mine] boxes, Charlotte schleps her laptop around the house, trying to get a grip on the erotic novel she's working on.

Examples in which *unpacked* means 'not unpacked' and 'unpacked' within a single sentence are particularly striking:

> Are you the kind of person who puts **unpacked** boxes in the basement of your new home to be **unpacked** at a later date (5 years later!)? [Emphasis mine, AS.]
> I finally got fed up that our office is a labyrinth of **unpacked** boxes from when we moved like five months ago, so to make a point, I hid the computer chair and stacked a bunch of boxes in front of the computer, so that we can't do anything on the computer until the boxes are **unpacked**. [Emphasis mine, AS.]

In turn, Jesse Sheidlower, Editor-in-Chief of the *Oxford Dictionary of the English Language,* noted that there are fairly numerous examples of the use of *unpacked* with the meaning 'not unpacked' among well-known authors and this should not be consequently considered to be a mistake. Moreover, the *Oxford Dictionary* gives, among others, the following meaning of the word *unpacked*: 'not taken out of a pack or parcel'. This meaning is illustrated by an example from a 1721 text: *Loads of ill Pictures, and worse Books..., lye unpacked and unthought of when they come into the Country* (Pryor 1907: 195–196). Still, as it turned out, many native speakers, including those who have used this expression themselves, consider it to be a mistake and, when it is pointed out to them, correct themselves. Curiously, after surveying consultants, Nunberg recognized that such usage may be considered correct and called it "autoantynomy",[20] saying furthermore that this is not the only case of "autoantynomy" ("Sanctioning something can mean either permitting it or setting penalties for it; renting an apartment can mean either being a tenant or being a landlord; and there are other examples."). He also pointed out that the idiomatic expression *couldn't care less* is equivalent to the same expression without negation (*could care less*); at the same time, it is easy to see that these examples of enantiosemic expressions are not connected with the pressure

---

19 http://158.130.17.5/~myl/languagelog/archives/002169.html
20 http://itre.cis.upenn.edu/~myl/languagelog/archives/002212.html

of surface negation but have a different source. (See also the discussion for the layman by Jan Freeman in his column in the *Boston Globe* of May 25, 2005.)

Nunberg connected such use of the word *unpacked* with haplology or the desire to avoid repeating the segment *un* (*ununpacked→unpacked*). The "correct" form, *ununpacked*, would involve the two different *un*-'s: the first *un-* is negative while the *un-* of *un-packed* is the reversative *un-*; being a past participle, it can have the negative *un-* prefixed to it, to give *ununpacked, meaning exactly 'not unpacked'. As is well known, speakers don't like such apparent doubling of morphemes, even when they are in fact two different (but homonymous) morphemes.

However, the following question remains: why speakers do not notice that *unpacked* in such contexts apparently means its opposite, that is, 'not unpacked' (if they did they could use the paraphrase *not unpacked* with no haplology). It seems to me that the cause may be a little more complex, though related. The speaker wants to express the meaning 'not unpacked', which involves the negation of an action related to packing, and uses a word including both the negative morpheme *un-* and the morpheme *pack*. The fact that one should express an action opposite to the action of "packing" goes unnoticed.[21]

A similar mechanism has resulted in the appearance and broad diffusion in contemporary Russian of the verb *razmorozit'* 'to defrost' in such expressions as *razmorozit' sistemu otoplenija* in which it paradoxically means 'to put the heating system out of order by letting the temperature fall to a critical point at which the system freezes' (i.e., the meaning of *razmorozit'* is 'to freeze'). It seems to me that the cause of such usage is the speaker's striving to express simultaneously the meaning 'to put out of order' (with the help of the prefix *raz-*) and the meaning 'low temperature, freezing' (with the help of the root *moroz*). At the same time, the speaker overlooks the fact that the dictionary meaning of the verb *razmorozit'* is opposite: 'to make something that is frozen melt by heating it' (Evgen'eva 1984a).

3.4.2 "Implied" negation

It is well known that certain words and expressions are used predominantly or exclusively in the context of negation. For this reason, the very presence of these

---

[21] Words such as *unshelled* as in *The eggs were unshelled*, which can mean 'The eggs had not been removed from their shells' (nobody shelled them) or 'The eggs were removed from their shells' (someone unshelled them) constitute similar but somewhat different variety of enantiosemy. For more details see below.

words suggests negation, so that it might seem unnecessary to express negation explicitly, and it is sometimes omitted. A case in point is the Russian word *otnjud'*: by the norms of the Russian literary language, it is used before a negation (*otnjud' ne* or *otnjud' net* 'not at all, by no means') in order to intensify the latter. At the same time, the solitary use of *otnjud'* has become widespread as a negative answer to a general question: *Vy ljubite syr? – Otnjud'* 'Do you like cheese? – Not at all'. This usage has evoked protests among purists of the Russian language. Nevertheless, the solitary use of *otnjud'* (in which it has virtually the same meaning as *otnjud' net*) has spread and is now widely used by writers (including well-known authors).

When such usage is conventionalized, we deal with "Jespersen's cycle" (Dahl 1979) whereby words that reinforce negation tend to take over the negating function themselves (then other intensifiers may be added and the cycle begins again). As a result of such phenomena, in which a word that is used predominantly or exclusively in the context of negation acquires a negative meaning itself, the negative meanings of the French words *personne*, *rien*, *plus*, and *jamais* have become conventionalized and are fixed in dictionaries. This has led to an enantiosemy in which the word *jamais*, for example, means 'never', while the expression *à jamais* means 'forever'. Such enantiosemy is not always eliminated by the context: for example, the isolated expression *plus de sucre* can mean both 'more sugar' and 'there is no more sugar'.

3.4.3 Negation with "minimizers"

In the fifth chapter (dedicated to the memory of James McCawley) of his *Skeptical Linguistic Essays*,[22] Postal described the paradoxical behavior of English "vulgar minimizers" (such words as *squat*). Phrases with these words mean the same regardless of the presence or absence of negation: the phrase *Eddie knows squat about phrenology* and the phrase *Eddie doesn't know squat about phrenology* both signify that Eddie does not know anything about phrenology. The semantic mechanism that generates this paradoxical effect is quite clear: the words and expressions in question indicate a negligibly small amount that is equivalent to zero; in the case of negation, the meaning is that even such a negligibly small amount is absent, which is once again equivalent to zero.

The situation with "vulgar minimizers" is similar (even if not entirely identical) in Russian: in a number of contexts in which such "minimizers" are used,

---

[22] http://www.nyu.edu/gsas/dept/lingu/people/faculty/postal/papers/skeptical/

phrases with negation and phrases without negation are synonymous (if one disregards a barely perceptible shift of semantic accent). *Xren pomenjaetsja* ≈ *Ni xrena-to ne pomenjaetsja* 'Nothing will change'; *Xren vozraziš'* ≈ *Ni xrena ne vozraziš'* 'You won't be able to object'. A similar mechanism explains the curious fact that the Russian expressions *Plevat' ja xotel!* (literally, 'I wanted to spit!') and *Plevat' ja ne zaxoču!* (literally, 'I won't want to spit!') express the same derogative attitude towards the object (they mean 'I don't care!').

Negation with "minimizers" has almost the same nature as the first stage of "Jespersen's cycle": words that reinforce negation are felt as the negative proper and may be used with no additional negation. However, they remain emphatic and are not found insufficient and requiring reinforcement; so, no cycle arise.

3.5 Asymmetry of action/process and result

Yet another type of "opposite" meanings derives from the opposite direction of actions (*come – leave*; *raise – lower*; *turn on – turn off*, *tie – untie*, etc.). These are antonyms of the type 'begin P' – 'begin not P' or Anti1 in Apresjan's terminology (Apresjan 1974: 288–292). This type of antonyms is not, as a rule, connected with enantiosemy.[23]

However, opposite meanings of this kind can also occur within a single word. They result from the fact that similar actions can lead to opposite results. For example, a strong stream of air can both augment and extinguish a flame. This results in the enantiosemy of the verb *zadut'*, which is seen in the collocations *zadut' domnu* 'to blow air into a blast furnace to increase flame intensity' and *zadut' sveču* 'to blow a candle out'.[24] Rakhilina has noted that the Russian verb *idti* 'to go' means 'to approach, come' in some contexts (*Iz Gonkonga idet novyj virus grippa* 'A new influenza virus is coming from Hong Kong'; *Oj! Moj tramvaj idet!* 'Oh! My tramcar is coming!') and 'to leave' in others (*Možete idti* 'You can go'; *Skažite, v kotorom času idet poezd na Lugu?* 'At what time does the train for Luga leave?') (Rakhilina 2000: 306–310). With regard to the verb *idti*, it is not entirely clear whether the verb's lexical meanings are truly opposite (although a potential source of enantiosemy clearly exists); nevertheless, a number of other lan-

---

[23] Consider, however, the pair *pack – unpack* discussed earlier. Since *unpacked* may mean 'not unpacked', it follows that *packed* under negation expressed by *un-* may mean *unpacked* (that is, its opposite of the type in question).

[24] Another important point here is the enantiosemy of the prefix *za-*, which can, as I noted above, indicate both the beginning and end of an action.

guages give "purer" examples of enantiosemy. For example, the Sanskrit verb *varj* (initial meaning 'to turn' [cf. Kočergina 1978: 567]) can be used "both for denoting 'drawing [a god] towards oneself' and 'repelling [something evil] from oneself'" (Ivanov and Toporov 1960: 129). An interesting example of interlanguage enantiosemy in Slavic languages is verbs arising from the development of the Common Slavonic **lǫčiti* (probably 'to bend'): Belorusian *lučyc'*, Polish *łączyć* 'to connect', on the one hand, and Bulgarian *lača*, Serbian *lučiti*, Czech *loučiti* 'to separate', on the other.[25] The same type of enantiosemy marks such examples as the Russian verbs *rubit'* <*izbu*> 'to build <a log house> (using an axe)' and *rubit'* <*mebel'*> 'to destroy <furniture> by hitting it with a sharp instrument'; *vyvesti* <*krolikov*> 'to breed, raise <bunnies>' and *vyvesti* <*tarakanov*> 'to destroy, exterminate <cockroaches>'.[26]

This type of enantiosemy is directly connected with the meanings 'beginning' and 'end' (because 'to begin not P' means 'to end P'). It is revealing that the Russian words *načalo* 'beginning' and *konec* 'end' have the same root historically. Let us cite a few more examples. If one leaves a certain place, s/he simultaneously stops being there ('to begin not P') and begins to be in a different place ('to begin Q'), which can serve as a source of enantiosemy. When A leaves B, A goes away and stops to be at the same place as B while B remains at that place. Accordingly, the form *left* means 'had gone' as a past tense verb, but 'remaining' as a participle.[27] As I have already mentioned, the Russian word *isxod*, which derives from

---

25 The English word *unbending* provides another instance of enantiosemy especially in its metaphoric meanings: it may mean both 'rigid, inflexible, refusing to yield or compromise; that cannot or will not relax' (*unbending will*) and 'becoming less tense, relaxing' (*unbending, he confided his secret*). Although it is related to the idea of 'bending' as well, the source of its enantiosemy is different from that of the Common Slavonic **lǫčiti*: in many cases *unbending* means 'firm', but if one speaks about bow, for example, it would mean 'released'.
26 The verb *vyvesti* is formed with the prefix *vy-* and can mean 'to take out' (in *vyvesti tarakanov*) and 'to bring out' (in *vyvesti krolikov*). A similar enantiosemy is characteristic of the English adverb *out*: the sentence *the lights are out* means that they are not shining, but *the stars are out* means that they are visible.
27 A similar type of enantiosemy may be exemplified with numerous English nouns verbed into distinct senses "add X to" and "remove X from", e.g. *to skin* ('to remove the skin of or from' as in *to skin a rabbit* and 'to cover with skin' as in *to skin a kayak*). The verb *to shell* means 'to remove the shell or covering from' as in *to shell peas, oysters*, etc.; the same meaning can be conveyed by the verb to *unshell* as in *How to unshell a Snow Crab Claw fast* (http://www.youtube.com/watch?v=_ttopAlWAKA). Hence, *unshelled* may mean both 'not extracted from its shell' (*un-* added to the past participle *shelled*) and 'removed from its shell' (past participle of the verb *to unshell*).

a Church Slavonic word meaning 'departure', signifies 'end', while the adjective *isxodnyj*, which contains the same morpheme, means 'initial'.

In numerous languages, the same word may be used for saying hello and saying goodbye (e. g. Italian *ciao*). The fact that one deals with the enantiosemy of the type in question here becomes clear not at the first sight but at the fourth stage of semantic analysis: (1) 'hello' means that A meets B; 'goodbye' means that A leaves B; (2) 'A meets B' = 'as a result of movement of A or B they begin to be at the same place at a certain time, and A acquires contact with B; 'A leaves B' = 'as a result of movement of A they stop being at the same place, and A loses contact with B; (3) 'to acquire' = 'to begin to have'; 'to lose' = 'to cease to have'; (4) 'to cease X' = 'to begin not X' (cf. Apresjan 1974: 289).

Enantiosemy of this type is sometimes related to cultural conventions. Thus, in many cultures admitting one's fault frees the person of blame. Accordingly, the Russian word *izvinenie* can refer both to an act of expressing regret for a fault and to an excuse, that is a reason for justification. Similarly, the English word *apology* refers to an act of expressing regret for a fault and to a formal spoken or written defense of something.

The asymmetry of action/process and result also manifests itself in a situation where the same result can be achieved by "opposite" actions or the "opposite" actions are directed towards the same object. For example, the opposite meanings of the Serbian *spor* 'slow' and the etymologically identical Russian *sporyj* 'fast' derive from the existence of two opposite ways of increasing work output: one can work longer or with greater efficiency. These are two paths of development of an adjective that clearly signified 'copious' initially: on the one hand, 'long' and thus 'slow' and, on the other, 'intensive; effective' and thus 'fast' (the 'more-less' opposition).[28]

3.6 Special cases

There are cases in which the source of enantiosemy is not fully clear (or, rather, involves several semantic shifts). Let us consider a well-known example of interlanguage enantiosemy: the Serbian word *vredno* 'good for you, worth' and the Russian *vredno* 'harmful'. It is widely believed that these words derive from

---

28 The English word *fast* has two "opposite" meanings itself. On the one hand, it means 'steady, not moving; not easily moved; stuck' as in *the ship was fast aground*; *the car stuck fast*; on the other hand, it means 'moving with high speed; quick, rapid' as in *he is a fast worker*; *my watch is fast*. Both meanings go back to the original meaning 'firm', then 'vigorous'.

a root with the meaning 'abscess' (cf. *beredit' (ranu)* 'to irritate, inflict pain by repeatedly touching a sore spot'). The semantic path to the meaning 'harm, damage' seems clear. A possible explanation of the emergence of the meaning 'good for you, worth doing' is as follows. The meaning 'pain, suffering' naturally transforms into the meaning 'work' (cf. a similar transition in the Russian word *strada* 'period of hard work' from *stradat'* 'to suffer'). This leads to the meaning 'hardworking, assiduous; strong; worthy' of the related adjective (these meanings indeed exist for the Serbian adjective *vredan*).[29] In predicative usage, such an adjective is naturally understood as 'good for you, worth' (for example, *to je vredno uraditi* 'this is worth doing').

Sources of enantiosemy may not be clear when loanwords are involved. Thus, the Russian borrowed adjective *original'nyj* 'original' in the most common reading refers to something unusual (as in *original'naja ideja* 'original idea'); hence, the phrase *original'naja vodka* would be understood as referring to unusually flavored vodka. However, recently the phrase *original'naja vodka* has started to be used as a calque of the English *original vodka* (that is, plain, unchanged vodka as opposed to flavored vodka). The Russian expression *igrat' v karty na interes* (with the borrowed word *interes* 'interest') formerly and more acceptably meaning 'to play cards for money' is now more commonly used to mean 'to play cards just for fun' (as in the alternative question *My budem igrat' na den'gi ili na interes?* 'Shall we play for money or just for fun?').

In any case, the difficulties and irregularities involved in the interpretation of individual examples do not contradict the overall conclusion: in most cases, the phenomena of "void" negation and enantiosemy have regular sources and typological parallels.

3.7 Conclusion

As has been shown, quite regular and well-known semantic shifts often result in enantiosemy. Among those shifts one may recognize the following.

Irony is the use of an expression to convey a meaning that is the opposite of its literal meaning; hence, it may be described as an occasional enantiosemy. If the ironic use of an expression is conventionalized in a language, enantiosemy occurs. Conventionalization of irony often produces implied negation and

---

29 Cf. the Bulgarian adjective *vreden*, which has the meanings 'harmful' and 'competent, capable'.

"good – bad" enantiosemy. Reevaluation most often leads to "good – bad" enantiosemy, but can also produce "more – less" enantiosemy.

A whole series of units acquire meanings that are opposite to their original meanings through the conventionalization of pragmatic inferences, which quite often results in implied negation.

The polarization of actants often involves conversive enantiosemy, which takes place when two actants (participants in a situation) begin to be perceived as "opposite," while the description of the situation from the standpoint of one of these participants is perceived as "opposite" to the description of the same situation from the standpoint of the other. Such "opposite" descriptions of a situation are metonymically connected.

Another metonymic source of enantiosemy (based on implied negation) is the fact that metonymy is actively used for denoting time. Periods of time that are conceptualized as being "opposite" are often contiguous and may involve transfer by "contiguity".

When one deals with "mixed feelings," i.e., with a situation in which the subject is a certain emotional state that combines the characteristic traits of two opposite emotional states ("good" and "bad"), depictions of such emotional states easily shift to contiguous emotions, leading to the appearance of semantic chains whose links can correspond to emotional states that are considered to be "opposite". This explains the enantiosemy of some "emotional terms".

A common source of enantiosemy is the presence of two opposite spatial metaphors of time in the metaphorical systems of many languages (one of them based on a notion that the world is stable and motionless, while time "goes by". the other based on a notion that time is constant and motionless, while the "observer" moves through time from the past to the future). As a result, both the past and the future can be seen as lying ahead. This leads to the enantiosemy of some temporal expressions with the same initial spatial meaning (the "more – less" opposition).

Various types of interaction between surface negation and implied negation can lead to enantiosemy as well. One should mention "Jespersen's cycle" in which a word that is used predominantly or exclusively in the context of negation acquires a negative meaning itself. "Mimimizers" often mean the same regardless of the presence or absence of negation: the words and expressions in question indicate a negligibly small amount that is equivalent to zero; in the case of negation, the meaning is that even such a negligibly small amount is absent, which is once again equivalent to zero.

Thus, in most cases, the phenomena of "void" negation and enantiosemy have regular sources and typological parallels.

The following table summarizes the different sources of enantiosemy.

Table 1: Sources of enantiosemy

Sources of enantiosemy	Intralanguage cases	Interlanguage cases
Irony	Russian *očen' nužno* ('there is a great need'; 'there is no need'); *xoroš* ('good'; 'bad')	
Re-evaluation	English *odor* ('aroma, fragrance'; 'bad smell')	Russian *von'* 'stink' vs. Church Slavonic *vonja* 'aroma, fragrance'
Pragmatic inferences	Russian *projti* ('to pass by'; 'to pass through'); *perepisat'* ('to copy or reproduce a text'; 'to write a text anew or differently')	
Polarization of actants	Russian *odolžit'* ('to grant a loan'; 'to contract a debt'); French *hôte* ('host'; 'guest'); English *to confess* ('to make confession; to tell one's sins to the spiritual father in the sacrament of penance'; 'to hear confession')	
Temporal metonymy	Russian *mjasopust* ('period of permission to eat dairy and meat products'; 'period of prohibition to eat dairy and meat products')	Italian *giorno feriale* 'working day' vs. French *jour ferié* 'holiday'
"Mixed feelings"		Russian *ljutost'* 'ferocity' vs. Polish *litość* ('compassion, empathy')
Spatial metaphors of time	Russian *vpered* ('before'; 'after, from now on')	
Pressure of surface negation	English *unpacked* ('unpacked'; 'not unpacked'); Russian *razmorozit'* 'to defrost'; 'to freeze')	
Implied negation and "minimizers"	French *plus* ('more'; 'no more'); English *squat*	
Asymmetry of action/process and result		Bulgarian *lǎča*, Serbian *lučiti*, Czech *loučiti* 'to separate' vs. Belorussian *lučyc'*, Polish *łączyć* 'to connect'; Serbian *spor* 'slow' vs. Russian *sporyj* 'fast'

3.8 References

Apresjan, Jurij D. 1974. *Leksicheskaia semantika (sinonimicheskie sredstva iazyka)* [Lexical semantics: Synonymic means of the language]. Moscow: Nauka. [English version: Apresjan, Jurij D. 1992. *Lexical semantics: User's guide to contemporary Russian vocabulary*. Ann Arbor: Karoma.]

Apresjan, Jurij D. 1995. Novyi ob"iasnitel'nyi slovar' sinonimov: kontseptsiia i tipy informatsii [A new synonym dictionary: the concept and types of information]. In Jurij D. Apresian (ed.), *Novyi ob"iasnitel'nyi slovar' sinonimov russkogo iazyka: prospekt* [A new explanatory dictionary of Russian synonyms: a prospectus], 7–118. Moscow: Russkie slovari.

Bally, Charles. [1944] 1950. *Linguistique générale et linguistique française*. 3rd edn. (Reprint of the 2nd edn.). Berne: A. Francke.

Bulygina, Tat'iana V. and Aleksei D. Shmelev. 1997. Referentsiia i smysl vyrazhenii *miasopust* (*miasopustnaia nedelia*) i *syropust* (*syropustnaia nedelia*) [Reference and meaning of the expressions *miasopust* (*miasopustnaia nedelia*) and *syropust* (*syropustnaia nedelia*)]. *Voprosy iazykoznaniia*, 3: 40–47.

Dahl, Östen. 1979. Typology of sentence negation. *Linguistics* 17, 1-2: 79–106.

Dal', Vladimir I. 1978. *Tolkovyi slovar' zhivogo velikorusskogo lazyka* [Explanatory dictionary of the living great Russian language]. Vol. 1. Moscow: Russkii iazyk.

Evgen'eva, Anastasiia P. (ed.). 1981. *Slovar' russkogo iazyka* [Dictionary of the Russian language]. Vol. 1. Moscow: Russkii iazyk.

Evgen'eva, Anastasiia P. (ed.). 1984a. *Slovar' russkogo iazyka* [Dictionary of the Russian language]. Vol. 3. Moscow: Russkii iazyk.

Evgen'eva, Anastasiia P. (ed.). 1984b. *Slovar' russkogo iazyka* [Dictionary of the Russian language]. Vol. 4. Moscow: Russkii iazyk.

Elistratov, Vladimir S. 1994. *Slovar' moskovskogo argo: materialy 1980–1994* [Dictionary of Moscow argot: 1980–1994 materials]. Moscow: Russkie slovari.

Filin, Fedot P. (ed.). 1982. *Slovar' russkogo iazyka XI-XVII vv. Vypusk 9 (M)* [Dictionary of the Russian language of 11–17th centuries: Issue 9 (M)]. Moscow: Nauka.

Iakovleva, Ekaterina S. 1994. *Fragmenty russkoi iazykovoi kartiny mira (Modeli prostranstva, vremeni i vospriiatiia)* [Fragments of the Russian linguistic worldview (models of space, time, and perception)]. Moscow: Gnozis.

Ivanov, Viacheslav V. and Vladimir N. Toporov. 1960. *Sanskrit* [Sanskrit]. Moscow: Izdatel'stvo vostochnoi literatury.

Kochergina, Vera A. 1978. *Sanskritsko-russkii slovar'* [Sanskrit–Russian dictionary]. Moscow: Russkii iazyk.

Lakoff, George and Mark Johnson. 1980. *Metaphors We Live by*. Chicago & London: The University of Chicago Press.

Larina, Tat'iana V. 2003. *Kategoriia vezhlivosti v angliiskoi i russkoi kommunikativnykh kul'turakh* [The category of politeness in the Anglo and Russian communicative cultures]. Moscow: Izdatel'stvo RUDN.

Levontina, Irina B. 1997. Zhalost'[The Russian word for 'pity']. In Jurij D. Apresian (ed.), *Novyi ob"iasnitel'nyi slovar' sinonimov russkogo iazyka. Pervyi vypusk* [A new explanatory dictionary of Russian synonyms: First issue], 107–112. Moscow: Shkola "Iazyki russkoi kul'tury".

Pryor, Matthew. 1907. The Writings of Matthew Prior: Volume 2, Dialogues of the dead and other works in prose and verse. In *Oxford Dictionary of the English Language*, 195–196. Oxford: Oxford Univeristy Press. Retrieved from: http://findwords.info/term/unpacked.

Pen'kovskij, Aleksandr B. 1995. Timiologicheskie otsenki i ikh vyrazhenie v tseliakh ukloniaiushchegosia ot istiny umaleniia znachimosti [Timiological evaluations and their expression in intentional deviation from the truth]. In Nina D. Arutiunova and Nadezhda K. Riabtseva (eds.), *Logicheskii analiz iazyka. Istina i istinnost' v kul'ture i iazyke* [Logical analysis of language: Truth and truth-value in culture and language], 36–40. Moscow: Nauka.

Pen'kovskij, Aleksandr B. 2004. *Ocherki po russkoi semantike* [Essays on the Russian semantics]. Moscow: Iazyki slavianskoi kul'tury.

Rakhilina, Ekaterina V. 2000. *Kognitivnyi analiz predmetnykh imen: semantika i sochetaemost'* [Cognitive analysis of concrete nouns: Semantics and combinability]. Moscow: Russkie slovari.

Shmelev, Aleksei D. 2002. *Russkaia iazykovaia model' mira. Materialy k slovariu* [The Russian linguistic model of the world: Materials for a dictionary]. M.: Iazyki slavianskoi kul'tury.

Wierzbicka, Anna. 1972. *Semantic primitives*. Frankfurt am Main: Athenäum.

Wierzbicka, Anna. 1992. *Semantics, culture, and cognition: Universal human concepts in culture-specific configurations*. New York & Oxford: Oxford University Press.

Zalizniak, Anna A. 1994. Prazdnik zhizni prokhodit mimo (Zametki o neodnoznachnosti nekotorykh russkikh slov) [Holiday of life passes by (Notes on the polysemy of some Russian words)]. *Wiener Slawistischer Almanach*, 34: 261–278.

Zalizniak, Anna A. 2000. O semantike shchepetil'nosti (*obidno, sovestno* i *neudobno* na fone russkoi iazykovoi kartiny mira) [On the semantics of scrupulousness (*obidno, sovestno* and *neudobno* against the background of the Russian linguistic worldview)]. In Nina D. Arutiunova, Tat'iana E. Ianko, and Nadezhda K. Riabtseva (eds.), *Logicheskii analiz iazyka. Iazyki ètiki* [Logical analysis of language: Languages of ethics], 101–118. Moscow: Iazyki russkoi kul'tury.

Ekaterina Rakhilina and Tatiana Reznikova
4. A Frame-based methodology for lexical typology

Abstract: The article deals with the methodology and techniques of lexical typological studies. It focuses on the cross-linguistic analysis of semantic areas that are deeply involved in semantic derivation processes, i.e. they either make a wide use of words coming from other semantic domains (as is the case with pain predicates) or frequently give rise to extended meanings (as e.g. rotation verbs, sound verbs, aqua-motion verbs, adjectives of quality). Based on these data, we propose a general approach to a lexical-typological study – a frame-based approach. It is argued that semantic comparison should rely on a set of conceptual frames that underlie the domains under examination and that can be revealed through the analysis of word combinability in natural texts (corpora, spontaneous speech, etc.). The results obtained by this approach can be easily visualized as semantic maps, in which nodes are associated with frames.

This technique is illustrated by several examples, which testify to its applicability not only to well-attested domains of semantic typology (like colors, body parts, cutting and breaking, etc.), but also to less observable and highly metaphorical domains. The typological analysis of these areas is appealing, as it allows not only to investigate their lexical organization, but also to compare, in a systematic way, the semantic shifts observed in different languages.

4.1 Introduction[1]

Lexical typology is gaining recognition as a sub-discipline of descriptive linguistics. Three major reviews (Rakhilina and Plungian 2007; Koptjevskaja-Tamm 2008; Evans 2010) have come out recently which show that an increasing number of researchers and research groups are comparing words not in two, but a dozen or two dozen, languages at a time (cf. Viberg 1983; Newman [ed.] 1998, 2002,

---

[1] This research was supported by the RFBR grant No. 14-06-00343a.

Ekaterina Rakhilina & **Tatiana Reznikova** (National Research University Higher School of Economics, Moscow)

2009; Blank and Koch 2000; Goddard and Wierzbicka [eds.] 1994, 2002, 2004; Levinson and Wilkins [eds.] 2006; Majid and Bowerman [eds.] 2007; Majid and Levinson [eds.] 2011; Koptjevskaja-Tamm and Vanhove [eds.] 2012, and others). The scope of such studies is also growing. Along with old favorites like color and kinship terms or names of body parts (see Koptjevskaja-Tamm 2008), attention is turning to such complex domains as perception verbs (Viberg 1983; Vanhove 2008), the predicates of position (Newman [ed.] 2002), movement (Maisak and Rakhilina [eds.] 2007), destruction (Majid and Bowerman [eds.] 2007), eating and drinking (Newman [ed.] 2009), putting and taking (Kopecka and Narasimhan [eds.] 2012), spatial relations (Levinson and Wilkins [eds.] 2006), memory (Amberber [ed.] 2007), among others.

Just as important, or perhaps even more so, as the findings about specific words and languages is the increasing realization that lexical typology needs a well-articulated method. Only when individual studies use the same theoretical framework, follow the same plan and method, can their results be fully compatible. They then reach their full worth and meaning, as typology ultimately addresses its main question: to what extent is the lexicon systematic and built on universal principles?

Some major steps have already been made in that direction. We will specifically discuss two approaches: the psycholinguistic studies at the Max Planck Institute in Nijmegen, and the method initially suggested by Anna Wierzbicka (Wierzbicka 1972, 1996). The first approach stems from research on color terms (Berlin and Kay 1969). In keeping with this tradition, the method is to collect the speakers' reactions to extralinguistic stimuli, be it color chips (Majid and Levinson 2007), samples of smells and tastes (Majid, Senft, and Levinson 2007; Senft, Majid, and Levinson 2007; Majid and Levinson [eds.] 2011), or video clips demonstrating different situations of cutting and breaking, such as tearing a rag or chopping a carrot (Majid and Bowerman [eds.] 2007). The second approach, represented by the works of Anna Wierzbicka, Cliff Goddard, and their colleagues and students (Goddard and Wierzbicka [eds.] 1994; Goddard [1998] 2011; Goddard [ed.] 2008; Gladkova 2010), is pursuing the old philosophic ideal of a natural semantic metalanguage – a small universal vocabulary of semantic primes sufficient to express any meaning in any language. Primes need to have lexical exponents in all languages. Other meanings can be explicated using these primes. Thus, meanings of words from different languages are compared with regard to which primes are needed in their respective explications. It should be noted that explicating word-meanings by primes is mostly an introspective process, but resulting definitions are supposed to predict the distribution (combinatorics, collocations, etc.) and entailments of the words being explicated, so textual examples are also used in NSM work. Recently, NSM linguists have proposed a more systematic approach to lexical typology using the notion of semantic template (Goddard 2012).

The principles and findings of both schools of thought are documented in detailed reviews (Apresjan 1995; Geeraerts 1988, 1993; Plungian and Rakhilina 1996; Goddard 2001a) and need not be repeated here.

In this paper we present an alternative approach to lexical typology that can be called the "frame method". It was developed and tested in the Moscow Lexical Typology Group (see http://lextyp.org)[2] and is currently used in all its projects, such as (Maisak and Rakhilina [eds.] 2007; Britsyn et al. [eds.] 2009; Kruglyakova 2010; Reznikova, Rakhilina, and Bonch-Osmolovskaya 2012).

Our main principle, taken from the Moscow semantic school of thought (Apresjan [1974]1992, 2000), is that lexical meanings can be studied and reconstructed by observing a word's "surroundings", or primarily collocation. They can then be compared using procedures similar to those used in grammatical typology. In the following sections we will describe how this works in detail.

We believe that this method has some advantages over the two approaches mentioned above. Namely that the psycholinguistic method, where extralinguistic stimuli need to be presented, is hardly suited for subjective, internal experiences such as emotions or pain. The disadvantage of the NSM method is that it seems to be less effective when dealing with large groups of near-synonyms. Above all, neither approach is suited to the study of semantic shifts.

Of course, the descriptive "weaknesses" are not coincidental, but arise from the particular goals each approach aims to achieve, as well as the theoretical views in which they are grounded. Still, it seems to us that lexical typology as a whole needs to have some means of describing any domain, as well as the ways in which domains relate to one another, i.e. semantic shifts, or, in synchronic terms, polysemy. Indeed, most words in a language are polysemous, and a typology that aims to compare words should account for possible (and impossible) combinations of meanings within one word.

This paper proposes to show that the frame method that we suggest is adequate to both tasks (namely, it has no limitations concerning semantic domains; it can be applied to, and is well suited for describing semantic shifts) and, therefore, compares favorably with the other approaches.

---

[2] The present members of the MLexT include A.Bonch-Osmolovskaya, E.Kashkin, L.Kholkina, L.Khokhlova, E.Kozlova, A.Kostyrkin, V.Kruglyakova, M.Kyuseva, E.Luchina, T.Maisak, S.Merdanova, L.Nanij, B.Orekhov, E.Pavlova, A.Panina, E.Parina, E.Rudnitskaya, D.Ryzhova, M.Shapiro, O.Shemanaeva, I.Stenin, M.Tagabileva, A.Vyrenkova.

The paper is structured as follows. Section I will explicate the goals of lexical typology as we see them in connection with our method, which will then be presented in more detail in Section II, as applied to some specific domains in specific languages. Section III discusses the importance of semantic shifts to lexical typology and reports on their study within the suggested framework.

4.2 Principles and goals of the Frame-based approach to lexical typology

As stated above, our aim is the synthesis of two schools of research, well-established in their own right: the Moscow semantic school with its methods of analyzing word-meanings; and grammatical typology. This section will show that such a synthesis is not only possible, but in a sense natural, since the fundamental assumptions about language (non-autonomous syntax, role of semantics in language modeling, etc.) in the two approaches have much in common. Going over the strong points and limitations of the Moscow semantic school in 4.2.1, we will then suggest some ways to overcome the limitations by adopting tools from the typology of grammatical categories.

4.2.1 The Moscow semantic school

Dating back to the 1960s, the Moscow semantic school has an internationally recognized standing in lexical semantics. Its main, and very powerful, method is comparing a word's surrounding constructions and collocations to those of its near synonyms (a major finding being that there is no such thing as full synonyms in any language), cf. (Apresjan 2000; Mel'čuk 2012; see also Wanner [ed.] 2008). Taking semantically related groups of words and exploring their differences proved an extremely effective lexicographic technique, as can be seen in some outstanding dictionaries, Russian and bilingual, produced within the approach (Apresjan and Rosenman [eds.] 1979; Mel'čuk and Zholkovsky 1984; Mel'čuk et al. 1999; Apresjan [ed.] 2004).

The core of the method is finding contexts in which a word cannot be replaced by a given near-synonym, and determining which properties prevent the substitution. Bilingual dictionaries treat translational equivalents as a simple extension of near-synonymy into another language. This means that the procedure is just as valid for a broad typological study, even though it would require proportionally more time and effort.

The Moscow semantic school itself does not venture into typology. Its members, lexicologists and lexicographers, maintain that the lexicon is a system which is highly motivated and structured on principles of human cognition (Apresjan 2009). However, their main practical goal is to create detailed descriptions, the so-called "lexicographic portraits", of individual lexemes. Still, if we look beyond the lexical system of one language and observe similar systems in others, a further task arises – to distill the typologically relevant features from the mass of features relevant intralinguistically.

4.2.2 Grammatical and lexical typology

The other field to which we turn in our search for methods is grammatical typology. It differs from lexical typology in being several decades older and has evolved its own standards of contrastive research, especially with regard to grammatical categories (see Comrie 1976, 1985; Bybee and Dahl 1989; Corbett 1991, 2000; Aikhenvald 2000, and others).

The common opinion is that there is a limited universal inventory of grammatical meanings (Bybee and Dahl 1989: 51–52; Plungian 2000: 233–238) from which each language "selects" a subset (for further discussion of this issue, see Croft 2001; Haspelmath 2010). The subsets can be quite different across languages. Further, it is common for multiple grammatical meanings to be explicated by a single marker or construction. Most typologists believe that the process is guided by a number of cognitive strategies, which also differ from one language to another, cf. (Plungian 2000; Haspelmath 2003).

Accordingly, the main goals of grammatical typology could be seen as 1) describing the set of universal atoms of grammatical meaning, and 2) determining the strategies that languages use when combining these meanings.

If we look at lexical typology as similar to grammatical typology the former should be in search of 1) a universal set of lexical meanings, and 2) the strategies of their combination in languages. We explore both topics in the following sections.

4.2.2.1 Universal features and oppositions

A grammatical category tends to have a limited number of elements – three persons, about two numbers (not many more even for the systems with dual and paucal), about three tenses etc. The structure of a category is usually highly visible, with clear-cut oppositions. A group of near-synonyms constituting a domain (=semantic field), on the other hand, is seldom so transparent; all the words in it have more or less the same meaning.

The closest thing to binary oppositions to be found in the lexicon are antonyms. Bringing antonyms into the picture often gives insight into a word's meaning; thus, *old* as opposed to *young* vs. *new* (*an old shoe/sailor* vs. *a young /*new sailor*) points towards animacy, or rather anthropocentrism, and we may reasonably expect a language to reflect the opposition by having two words for 'old'[3] (see Paradis, this volume).

However, a vastly larger number of words have near-synonyms than they have antonyms. It is difficult to imagine lexical antonyms for *grass* or *house*, *golden* or *striped*, *embellish* or *burrow* etc. Even words that do pair up rarely mirror one another's semantics perfectly. For example, taking the adjectives *live/dead* we find that they highlight different aspects of the opposition – while *dead* means biological death (*a dead cat, dead trees* etc.), *live* seems to be the default state for everything it is applicable to, so that when it is specifically mentioned, the resulting meaning is non-trivial, as in *a live performance* (not a recording), *live snakes* (not toys), etc.[4]

We have to admit that lexical and grammatical typology deal with different enough objects that the methods of one cannot be adopted into the other without some modification.

There is an additional difficulty surrounding the usage of grammatical markers vs. lexemes. Grammatical markers tend to occur in texts with a much greater frequency. While a corpus of 200–300 thousand words should yield all the relevant contexts for reasonably common markers, 100 million is not always enough to illustrate the behavior of a lexeme. With rare words billion-word corpora may be required.

4.2.2.2 Combination of meanings

It is well known that a grammatical marker in a given language generally has several functions, each realized in a particular context, and that the sets of contexts differ across languages. Grammatical typologists collect relevant contexts from known languages to check new data against them. When a context proves

---

3 Indeed, Cusco Quechua lexicalizes the opposition – it uses *thanta* for artefacts vs. *machu* and *paya* for men and women respectively, see (Cusihuamán [1976] 2001); we thank Paul Hegarty for bringing this to our attention.
4 On the assymetry of the Russian adjectives *živoj* 'live' / *mertvyj* 'dead', see Podlipentseva (2011).

relevant to the category in question in a language, it receives a place in the typological questionnaire. When some of the contexts in a given language are found to have the same explication, this pattern is what characterizes the language typologically.

The same procedure can be used for a semantic domain, listing the relevant contexts and observing the patterns in their lexical explications in different languages. If we take this approach, the main problem is technical: how to select the vocabulary, contexts and languages. The next section presents our process in detail, using examples from some of our completed and ongoing projects.

4.3 Methodological foundations

4.3.1 Selection of languages

The work starts with defining a semantic domain for the analysis. This is in itself a non-trivial task because the researcher has to decide where to draw the domain boundaries, i.e. which words should be considered relevant for the domain in question. This decision is first made with respect to the native language of the researcher and may then undergo changes as other languages are included in the study.

The number and choice of these languages is another point in which lexical typology is different from grammatical typology. Grammatical typology requires several hundred languages, usually 200–400, which, furthermore, need to be distributed equally among genetic and areal groups (Bybee 1985; Bybee, Perkins, and Pagliuca 1994). Closely related languages are almost never used, lest their similarities distort the general picture[5].

The striking difference of lexical typology in this respect is that related languages tend to be just as valuable to it as unrelated ones (cf. Rakhilina and Prokofieva 2004; Rakhilina 2010a). While grammatical constructions take centuries to evolve, vocabulary is much more fluid. A single generation of speakers may witness words falling in and out of use and word meanings changing dramatically. As a result, even such close relatives as Russian and Polish do not necessarily have many cognates in a given domain, and even when they do, such words tend to have meanings quite dissimilar to those of their "cousins".

---

[5] Kibrik 1992, 1998, however, claims that related languages are also suited for grammatical typology.

Verbs of rotation provide a good example. Russian has *krutit'sja, vertet'sja, vraščat'sja,* and *kružit'(sja),* and Polish *kręcić się, wiercić się, obracać się, krążyć,* and *wirować.* Although most of these verbs are cognates (except for Polish *wirować*), they structure the semantic domain of rotation in completely different ways. For example, Russian *vertet'sja* applies both to animate and inanimate subjects, whereas Polish *wiercić się* describes only animate subjects. The scope of Polish *kręcić się* can include, unlike Russian *krutit'sja,* long and flexible objects, such as curved hair or a meandering road. Russian *kružit'* presupposes that the Trajector is situated above the Landmark (typical examples are eagles or hawks flying above prey), while Polish *krążyć* is not sensitive to this restriction and tolerates the Trajector and the Landmark located at the same level (a boat going around an island, etc.) (Rakhilina 2010a).

As to the number of languages on the list, it does not seem realistic for lexical typology to imitate the scope of grammatical typology, especially since preexisting resources such as dictionaries are seldom sufficient, and often not available. Still, we believe that for lexical typology method takes precedence over scope. If the angle is typological, i.e. suited to accommodating different languages, a study can be considered typological even if the data is limited. The most extensive of our own projects, the domain of swimming and floating, covers 50 languages; the vocabulary of pain 30, rotation 17, and sharpness and bluntness 15. We find that even a study of 15 languages allows for some non-trivial generalizations (it is worth noting that a dozen languages is also considered a valid sample for a general sketch of a grammatical category – see Haspelmath 2003).

Naturally a typological hypothesis, even if based on a small initial sample, serves as a framework which facilitates dealing with each additional language.

4.3.2 Dictionaries, corpora and questionnaires

Having determined the rough outlines of the domain in question in one's native language, the next step is to consult bilingual dictionaries for translational equivalents. Any of the source words can be expected to have more than one translation into a given language, and it is equally common for several words to have the same equivalent. For example, Russian *ostryj,* 'sharp' corresponds to two Komi adjectives – *lečyd,* 'sharply edged' (*lečyd purt* 'a sharp knife'), and *jos',* 'sharply pointed' (*jos' pu* 'a sharp stick').

Sometimes the dictionaries are outdated or incomplete, so the data needs to be rechecked. The quickest way to do this is a corpus search, provided there is a corpus for the language. If the words are reasonably common and the corpus large, their typical collocation and differences in usage should become clear.

A corpus may still contain outdated, peculiar or otherwise non-standard examples, so it is best to have them verified by a native speaker. For languages without other resources, interviewing speakers is the only way to gather data. Experience shows that the most efficient way is to leave such languages for later, so as to have a list of questions ready for the interview. In this sense, examples from corpora are valuable not simply as illustrations of word usage, but as a source of contexts potentially relevant to other languages. These contexts provide the basis for a questionnaire that is then used to collect data from under-resourced languages.

4.3.3 Semantic features

Groups of contexts from the corpus are analyzed in the tradition of the Moscow semantic school to find the differences. For predicates, one of the key factors of their distribution is the semantic type of the subject (for verbs) or the qualified entity (for adjectives). The distinction made most often and most consistently is that of animate (especially human) vs. inanimate subjects. Many languages have predicates specifically designated for one or the other.

Motion verbs are often found in such pairs – cf. the English *swim* (=voluntary motion) vs. *float* (=being passively moved around) and their numerous equivalents – Persian *šenā kardan* vs. *šenāvar budan*, Tamil *nīntu* vs. *mita*, Manyika *námún* VS. *fún*, etc., see (Maisak and Rakhilina [eds.] 2007). Active vs. passive motion can be present as distinct concepts at high levels of abstraction (Plungian and Rakhilina 2007). Verbs of rotation appear to be a rare exception, divided not by the animacy of the subject but by whether the axis of rotation is inside or outside of the rotating object: Polish *wiercić się* vs. *krążyć*, Koryak *kamlil* vs. *kavaljil* etc.

The more participants there are in a situation, the more factors a researcher needs to take into account. For example, verbs of eating and drinking are structured around the type of subject (such as human vs. animal), object (in particular solid vs. liquid), and presence or absence of specific instruments or quasi-instruments (teeth, tongue, spoon, etc.). Thus in Russian we have *est'* (solid food), *glodat'* ('gnaw' – animal agent, hard object such as a bone, teeth), *lakat'* ('lap' – animal agent, liquid, tongue), etc.

Even more intricate is the domain of cutting and breaking (Bowerman and Majid [eds.] 2007). Apart from the subject being in control, or not in control, of the situation, the lexical choice is affected by at least three other variables: the type of object being destroyed, presence and type of instrument, and the end results such as size and quantity of pieces. The Russian language distinguishes, among others, *rvat'* ('tear' – soft object, by hand); *rubit'* ('hew' – hard object, an axe or similar instrument, in half or into big pieces); *rezat'* ('cut' – moderately soft object, blade-like instrument, esp. knife or scissors); *toloč* ('grind; pound' – small hard objects, using millstones or mortar, into a homogeneous mass); *šinkovat'* (vegetables, knife or hatchet, very small pieces), and many others. Komi has the verb *jukavny* meaning 'to splinter planks', which leaves no choice of object (wood), instrument (axe or knife), or result (splinters). Another Komi verb, *šarsköbtyny*, is an otherwise ordinary verb of breaking, but with an interesting addition: a ringing sound (Kashkin 2010).

With types of arguments and other relevant parameters listed like this, it may seem that we reduce each domain to a set of oppositions, as in component analysis, cf. (Katz and Fodor 1963; Lehrer 1974). Indeed, we use semantic features to compare and contrast words across languages – e.g. verbs of rotation are classified by the following characteristics:
– internal/external axis
– elevation over the landmark
– control
– single/repeated turn, etc.

The approach seems essentially the same as the features Lehrer (Lehrer 1974: 61–63) uses to describe the vocabulary of cooking:
– use of liquids
– use of fat
– use of steam
– high/low heat
– long/short duration, etc.

However there is a crucial difference. Component analysis assumes features to be independent – hence the tendency, popular from the 1960's and onwards, to describe both semantic fields and grammatical categories by exhaustively listing their features (Mel'čuk and Kholodovich 1970; Khrakovsky [ed.] 1989).

Our approach, on the other hand, is to view features as interdependent. They fall into gestalts, often so closely knit together that selecting one argument restricts the others. Thus, if the subject of rotation is a bird, the axis is going to be external. Furthermore, a flying agent is moving not just around the landmark, but above it (e.g. a hawk circling over its prey), while for other kinds of subjects elevation is usually irrelevant.

Verbs of cooking (Lehrer 1974) also demonstrate the interdependency of features quite clearly. Intense heating can only last for a short time, otherwise the food will burn; water, but not fat, is used in steaming; and so on.

Translating the idea into component-analytical terms, it can be said that along with truly equipollent oppositions (+/−), we find some features better represented as +/0. They are irrelevant for most of the domain and true for one or a few lexemes. E.g. *šarsköbtyny* is the only verb of breaking in Komi for which sound is relevant (e.g. constitutes a part of its meaning), even though other actual situations of breaking may involve sound.

It naturally follows that the entries in a lexical typological questionnaire must represent not all features multiplied by all values, but all gestalts – all meaningful clusters of features, cf. in this respect (Goddard and Wierzbicka 2009).

Individual features are still of great importance when we determine what exactly constitutes each particular gestalt, lest some aspect of the meaning get ignored. This is especially true for predicates with three or more arguments. The study of the verbs of cutting and breaking mentioned above (Majid and Bowerman [eds.] 2007) uses 61 video clips to represent various situations in the domain, yet even this was not enough to cover the full range of possibilities. Among the situations that were overlooked are the use of a stationary background object as an instrument (e.g. smashing things against a wall) and crushing or grinding into small pieces (see Kashkin 2010).

4.3.4 Frames

The gestalts or prototypical situations discussed above appear to be so closely related to the predicate's argument types that a full set of arguments can serve as a sufficient representation of the situation. We believe that these sets, which we shall call semantic frames, constitute a relevant unit of lexical typological description.

To describe a domain, then, is to list all the frames covering it, and for each frame to find its explication in all of the chosen languages.

For the domain of swimming and floating the relevant frames are 1) active swimming, 2) passively drifting with the current, 3) floating on the surface, 4) the movement of vessels and people on vessels. The domain of oscillation is richer; its frames include 1) the swinging of a suspended object (e.g. a pendulum), 2) rocking, 3) the bending of a tall object, 4) an object being deformed by an external force (a shaky bridge), 5) the undulating movement of the surface of a liquid, and some others.

Note that these situations differ from the traditional understanding of frames (Fillmore 1976, 1982), currently used in FrameNet (see framenet.icsi.berkeley.edu). Traditionally a frame is defined as a set of participants with their assigned syntactic roles. Valence as such, however, proves to be of little use in cross-linguistic lexical studies. Adjectives, for example, are mostly one-place predicates with next to no variation in the marking of their only argument. Therefore, if their meanings are to be compared, the distinction has to be based also on the semantic, and not merely on the syntactic, properties of the argument.

The same is often true for verbs. Verbs of swimming and drifting are nearly indistinguishable in the case marking of their arguments; the difference lies in the semantic class of the arguments. Therefore, our concept of frame, as opposed to the traditional one, includes information on the semantic types of the arguments.

Our approach also differs from the NSM theory in how frames are treated. The Lexico-Syntactic Frames of NSM are rather general and are defined for an entire semantic class, as illustrated in Goddard (2012: 726), with three subclasses of physical activity verbs – locomotion, routine physical activities and complex physical activities. Each of these subclasses includes a number of lexical units (cf. *walk, run*, etc. for locomotion, *eat, drink* etc. for routine physical activities and *cut, chop,* etc. for complex physical activities) encompassing a wide range of specific situations, which we regard to be frames.

So far we have discussed frames as if they were ready-to-use tools for comparing word meanings in different languages. Yet this is not the case; frames need to be identified for each semantic domain that is being researched.

4.3.5 Frames and micro-frames

Grammatical typology, especially when searching for universals, has developed a procedure for working with questionnaires (Dahl 1985). It starts with a model of the category, such as the passive voice or subjunctive mood, already well-known from the previous studies. The category is associated with a set of grammatical contexts in which it usually appears cross-linguistically. These contexts are represented by the questionnaire entries. Going through them, the researcher looks for the corresponding marker or construction in a particular language. The more entries the marker covers, the closer the language is to the prototypical model.

Lexical typology, unfortunately, cannot make use of previously developed sets of prototypical situations (i.e., in our terminology, semantic frames) and check lexical units from a particular language against them. Such lists emerge only gradually from the typological data. As mentioned above, the starting point for data collection is contexts, as detailed as dictionaries and corpora can make them, with the additional subtleties added precisely because we do not know beforehand which distinctions may be relevant to lexicalization. The contexts are tested with data from different languages.

As a result, some of the contexts will systematically turn out not to be distinguished in any of the target languages. They are then collapsed, not yet into a frame but into what we call a micro-frame. Often these contexts are metonymically related, such as 'sound of wind/sound of trees in the wind' or 'stream flowing/something drifting with the current'. Micro-frames are still more specific than typical word-meanings. The way they are grouped into word-meanings need not be similar in all languages, yet often several languages group them similarly. These tendencies in lexicalization show which features are more important for the domain.

Micro-frames can be compared to the units in the universal grammatical inventory: just as most languages group several of them together to be explicated by a single marker, micro-frames are clustered into frames so that for each frame a word exists in at least one language (and usually, more than one). Triple number, distinct from plural, is rare; likewise, "waterfowl swimming" does not warrant its own frame and is conceptualized as similar to either swimming or the motion of vessels, in the same way that flying insects (e.g. moths circling around a candle) are grouped together with either birds or eddies of wind.

Thus, micro-frames are rather peripheral situations that, although they exhibit variation in lexical patterning across languages, are not expressed by a dedicated lexical unit (cf. waterfowl swimming or flying insects). By contrast, frames represent the core situations of a domain and may be distinctly lexicalized in a certain language. While micro-frames must be relevant to the more detailed contrastive studies of languages, such as compiling a typologically oriented dictionary, broader frames are better suited to the task of comparing semantic fields.

4.3.6 Semantic maps

Semantic maps are another tool of grammatical typology that can be adapted to the needs of lexical typology. Grammatical maps represent an area of the grammatical system, such as modality or interrogative pronouns; the universal inventory of meanings forms the map's nodes, and several nodes can be marked with a similar color to show that in a given language the meanings are expressed by the same marker. The pictures are then easy to compare across languages, see (van der Auwera and Plungian 1998; Haspelmath 2003; Tatevosov 2004).

In our lexical typological studies we build maps for larger entities – domains, or semantic fields, which would be similar to whole grammatical categories. The nodes, too, are larger – frames, rather than micro-frames. This is due to the fact that lexical meanings vastly outnumber grammatical meanings. A map built from micro-frames would be too clustered by differences between individual lexemes, swallowing any useful generalizations. Therefore we intentionally omit some finer nuances (such as the insects from the previous section) and operate at the level of entire lexical systems.

As with grammatical maps, the nodes that are often realized by the same linguistic means are placed closely on the map. Two frames with a similar lexicalization cannot be separated by a third if it corresponds to a different word.

Lexical data is then placed on the map to show how the domain is divided into individual words in a given language, for further comparison between languages[6]. As an example, let us take the domain of emptiness (Tagabileva and Kholkina 2010; Tagabileva 2011). The relevant frames for it were found to be 'hollow shape', 'empty container', 'location empty of people', 'large space without objects on it' (cf. 'a field without buildings'), small flat surface without things on it' (cf. 'an empty table'), and 'empty hanger' (Fig. 1). None of the surveyed languages lexicalized all of them, but at least one frame was lexicalized in each. Chinese and Russian (Fig. 2), with *kong* vs. *kongxin* and *pustoj* vs. *polyj* respectively, have only the opposition of functional emptiness vs. hollow shape (it is worth noting that, while *kongxin* is a derivate of *kong*, *polyj* and *pustoj* do not share any common roots).

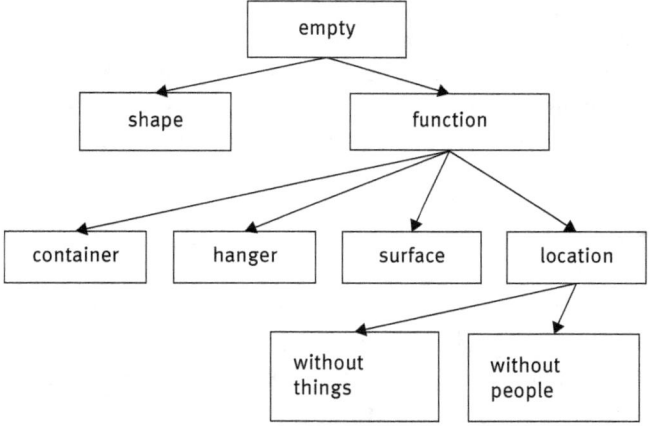

Fig. 1: Semantic map: domain of 'empty'

---

[6] For another technique for visualization of lexical typological data see multidimensional scaling plots as used in the Nijmegen School (cf. Majid et al. 2007, 2011).

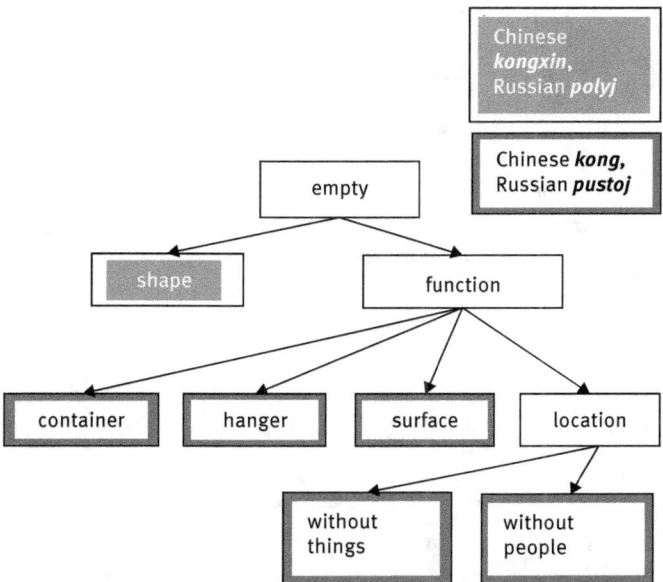

Fig. 2: Semantic map: domain of 'empty' in Russian and Chinese

Serbian (Fig. 3), in addition to emptiness (*prazan*) and hollowness (*šupalj*), has a word specifically for absence of people – *pust*, at least in the dictionaries; speakers and corpora appear to testify that the current usage is shifting. According to Tolstaya (2008), the distinction, present in Serbian until recently, at an earlier time was common to all Slavonic languages. The corresponding word in modern Russian, *prazdnyj*, has shifted its meaning from 'unoccupied' to 'idle' and is generally fading out of active use.

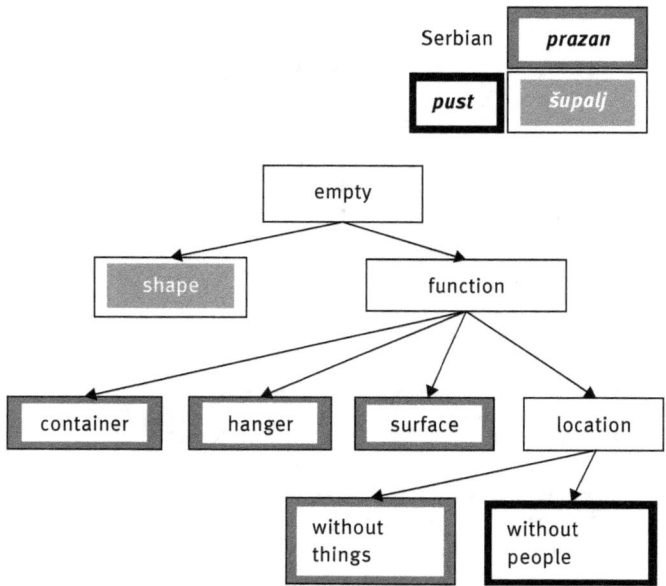

Fig. 3: Semantic map: domain of 'empty' in Serbian

Korean (Fig. 4) distributes words between frames more evenly. There is no distinction of hollow object vs. empty container – an empty glass and a hollow gourd would both be described as *thengpita*. The situation is distinguished, on the one hand, from locations, *konghehata*, irrespective of whether they are empty of people or things, and on the other from working surfaces and hangers, *pita*.

Maps offer a ready and intuitive way to grasp the domain as a whole and how different languages structure it. A lexical system can be rich, in extreme cases lexicalizing every frame separately, or poor, with one word for the whole domain. Even the poorer systems, however, along with the dominant word tend to have a periphery of less common specific expressions. The Armenian domain of swimming and floating is one of these; there is the dominant verb *loyal*, which can cover all situations of swimming and floating. The others, *navel* and *navarkel*, are marginal for the domain – they are less frequent and have narrower meanings.

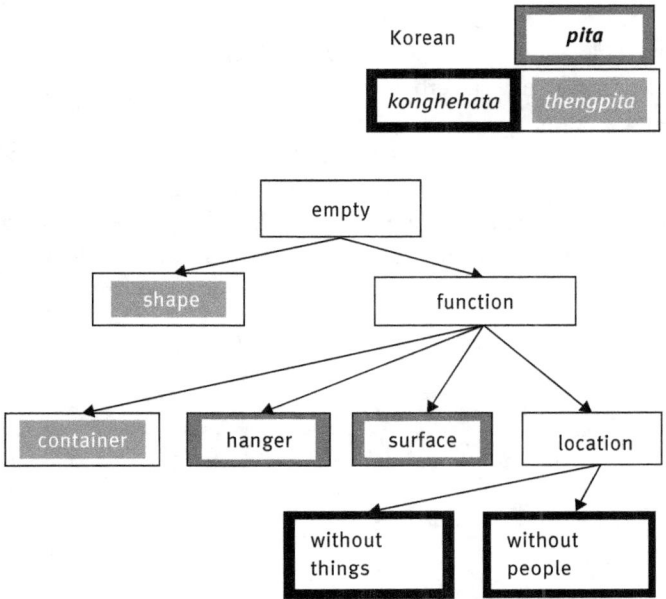

Fig. 4: Semantic map: domain of 'empty' in Korean

Thus, lexical typology can deal not just with lexemes but with lexical systems. The ambition is similar to that of the WALS (http://wals.info) at the Max Planck Institute that is recording the distribution of grammatical systems of different types over the world.

A working typology must have some predictive value – it should not just observe the existing systems, but judge which configurations are common and which less expected or outright impossible. In the domain of swimming and floating, for example, the frames can be ranked according to how active the subject is: *swim > travel by vessel > drift > float*. Seeing that vessels are usually lexicalized together with drifting (sometimes with swimming), we can expect that the most natural tendency would be to distinguish active swimming from passive drifting and floating (as in Persian, Korean etc.). Another strategy, also found empirically, is based on control and contrasts uncontrolled drifting to both swimming and floating, which are grouped together (e.g. Hindi and Khakas). Some languages make further distinctions without disrupting the overall pattern[7], but the absence

---

[7] Floating in a small container, such as vegetables in a stew, often gets special explication – usually with a verb of existence rather than a *float*-type verb.

of contradicting tendencies is remarkable and can be taken in support of our model of the domain. This allows us to predict with a high degree of certainty that no language is expected to have a verb for swimming and drifting opposed to another for vessels and floating.

Semantic maps express these restrictions by the placement of nodes. In grammatical typology (van der Auwera and Plungian 1998; Haspelmath 2003; also Tatevosov 2004) a similar explication for two nodes is only possible if the nodes are neighbors. Fig. 5–6 show how it works for the domain of swimming and floating:

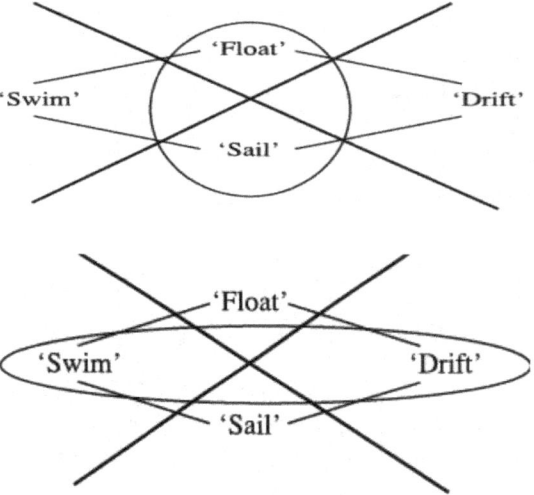

Fig. 5–6: Improbable (impossible?) systems: swimming and drifting vs. vessels and floating; vessels and drifting vs. swimming and floating.

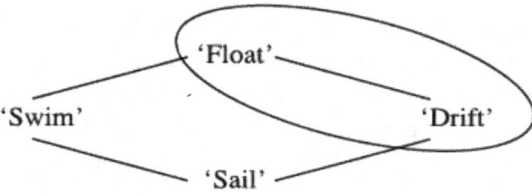

Fig. 7: An existing system: floating and drifting vs. vessels vs. swimming (cf. Tamil).

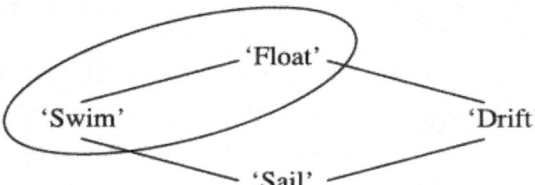

Fig. 8: An existing system: swimming and floating vs. drifting vs. vessels (cf. Komi)

4.4 Semantic shifts

An important difference between grammatical and lexical typology maps is their relation to the history of language. Grammatical markers often derive from one another, and their proximity on the map correlates with their diachronic relations. Historical relations between lexical meanings, on the other hand, are much more complex and difficult to observe, which makes our map a strictly synchronous device.

Exactly to what extent historical and etymological data is relevant to lexical typology is far from self-evident. For some researchers who focus specifically on the evolution of word-meanings, the answer is 'a great deal' (e.g. Blank and Koch 2000; Gévaudan, Koch, and Neu 2003; Dybo 1994, 1996, and others). Zalizniak (2009) is also to a large extent diachronically oriented. Others, such as the Nijmegen psycholinguistic school, make no use of historic data; nor is Goddard and Wierzbicka's metalanguage suited to describing semantic shifts (except for historical and diachronic changes, cf. Bromhead 2009; Wiezbicka 2006, 2010a, 2010b).

Our view is that meaning shifts should be studied, by lexical typology especially, for the following reasons:
– In some domains there are meanings explicated only by metaphors.
– The way a polysemous word combines several meanings is not identical, but in important ways similar, to a word expressing several frames in a domain.
– The typology of shifts sheds light on the shifts themselves, in particular on the difference between metaphor and metonymy.
– Meaning shifts can help determine the extent of a domain.
– From a theoretical perspective, shifts bring current and historical phenomena together.
– From the point of view of lexicological practice, metaphors provide an opportunity to look at constructions rather than isolated lexemes. It is important

to compare the syntactic properties of a word's main and metaphoric senses and explain the differences.

In the following sections we will discuss each point in detail.

4.4.1 Metaphoric domains

Metaphor, by definition, involves a word shifting from one semantic domain into another. Most of the existing approaches to lexical typology focus on a specific semantic field. It may thus seem that, since metaphoric senses lie outside these fields, they are of no interest to typologists. However there are some domains which in most, if not all, languages are predominantly populated by metaphoric usages – in these cases, metaphors simply cannot be neglected.

One such example is the domain of pain and unpleasant physical sensations. The vocabulary used to describe a variety of sensations in different body parts may number as many as 50 words. Of these only a small minority, such as *hurt*, *ache* in English or *bolet'* in Russian, are the so-called primary pain predicates, and the rest originate from other domains – e.g. English *My eyes are burning, The wound is stinging*; Crimean Tatar *başım uvulday*, lit. 'my head is hooting'; Erzya *kar'az aj s'iž't'e* lit. 'the back is tearing'; Aghul *ze jak̄-ar ar ʕ.u-naa* 'my muscles are smashed (aching from fever)' etc., see Reznikova, Rakhilina, and Bonch-Osmolovskaya (2012).

Of course, it must be noted that such domains are the exception rather than the rule. For non-metaphoric fields it is more efficient to ignore metaphors until after the main senses are described. The representation of metaphoric shifts in dictionaries is sporadic, and corpora present the additional challenge of separating established usages from occasional word-play by individual authors. Even interviewing speakers is not an easy way to collect metaphors. Some speakers are insensitive to semantic shifts (which is an interesting psycho-linguistic problem in itself), and when presented with a metaphoric expression tend to translate it word for word, instead of remembering a differently-worded equivalent from their native language. Calques have little value in a lexical typological study.

When we have a general picture of the domain, on the other hand, metaphoric shifts within the source domain make for an interesting follow-up study. Therefore our project on sound verbs (Rakhilina 2010b) largely focused on the verbs that have animal sounds as their main sense and sounds made by humans, nature, machinery etc. as metaphoric usages. While there is a considerable variety among languages – laughter < noise made by geese (Russian) and crickets (Armenian), hoarse speech and malfunctioning audio < crows (German), pleased grunting < pigs (Bulgarian) etc. – there are some observable tendencies in the mapping of different kinds of animals to human behavior, and of artifacts to the sound they make.

4.4.2 Metaphor and metonymy as a combination of senses

When several frames in a domain are covered by a single lexeme, it can be viewed as vagueness or a broader meaning compared to the languages that have separate words for the frames. When a word explicates frames from different domains, it is a case of polysemy – usually metaphor. It is well-known that the so-called primary metaphors (Lakoff and Johnson 1980; Grady 1999) have considerable similarity across languages, so their patterns and typological consistency could be an appealing subject for cross-linguistic lexical studies.

It is remarkable that even closely related frames differ in the direction of their "cross-domain relationships". Active horizontal motion through the air (prototypically self-propelled flight, as of birds) is often combined with the frame of jumping – East-Armenian *tʰəṙčʰel*, Persian *päridän* etc., and passive motion (arrows and other projectiles) with the frame of falling – Sanskrit *pat-*, but never the opposite (Plungian and Rakhilina 2007). In languages that classify sharp objects into sharply pointed and sharply edged, the former frame is a typical source of metaphors for keen senses (sharp sight, hearing etc.), and the latter for speed (see Kyuseva 2012). Another such pair of systematic shifts can be seen in the domain of hardness and firmness: such negative human traits as cruelty or meanness often borrow the adjective that signifies hardness experienced directly (such as hard bedding or tough undercooked meat), and positive traits such as loyalty are usually associated with firmness attested by touching with the hand or an instrument (Pavlova 2014).

What is more interesting in the examples above is not the fact that similar metaphoric shifts occur systematically in different languages, nor even the underlying semantic and cognitive factors, but the way metaphors structure the source domain. We will come back to this after pointing out some cases of typologically relevant metonymy.

The most widespread metonymy – "part > whole" – is the least typologically interesting: in such pairs as *blunt edge > blunt scissors*, *hard cushion > hard chair*, *lock the door* > *lock the house* both usages explicate the same semantic frame and are not lexically opposed to each other in most languages[8].

Other types of metonymy, however, may show greater typological variation. Travel by vessel can be lexicalized separately from the movement of the vessel itself – this is the case with denominatives in Indonesian: *berkapal* 'go by ship', *berperahu* 'go by boat' etc., which cannot refer to ships and boats themselves (Lander and Kramarova 2007: 679). For the Persian AQUA-motion verb *šenā kardan* vessels are acceptable subjects, but passengers are not – with an animate subject it can only mean swimming (Kuznetsova 2007). Several languages, such as Russian and Tamil, have different words for the motion of a single fish vs. that of a shoal of fish – *plyt'*, *nīntu* 'swim' vs. *idti*, *cēl* 'go' respectively (Smirnitskaya 2007). In other words, meanings that in some languages are expressed by the same lexical item, and stand in a metonymic relation, may in others be lexically opposed to each other.

Another non-trivial metonymy can be found in the domain of speed. Russian *bystryj*, English *quick*, German *schnell* all combine two meanings: speediness of a process and shortness of the interval between the point of reference and an instantaneous event: *walk quickly* vs. *decide quickly*. These are in fact different frames which can be lexicalized separately – cf. Russian *medlenno* 'slowly' (as in *medlenno idti* 'walk slowly') vs. *dolgo* 'for or after a long time' (as in *dolgo ne otvečat'* 'not to answer for a long time').

A remarkable metonymic shift occurs when the same word means 'drifting on the current' and 'flow of the current itself'. This metonymy is by no means universal, e.g. English and Russian lack it, but it can be observed in more than 15 languages of our sample including Chinese, Japanese, Italian, Swedish, Lithuanian, Polish, Khakas and others.

Even more typologically relevant is the so-called "end-point metonymy" (Lakoff 1987; Brugman and Lakoff 1988; Paducheva 2004; Kustova 2004) that combines the meanings of a process and its result (*he surrounded the house with a fence* > *a fence surrounded the house*). Another well-known example is the polysemy of the English preposition *over*, as in *fly over the hill* (movement) vs. *live over the hill* (location at the end point of the movement). In some languages, horizontal and vertical movement through water are also united in process-result metonymy: 'rising to the surface > floating on the surface', as in Indonesian *mengam-*

---

[8] This does not mean that part-whole metonymy presents no possibilities for lexical typology. An interesting task, for example, would be to find if any shifts of this kind are impossible. A likely impossible metonymy is 'a person moving > body part moving', as in *a skater glides by* / **a skater's legs glide by*.

bang (also Chinese, Japanese, Hindi, Karachay-Balkar and others, see Maisak and Rakhilina [eds.] 2007).

4.4.3 Shifts and the borders of semantic domains

Since metaphor and the special cases of metonymy discussed above involve more than one domain, semantic maps are no longer a good illustration. Maps of the source and target domains together with the graphic representation of the shift can only be visualized as a three-dimensional structure, and overlaying several of them to compare languages would be nearly impossible. Fortunately, for metaphoric and metonymic usages, maps are largely unnecessary, since, as discussed above, semantic shifts are defined more by the specific source situation within the domain (=frame) than by the source domain as a whole.

Since different frames tend to give rise to different shifts, a semantic shift can be seen as strong evidence that its source situation exists as a separate frame. Taking the domain of swimming and floating, we find that drifting on the current in most languages is combined either with travel of vessels or with stationary floating on the surface. This might suggest that moving with the current does not constitute a frame, unless we consider metaphoric data – this situation serves as a source for a distinct group of metaphors of 'unimpeded movement': effortlessly gliding over a surface, moving through the air, slipping inside something etc. (see Rakhilina 2007 for details).

Sometimes the precise source of a shift becomes evident only in typological perspective, while a particular language may seem confusing and even contradictory to the general tendency. This is often the case when the source sense of the polysemous word is itself a combination of multiple frames. The sense 'passage of time' for such verbs as the Japanese *nagareru* seems to derive from the above-mentioned 'drifting with the current' if we look at it isolated from the other languages. In fact, the source of this metaphor is not the situation of drifting but the flow of the current itself, metonymically expressed by the same verb (cf. Panina 2007). Both the metonymy of flowing/drifting and the metaphor of TIME as a STREAM (cf. English *the flow of time*) are much more in keeping with typological evidence than 'time as a drifting object', and it turns out, the metaphor is not related to the domain of swimming and floating.

An interesting question is whether some shifts could have abstract sources which subsume several frames from different domains, especially for metaphors with a very abstract target. For example, the idea of approximation can be expressed by verbs of oscillation (Russian *kolebat'sya*), rotation (Spanish *rondar*), and even floating (English *floating exchange rate* and its calques in other languages, see Rakhilina 2007).

4.4.4 Shifts and etymologies

The examples above deal with the current state of language, but evolution of lexical meanings in its essence is nothing but a semantic shift where the source and target belong not just to different domains, but to different time periods.

From this point of view it is theoretically possible to use typological data to evaluate etymological hypotheses once lexical typology has covered enough languages and domains for such an application. Likewise, etymological dictionaries are already valuable sources of additional information for lexical typology and were used extensively in Plungian and Rakhilina (2007) and Rakhilina and Plungian (2013). Even if we differ from Zalizniak's approach in not giving historical data a more central role, sometimes the historical approach can produce interesting methodological results.

In the previous section we have mentioned the regular combination of the senses 'jumping/self-propelled flight'. In Plungian and Rakhilina (2007) it is examined synchronously in a number of languages, some of which have one verb for both situations (Rutul *la=w=č-*), and others which have cognates, diverging into different senses completely or partially (Lithuanian *lėkti* 'to fly' vs. Latvian *lekt* 'to jump'; Polish *latati* 'to fly' covers some contexts of the Russian *prygat'* 'to jump', as in *usta mu latają* 'his lips quiver'). The direction of this shift is not evident. Usually the more abstract of the two meanings is assumed to be the target, but in this case both meanings are physical and fairly specific.

Turning to etymological data, then, we see that the Baltic root is related to Slavonic **let-* / **lět-*, and more traces are observed in other Indo-European languages, usually with the meaning 'to jump, hop', but sometimes also 'to kick', 'to step on' and some others (Fasmer 1986, 2: 488). This leads us to believe that for the metonymical pair in question jumping was the source and active flight the target of the shift, while 'projectile flight > falling' is probably a later development.

4.4.5 Lexical typology as construction typology

Cataloguing every source and target of semantic shifts is an engrossing, but so far unfinished, task. Both Heine and Kuteva's dictionary of lexical sources of grammaticalization (Heine and Kuteva 2002) and the Database of semantic shifts

(Zalizniak 2009), mentioned above, are far from complete, and may take years to reach their goals. The former, for example, covers only two adjectival meanings: 'bad' and 'true'.

Even when completed, however, such a catalogue would be insufficient for typological generalizations, because a semantic shift is more than just its source and target.

Two other properties essential to a semantic shift are its type (metaphor or metonymy, i.e. similarity of frames vs. contiguity within a frame); and syntactic constructions by which the source and target are expressed, especially the similarity or dissimilarity of the source and target syntax. This last can be studied as such (see Apresjan 1967 and many others), but typological studies also exist (Haspelmath and Buchholz 1998; Shemanaeva 2008; Koch 2012, and the cross-linguistic project *Valency Classes in the World's Languages* at the Max Planck Institute Leipzig[9]), see also (Britsyn et al. [eds.] 2009).

The object of typological comparison in this case is the process which is triggered as a word meaning crosses into another, differently structured, domain. Sometimes the transition is accompanied by a dramatic change in syntax – indeed, this change is one of the linguistic markers of the semantic shift. On the other hand, syntactic constructions may be preserved if the source and target frames are isomorphic.

Source frame mapping directly onto target is typical for abstract notions which cannot be experienced directly. Emotions often "borrow" frames from simpler and more straightforward physiological states, usually preserving the constructions in which the source word participates and its valency behavior – e.g. Russian *mne bol'no smotrjet' na svet* 'It hurts me to look at the light' (physical pain) vs. *mnje bol'no (strašno / grustno) videt' èto* 'It pains (frightens/saddens) me to see this' (emotions), or English *the fire seared his skin* vs. *jealousy seared him*.

More typologically interesting are cases where source and target frames are extremely dissimilar, as with various idioms describing luck. Here Russian uses a verb with the main sense 'to carry', *vezti*, lit. 'it transports to one', and Japanese – 'to stick', *tsuku*, lit. 'one has it attached', cf. also slang expressions such as the English *dig* 'excavate; enjoy'. Such examples, which cannot be reduced to the mapping of one situation onto another, are largely ignored by the theories of metaphor (Lakoff and Johnson 1980; Croft 1993), or of mental spaces (Fauconnier 1985). Both models are primarily concerned with direct similarities in the conceptualization of the source and target. Discussion of the famous examples, such as

---

9 http://www.eva.mpg.de/lingua/valency/index.php

ARGUMENT IS WAR (Lakoff and Johnson 1980) or SURGEONS ARE BUTCHERS (Grady, Oakley, and Coulson 1999; Fauconnier and Turner 2002), focuses mainly on the opposing parties in one, or the agent, patient and instrument in the other, i.e. the common elements identifiable due to the structural similarities of the situations. The differences between source and target, such as quarrels being non-lethal, or surgeons dealing with people and not meat, are dismissed with the explanation that no metaphor can be complete. (Indeed, looking at the Russian *kačat'* 'to pump > to download' we find that some components, in particular 'manual labor and/or use of heavy machinery', of the source sense are lost, while some new properties appear: even when conceptualized as a liquid, information still exists in countable chunks such as files etc.). But the dissimilar examples, like 'carry > be lucky', are different from these cases in that almost everything needs to be changed in order to produce *Mne vezet* 'I am lucky', lit. 'It carries to me', from *Mul vezet poklažu* 'A mule carries baggage'. The Agent and Patient must be omitted, an Experiencer added, and the initial situation generally becomes unrecognizable.

We have encountered many such shifts when studying the typology of predicates denoting pain. Most of them are derived from physical actions, e.g. Russian *sxvatit'* 'to grab' or Japanese *sashikomu* 'to stab' used to describe a pain in the stomach. The shifts are often accompanied by dramatic changes in valency (*sashikomu* becomes intransitive), syntax (*sxvatit'* is used in an impersonal construction), or sometimes even morphological limitations. We view the process as a special type of semantic shift, separate from both metaphor and metonymy and related to grammaticalization in the amount of fundamental change on all levels that it entails. For details on this type of shift, that we term "rebranding", see Rakhilina, Reznikova, and Bonch-Osmolovskaya (2010); Reznikova, Rakhilina, and Bonch-Osmolovskaya (2012). The study of it appears to be one of the most promising tasks for lexical typology, bringing it closer to more general linguistic issues concerning the structure and function of language constructions.

4.5 Conclusion

Different approaches to lexical typology give this new branch of linguistics different goals; theoretical and practical, and all equally fascinating.

The Nijmegen school views the lexicon as a reflection of psychological reality – do speakers of different languages react to the same stimuli similarly or differently? The stimuli need not exhaust all the possibilities, and the verbal response is viewed mainly as behavior. Morphology, syntax, semantic shifts and other purely linguistic phenomena do not always get enough attention even in such outstanding works as Levinson (2003); Levinson and Wilkins [eds.] (2006), among others. The primary search is for the universal cognitive basis underlying and transcending linguistic experience.

Cliff Goddard and Anna Wierzbicka, leaders of another lexical typological school, are working on a venerable logic problem: is it possible to reduce all meanings in all languages to a small set of semantic primes, supposedly omnipresent? Words are contrasted not with words from other languages directly, but via this meta-vocabulary (Wierzbicka 1997; Goddard 2001b; Goddard and Wierzbicka 2008, 2009; Ye 2010, and many others). Success in this task, aside from showing the limits of linguistic variation, would have a tremendous impact on cross-cultural communication, enabling mutual understanding at unprecedented depth and scale.

Our own approach to lexical typology focuses on actual word-senses, semantic domains and lexical systems as they are. The end result may take the shape of a multilingual (ideally universal) dictionary with situations, or semantic frames, as entries. Obviously, the sheer scope of this task makes its significance theoretical rather than practical.

We believe that semantic fields are structured after a limited number of basic patterns, and we hope to gradually learn to extract these patterns even from a small initial selection of languages. After this a thorough study of structures would help us predict the behavior of words as new languages are observed or as known meanings evolve and change, which has always been a fascinating target for linguistic studies.

4.6 References

Aikhenvald, Alexandra Y. 2000. *Classifiers: A typology of noun categorization devices*. Oxford: Oxford University press.
Amberber, Mengistu (ed.). 2007. *The language of memory in a crosslinguistic perspective*. Amsterdam: John Benjamins.
Apresjan, Jurij D. 1967. *Èksperimental'noe issledovanie semantiki russkogo glagola*. [Experimental research in the semantics of the Russian verb]. Moscow: Nauka.
Apresjan, Jurij D. 1992. *Lexical semantics: User's guide to contemporary Russian vocabulary*. English translation, Ann-Arbor: Karoma Publishers. Original edition in Russian, 1974, *Leksičeskaja semantika: Sinonimičeskie sredstva jazyka*. Moscow: Nauka.
Apresjan, Jurij D. 1995. O jazyke tolkovanij i semantičeskix primitivax [On the language of explications and semantic primitives]. In Jurij D. Apresjan (ed.), *Izbrannye Trudy, Vol. II: Integral'noe opisanie jazyka i sistemnaja leksikografia*, 466–484. Moscow: Škola "Jazyki Russkoj Kultury".

Apresjan, Jurij D. 2000. *Systematic lexicography*. Translated by Kevin Windle. Oxford: Oxford University Press.
Apresjan, Jurij D. 2009. *Issledovanija po semantike i leksikografii. T. I. Paradigmatika* [Research in semantics and lexicography: Volume 1: Paradigmatics] (Studia philologica). Moscow: Jazyki Slavjanskoj Kul'tury.
Apresjan, Jurij D. (ed.). 2004. *Novyj ob"jasnitel'nyj slovar' sinonimov russkogo jazyka* [New explanatory dictionary of synonyms of Russian language]. Moscow, Vienna: Yazyki slavjanskoj kultury, Wiener Slawistischer Almanach.
Apresjan, Jurij D. and Abram I. Rosenman (eds.). 1979. *Anglo-russklj sinonimičeskij slovar'* [English-Russian dictionary of synonyms]. Moscow: Russkij Jazyk.
Auwera, Johan van der and Vladimir A. Plungian. 1998. Modality's semantic map. *Linguistic typology* 2 (1): 79–124.
Berlin, Brent and Paul Kay. 1969. *Basic Color Terms: Their Universality and Evolution*. Berkeley: University of California press.
Blank, Anreas and Peter Koch. 2000. La conceptualisation du corps humain et la lexicologie diachronique romane. In Hiltraud Dupuy-Engelhardt and Marie-Jeanne Montibus (eds.), *La lexicalisation des structures conceptuelles*, 43–62. Reims: Presses Universitaires.
Boas, Hans C. 2011. Constructing parallel lexicon fragments based on English FrameNet entries: Semantic and syntactic issues. In Hanna Hedeland, Thomas Schmidt, and Kai Wörner (eds.), *Multilingual resources and multilingual applications. Proceedings of the German Society for computational linguistics and language technology* (GSCL) 2011, Hamburg, 9–18. University of Hamburg: Center for Language Corpora.
Britsyn, Viktor M., Ekaterina V. Rakhilina, Tatiana I. Reznikova, and Galina M. Yavorska (eds.). 2009. *Koncept boli v tipologičeskom osveščenii* [The concept of PAIN in typological context]. Kiev: Dmitri Burago's Publishing House.
Bromhead, Helen. 2009. *The reign of truth and faith: Epistemic expressions in 16th and 17th century English*. Berlin: Mouton de Gruyter.
Brugman, Claudia and George Lakoff. 1988. Cognitive topology and lexical networks. In Garrison W. Cottrell, Steven L. Small, and Michael K. Tanenhaus (eds.), *Lexical ambiguity resolution: Perspectives from psycholinguistics, neuropsychology and artificial Intelligence*, 477–508. San Mateo (CA): Morgan Kaufmann.
Bybee, Joan L.1985. *Morphology: A study of the relation between meaning and form*. Amsterdam: John Benjamins.
Bybee, Joan L. and Östen Dahl. 1989. The creation of tense and aspect systems in the languages of the world. *Studies in Language* 13: 51–103.
Bybee, Joan L., Revere Perkins, and William Pagliuca. 1994. *The evolution of grammar: Tense, aspect and modality in the languages of the world*. Chicago: University of Chicago Press.
Comrie, Bernard. 1976. *Aspect*. Cambridge: Cambridge University Press.
Comrie, Bernard. 1985. *Tense*. Cambridge: Cambridge University Press.
Corbett, Greville G. 1991. *Gender*. Cambridge: Cambridge University Press.
Corbett, Greville G. 2000. *Number*. Cambridge: Cambridge University Press.
Croft, William. 1993. The role of domains in the interpretation of metaphors and metonymy. *Cognitive Linguistics*, 4: 335–370.
Croft, William. 2001. *Radical construction grammar*. Oxford: Oxford University Press.
Cusihuamán, Antonio. 2001. Diccionario Quechua: Cuzco-Collao 2nd ed. Lima: Centro Bartolomé de las Casas. Original edition 1976. Lima: Instituto de Estudios Peruanos.
Dahl, Östen. 1985. *Tense and aspect systems*. Oxford & New York: Basil Blackwell.

Dybo, Anna V. 1994. On the history of traditional anthropometric terms: Qarï and other Central Asian linear measures. In Vitaly V. Naumkin (ed.), *Russian Oriental Studies*, 195–210. Leiden, Boston: Brill.

Dybo, Anna V. 1996. *Semantičeskaja rekonstrukcija v altajskoj ètimologii. Somatičeskie terminy (plečevoj pojas)* [Semantic reconstruction in altaic etymology. Somatic terms (shoulders area)]. Moscow: Jazyki Russkoj Kul'tury.

Evans, Nicholas. 2010. Semantic typology. In Jae Jung Song (ed.), *The Oxford handbook of linguistic typology*, 504–533. Oxford, New York: Oxford University Press.

Fauconnier, Gilles. 1985. *Mental spaces: Aspects of meaning construction in natural languages.* Cambridge (MA): MIT Press.

Fauconnier, Gilles and Mark Turner. 1996. Blending as a central process in grammar. In Adele Goldberg (ed.), *Conceptual structure, discourse and language*, 183–203. Stanford: CSLI.

Fauconnier, Gilles and Mark Turner. 2002. *The way we think: Conceptual blending and the mind's hidden complexities.* New York: Basic Books.

Fillmore, Charles J. 1976. Frame semantics and the nature of language. *Annals of the New York Academy of Sciences: Conference on the Origin and Development of Language and Speech* 280: 20–32.

Fillmore, Charles J. 1982. Frame semantics. In *Linguistics in the Morning Calm*, 111–137. [The Linguistic Society of Korea]. Seoul: Hanshin Publishing Co.

Ganenkov, Dmitrij S. 2005. *Kontaktnye lokalizacii v naxsko-dagestanskix jazykax* [Contact localizations in Nakh-Daghestanian languages]. Moscow: Moscow State University Ph.D. dissertation.

Geeraerts, Dirk. 1988. Review of Wierzbicka (1985). *Language in Society* 17: 449–455.

Geeraerts, Dirk. 1993. Vagueness's puzzles, polysemy's vagaries. *Cognitive Linguistics* 4: 223–272.

Gévaudan, Paul, Peter Koch, and Antonia Neu. 2003. Hundert Jahre nach Zauner: Die romanischen Namen der Körperteile im DECOLAR. *Romanische Forschungen* 115: 1–27.

Gladkova, Anna N. 2010. *Russkaja kul'turnaja semantika: èmocii, cennosti, žiznennye ustanovki.* [Russian cultural semantics: Emotions, values, and attitudes]. Moscow: Jazyki Slavjanskix Kul'tur.

Goddard, Cliff. 2001a. Lexico-semantic universals: a critical overview. *Linguistic typology.* 5(1): 1–65.

Goddard, Cliff. 2001b. *Sabar, ikhlas, setia*—patient, sincere, loyal? A contrastive semantic study of some "virtues" in Malay and English. *Journal of Pragmatics* 33: 653–681.

Goddard, Cliff. 2011 [1998]. *Semantic analysis: A practical introduction.* 2nd edn. Oxford: Oxford University Press.

Goddard, Cliff. 2012. Semantic primes, semantic molecules, semantic templates: Key concepts in the NSM approach to lexical typology. *Linguistics* 50(3): 711–743.

Goddard, Cliff (ed.). 2008. *Cross-linguistic semantics.* Amsterdam & Philadelphia: John Benjamins.

Goddard, Cliff and Anna Wierzbicka. 2008. Universal human concepts as a basis for contrastive linguistic semantics. In María de los Ángeles Gómez-González, Lachlan Mackenzie, and Elsa Gonzáles Álvarez (eds.), *Current trends in contrastive linguistics: Functional and cognitive perspectives,* 205–226. Amsterdam & Philadelphia: John Benjamins.

Goddard, Cliff and Anna Wierzbicka. 2009. Contrastive semantics of physical activity verbs: 'cutting' and 'chopping' in English, Polish, and Japanese. *Language Sciences* 31: 60–96.

Goddard, Cliff and Anna Wierzbicka (eds.). 1994. *Semantic and lexical universals – Theory and empirical findings*. Amsterdam: John Benjamins.
Goddard, Cliff and Anna Wierzbicka (eds.). 2002. *Meaning and universal grammar: Theory and empirical findings* (2 volumes). Amsterdam & Philadelphia: John Benjamins.
Goldberg, Adele. 1995. *Constructions: A construction grammar approach to argument structure*. Chicago: University of Chicago Press.
Grady, Joseph. 1999. A typology of motivation for conceptual metaphor: Correlation vs. resemblance. In Raymond W. Gibbs, Jr., and Gerard J. Steen (eds.), *Metaphor in cognitive linguistics*, 79–100. Amsterdam, Philadelphia: John Benjamins.
Grady, Joseph, Todd Oakley, and Seana Coulson. 1999. Conceptual blending and metaphor. In Raymond W. Gibbs, Jr. and Gerard J. Steen (eds.), *Metaphor in cognitive linguistics*, 101–124. Amsterdam & Philadelphia: John Benjamins.
Haspelmath, Martin. 2003. The geometry of grammatical meaning: Semantic maps and cross-linguistic comparison. In Michael Tomasello, (ed.), *The new psychology of language*, vol. 2, 211–242. Mahwah, NJ: Lawrence Erlbaum.
Haspelmath, Martin. 2010. Comparative concepts and descriptive categories in crosslinguistic studies. *Language* 86: 663–687.
Haspelmath, Martin and Oda Buchholz. 1998. Equative and similative constructions in the languages of Europe. In Johan van der Auwera (ed.), *Adverbial constructions in the languages of europe* (Empirical Approaches to Language Typology/EUROTYP, 20–3), 277–334. Berlin: Mouton de Gruyter.
Heine, Bernd and Tania Kuteva. 2002. *World lexicon of grammaticalization*. Cambridge: Cambridge University Press.
Janda, Laura A. and Valery D. Solovyev. 2009. What constructional profiles reveal about synonymy: A case study of Russian words for SADNESS and HAPPINESS. *Cognitive Linguistics*, 20 (2): 367–393.
Kashkin, Egor V. 2010. *Semantika glagolov razdelenija ob"ekta na časti v èrzjanskom i komi-zyrjanskom jazykax (prjamye i perenosnye upotreblenija)* [Semantics of verbs of cutting and breaking in Erzya and Komi-Zyryan (basic and derived meanings)]. Moscow: Moscow State University Diploma paper.
Katz, Jerrold J. and Jerry A. Fodor. 1963. The structure of a semantic theory. *Language* 39: 170–210.
Khrakovsky, Viktor S. (ed.). 1989. *Tipologija iterativnyx konstrukcij* [Typology of iterative constructions]. Leningrad: Nauka.
Kibrik, Alexandr E. 1992. *Tipologija rodstvennyx jazykov: sinxronija i èvoljucija* [Typology of genetically related languages: synchrony and evolution]. In Tatiana N. Mološnaja, Tatiana M. Nikolaeva, Lev N. Smirnov, and Anna F. Litvina (eds.), *Tipologičeskoe i sopostavitel'noe izučenie slavjanskix i balkanskix jazykov*. Moscow: ISB RAN.
Kibrik, Alexandr E. 1998. Does intragenetic typology make sense? In Winfried Boeder, Christoph Schroeder, Karl H. Wagner, and Wolfgang Wildgen (eds.), *Sprache in Raum und Zeit: in memoriam Johannes Bechert*, Bd. 2: Beiträge zur empirischen Sprachwissenschaft, 61–68. Tübingen: Narr.
Koch, Peter. 2012. Location, existence, and possession: A constructional-typological exploration. *Linguistics* 50: 533–603.
Kopecka, Aneta and Bhuvana Narasimhan (eds.). 2012. *Events of putting and taking: A crosslinguistic perspective*. Amsterdam: Benjamins.

Koptjevskaja-Tamm, Maria. 2008. Approaching Lexical typology. In Martine Vanhove (ed.), *From polysemy to semantic change: Towards a typology of lexical semantic associations*, 3–52. Amsterdam & Philadelphia: John Benjamins.

Koptjevskaja-Tamm, Maria and Martine Vanhove (eds.). 2012. New directions in lexical typology. [Special Issue] *Linguistics* 50(3).

Koptjevskaja-Tamm, Maria, Dagmar Divjak, and Ekaterina V. Rakhilina. 2010. Aquamotion verbs in Slavic and Germanic: A case study in lexical typology. In Victoria Driagina-Hasko, and Renee Perelmutter (eds.), *New approaches to slavic verbs of motion*, 315–341. Amsterdam & Philadelphia: John Benjamins.

Kretov, Alexej A., Inna A. Merkulova, and Vladimir T. Titov. 2011. Problemy kvantitativnoj leksikologii slavjanskix jazykov [Issues in Slavic Quantitative Lexicology]. *Voprosy jazykoznanija* 1: 52–65.

Kruglyakova, Victoria A. 2010. *Semantika glagolov vraščenija v tipologičeskoj perspektive* [Semantics of rotation verbs in a typological perspective]. Moscow: Russian State University for Humanities Ph.D. dissertation.

Kustova, Galina I. 1998. Proizvodnye značenija s èksperiencial'noj sostavljajuščej [Derived meanings containing an experiential component]. *Semiotika i Informatika*, 36.

Kustova, Galina I. 2004. *Tipy proizvodnyh značenij i mehanizmy jazykovogo rasširenija* [Types of derived meanings and mechanisms of language extension]. Moscow: Jazyki slavjanskoj kul'tury.

Kuznetsova, Julia L. 2007. Glagoly peremeščenija v vode v persidskom jazyke [Verbs of aqua-motion in Persian]. In Timur A. Maisak and Ekaterina V. Rakhilina (eds.), *Glagoly dviženija v vode: leksičeskaja tipologija* [Verbs of AQUA-motion: lexical typology], 335–350. Moscow: Indrik.

Kyuseva, Maria V. 2012. *Leksičeskaja tipologija semantičeskix sdvigov nazvanij kačestvennyx priznakov 'ostryj' i 'tupoj'* [Lexical typology of semantic shifts in adjectives 'sharp' and 'blunt']. Moscow: Moscow State University Diploma paper.

Lakoff, George. 1987. *Women, fire, and dangerous things. What categories reveal about the mind*. Chicago & London: The University of Chicago Press.

Lakoff, George and Mark Johnson. 1980. *Metaphors we live by*. Chicago: University of Chicago Press.

Lakoff, George and Mark Turner. 1989. *More than cool reason: A field guide to poetic metaphor*. Chicago: University of Chicago.

Lander, Jurij A. and Svetlana G. Kramarova. 2007. Indonezijskie glagoly plavanija i ix sistema [Indonesian aqua-motion verbs and their system]. In Timur A. Maisak and Ekaterina V. Rakhilina (eds.), *Glagoly dviženija v vode: leksičeskaja tipologija* [Verbs of AQUA-motion: lexical typology], 664–693. Moscow: Indrik.

Lehrer, Adrienne. 1974. *Semantic fields and lexical structure*. Amsterdam: North Holland.

Levinson, Stephen C. 2003. *Space in language and cognition: Explorations in cognitive diversity*. Cambridge: Cambridge University Press.

Levinson, Stephen C. and David P. Wilkins (eds.). 2006. *Grammars of space: Explorations in cognitive diversity*. Cambridge: Cambridge University Press.

Majid, Asifa, and Melissa Bowerman (eds.). 2007. Cutting and breaking events: A crosslinguistic perspective. [Special Issue] *Cognitive Linguistics* 18(2).

Majid, Asifa, Melissa Bowerman, Miriam van Staden, and James S. Boster. 2007. The semantic categories of cutting and breaking events: A crosslinguistic perspective. In Asifa Majid

and Melissa Bowerman (eds.), Cutting and breaking events: A crosslinguistic perspective. [Special Issue] *Cognitive Linguistics* 18(2): 133–152.
Majid, Asifa and Stephen C. Levinson. 2007. The language of vision I: Color. In Asifa Majid (ed.), *Field Manual, Volume 10*, 22–25. Nijmegen: Max Planck Institute for Psycholinguistics.
Majid, Asifa and Stephen C. Levinson (eds.). 2011. The senses in language and culture. [Special Issue] *The Senses & Society* 6(1).
Majid, Asifa, Gunter Senft, and Stephen C. Levinson. 2007. The language of olfaction. In Asifa Majid (ed.), *Field Manual, Volume 10*, 36–41. Nijmegen: Max Planck Institute for Psycholinguistics.
Majid, Asifa, Nicholas Evans, Alice Gaby, and Stephen C. Levinson. 2011. The grammar of exchange: A comparative study of reciprocal constructions across languages. *Frontiers in Psychology* 2: 1–15.
Maisak, Timur A. and Ekaterina V. Rakhilina. 2007. Glagoly dviženija i nahoždenija v vode: leksičeskie sistemy i semantičeskie parametry [Verbs of moving and standing in water: lexical systems and semantic parameters]. In Timur A. Maisak and Ekaterina V. Rakhilina (eds.), *Glagoly dviženija v vode: leksičeskaja tipologija* [Verbs of AQUA-motion: lexical typology], 27–75. Moscow: Indrik.
Maisak, Timur A. and Ekaterina V. Rakhilina (eds.). 2007. *Glagoly dviženija v vode: leksičeskaja tipologija* [Verbs of AQUA-motion: lexical typology]. Moscow: Indrik.
Mel'čuk, Igor A. 2012. *Semantics: From meaning to text*. Amsterdam: John Benjamins.
Mel'čuk, Igor A. and Alexandr A. Kholodovich. 1970. K teorii grammatičeskogo zaloga [Towards a theory of grammatical voice]. *Narody Azii i Afriki*, Vol. 4: 111–124.
Mel'čuk, Igor A. and Alexandr K. Zholkovsky. 1984. *Tolkovo-kombinatornyj slovar' sovremennogo russkogo jazyka* [Explanatory Combinatorial Dictionary of Modern Russian]. Vienna: Wiener Slawistischer Almanach.
Mel'čuk, Igor A., Nadia Arbatchewsky-Jumarie, André Clas, Suzanne Mantha, and Alain Polguère. 1999. *Dictionnaire explicatif et combinatoire du français contemporain. recherches lexico-sémantiques, tome IV*. Montréal: Les Presses de l'Université de Montréal.
Narrog, Heiko. 2010. A diachronic dimension in maps of case functions. *Linguistic Discovery* 8(1): 233–254.
Newman, John. (ed.). 1998. *The linguistics of giving* [Studies in Typological Linguistics 36]. Amsterdam & Philadelphia: John Benjamins.
Newman, John. (ed.). 2002. *The linguistics of sitting, standing, and lying* [Studies in Typological Linguistics 51]. Amsterdam & Philadelphia: John Benjamins.
Newman, John. (ed.). 2009. *The linguistics of eating and drinking* [Studies in Typological Linguistics 84]. Amsterdam & Philadelphia: John Benjamins.
Paducheva, Elena V. 2004. *Dinamičeskie modeli v semantike leksiki* [Dynamic models in lexical semantics]. Moscow: Jazyki slavjanskoj kultury.
Panina, Anna S. 2007. Vyraženie peremeščenija i nahoždenija v vode v japonskom jazyke [Verbs of moving and standing in water in Japanese]. In Timur A. Maisak and Ekaterina V. Rakhilina (eds.), *Glagoly dviženija v vode: leksičeskaja tipologija* [Verbs of AQUA-motion: lexical typology], 617–640. Moscow: Indrik.
Pavlova, Elizaveta K. 2014. *Kačestvennye priznaki 'mjagkij' i 'tverdyj' v tipologičeskoj perspektive* [Qualities 'soft' and 'hard' in a typological perspective]. Moscow: Moscow State University Diploma paper.
Plungian, Vladimir A. 2000. *Obščaja morfologija* (Common morphology). Moscow: URSS.

Plungian, Vladimir A. and Ekaterina V. Rakhilina. 1996. Book review: Cliff Goddard, and Anna Wierzbicka (eds.). Semantic and lexical universals: Theory and empirical findings. Amsterdam, 1994. *Voprosy Jazykoznanija*, 3: 139-143.
Plungian, Vladimir A. and Ekaterina V. Rakhilina. 2007. K tipologii glagolov 'letat' i 'prygat' [Towards a typology of verbs 'to fly' and 'to jump']. In Timur A. Maisak and Ekaterina V. Rakhilina (eds.), *Glagoly dviženija v vode: leksičeskaja tipologija* [Verbs of AQUA-motion: lexical typology], 739-748. Moscow: Indrik.
Podlipentseva, Anna A. 2011. «Živoj» i «mertvyj» kak istočniki priznakovyx metafor (v tipologičeskom osveščenii) ["Dead" and "alive" as sources for metaphors (in a typological perspective)]. Moscow: Russian State University for Humanities Diploma paper.
Rakhilina, Ekaterina V. 2007. Tipy metaforičeskix upotreblenij glagolov plavanija [Types of metaphorical uses of aqua-motion verbs]. In Timur A. Maisak and Ekaterina V. Rakhilina (eds.), *Glagoly dviženija v vode: leksičeskaja tipologija* [Verbs of AQUA-motion: lexical typology], 76-105. Moscow: Indrik.
Rakhilina, Ekaterina V. 2010a. Verbs of rotation in Russian and Polish. In Victoria Driagina-Hasko and Renee Perelmutter (eds.), *New approaches to slavic verbs of motion*, 291-316. Amsterdam, Philadelphia: John Benjamins.
Rakhilina, Ekaterina V. 2010b. Zvuki Mu. In Valentin F. Vydrin, Sergej. Ju. Dmitrenko, Natalia M. Zaika, Sergej S. Saj, Nina R. Sumbatova, and Viktor S. Khrakovskij (eds.), *Problemy grammatiki i tipologii: sbornik statej pamjati V.P. Nedjalkova*, 283-302. Moscow: Znak.
Rakhilina, Ekaterina V. and Vladimir A. Plungian. 2007. O leksiko-semantičeskoj tipologii [on Lexical Semantic Typology]. In Timur A. Maisak and Ekaterina V. Rakhilina (eds.), *Glagoly dviženija v vode: leksičeskaja tipologija* [Verbs of AQUA-motion: lexical typology], 9-26. Moscow: Indrik.
Rakhilina, Ekaterina V. and Vladimir A. Plungian. 2013. TIME and SPEED: Where do speed adjectives come from? *Russian Linguistics* 37 (3): 347-359.
Rakhilina, Ekaterina V. and Irina A. Prokofieva. 2004. Rodstvennye jazyki kak ob"ekt leksičeskoj tipologii: russkie i pol'skie glagoly vraščenija [Genetically related languages in linguistic typology: Russian and Polish verbs of rotation]. *Voprosy jazykoznanija* 1: 60-78.
Rakhilina, Ekaterina V., Tatiana I. Reznikova, and Anastasia A. Bonch-Osmolovskaya. 2010. Tipologija preobrazovanija konstrukcij: predikaty boli [A typology of construction modifications: Pain predicates]. In Ekaterina V. Rakhilina (ed.), *Lingvistika Konstrukcij*, 456-540. Moscow: Azbukovnik.
Reznikova, Tatiana I., Ekaterina V. Rakhilina, and Anastasia A. Bonch-Osmolovskaya. 2012. Towards a typology of pain predicates. *Linguistics* 50 (3): 421-465.
Senft, Gunter, Asifa Majid, and Stephen C. Levinson. 2007. The language of taste. In Asifa Majid (ed.), *Field Manual, Volume 10*, 42-45. Nijmegen: Max Planck Institute for Psycholinguistics.
Shemanaeva, Olga Ju. 2007. Vyraženie peremeščenija v vode v nemeckom jazyke [Aqua-motion in German]. In Timur A. Maisak and Ekaterina V. Rakhilina (eds.), *Glagoly dviženija v vode: leksičeskaja tipologija* [Verbs of AQUA-motion: lexical typology], 175-197. Moscow: Indrik.
Shemanaeva, Olga Ju. 2008. *Konstrukcii razmera v tipologičeskoj perspective* [Constructions for size and measure in a typological perspective]. Moscow: Russian State University for Humanities Ph.D. dissertation.
Smirnitskaya, Anna A. 2007. Glagoly peremeščenija v vode v tamil'skom jazyke [Verbs of aqua-motion in Tamil]. In Timur A. Maisak and Ekaterina V. Rakhilina (eds.), *Glagoly*

dviženija v vode: leksičeskaja tipologija [Verbs of AQUA-motion: lexical typology], 582–594. Moscow: Indrik.

Sorokina, Anna S. 2010. *Semantika kačestvennyx prilagatel'nyx so značeniem 'ostryj', 'tupoj', 'polnyj' i 'pustoj' v korejskom jazyke* [The semantics of adjectives 'sharp', 'blunt', 'full' and 'empty' in Korean]. Moscow: Russian State University for Humanities Diploma paper.

Sweetser, Eve. 1990. *From etymology to pragmatics: Metaphorical and cultural aspects of semantic structure.* Cambridge, New York: Cambridge University Press.

Tagabileva, Maria G. 2011. Kačestvennye priznaki 'pustoj', 'polnyj': k postroeniju semantičeskoj tipologii [Qualities 'empty' and 'full': towards a semantic typology]. Moscow: Moscow State University Term paper.

Tagabileva, Maria G. and Kholkina, Lilia S. 2010. Kačestvennye priznaki «pustoj» i «polnyj» v tipologičeskom osveščenii [Qualities "empty" and "full" in a typological perspective]. In Nikolaj N. Kazanskij (executive ed.), *Materialy Sed'moj Konferencii po Tipologii i Grammatike dlja Molodyx Issledovatelej*, 167–169. St.-Petersburg: Nauka.

Tatevosov, Sergej G. 2004. Semantičeskoe kartirovanie: metod i teorija [Semantic maps: a method and a theory. *Vestnik Moskovskogo universiteta, Ser. 9: Filologija* 1: 123–141.

Titov, Vladimir T. 2002. *Obščaja kvantitativnaja leksikologija romanskix jazykov* [Quantitative lexicology of Romance languages]. Voronezh: VGU.

Tolstaya, Svetlana M. 2008. *Prostranstvo slova. Leksičeskaja semantika v obščeslavjanskoj perspektive* [Extent of a word. Lexical semantics in a general Slavic perspective]. Moscow: Indrik.

Vasmer, Max. 1986–1987. *Ètimologičeskij slovar' russkogo jazyka* [Etymological dictionary of the Russian language]: 4 Vols. Moscow: Progress.

Vanhove, Martine. 2008. Semantic associations between sensory modalities, prehension and mental perceptions: A crosslinguistic perspective. In Martine Vanhove (ed.), *From polysemy to semantic change: Towards a typology of lexical semantic associations*, 342–370. Amsterdam & Philadelphia: John Benjamins.

Viberg, Åke. 1983. Verbs of perception: A typological study. *Linguistics* 21: 123–162.

Wanner, Leo (ed.). 2008. *Selected lexical and grammatical issues in the meaning-text theory.* Amsterdam: Benjamins.

Wierzbicka, Anna. 1972. *Semantic primitives.* Frankfurt (M): Athenäum.

Wierzbicka, Anna. 1985. *Lexicography and conceptual analysis.* Ann Arbor: Karoma.

Wierzbicka, Anna. 1996. *Semantics: Primes and universals.* Oxford: Oxford University Press.

Wierzbicka, Anna. 1997. *Understanding cultures through their key words: English, Russian, Polish, German, Japanese.* New York: Oxford University Press.

Wierzbicka, Anna. 2006. *English: Meaning and history.* New York: Oxford University Press.

Wierzbicka, Anna. 2010a. *Experience, evidence and sense: The hidden cultural legacy of English.* New York: Oxford University Press.

Wierzbicka, Anna. 2010b. The "History of Emotions" and the future of emotion research. *Emotion Review* 2(3): 69–273.

Ye, Zhengdao. 2010. Eating and drinking in Mandarin and Shanghainese: A lexical-conceptual analysis. In Wayne Christensen, Elizabeth Schier, and John Sutton (eds.), *ASCS09: Proceedings of the 9th Conference of the Australasian Society for Cognitive Science*, 375–383. Sydney: Macquarie Centre for Cognitive Science.

Zalizniak, Anna A. 2009. O ponjatii semantičeskogo perexoda [On the notion of semantic shift]. In Aleksandr E. Kibrik (editor-in-chief), *Lingvistika i intellektual'nye tehnologii: Po materialam ežegodnoj Meždunarodnoj konferencii "Dialog'2009"*, 107–112. Moscow: RGGU.

Carita Paradis
5. Corpus methods for the investigation of antonyms across languages

Abstract: This chapter proposes an onomasiological research methodology for cross-linguistic investigations of antonyms. The basic assumption is that there is a number of strongly opposable lexical semantic pairings in all languages, whose meanings are central to human existence, e.g. SPEED *slow–fast*, LUMINOSITY *dark–light*, STRENGTH *weak–strong*, SIZE *small–large*. There is also a large number of other pairings that are frequently used as antonyms in discourse, but for various different reasons they are not as strongly coupled as the canonical ones. The meaning dimensions of the canonical pairings, e.g. SPEED, LUMINOSITY, STRENGTH, SIZE, are used as the point of departure for the typological research program to identify the use of the antonymic words in different combinations and in different semantic frames in a principled way across languages and cultures. Large scale studies carried out along the lines proposed will make it possible to produce a typological antonym atlas of the formal realization of antonym pairs and their usage patterns, at the same time as it will allow us to make statements about the role of binary opposition in language and cognition more generally.

5.1 Introduction[1]

The aim of this chapter is to propose corpus based as well as corpus driven techniques for the investigation of antonyms cross-linguistically. The techniques capture the co-occurrence patterns of antonymic partners within sentences, i.e. antonym use in discontinuous constructions, as well as antonym use in continuous constructions, or contrastive frames, such as *young and old alike, neither long nor short*. The basic assumption is that all languages feature a number of strongly opposable lexical semantic pairings expressing binary opposition. Such pairings

---

[1] I would like to thank two anonymous reviewers and the editors of this volume for helpful comments. I would also like to thank Sara Farshchi very much for proof-reading the manuscript and for her comments on the final draft.

Carita Paradis (Lund University)

are expressions of particularly salient meaning dimensions, which are central to human existence, such as *small–large, low–high, narrow–wide, slow–fast, long–short, good–bad* as expressions of the dimensions of SIZE, HEIGHT, WIDTH, SPEED, LENGTH, and MERIT, respectively. In addition, there are a large number of opposable pairings with more restricted contextual applicability, such as *open–laparoscopic* in the context of surgery, *lean–fat* about bacon, *dull–exciting* about events, as opposed to *dull–bright* for colours. The methods described in this chapter are suitable for investigations of all types of antonym pairings across languages for which machine readable data are available. These methods allow analysts to be able to identify the different senses or readings that the members of the pairings have as properties of different dimensions, such as the meanings of, say, *light* in the cases of LUMINOSITY (*light–dark*) and WEIGHT (*light–heavy*). Work has already been done using these techniques on a limited set of languages (Jones et al. 2012). The proposal is that the results of these studies make good starting-points for further studies of more languages.

The structure of the chapter is as follows. Section 5.2 provides a rationale for using antonym pairs as the object of study across languages. Section 5.3 explores the notion of dimensions and the opposable properties of such dimensions as well as their expressions in English from the point of view of Cognitive Linguistics. Section 5.4 describes various typological issues relating to investigatory designs and different types of data. Section 5.5 is concerned with the proposal of two different research methodologies based on the results of a number of corpus investigations in different languages and the expressions of such dimensions. The chapter is summarized in Section 5.6.

5.2 Rationale

Bipolar organization in cognition and evaluative polarity in language are pervasive phenomena that have been observed and studied for a very long time by among others Aristotle (Ackrill 1963; Lloyd 1966), Ogden (1932), Osgood, Suci, and Tannenbaum (1957), and Osgood and Richards (1973). The latter scholars report on the dynamics of the interaction among cognitive structures. Already some 4000 years ago ancient Chinese metaphysics stated that human cognition relies on three fundamental structures: (i) the bipolar organization of human cognition; (ii) the attribution of positive polarity to the Yang and negative polarity to the Yin, and finally the (iii) parallelism of dimensions in terms of underlying positiveness and negativeness. They say that the "underlying polarity of Yang and Yin begins with light *vs.* dark and extends into high *vs.* low, creative *vs.* receptive, firm *vs.* yielding, moving *vs.* resting, and feminine *vs.* masculine, but also into many other areas of human concern, including the sun and the moon, the weather, the parts of the body, and even the distinction between gods (all Yang) and ghosts (all Yin)" (Osgood and Richards 1973: 380).

What this pervasive conceptual organization translates into in language is antonymy, i.e. expressions of binary opposition (Paradis, Willners, and Jones 2009). Of all lexical semantic relations in the linguistics literature, the binary relation of antonymy, or lexical oppositeness, appears to be the most readily apprehended by speakers of all ages. Most speakers have strong intuitions about how antonyms are used and that some antonyms are considered to be better exemplars than others. Using a combination of textual, psycholinguistic and neurolinguistic techniques, recent research, within the Cognitive Linguistics framework, has established that there are a number of opposable word pairs that have special status as canonical antonyms. It has been suggested that antonym canonicity is determined by factors such as the degree of conventionalization as form–meaning pairs in discourse, the degree of entrenchment as antonymous words in memory, and the salience of the dimensional domain they express, e.g. SPEED *slow–fast*, LUMINOSITY *dark–light*, STRENGTH *weak–strong*, SIZE *small–large*, WIDTH *narrow–wide*, MERIT *bad–good* and THICKNESS *thin–thick* (Jones et al. 2007; Muehleisen and Isono 2009; Murphy et al. 2009; Willners and Paradis 2010; Paradis and Willners 2011; van de Weijer et al. 2014). Furthermore, it has also been shown that the meaning dimension is the *cause* of of the strength of the lexical relation rather than the *effect* of the frequency of these words in language (Murphy and Andrew 1993; van de Weijer et al. 2012). The content of the dimensions that form the base of canonical antonyms coincides with the core of semantic types that are central to all human activities, and as noted by Dixon (2009), to adjective classes in the world's languages. If a language has adjectives, they are associated with the dimensions of the canonical antonyms that have been identified in the works above.

In spite of the role of binary opposition as an extremely powerful construal in human thinking, important both to the mental organization of languages' vocabularies and to the organization of coherent discourse, only few attempts have been made to describe variation and polysemy across opposable meanings along dimensions such as the above ones cross-linguistically. The contribution of this chapter is therefore to point to the fundamental cognitive role of meaning dimensions that readily lend themselves to binary opposition in language and cognition as powerful structuring forces. The chapter proposes an onomasiological research methodology for lexical typology (cf. Geeraerts, Grondelaers, and Bakema 1994; Geeraerts 1997; François 2008) on the basis of research carried out on expressions of core meaning dimensions in English, Swedish, Dutch, Japanese and Russian (e.g. Koptjevskaja-Tamm and Rakhilina 2006; Mohammad, Dorr, and Hirst 2008; Muehleisen and Isono 2009; Murphy et al. 2009; Paradis, Willners, and Jones 2009; Willners and Paradis 2010; Lobanova, van der Kleij, and Spenader 2010). The identification of canonical antonyms cross-linguistically and the subsequent description of their usage patterns in different semantic frames and in different linguistic constructions will allow us to draw maps of lexicalization patterns. The onomasiological dimensions will be used as the points of departure from which contextually motivated lexical semantic variation will emerge across domains as well as within domains (Paradis 2008, 2011; Geeraerts and Peirsman 2011). Not only will a research program carried out along these lines make it possible for us to produce a typological antonym atlas of the formal realization of antonym pairs and their usage patterns in discourse, but it will also allow us to make even stronger statements about the role of binary opposition in language and cognition more generally.

5.3 Lexical meanings in theory and practice

A number of textual and experimental studies of antonymy have been carried out using a whole range of different techniques (Jones et al. 2012). The results of those studies are explained within the framework of Lexical Meaning as Ontologies and Construals (LOC, for short, Paradis 2005). They paint a picture of word meaning in general and antonymy in particular as both constrained and dynamic. It is obvious, in particular from elicitation experiments, that participants envisage very different scenarios and different styles and genres, when they offer antonyms to adjectives (Paradis, Willners, and Jones 2009; Willners and Paradis 2010). These elicitation experiments, carried out in English and Swedish (on 85 unique words for English and 77 for Swedish), indicate that there is a continuum of antonym affinity between antonym pairs. At the top end of the list we find test words for which all 50 participants suggested one and the same antonym, given in brackets: *bad* (*good*), *beautiful* (*ugly*), *clean* (*dirty*), *heavy* (*light*), *hot* (*cold*), *poor* (*rich*) and *weak* (*strong*). From this end, the elicitations form a slope of increasingly more suggestions up to the items with the most suggestions. The very last item in the English data is *calm*, for which 29 different antonyms were suggested by the 50 participants. The shape of the list of elicited antonyms across test items suggests a scale of canonicity from very good matches to test items with no preferred partners. The very best matches were translation equivalents in English and Swedish and what they all have in common is a salient meaning dimension such as MERIT, CLEANLINESS, WEIGHT, TEMPERATURE, WEALTH and

STRENGTH. The dimension along which *calm* expresses an opposable property is less straightforward, which gave rise to many suggestions and little unanimity. The interpretation of these results is that the participants had many different meaning dimensions in mind, e.g. ANXIETY *calm–nervous*, WORRY *calm–troubled*, ANGER *calm–angry*.

In the Cognitive Linguistics framework, the couplings between lexical items and meanings are partly conventionalized and routinized and partly constantly negotiated by speakers and addressees at the time of use. The basic assumptions made are that meaning is grounded in how we as humans both perceive and understand the world around us. Lexical elements 'evoke' meanings rather than 'have' meanings (Cruse 2002; Paradis 2015a). Different readings in different contexts emerge from the motivations that activate the expressions in human communication in order to obtain socially viable mappings between words and concepts. Cognitive processes (construals) operate on the conceptual structures on all occasions of use in the creation of discursive meanings. The view taken is that antonymy is a construal of a relation of binary opposition in context, rather than a fixed relation of opposition between words (Croft and Cruse 2004; Paradis and Willners 2011). As suggested by Murphy (2006) and Paradis and Willners (2011), strongly associated antonyms are modelled as discontinuous constructions (expounded on in Section 5.1 of this chapter) in the technical sense of Construction Grammar (Jones et al. 2012: 102–105). The notion discontinuous refers to the fact that the members form pairs of opposite meanings. They co-occur in a linear sequence with other language elements between them, as in [x [...| y]. Their order in these discontinuous constructions as well as the constructions within which they co-occur may differ. Such word pairs form natural anchor points for the identification of meaning dimensions in onomasiological typology research, whose goal is to identify what words are used to express what meaning domains/dimensions. Also, such pairs have been shown to be attracted by constructions of opposition, i.e. there is a tendency of antonyms to favour certain contrastive constructions in discourse (expounded on in Section 5.2 of this chapter), such as *X and Y alike, between X and Y, both X and Y, either X or Y, from X to Y, X versus Y* and *whether X or Y* (Jones 2002). Since the present Cognitive Linguistics approach encompasses antonymy as a lexical-semantic discourse phenomenon, the definition of *antonymy* is broad and inclusive. It is an account that potentially extends to all kinds of antonym pairs in natural language use. However, most importantly for lexical typology, some of them are strongly associated as word pairs too (Paradis and Willners 2011). The next section raises some issues relating to the rationale of programmes for typological research.

5.4 Lexical typology

In the setting-up of a design of a lexical typological methodology, analysts have to make two fundamental decisions. The first decision is methodological in nature and concerns the starting-point and the basic object of study. The other decision is theoretical and concerns the view of the nature of linguistic meaning and the issue of multiple interpretations. These considerations are by no means specific to lexical typology but are equally important for grammatical typology, which has a much longer tradition capitalizing on functional grammaticalized categories such as tense and aspect, negation, classifiers, indefiniteness, deixis, animacy and evidentiality (e.g. Dahl 1985; Aikhenvald 2003; van der Auwera and Nuyts 2007; Horn 2010; Croft 2012). Lexical typology is a much more recent line of research. It is still in its infancy and work is currently being carried out to create robust models for the investigation of expression of contentful (lexical) rather than configurational (grammatical) meanings in language (François 2008; Koptjevskaja-Tamm, Vanhove, and Koch 2007; Koptjevskaja-Tamm 2012).

The design of a robust mode of procedure to ascertain comparability across languages is considered to be a more challenging enterprise in lexical typology than in grammatical typology, because the identification of a grammatical function and the identification of grammatical elements expressing that function may be an easier task for the analyst than the identification of a semantic domain and the subsequent identification of its exponents. The reason given for this is that they are semantically richer than grammatical elements. The distinction between grammatical and lexical expressions in language is by no means a straightforward one which much recent research in particular within usage-based accounts has shown. A case in point is the English adjective class or the class of adverbials (Paradis 2003, 2005, 2008), and the case of antonyms viewed as dimensional constructions may have a stronger structural potential than has previously been considered to be the case (Jones et al. 2012: Chapters 6 and 7). Croft (2012) is one of the most ardent advocates for an approach to typology in general that does not rely on preconceived conceptions of the existence of universal categories but an open-minded empirically-based research endeavour where meaning is key.

This chapter takes the research agenda for lexical typology proposed by François (2008), also advocated by Croft (2012), as its point of departure offering a direction for a proposal of a research strategy for bipolar conceptual dimensions employed in language to express opposition in text and discourse. François' (2008) approach is natural in the context of a usage-based Cognitive Linguistics framework where meaning in language is at the heart of all analyses. Meanings of words are not fixed, but words have a meaning potential from which more specific readings are evoked on the occasion of use in text and discourse (Paradis

2005, 2015a). Given that words and constructions are couplings of form and meaning, lexical typologists are confronted with a choice between a semasiological approach and an onomasiological approach to the design of an investigation. The semasiological approach takes *form* as its starting point, asking questions such as "Given word X, what meanings does it express?", while the onomasiological approach is essentially the opposite taking meaning as its starting point, i.e. "Given concept Y, what words can be used to express it?". The semasiological approach directly tackles the problem of multiple readings of words, while the onomasiological approach is concerned with multiple readings via the lexical expressions and/or their synonyms. In a sense, typological research is strongly onomasiological in that various domains, configurational (grammatical) or contentful (lexical), form the point of departure, i.e. analysts start from specific domains, e.g. evidence, aspect, body parts or sensory perceptions. Koptjevskaja-Tamm (2012) offers a detailed and useful presentation of previous typological research and future avenues, comprising many onomasiological domains both contentful such as CUTTING-AND-BREAKING EVENTS, TEMPERATURE, TASTE etc. and more configurational or grammatical such as spatial relations and reflexive-middle-reciprocal configurations.

In his proposal, François (2008) takes a radical polysemy view, taking individual meanings to be the primary object of investigation rather than word forms. In order to get a clearer picture of the organization of languages' vocabularies, an important component in his model is the notion of colexification through which his purpose is to account for empirically-based systems of polysemy across languages, also paving the way for possible language universals. The typological prospect of his research agenda is that if two senses are colexified in at least one language, this may be a sign of there being some sort of meaning connection between them, and this connection may be explainable through general cognitive construals of conceptual structures such as metonymization, metaphorization, hyponymization etc. An example given by François (2008) concerns the spatial notion of 'straightness', as in *a straight line,* which is metaphorically associated with social normality as in *keep to the straight and narrow path* or *the straight and the gay.*[2] The more widespread the colexification patterns are across the world's

---

[2] The latter example explicitly sets up the opposition between two different sexual inclinations. In this context it should be noted that the meaning dimension along which the antonym pairing is one of SEXUAL INCLINATION, which is different from say *straight* and *crooked*, in which case the dimension is SHAPE. The antonym pairings and the identification of the meaning dimensions guide us in determining differences between readings as well as polysemies within and across languages, which is the point made in this chapter.

languages, the stronger the semantic connection and the way of construing information. Another example concerns the domain of sensory perceptions. François (2008) states that the senses 'hear', 'smell', and 'feel' are colexified in several areas of the world, e.g. Catalan *sentir*, Italian *sentire*, Mwotlap *yoŋey*, Bislama *harem*. This is also the case in Swedish (Viberg 2015). In a corpus of descriptions of sensory perceptions in English, we also see this very clearly. There are descriptors of wine such as *white aromas* as well as the use of some dimensional properties such as SOFT, as in *soft smells, soft tastes* and *soft textures* where several descriptors are used across domains and cultures (Caballero and Paradis 2013, 2015; Paradis and Eeg Olofsson 2013; Paradis 2015b). This lexical syncretism is grounded in how the conceptualization of our sensorium functions. Under normal circumstances, we cannot taste something without smelling something and we cannot taste something without feeling something and over and above everything is the sight of this something (Paradis and Eeg Olofsson 2013).

In order to discover and empirically determine patterns of use and complex variation both within and across languages, we need to collect large sets of natural data in machine-readable form to be put under the magnifying glass and analyzed both automatically and manually along a number of variables. Obviously, this is a methodology that is not available to all the languages of the world because of the lack of textual data. However, there will be a sufficient number of languages in different parts of the world that can be used as a starting-point. With the rapid development of new computational techniques and the possibilities offered by the WorldWideWeb, the prospects are promising for cross-linguistic discourse research through various distributional techniques (Geeraerts, Grondelaers, and Bakema 1994; Sahlgren 2008; Glynn and Fisher 2010; Wälchli and Cysouw 2012; Paradis et al. 2015) and visual text analytics of linguistic data (Kerren, Prangova, and Paradis 2011, 2012). Similar to Croft (2012: 129), the approach does not assume presupposed universal linguistic categories, rather it abandons universal claims about categories in language in favour of comparisons based on meaning structures. What meanings are expressed through what words and constructions in languages is basically a probabilistic, variationist, distributional approach. If there are universal linguistic constraints of patterning on conceptual structures, this will show in the results of cross-linguistic comparisons. The next section presents the methods of analysis to be used within the research program outlined above.

5.5 Methods for cross-linguistic comparisons of antonyms

The relation of antonymy is a particularly interesting area for typological research because antonyms always express opposite properties of simple conceptual dimensions and a pair of antonyms in use are always configured as a bounded partition in twos, irrespective of whether the dimensions are scalar, e.g. HEIGHT (*high–low*), *long–short*, or not, e.g. EXISTENCE *dead–alive* (Paradis and Willners 2011). Some antonymic words tend to elicit one another more strongly than others. They are expressive of dimensions such as LENGTH (*long–short*), SIZE (*small–large*) MERIT (*good–bad*) and STRENGTH (*strong–weak*), all of which are central to human life and way of living in all parts of the world, and the content of these dimensions coincide with the core of the semantic types that are associated with both very small and large adjective classes in the world's languages (Dixon 2009). In a large number of different investigations, using both experimental and textual techniques, a number of pairings, such as the ones above, have been shown to be particularly strong couplings in languages such as English, Swedish, Japanese, Dutch, Russian (Koptjevskaja-Tamm and Rakhilina 2006; Jones et al. 2007; Muehleisen and Isono 2009; Murphy et al. 2009; Paradis, Willners, and Jones 2009; Willners and Paradis 2010; Jones et al. 2012). With the aim of implementing an onomasiological starting-point, such dimensions are of particular interest, both in their own right (Section 5.5.1) and as springboards for further investigations using those dimensions as nodes for the investigation of lexical semantic patterns (Section 5.5.2). The reader is reminded that the onomasiological approach takes an interest in the lexical items that express a given concept (dimensions of domains), while the semasiological approach takes the lexical items as the starting-point in order to investigate what concepts/properties they express in what domains or dimensions. Thus, for a typological investigation of antonymy, we have two different ways of shedding light on antonymic dimensions and antonym use and their different couplings across languages.

This section suggests two main ways of investigating the discursive usage pattern of word pairs that are most strongly associated with the opposite properties of such central dimensions across languages. The techniques for the identification of the most strongly affiliated word pairs along such dimensions are described in order to determine their usage patterns and relations of these canonical antonyms with other opposable word meanings along other dimensions, with the prospect of being able to describe and explain what contentful domains are employed by these word forms in what languages.

5.5.1 Conceptual dimensions and discontinuous antonymic constructions

As has been pointed out, various observational techniques have shown that there are a number of opposable adjectives that have special status as canonical antonyms. It has also been pointed out that antonymous word pairs that have been shown to be strongly canonical are expressive of properties of salient dimensions. Whereas most studies have been carried out using adjectives, word class membership is irrelevant for any study of opposites, since the onomasiological basis of a pair of antonyms is always a simple dimensional structure which may be the only meaning of some words, such as *good–bad*, or an aspect of richer concepts such as *man–woman*, zooming in on the dimension of gender (for a more detailed description of zone activation, see Paradis 2004). This section reports on two corpus methods that can be used across languages to establish usage patterns and meaning variation patterns for canonical antonym pairs in the first place and their extended antonymic patterns after that.

Following Charles' and Miller's (1989) proposal that lexical associations between adjectival antonyms are formed through co-occurrence in sentences rather than substituting for one another in the same syntactic context, Justeson and Katz (1991, 1992) showed that very high co-occurrence rates appear for antonymic adjective pairs. They claim that strength of co-occurrence is to be seen as the precondition for the formation of associations between words as shown experimentally by for example Deese (1964, 1965). Like Justeson and Katz, Willners (2001) established that antonyms tend to co-occur at higher-than-chance rates in sentences, and that the 'direct' antonyms of Princeton WordNet co-occur significantly more often than the 'indirect' antonyms and also significantly more often than other semantic relations such as synonyms. The added value of using Willners' algorithm is that it also takes sentence length into account in the calculations (Willners and Holtsberg, 2001). Based on both English and Swedish data, Paradis, Willners, and Jones (2009) and Willners and Paradis (2010) show that not only do antonyms co-occur sententially more often than chance but some pairings stand out as exceptionally strongly affiliated in this respect and these pairs evoke opposite meanings along core dimensions, as in Table 1.

Table 1: Seven dimensions and their canonical antonym pairs in English and Swedish

DIMENSIONS	English antonyms	Swedish antonyms
SPEED	slow–fast	långsam–snabb
LUMINOSITY	light–dark	ljus–mörk
STRENGTH	weak–strong	svag–stark
SIZE	small–large	liten–stor
WIDTH	narrow–wide	smal–bred
MERIT	bad–good	dålig–bra
THICKNESS	thin–thick	smal–tjock

The word pairs in Table 1 were searched in the BNC (British National Corpus) and SUC (Stockholm-Umeå Corpus) using *Coco*, the computer program developed by Willners (2001: 83). Coco calculates expected and observed sentential co-occurrences of words and their levels of probability in a given sentence. The results of using Coco on the seven word pairs in the BNC are shown in Table 2 (the corresponding figures for Swedish can be found in Willners and Paradis 2010). $N1$ and $N2$ are the numbers of times that the two words occur in the corpus. *Co* is the number of times they co-occur in the same sentence, while *ExpctCo* is the number of times they are expected to co-occur in a way that chance would predict. The calculations were made under the assumption that all words are randomly distributed in the corpus and the *p-values* are all lower than 10^{-4}. Translation equivalents of the strongly canonical antonyms already established can be used since very robust results for the basic expressions of conceptual dimensions in both English and Swedish have already been obtained.

Table 2: Sentential co-occurrence of the canonical antonyms in the the BNC.

		Word frequency		Co-occurrence frequency	
Word 1	Word 2	N 1	N 2	Co	Expct Co
slow	fast	5760	6707	163	9.6609
dark	light	12907	12396	402	40.0103
strong	weak	19550	4522	455	22.1076
large	small	47184	51865	3642	611.9756
narrow	wide	5338	16812	191	22.4421
bad	good	26204	124542	1957	816.1094
thick	thin	5119	5536	130	7.0867

Synonyms of the members of each pair were also collected from Princeton WordNet. For the dimension of SPEED, for instance, *slow–fast* represent the strongest co-occurrence pair. The synonyms of the members of canonical pairs were searched and combined in all possible constellations in the same way as the canonical pairing, resulting in much less strong figures of co-occurrence, but still co-occurring with *p*-values lower than 10^{-4}. Examples of combinations that were thrown up using this method are *rapid–slow, delayed–immediate, gradual–immediate, gradual–sudden* and *quick–slow*. For a full report of this see Paradis, Willners, and Jones (2009) and Willners and Paradis (2010).

In contrast to the idea that antonymy is a lexical relation based on associations of words in language, as in Structuralism, our investigations show that the strength of opposability of antonyms is not first and foremost a lexical relation between antonyms but a conceptual relation between opposite meanings. The strength of the relation is caused by the salience of the meaning dimension (the onomasiological basis) construed according to a basic configurations of SCALE or BOUNDARY (Paradis and Willners 2011). In a lexical decision task using 'strength-of-conceptual-coupling' and 'frequency-of-co-occurrence' as experimental conditions, van de Weijer et al. (2012) show that the antonyms earn their canonical status through the clarity of the meaning structure evoked by the opposite properties, rather than through the co-occurrence frequency of the pairings of the lexical items in text and discourse. Using the converging results from experiments and corpus methodologies, the textual technique of investigating co-occurrence patterns is useful in the study of semantic dimensions and their expressions in language and the typological patterns of these conceptual dimensions across languages. Examining patterns of canonical antonyms through corpus-driven methods has the potential of contributing to our understanding of lexical semantic variation across languages.

The usage-based investigations described above could be replicated in other languages to address broader, cross-linguistic questions about these particular dimensions and the pairings that express their opposite properties in language (Jones et al. 2012: 150). They can subsequently be extended through detailed corpus-based analyses of multiple variables involved in the semantic patterns of these pairs in terms of what meanings they modify and if and how they are used with respect to reference points and in metaphorizations and metonymizations etc. (Koptjevskaja-Tamm and Rakhilina 2006; Tribushinina 2008; Marková 2010). Paradis et al. (2015) have conducted a detailed corpus study comprising 21 dimensions expressed by their most canonical antonym pairs in English, as shown in Table 3.

Table 3: Meaning dimensions and antonym pairs expressing opposite properties of the dimensions.

DIMENSIONS	antonym pairs		DIMENSIONS	antonyms pairs	
AGE	young	old	SIZE	little	big
APERTURE	closed	open	SPEED	slow	fast
BEAUTY	ugly	beautiful	STRENGTH	weak	strong
EXISTENCE	dead	alive	TEMPERATURE	cold	hot
FULLNESS	empty	full	TEMPERATURE	cool	warm
HARDNESS	soft	hard	TEXTURE	smooth	rough
HEIGHT	low	high	THICKNESS	thin	thick
LENGTH	short	long	WEALTH	poor	rich
LUMINOSITY	light	dark	WEIGHT	light	heavy
MERIT	bad	good	WIDTH	narrow	wide
SIZE	small	large			

Paradis et al. (2015) have scrutinized almost 20,000 occurrences of individual uses of adjectives (i.e. separate uses of these words when they were not used to express opposition) that previously have been shown to be strongly opposable (Paradis, Willners and Jones 2009). A comprehensive semantic coding schema was used on these corpus data to determine similarity patterns and differences across the uses of such antonymic adjectives. One important result of this study is *light* which clearly has two senses in English – *light* as opposed to *dark*, as properties of LUMINOSITY, and *light* as opposed to *heavy*, as properties of WEIGHT. Correspondence analysis was used to identify similarities and differences. The antonymic adjectives pattern in a similar way, which in the case of *light* means that it shared its semantics both with *dark* and *heavy* in different places of the correspondence plot.

Boundaries between senses in conceptual space in language understanding equal meaning *autonymy*. In the case of antonymous adjectives such as *thin* and *thick*, or *good* and *bad*, the symptoms of autonymy become evident by the fact that they resist unification in constructions that force sameness of meaning. For instance, the construction [the book was X and so was the voice], i.e. ?*the book was thick and so was the voice*, forces identity of the two interpretations of *thick* in *thick book* and *thick voice*. Since the two uses of *thick* resist unification because they are too different from one another, a zeugma is created and the expression comes across as infelicitous. The autonomy effect then is a result of the fact that senses can only be conceptualized one at a time. We can flicker between two senses but not interpret both simultaneously (Paradis 2012). Such constraints of focus of attention provide evidence for sense boundaries in conceptual space, or in other words, as related, but different, dimensions at a certain distance form one another in conceptual space – the further away the stronger the sense boundary. Another reflex of two senses that can be uncovered is to exploit ambiguity. Instead of using constructions such as [the book was X and so was the voice], which force sameness, the inverse strategy can be used to identify polysemy. Again this method makes use of constructions where the elements modify one and the same entity where both senses are indeed possible. For instance, *thick* in 'he thinks I am thick' may refer to either body size or intelligence, and out of global context, we do not know which one of the two meanings is the intended meaning. A third way of identifying sense boundaries and polysemy may be that different senses of, say, *thick*, have different antonym partners in language. The antonym of *thick* referring to body size may be *thin* or *slim*, while the antonym of *thick* in the domain of intelligence of intelligence may be *clever* or *intelligent*. Antonyms form discontinuous constructions along one dimension (Jones, et al. 2012 Chs 6–7), and in the case of the above examples sameness of the dimension is the connecting link that makes testing possible. This brings us into the next section where we take a closer look at a method of investigation where sameness is kept constant through continuous construction.

5.5.2 Corpus methodologies: continuous constructions

The second method proposed for the investigation of dimensions and antonymic words is to make use of contrastive constructions that interact with antonym pairs. Murphy et al. (2009), Muehleisen and Isono (2009), Kostić (2011) and Wu (2014) took the first steps in the cross-cultural study of antonym co-occurrence across English, Swedish, Japanese, Serbian and Chinese respectively. The first investigations opened up for a description of antonyms as constructions, in the technical sense (Murphy 2006). The construction approach was further developed and subsequently incorporated into the framework of Cognitive Linguistics (Paradis and Willners 2011; Jones et al. 2012) and accounted for both in terms of discontinuous constructions of antonyms expressing the opposable meaning dimension (reported in Section 5.5.1) and continuous constructions (in this section), i.e. contrastive constructions with two slots to filled by words expressing antonymic content. This section complements the cross-linguistic investigations of antonyms and contrastive constructions with a description using the WorldWideWeb as corpus.

Jones (2002) provided the initial account of antonym functions in discourse by searching for sentential co-occurrences of 56 antonym pairs in a corpus composed of eight years of the British newspaper *The Independent*. He categorized the antonym co-occurrences according to the functional relations between the members of the pairs in each sentence, using a sample of 3,000 sentences. In so doing, he was able to identify a number of constructions hosting antonym pairs, e.g. *X and Y alike* as in *hot and cold alike*, and found that the majority of English antonym pairs, some 77 % in his corpus, occur in one of two major constructional frames, described below. He identified a number of minor constructional frames too that account for most of the rest of antonym co-occurrences. This finding was used as a basis for systematic comparison between English and Swedish (Murphy et al. 2009) and also a more limited study was performed using Japanese pairs (Muehleisen and Isono 2009). The set of antonym pairs in both languages are shown in Table 4.

Table 4: English and Swedish search terms.

English		Swedish		
Word1	Word2	Word1	Word2	Word class
active	passive	aktiv	passiv	ADJ
advantage	disadvantage	fördel	nackdel	N
agree	disagree	enig	oenig	ADJ
alive	dead	levande	död	ADJ
attack	defend	angripa	försvara	V
bad	good	dålig	bra	ADJ
badly	well	illa	väl	ADV
begin	end	börja	sluta	V
boom	recession	högkonjunktur	lågkonjunktur	N
cold	hot	kall	varm	ADJ
confirm	deny	bekräfta	förneka	V
correct	incorrect	korrekt	felaktigt	ADJ
difficult	easy	svår	lätt	ADJ
directly	indirectly	direkt	indirekt	ADV
discourage	encourage	avskräcka	uppmuntra	V
dishonest	honest	oärlig	ärlig	ADJ
disprove	prove	motbevisa	bevisa	V
drunk	sober	full	nykter	ADJ
dry	wet	torr	blöt	ADJ
explicitly	implicitly	explicit	implicit	ADJ
fact	fiction	verklighet	dikt	N
fail	succeed	misslyckas	lyckas	V
failure	success	misslyckande	framgång	N
false	true	falsk	sann	ADJ
fast	slow	snabb	långsam	ADJ
female	male	kvinnlig	manlig	ADJ
feminine	masculine	feminin	maskulin	ADJ
gay	straight	homosexuell	heterosexuell	ADJ

Tab. 4 (continued)

English		Swedish		
Word1	Word2	Word1	Word2	Word class
guilt	innocence	skuld	oskuld	N
happy	sad	glad	ledsen	ADJ
hard	soft	hård	mjuk	ADJ
hate	love	hata	älska	V
heavy	light	tung	lätt	ADJ
high	low	hög	låg	ADJ
illegal	legal	olaglig	laglig	ADJ
large	small	stor	liten	ADJ
long	short	lång	kort	ADJ
lose	win	förlora	vinna	V
major	minor	större	mindre	ADJ
married	unmarried	gift	ogift	ADJ
new	old	ny	gammal	ADJ
officially	unofficially	officiellt	inofficiellt	ADV
old	young	gammal	ung	ADJ
optimism	pessimism	optimism	pessimism	N
optimistic	pessimistic	optimistisk	pessimistisk	ADJ
peace	war	fred	krig	N
permanent	temporary	permanent	tillfällig	ADJ
poor	rich	fattig	rik	ADJ
private	public	privat	offentlig	ADJ
privately	publicly	privat	offentligt	ADV
punishment	reward	straff	belöning	N
quickly	slowly	snabbt	långsamt	ADV
right	wrong	rätt	fel	ADJ
rightly	wrongly	riktigt	oriktigt	ADV
rural	urban	lantlig	urban	ADJ
strength	weakness	styrka	svaghet	N

The various constructions, exemplified below in (1)–(14), were used to gather cross-linguistic data seeded with translation equivalents of Jones' (2002) antonym pairs. Because the subsequent studies took as their starting point the comparison of Swedish data with Jones' findings for English, they make use of Jones' categories. In his study they are considered as purely functional categories. This means that, although instances of these categories are often expressed using particular lexico-grammatical frames, they were not defined by them. For instance, while many instances of the so-called coordinated antonymy include instances of the *X and Y* frame, it is not the occurrence of antonyms within that frame that make them coordinated antonymy, but the functional relation between the antonyms.

In this chapter, the proposal is to use the discourse constructions seeded with antonym expressions of dimensions for cross-linguistic investigations.

The first of the two major categories, ancillary antonymy, involves the use of an antonym pair in order to highlight a secondary contrast, as in (1) and (2), which is the most frequent one in the English data.

1) I **love** to *cook* but **hate** *doing the dishes*.

2) Archer was a formal, eccentric man, **long** on *acquaintances* and **short** on *friends*

The antonym pair in bold represents the pair that Jones had searched for, termed the "A-pair", and the italicized elements, or the "B-pair", are in a contrast relation that has been highlighted by their co-occurrence with the A-pair. There is of course not much support for the claim that the A-pair has the function of promoting the B-pair. This is a mere stipulation, which can be accepted for methodological reasons but not for any other reason.[3] In spite of the shortcomings, these contrasting frames are useful tools in cross-linguistic searches for expressions of dimensional meanings and antonym patterns across languages. The second major antonym function, coordinated antonymy, is just slightly less common. The distinction between the antonyms is here neutralized, as in (3) and (4).

3) He played numerous cameo roles both on the **large** and the **small** screen.

4) We may **succeed**, we may **fail**—but we will at least give it a whirl

The minor categories account among themselves for the remainder of the instances, i.e. around 33 %. In order of frequency, the most important ones are comparative antonymy, (5) and (6), distinguished antonymy, (7) and (8), transitional antonymy, (9) and (10), negated antonymy (11) and (12), extreme antonymy, (13) and (14).

---

3 Due to the fact that these categories do not form a coherent intelligible patterning and due to the fact that not all of these categories are at the same taxonomic level, they are in need of some more work to form a systematic model of discourse meaning. For instance, the Ancillary category does not address how the members of the antonymous pairs relate to one another but only focuses on how the more canonical pair allows for a secondary contrasting pair (Murphy et al. 2009). Improvements have been suggested by other scholars too, e.g. Panther and Thornburg (2012).

5) [S]ome living composers are more **dead** than **alive**.

6) All fat, **unsaturated** no less than **saturated**, is fattening.

7) [H]e still doesn't know the difference between **right** and **wrong**.

8) You'll struggle to find a better delineation of the no-man's land between **love** and **hate**.

9) Inflation is a tax which redistributes wealth to the **sophisticated** from the **unsophisticated**.

10) Economic **optimism** has given way to economic **pessimism**.

11) However, the citizen pays for public services to work **well**, not **badly**

12) That's not making it **clean,** that's making it **dirty**.

13) For thousands of years in Britain, food had to be either very **cold** or very **hot**, but now they are accepting warm salads.

14) I am not completely **afraid** and not completely **unafraid**.

The comparisons across English, Swedish and Japanese return similar patterns of interaction between discourse frames and antonyms. There were distributional differences across the categories cross-linguistically. Ancillary antonymy and coordinated antonymy figure as the two main functions in all three languages, which means that the attraction of the constructions on antonym pairs was clear across all three languages. Based on a smaller number of sentences and burdened by a more complex translation process due to the morphological, syntactic and orthographic differences between English and Japanese, the main result of the investigation of Japanese pairings identified through discourse constructions is clearly not as robust as the one between English and Swedish. This said, it deserves to be pointed out that the translation process into Swedish was not entirely straightforward either. It was at times difficult to find corresponding words with the same meaning, register, word class and approximately the same frequency rank. Although the similarities between English and Swedish are strong, the distribution of the categories was significantly different, but the statistical difference is largely the result of a small number of trends in particular categories. For instance, while the coordinated category was less frequent in Swedish than in English, Swedish had greater proportions of ancillary constructions. On closer inspection, the general trend toward coordinated antonyms in English was particularly supported by a small number of antonyms that had much higher rates of the coordinated function in English (Murphy et al. 2009).

All the searches in the above studies were employed on the basis of the antonym pairs selected, and the types of discourse functions were determined on the basis of the occurrences. The study was geared towards cross-linguistic comparisons of antonymy use in these specific constructions as well as across the constructions. In another study, the World-Wide-Web was used as corpus for the identification of strength of antonym couplings (Jones et al. 2007). The issue of antonym canonicity and antonym diversity was approached by building specifically on the research described above which has demonstrated the tendency of antonyms to favour certain constructions in discourse, such as *X and Y alike*, *between X and Y*, *both X and Y*, *either X or Y*, *from X to Y*, *X versus Y* and *whether X or Y*. In this study, the method was reversed compared to the previously described investigations in the sense that the discourse constructions were used as the starting point and the two open slots were subsequently seeded with one or the other of a number of antonym partners. Seven discourse constructions, making 14 search frames, were used. The constructions and the system of seeding of antonyms, abbreviated as ANT in combination with wildcard is shown in Table 5.

Table 5: The fourteen search frames used in Jones et al. (2007).

Wildcard-first frame	Wildcard-second frame
* and ANT *alike*	ANT *and* * *alike*
between * *and* ANT	*between* ANT *and* *
both * *and* ANT	*both* ANT *and* *
either * *or* ANT	*either* ANT *or* *
from * *to* ANT	*from* ANT *to* *
* *versus* ANT	ANT *versus* *
whether * *or* ANT	*whether* ANT *or* *

The antonyms used as seed words for this study were the high-scoring pairings from the previously described textual and the experimental studies. The fourteen contrastive constructions were used for the identification of the range of contrast items, i.e. the range of dimensions, across a number of seed words. Strong correlations emerged between those antonymic words that were found to be as 'good opposites' in the previously described elicitation experiments (Paradis et al. 2009). As a matter of fact, in the case of nine of the ten seed words selected as a starting point for the web searches, i.e. *beautiful, poor, open, large, rapid, exciting, strong, wide, thin* and *dull*, the antonyms retrieved most often in these searches were the same as the adjectives that were suggested by the participants in the elicitation experiment.

Also, it is a useful way of investigating dimensional variation across the antonyms selected for investigation. Jones et al. (2007) reports the results (one example from each frame) for *dull* in the 14 discourse frames. The examples are repeated in (15)–(28) below. The search-construction appears in bold and the word retrieved in wildcard position is italicized.

15) I would gladly hear your musings, **dull and** *dreary* **alike**.

16) Most young women, *intelligent* **and dull alike**, feel the same way.

17) **Both dull and** *bright* colors are used in impressionistic paintings.

18) Senses become **both** *acute* **and dull** at the same time.

19) The outer surface of the shell may be **either dull or** *shiny*.

20) You'll probably find this **either** *amusing* **or dull**, depending on your politics.

21) Intensity refers to a color's strength **whether dull or** *bright*.

22) Other art meetings, **whether** *fun* **or dull**, were strained.

23) The 5,000sq.km salt lake ranges **from dull to** *technicolour* depending on the weather.

24) The amethyst surface luster varies **from** *glassy* **to dull**.

25) It's **dull versus** *bright*, what with bland hues thrown in.

26) Choose between types of pain: new versus old, *sharp* **versus dull**, local versus radiating.

27) "The Three Sisters" precariously walks the line **between dull and** *compelling*.

28) For me the difference **between** *interesting* **and dull** is the sincerity of the preacher.

All in all, 2,760 contexts were retrieved for *dull* and, as the examples above show, many different words were found in the wildcard position. The frequencies for the 14 discourse constructions were combined and a ranked list was created, where the ten most commonly retrieved words in the wildcard slot were recorded. Table 6 shows the frequencies for *dull* expressed both in absolute terms and as a percentage of all output as well as the number of discourse constructions in which each word appeared. It should be pointed out that all contexts were manually scrutinized in this study in order to make sure that the words were used as antonyms.

Table 6: The top ten frequencies antonymic partners of *dull* in their discourse frames.

Antonyms of *dull*	frequency	%	frames
1. bright	103	3.73	11
2. dynamic	83	3.01	3
3. sharp	73	2.64	8
4. dazzling	60	2.17	2
5. shiny	50	1.81	8
6. boring	28	1.01	4
7. brilliant	22	0.80	5
8. delightful	21	0.76	1
9. exciting	19	0.69	6
10. interesting	19	0.69	6

This method sheds light on the various dimensions from the starting point of a given item, i.e. various readings related to LUMINOSITY, CLARITY and BRIGHTNESS (*dull–bright/sharp/dazzling/shiny*) and another set of partners related to INTELLIGENCE and EXCITEMENT (*dull – sharp/boring/brilliant/delightful/exciting/interesting*). It paints a picture of meaning variation of individual antonymic words, which can be used as a point of departure for the retrieval and comparison of the different senses and readings cross-linguistically. This then is directed towards the most challenging and at the same time most intriguing problem for lexical typology, which is the malleability of word meaning and its sensitivity to context and discursive considerations. This constitutes a challenge both for the description and for the explanation of word meaning variability, i.e. how and where words are used, their combinatorial couplings in constructions and their relations to other word meanings in the context and in the vocabulary of languages. Such factors are most pertinent to the investigation of lexical semantic couplings within languages as well as across languages and through time. Given the distributional similarity of antonym discourse functions across different corpora and in a WorldWideWeb corpus, it is reasonable to expect any strongly co-occurring, lexically enshrined pair of antonyms to serve most or all of these functions at relatively high rates. This raises the possibility that canonicity may therefore be operationalized according to a pair's rates of co-occurrence in the discourse frames that are most closely associated with these functions in different languages.

5.6 Summary

The main aim of this chapter has been to suggest different corpus techniques, corpus driven as well as corpus based, and to show how they can be useful for cross-linguistic comparisons of lexical semantic construals such as expressions of binary opposition through antonymic pairs in lexical typology. It is assumed that all languages express binary opposition and it is also assumed that all languages have a set of particularly felicitous couplings of words that express opposite properties along salient meaning dimensions such as SIZE, LUMINOSITY, STRENGTH, MERIT, WIDTH. Such pairings can be compared across languages. They can also be taken as points of departure, as seed words, for extractions of other possible antonym partners, either along different meaning dimensions (LUMINOSITY (*light–dark*) WEIGHT (*light–heavy*) in which case we determine that *light* is polysemous, or along fairly similar dimensions such as LUMINOSITY, CLARITY and BRIGHTNESS (*dull– bright/sharp/dazzling/shiny*) and another set of partners related to INTELLIGENCE and EXCITEMENT (*dull–sharp boring/brilliant/delightful/ exciting/interesting*), which are related within their different groupings and metaphorically also across the grouping from visual experiences of light to emotional reactions and mental abilities. The methodologies presented have previously been put to use in English and Swedish and a couple of other languages. Given the results of those studies, it is reasonable to assume that they can, successfully, be more widely and more systematically used for cross-linguistic comparisons.

5.7 References

Ackrill, J.L. 1963. *Aristotle: Categories and De Interpretaione*. Oxford: Clarendon Press.
Aikhenvald, Alexandra J. 2003. *Classifiers: A typology of noun categorization devices*. Oxford: Oxford University Press.
Auwera, Johan van der and Jan Nuyts. 2007. Cognitive linguistics and linguistic typology. In Dirk Geeraerts and Hubert Cuyckens (eds.), *The Oxford handbook of cognitive linguistics*, 1075–1091. New York: Oxford University Press.

Caballero, Rosario and Carita Paradis. 2013. Perceptual landscapes from the perspective of cultures and genres. In Rosario Caballero and Javier E. Díaz-Vera (eds.), *Sensuous cognition: Explorations into human sentience: Imagination, (E)motion and Perception*, 77–105. Berlin: de Gruyter Mouton.

Caballero, Rosario and Carita Paradis. 2015. Making sense of sensory perceptions across languages and cultures. *Functions of language*, 22(1): 1–19.

Charles, Walter G. and George A. Miller. 1989. Contexts of antonymous adjectives. *Applied psycholinguistics* 10: 357–75.

Croft, William. 2012. *Verbs: Aspect and causal structure*. Oxford: Oxford University Press.

Croft, William and Alan Cruse. 2004. *Cognitive linguistics*. Cambridge: Cambridge University Press.

Cruse, Alan. 2002. The construal of sense boundaries. *Revue de Sémantique et Pragmatique* 12: 101–19.

Dahl, Östen. 1985. *Tense and aspect systems*. Oxford: Blackwell.

Deese, James. 1964. The associative structure of some common English adjectives. *Journal of Verbal Learning and Verbal Behavior* 3: 347–57.

Deese, James. 1965. *The structure of associations in language and thought*. Baltimore: John Hopkins University Press.

Dixon, Robert M. W. 2009. Adjective classes in a typological perspective. In Robert M.W. Dixon and Alexandra Y. Aikhenvald (eds.), *Adjective classes: A cross-linguistic typology*, 1–49. Oxford: Oxford University Press.

Firth, John R. 1957. Modes of Meaning. *Papers in Linguistics* 1934 (51): 190–215. Oxford: Oxford University Press.

François, Alexander. 2008. Semantic maps and the typology of colexification: intertwining polysemous networks across languages. In Martine Vanhove (ed.), *From polysemy to semantic change*, 163–215. Amsterdam: John Benjamins.

Geeraerts, Dirk. 1997. *Diachronic prototype semantics*. Oxford: Clarendon Press.

Geeraerts, Dirk, Stefan Grondelaers, and Peter Bakema. 1994. *The structure of lexical variation: Meaning, naming and context*. Berling & New York: Mouton de Gruyter.

Geeraerts, Dirk and Yves Peirsman. 2011. Zones, facets and prototype-based metonymy. In Réka Benczes, Antonio Barcelona and Francisco Ruiz de Mendoza Ibáñez (eds.), *What is metonymy? An attempt at building a consensus view on the delimitation of the notion of metonymy in Cognitive Linguistics*. 89–102. Amsterdam: John Benjamins.

Glynn, Dylan and Kerstin Fischer (eds.). 2010. *Corpus-driven cognitive semantics*. Berlin: de Gruyter Mouton.

Horn, Laurence (ed.). 2010. *The expression of negation*. Berlin: de Gruyter Mouton.

Jones, Steven. 2002. *Antonymy: a corpus-based perspective*. London: Routledge.

Jones, Steven, Carita Paradis, M. Lynne Murphy, and Caroline Willners. 2007. Googling for opposites: a web-based study of antonym canonicity. *Corpora* 2: 129–154.

Jones, Steven, M. Lynne Murphy, Carita Paradis, and Caroline Willners. 2012. *Antonyms in English: Construals, constructions and canonicity*. Cambridge: Cambridge University Press.

Justeson, John S. and Slava M. Katz. 1991. Co-occurrence of antonymous adjectives and their contexts. *Computational Linguistics* 17: 1–19.

Justeson, John S. and Slava M. Katz. 1992. Redefining antonymy: the textual structure of a semantic relation. *Literary and Linguistic Computing* 7: 176–84.

Kerren, Andreas, Mimi Prangova, and Carita Paradis. 2011. Visualization of sensory perception description. In *Proceedings of the 15th International Conference on Information Visualisation (IV '11)*, 135–144. London, UK. IEEE Computer Society Press.

Kerren, Andreas, Mimi Prangova, and Carita Paradis. 2012. From culture to text to interactive visualization of wine reviews. In Francis T. Marchese and Ebad Banissi (eds.), *Knowledge visualization currents. From text to art to culture*, 85–110. London: Springer Verlag.

Koptjevskaja-Tamm, Maria. 2012. New directions in lexical typology. *Linguistics* 50 (3): 373–394.

Koptjevskaja-Tamm, Maria. 2008. Approaching lexical typology. In Martine Vanhove (ed.), *From polysemy to semantic change*, 3–52. Amsterdam: Benjamins.

Koptjevskaja-Tamm Maria and Ekaterina Rakhilina. 2006. "Some like it hot": on the semantics of temperature adjectives in Russian and Swedish. [Special Issue, Torsten Leuschner & Giannoula Giannoulopulou (eds.)]. *Sprachtypologie und Universalienforschung*, STUF, 2–59.

Koptjevskaja-Tamm, Maria, Martine Vanhove, and Peter Koch. 2007. Typological approaches to lexical semantics. *Linguistic Typology* 11 (1): 159–186.

Kostić, Nataša. 2011. Antonymous frameworks in Serbian written discourse: Phrasal contexts of antonym co-occurrence in text. *Poznań Studies in Contemporary Linguistics* 47(3): 509–537.

Lehrer, Adrienne and Keith Lehrer. 1982. Antonymy. *Linguistics and Philosophy* 5: 483–501.

Lloyd, Geoffrey E.R. 1966. *Polarity and analogy: two types of argumentation in early Greek thought*. Cambridge: Cambridge University Press.

Lobanova, Anna, Tom van der Kleij, and Jennifer Spenader. 2010. Defining antonymy: a corpus-based study of opposites by lexico-syntactic patterns. *International Journal of Lexicography* 23 (1): 19–23.

Marková, Věra. 2010. *Zur Ermittlung der lexikalischen Beziehungen zwischen semantisch nahen Adjektiven*. Prague: Univerzita Karlova (Charles University) Ph.D. dissertation.

Mohammad, Saif, Bonnie Dorr, and Graeme Hirst. 2008. Computing word-pair antonymy. *Proceedings of the 2008 conference on empirical methods in natural language processing*, 982–991, Honolulu: Association for Computational Linguistics.

Muehleisen, Victoria and Maho Isono. 2009. Antonymous adjectives in Japanese discourse. *Journal of Pragmatics* 41: 2185–2203.

Murphy, Gregory, L. and Jane M. Andrew. 1993. The conceptual basis of antonymy and synonymy of adjective. *Journal of memory and language* 32: 301–319.

Murphy, M. Lynne. 2006. Antonyms as lexical constructions: or, why paradigmatic construction is not an oxymoron. *Constructions* 1 (8): 1–37.

Murphy, M. Lynne, Carita Paradis, Caroline Willners, and Steven Jones. 2009. Discourse functions of antonymy: a cross-linguistic investigation of Swedish and English. *Journal of Pragmatics* 41: 2159–2184.

Ogden, Charles K. 1932. *Opposition: A linguistic and psychological analysis*. Bloomington: Indiana University Press.

Osgood, Charles E., Suci, George J., and Percy H. Tannenbaum. 1957. *The measurement of meaning*. Urbana, IL: University of Illinois Press.

Osgood, Charles E. and Meredith M. Richards. 1973. From Yang and Yin to and or but. *Language* 49 (2): 380–412.

Panther, Klaus-Uwe and Linda Thornburg. 2012. Antonymy in language structure and use. In Mario Brdar, Ida Raffaelli, and Milena Žic Fuchs (eds.), *Cognitive linguistics between universality and variation*, 161–188. Newcastle, UK: Cambridge Scholars.

Paradis, Carita. 2001. Adjectives and boundedness. *Cognitive Linguistics* 12 (1): 47–65.

Paradis, Carita. 2003. Is the notion of linguistic competence relevant in Cognitive Linguistics? *Annual Review of Cognitive Linguistics* 1: 247–271.

Paradis, Carita. 2004. Where does metonymy stop? Senses, facets and active zones. *Metaphor and symbol* 19: 245–264.

Paradis, Carita. 2005. Ontologies and construals in lexical semantics. *Axiomathes* 15 541–573.

Paradis, Carita. 2008. Configurations, construals and change: expressions of DEGREE. *English Language and Linguistics* 12: 317–343.

Paradis, Carita. 2011. Metonymization: a key mechanism in language change. In Réka Benczes, Antonio Barcelona, and Francisco Ruiz de Mendoza Ibáñez (eds.), *What is metonymy? An attempt at building a consensus view on the delimitation of the notion of metonymy in Cognitive Linguistics*, 61–89. Amsterdam: John Benjamins.

Paradis, Carita. 2012. Lexical semantics. In C. A. Chapelle (ed.), *The encyclopedia of applied linguistics*, 3357–3356. Oxford: Wiley-Blackwell.

Paradis, Carita. 2015a. Meanings of words: Theory and application. In Ulrike Hass and Petra Storjohann (Eds.) Handbuch Wort und Wortschatz (Handbücher Sprachwissen-HSW Band 3) Mouton de Gruyter, Berlin (274–294) DOI (Chapter): HYPERLINK "http://dx.doi.org/10.1515/9783110296013-012" 10.1515/9783110296013-012.

Paradis, Carita. 2015b. Conceptual spaces at work in sensory cognition. Domains, dimensions and distances. In Frank Zenker and Peter Gärdenfors (eds.), *Applications of conceptual spaces: The case for geometric knowledge representation*, 33–55. Dordrecht: Springer Verlag.

Paradis, Carita and Caroline Willners. 2011. Antonymy: from conventionalization to meaning-making. *Review of Cognitive Linguistics* 9 (2): 367–391.

Paradis, Carita and Mats Eeg-Olofsson. 2013. Describing sensory experience: The genre of wine reviews. *Metaphor & Symbol* 28 (1): 1–19.

Paradis, Carita, Caroline Willners and Steven Jones. 2009. Good and bad opposites: using textual and psycholinguistic techniques to measure antonym canonicity. *The Mental Lexicon* 4: 380–429.

Paradis, Carita, Joost van de Weijer, Caroline Willners, and Magnus Lindgren. 2012. Evaluative polarity of antonyms. *Lingue e Linguaggio*, 2: 199–214.

Paradis, Carita, Simone Löhndorf, Joost van de Weijer, and Caroline Willners. 2015. Semantic profiles of antonymic adjectives in discourse. *Linguistics*, 53.1, 153–191.

Sahlgren, Magnus. 2008. The distributional hypothesis. *Rivista di Linguistica*, 20 (1): 3–53.

Tribushinina, Elena. 2008. *Cognitive reference points: semantics beyond the prototypes in adjectives of space and colour* [Dissertation Series 192] Utrecht: Landelijke Onderzoekschool Taalwetenschap Ph.D. dissertation.

Viberg, Åke. 2015. Sensation, perception and cognition. Swedish in a typological-contrastive perspective. *Functions of Language*: 22 (1) 96–131.

Wälchli, Bernhard and Michael Cysouw. 2012. Lexical typology through similarity semantics: Toward a semantic map of motion verbs. *Linguistics,* 50(3): 671–710.

Weijer, Joost van de, Carita Paradis, Caroline Willners, and Magnus Lindgren. 2012. As lexical as it gets: the role of co-occurrence in a visual lexical decision experiment. In Dagmar

Divjak and Stefan Th. Gries (eds.), *Frequency effects in language: linguistic representation*, 255–279. Berlin: Mouton de Gruyter.

Weijer, Joost van de, Carita Paradis, Caroline Willners, and Magnus Lindgren. 2014. Antonym canonicity temporal and contextual manipulations. *Brain & Language* 128 (1): 1–8.

Willners, Caroline. 2001. *Antonyms in context: A corpus-based semantic analysis of Swedish descriptive adjectives. Travaux de l'Institut de Linguistique de Lund,* 40. Lund: Lund University, Department of Linguistics Ph.D. dissertation.

Willners, Caroline and Anders Holtsberg. 2001. Statistics for sentital co-occurrence. *Working papers* 48: 135–48. Lund University, Department of Linguistics.

Willners, Caroline and Carita Paradis. 2010. Swedish opposites: a multi-method approach to antonym canonicity. In Petra Storjohann (ed.), *Semantic relations: Theoretical and practical perspectives,* 15–47. Amsterdam: John Benjamins.

Wu, Shuqiong. 2014. The metonymic interpretation of Chinese antonym co-occurrence constructions: the case of *you x you y*. *Language Sciences* 45: 189–201.

Robert Östling
6. Studying colexification through massively parallell corpora

Abstract: Large-sample studies in lexical typology are limited by whatever lexical information is available or can be obtained for all the languages in the study. Various types of word lists, from simple Swadesh lists to large dictionaries, can be used for this purpose. Unfortunately, these resources often present only a very fragmentary view of a given language's vocabulary. As a complement, we propose an additional source of lexical information: parallel texts. Books such as the New Testament have been translated into thousands of languages, and it is possible to automatically extract word lists from their vocabulary, which can then be applied to lexical typological studies. In particular, we focus on studying colexification using a sample of 1 001 different languages, based on 1 142 translations of the New Testament. We find that although the automatically extracted word lists contain errors, their quality can be sufficiently good to find real areal patterns, such as the 'tree'/'fire' colexification that is widespread in the Sahul area.

6.1 Introduction

The purpose of this work is to develop automatic methods for investigations in lexical typology, by utilizing parallel texts that have translations into hundreds or even thousands of languages, but without any linguistic annotation for all languages. In this case translations into 1 001 languages of the New Testament are used as source material. To evaluate the methods presented, we focus on the specific phenomenon of *colexification*. François (2008: 170) defines colexification in the following way:

> A given language is said to colexify two functionally distinct senses if, and only if, it can associate them with the same lexical form.

This definition intentionally circumvents the often difficult distinction between polysemy and semantic vagueness, and provides an operationalizable way to

---
Robert Östling (Stockholm University)

explore the lexical structure of languages without having to consider the actual forms of words.

Colexification provides a way of studying the lexica of languages without considering the actual forms of the lexical items, the only thing that needs to be known is whether the forms of two given semantic concepts are equal or not. These equalities or non-equalities characterize a language in the same way that, say, the basic word order or the number of genders do. Like those well-studied typological features, the colexification profile of a language tends to be similar to those of languages that are related or in contact with it.

Two different examples can be found in Figure 1 and Figure 2, showing languages with DIE-BLOOD and STONE-MOUNTAIN colexification. Both cases are localized to one or a few regions, while almost unattested in most of the world. Each shape/shade combination represents a particular language family, according to the top-level classification of Hammarström et al. (2014). In the case of DIE-BLOOD, although a fairly large geographical area is covered, all of the languages are Sino-Tibetan and the actual word forms are similar (e.g. Dafang /si/, Lahu /si/, Jino /S i/)[1]. This indicates either a genetic explanation or possibly borrowing. For STONE-MOUNTAIN, the situation is different. There are a few different areas (in central Africa, southern Africa, Australia, parts of South America) where this colexification is frequent, but in all these cases there is a broad representation of language families and word forms, which suggests that this is an areal phenomenon (or rather, several independent such phenomena).

Since the focus in this chapter is on methods for identifying colexification patterns, rather than analyzing the underlying reasons for these patterns, we will not dwell upon this subject. The interested reader may refer to the study of Koptjevskaja Tamm and Liljegren (forthcoming) on areal aspects in lexical typology.

---

[1] There is only a single case attested outside this area: Sumerian, an extinct isolate.

Fig. 1: Languages (28) with DIE-BLOOD colexification. Shape/shade represents language family, according to the Glottolog classification (Hammarström et al. 2014). The purpose of this map is to illustrate the geographic and genealogical distribution of colexification, and the data is taken from ASJP (Wichmann et al. 2013) rather than from the method presented here.

Fig. 2: Languages (139) with STONE-MOUNTAIN colexification. Shape/shade represents language family, according to the Glottolog classification (Hammarström et al. 2014). The purpose of this map is to illustrate the geographic and genealogical distribution of colexification, and the data is taken from ASJP (Wichmann et al. 2013) rather than from the method presented here.

Most of the colexifications discussed here have been previously studied, TREE-FIRE(-FIREWOOD) is discussed in depth for a large sample of Papuan and Australian languages by Schapper, San Roque, and Hendery (this volume). Aikhenvald (2009) similarly discusses EAT-DRINK-SMOKE colexification in Manambu (a Sepik language spoken in Papua New Guinea) and in other languages of the area. Urban (2012) covers patterns of colexifications for a large number of concepts and languages. ARM-HAND and HAND-FINGER colexification has been studied by Brown (2013b, a), who has also made public the data sets. Other studies focus on how different parts of the color space are colexified (Kay and Maffi 2013a, b).

6.2 Resources

We begin with a brief survey of some resources available for studies of colexification. The deficiencies of these resources are then used as justification for our proposed method.

6.2.1 WALS

The World Atlas of Language Structures, WALS (Dryer and Haspelmath 2013), contains four chapters on what may be termed colexification. Two concern body parts, HAND-ARM (Brown 2013b) and HAND-FINGER (Brown 2013a), while two concern color terms GREEN-BLUE (Kay and Maffi 2013a) and RED-YELLOW (Kay and Maffi 2013b). The samples of the body part chapters are fairly large and balanced, with about 600 languages each, while the color term chapters use a smaller sample of 120 languages.

6.2.2 CLICS

The CLICS database of cross-linguistic colexifications (List et al. 2014) uses a smaller sample than WALS, only 221 languages with a bias towards certain areas such as the Caucasus, South America and Europe. This is problematic since large areas are covered very sparsely or not at all, which for instance results in the omission of the fire-tree colexification attested from dozens of languages in Papua and Australia. However, the number of semantic concepts covered (1 280) is large and fine-grained compared to the other resources.

6.2.3 ASJP

The database of the Automated Similarity Judgement Program, ASJP (Wichmann et al. 2013), contains wordlists covering 40 basic concepts in 6 895 languages or language varieties. While colexifications are not explicitly marked in the database, it is trivial to compute them based on the word lists. There are several pairs of concepts that show interesting colexification patterns, such as TREE-FIRE and STONE-MOUNTAIN. For these pairs, a very large sample of languages can be used.

6.2.4 The New Testament

Parts of the Christian Bible, particularly the New Testament, have been translated into thousands of languages and have previously been used for typological studies (Cysouw and Wälchli 2007; Dahl 2007; Wälchli and Cysouw 2012). We have access to 1 142 translations of the New Testament into 1 001 different languages, and propose to use these in order to extract the wordlists necessary for identifying instances of colexification.

The WALS and ASJP databases both contain large samples of languages, but few concepts. CLICS instead contains many concepts, but for a small sample of languages. The New Testament combines the best features of both: a large sample of languages, and many concepts.

Unfortunately, it is much less straightforward to use a parallel text without any type of linguistic annotations, than it is to use the other databases. The way we propose to do this is through word alignment, and transfer of morphological analysis in order to identify the lexeme(s) in a language which most closely corresponds to a given semantic concept.

Although the New Testament corpus covers a large number of languages, the sample is somewhat biased to those languages where there has been incentives for translation. This disproportionately excludes languages with few speakers, which unfortunately leaves large areas almost uncovered, in particular Australia and North America.

6.3 Word alignment

Automatic word alignment of parallel texts has long been used as an intermediate step in statistical machine translation (Brown et al. 1990, 1993) and lexicon construction (Klavans and Tzoukermann 1990; Wu and Xia 1994; Fung and Church 1994).

The problem is basically this: given a set of sentences in different languages[2], assumed to be translation equivalents, find out which words correspond to each other.

A variety of different algorithms have been applied to the problem of word alignment, including simple co-occurrence based methods (Gale and Church 1991; Melamed 2000), methods based on the Expectation-Maximization (EM) algorithm (Brown et al. 1993; Och and Ney 2003) and more recently, variational Bayesian methods (Riley and Gildea 2012) or Gibbs sampling (DeNero, Bouchard-Côté, and Klein 2008; Mermer and Saraçlar 2011; Mermer, Saraçlar, and Sarikaya 2013; Gal and Blunsom 2013).

Below, the algorithm of Mermer and Saraçlar (2011) will be presented in a simplified manner to illustrate how one goes about learning word alignments for IBM Model 1 (Brown et al. 1993) using Gibbs sampling.

6.3.1 Word alignment through Gibbs sampling

The basic idea behind Gibbs sampling is to repeatedly *sample* (that is, select randomly) each variable conditioned on the present values of all other variables. After a number of repetitions, the alignments become increasingly consistent as the possible translation(s) of each word become established[3].

To illustrate this, consider Fig. 3. This parallel sentence contains two sets of *observed variables*: English words (e_1, e_2, ...) and German words (f_1, f_2, ...). We also postulate a set of *latent* alignment variables (a_1, a_2, ...) which are used to link the English and German words. Specifically, a_j gives the index of the word linked to f_j. If the value of, say, a_3 is 1, this indicates that word f_3 (*es*) is aligned to with e_1 (*it*). These alignment variables are what we want to compute.

At the core of a Gibbs sampling algorithm is the *sampling distribution* for each variable, which describes the probability of each possible alignment for a given target word. These distributions can be illustrated by pie charts, for the varia-

---

[2] There is of course nothing that prevents parallel texts with different dialects of the same language from being aligned, or even independent translations of the same language variety. This can be used to study within-language variation, both synchronically and diachronically.

[3] Technically, the samples of the whole set of alignment variables a obtained through Gibbs sampling are (in the limit) guaranteed to be unbiased samples under the model. At any given time during sampling, a contains sampling noise and one typically uses multiple samples to estimate each variable a_j as e.g. the mode among all individual samples of a_j.

ble *a*3 this is illustrated in in Fig. 4 (for a vague distribution, as is typically seen early during the sampling process) and in Fig. 5 (for a more specific distribution, typical after correct alignments have been chosen for most other words).

Fig. 3: Example of a parallel sentence. The source language is English, and the target language is German.

When comparing the two figures, it is important to remember that in a typical corpus there are thousands if not millions of other sentences, with many instances of each of the words in our example sentence. In the beginning, *es* might only be correctly aligned in about 5 % (1/20) of cases due to random chance, if a sentence is on average about 20 words long. A small initial bias towards the correct translation (in this case, *it*, as seen in Fig. 4) will gradually be reinforced, until most instances of *es* are linked to *it*. Once this has happened, the sampling distribution might look like in Fig. 5, which ensures that most instances of *es* will be linked to *it* during the following iterations[4].

The Gibbs sampling algorithm consists of the following steps:

1. Choose random values for each alignment variable a_j. This results in a mostly incorrect alignments, but since English words can only be aligned to German words in the same sentence, there will also be a significant number of *correct* alignments produced. For instance, *es* and *it* might occur as translations in 1000 sentences, and in say 40 of those they might actually be aligned to each other by chance (whereas the remaining 960 are incorrectly aligned to random words).

2. For each alignment variable a_j:

    (a) Compute for each English word in the sentence e_i the sampling probability $p(a_j = i | \boldsymbol{a}^{(-j)}, \boldsymbol{e}, \boldsymbol{f})$, which is the probability given all *other* alignments that $a_j = i$. For instance, in Figure 4 the value of $p(a_3 = 2 | \boldsymbol{a}^{(-j)}, \boldsymbol{e}, \boldsymbol{f}) = 0.15$, meaning that there is a 15 % chance that *es* should (incorrectly) be linked to *rained*.

    (b) Sample a_j randomly from this distribution. This corresponds to throwing a dart at the pie chart and letting the German word *es* be linked to

---

[4] This is not true, strictly speaking, because if the sampling is run long enough all possible alignments will be sampled eventually.

the English word that the dart hits. Perhaps counter-intuitively, this randomness is an essential part of the algorithm, and simply choosing the word with the highest probability all the time will in general lead to poor results.
3. When sampling is finished, we select the final alignment by linking each German word to the English word that was most often chosen during the sampling (dartthrowing) process.

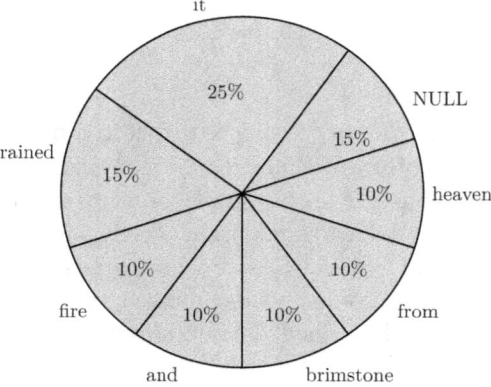

Fig. 4: Sampling distribution of a_3 (link to German *es*) at an early stage of the Gibbs sampling procedure. Constructed example with imaginary but realistic percentages.

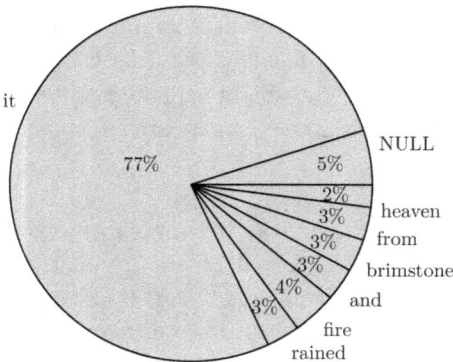

Fig. 5: Sampling distribution of a_3 (link to German *es*) after a number of Gibbs sampling iterations. Constructed example with imaginary but realistic percentages.

The crucial step is to find the sampling distribution. Deriving this equation is beyond the scope of this article, but details can be found elsewhere (Mermer,

Saraçlar, and Sarikaya 2013; Östling 2015). Given a Bayesian version of IBM Model 1, with symmetric Dirichlet priors, the sampling distribution becomes:

$$p(a_j = i | \boldsymbol{a}^{(-j)}, \boldsymbol{e}, \boldsymbol{f}) = \frac{n^{(-j)}_{e_i, f_j} + \alpha}{\sum_k n^{(-j)}_{e_i, f_k} + \alpha |F|} \tag{1}$$

where α is a small constant,[5] $|F|$ is the size of the target language (German) vocabulary, and $n^{(-j)}_{e,f}$ is the number of times English word e is aligned to German word f, *excluding* the word f_j itself and whatever word it is currently linked to. That is, we should only consider *other* contexts of the word, avoiding the one we are currently sampling.

Note that Equation (1) assigns a probability that is roughly proportional to the number of times a given pair of English and German words are linked elsewhere, which intuitively makes the algorithm prefer consistent translations, as expected. Another essential point is that when using a small value of α (typically less than 0.01), the algorithm is very unlikely to link words that are not linked elsewhere. Again, this makes intuitive sense. If *Katze* 'cat' is only linked to *cat* elsewhere in the text, we would be very hesitant to suddenly propose linking *Katze* to some other word if *cat* is available as a candidate.

6.3.2 Part of speech transfer

Toutanova, Ilhan, and Manning (2002) showed that by also making sure parts of speech are consistently aligned, word alignment accuracy can be increased. There is one issue that prevents their approach from being useful for aligning e.g. the New Testament corpus: it assumes that part of speech (PoS) annotations are available for the languages which are to be word aligned. Accurate automatic tools for PoS annotation exist for a number of languages, but those are a diminishingly small minority among the thousand languages in the New Testament corpus.

Therefore, we use *annotation transfer*, where linguistic annotation from one language is transfered to other languages through a parallel text. Much has been written about this topic (see e.g. Yarowsky and Ngai 2001; Hwa et al. 2002; Spreyer 2011; Täckström 2013), but some of the assumptions behind these techniques deserve to be made explicit. First of all, methods for annotation transfer typically assume a more or less strict correspondence between languages with respect to

---

[5] This is the Dirichlet prior parameter.

whatever is being annotated. For parts of speech, this means that for instance a noun in one language assumed to be generally translated with a noun in another language. Given both the theoretical arguments against cross-linguistically valid categorizations (Croft 2001; Haspelmath 2007) and the fact that there are numerous counter-examples, one could certainly question the linguistic usefulness of annotation obtained through transfer from another language.

Our justification is simply that using PoS annotations has been shown to improve the accuracy of automatic word alignment algorithms (Toutanova, Ilhan, and Manning 2002). Normally word alignment is performed first, and the result is used by the annotation transfer algorithm. In this case, however, we perform these tasks simultaneously in order to allow the word alignment algorithm benefit from the transfered PoS annotations. Further details and an empirical evaluation of this algorithm can be found elsewhere (Östling 2015, chapter 4).

6.3.3 Lemmatization transfer

One important difference between using word lists and raw parallel text without annotations is that the former generally contain lemmas, whereas in a normal text only word forms are given. For a few languages there are high-quality lemmatization systems based on dictionaries, such is the case for e.g. English (Manning et al. 2014) and Swedish (Östling 2013). Some languages, such as Chinese and Vietnamese, are highly analytic and word forms coincide with lemmas in nearly all cases.

Unfortunately, for the vast majority of languages in the New Testament corpus, we are still faced with the problem of identifying lemmas. Like part of speech annotations, this is a problem which has been successfully approached using word-aligned parallel texts (Yarowsky and Wicentowski 2000). We use a fairly simple method which assumes concatenative morphology, with at most one prefix and one suffix per word form. This assumption is clearly much too strong, but note that for the purpose of lemmatization it is no problem if several affixes are lumped into one – as long as they can be separated from the stem. Phenomena like stem alteration can however not be modeled by the approach we use in this work, and due to time constraints it has not been possible to use more flexible morphological models.

Lemmatization is performed in tandem with word alignment, so that the word alignment algorithm could potentially benefit from having access to the lemmatized word forms. Further details on this algorithm can be found in Östling (2015, section 4.4).

6.4 Word list generation

Given word alignments and lemmas, it is straightforward to generate a word list for each language in the corpus. We begin by defining concepts[6] using lemmas from languages where we have access to high-quality lemmatizers (English and Swedish) or languages that are highly analytic (Mandarin Chinese and Vietnamese).

Table 1: Example definitions of four concepts.

Language	mountain	stone	tree	fire
English	mountain	stone	tree	fire
Swedish	berg	sten	träd	eld
Mandarin	shān	shítou	(shù)	huǒ

In case of close synonyms, more than one lemma may be specified for each language, or conversely, some of the languages may not be used for the definitions of certain concepts if the word form is polysemous and the unintended meanings are too frequent – a decision made by the author based on corpus searches and lexica. This is the case with Mandarin[7] *shù* ('tree', 'number', 'method', etc.)

Then, for each translation of the New Testament we compute a table containing the number of instances in which each lemma is linked to one of the lemmas in the concept definitions. The lemma(s) with a sufficiently large number of links is accepted as a translation, and included in the word list for that language. In our experiments, we require that a lemma be linked to at least 50 % of concept definition instances, but by varying this threshold one can adjust the balance between precision and recall – that is, whether false negatives (i.e. colexifying languages that are missed by the algorithm) are to be preferred to false positives (languages incorrectly claimed to be colexifying by the algorithm), or the other way around.

---

[6] This way of defining semantic concepts will leave some readers dissatisfied, but since all we have is a parallel text, our options are limited.
[7] This would not have been a problem in this case if a translation with Chinese characters had been available, but the only word-segmented versions are romanized.

6.5 Summary of the method

The basic goal of our method is to generate a table, which for each language and semantic concept under consideration gives a list of lemmata used for that concept in that language. Thus, our goal is essentially the same as that of a linguist trying to elicit a word list, but the means are different. Given such a table, we can directly read out the colexifications of each language by checking for overlapping entries in the table. To summarize the preceding sections, the way we create this table is as follows:

1. Prepare a parallel text with translations into the languages of study. In our case the New Testament is used since translations into a large number of languages (1 001) are available.
2. Define the semantic concepts using some subset of the languages in the corpus. We use English, Swedish, Mandarin Chinese and Vietnamese. Examples are given in Table 1.
3. Perform word alignment between the translations used to define the concepts and all other translations. For this, the alternating alignment-annotation algorithm (Östling 2015, chapter 4) is used, of which a simplified version is sketched above in Section 6.3.1.
4. Perform *lemmatization*, i.e. try to identify the lemma of each word form in each of the translations. Again, a sketch of the method is given above in Section 6.3.3, but for full details consult Östling (2015, section 4.4).
5. For each concept, find the lemmata in each language that are most often linked (in step 3) to the words defining the concepts. These are what we are looking for.

6.6 Results

There are three interesting colexification patterns that occur in a sufficient number of languages (at least ten) which are both in the New Testament corpus, and in either the ASJP or WALS databases: STONE-MOUNTAIN, TREE-FIRE and HAND-ARM.

For these cases, we generate wordlists using the method described above, and identify the languages for which there is any overlap in translations between the two concepts in each pair. Table 2 shows how many languages were identified as colexifying each pair of these concepts (and how many of those identifications are correct, according to the given reference). The total number of colexifying languages in the reference is also given.

These results are clearly not perfect, but sufficient to identify a likely set of candidates which can be explored in greater depth through other means. It can also be sufficient to draw preliminary conclusions, such as that the languages identified as colexifying tree and fire are mostly spoken in Papua New Guinea and belong to different families, indicating an areal phenomenon (cf. Figures 6 and 7). The patterns discovered can then be explored using more precise – and much more timeconsuming – methods.

When interpreting the figures in Table 2, it is important to keep in mind that the total samples with information from both the New Testament corpus and the reference are much larger (821 for ASJP, and 225 for WALS), but that the majority of languages distinguish between these concepts, and nearly all of those are correctly identified as such by the algorithm. So although the number of false positives is minute with respect to all the languages investigated, since the true positives (actually colexifying languages) are so few, these numbers are comparable.

Table 2: Agreement between algorithm and ASJP/WALS. Precision is the ratio between correctly identified colexifying languages, and all languages reported by the algorithm. Recall is the ratio between correctly identified colexifying languages and all colexifying languages in the given data.

Concepts	Identified	(Correctly)	Total	Precision	Recall
stone-mountain	24	(9)	12	38 %	75 %
tree-fire	15	(11)	14	73 %	79 %
hand-arm	51	(27)	92	53 %	29 %

6.7 Error analysis

While our method is highly accurate when it comes to excluding languages that are *not* colexifying a particular pair of concepts, and the results above show that it can deliver useful results when asked to pick out the languages that do, the method also makes numerous mistakes. There are three main causes behind these mistakes: word alignment errors, multi-word expressions, and morphology.

6.7.1 Word alignment errors

If the word alignment algorithm mistakenly links two unrelated words a sufficient number of times, this will introduce spurious items into the wordlists generated. This is fairly common, for three major reasons:
1. it is difficult to reliably link words that occur only a few times in a corpus, because of insufficiently strong statistics;
2. words that occur frequently together (such as *hand* and *arm*) can be difficult to tell apart, and the alignment algorithm might decide that *arm* should be translated with a word that actually means *hand*. This turned out to be a particular problem in the New Testament, and a manual analysis indicates that this is the reason for the large share of false positives reported by the algorithm in the HAND-ARM task;
3. translation is rarely one-to-one, and phenomena like synonymy, homophony or polysemy ensure that even for relatively common words there will be unusual word combinations that are difficult to link correctly.

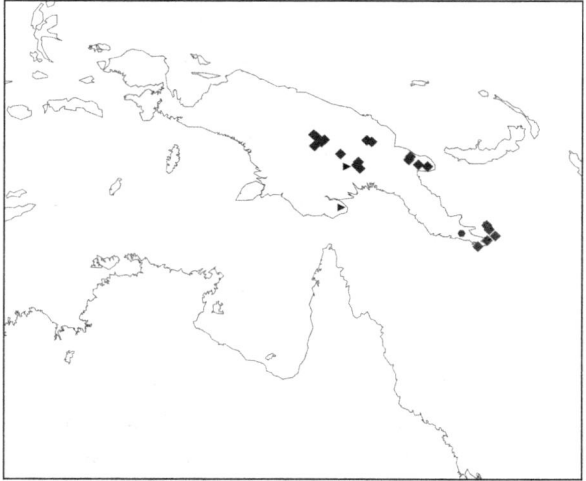

Fig. 6: Languages (23) with TREE-FIRE colexification, according to our algorithm. Shape/shade represents language family, according to the Glottolog classification (Hammarström et al. 2014). All languages are contained in Papua.

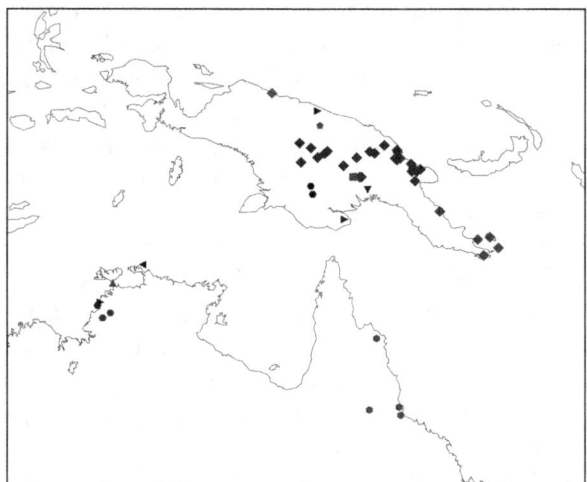

Fig. 7: Languages (64) with TREE-FIRE colexification, according to ASJP (Wichmann et al. 2013). Shape/shade represents language family, according to the Glottolog classification (Hammarström et al. 2014). Only a handful of languages are outside Papua/northern Australia, scattered around the world.

6.7.2 Multi-word units

Since a strictly word-based alignment algorithm is used, it can be confused when a multi-word unit (e.g. a compound or a whole phrase) is used to translate a particular word. In these cases, any or all of the words in the multi-word unit may show up as candidate translations.

This is a particular problem in colexification studies, since our goal is to identify concepts that are expressed in *the same* way, not where one term may be somehow derived from the other. For instance, the English *pear* and *prickly pear* ought to be considered distinct, even through both contain the word *pear*. The algorithm presented could in this case report a false positive: CACTUS.FRUIT-PEAR.

6.7.3 Morphology

One of the basic assumptions made by the algorithm is that identical lexical items can be identified by comparing sequences of letters from the texts, but this is clearly a simplification. There are a number of things that can, and do, go wrong:

1. Mistakes in the lemmatization transfer. This could be because of words that occur only in a single inflectional form, which could potentially be interpreted either as zero-marked or as having an affix. The simple lemmatization method used for this work is only able to handle simple concatenative morphology, and does not deliver correct results given phenomena like fusion, stem alterations or vowel harmony. Normally the effect of this would be false negatives, where actual colexifications are missed.
2. Derivational morphology, which might be misidentified as inflectional. Since semantically related words are frequently derived from one another using some kind of derivational affixes, if these affixes are mistakenly removed as mere inflections, we might be led to believe that two words which are actually distinct (although related) are equal. In the end we are faced with the same problem as was discussed above for the case of multi-word units, resulting in a colexification that in in fact a false positive.
3. Noun incorporation, which could prevent the algorithm from even detecting the noun, so that even if the noun is colexified with another there is no chance of detecting this. This could lead to false negatives.

6.7.4 Homophones

Homophones create a problem which is shared by many colexification databases, including CLICS (List et al. 2014). In languages with many homophones, a number of them will be semantically related and these can be difficult to separate from true colexifications, lacking historical data. Fortunately these types of homophones are not common enough to create a major distraction when looking at individual colexifications, but if one tries to e.g. find common colexifications automatically then a number of those found will be accidental homophones.

6.8 Discussion

I have demonstrated that the method proposed can serve as a useful exploratory tool in lexical typology, but it is important to be aware of its limitations. First of all, it is highly dependent on the particular text used as source material. If a concept does not occur in the text, it is impossible to investigate it. Even concepts that do occur can be difficult to investigate, if they occur so rarely that it is difficult to accurately identify them, or if they frequently co-occur with other concepts. For instance, it is very difficult to study EAT-DRINK colexification with the New Testament since these are often expressed in the same sentences, which makes it difficult to differentiate between words expressing them, which in turn leads to a high rate of false positives. This particular problem could in some cases be alleviated by excluding verses where both concepts occur, but then there might not be a sufficient number of instances left to make a reliable match.

Furthermore, our method rests on the assumption that we can define a concept using lemmas from a few languages, and that we can identify equivalent words in other languages through the parallel text. There are many cases in which this assumption is broken. For instance, where one English version might have "eat", another has "take food", and this complicates automated studies of EAT-FOOD colexification.

Biases in the translations will also affect the result. With the New Testament, this results in very poor coverage for among others the native languages of Australia and North America. In the case of TREE-FIRE (Fig. 6) this means that our method does not discover that the pattern actually extends beyond Papua, into the Australian continent (Fig. 7, see also Schapper, San Roque, and Hendery, this volume).

Given the reservations above, our method allows us to give a preliminary answer to questions such as "where, if at all, does TREE-FIRE colexification occur?" within seconds, a question which (unless all the source material is already compiled) would require a large amount of work to answer.

Bibliography

Aikhenvald, Alexandra Y. 2009. The linguistics of eating and drinking. In John Newman (Ed.), *'Eating', 'drinking' and 'smoking': A generic verb and its semantics in Manambu* pp., 91–108. Amsterdam: John Benjamins.

Brown, Cecil H. 2013a. Finger and hand. In Matthew S. Dryer and Martin Haspelmath (Eds.), *The world atlas of language structures online*. Leipzig: Max Planck Institute for Evolutionary Anthropology.

Brown, Cecil H. 2013b. Hand and arm. In Matthew S. Dryer and Martin Haspelmath (Eds.), *The world atlas of language structures online*. Leipzig: Max Planck Institute for Evolutionary Anthropology.

Brown, Peter F., John Cocke, Stephen A. Della Pietra, Vincent J. Della Pietra, Fredrick Jelinek, John D. Lafferty, Robert L. Mercer, and Paul S. Roossin 1990. A statistical approach to machine translation. *Computational Linguistics*, 16(2), 79–85.

Brown, Peter F., Vincent J. Della Pietra, Stephen A. Della Pietra, and Robert L. Mercer 1993. The mathematics of statistical machine translation: Parameter estimation. *Computational Linguistics*, 19(2), 263–311.

Croft, William. 2001. *Radical construction grammar: Syntactic theory in typological perspective*. Oxford University Press.

Cysouw, Michael and Bernhard Wälchli. 2007. Parallel texts: Using translational equivalents in linguistic typology. *STUF – Language Typology and Universals*, 60(2), 95–99.

Dahl, Östen. 2007. From questionnaires to parallel corpora in typology. *STUF – Language Typology and Universals*, 60(2), 172–181.

DeNero, John, Alexandre Bouchard-Côté, and Dan Klein. 2008. Sampling alignment structure under a Bayesian translation model. In *Proceedings of the 2008 Conference on Empirical Methods in Natural Language Processing*, 314–323. Honolulu, Hawaii: Association for Computational Linguistics.

Dryer, Matthew S. and Martin Haspelmath. 2013. *The World Atlas of Language Structures Online.* http://wals.info.

François, Alexandre. 2008. Semantic maps and the typology of colexification: Intertwining polysemous networks across languages. In Martine Vanhove (Ed.), *From polysemy to semantic change*, 163–215. Amsterdam: Benjamins.

Fung, Pascale and Kenneth Ward Church. 1994. K-vec: A new approach for aligning parallel texts. In *Proceedings of the 15th Conference on Computational Linguistics – Volume 2*, COLING '94, 1096–1102). Stroudsburg, PA, USA: Association for Computational Linguistics.

Gal, Yarin and Phil Blunsom. 2013. A systematic Bayesian treatment of the IBM alignment models. In *Proceedings of the 2013 Conference of the North American Chapter of the Association for Computational Linguistics: Human Language Technologies* Stroudsburg, PA, USA: Association for Computational Linguistics.

Gale, William A. and Kenneth W. Church. 1991. Identifying word correspondence in parallel texts. In *Proceedings of the Workshop on Speech and Natural Language*, HLT '91, 152–157. Stroudsburg, PA, USA: Association for Computational Linguistics.

Hammarström, Harald, Robert Forkel, Martin Haspelmath, and Sebastian Nordhoff. 2014. *Glottolog 2.3.* Leipzig: Max Planck Institute for Evolutionary Anthropology. http://glottolog.org.

Haspelmath, Martin. 2007. Pre-established categories don't exist: Consequences for language description and typology. *Linguistic Typology*, 11(1), 119–132.

Hwa, Rebecca, Philip Resnik, Amy Weinberg, and Okan Kolak. 2002. Evaluating translational correspondence using annotation projection. In *Proceedings of the 40th Annual Meeting on Association for Computational Linguistics*, ACL '02, 392–399. Stroudsburg, PA, USA: Association for Computational Linguistics.

Kay, Paul and Luisa Maffi. 2013a. Green and blue. In Matthew S. Dryer and Martin Haspelmath (Eds.), *The world atlas of language structures online*. Leipzig: Max Planck Institute for Evolutionary Anthropology.

Kay, Paul and Luisa Maffi. 2013b. Red and yellow. In Matthew S. Dryer and Martin Haspelmath (Eds.), *The world atlas of language structures online*. Leipzig: Max Planck Institute for Evolutionary Anthropology.

Klavans, Judith and Evelyne Tzoukermann. 1990. The bicord system: Combining lexical information from bilingual corpora and machine readable dictionaries. In *Proceedings of the 13th Conference on Computational Linguistics – Volume 3*, COLING '90, 174–179. Stroudsburg, PA, USA: Association for Computational Linguistics.

Koptjevskaja Tamm, Maria and Henrik Liljegren (forthcoming). Semantic patterns from an areal perspective. In Raymond Hickey (Ed.), *The Cambridge handbook of areal linguistics*. Cambridge University Press.

List, Johann-Mattis, Thomas Mayer, Anselm Terhalle, and Matthias Urban. 2014. CLICS: Database of Cross-Linguistic Colexifications. http://clics.lingpy.org.

Manning, Christopher D., Mihai Surdeanu, John Bauer, Jenny Finkel, Steven J. Bethard, and David McClosky. 2014. The Stanford CoreNLP natural language processing toolkit. In *Proceedings of 52nd Annual Meeting of the Association for Computational Linguistics: System Demonstrations*, 55–60. Baltimore, Maryland: Association for Computational Linguistics.

Melamed, I. Dan. 2000. Models of translational equivalence among words. *Computational Linguistics*, 26(2), 221–249.

Mermer, Coşkun and Murat Saraçlar. 2011. Bayesian word alignment for statistical machine translation. In *Proceedings of the 49th Annual Meeting of the Association for Computational Linguistics: Human Language Technologies: short papers – Volume 2*, HLT '11, 182–187. Stroudsburg, PA, USA: Association for Computational Linguistics.

Mermer, Coşkun, Murat Saraçlar, and Ruhi Sarikaya. 2013. Improving statistical machine translation using Bayesian word alignment and Gibbs sampling. *IEEE Transactions on Audio, Speech, and Language Processing*, 21(5), 1090–1101.

Och, Franz Josef and Hermann Ney. 2003. A systematic comparison of various statistical alignment models. *Computational Linguistics*, 29(1), 19–51.

Östling, Robert. 2013. Stagger: An open-source part of speech tagger for Swedish. *North European Journal of Language Technology*, 3, 1–18.

Östling, Robert. 2015. *Bayesian models for multilingual word alignment*. Stockholm: Stockholm University PhD dissertation.

Riley, Darcey and Daniel Gildea. 2012. Improving the IBM alignment models using variational Bayes. In *Proceedings of the 50th Annual Meeting of the Association for Computational Linguistics: Short Papers – Volume 2*, ACL '12, 306–310. Stroudsburg, PA, USA: Association for Computational Linguistics.

Spreyer, Kathrin. 2011. *Does it have to be trees? Data-driven dependency parsing with incomplete and noisy training data*. Potsdam: University of Potsdam PhD dissertation.

Täckström, Oscar. 2013. *Predicting linguistic structure with incomplete and cross-lingual supervision*. Uppsala: Uppsala University, Department of Linguistics and Philology PhD dissertation.

Toutanova, Kristina, Tolga H. Ilhan, and Christopher Manning. 2002. Extensions to HMM-based statistical word alignment models. In *2002 Conference on Empirical Methods in Natural Language Processing (EMNLP 2002)*, 87–94.

Urban, Matthias. 2012. *Analyzability and semantic associations in referring expressions: A study in comparative lexicology*. Leiden: Leiden University PhD dissertation.

Wälchli, Bernhard and Michael Cysouw. 2012. Lexical typology through similarity semantics: Toward a semantic map of motion verbs. *Linguistics*, 50(3), 671–710.

Wichmann, Søren, André Müller, Annkathrin Wett, Viveka Velupillai, Julia Bischoffberger, Cecil H. Brown, Eric W. Holman, Sebastian Sauppe, Zarina Molochieva, Pamela Brown, Harald Hammarström, Oleg Belyaev, Johann-Mattis List, Dik Bakker, Dmitry Egorov, Matthias Urban, Robert Mailhammer, Agustina Carrizo, Matthew S, Dryer, Evgenia Korovina, David Beck, Helen Geyer, Pattie Epps, Anthony Grant, and Pilar Valenzuela. 2013. *The ASJP Database (version 16)*. Leipzig. http://email.eva.mpg.de/~wichmann/languages.htm.

Wu, Dekai and Xuanyin Xia. 1994. Learning an English-Chinese lexicon from a parallel corpus. In *Proceedings of the First Conference of the Association for Machine Translation in the Americas*, 206–213.

Yarowsky, David and Grace Ngai. 2001. Inducing multilingual POS taggers and NP bracketers via robust projection across aligned corpora. In *Proceedings of the Second Meeting of the*

North American Chapter of the Association for Computational Linguistics on Language Technologies, NAACL '01, 1–8. Stroudsburg, PA, USA: Association for Computational Linguistics.

Yarowsky, David and Richard Wicentowski. 2000. Minimally supervised morphological analysis by multimodal alignment. In *Proceedings of the 38th Annual Meeting on Association for Computational Linguistics*, ACL '00, 207–216. Stroudsburg, PA, USA: Association for Computational Linguistics.

Åke Viberg
7. Polysemy in action: The Swedish verb *slå* 'hit, strike, beat' in a crosslinguistic perspective

Abstract: The chapter analyses the pattern of polysemy of the Swedish verb *slå* 'hit, strike, beat'. The major hypothesis is that a large proportion of the many meanings of this verb are best understood as extensions (semantic shifts) from a prototype representing *slå* as a hand action, which can be described as a goal-directed physical action sequence. The meaning of the verb interacts with the meaning of nouns serving as arguments to produce new meanings in context and recurrent thus inferred meanings are lexicalized and serve as the source of further meaning shifts. Meanings are related in networks. Shifts are studied primarily synchronically but examples are given of how meanings are lost over time in a way that breaks the links between related meanings leaving idiom-like expressions behind. However, the distinction between synchrony and diachrony forms a continuum, due i.a. to register variation. The analysis is based on a multilingual translation corpus, which makes it possible to see how the meanings of the Swedish verb are reflected in translations. Crosslinguistic data are also presented from earlier studies of verbs of hitting

7.1 Introduction

Across languages, a verb with the basic meaning HIT has a tendency to be among the most frequent verbs and to have many extended meanings. It is often represented among the simple verbs in languages with a very restricted number of such verbs (see McGregor 2002 on Australian languages) and it appears as a light or support verb in complex predicates (see Hook, Pardeshi, and Liang 2012 on four Asian languages). This paper presents a study of the polysemy of the Swedish verb *slå* 'hit, strike, beat' based on data from a multilingual parallel corpus, which is used to contrast Swedish to a number of genetically and/or areally related languages. It represents a substantially extended analysis of *slå* in Viberg (1999) which presented a general study of the semantic field of physical contact verbs

---

Åke Viberg (Uppsala university)

in Swedish. Since then, studies of the verbs of hitting in several typologically different languages have been published, and these will be reviewed in Section 7.2.

The relations between various meanings of a polysemous word can be described as a set of semantic shifts. The study of semantic shifts can be concerned with *general mechanisms* such as metaphor and metonymy (Barcelona 2000) and the mechanisms proposed by Pustejovsky (1995) in the generative lexicon such as selective binding and coercion. However, the major focus in this paper will be on *substantive semantic shifts* related to specific lexical concepts and to semantic fields. Verbs of perception, for example, tend to shift (extend) their meaning according to the sense modality hierarchy for verbs of perception: SEE > HEAR > TOUCH/TASTE/SMELL (Viberg 1983). This is an example of a field-internal shift. Field-external substantive shifts from perceptual to cognitive meanings such as SEE > KNOW or UNDERSTAND, HEAR > KNOW or UNDERSTAND have been heatedly debated (Sweetser 1990; Evans and Wilkins 2000; Vanhove 2006; Aikhenvald and Storch 2013; Viberg 2015a.)

One important factor underlying substantive shifts is human biology. To a great extent, the semantics of the verbs of perception and indirectly also of several verbs of cognition is biologically grounded in the structure and function of the human sense organs. Several semantic fields contain verbs describing physical actions (i.e. goal-directed bodily actions carried out by humans). Viberg (2010) discusses the relationship between physical manipulation and more abstract meanings of verbs of possession. The title *Polysemy in action* is motivated by the assumption that the many extended meanings of *slå*, which tend to form chains, usually originate in various aspects of the hand actions and their goals that the verb can refer to. There is also a close relationship between hand actions and tools and other artefacts that are designed to allow for optimal manipulation. Linguistically, this is reflected in the semantic interplay between the verb and its arguments.

7.2 Verbs of hitting as a field of study

The following review of earlier studies of verbs of hitting will focus on aspects that are particularly relevant to the present study.

7.2.1 Riemer's four general mechanisms in a study of English and Warlpiri

Riemer (2005) presents a theoretically very well-argued and interesting cognitive linguistic model of polysemy, which is tested on an analysis of physical contact verbs in English and Warlpiri, a Pama-Nyungan language spoken in Central Australia. The semantic analysis is based on a core meaning and four general mechanisms of shift which account for the non-core meanings: metaphor and three types of metonymy. The core meaning is based on the idealized percussion/impact (P/I) scenario (Riemer 2005: 129–130). In a simple example such as *The stick hit the fence*, a moving entity called impactor (the stick) comes into contact with an object surface (the fence) at a particular point of impact (e.g. the head in *He hit me in the head*). The first type of the processes that account for the non-core meanings is *metaphorical application*. A metaphorical application is not strictly speaking an extension. All that distinguishes a metaphorical use from a core use is the denotation of the arguments: "the impactor is predicated of a less than prototypical impactor and object surface." (Riemer 2005: 184). In *a thought has struck me*, the thought is treated as an impactor and consciousness as the object surface. There are three major types of metonymy. The first, *effect metonymy*, refers to metonymic extension to the effect of the action of the verb, for example *strike fire*. The second type of extensions, *context metonymy*, "names the event that forms the context in which the act occurs" (Riemer 2005: 347), for example *smite the harp* 'strike/touch to make musical sounds'. Finally, the third type, *constituent metonymy*, refers to the case where only some parts of the core meaning apply. One example is when the meaning only refers to the movement of a body part as in *He [a preacher] thrashed with his arms* (Riemer 2005: 292–293). Riemer shows that the same general mechanisms apply to English and Warlpiri.

Basically, Riemer shows how a number of specific extended meanings, which I will refer to as substantive semantic shifts, can be derived with the four general types of shift. For example, the core meaning of Warlpiri *pakarni* 'hit' in (1) is related to the use of *pakarni* as a verb of creation (glossed 'make by *paka*') via effective metonymy in (2).

(1) *karnta-ngku*   *ka*   *maliki*   *paka-rni*
woman-ERG   AUX   dog   hit-NPST
watiya-kurlu-rlu
stick-PROP-ERG
'The woman is hitting the dog with a stick' (core meaning)
(Riemer 2005: 343)

(2) Karli   ka-lu   paka-rni   manja
    boomerang   AUX-333S   hit-NPST   mulga
    'They chop (wood for) boomerangs from mulga trees'
    (Riemer 2002: 62)

Effective metonymy also explains other substantive shifts as 'hit' > 'kill', 'hit' > 'paint' and 'hit' > 'perform (dance, ceremony)'. Another type of substantive shift refers to how diseases adversely affect humans (see 3). Since the verb in this case has a non-prototypical impactor, this is an example of metaphorical application.

(3) Kuntulpa-rlu   kurdu   wita   paka-rnu
    cold-ERG   child   small   hit-PST
    'The baby has a cold'
    (Riemer 2005: 343)

In another study comparing the meaning extensions of hit and other P/I verbs in Warlpiri and ten other Central Australian languages, Riemer (2002) found a high degree of semantic uniformity.

7.2.2 Schultze-Berndt's study of Jaminjung, a language with a minimal system of simple verbs

One of the Australian languages with a very restricted number of simple verbs is Jaminjung (Schultze-Berndt 2000). In this language, there are only 35 frequent simple verbs that can be inflected for tense and one of these verbs is *ma-* 'hit', which is described in rather great detail. In addition to simple verbs, there is an open class of complex verbs consisting of a simple verb and another element referred to as a coverb. Coverbs do not inflect and cannot function as verbs on their own. The simple verb *-ma* 'hit' together with various coverbs has developed a grammatical meaning and can be used in complex verbs to describe complete affectedness without any implication of contact or impact. A coverb such as *walig* can be used in combination with a number of different motion verbs to describe motion around something in a (semi-)circle but together with *–ma* 'hit' it refers to complete encircling. In (4), the complex verb means 'to walk around something completely'.

(4) walig   gani-ma-m   gururrij
    around   3sg:3sg-HIT-PRS   car
    'he walks around the car'
    (Schultze-Berndt 2000: 314)

Another set of generalized meanings refers to emergence, but that meaning is not quite as general. The system of extensions in Jaminjung are summarized in Figure 1.

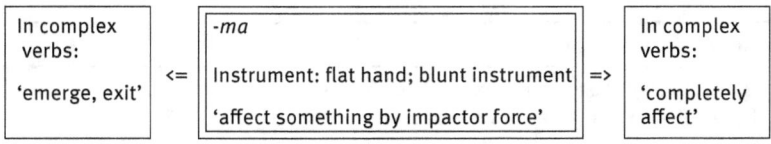

Figure 1: The extensions of *–ma* hit in Jaminjung (based on Schultze-Berndt 2000)

7.2.3 HIT as a verbal operator in Asian languages

In many Asian languages, HIT can be combined with an abstract noun (often the nominal form of a verb) to form a very frequent type of complex predicates (CPs) studied in Hook, Pardeshi, and Liang (2012). In these languages, HIT together with a small set of other verbs functions as a kind of verbal operator with a very general meaning. In particular, CPs with HIT as an operator contrast with antonymous CPs with a verb basically meaning EAT as an operator. In examples of paired CPs such as Chinese *dǎ guan.sī* (HIT lawsuit) 'sue someone' and *chī guan.sī* (EAT lawsuit) 'be sued', the subject of HIT refers to the Agent that delivers the damage, whereas the subject of EAT refers to the Undergoer (Hook et al. 2012: 613). It appears that HIT even in these highly generalized uses has kept some trace of its basic meaning. Only in certain intransitive constructions ("unintransitives") characteristic of Indo-Aryan languages is the contrast between EAT and HIT neutralized.

7.2.4 Family's study of islands of productivity in Persian

Family (2011) presents a detailed study based on construction grammar of the polysemy of *zædæn* 'hit' in Persian, which is another language with a restricted number of verbs. There are only around 200 full verbs, but a small set of the full verbs (around a dozen) can serve as light verbs and form a very large number of light verb constructions in combination with a more or less open set of preverbal elements (cf. coverb above). Often light verb constructions are the only option for expressing a verbal notion. A light verb together with various sets of preverbs with a related meaning form verbal islands. Such constructions form clusters referred to as *islands of productivity* which express similar verbal notions. Two examples are shown in Table 1 (cf. visible emission and emergence in Jaminjung).

Table 1: Islands of productivity in Persian (Family 2011)

1a. The Hand-held weapons island		
– Meaning: wound or penetrate another entity with a weapon		
– Preverbal element (PV): a sharp, penetrating weapon		
xænjær zædæn	scythe HIT	'hit with a scythe'
tʃaqu zædæn	knife HIT	'stab with a knife'
ʃæʃir zædæn	sword HIT	'stab with a sword'
1b. The Visible emission island		
– Meaning: emit a bright visible stimulus		
– Preverbal element (PV): bright shimmer or flash		
jæræqe zædæn	spark HIT	'spark'
tʂeʂmæk zædæn	wink HIT	'blink' (as in a light)
zæbane zædæn	flame HIT	'flare up' (as in a fire)

Family (2011) accounts for around 50 such islands formed around *zædæn* 'hit' and their relatedness.

7.2.5 Gao Hong's study of Chinese *dǎ* and the role of hand actions

Gao Hong's (2001) study of the Chinese verb *dǎ* 'hit, strike, beat' is particularly relevant to the present paper, because it is focused around the idea of *dǎ* 'hit' as a hand action verb. The centrality of the hand for the prototypical meaning of the verb is even represented in the Chinese character for *dǎ* which consists of a combination of the character for 'hand' and the character for 'man' (Gao 2001: 157). The verb, which belongs to one of the around 20 most frequent verbs in Chinese, has a very wide range of extended uses where it refers to hand actions of a more general type that are increasingly more removed from the prototype and less specific. Based on the remoteness from the prototype five categories of meanings of dǎ are distinguished as shown in Table 2.

Table 2: Five major categories of meaning of Chinese *dǎ* (Gao 2001)

1)	Physical Action Focusing on Hand Contact
2)	Hand Action (mostly with Instrument)
3)	Physical Action with Physical Contact Unspecified
4)	Metaphorical Uses (Hand Action Traceable)
5)	Metaphorical Uses (Hand Action Untraceable)

7.2.6 Generalized hand actions in Swahili

The introduction of new artefacts requires naming the typical hand actions that are needed to put these objects into use. This is clearly illustrated in Johnson's (1939) dictionary of Swahili (the entry: *piga* 'hit, strike, beat'). The frequency of *piga* is high: 460 occurrences per million words.[1] A selection of the examples provided in the entry *piga* in Johnson's dictionary is shown in Table 3 grouped into five numbered senses. (The brief characterization after the number of each sense in Table 3 follows the wording of the dictionary.)

Table 3: Swahili: *piga* (based on Johnson 1939)

1. The basic ("definite") meaning		
piga		'hit, strike', 'give a blow'
2. the proper use of a tool		
piga bomba	HIT pump	'work a pump'
piga pasi	HIT iron (for ironing clothes)	'iron clothes'
piga picha	HIT picture	'photograph'
piga kinanda	HIT string instrument	'play an organ, piano'
piga kengele	HIT bell	'ring a bell'
piga chapa	HIT book	'print a book'
3. construction, execution, giving form to something		
piga fundo	HIT knot	'tie a knot'
piga kilemba	HIT turban	'wear a turban'
4. of a sudden forceful action		
piga mbio	HIT (a) run	'run'
piga kelele	HIT noise	'shout'

---

[1] The Helsinki corpus of Swahili, see Electronic sources.

Tab. 3 (continued)

5. of producing a showy, sensational effect		
piga nguo	HIT cloth(es)	'show off clothes'
piga ubwana	HIT master	'domineer, tyrannize'

The first extended sense (2 in Table 3) is related to the proper use of a tool and refers to a variety of generalized hand actions. According to Johnson, *piga kinanda* originally referred to playing an indigenous string instrument but was extended to refer to playing an organ or a piano. Today, (Abdulaziz Lodhi p.c.), *piga* can be used with nouns referring to a wide range of instruments and even to instruments such as a trumpet, where hand actions are not as prominent as with string instruments. A related use is the launching of projectiles with a weapon (Abdulaziz Lodhi p.c.): *piga mshale* 'shoot (with bow and) arrow', *piga bunduki* 'shoot (with a) gun'. Some of the examples of sense 2 such as 'HIT picture' and 'HIT book' overlap with the following sense since the syntactic objects refer to the result rather than the tool (even if specific tools are understood). Sense 3 which is related to the use of HIT as a verb of creation (see Section 7.5.5) in many cases can also be interpreted as a generalized hand action. Wearing clothes is a productive sense. Often the object is a loan word: *piga tie* 'wear a tie', *piga koti* 'wear a blazer', *piga suti* 'wear a suit, dress up' (Abdulaziz Lodhi p.c.). Swahili appears to have several parallels to Family's (2011) "islands of productivity". The last two senses 4 and 5 also have parallels in other languages but do not refer to hand actions but rather to the way the action is carried out (forcefully, swiftly etc.) or the psychological impact on an observer or experiencer.

7.2.7 Summary

It is difficult to sum up the result from earlier studies as a set of generalizations, since they are based on different theories and different types of data. The analysis in the following sections will rather pick important ideas from each. Riemer presents a general model for semantic shifts (even if he does not use that term), which is interesting and elegant but does not address the question of what is characteristic of verbs of hitting in relation to other verbs. Gao Hong stresses the importance of verbs of hitting as hand actions, which is central for the following account. Family's islands of productivity point to the important interaction between the verb and the semantic properties of its arguments. The Swahili data point in the same direction. The analysis of HIT as verbal operator by Hook et al. and the grammaticalization of HIT by Schulze-Bernt appear to represent later stages of development than those that will be accounted for in Swedish.

7.3 A corpus-based study of Swedish *slå*: Overview

7.3.1 The data

Two parallel (translation) corpora will be used. Primarily data will be taken from the Multilingual Parallel Corpus (MPC), which at present consists of extracts from 22 Swedish novels and their translations into English, German, French and Finnish (around 610 000 words in the Swedish originals. See Appendix 1 in Viberg (2013) for a list of the novels and an index of the texts.[2] In addition, there are translations of a limited number of the texts into other languages which will be referred to in some cases. Data will also be included from the English Swedish Parallel Corpus (ESPC), which was used in an earlier contrastive study of *slå* in comparison to its English correspondents (Viberg 2004). The ESPC contains original texts in English and Swedish and their translations (see Altenberg and Aijmer 2000, and electronic sources).

7.3.2 Hitting as a physical action sequence

The polysemy of *slå* and of verbs meaning HIT across languages is based to a great extent on the fact that hitting is one of the most basic physical actions, and this forms the point of departure for the analysis. Physical actions can be divided into sequences of more elementary actions: Intention or Goal, a sequence of bodily movements of some body part(s) and a result which is congruent with the goal (in the unmarked case). Different types of goals are actualized depending on whether the action is directed towards another human or towards a physical object. For that reason, uses when both the subject and the object are human will be treated separately in Section 7.4 and uses where a human acts on a physical object in Sections 7.5 and 7.6. Non-human subjects will be more briefly treated in Section 7.7.

---

[2] An extract from one more text has been added to the 21 texts listed there: Fagerholm, Monika. 2005. *Den amerikanska flickan*. Stockholm: Albert Bonniers Förlag.[MoFa]

The sequence of bodily actions involved in hitting are schematically shown in Figure 2. (Strictly speaking, the Goal should appear before the bodily actions, but since there is a close connection between Goal and Result they appear together in the figure.)

Sequence of bodily actions		Goal/Result
Bodily movement	Contact and Impact	Human object
Swiftly extend arm making hand (and Instrument held in hand) move towards object (Target)	Forceful contact between hand (Instrument) and Target resulting in Impact	Hurt Defeat Punish Kill

Figure 2: Hitting as a goal-directed action sequence directed towards another human

Example (5) shows a typical example with translations into English, German, French and Finnish.

(5) Mor **slog** far i ansiktet [Mother struck father in face-DEF.Neut]
    She **struck** him in the face
    Mutter **schlug** Vater ins Gesicht [ins < in das DEF.Neut.Acc face]
    Mère **a frappé** père au visage
    Äiti **löi** isää kasvoihin [Mother struck father-Partitive face-Illative]
    (IB)[3]

In (5), the mother swiftly and forcefully extends her arm making the hand move towards the father's face until it makes contact. Unless something else is implied by the context, *slå* indicates that the contact results in a forceful impact (and transmission of energy) and is carried out with a hostile (in some sense) intent and has a negative impact on the other human such as hurting, defeating of even killing that person. If the intent is positive (and the contact is lighter) another verb than *slå* should be used, such as *klappa* (*klappa någon på kinden* 'pat s. o.'s cheek') or *stryka* (*stryka någon över kinden* 'stroke s. o.'s cheek'). The verb *slå* does not indicate the shape of the hand; it can be open (cf. *slap*) or clenched (cf. *knock*) or even involve a hand-held instrument (e.g. a stick). Such distinctions can be inferred from the context or indicated with an instrumental PP (*Mor slog far i*

---

[3] IB refers to a text code based on the author's name given in the index of MPC mentioned in Section 7.3.1.

ansiktet med handflatan/knytnäven/en käpp 'Mother struck father in the face with the palm of her hand/her fist/a stick').

It is convenient to be able to talk about the roles of the arguments involved. In examples like (5), the direct object can be said to play the role of an Opponent, which subsumes more specific roles like Victim or Loser. Table 4 serves as a reference point for the syntactic description, which, however, is not discussed in any detail in this paper.

Table 4: The role structure and its realization

Roles	Agent	(Verb)	Opponent	Impactee	Impactor
Phrase str.	NP	V	NP	Prep^{Spatial} + NP	Prep^{Instr} + NP
Relations	Subject	Predicate	Direct object	Adjunct	Adjunct
Example	*Mor* Mother	*slog* struck	*far* father	*(i ansiktet)* (in the face)	*(med knytnäven)* (with the fist)

Note, that in simple textbook examples such as *Bill slog Harry* 'Bill hit/beat Harry', all of the more specific roles are implicit, for example the Impactee and Impactor referred to by Riemer (see Section 7.2.1.). A rich and open-ended semantic representation of the verb is necessary to make it possible to fill out some of the more specific parts of the interpretation from clues in the context. When there is no Opponent in Swedish, the Impactor (usually a body part or an instrument) can be realized as a direct object: *Bill slog näven/klubban i bordet.* 'Bill hit the fist/the club in the table'. In Swedish, the Impactee is in general not realized as a direct object (unless a result is indicated, see Section 7.5.1): *Bill slog på den tomma lådan* 'Bill hit at the empty box' (cf. **Bill slog lådan*). Another verb, *träffa* 'hit (a target)', must be used in that case: *Bill träffade hakan (med ett välriktat slag)* 'Bill hit the chin (with a well-aimed punch)'. (*Träffa* is the major equivalent of the projectile uses of hit: *Bollen/Kulan träffade väggen* 'The ball/bullet hit the wall.' See Viberg 2004: 331–332).

7.3.3 An overview of the contrastive relationships

As a starting point for the analysis, the case where both an agent and an opponent (usually the subject and the object) are involved and the verb refers to a movement of the hand that ends with contact and impact is regarded as the prototypical use, at least for the case when both the subject and the object are human. This will be called the human prototype, leaving it open for the time being whether this should be regarded as the prototype when the object is inanimate. There is no simple objective test that can be used to identify the prototype. Frequency will not work since it varies a lot across speech activities and registers. The total number of prototypical uses in the MPC corpus is only 30 out of 465 occurrences, which only amounts to 6 %. The analysis is based on the meaning that intuitively is felt as most basic, and that is the best starting point for a systematic account of the many extended meanings of *slå* and provides a motivation for the extensions.

In example (5), one of the major equivalents of *slå* is used as a translation. As can be observed in Table 5a, which shows the verbs of hitting that are most frequently used as translations of *slå* in its prototypical meaning, there is one dominant translation only in German, which uses *schlagen*, a cognate of *slå*, as a translation in 87 % (26 of 30) of the cases. In Finnish, *löydä* is used as a translation in 67 % of the cases, which is relatively high, whereas in French *frapper* accounts only for 37 %. In English, several verbs are used with approximately equal frequency. (The absolute numbers are too small to rank the alternatives, but see Viberg 2004.)

Table 5a: The most frequent verbs of hitting as translations of Swedish *slå* in the MPC corpus: the human prototype

	Swedish		**English**		**German**		**French**	
	slå	30	strike	4	schlagen	26	frapper	11
			hit	8			battre	3
			beat	7			cogner	1
			knock	4				
Total: N		30		23		26		15
Total: %		100		77		87		50
	Finnish							
	lyödä	20						
	iskeä	2						
Total N		22						
Total %		73						

Table 5b shows the frequency of the same verbs as in Table 5a, when all meanings are taken into consideration. The result can serve as an indication of the degree to which the pattern of polysemy of *slå* is language-specific. When all meanings are included, German *schlagen* is used as a translation only in 36 % of the cases and the major equivalents of the other languages account for a considerably lower proportion in spite of the fact that several verbs are involved. Among individual verbs, Finnish *lyödä* comes second but accounts for only 14 %. This low degree of agreement between genetically and/or areally closely related languages should be kept in mind when we discuss the parallels that exist between Swedish and remotely related languages.

Table 5b: The most frequent verbs of hitting as translations of Swedish *slå* in the MPC corpus: All meanings

	Swedish		English		German		French	
	slå	465	strike	38	schlagen	169	battre	32
			hit	22			frapper	24
			beat	16			heurter	9
			knock	9			cogner	8
			punch	6			taper	7
Total: N		465		91		169		80
Total: %		100		20		38		17
	Finnish							
	lyödä	64						
	iskeä	19						
Total N		83						
Total %		18						

Ideally, comparisons should be made with translations in the other direction as well, where Swedish is the target language. Such data were used in an earlier study based on the English-Swedish parallel corpus (Viberg 2004) and confirms the general picture of the relationship between Swedish and English.

7.4 Human acting on human

7.4.1 Overview

Figure 3 gives an overview of the meanings describing the interaction between two humans playing the roles of agent and opponent. (The meaning *Body movement* does not involve an opponent but rather an implicit addressee, see below.)

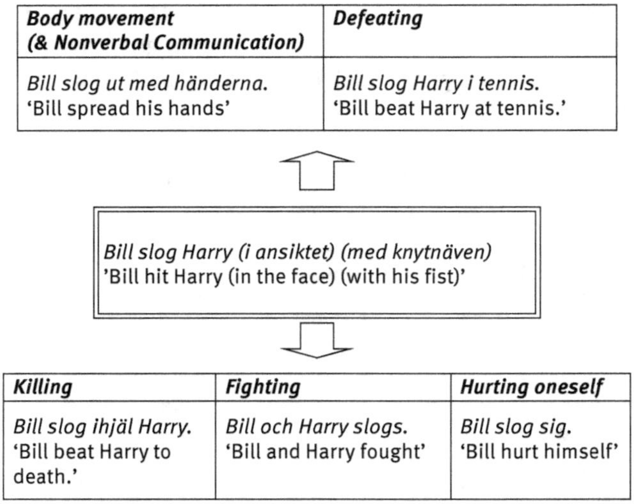

Body movement **(& Nonverbal Communication)**	**Defeating**
Bill slog ut med händerna. 'Bill spread his hands'	*Bill slog Harry i tennis.* 'Bill beat Harry at tennis.'

⇑

Bill slog Harry (i ansiktet) (med knytnäven) 'Bill hit Harry (in the face) (with his fist)'

⇓

Killing	**Fighting**	**Hurting oneself**
Bill slog ihjäl Harry. 'Bill beat Harry to death.'	*Bill och Harry slogs.* 'Bill and Harry fought'	*Bill slog sig.* 'Bill hurt himself'

Figure 3: *Slå* referring to human interaction

The prototype serves as a point of departure for two major types of extensions: 1) extensions which basically consist in foregrounding part of the prototypical meaning and backgrounding or totally suppressing the rest of it and 2) various types of what broadly can be referred to as specialization or strengthening which add information to the prototypical meaning. The former type, which is placed above the prototype in Figure 3, was referred to as focusing in Viberg (1999) and corresponds to what Riemer (2005) refers to as constituent metonymy. The second type (placed below the prototype) was referred to as resultative strengthening in Viberg (1999) and most closely resembles Riemer's (2005) effect metonymy, the major difference being that the former emphasizes the role of the discourse context (cf. The Invited Inferencing Theory of Semantic Change Model, Traugott and Dasher 2005: 34–40). These two types of extension seldom appear in pure form, but they indicate the basic nature of an extension and provide a convenient way to achieve a broad classification of the extensions. (Riemer's [2005] context metonymy does not have any parallel in Viberg 1999.)

7.4.2 Killing

Across languages, the verb meaning 'hit' often also can mean 'kill' (cf. the English cognate *slay* of *slå*). In Swedish, *slå* usually is combined with the particle *ihjäl* when it has this meaning as in (6).

(6) De hade kommit för att **slå ihjäl** honom.
They had come to **kill** him.
(JG)

In this use, *slå* primarily has its basic meaning and indicates the manner of the killing, whereas the result is indicated explicitly by the particle *ihjäl*, which etymologically is derived from 'into Hel', the kingdom of the dead in old Norse mythology, in Christian times reinterpreted as Hell (Swed. *helvetet*). In historical texts, *slå* in specific contexts incorporates the meaning 'kill' and is used without this particle as in (7) from a medieval Swedish rhymed chronicle (quoted in Söderwall, 1884–1918).

(7) the sörgde syna wener swåre som i then striidhen **slagne wåre**
they mourned profoundly for their friends who **were struck** (slain) in that fight

The particle *ihjäl* was used as early as Medieval times and in present-day Swedish the particle (or an equivalent such as *till döds* 'to death') must be used except with certain animal subjects as in *Björnen slog ett får* 'The bear got ('struck') a sheep'. Another function of *slå*, which has also become more or less obsolete, is as a verb of punishment.

7.4.3 Fighting

In a lexicalized passive form *slåss*, the verb *slå* has the meaning 'to fight'. The passive in this case has a reciprocal meaning and basically refers to a fist-fight 'to hit one another'. The meaning is generalized and can refer to a wide variety of forms of vigorous and usually hostile competition. In (8), the fight is still physical.

(8) När de sedan **slagits** om degen och kladdat ner hela köket började hennes tålamod tryta.
By the time they'd **fought** over the dough and messed up the whole kitchen, her patience would be giving out.
Als sie **sich** dann um den Teig **prügelten**/---/['beat' + Reflexive]
Mais quand ensuite ils **se battaient** pour la pâte ['beat' + Reflexive]
Kun he olivat **tapelleet** taikinasta ['fight']
(LM)

In (9), the meaning is further generalized and does not involve any physical fight.

(9) *Om du får välja kommer du att **slåss mot** Wennerströms advokater till dess att också din trovärdighet är borta.*
*If you had to choose, you'd keep **fighting against** Wennerström's lawyers until your credibility was gone too.*
(SL)

The passive form *slåss* is partly irregular (the regular form is *slås*) and on the way to being lexicalized and established as a separate lexical item, but the relatedness with *slå* is still rather transparent both with respect to the form and the meaning.

7.4.4 Hurting oneself

In combination with a reflexive pronoun (*sig*) as object, *slå* usually indicates that the physical contact was unintentional, and a prominent part of the meaning is usually that the physical contact resulted in pain. This is often reflected in the translations as in example (10) from the MPC corpus.

(10) *Har pojken fallit och **slagit sig**?*
*Has the boy fallen and **hurt himself**?*

*Ist der Junge gefallen? Hat er **sich wehgetan**?* ['do oneself pain/ache']
*Le garçon est tombé ? Il **s'est fait mal**?* ['do oneself bad']
*Onko poika kaatunut ja **satuttanut itsensä**?* ['hurt oneself']
(MoFa)

Besides being unintentional, *slå* in this meaning does not have the hand as a default, and any body part can be involved. The infliction of pain is a prominent part of the meaning also in another construction where a body part appears as object of *slå* as in (11).

(11) *Men på samma gång halkade hon och tappade balansen och **slog huvudet** i toalettskålens kalla kakel.*
*But at the same time she slipped and lost her balance and **hit her head** on the cold porcelain of the toilet bowl.*
(MoFa)

7.4.5 Expressing the abstract goal: 'defeat'

The intent to hurt or defeat another human is a vital part of the prototypical meaning of *slå*. This is particularly prominent with reference to a fist fight. The sentence *Cassius Clay slog Liston* 'CC hit/defeated L' is potentially ambiguous in Swedish, but often, especially in the context of sports competition *slå* simply means 'defeat' as in (12), where only the abstract result is a relevant part of the meaning.

(12) *He was quick and good at tic-tac-toe and checkers, and cunning and aggressive; he easily **beat** me.*
*Han var snabb och duktig i luffarschack och damspel, och listig och offensiv; han **slog** mig utan besvär.*
(ESPC:OS1)[4]

In this type of use, *slå* simply has the abstract meaning 'defeat'. This might be regarded as a metaphor since it refers to an abstract domain, but even if there is no reference to the concrete part of the prototypical meaning (body movement), the intention to defeat (or some related notion such as hurting or killing) is already part of the prototypical meaning. Even if 'defeat' thus can be regarded as part of the prototypical meaning, a certain degree of conventionalization is also involved. The meaning 'defeat' has a very high frequency in the sports pages.

7.4.6 Extended meanings profiling the limb movement

In Swedish, the first part of the action sequence, the bodily movement, is profiled in several examples where *slå* is used to describe a limb movement that does not result in any type of contact with the hand (or other body part). In (13), the English translation describes the movement of the arms.

(13) *Han **slog ut** med armarna.* ['He struck out with the arms']
He spread his arms out wide.
(SL)

---

[4] ESPC:OS1 refers to the ESPC corpus followed by the text code used in that corpus (see electronic sources)

(13) is a good example of constituent metonymy (Riemer 2005), but usually, *slå* is not used to describe the limb movement in pure form. Such limb movements often represent gestures with a symbolic or indexical meaning in the sense of C. S. Peirce (1932). The limb movement should be interpreted as a symbol, when a character in a novel consciously uses it to communicate something non-verbally, whereas it has an indexical function when it simply expresses a non-intended emotional reaction. (It is not always clear which alternative the author of the novel intends to communicate to the reader.) In (14), the translator has felt the need to spell out the symbolic meaning which is implicit in the Swedish original.

(14) *Danielsson **slog ut** med händerna.*
[lit. 'Danielsson struck out with the hands']
*Danielsson **flung** his hands out to the sides in a gesture of helplessness.*
(LM)

In (15), only the symbolic (or indexical) meaning is expressed in the translation.

(15) *En kort stund senare fick han tag på Broder Lucien som förskräckt **slog ifrån sig med båda händerna**.*
[who frightened struck from himself with both hands]
*A short time later he spoke to Brother Lucien, who **vehemently rejected the idea** in fright.*
(JG)

There are also several examples that describe movement of the arms and also involve contact with the arms wrapped around someone as in (16) and also in such examples the emotional reaction is central.

(16) *Hon blir rädd, **slår armarna om** hans ben,* ['She...strikes the arms round his leg(s)'].
*She's scared and **flings her arms round** his leg.*
(MF)

Authors of fiction often depict emotional reactions implicitly in this way, and verbs of physical contact in general often have this function.

7.5 Manipulation of physical objects based on the prototypical hand action

7.5.1 Hand actions directed at physical objects: overview

When the hitting is directed at physical objects, another set of goals are relevant than when the target is human. There are very few examples of this type that simply describe the physical contact and impact without indicating a specific result. Typically, as in (17), the impactee (the stone) is marked with a preposition, which makes the sentence atelic. An example of this kind describes the same type of hand action as when there is a human direct object, but the use of a PP makes examples with a human object feel more prototypical in Swedish, even if it is left open whether several prototypes should be recognized.

(17) *För nu började de **slå mot stenen** med klubbor och påkar.*
   For now they were beginning to **beat on the stone** with sticks and clubs.
   (AL)

Figure 4 gives an overview of uses of *slå* describing humans acting on concrete physical objects.

Pure physical contact:
Bill *slog på* dörren (med en käpp).
'Bill *hit at* the door (with a stick)'

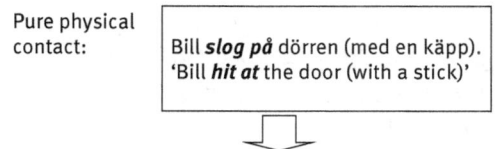

Resultative extensions based on the prototypical hand action			
Motion	**Creation**	**Sound production**	**Disconnection**
Bill slog bollen över nät. 'Bill hit the ball over the net'	Bill slog tegel. 'Bill produced ('struck') bricks'	Bill slog på trumman. 'Bill beat the drum'	Bill slog gräset. 'Bill cut the grass'

Generalized hand actions (based on the affordances of objects)						
Pour	**Open/Close**	**Switch on/off**	**Wrap**	**Join**		**Dial**
slå upp/i/ut...	slå upp/igen	slå av/på	slå in	slå ihop/ samman		slå ett nummer

Figure 4: *Slå* expressing prototypical and generalized hand actions on physical objects

In many extended uses, *slå* has kept most of its basic meaning at the same time as an additional meaning has been added which describes the result of the act of hitting. Such uses are referred to as resultative extensions based on the prototypical hand action in Figure 4 (cf. Riemer's 2005 effect metonymy). These uses will be commented on in the rest of Section 7.5. In Section 7.6, a number of generalized hand actions will be discussed which are further removed from the prototype. (The dotted arrow indicates that these senses are further removed from the prototype than the resultative meanings, but does not imply that they are derived from these meanings.)

7.5.2 Motion induced by hitting

A natural result of hitting a physical object is setting it in motion. Not very many examples of this type are found in the novels, but such examples are frequent in sports reports. A simple made-up example such as *Bill slog bollen över nät* 'Bill hit the ball over (the) net', which could be used to describe part of a tennis match, is closely related to the prototypical meaning. The ball is hit with an instrument held in the hand which causes it to move. The basic meaning of *slå* is turned into a manner component: 'Cause to move by hitting'. Often *slå* is constructed as a motion verb and combined with directional complements such as spatial particles and PPs in this use.

In sport reports, hand actions are not necessarily involved, since *slå* can freely be used when the foot instead of the hand is used as in football, in spite of the fact that Swedish has a verb *sparka* which means 'kick'. In some examples, the ball is explicitly mentioned in combination with a directional phrase as in (18), where *slå* is constructed as a motion verb and the caused motion can be induced from the syntactic construction.

(18) /---/John Clark/---/**slog bollen** i nät.
John Clark hit the ball in(to) (the) net [My translation, ÅV].
(SLB: DN87)

The major information conveyed in (18) is that John Clark scored a goal ('score a goal by hitting the ball with the foot causing it to move into the goal'). Most of the examples are less straightforward. Often a phrase describing different moves in the game serve as objects such as 'penalty' 'corner', 'cross centre' or a specific score (*slå in 2–1* [lit. 'strike in 2–1'] 'score 2–1'. For an example, see (19). This is a kind of resultative strengthening (effect metonymy).

(19) Kent Nilsson **slog in 'fyran'** i spel fyra mot fyra.
Kent Nilsson struck in "the four" (goal number four) in play four against four
[My translation, ÅV].
(SLB: DN87)

With an abstract object, there are several well-established mental meanings based on *slå* as a motion verb through metaphorical applications. Both (20) and (21) describe the intentional suppression of thoughts which requires effort. In (20), all the translations are based on motion metaphors that treat thoughts as things, but different motion verbs have been chosen as sources for the metaphor.

(20) Erica **slog bort** tanken.
Erica **pushed away** the thought.
Erica **verjagte** ihn ['chase away'].
Erica l'écartait ['move away, separate'].
Erica koetti **sysätä** ajatuksen mielestään
['Erica tried to **push** the thought out of her mind'].
(CL)

(21) Robert som **slagit** amerikaplanerna **ur hågen**.
['Robert who had struck the plans for America out of the mind'].
Robert had **given up** his plans for America.
(MF)

7.5.3 Creation

In (22), *slå* functions as a verb of creation similar to verbs such as *build* (a house). This example refers to a historical state of affairs and this is true of most examples of this use, which once was very productive.

(22) I denna stad hade kungen sin gård, och i Sigtuna **slogs** också de äldsta daterbara mynten i landet. ['the coins were struck']
The King had his residence in that town, and the oldest dated coins **were minted** there.
(ESPC: AA)

When the original meaning of a certain phrasal combination is lost, it often is experienced as an idiom that cannot be further analysed. The use of *slå* as a concrete verb of creation, which is on its way to becoming obsolete in present-day

Swedish, is a good example of this. *Slå mynt av* today is primarily used with the abstract meaning 'take advantage of' as in (23).

(23) *"You'll pay for this,"* Con said, already seeing opportunities for **cashing in on** this young fool's misfortune.
„Det här ska du få betala för", sa Con, som redan hade insett att det gick att **slå mynt av** den unge klåparens misslyckade försök. ['strike coins from']
(ESPC: JC)

It must be left open to what degree present-day speakers of Swedish relate examples of this type to the use of *slå* as a verb of creation, but once the concrete meaning was productive and *slå* could be used with a flexible range of objects and syntactic constructions.[5] Another example is *slå en bro* (lit. 'strike a bridge'), which still can be used concretely to refer to the creation of a bridge but more frequently is used metaphorically as in (24).

(24) *Ni har en betydelsefull roll för att **slå broar** mellan öst och väst.*
You have a significant role in **building bridges** between East and West.
(ESPC: MAU)

The verb *slå* functions as a verb of creation when the object of *slå* refers to an artefact which has been created by hitting with a tool (hammer, club, sledgehammer) at some material (cf. *smida* 'forge', the Swedish cognate of *smite* 'hit something hard'). In pre-industrial times, this manner of producing artefacts must have been very salient. Not only because striking with sledges and hammers etc. was involved to a great extent in the production of many artefacts (often accompanied by constant noise), but also because such production took place in rather small units (such as a forge or a workshop) that were familiar to everyone and not in factories or plants far removed from the stores and supermarkets where artefacts are acquired today.

---

5 Several examples of the flexible use of *slå* as a creation verb with special reference to the production of coins appear in Peder Swart's Chronicle from 1560. The following examples are taken from the Bank of Old Swedish (see Electronic sources):
Han lett j Wisby **slå sitt eget mynt**,/---/ther war på een sidan **slagit hans egit wapen**,
Widh samma tijdh lett Her Götstaff vpretta ett mynte j Vpsale (·förutan them han tilförende hade j Westrårs och Suderköping·) **thär begynte slåes rundstycke**, hwilket som war ett ganska godt och fedtt mynt, **the sloges först på halffannen öre**, men sedan lett Her Götstaff then halffua ören falla, och lett giffua them vth för en öre stycket.

Actually, the use of *slå* as a creation verb is well attested in the historical dictionary produced by the Swedish Academy (SAOB; see Electronic sources). One example is *slå tegel* (lit. 'strike bricks') with the meaning 'to produce bricks'. Originally, the clay was hit with clubs to obtain the appropriate shape. The expression *slå tegel* 'strike bricks' was maintained after the introduction of moulds to give the clay its shape. Today, the term does not appear to be known by people in general but is used primarily by experts.[6] As a verb of creation, *slå* is also well attested in SAOB with reference to building various types of military defences such as *slå ett plank* 'build (strike) a fence' and *slå en skans* 'build (strike) a fort/redcubt'.[7] The expression *slå läger* (lit. strike camp 'to camp') originally referred to a military camp, where defences were built ('struck') but is today used with reference to setting up a camp in general. Another well-attested expression that is now obsolete was *slå ett skepp* 'build (strike) a ship'.[8]

The decline of *slå* as a verb of creation in modern Swedish is a clear example of a semantic shift caused by cultural change. Isolated expressions of this type survive more or less as idioms. Only a systematic study of historical corpora could give a more exact picture of how common the use as a creation verb once was, but it appears to have been prominent. Even if this use is more or less obsolete, historical examples of this type are still transparent when they are presented in context, since they represent *natural* extensions from the prototype.

7.5.4 Sound production

Hitting something often produces a sound. Both in Swedish and English, there are a number of verbs of hitting that incorporate a reference to the emergence of a sound such as *banka* 'bang' and *dunka* 'thump' (see Viberg 1999, Section 7). In Swedish, *slå* can also refer to the production of a sound. In example (25), *ljudet* 'the sound' is introduced in definite form in the second clause, since it is implicit in *slå på trumma* (lit. 'strike on drum') 'beat a drum'.

---

6 The following is part of a presentation of a modern brick factory found by googling *slå tegel*: *Konsten att **slå tegel** är ett hantverk som i den här bygden utvecklats och gått i arv från generation till generation.* (Vittinge tegelbruk).

7 For example: *att Så snart . . (de svenska sändebuden* **1569**) *ankommit til Novogrcd,* **slogs et plank** *omkring deras härberge.* DALIN *Hist*. III. (1762). (SAOB: slå) *då Fältmarskalken kommer i Mecklenburg, att han då låter* **slå en fast skans** *vid Damgarten.* (1631) (SAOB:slå)

8 For example: *Rijkz-Cantzlern frågade, om thet voro rådeligare* **slåå skeppen** *(som skulle byggas av pommerskt virke) ther in loco (dvs. i Pommern) eller och föra verket hijt öffver.* RP 8: 104 (1640). (SAOB: slå)

(25) *Det märkliga är att jag aldrig sett någon **slå på trumma** här i Afrika. Ändå har jag hört **ljudet** otaliga gånger.*
The curious thing is that I've never seen anyone **beating a drum** here in Africa, even though I have heard **the sound** countless times.
(ESPC: LH)

The expression *slå på trumma* can also be further extended (see 26) and refer to an attempt to draw positive attraction to oneself (cf. *to blow one's horn*).

(26) *Han kunde liksom inte **slå på trumma för sig**.*
['strike on drum for himself']
He could not so to speak **blow his horn**. [My translation, ÅV]
[SLB: NEWS]

The chain of extensions goes from beating as a concrete activity, to a concrete activity profiling a certain result (sound production), to the introduction of an abstract goal (draw attention by producing the sound) to a use where only the abstract goal is expressed. These extensions are all metonymic rather than metaphorical. In Riemer's (2005) model, the production of the sound is based on effect metonymy, whereas (26) represents a further extension.

7.5.5 Disconnection (cutting and breaking)

The verb *slå* plays an important role among Swedish verbs of cutting and breaking or disconnection as they are called here. A frequent translation of English *break* used as a transitive verb is *slå sönder* 'strike asunder'. The particle *sönder* is resultative and means approximately 'into pieces' and/or 'broken, not possible to use'. A typical example is given in (27).

(27) *Han såg att någon **slagit sönder** en av rutorna i det rundade burspråksfönstret.*
He saw that someone had **broken** one of the panes in a bow window.
(ESPC: RR)

The meaning of *slå* in (27) is close to the prototype: someone had broken the window by (intentionally or unintentionally) hitting it with the hand or something held in the hand. It could also refer to a situation where someone breaks the pane by throwing something, for example a ball. In combination with *sönder* and other particles indicating disconnection, *slå* is generalized, but some type of impact by contact is obligatory. An utterance such as *Bill slog sönder vasen* 'Bill broke the vase' can be used even it the vase is broken by accidentally dropping it, but *slå* cannot be used if a sudden physical contact is not involved, for example if something is broken by bending it. In that case another verb *bryta* must be used: *Han bröt itu pennan* 'He broke the pencil in two (by bending it)'.

There is another use of *slå* as a disconnection verb, where the only clue to the interpretation is the semantic type of the object. In *Bill slog höet* 'Bill cut (literally: 'struck') the hay', *slå* means 'cut grass by hitting it with a scythe'. By metonymy, the object does not have to contain the word 'grass' (or 'hay' etc.) but can be any word that refers to a place containing grass such as 'meadow' in example (28). Literally, the Swedish example says that the meadows were not 'struck' anymore without mentioning the grass.

(28) *Men sedan en tid tillbaka **slogs** inte ängarna längre.*
But the grass in the meadows had not been **harvested** for years.
(MN)

Not very long ago, when Sweden was predominantly a traditional agricultural society, the cutting of hay with scythes was an annual event of great importance. This explains why so much information could be understood from context.

Slå can also be used with a number of other particles related to disconnection such as *slå av* 'strike off' as in *Bill slog av foten på glaset* 'Bill broke ("struck off") the base off the glass'. If some part is broken off an object it is physically reduced. This use of *slå av* serves as a point of departure for metaphorical extensions with abstract arguments, where *slå av* simply means 'reduce': *slå av på farten* (strike off on the speed) 'reduce the speed', *slå av på priset* (lit. 'strike off on the price') 'reduce the price', 'bargain'. An expression that can be used concretely but that is often used abstractly is *slå hål på* 'strike (punch) a hole in', where *hål* is used as a bare noun which makes it function as a kind of verbal particle. Expressions such as *slå hål på isen* 'strike a hole in the ice' and *slå hål i väggen* 'strike a hole in the wall' have a concrete meaning. Examples of metaphorical expressions based on this use are *slå hål på myten/fördomen/klichéerna* 'dispel ('strike hole on') the myth/the prejudice/the clichés'. The combination *slå igenom* ('strike through') can be used concretely but is primarily used metaphorically with reference to the breaking of some abstract barrier 'make a breakthrough', 'become established'. For example, *slå igenom* can be used about an actor who has made a breakthrough but is also frequently used – in particular in non-fiction – with abstract subjects as in (29).

(29) *Införandet av miljöledningssystem börjar nu också **slå igenom** på allvar.*
*The introduction of environmental management systems is now beginning to **have a** marked **impact**.*
(ESPC: ASSI1)

7.5.6 Summary of *slå* as a hand action

Sections 7.4 and 7.5 have analysed the meanings of *slå* that are close to the prototype based on the assumption that the prototypical meaning is based on the characteristic hand action that the verb refers to. In Figure 5, the analysis of *slå* as a goal-directed action sequence (compare Figure 2 above) is expanded to cover the meanings discussed so far. As discussed in Section 7.4.6, *slå* can be used with reference only to the movement of the arm and hand (indicated in the left box at the top). Usually, this has as a goal to communicate attitudinal or emotive information non-verbally as indicated in the box below. In most cases, the bodily movement deviates somewhat from the prototype, and a particular target is often missing. In its basic uses, *slå* refers to a movement with the hand that results in contact and impact. An essential part of the meaning is the result of this impact and as has been demonstrated above, the basic meaning of *slå* is often reduced to a kind of manner component in such uses. When the target is a concrete physical object the meaning is something like 'to cause something to move/to come into existence/to break etc. by hitting it'. The goal/result of such physical actions forms the point of departure for more abstract uses and metaphorical applications.

When the target is human, it is regarded as an Opponent or a Victim and a completely different set of goals and results are relevant, such as Hurt, Defeat, Punish and Kill. The metaphorical uses of *slå* are not included in Figure 5. Most of the concrete meanings shown in the figure can serve as the source of various such meanings in a chain of extensions that add further complexity to the semantic representation. As a general model, the analysis is simplified in many respects. For example, the Goal of an action should rather be placed to the left in the upper line since it is what initiates the bodily action sequence. The last step (the lower boxes) rather represents an evaluation of the Goal, whether it has been achieved (intended Result) or not. (A sentence like *Bill didn't manage to beat Harry* refers to the same Goal as *Bill beat Harry* but the Result has not been achieved.)

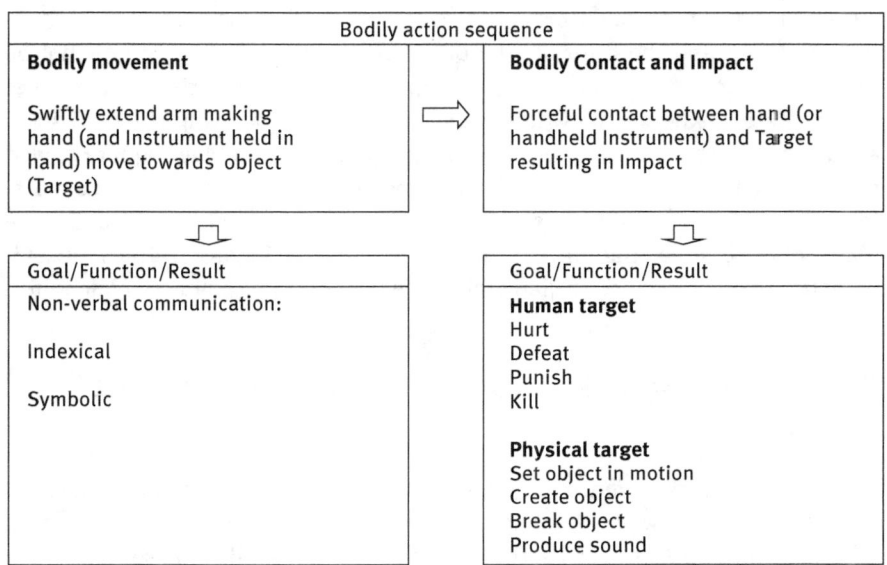

Figure 5: A characterization of *slå* as a goal-directed action sequence

The view of meaning is inspired by theories of the embodied mind which are supported by brain imaging of neural activity: "Understanding language about perceiving and moving involves much of the same neural circuitry as do perceiving and moving themselves" (Feldman 2006: 5). Related to this is Barsalou's (1999, 2003) situated simulation theory, according to which conceptual representations are multi-modal simulations that are distributed across modality-specific systems and prepare an agent for situated action. That the meaning of physical action verbs includes sensorimotor information has been supported most clearly in neuroscientific studies. Damasio and Tranel (1993) have shown that verbs activate motor control regions, while nouns do not. More specifically, Pulvermüller (2001) has shown that words like *kick*, *pull* and *lick* activate appropriate areas in the motor strip specialized for actions with the foot, hand and tongue, respectively.

Figure 5 is intended only as a summary of the meanings of *slå* regarded as a hand action, but a few remarks will be made about its relation to the view that concepts are multi-modal simulations. Hitting can be experienced from within as a sensorimotor activity perceived via proprioception or via the sensory modalities of touch and pain ('to hurt oneself by hitting'). Hitting can also be experienced from outside as motion through space when observing others performing the action. Contact is basically a spatial concept, and contact between two physical objects is the judgment that the distance between them is zero (contact as zero distance). Impact, on the other hand, is a concept which is based on mechanical reasoning and the transmission of force. Mechanical reasoning cannot be reduced to mere spatiotemporal patterning. Michotte (1963) carried out a number of now classic experiments where subjects were shown moving coloured spots and asked to describe what they saw. In one experiment, a black square moved towards a stationary red square. When it came into contact with the red square, it stopped moving and the red square started moving. Subjects reported that the black square bumped into the red square and launched it, gave it a push or set it in motion. This was called the launching effect (l'effect lancement) by Michotte.

7.5.7 Register variation and the development of abstract meanings

The frequency of occurrence of *slå* varies markedly across registers. In the MPC corpus, the frequency is 603 pm (i.e., per million words). This can be compared to some of the registers found in the Swedish Language Bank (SLB, see Electronic sources): Fiction[9]: 660 pm, News: 463 pm, Academic prose: 108 pm, Legal: 2.4 pm. The differences are even more pronounced with respect to the frequencies of the various senses or uses. Concrete meanings such as prototypical hitting, bodily movement, generalized hand actions and the use of *slå sig ner* 'sit down' (see Section 7.1) are characteristic of fiction.[10] Meanings such as 'defeat' and 'setting a ball in motion' are very frequent in the sports sections of newspapers, but not very frequent in fiction. In news media and especially in academic prose, certain combinations of *slå* + particle with an abstract meaning account for a high proportion of the uses of *slå*. This tendency will be briefly commented on in academic texts, where it is most pronounced. The four verb-particle combinations *slå igenom* (treated in Section 7.5.5), *slå fast*, *slå samman* and *slå ihop* account for 30 % (33 pm) of all the occurrences of *slå* in Academic prose. Examples of the abstract uses can be found in the non-fiction part of the ESPC corpus and will be used as illustrations.

---

9 Fiction contains five sub-corpora, one of which comprises older texts and some of which contain translated texts. In Bonniersromaner II (4.3 million words), which only contains original Swedish novels from 1980–1981, the frequency is 604 pm.
10 The brief characterization is based on a coding of 500 examples from each of the corpora Fiction, News and Academic prose in SLB. Space does not allow a systematic account backed with statistical tables.

As an adjective or adverb *fast* means 'firm(ly)'. In *slå fast*, it is used as a stressed verbal particle and is usually translated with mental or verbal communication verbs such as *decide*, *establish* and *note* (see 30).

(30) *Jag tycker också att man här borde ha tagit chansen att **slå fast** att parlamentets ordförande skall utses på fem år.*
*In my view, we should have used this opportunity to **establish** that the President of Parliament should be elected for five years.*
(ESPC: ESJO)

The degree to which the abstract meaning of *slå fast* has been established is reflected also in its use as a compound verb *fastslå*, which can be used as an alternative to *slå fast* when it has an abstract meaning (see 31). In Swedish, verbal particles can be prefixed to the verb primarily when the resulting expression has an abstract meaning. (Otherwise this construction sounds extremely formal in most cases.)

(31) *Redan i konventionens ingress **fastslås** att varje stat har rätten till sina biologiska resurser, däribland de genetiska resurserna.*
*It **is** already **laid down** in the preamble to the Convention that every state has the right to its own biological resources, including genetic resources.*
(ESPC: ESJO)

In the ESPC and MPC corpora, there is no occurrence of *slå fast* with a concrete meaning, but it is possible to use the phrase with reference to a hand action 'to fasten something by hitting': *Peter slog fast brädan med en hammare.* 'Peter fastened [hit "firm"] the board with a hammer'.[11] Thus, this frequent abstract metaphorical use can be traced to a hand action.

Characteristic of academic prose are also the two phrases *slå ihop/slå samman* 'join' (literally 'strike together'), which have similar concrete and abstract meanings. One of the few examples from the MPC corpus shows how *slå ihop* can be used concretely, when the hands (or objects held in the hands) are joined together (see 32).

---

[11] A couple of current examples: *Slå fast nästa bräda med bred slagkloss.* http://www.baseco.se/wp-content/uploads/2011/02/montering_sv.pdf; *Till sist slog han fast en hake på utsidan av dörren.* SLB: Bonniersromaner I.

(32) *Hur han hänfört* **slog ihop händerna** *när hon hade klippt håret eller köpt en ny blus.*
How he **clapped his hands** *with pleasure when she'd had her hair cut, or bought a new blouse.*
(ÅL)

In uses of this kind, *slå* has kept most of its basic meaning, even if it also involves non-verbal communication (cf. Section 7.4.6). However, in non-fiction, *slå ihop* is used with the abstract meaning 'join, unite' in the majority of the cases and is a frequent alternative to the abstract verb *förena* 'make one, unite' (see 33).

(33) *Över hela Europeiska unionen ser vi nu hur man* **slår ihop** *ägarskapet till de gamla, offentligägda verken.*
All over the European Union we are seeing a **merging** *of the ownership of the old, publicly owned utilities.*
(ESPC: ERA)

In such uses, *slå* has lost all concrete meaning, but the joining together of concrete objects by hitting appears to be the source of this abstract use. There is a colloquial expression *slå sina påsar ihop* (lit. 'hit one's bags together'), which originally referred to a couple who married and moved together but has generalized its meaning so it comes close to the more abstract (and stylistically more formal) expression *slå ihop sina resurser* 'pool one's resources' (see 34).

(34) *Två företag som arbetar med läkemedels- och hälsorådgivning* **slår sina påsar ihop.**
Two companies working with drug counseling and health advice **join forces/ merge** (lit. 'hit their bags together'). [My translation, ÅV]
(UNT.se 2012-06-01)

There is a very great variation between different registers with respect to several of the senses of *slå*. In particular in non-ficion, several combinations of *slå* and a particle or a bare noun are today most frequently used with a non-literal meaning and thus might be regarded as phraseological units (or idioms) of various types. The status of such phrases probably varies among native speakers with respect to the degree to which the expression is experienced as an extension from the prototypical meaning of *slå*. Often an extended meaning is the result of a chain of extended meanings. For a non-literal meaning to be experienced as an extension from the prototype, it is a necessary (but not always sufficient) condition that the major links are still represented in language use. There is a continuum between synchrony and diachrony. In some cases, the concrete meaning serving as a source is well on the way to being obsolete. The use of *slå* as a verb of creation is a good example of that.

7.6 Generalized hand actions

The extensions that will be described in this section are more vaguely related to the basic meaning but still describe goal-directed bodily action sequences, where *slå* has a number of concrete meanings that refer to bodily action but where the action with the hand has been generalized to include a variety of other movement patterns than striking. The term "generalized hand action" refers to the fact that the meaning of *slå* no longer refers to the prototypical hand action and does not focus contact and impact, but each of the actions referred to below usually involve very specific hand movements.

7.6.1 Pouring liquids

In (35), *slå* refers to the pouring of a liquid. Pouring is a hand action different from striking and refers to a situation where someone is holding a container with a liquid and causing the liquid to move by tilting the container.

(35) *Jag **slog upp** en kopp ljummet kaffe.*
     ['I struck up a cup of lukewarm coffee']
     *I **poured** myself a cup of lukewarm coffee.*
     *Ich **schenkte** eine Tasse lauwarmen Kaffee **ein**.*
     *Je me **servis** une tasse de café tiède.*
     ***Kaadoin** itselleni kupin haaleaa kahvia.* ['I poured to myself a cup.']
     (KÖ)

The major English translation of *slå* with this meaning is *pour*, and actually there is a more direct equivalent in Swedish, namely *hälla* 'pour'. When *slå* is used with a beverage as object as in (35), the goal of the action is to 'serve' the beverage and this more abstract goal is reflected in the German (*einschenken*) and the French (*servir* 'serve') translations. In addition, the receiver or beneficiary ('myself') is explicitly mentioned in all but the German translations, in spite of the fact that this argument is not explicitly mentioned in the original. It should be noted that the object does not always refer directly to the liquid that is moved from the container but could also refer to a kind of resultative object as in (36).

(36) Henry **slog upp** ett par rejäla värmare.
Henry **poured** a couple of healthy pick-me-ups.
(KÖ)

When used to refer to pouring, *slå* is combined with a spatial particle such as *upp* 'up' or with a spatial preposition, but it would be wrong to refer to *slå upp* simply as an idiom, since the same particle can be combined with *slå* when several other meanings are expressed (see e.g. Section 7.6.2). In this particular use, *upp* refers to the rising of the liquid in the target container. In addition, *slå* still has a rather specific meaning (a hand action) related to its basic meaning. The choice of particle or preposition is also flexible, and *slå* can be combined with a number of different particles and prepositions when it refers to pouring.

7.6.2 Open/Close

In (37), *slå* in combination with the particle *upp* 'up' means 'open' and this is the meaning of the translations used in all the other languages except German which uses the cognate *schlagen* in combination with the preverb *auf* (*aufschlagen*).

(37) Hon **slog upp** loggboken.
She **opened** the ledger
Sie **schlug** das Journal **auf**
Elle **ouvrit** le registre,
Hän **avasi** muistikirjan
(HM)

Swedish also has a more direct equivalent to *open*, namely *öppna*. With *slå*, the meaning 'open' is primarily signalled with the particle *upp* 'up' which can contribute this meaning also with other verbs signalling the manner of opening. For example, in addition to *slå upp dörren* 'open (hit up) the door', there is *kasta upp dörren* 'throw the door open' and *sparka upp dörren* 'kick the door open'. *Slå* in this use still refers to a hand action and tends to signal that the action was carried out suddenly or in a forceful way, even if this specific modulation of the meaning (in relation to the neutral *öppna* 'open') has been weakened and the manner component is not always obvious. There are 25 occurrences where *slå upp* refers to opening. The dominant translation (18 occurrences) in German is *aufschlagen* (*auf-* 'up' + 'hit'). In the other languages, the dominant translation simply means 'open' (English *open*: 18, French *ouvrir*: 21, Finnish *avata*: 22). Only in a few cases is a verb marked for manner used as a translation (e.g. *throw open* and *fling open* in English and *räväyttää auki* 'throw open' and *tempaista auki* 'jerk/pull open' in Finnish.

Primarily, two classes of nouns are used as objects. One is books cr journals or any other publications that are folded, such as menus. The other class is doors, windows or other barriers (e.g. lids) used to close openings. A further possibility is *slå upp ögonen* 'open the eyes'. *Slå upp* forms an antonymous pair with *slå igen*, which signals closing with the same classes of objects (except eyes). This expression often indicates that the closing was violent and is also associated with a strong sound as in (38), where this element is reflected in the English (*slam*) and French (*claquer*) translations. German even in this case uses the cognate verb (*zuschlagen* with the preverb *zu-* 'to').

(38) *Däruppe **slog** hon **igen** dörren så att det skallrade i rutan.*
Upstairs she **slammed** the door behind her so that the windows rattled.
*Oben **schlug** sie die Tür **zu**.*
*En haut, elle **claqua** la porte.*
*Ylös päästyään hän **paukautti** oven **kiinni**.*
(KE)

There are 13 occurrences of *slå* + Particle referring to closing (*slå igen/samman/ihop*). Except for German (*zuschlagen*, *zu-* 'to' + 'hit'), a verb lacking the manner component is dominant as a translation (English *close, shut*: 10, French (*re*)*fermer* 'close (again): 6, Finnish *sulkea* 'close': 6). The production of a loud sound is also a prominent component in the case of *slå igen*, and this is reflected in several of the manner verbs that do occur as translations, e.g. English *slam, bang*. German *zuknallen* and *zuschnappen*, French *claquer* and Finnish *heittää kiini* 'throw shut', *paukauttaa kiinni* 'slam shut' and *läimäyttää kiinni* 'slam shut'.

The use of *slå upp* has a relatively frequent metonymical extension, which means 'open a book to find written information' (see 39).

(39) *Sedan hämtade hon Statskalendern och **slog upp** namnet på skattechefen i Tyresö.* ['hit up the name']
Then she went and picked up a copy of the Government's official yearbook and **looked up** the name of the director of the local tax office in Tyresö.
*Dann holte sie das Beamtenregister hervor und **schlug** den Namen des Steuerchefs in Tyresö **nach**.*
(LM)

The set of verbs used as translations of this meaning differ from the ones used to translate *slå upp* meaning 'open' except in German. The most frequent English translation is *look up*. German uses the cognate verb even in this case (*nachschlagen* with the preverb *nach-*). In (39), a verb meaning 'search/find' is used as a translation in both French (*chercher*) and Finnish (*etsiä*). In many uses, the meaning of *slå upp* still includes the concrete part 'open a book', but the expression can today also refer to looking up information on a computer. (Microsoft Help: *Slå upp ord med användarstöd för engelska* 'Look up words with user support for English'). In that case only the abstract part of the meaning ('find information') is left, and there is no longer any trace of the hand action. When an action is carried out, there are goals at different levels. To stretch out the hand to open a book is a goal at a lower level than searching for information. When a higher-level, abstract goal is lexicalized as part of the meaning, the concrete part is backgrounded as a kind of manner component ('search for information by opening a book') and may finally be dropped completely from the semantic representation.

7.6.3 Switch on/off

There is another set of combinations of *slå* and particle that forms an antonymous pair *slå på* vs. *slå av* 'switch/turn on vs. off'. These expressions are primarily used with various machines and appliances as in (40).

(40) **Slagit på** *radion och diskmaskinen.*
 Switched on *the radio and the dishwasher.*
 Hatte Radio und Spülmaschine **eingeschaltet.** ['in-connected ']
 avait **allumé** *la radio et* **mis en marche** *le lave-vaisselle.* ['lighted'...'set in motion']
 Avannut *radion ja* **käynnistänyt** *tiskikoneen.* ['opened' ... 'started']
 (ÅL)

A variety of verbs with a wide range of basic meanings are used as translations in (40) and several other alternatives appear in the rest of the 13 examples of this type in the MPC corpus. The combination Verb + *på/av* similar to *on/off* in English forms a minor pattern signalling the (de)activation of various appliances. A rather frequent alternative is *sätta på* 'set on' – *stänga av* 'close off'. In this use, *slå* refers to a broad variety of hand actions involving different motor patterns (press a button, turn a switch). The hand action is usually backgrounded, which is why it is often not reflected in the translations. Only the goal is shared across languages (see 41).

(41) *Med fjärrkontrollen* **slog** *han* **av** *teven.*
   With the remote he **clicked off** the TV.
   (ESPC: HM1)

It seems that this is an area where there is rather great variation even between related languages with respect to the range of verbs that are used, although English and German, like Swedish, have a productive minor pattern using antonymous particles to signal this set of meanings (Swed. *på/av*; Eng. *on/off*; Germ. *ein-, an-/aus-* as in *einschalten/ausschalten* '(dis)connect'). Since new artefacts are being introduced continuously, expressions referring to their use must be constantly renewed, usually by adapting already existing words and phrases (cf. the expression of 'to dial a telephone number' in Section 7.6.5).

The use of *slå på* and *slå av* has generalized to cases where no hand action is involved and can be applied when an appliance appears as subject (see 42).

(42) *Klockradion* **slog på.**
   The radio alarm **switched itself on.**
   (ESPC: FW)

Together with the particle *om*, *slå* can be used in a rather abstract way to refer to a change as in (43).

(43) *Ljusen hade* **slagit om** *till rött igen.*
   The lights had **changed** again to red.
   (ESPC: PDJ)

Further removed examples are *Vädret hade slagit om* 'The weather had changed', *Kärleken slog om till hat* 'Love turned into hate'. The only trace of the basic meaning of *slå* in such examples is that *slå om* tends to refer to a sudden change

7.6.4 Wrap

Slå together with the preposition *om* 'around' is also used to describe how the hands are used to wind cloth or paper (or a rope or a string) around something as in (44). This use is related to the limb movement in example (13) in Section 7.4.6.

(44) *Han* **slog** *en filt* **om** *benen.*
   He **wrapped** a blanket **round** his legs.
   (KE)

The same movement of the hands is involved in forming a parcel of some kind by winding paper around an object. *Slå* in this use is combined with the particle *in* 'in', which refers to the fact that the object is enclosed in the parcel (see 45). This is one more use where rather much information is signalled in a compact way, since the paper is typically not explicitly mentioned, even if that is possible: *Han slog in vasen i silkespapper* 'He wrapped up the vase in tissue paper'.

(45) *Vi kunde inte konversera, inte deklamera, inte* **slå in presenter** *eller hålla tal.*
We were useless at conversation, reciting poems, **wrapping up presents** and giving speeches.
...Geschenke einwickeln...['wind in presents']
...faire des paquets-cadeaux...['make presents']
..paketoida lahjoja...['to packet presents']
(MN)

7.6.5 Dial a telephone number

Dialling a telephone number is also a hand act, which in Swedish primarily is expressed with *slå*. The object in this use refers to a telephone number as in (46). Often only a number is indicated: *Slå 00 till receptionen* 'Dial 00 for the reception'.

(46) *Sedan* **slog** *hon numret hon antecknat från klisterlappen på entrén.*
She then **dialed** the number she had found on the sticker on the entrance doors.
Dann **wählte** *sie die Nummer,/---/*['choose']
Puis elle **composa** *le numéro/---/*['compose, make up']
Sitten hän **soitti** *numeroon,/---/*['ring']
(LM)

A further extension is found in the expression *slå (någon) en signal* (lit. 'strike (someone) a signal') 'call (someone)' which is based on the idea that someone contacts someone else by dialling a telephone number which causes a signal to emerge from the receiving telephone (see 47).

(47) *Francine är säkert på galleriet, jag* **slår henne en signal.**
Francine is probably at the gallery. I'll **give her a ring.**
(CL)

7.6.6 Summing up generalized hand actions

The interpretation of verbs of hitting, in particular when they describe various generalized hand actions, depends to a great extent on the meaning of nouns referring to physical objects involved in the action, as has been demonstrated both for Swedish and Swahili (see Section 7.2.6).

That particular objects suggest specific actions known as affordances is a central assumption in Gibson's (1979) affordance theory of perception. Many of the examples in Section 7.6 are concerned with the manipulation of artefacts which are designed to have specific functions and show how knowledge of such interactions influences the semantic representation of lexical elements. Gibson's original theory was more general and claimed that humans automatically (and not necessarily consciously) could spot "action possibilities" latent in the environment. More recent psychological experiments indicate that there is a close relationship between the perception of objects and their affordances (Kaschak and Glenberg 2000) and, more specifically, that viewing an object activates the appropriate hand shape for using it (Klatzky et al. 1989). Borgi (2005) reviews both neuroimaging and behavioural studies supporting the idea that noun concepts activate motor responses automatically. "In the presence of objects and when objects are referred to by words they activate action simulations to facilitate interaction with objects." (Borgi 2005: 29). Within formal linguistics, the view that the interpretation of the meaning of verbs is dependent on the nouns appearing as arguments is related to Pustejovsky's (1995) theory of qualia roles, in particular the telic role.

7.7 Beyond *slå* as a hand action verb

A large part of the many senses of *slå* – even abstract ones – can be traced back to the use of *slå* as a hand action verb via a chain of meanings which in many cases involves several steps. There are, however, certain meanings which originate in other aspects of meaning, especially when the subject is non-human. The meaning of *slå* in such examples tends to be related to the usually very sudden and forceful impact that is a prominent part of the prototypical meaning.

7.7.1 Body contact not involving the hand: *slå sig ner* 'sit down

One frequent but very language-specific use of *slå* in Swedish is the use as a postural verb meaning 'sit down' in the combination *slå sig ner* ('strike oneself down'). This use is shared only with Norwegian and Danish (se 48).

(48) Swedish   *Erica **slog sig ner** på den ena.*
                   ['Erica struck herself down on one (of the chairs)'].
    Norwegian *Erica **slo seg ned** på den ene.*
    Danish   *Erica **slog sig ned** på den ene.*
    English   *Erica **sat down** [on one of the chairs].*
    (CL)

This use is probably motivated by the fact that sitting down results in contact between the buttocks and the seat, but the expression is completely conventionalized and the concept of body contact is probably not an active part of the meaning. *Slå sig ner* has developed a further sense 'settle down' (see 49), which is characteristic of verbs meaning 'sit (down)' (Newman 2002). In Swedish, *sätta sig* 'sit down' cannot be used with this meaning. This is an example how an expression once it has been established in an extended use can shift in a way that is characteristic of the new rather than the original meaning.

(49) Swedish   *Först måste jag hitta en plats, där vi utan fara kan **slå oss ner**.*
    Norwegian *Først må jeg finde et sted der vi kan **slå oss ned** uten fare.*
    Danish   *Først må jeg finde et sted, hvor vi kan **slå os ned** uden at være i fare.*
    English   *First I have to find a place where we can **settle down** out of danger.*
    (AL)

7.7.2 Thoughts and other non-human subjects

The subject of *slå* is to a great extent human, but a wide range of other subjects are possible. For physical objects a degree of dynamicity is required (e.g. balls and bullets and other projectiles set in motion by humans). Natural forces such as rain, wind and lightning, as well as sense impressions such as heat and smell can also appear as subject (see Viberg 1999, Section 4). Such examples are related to the prototype via concepts such as motion, contact and (usually violent) impact.

One type of subject that reaches a relatively high frequency in the MPC corpus and therefore will be treated here is the abstract category thought. In (50), a noun meaning 'thought' (*tanke*) appears as subject.

(50) Den första tanken **slog** mig när jag vaknade nästa morgon.
That thought **struck** me the following morning when I woke up.
(ESPC: RJ)

Usually the thought represents a full proposition and is realized as an *att*-('that')-S-complement, which appears in an extraposed position with a dummy *det* 'it' in the ordinary subject slot (see 51).

(51) Det **slog** honom att hon visste allting om honom.
Ihm **ging** durch den Kopf, daß sie alles über ihn wußte.
It **struck** him that she knew everything about him.
L'idée le **frappa** qu'elle savait tout de lui.
Johan **tajusi** että Gudrun tiesi hänestä kaiken.
(KE)

Verbs of hitting are relatively frequently used in the MPC corpus as translations of *slå* in this use in English and French, whereas this is not the case in German and Finnish. In German, the most frequent type of translation is a motion verb meaning 'fall' or 'come' (or occasionally 'go' as in example 51) with the human experiencer in the dative case. Finnish also uses spatial metaphors *tulla mieleen* 'come into mind'; *juolahtaa mieleen* 'fall into mind' in addition to mental verbs such as *tajuta* 'realize'. Examples such as (50) and (51) are conventionalized to a high degree. There are, however, related uses with abstract subjects that are more directly linked to concrete uses of *slå*. The phrase *slå ner* 'strike down' is used concretely with subjects such as 'lightning' and 'bomb'. In (52), *slå ner* is used metaphorically with explicit reference to the lightning. Examples of this type form a bridge to examples like (53), where there is no overt such reference. There are parallel examples with other subjects: *Nyheten slog ner (som en bomb)* 'The news struck down (like a bomb)'.

(52) Den avsikten hade alltså **slagit ner i** henne som en blixt. ['struck down in']
That purpose **hit** her like a bolt of lightning.
(MoFa)

(53) *Nu var den framför allt en känsla och den* **slog ner i** *henne med en kraft som var bedövande.*
Now it was above all a feeling and it **struck down in** her with a deafening force.
(MoFa)

7.8 Conclusion and discussion

The major aim of the analysis proposed in this paper has been to find motivations why *slå* has developed various senses or uses. Once a certain use has been established and appears frequently, it is possible that the motivation is lost and the new use develops a certain degree of autonomy. This applies in particular to multiword units such as *slå mynt av* 'strike a coin/take advantage of' which may have an idiom status for many users. This section will discuss the relationships between semantic shifts, contextual elements motivating the shift and the meaning potential.

7.8.1 The semantic shifts

Many of the extensions of *slå* can be described with the general model proposed by Riemer (2005) as derived via three metonymic processes and metaphorical application, often in reiterated combinations. The strength of that model is that it is general and can be applied to words belonging to other semantic fields. On the other hand, such a general model cannot explain why certain types of extensions tend to be characteristic of specific semantic fields (or domains etc.)

The major focus of this paper is the substantive semantic shifts characteristic of verbs of hitting and to what extent is it possible to characterize the typical patterns of polysemy in such a way that it is possible to distinguish these patterns from those of other hand actions, such as grasping and holding. An extended use must – at least when it first appears – correspond to a plausible simulation (cf. Barsalou 2003). The act of hitting has certain general effects which follow from folk models of biology ('hurt', 'kill' etc.) and naïve physics ('set in motion', 'produce sound', 'break' etc.). With a human subject, the verb tends to incorporate various types of goals which are constrained by what is biologically and physically possible, but which extensions are lexicalized also to a great extent is culture-specific and depends on what types of goals are salient in a certain culture at a certain time. The historical development of *slå* as a verb of creation is a good example of that. In particular, the role of the affordances of physical objects is often culture-specific since it tends to apply to artefacts. Generalized hand actions can be regarded as one step in a series of general steps in the semantic shifts of verbs of hitting based on the distance from the prototype as illustrated in Figure 6.

(1) Motion – Contact – Impact (prototype)

⇩

(2) Resultative strengthening: Lexicalization of the result of the impact
(Motion, Creation, Sound emission, Breaking...)

⇩

(3) Generalized hand actions related to the affordances and conventional use of objects

⇩

(4) Generalization. (No trace of hand action)

⇩

Verbal operator, Light verb
Grammaticalization (complete affectedness)

Figure 6: General types of substantive semantic shifts characteristic of HIT

Verbs of hitting represent one type of hand action verbs. Another important group of such verbs is verbs of holding and grasping, which in several languages have developed into verbs of possession. Basic verbs of possession in their turn are a frequent source of a broad range of grammatical meanings (Viberg 2010). Many of the verbs that refer to induced object motion are also hand action verbs such as verbs of putting, pouring, throwing, pulling, pushing and carrying (see Viberg 2015b). To what extent are such contrasts basic in non-European languages? Much more work is required to present substantive universals based on basic hand actions, but it is a fruitful question to ask. Examples of *slå* with an inanimate or abstract subject have been discussed rather briefly, but as mentioned in Section 7.2, the meaning of *slå* in such examples tends to be related to the usually very sudden and forceful impact that is a prominent part of the prototypical meaning.

As has been demonstrated repeatedly above, once a new meaning has been established, that meaning serves as the source of other new meanings and after several steps in such a chain have been passed, it may be difficult to trace the association to the prototype, in particular if some of the earliest links have been lost via historical change. It is also the case that once HIT has been extended into a new semantic field, it can serve as a source of meanings that typically extend from the new field. In Swedish, a large portion of the extensions are still relatively transparently related to the prototype. This is probably less so in a language such as Persian where HIT has been generalized to a greater extent, but in spite of this many of the islands of productivity described by Family (2011) have parallels in Swedish. In Swedish, *slå* in combination with a number of different particles has developed phrases with abstract meanings in registers more or less removed from everyday language, such as news reports and in particular academic prose. Even if many of those combinations can be related to concrete uses with clear links to the prototype, such phrases appear to be on their way to developing into independent lexical units that organize a set of related abstract meanings and fulfil the special expressive needs (often of an abstract kind) in the registers where these phrases are primarily used.

7.8.2 Semantic shifts and the meaning potential of a word

Semantic shifts build expanding networks of new senses. A basic assumption is that all senses of a word are organized as a meaning potential which indicates the relations between all the senses (cf. Viberg 2012, Section 10.1 and references there. See also Allwood 2003). The alternative would be to distinguish a number of semantically unrelated items. To begin with, what speaks in favour of the meaning potential is that there is great overlap between the representations of the various senses of a word, whether this is modelled as a structured set of components partly shared by related meanings (see Viberg 1999 for an attempt to describe *slå* in this way) or a neural network where different senses are modelled as patterns of activation of various links in a complex network. This view has consequences also for language learning; the acquisition of new meanings of a word is facilitated if the already acquired uses are organized as a structured meaning potential rather than a list of unrelated uses.

The concept of meaning potential appears to be fruitful for psycholinguistic approaches. Obviously, the meaning potential in several respects must be organized and accessed differently for production and reception in a way that goes beyond the analysis presented in this paper. Even if many of the uses discussed in this paper are already established and do not necessarily need to be derived via meaning shifts each time they are used, in many cases the meaning potential is important for interpretation in order to select the intended meaning. When the verb *slå* appears in a text, the intended meaning is easier to identify if all the potential meanings of the word are systematically organized rather than just listed. This has to do with the important role of context in the identification of word meanings ("lexical disambiguation").

7.8.3 The role of context

The role of context has been stressed throughout this paper, and the interaction between *slå* and the semantics of its arguments and particles and prepositions. Both the situational and the linguistic context are important for the emergence of extended senses via inferencing and pragmatic strengthening (cf. "The Invited Inferencing Theory of Semantic Change Model", Traugott and Dasher 2005: 34–40). Once a certain sense has been established, *slå* may be used with this meaning with less contextual support, but several elements in the original contexts where the sense emerged may still be important as linguistic cues for the interpretation and the selection of the intended sense, as can be illustrated with simple idealized examples. For *slå*, a wide variety of semantic classes of nouns serving as objects of verbs are important. Reference to a lawn evokes the 'cut grass' interpretation in an example such as *Per slog gräsmattan* 'Per mowed (lit. struck) the lawn', whereas the reference to a number evokes the sense 'dial' in *Per slog numret* 'Per dialed (struck) the number'. Verbal particles are also important cues. In *Per slog upp boken* 'Per opened (lit. 'struck up') the book', it is primarily the particle *upp* that conveys the meaning 'open', but the verb is also involved (cf. *Per tog upp boken* 'Per picked up the book'). In an example such as *Per slog upp en grogg* 'Per poured (lit. struck up) a drink', the semantic class of the object (a beverage) leads to a different interpretation of both the verb ('pour') and the particle, which in this example refers to upwards motion of the liquid in a container. Linguistic cues will not always be enough for disambiguation. In a sentence such as *Djokovic slog Federer* 'Djokovic beat Federer', *slå* is interpreted as 'defeat' when we see it in headlines or on news bills, since the names refer to two tennis stars. A headline such as *Lärare slog elev* 'Teacher beat pupil', would rather evoke a scenario of hurting and battery, unless an adjunct is added: *Lärare slog elev i schack* 'Teacher beat pupil at chess', though this does not sound like a selling story. The meaning potential constantly interacts with the speech situation.

7.9 References

Aikhenvald, Alexandra Y. and Anne Storch (eds.). 2013. *Perception and cognition in language and culture*. Leiden: Brill.

Allwood, Jens. 2003. Meaning potential and context. Some consequences for the analysis of variation in meaning. In Hubert Cuyckens, René Dirven, and John A. Taylor (eds.), *Cognitive Approaches to Lexical Semantics*, 29–65. Berlin: Mouton de Gruyter.

Altenberg, Bengt and Karin Aijmer. 2000. The English-Swedish Parallel Corpus: A resource for contrastive research and translation studies. In Christian Mair and Marianne Hundt (eds.), *Corpus Linguistics and Linguistic Theory*, 15–33. Amsterdam & Atlanta/GA: Rodopi.

Barcelona, Antonio (ed.). 2000. *Metaphor and metonymy at the crossroads. A cognitive perspective.* Berlin: Mouton de Gruyter.

Barsalou, Lawrence W. 1999. Perceptual symbol systems. *Behavioral and Brain Sciences*. 22: 577–660.

Barsalou, Lawrence W. 2003. Situated simulation in the human conceptual system. *Language and Cognitive Processes* 18(5/6): 513–562.

Borgi, Anna M. 2005. Object concepts and action. In Diane Pecher and Rolf A. Zwaan (eds.), *Grounding cognition. The role of perception and action in memory, Language and thinking*, 8–34. Cambridge: Cambridge University Press.

Damasio, Antonio R. and Daniel Tranel. 1993. Nouns and verbs are retrieved with differently distributed neural systems. *Proceedings of The National Academy of Sciences* 90: 4757–4760.

Evans, Nicholas and David Wilkins. 2000. In the mind's ear: The semantic extension of perception verbs in Australian languages. *Language* 76: 546–592.

Family, Neiloufar. 2011. Verbal islands in Persian. *Folia Linguistica* 45(1): 1–30.

Feldman, Jerome A. 2006. *From molecule to metaphor. A neural theory of language*. Cambridge, MA: MIT Press.

Gao, Hong. 2001. *The physical foundation of the patterning of physical action verbs. A study of Chinese verbs*. [Travaux de l'institut de linguistique de Lund, XLI]. Lund: Lund University PhD dissertation.

Gibson, James J. 1979. *The ecological approach to visual perception*. Boston, MA: Houghton Mifflin.

Hook, Peter, Prashant Pardeshi, and Hsin-Hsin Liang. 2012. Semantic neutrality in complex predicates: Evidence from East and South Asia. *Linguistics* 50(3): 605–632.

Johnson, Frederick. 1939. *A standard Swahili-English dictionary*. Oxford University Press.

Kaschak, Michael P. and Arthur M. Glenberg. 2000. Constructing meaning: the role of affordances and grammatical constructions in sentence comprehension. *Journal of Memory and Language* 43: 508–529.

Klatzky, Roberta L., James W. Pellegrino, Brian P. McCloskey, and Sally Doherty. 1989. Can you squeeze a tomato? The role of motor representations in semantic sensibility judgments. *Journal of Memory and Language* 28(1): 56–77.

McGregor, William B. 2002. *Verb classification in Australian languages*. Berlin & New York: Mouton de Gruyter.

Michotte, Albert. 1963. *The perception of causality*. London: Methuen & Co. (Original in French 1946.)

Newman, John (ed.). 2002. *The linguistics of sitting, standing, and lying*. Amsterdam: Benjamins.

Peirce, Charles Sanders. 1932. The icon, index and symbol. In Charles Hartshorne and Paul Weiss (eds.), *Collected papers of Charles Sanders Peirce*. Vol. 2, 156–173. Cambridge, MA: Harvard University Press.

Pulvermüller, Friedemann. 2001. Brain reflections of words and their meanings. *Trends in Cognitive Sciences* 5: 517–24.
Pustejovsky, James. 1995. *The generative lexicon*. Cambridge, MA: MIT Press.
Riemer, Nick. 2002. Verb polysemy and the vocabulary of percussion and impact in Central Australia. *Australian Journal of Linguistics*. Vol. 22(1): 45–96.
Riemer, Nick. 2005. *The semantics of polysemy: Reading meaning in English and Warlpiri*. [Cognitive Linguistics Research] Berlin: Walter de Gruyter.
Schultze-Berndt, Eva Friederike. 2000. *Simple and complex verbs in Jaminjung. A study of event categorisation in an Australian language*. MPI Series in Psycholinguistics 14. Nijmegen: University of Nijmegen PhD dissertation.
Söderwall, Knut F. 1884–1918. *Ordbok öfver svenska medeltidsspråket. Vol I–III*. http://spraakbanken.gu.se
Sweetser, Eve. 1990. *From etymology to pragmatics. Metaphorical and cultural aspects of semantic structure*. Cambridge: Cambridge University Press.
Traugott, Elisabet and Richard Dasher. 2005. *Regularity in semantic change*. Cambridge: Cambridge University Press.
Vanhove, Martine (ed.). 2008. Semantic associations between sensory modalities, prehension and mental perceptions: A crosslinguistic perspective. In Martine Vanhove (ed.), *From polysemy to semantic change. Towards a typology of lexical semantic associations.*, 341–370. Amsterdam: Benjamins.
Viberg, Åke. 1983. The verbs of perception: a typological study. *Linguistics* 21: 123–162.
Viberg, Åke. 1999. Polysemy and differentiation in the lexicon. Verbs of physical contact in Swedish. In Jens Allwood and Peter Gärdenfors (eds.), *Cognitive semantics. Meaning and cognition*, 87–129. Amsterdam: Benjamins.
Viberg, Åke. 2004. Physical contact verbs in English and Swedish from the perspective of crosslinguistic lexicology. In Karin Aijmer and Bengt Altenberg (eds.), *Advances in Corpus Linguistics*, 327–352. Amsterdam/New York: Rodopi.
Viberg, Åke. 2010. Basic verbs of possession. In Maarten Lemmens (ed.). Unison in multiplicity: Cognitive and typological perspectives on grammar and lexis, *CogniTextes* 4. http://Cognitextes.revues.org/308.
Viberg, Åke. 2012. Language-specific meanings in contrast. A corpus-based contrastive study of Swedish *få* 'get'. *Linguistics* 50(6): 1413–1461.
Viberg, Åke. 2013. Seeing the lexical profile of Swedish through multilingual corpora. The case of Swedish *åka* and other vehicle verbs. In Karin Aijmer and Bengt Altenberg (eds.), *Advances in Corpus-Based Contrastive Linguistics. Studies in Honour of Stig Johansson*, 25–56. Amsterdam: Benjamins.
Viberg, Åke. 2015a. Sensation, perception and cognition. Swedish in a typological-contrastive perspective. *Functions of Language* 22(1).96–131.
Viberg, Åke. 2015b. Motion verb typology and the expression of endpoint of motion in Swedish. In Maria Bloch-Trojnar, Anna Malicka-Kleparska, and Karolina Drabikowska (eds.), *Concepts and structures – Studies in semantics and morphology* in the series Studies in Linguistics and Methodology (SLAM), 209–229. Lublin: Wydawnictwo KUL.

Electronic sources

ESPC: The English Swedish Parallel Corpus (ESPC). For a description, see: http://www.sol.lu.se/engelska/corpus/corpus/espc.html

Helsinki Corpus of Swahili: http://www.aakkl.helsinki.fi/cameel/corpus/intro.htm (Data obtained from Arvi Hurskainen September 2009)

The Bank of Old Swedish (Fornsvenska textbanken): http://project2.sol.lu.se/fornsvenska/ Peder Swart's Chronicle

SLB: Corpora from the Swedish language bank (Språkbanken) http://spraakbanken.gu.se/

The following corpora have been accessed (Summer 2014):
– Fiction: Skönlitteratur: 22.4 M(illion words)
– News: Tidningstexter: 575.6 M
– Academic prose: Akademiska texter: 25.3 M
– Legal: Svensk författningssamling: 8.3 M

Päivi Juvonen
8. Making do with minimal lexica. Light verb constructions with MAKE/DO in pidgin lexica

Abstract: One of the most characteristic features of pidgin languages is the small size of their lexica. Normally, a pidgin makes do with less than 2000 common lexical items. How can one make do with so few words? The present study focuses on how pidgin lexica may allow for a systematic expansion of their minimal lexica by using a light verb meaning 'make' or 'do', or both, and investigates the polysemy that arises as a result of semantic shifts in 30 mostly unrelated pidgin varieties. The main results of the semantic analysis show that 1) two thirds of the analysed varieties make use of the light verb construction studied and, 2) those that make use of it are distributed all over the world, represent different combinations of languages in contact, favour effect metonymies and context metonymies over other types of semantic shifts and, use the construction to different degrees. These results are discussed mainly in terms of grammaticalization: in some of the languages the light verb MAKE/DO is argued to have become a verbaliser, in others, the constructions (if attested) are best described as conventionalised idiomatic expressions, i.e. verb idioms.

8.1 Introduction[1]

A pidgin is a variety of language that may emerge in language contact situations. One of the most characteristic features of pidgin languages is the small size of their lexica. Normally, a pidgin makes do with less than 2000 common lexical items (Bakker and Parkvall 2013: 33). Thus, their mere size makes their study

---

[1] I would like to thank the two anonymous reviewers and my co-editor Maria Koptjevskaja Tamm for helpful comments and suggestions. Mikael Parkvall has not only compiled the corpus used as data in the present study, he has also made helpful comments and suggestions for improvement of the paper, created the map in Figure 1 and supported the writing of this paper in all possible ways. Mahsie! Also thanks to Anne Reath Warren for polishing my English.

Päivi Juvonen (Stockholm university)

interesting from the point of view of lexical semantics. How can one make do with so few words?

Usually, most of the lexicon of a pidgin comes from one single language, referred to as the lexifier. This, together with the main area where the language was/is spoken, is often reflected in the names of these contact languages as used by linguists. We, thus, speak about Hawaiian Pidgin English (English-lexified pidgin spoken in Hawaii), about Gulf Pidgin Arabic (Arabic-lexified pidgin spoken in the Persian Gulf area), etc. Until recently, the study of pidgin lexica has mainly concentrated on the question of the etymological sources of lexical items. Hence, we know quite a lot about the relative contributions different languages have made to the vocabularies of pidgin languages all over the world. Also, as the use of pidgin languages is typically confined to specific domains of use (a common categorisation of them is based on their use as military pidgins, trade pidgins, plantation pidgins etc.), one finds mentions of there being a lot of lexical elements that belong to the domain(s) the pidgin language in question is mainly used in. This is to be expected: a military pidgin needs vocabulary to talk about weapons etc., a pidgin used on a plantation needs items to talk about crops and plants and, thus, words belonging to these domains tend to be present in their vocabularies. However, this focus on the ancestry and the different domains of use has also led to a situation where little is known about what, if any, regularities and lexicon-grammar interaction exist in pidgin lexica, irrespective of their ancestry or main domain of use (Bakker and Parkvall 2013: 33–35).

The present paper aims to contribute to our knowledge of pidgin lexica by describing the patterns of polysemy[2] of the basic or nuclear verb (Stubbs 1986; Viberg 1993: 247) meaning MAKE/DO in pidgin languages with different lexical affiliations and domains of use, when used in a light verb construction. It describes patterns of polysemy which, it is argued, have led to the grammaticalization of MAKE/DO as an auxiliary (Heine and Kuteva, 2002: 52–3), more specifically a verbaliser, in some of the analysed languages. In yet some of the analysed languages, however, the constructions (if attested) are best described as conventionalised idiomatic expressions, i.e. verb idioms (Booij 2002; Nunberg, Sag, and Wasow 1994). Hence, the paper addresses the question of lexicon-grammar interaction in pidgin languages, both from the point of view of lexical semantics and the point of view of grammaticalization.

---

2 "Colexification" (cf. Östling, this volume; Schapper, San Roque, and Hendery, this volume) might be a more appropriate term. However, I will here follow the tradition of Pidgin studies and talk about polysemy.

8.2 MAKE/DO in Tay Boi

In order to set the scene, this section illustrates how the verb meaning MAKE/DO is used in the French-lexified, Vietnamese-substrate pidgin Tay Boi. To begin with, it is used as a main verb in sentences such as (1), i.e. in the same fashion the corresponding lexical item can be used in many languages, among them French (*Qu'est-ce que vou faites dans votre village?*) and Vietnamese (*Những gì bạn làm trong ngôi làng của bạn?*, where *làm* is the equivalent of MAKE/DO).

(1) Toi   y en a   faire   quoi   dans   village   toi?
    2SG   YENA³   MAKE/DO   what   in   village   2SG
    'What do you do in your village?'
    Nolly (1908: 73), via PaCo.⁴

Frequent basic verbs may develop into auxiliaries, for instance, DO often develops into a causative marker in the languages of the world (Heine and Kuteva 2002: 320, 328). Example (2) illustrates how the verb MAKE/DO is used with a causative meaning in Tay Boi. The same pattern of use is also found both in French (*Il me fait aller*) and in Vietnamese (*Ông đã làm cho tôi đi*).

(2) Lui   faire   moi   aller.
    3SG   MAKE/DO   1SG   go
    'He makes me go.'
    Liem (1979: 241), via PaCo.

Besides the use of the lexical item *faire* as a main verb as in (1) or as a causative as in (2), Tay Boi also combines *faire* with nouns in cases not attested in French with the same meaning, as in examples (3–5). French has lexicalised the word *marier*, 'to marry' and the construction in (3) is not used to convey this meaning. *Faire papier* in (4) does exist in French (with an additional partitive article), but means to 'manufacture or produce paper' rather than to 'to write, work with written documents'. And, from a French horizon, you do not *faire rizière* (5), you *cultivez*

---

3 This item has not been sufficiently analysed in the source and is therefore left unanalysed here.
4 The examples used here come from a corpus of pidgin examples compiled by Mikael Parkvall, henceforth The Parkvall Corpus, or, PaCo, for short. For the sake of transparency, the sources referred to are listed in the list of references. For more information about or access to the corpus, please contact parkvall@ling.su.se.

du riz. By and large, the same appears to hold for Vietnamese as regards these constructions.

(3) *Toi   vouloir   faire   congaï   moi?*
    2SG   want   MAKE/DO   girl/woman   1SG
    'Would you like to marry me?'
    Léra (1896: 67), via PaCo.

(4) *Y en a   faire   beaucoup   papier,   même chose   resident civil?*
    YENA   MAKE/DO   much   paper   same thing   administrator
    'Is there a lot of paperwork (writing), as an administrator?'
    Léra (1896: 77), via PaCo.

(5) *Moi   y en a   faire   rizière.*
    1SG   YENA   MAKE/DO   rice.field
    'I grow rice.'
    Nolly (1908: 73), via PaCo.

Obviously, then, MAKE/DO is in Tay Boi used also in contexts where the main contributing languages have other, lexicalised means of expressing the content. Example (1) is here analysed as an example of one of the core meanings of the polysemous verb MAKE/DO as a GENERAL DYNAMIC verb (the other being PRODUCTION). Examples (2)–(5) are here all analysed as instances of a light verb construction. Lehmann (2012: 473) describes light verb constructions as "verbal constructions whose structural head is a rather empty verb taking a dependent which semantically enriches the situation core". The light verb and the dependent together have one meaning and function as the main verbal (i.e. dynamic relational) element in an utterance. In example (2) above, the meaning of the MAKE/DO construction is clearly causative and we would usually consider MAKE/DO as an auxiliary in this kind of construction. However, in order to account for all possible light verb constructions in the pidgin languages studied, I consider examples with any kind of dependent as light verb constructions. The questions of degree of grammaticalization will be briefly discussed below in 8.4 and 8.7.

8.3 Semantic shifts in verbs

All languages may expand the size of their lexicon by inventing new words or by borrowing existing words from other varieties. All languages may also change the meaning of existing words or constructions, and expand (or reduce) the number of lexemes (Koch, this volume[5]). The present study focuses on how pidgin lexica may allow a systematic expansion of their minimal lexica by using a light verb construction, and investigates the polysemy that arises as a results of semantic shifts in these constructions.

Riemer (2002, 2005) studies verbs of PERCUSSION and IMPACT ('hit', 'strike' etc.) in Central Australian languages and English in terms of their semantics, and proposes a cognitive linguistic model of polysemy. He sees "meaning as interpretative, multifaceted and translational" and consequently, the goal of a semantic analysis cannot be to once and for all "uniquely specify *the* meaning of a lexeme, but instead as many as possible of its salient and interesting features" (Riemer 2002: 48). He argues convincingly that the polysemy of the studied verbs in Warlpiri and other Central Australian languages as well as in English can be described in terms of a core, prototypical meaning and four major types of non-core meanings. In metaphorical application, the verb is used of non-typical referents as in *"The virus will strike many Australians this year"* (Riemer 2005: 233). A metonymic extension to the effect of the action of the verb is called effect metonymy, as in *"He kicked the cat out of the house"* (Riemer 2005: 246, cf. "causative metonymy" in Koch, this volume). In context metonymy, the interpretation of the verb depends on the larger context of the utterance as in *"Rosa [...] savagely slamming around the kitchen"* (Riemer 2005: 288), where the violent motion, rather than any percussion or impact on a non-present surface, is highlighted. Finally, in constituent metonymy, only a part of the basic meaning of the verb is activated as in *"He [a preacher] thrashed with his arms"* (Riemer 2005: 293). Metaphorical application is seen not as a semantic shift, but as the application where the core sense of the verb is predicated of referents not typically occurring with the verb, but the metonymies are seen as semantic shifts from the core meaning of the verb. (See also Viberg, this volume.)

Riemer's description of polysemy as an effect of metaphorical applications and metonymic shifts is appealing. However, whereas Riemer studies the polysemies of verbs with a lot of lexical meaning, the present study analyses the semantic relationship between the dependent in a light verb construction to the meaning of the whole light verb construction. Therefore, the analysis and the categories of metonymy are somewhat adapted to suit the present enterprise.

The semantic relation between the dependent and the meaning of the light verb construction in examples (2–5) above is metonymy. In (2) the relation between the dependent verb 'go' and the meaning of the whole construction is

---

[5] Koch (this volume) is an excellent introduction to meaning change in general.

that of effect metonymy, the paradigm case of which I consider to be causative meaning (Riemer 2002, 2005 does not talk about causatives, but gives plenty of typical examples). Examples (3) to (5) are all analysed as context metonymy, where the dependent is a salient part of the event frame in which the construction occurs. Example (3) can be understood in terms of a frame (or an idealised cognitive model) of getting married: a woman who acts as a bride is a crucial participant in the act of getting married (cf. AGENT FOR ACTION-metonymy in Radden and Kövecses 1999: 37). Writing is an activity that uses a pen or a pencil, paper or papyrys or the like. Hence, the dependent *papier* in (4) is selected to stand, together with the light verb MAKE/DO, for the whole event of writing.[6] Last, in (5) the context of growing something in Vietnam most probably includes a rice field, and, thus, even this example is here analysed as an example of context metonymy (see also RESULT FOR ACTION-metonymy in Radden and Kövecses 1999: 37).

From a slightly different angle, Family (2008) examines the use of the Persian light verb *xordæn*, 'to eat' within a cognitive, Construction Grammar framework. She develops an interesting analytical tool for crosslinguistic comparisons, where semantic regularities (groups of light verb constructions that express similar notions such as 'affected' or 'motion', where the light verb combines with a restricted but large set of dependents) are mapped into semantic spaces. Her analysis shows, that these "notional islands", i.e. groups of light verb constructions, are important, as they are argued to allow for intuitive disambiguation.

Within another branch of cognitive linguistics, Langacker (2002: 3) talks about what resembles the notional islands of Family (2008) as domains of use. In the present study, even though inspired by the method applied in Family (2008), I will apply a combination of Riemer's (2002, 2005) model of polysemy and domains of use as the analytical tool. First, however, a brief overview of previous studies of polysemy, multifunctionality and grammaticalization in pidgin languages.

8.4 Polysemy, multifunctionality and grammaticalization in pidgin languages

The present study presents a semantic analysis of pidgin lexica in several, mostly unrelated pidgin languages. Pidgin lexica have hitherto seldom been subject to

---

6 Incidentally, the verb meaning 'pierce' is in several Central Australian languages used in the extended meaning 'to write' (Riemer 2002: 81), analysed as an instance of context metonymy.

any lexical semantic analyses, nor are there any typological studies of pidgin lexica[7]. Several authors mention that pidgins rely heavily on polysemy and multifunctionality, i.e. that the part-of-speech category of a pidgin lexeme is often context dependent as demonstrated in example (6) (see e.g. Holm 1989: 599, 2000; Johnson 1978: 222; Silverstein 1972). Some authors also discuss the use of lexical items as general dynamic verbs, verbalisers or causatives (notably in connection to Chinook Jargon, see e.g. Grant 1996; Jacobs 1932; Juvonen 2008; Robertson 2011; Silverstein 1972; Thomason 1983), but to date, studies of the way pidgin lexica are composed in terms of meaning and use, especially in cross-linguistic terms, are sparse. Apart from a brief overview of the observations on the organisation of pidgin lexica from a structural point of view made in different studies in Mühlhäusler (1997: chapter 5) and his own observations of the semantic organisation of Tok Pisin (Mühlhäusler 1997: 156–158), not much attention has been paid to the semantic organisation or the cross-linguistic patterns of lexicon-grammar interaction in pidgin lexica (cf. Koptjevskaja-Tamm [2008: 6] about the sparseness of studies of this latter kind in any languages). There are, however, some exceptions.

Juvonen (2008) studies the use of multifunctional lexical items, among them the use the verb *mamook*, 'make/do', in a doculect[8] of Chinook Jargon in comparison to English in terms of complexity and simplicity. Juvonen describes the light verb MAKE/DO as a general dynamic verb that can be attached to several other part-of-speech categories to form multiword verb phrases. *Mamook* is by no means the only light verb in Chinook Jargon, but it is by far the most frequent. Mühlhäusler (2008) studies the multifunctionality of lexical items in Pitkern-Norf'k and Tok

---

[7] There are only a few typological studies of pidgin languages from any point of view. Besides an areal typological study of Sub-Saharan pidgins in Africa (Heine 1973), the inflectional morphology (Bakker 2003a, 2003b; Roberts and Bresnan 2008) and phonology (Bakker 2009) of pidgins has been studied from a typological point of view. Bakker (2003a) shows that reduplication is not a productive morphological device in his sample of 30 pidgins studied. Bakker (2003b) studies morphology in a large sample of pidgins and concludes that pidgins both preserve some morphological markers from the languages in contact and develop new markers. He proposes two implicational hierarchies to account for how nominal and verbal inflections, respectively, are retained in pidgins (Bakker 2003b: 23):
Nominal inflections: number > case > gender
Verbal inflections: TMA > valence > number > person > gender
These findings are also confirmed by Roberts and Bresnan (2008), who compare inflectional morphological categories in 29 pidgins with those found in their lexifieres. The phonological inventories of pidgins is in Bakker (2009) found to resemble that of any language.
[8] A doculect refers to any documented variety of a pidgin language.

Pisin. Among these, he discusses the use of *mek* (< English 'make') in Tok Pisin as a means to make maximal use of a limited number of lexical items.

Keesing (1988, 1991) studies several different varieties of Melanesian Pidgin English (Bislama, Tok Pisin and Solomon Pijin) and argues that these languages have, under the influence of and modelling structures in the local languages spoken by the pidgin users (referred to as the substrate languages), developed several grammatical markers from lexical items. Among these, there is the perfect marker *bin* in Bislama and Tok Pisin (< English *been*, Keesing 1991: 330–31), the transitive/causative suffix *-im* (< English *him*, Keesing 1991: 318–19) and the development of the English *by and by*, *just*, *now* and others as markers of aspect, mood and modality in Melanesian Pidgin (Keesing 1991: 325).

Heine and Kuteva (2005), who review cases of contact induced language change in general often use pidgin languages as examples of language contact. They argue that language contact commonly includes the replication of pre-existing grammatical and/or semantic patterns from the languages in contact. They do not rule out the possibility that language contact may result in new usage patterns (Heine and Kuteva 2005: 44; 2010), but their main argument is that in language contact situations, a pragmatically motivated use of a collocation, a less frequent and optional minor usage pattern, may be replicated and become a fully grammaticalized, frequent and obligatory, major usage pattern in the contact language(s). With regard to pidgin languages, this is demonstrated to be possible when the substrate languages provide the speakers of the pidgin with the same usage pattern. The Melanesian Pidgin transitive/causative marker *-im* (< English *him*) may, thus, have been replicated from a pre-existing pattern in many of the Eastern Austronesian substrate languages (Heine and Kuteva 2005: 111). However, the suggestions made by Keesing (1988, 1991) and Heine and Kuteva (2005, 2010) with regard to Melanesian pidgin can be questioned. Baker (1993) argues convincingly that many such features in fact arose in Australia only to later be exported to Melanesia. Also, as Parkvall (1999) has shown, the same items are found in several English lexified pidgins (and creoles), not only in pidgins with Melanesian substrate[9].

---

9 Hence, the items discussed may have been borrowed rather than grammaticalized. As for light verbs, Wichmann and Wohlgemuth (2008) propose "the light verb strategy" (2008: 92) as one of the main strategies in verb borrowing across languages; a strategy that according to them indicates a lesser degree of bilingualism and a less intense language contact situation (Wichmann and Wohlgemuth 2008: 112). As the main aim of the present paper is to study the semantics of the MAKE/DO light verb construction, the borrowing of items will, however, not be discussed further here.

Heine and Kuteva (2005, also 2010) discuss cases of lexicon-grammar interaction as contact-induced grammaticalization in language contact situations. Grammaticalization as such is of course not confined to language contact situations, nor is the use of pro-verbs or light verbs[10], but it is argued to function as the motivation for these changes in language contact situations: the existence of model categories in the languages in contact may lead to the replication of the model in the contact language (replica language in their terminology). The present study aims not to settle the question of replication; rather, it discusses the use of the light verb construction in terms of grammaticalization in general. With regard to frequently used verbs Heine and Kuteva state:

> A fairly common strategy to be observed in situations of language contact is to extend the use of some basic verb by allowing it to take new complements in order to express new concepts. This strategy may have the effect that the semantic content of the relevant verb is generalised, and the verb retains its status as a lexical category. Still, the verb also assumes properties of a functional category, namely that of serving as a pro-verb whose meaning can be determined only with reference to the complement it is associated with. This evolution is in accordance with a universal process of grammaticalization whereby verbs occurring regularly in collocation with some specific type of complement tend to assume functions of auxiliaries. (Heine and Kuteva 2005: 52–53)

To summarise, pidgin lexica are sparsely studied from the point of view of their semantic organisation. Most descriptions of pidgin languages do mention that they are highly polysemous and multifuntional. The few comparative studies of pidgin languages have identified a basic verb glossed as having the meaning 'make' or 'do', or both, i.e. MAKE/DO, that quite regularly combines with a dependent in a light verb construction to create new meanings. Hence, it seems to have acquired a new function that paves the way for grammaticalising it as a verbalizer.

8.5 Data and procedure

The data analysed in the present study consist of mostly published text examples of 32 doculects of pidgin languages. These have been collected and glossed in a corpus, the Parkvall Corpus (PaCo), by Mikael Parkvall of Stockholm University. Most pidgin languages are very poorly documented, while a few are slightly better known. The corpus used in the present study included all documented

---

[10] See e.g. Butt 2003, 2010; Lehmann 2012; Liljegren 2010.

data for some of the poorly documented languages, such as Herschel Island Pidgin Eskimo or Yokohamese, but not all data of the richly documented languages, such as Chinook Jargon, were included in their entirety. However, the corpus has good coverage of many languages (for example, the more than 2300 sentences in Français-Tirailleur are collected from over 148 different documents by 130 authors, the earliest published in 1864 and the most recent in 2008). In its current state, the corpus does not include text examples of all known pidgin languages. It is not a balanced corpus, nor is it a total corpus. It is, however, the first ever glossed compilation of pidgin texts, and as such, a rich source of data. The map in Figure 1 shows where the analysed languages were used.

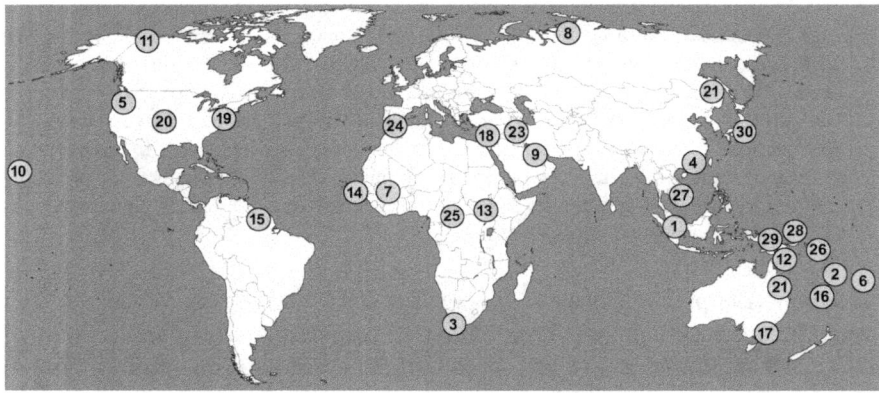

Figure 1: The distribution of the pidgin languages analysed. 1=Bazaar Malay, 2= Bislama (two doculects), 3=Cape Pidgin Dutch, 4=Chinese Pidgin English, 5=Chinook Jargon, 6= Fiji Pidgin Hindustani, 7=Français-Tirailleur, 8=Govorka, 9=Gulf Pidgin Arabic, 10=Hawaiian Pidgin English, 11=Herschel Island Pidgin Eskimo, 12=Hiri Motu, 13=Juba Arabic (two doculects), 14=Língua do Preto, 15=Ndyuka-Trio Pidgin, 16=New Caledonian Pidgin French, 17=New South Wales Pidgin English, 18=Pidgin Madame, 19=Pidgin Delaware, 20=Plains Indian Sign, 21=Primorye Pidgin Russian, 22=Queensland Pidgin English, 23=Romanian Pidgin Arabic, 24=Roquetas Pidgin Spanish, 25=Sango, 26=Solomon Pijin, 27=Tay Boi, 28=Tok Pisin, 29=Yimas-Arafundi Pidgin, 30=Yokohamese.

For the present study, all the data in PaCo was manually searched for examples of MAKE/DO-constructions. In a first step, the English glosses were searched and all examples that were glossed with either *do* or *make* were collected. The second step was to examine all such examples and to search for and identify pidgin equivalent(s). Then, in the third step, the corpus was searched for further instances of such pidgin item(s) that did not correspond to *do* or *make* in the translation, and remaining examples were included. This way, even examples glossed or translated as *work, be, create* or *produce* or the like were found. If no examples were found in the first step, the pidgin data was examined directly without the second step. This procedure resulted, after seven examples were removed due to insufficient glossing, in 870 examples. 619 of these were examples of the MAKE/DO-construction (cf. 8.6).

The item searched for was not identified and attested among the following doculects/pidgins studied: Arabic lexifier Juba Arabic (two separate doculects), Pidgin Madame, Romanian Pidgin Arabic, New Caledonian Pidgin French, Japanese lexified Yokohamese, Motu lexified Hiri Motu, Ndyuka (and Trio) lexified Ndyuka-Trio Pidgin, Roquetas Pidgin Spanish and, Yimas lexified Yimas-Arafundi Pidgin[11]. The doculects that rendered examples are listed, together with information about the main lexifier, the item(s) identified and the type of dependents found to co-occur with them in Table 1. Table 2 will show numerical data.

As Table 1 reveals, most but not all the languages that render examples of the light verb construction studied list the light verb item(s) as polysemous: in for example Língua do Preto it is in the sources listed as meaning 'to make' and nothing else. Bazaar Malay has two lexical items, one of which is listed as polysemous, one of which is not (*bikin*, 'do, make' *buat*, 'make'). I will, however, in what follows, use the more general term MAKE/DO to cover all these different cases, i.e. even when talking about the languages that have not been listed to have a polysemous light verb with both or one of the meanings or, when talking about languages where several forms/items have been identified.

Besides the fact that many lexical items in pidgin languages have several related meanings, the part-of-speech (PoS) category of a lexical item may also vary rather freely (i.e. the lexical items are multifunctional or heterosemantic, cf. Enfield 2006). In Tay Boi (6), cooking or feeding can be expressed by means of the multi-word phrase *faire manger*, 'MAKE/DO eat/food'.

---

[11] MAKE/DO is not the only lexical item in these languages that can be used in several constructions either in idiomatic fashion or as incipient light verbs: e.g. 'travailler' in New Caledonian Pidgin French, 'do, give' in Bazaar Malay, 'take' in Ndyuka Trio Pidgin, 'take' and 'come' in Chinook Jargon seem to function in this way. These are, however, not discussed further here.

Table 1: Overview of the pidgin languages/doculects that render light verb constructions with MAKE/DO in the data. N=nominal dependent as in Chinook Jargon *mamook pipa*, 'to write' (literally 'make/do paper'), A=adjectival dependent as in Plains Indian Sign *make bad*, 'to insult', V=verbal dependent as in New South Wales Pidgin English *make cry*.

Language/doculect	Lexifier	Item and gloss(es) in PaCo	N	A	V
Bazaar Malay	Malay	*bikin*, 'do, make' *buat*, 'make'	x	x	x
Bislama	English	*mekem*, 'make'	x	x	0
Bislama (early)	English	*make_im*, 'make, do'	x	0	x
Cape Pidgin Dutch	Dutch	*maak*, 'make'; *doen*, 'do'	0	x	0
Chinese Pidgin English	English	*do*, 'do, make'	x	0	0
Chinook Jargon	Chinook	*mamook*, 'do, make, work'	x	x	x
Fiji Pidgin Hindustani	Hindustani	*karo*, 'do, make'	x	0	x
Français-Tirailleur	French	*faire*, 'do, make'	x	x	x
Govorka	Russian	*delat*, 'do, make'	x	0	0
Gulf Pidgin Arabic	Arabic	*sawwi*, 'do, make'	x	x	0
Hawaiian Pidgin	Hawaiian	*han*, 'do, make, work'	x	x	x
Herschel Island Pidgin Eskimo	Eskimo	*ʃabakto*, 'make'	x	0	x
Língua do Preto	Portuguese	*fazer*, 'make'	x	x	0
New South Wales Pidgin English (early)	English	*make, make_him*, 'do, make'	x	x	x
Pidgin Delaware	Unami	*maranijto*, 'do, make'	x	0	0
Plains Indian Sign	–	*do, make, work* 'do, make, work'	x	x	x
Primorye Pidgin Russian	Russian	*delat*, 'do, make'	x	x	x
Queensland Pidgin English (early)	English	*make, make_em*, 'make'	x	x	x
Sango	Ngbandi	*sara*, 'do, make'	x	0	0
Tok Pisin (early)	English	*make_him, make*, 'make'	x	x	x
Tay Boi	French	*faire*, 'do, make'	x	x	x

(6) *No,   madame retter   maison coucher   faire   petit petit   manger.*
    no   missus   stay   house   lie.down MAKE/DO   small small   eat/food
    'No, missus is staying at home preparing food for/feeding the children.'
    Schuchardt (1888: 230), via PaCo.

It is not clear, what part-of-speech category *manger* belongs to, and thus, what the most plausible meaning of the sentence is – if interpreted as a noun, the meaning 'to cook' seems the most reasonable, if interpreted as a verb, the causative meaning 'make somebody eat' seems the most plausible. Multifunctional items are probably found in all languages (the same indeterminacy as in (6) yields the French equivalent of *faire manger*), but as argued in Juvonen (2008) with respect to a doculect of Chinook Jargon in comparison to English texts, they are more common in Chinook Jargon than in English (10 % vs. less than 1 %). Hence, interpreting pidgin clauses relies heavily on their context. For the present purposes, I have chosen not to settle on a specific PoS-category for the clearly multifunctional and context-dependent examples, i.e. only (relatively) certain cases are accounted for in Table 1. The syntactic distribution of MAKE/DO construction will, however, not be explored further here.

8.6 Results: making and doing in pidgin languages

MAKE/DO is a polysemous lexical item in most of the pidgin languages where it was attested in these data (see Table 1 above). Besides the GENERAL DYNAMIC meaning exemplified in (1) above, it is rather regularly used as a verb of PRODUCTION, often glossed as 'to make, to build, to work'. Both these meanings are found in Chinook Jargon, as seen in (7)–(9).

(7) *Wik-kata   naika   ikta   mamook*
    NEG   1SG   what   MAKE/DO
    'I can't do anything.'
    Robertson (2011: 152)[12], via PaCo.

---

[12] The corpus in Robertson 2011 dates from around the turn of the century 1800/1900.

(8) *Alta   nsaika trai   pus   mamook   sondi   haws*
    PRES   1PL   try   IRR   MAKE/DO   Sunday   house
    'Now we're trying to build a church.'
    Robertson (2011: 107), via PaCo.

(9) *Mika   tikeh   mamook*
    2SG   want   MAKE/DO
    'Do you want (to) work?'
    Gill (1889: 55), via PaCo.

Both these meanings, i.e. as a GENERAL DYNAMIC verb and as a verb of PRODUCTION, are here analysed to be prototypical or core meanings of MAKE/DO. 251 of the 870 tokens rendered (29 %) were classified as basic. Both these meanings may be extended into new contexts by means of metonymical semantic shifts, or by means of metaphorical applications in the sense of Riemer (2002: 54, 2005: 181–183). In the following sections, the most pervasive constructions, found in several languages/doculects, are exemplified and discussed.

8.6.1 Effect metonymies

Out of the 21 doculects including examples of the light verb construction analysed, only three do not render any examples of effect metonymies (i.e. causative metonymy). These are Chinese Pidgin English, Govorka and Fiji Pidgin Hindustani – all of which are so far sparsely documented in PaCo. There are 257 tokens (42 % of all light verb constructions) analysed as effect metonymies in the corpus. Most of them can be further analysed as belonging to the domains of use *Emotions, Change of mental state, Change of physical state, Domestic activities, Interpersonal relations and social interaction* and *Motion* (cf. Langacker 2002: 3). Effect metonymies are the most widely spread type of metonymies over the pidgin languages studied. However, as also discussed shortly, some of the doculects render far more examples than others. The next sections discuss the use of effect metonymies in the data.

8.6.1.1 Emotions

In eight of the doculects (Bazaar Malay, Chinook Jargon, Gulf Pidgin Arabic, New South Wales Pidgin English, Plains Indian Sign, Queensland Pidgin English,

Sango and Tai Boy) we find examples where the dependent of the light verb MAKE/
DO expresses an emotion such as being afraid, angry, crazy, happy, lucky or silly.
The light verb construction, thus, expresses that these emotions are caused into
being.

8.6.1.2 Change of mental state

In Chinook Jargon, New South Wales Pidgin English and Tay Boi we also find
expressions of change of mental state in the realm of cognition: MAKE/DO *know*
is in these doculects used to mean 'to teach'. In Chinook Jargon it also renders
translations with *to let know, to inform* and *to report*.

8.6.1.3 Change of physical state

The single most common effect metonymy in these data is MAKE/DO *die/dead*
meaning 'to kill' or 'to die' (Bislama, Cape Pidgin Dutch, Chinook Jargon, Gulf
Pidgin Arabic, New South Wales Pidgin English, Tay Boi, Tok Pisin, Early Bislama),
i.e. both the causative and the inchoative meaning is possible and sometimes rendered in one and the same doculect. The same kind of meaning alternation is also
found in the construction MAKE/DO *sleep*. In Français-Tirailleur, Primorye Pidgin
Russian and Plains Indian Sign the construction may simply mean 'to sleep', but
in Français-Tirailleur the same construction also means 'to make sleep', 'to put
to sleep'. Hence, MAKE/DO seems not to be used as a simple causative marker;
rather, it signifies the change of the agents physical state and may, but need not,
have a causative meaning. Whether or not it receives a causative reading remains
a matter of the context of utterance. If indeed causative meaning is the paradigm case of effect metonymy, as suggested above, these inchoative cases could
be seen as post-metonymic, i.e. as cases where the original metonymic link of
causing or bringing a state into being has been lost, and the construction is used
to signify the inchoative being in a physical state (cf. Riemer 2005: 198–199).

Within this category we also find dependents such as 'healthy' (i.e. 'to cure',
Cape Pidgin Dutch), 'big' (Bazaar Malay), 'thin' (Língua do Preto), 'hurt' (Hawaiian Pidgin) and 'drunk' (Chinook Jargon, New South Wales Pidgin English).

8.6.1.4 Domestic activities

Domestic chores such as making fire (Chinook Jargon, Français-Tirailleur, New South Wales Pidgin English, Pidgin Delaware, Plains Indian Sign, Queensland Pidgin English), chopping wood (Chinook Jargon, New South Wales Pidgin English, Pidgin Delaware), cultivating rice (Tay Boi, see example 5), herding cattle (Chinook Jargon), cooking or frying and boiling (Bazaar Malay, Chinook Jargon, Gulf Pidgin Arabic, Early Tok Pisin, Plains Indian Sign, Sango, Tay Boi, Early Bislama), cleaning (Français-Tirailleur, Gulf Pidgin Arabic), sewing (Tay Boi), washing (Bazaar Malay, Early Bislama) and making beds (Tay Boi), and then some, are all expressed by means of the light verb construction studied. The semantic relationship between the light verb and the meaning of the construction is effect metonymy: the chopping of wood has an effect on the 'wood' in the construction MAKE/DO 'wood'; the cooking has an effect on the 'food/eat' in the construction MAKE/DO 'food/eat' etc.

8.6.1.5 Interpersonal relations and social interaction

Eight of the doculects render light verb constructions with effect metonymies in the domain of *Interpersonal relations and social interaction* (Français-Tirailleur, Gulf Pidgin Arabic, Hawaiian Pidgin, New South Wales Pidgin English, Plains Indian Sign, Sango, Early Tok Pisin and Early Bislama). Gifts are given (Tay Boi, Français-Tirailleur), complaints and promises are made and taboos proclaimed (Français-Tirailleur, Gulf Pidgin Arabic, New South Wales Pidgin English, Early Tok Pisin), games played (Français-Tirailleur) and songs sung (Early Tok Pisin, Early Bislama).

8.6.1.6 Motion

The effect metonymies already discussed are present in several pidgin languages with different ancestry and geographical distribution. This is also the case within the domain of *Motion*. Bazaar Malay, Chinook Jargon, Français-Tirailleur, Hawaiian Pidgin, New South Wales Pidgin English, Plains Indian Sign, Tai Boy and Early Bislama all render light verb constructions with meanings such as 'to come', 'to go', 'to enter', 'to leave', 'to turn', 'to return', 'to kneel', 'to throw', 'to rush', or 'to rise'. Often, but not always, the dependent in the construction is a verb itself (*go, walk, enter*), and the construction could, thus, at least in some cases, be argued to be a serial verb construction. In e.g. Tai Boy, the construction meaning both 'to return' and 'to leave' is expressed by *faire divé* < Vietnamese *đi về*, 'to go back' – a verb phrase with both these meanings already in Vietnamese.

8.6.2 Context metonymies

As previously mentioned, the category of context metonymies is used by Riemer (2005: 182) to refer to "metonymic extensions to the context in which the action of the verb occurs". I take this to imply the larger context of the event; i.e. the whole frame (Koch 1999: 145–149; this volume) or the highest level idealised cognitive model within which the metonymy operates (Radden and Kövecses 1999: 19–21).

222 tokens or 36 % of all light verb constructions with MAKE/DO in the data have been analysed as context metonymies. Most of these are used within several subdomains of the domain Interpersonal relations and social interaction. The next sections discuss the use of context metonymies in the data.

8.6.2.1 Interpersonal relations and social interaction: Communication

Forms of both oral and written communication are often denoted by a context metonymy in the sense of a contiguity relation within a frame. As regards written communication, eight doculects denote writing by means of a MAKE/DO construction. The dependent in these is either the equivalent of *paper* (Chinook Jargon, Herschel Island Pidgin Eskimo, New South Wales Pidgin English, Sango, Tay Boi), *letter* (Français-Tirailleur, Early Bislama, Queensland Pidgin English) or *spots* (Chinook Jargon), and MAKE/DO 'newspaper' means publishing it in Chinook Jargon. Written communication is also at work when you sign something; in Early Bislama and Early Tok Pisin this is accomplished by MAKE/DO *mark*.

Creating new lexical items by giving them names or calling them something is accomplished by MAKE/DO 'name' in both Chinook Jargon and Early Bislama, whereas speakers of Govorka MAKE/DO 'riddles' and chatting is considered a pleasure in Sango (MAKE/DO 'pleasure').

8.6.2.2 Interpersonal relations and social interaction: Social order

Marriage is sometimes considered to be a corner stone of social organization. As already seen in example (3) above, Tay Boi, as also Gulf Pidgin Arabic, expresses the act of marrying by means of the light verb construction studied. In both languages there is some variation as to the dependent: it may be a 'girl/woman', a 'bride' or the 'wedding' itself, all elements of the marriage frame.

Seven of the doculects make use of the MAKE/DO construction in creating and maintaining social order by means of a context metonymy. Somebody may MAKE/DO 'trouble/problems' (Gulf Pidgin Arabic, Hawaiian Pidgin), perhaps by making enemies (MAKE/DO 'opponent', Français-Tirailleur) or because of cheating (MAKE/DO 'whore', Français-Tirailleur), be prosecuted and judged (MAKE/DO 'court house', Chinook Jargon), end up guarded (MAKE/DO 'guard', Fiji Pidgin Hindustani) and imprisoned (MAKE/DO 'jail house', Chinook Jargon), and, in the worst case scenario, no praying (MAKE/DO 'medicine', Plains Indian Sign) will save him from his funeral (MAKE/DO 'burial', Tay Boi).

8.6.2.3 Interpersonal relations and social interaction: Conflict

Only two pidgins in the corpus, Français-Tirailleur and Tay Boi, MAKE/DO 'war' in these data. MAKE/DO 'fight' is expressed also in Bislama, Chinook Jargon, New South Wales Pidgin English, Plains Indian Sign (MAKE DO 'strong medicine', cf. above in 8.6.2.2.), Early Tok Pisin and Early Bislama, and shooting is referred to in Chinook Jargon by one of the few dependents that denote the sound made by the action described by the construction (MAKE/DO *pooh*).

8.6.2.4 Miscellaneous

The corpus also includes examples of context metonymies in other domains, as already seen in example (5). Some more are worth mentioning: in Fiji Pidgin Hindustani you MAKE/DO 'eye' and in New South Wales Pidgin English and Queensland Pidgin English 'a light', 'to look, see' and in Chinook Jargon you MAKE/DO 'paddle', 'to paddle' or 'stick', 'to poke, dig'.

8.6.3 Constituent metonymies and metaphorical applications

I have not been able to identify any constituent metonymies in the corpus, but a group of 52 expressions are here considered to be metaphorical applications, i.e. cases where the verb is used of atypical referents. In many of the doculects in the corpus, MAKE/DO has 'to work' as one of its core meanings. You may thus work as a missionary (Early Bislama), a lawyer, a driver, a soldier, an electrician (Français-Tirailleur and Tay Boi) and so on. For example the following examples are here analysed as metaphorical applications of this meaning of the verb: MAKE/DO 'batman', 'Christian', 'deserter', (member of) 'institute' (Français-Tirailleur), MAKE/DO 'Catholic', 'liar', 'thief', 'leader' (Tay Boi) and 'Navaho' (MAKE/DO *striped blanket*, Plains Indian Sign). In these uses you do not work as a liar or a catholic, you rather are or become one.

8.6.4 Miscellaneous

Due to space limitations, it is not possible to account for each and every interesting example in the corpus. There is, however, one last group of 87 tokens that needs to be mentioned. This is a group of constructions that express the manner of the activity or event the verb phrase expresses, sometimes in a simile-like fashion, i.e. there is an explicit cross-domain comparison with comparative markers such as *like* or *fashion* (*Toujours ya faire manière ya pas arrêter son camarades*. 'He must never stop his comrades', literally 'MAKE/DO manner' in Français-Tirailleur), sometimes directly by evaluating the manner (MAKE/DO *bad*, 'misbehave', Chinook Jargon, Français-Tirailleur). These examples do not lend themselves easily to a unified classification in terms of metonymical extensions or metaphorical application. Due to time and space limitations, I will leave these examples for future analysis.

8.6.5 Summary of the results

Two thirds (21/32) of the doculects in the corpus were found to use light verb constructions with MAKE/DO. The majority of these uses (78 %) could be analysed in terms of effect metonymies and context metonymies of the basic meanings of the verb. However, as displayed in Table 2, these are unevenly distributed among the doculects studied.

Table 2 displays the number of types and tokens of metaphorical applications and metonymic shifts in the different doculects that rendered examples of the light verb construction studied. It also gives the number of words in the corpus and the relative frequency of the constructions in the doculects.

Table 2: Size of corpus, relative frequency and types and tokens of semantic shifts in the data.

Language/doculect	Words in corpus	Tokens /100 words	Effect type	Effect token	Context type	Context token	Manner type	Manner token	Metaphor type	Metaphor token	Type total	Token total
Bazaar Malay	14643	0,07512	8	10			1	1			9	11
Govorka	561	0,17825	1		1	1					1	1
Bislama	1609	0,18645	1	1	1	1	1	1			3	3
Sango	2869	0,24399	2	2	4	5					6	7
Hawaiian Pidgin	1520	0,26316	3	3	1	1					4	4
Early QLD Pidgin English	34735	0,28789	25	46	21	45	4	9			50	100
Primorye Pidgin Russian	678	0,44248	2	3							2	3
Chinese Pidgin English	219	0,45662					1	1			1	1
Early Bislama	10659	0,50661	17	24	7	23	3	6	1	1	28	54
Fiji Pidgin Hindustani	376	0,53191			2	2					2	2
Lingua do Preto	523	0,57361	3	3							3	3
Early Tok Pisin	1762	0,62429	6	8	3	3					9	11
Cape Pidgin Dutch	597	0,67002	3	3			1	1			4	4
Early NSW Pidgin English	8227	0,70499	17	28	3	28	1	1	1	1	22	58
Pidgin Delaware	393	0,76336	2	3							2	3
Tay Boi	9535	0,80755	20	28	12	14	7	14	13	21	52	77
Gulf Pidgin Arabic	1884	0,95541	6	7	7	11					13	18
Français-Tirallieur	11382	1,10701	26	31	12	31	10	35	15	29	63	126
Herschel Island Pidgin Eskimo	225	1,33333	1	1	2	2					3	3
Chinook Jargon	6822	1,45119	21	42	10	43	7	14			38	99
Plains Indian Sign	1058	2,93006	10	14	8	12	2	4	1	1	21	31
Total	110277		257		222		87		52		619	

The main findings of the present study can be summarised as follows:
1. Not all the pidgins studied make use of the light verb construction studied.
2. The languages that do make use of the construction:
    2.1. are distributed all over the world
    2.2. represent languages of varying lexical affiliation
    2.3. favour two types of metonymic shifts: effect metonymies and context metonymies
    2.4. do so unevenly, i.e. some doculects yield only a few examples, while others display plenty of them.

The next section discusses these findings and suggests a way to interpret them.

8.7 Discussion

The most general question asked in the beginning of this paper was how pidgin languages can make do with a vocabulary with less than two thousand lexical items, sometimes even less. One quite widely spread idea, besides polysemy, is that their exceptional analyticity is part of the answer. It is often quite easy to see how new meaning is composed in pidgin languages or, as one of the reviewers suggested, there seems to be a "tendency to transparent packaging" in pidgin languages. The reviewer also gave me a nice additional example of this tendency: in pidgin Bislama you may say *Klos we i luk olsem kras* 'clothes that look like grass' (i.e. 'camouflage'). Pidgin languages are indeed analytic, allow creativity in language use and are highly context sensitive. It is unlikely that an established word for 'camouflage' would be this long in any language variety with stability enough to develop into a creole, and, indeed, the anonymous reviewer has attested the word *kamuflas* in young creole speakers of Bislama.

The present paper offers a different, but possible (partial) answer to this question with regard to pidgin languages with different geographical distribution and lexical affiliation. The answer includes two different but, it is argued, interrelated processes: semantic shifts and grammaticalization.

The first major finding of the study is that only two thirds of the pidgin languages in the corpus studied made use of the verb MAKE/DO in light verb constructions. That not all the languages did so could of course depend on the different amounts of data available for analysis in the corpus. However, the 62 sentences in PaCo for Herschel Island Pidgin Eskimo contain several examples, whereas the 67 examples for Ndyuka-Trio Pidgin do not include a single one. The results are, thus, not necessarily explainable only with reference to the size of the sub-corpora, even if a balanced corpus would be desirable. This result may also depend on the fact that a single lexical item was chosen for the study. As mentioned in footnote 11, several of the studied languages make use of light verbs other than MAKE/DO. Hence, if several light verbs had been studied, the results could have been at least partly different.

Light verbs are also typically an areal feature of the world's languages. The present study has not specifically addressed this question, but it can be mentioned, that whereas the languages that are in contact with Gulf Pidgin Arabic favour light verb constructions, as does Gulf Pidgin Arabic, the languages of North America in contact with Chinook Jargon, a light verb-heavy pidgin, do not favour light verb constructions (Mithun 2010). Even though more in-depth studies are needed to this end, in light of the results of this study, contact with languages that host the construction do not automatically imply that a pidgin makes use of the construction. The occurrence or non-occurrence does, thus, not lend itself to be explained solely as replication on this general level (but see Heine and Kuteva 2005; 2010 for more specific level examples). Rather, the usage patterns described are best characterised either as idiomatic expressions or as grammaticalization – a question I will return to shortly.

The rest of the major findings concern languages that make use of the light verb construction. In 2.1 and 2.2 it was underlined, that the languages that make use of the MAKE/DO construction are geographically distributed all over the world and of differing lexical affiliation. This finding suggests that there is something in common in pidgin lexica. Typological studies of the kind conducted here can, thus, shed new light on the common traits in pidgin lexica.

The results show that effect metonymies and context metonymies together cover 78 % of all semantic shifts in the data (2.3) or, if we leave out the miscellaneous cases discussed in section 8.6.4., they cover 85 % of the cases. Only 52 or 8 % of all shifts were metaphorical applications; all of the type MAKE/DO 'Catholic/Christian/thief', attested in five of the languages (Early Bislama, Early New South Wales Pidgin English, Français-Tirailleur, Plains Indian Sign and Tay Boi). As argued in Marzo and Umbreit (this volume) in connection with the motivatedness and motivatability in the lexicon of French and Italian, this might be due to the relatively less cognitive load of relations that operate within one and the same frame (contiguity relations) as compared to relations that operate over different frames (metaphors). Hence, the most common metonymical extensions in these data may be the easiest and first to appear when constructions gain new uses.

The last major finding (in 2.4) is that the languages that make use of the MAKE/DO construction, do so to varying degrees. As the second column in Table 2. displays, the relative textual frequency of the light verb construction varies from very low in Bazaar Malay to quite high in Plains Indian sign. However, even though the corpus includes all data known for e.g. Herschel Island Pidgin Eskimo, the figures for languages with less than 1000 words analysed should be interpreted with great caution. For this reason, I will in what follows only refer to languages where texts with more than 1000 words have been available.

Also, only the five languages that also employ the light verb construction in metaphorical application give examples of all types of semantic shifts analysed. Chinook Jargon lacks examples of metaphorical application, but comes otherwise close in terms of both types and tokens of different semantic shifts attested in the corpus, followed by Gulf Pidgin Arabic and Early Tok Pisin. These languages also produce examples of the kind discussed above in 8.6.1.2, where the light verb combined with a verbal dependent could be interpreted either as a causative verb or an inchoative verb; as in MAKE/DO 'sleep'. It makes sense to mark the difference between sleeping and putting somebody to sleep – however, these pidgins are blurring the boundary. The meaning of the light verb has in these languages partly lost its original meaning and come to mark the status of the construction as a verb phrase – i.e. it has begun to grammaticalize as a verbalizer.

In grammaticalization, both the frequency and the functional range of the item grammaticalizing increases. Tables 1 and 2 suggest, that there is good reason to believe that these pidgins, i.e. Plains Indian Sign, Chinook Jargon, Français-Tirailleur, Gulf Pidgin Arabic, Tay Boi, Early New South Wales Pidgin English Pidgin English, Early Tok Pisin and Early Bislama, have indeed developed a category of a pro-verb (Heine and Kuteva 2005) or a verbalizer, that greatly expands the possibilities of making use of a minimal lexicon.

8.8 Concluding remarks

The kind of typological study conducted here suggests, that the patterns of polysemy in pidgin lexica may indeed be described in terms of metonymic semantic shifts and metaphorical applications. Further, I hope to have demonstrated that analysing the polysemy of a single lexical construction may indeed shed light on the question of lexicon-grammar interaction in pidgin languages, both from the point of view of lexical semantics and the point of view of grammaticalization.

8.9 References

Baker, Philip. 1993. Australian influence on Melanesian Pidgin English. *Te Reo* 36: 3–67.
Bakker, Peter. 2003a. The absence of reduplication in pidgins. In Silvia Kouwenberg (ed.), *Twice as meaningful. Reduplication in pidgins, ceoles, and other contact languages*, 37–46. [Westminster Creolistic Series 8]. London: Battlebridge.
Bakker, Peter. 2003b. Pidgin inflectional morphology and its implications for creole morphology. In Ingo Plag (ed.), *Yearbook of morphology 2002*, 3–33. [Special section on pidgins and creoles]. Dordrecht: Kluwer.
Bakker, Peter. 2009. Phonological complexity in pidgins. In Nicholas Faraclas and Thomas Klein (eds.), *Simplicity and complexity in creoles and pidgins*, 7–27. [Westminster Creolistics Series 10]. London: Battlebridge.
Bakker, Peter and Mikael Parkvall. 2013. Pidgins. In Peter Bakker and Yaron Matras (eds.), *Contact languages: A comprehensive guide*, 15–64. [Language Contact and Bilingualism Nr. 6.] Berlin: Mouton de Gruyter.
Booij, Geert E. 2002. Constructional idioms, morphology, and the Dutch lexicon. *Journal of Germanic Linguistics* 14: 301–329.
Butt, Miriam. 2003. The light verb jungle. *Harvard Working Papers in Linguistics* 9: 11–49.
Butt, Miriam. 2010. The light verb jungle: still hacking away. In Mengistu Amberber, Brett Baker, and Mark Harvey (Eds.), *Complex predicates: Cross-linguistic perspectives on event structure*, 48–78. Cambridge: Cambridge University Press.
Enfield, Nicholas J. 2006. Heterosemy and the grammar-lexicon trade-off. In Felix Ameka, Alan Dench, and Nicholas Evans (eds.), *Catching language: The standing challenge of grammar writing*, 1–24. Berlin: Mouton de Gruyter.
Family, Neiloufar. 2008. Mapping semantic spaces: A constructionist account of the "light verb" *xordæn* "eat" in Persian. In Martine Vanhove (ed.), *From polysemy to semantic change*, 139–161. Amsterdam & Philadelphia: Benjamins.
Gill, John Kaye. 1889. *Gill's Dictionary of the Chinook Jargon: With examples of use in conversation and notes upon tribes and tongues*. Portland, Oregon: J.K. Gill Company.
Grant, Anthony, P. 1996. The evolution of functional categories in Grand Ronde Chinook Jargon: ethnolinguistic and grammatical considerations. In Philip Baker and Anand Syea (eds.), *Changing meanings, changing functions. Papers relating to grammaticalization in contact languages*, 225–242. [Westminster Creolistics Series 2] London: University of Westminster Press.
Heine, Bernd. 1973. *Pidgin-Sprachen im Bantubereich*. [Pidgin languages in the *bantu area*.] [Kölner Beiträge zur Afrikanistik, vol. 3]. Berlin: Dietrich Heimer Verlag.
Heine, Bernd and Tania Kuteva. 2002. *World lexicon of grammaticalization*. Cambridge: Cambridge University Press.
Heine, Bernd and Tania Kuteva. 2005. *Language contact and grammatical change*. Cambridge: Cambridge University Press.
Heine, Bernd, and Tania Kuteva. 2010. Contact and grammaticalization. In Raymond Hickey (ed.), *The handbook of language contact*, 86–105. Singapore: Wiley-Blackwell.
Holm, John. 1989. *Pidgins and creoles*. Vol II. Cambridge: Cambridge University Press.
Holm, John. 2000. *Introduction to pidgins and creoles*. Cambridge: Cambridge University Press.
Jacobs, Melville. 1932. Notes on the structure of Chinook Jargon. *Language*, 8(1): 27–50.

Johnson, Samuel V. 1978. *Chinook Jargon: A computer assisted analysis of variation in an American Indian Pidgin.* Kansas City: University of Kansas Ph.D. dissertation.
Juvonen, Päivi. 2008. Complexity and simplicity in minimal lexica: the lexicon of Chinook Jargon. In Fred Karlsson, Matti Miestamo, and Kaius Sinnemäki (eds.), *Language complexity: Typology, contact, change,* 321–340. Amsterdam: John Benjamins.
Keesing, Roger M. 1988. *Melanesian Pidgin and the oceanic substrate.* Stanford, California: Stanford University Press.
Keesing, Roger M. 1991. Substrates, calquing and grammaticalization in Melanesian Pidgin. In Elizabeth Closs Traugott and Bernd Heine (eds.), *Approaches to grammaticalization, Vol. 1,* 315–42. [Typological Studies in Language]. Amsterdam & Philadelphia: John Benjamins.
Koch, Peter. 1999. Frame and Contiguity. In Klaus-Uwe Panther and Günter Radden (eds.), *Metonymy in language and thought,* 139–165. Amsterdam & Philadelphia: John Benjamins.
Koptjevskaja Tamm, Maria. 2008. Approaching lexical typology. In Martin Vanhove (ed.), *From polysemy to semantic change,* 3–52. Amsterdam & Philadelphia: John Benjamins.
Langacker, Ronald W. 2002. *Concept, image and symbol. The cognitive basis of grammar.* 2nd edn. Berlin/New York: Mouton de Gruyter.
Lehmann, Christian. 2012. Converse categorization strategies. *Linguistics* 50–3, 467–494.
Léra, Jean. 1896. *Tonkinoiseries. Souvenirs d'un officier.* Paris: H. Simonis Empis.
Liem, Nguyen Dang. 1979. Cases and verbs in pidgin French (Tay Boi) in Vietnam. *Papers in Pidgin and Creole Linguistics* 2: 217–246.
Liljegren, Henrik. 2010. Where have all the verbs gone? On verb stretching and semi-words in Indo-Aryan Palula. *Himalayan Linguistics,* Vol. 9(1): 51–79.
Mithun, Marianne. 2010. Contact and North American languages. In Raymond Hickey (ed.), *The handbook of language contact,* 673–694. Singapore: Wiley-Blackwell.
Mühlhäusler, Peter. 1997. *Pidgin and creole linguistics,* expanded and revised edition. London: University of Westminster Press.
Mühlhäusler, Peter. 2008. Multifunctionality in Pitkern-Norf'k and Tok Pisin. *Journal of Pidgin & Creole Languages.* 23(1): 75–113.
Nolly, Émile. 1908. *Hiên le Maboul.* Edinburgh: Nelson.
Nunberg, Geoffrey, Ivan A. Sag, and Thomas Wasow. 1994. Idioms. *Language* 70(3): 491–538.
Parkvall, Mikael. 1999. Feature selection and genetic relationships among Atlantic Creoles. In Magnus Huber and Mikael Parkvall (eds.). *Spreading the word. The issue of diffusion among the Atlantic Creoles.* [Westminster Creolistics Series – 6]. London: Battlebridge Publications.
Radden, Günter and Zoltán Kövecses. 1999. Towards a theory of metonymy. In Klaus-Uwe Panther and Günter Radden (ed.), *Metonymy in language and thought,* 17–59. Amsterdam & Philadelphia: John Benjamins.
Riemer, Nick. 2002. Verb polysemy and the vocabulary of percussion and impact in Central Australia. *Australian Journal of Linguistics* 22(1): 45–96.
Riemer, Nick. 2005. *The semantics of polysemy.* [Cognitive Linguistics Reasearch 30]. Berlin & New York: Mouton de Gruyter.
Roberts, Sarah and Joan Bresnan. 2008. Retained inflectional morphology in pidgins: A typological study. *Linguistic Typology* 12: 269–302.
Robertson, David. 2011. *Kamloops Chinuk Wawa, Chinuk pipa, and the vitality of pidgins.* Victoria, BC: University of Victoria PhD dissertation.
Schuchardt, Hugo. 1888. Kreolische Studien 8: Über das Annamito-Französische. *Sitzungsberichte der Wienische Akademie von Wissenschaften* 116 (1), 227–234.

Silverstein, Michael. 1972. Chinook Jargon: Language contact and the problem of multi-level generative systems. *Language* 48: 378–406.
Stubbs, Michael. 1986. *Educational linguistics*. Oxford: Blackwell.
Thomason, Sarah G. 1983. Chinook Jargon in areal and historical context. *Language* 59: 820–870.
Viberg, Åke, 1993. Crosslinguistic perspectives on lexical organization and lexical pro gression In Kenneth Hyltenstam and Åke Viberg (eds.), *Progression and regression in language*, 340–383. Cambridge: Cambridge University Press.
Wichmann, Sören and Jan Wohlgemuth. 2008. Loan verbs in a typological perspective. In Thomas Stolz, Dik Bakker, and Rosa Salas Palomo (eds.), *Empirical approaches to language typology: Aspects of language contact: New theoretical, methodological and empirical findings with special focus on romancisation processes*, 89–121. [Empirical Approaches to Linguistic Typology 35]. Berlin & New York: Mouton de Gruyter.

Susanne Vejdemo and Sigi Vandewinkel
9. Extended uses of body-related temperature expressions

Abstract: The chapter presents the results of a cross-linguistic study where we examined body-related temperature expressions (BRTEs), like "warm heart" and "cold eyes", in English, Ibibio, Japanese, Kannada, Mandarin Chinese, Ojibwe, and Swedish. We found that all the studied languages have BRTEs, even metaphor-poor Ojibwe, and that certain body related expressions recur in the BRTEs, mostly 'heart', 'head', 'voice', 'smile' and 'eyes'. We found support for two conceptual metaphors: CONTROL IS COLD/LACK OF CONTROL IS HOT and CARING IS WARM/UNCARING IS COLD. The temperature scales were found to be translated to scalar target domains, mostly emotions. However, we found little support for the hypothesis that local cultural/climate factors, such as the temperature related humoral theory or the mean temperature of a region, would affect the BRTEs.

9.1 Introduction[1]

> 'A warm heart is important in love, but a cool head is better in this sort of work.' The old conundrum emerged into my consciousness: Which is best? Cold heart and hot head, cold heart and cold head, hot heart and cold head or hot heart and hot head? Or should we avoid the extremes of hot and cold, and deal only with warm and cool? (Craig 2003: 77)

This quote, taken from a crime novel, introduces the reader to a great number of hearts and heads of different temperatures, and invites us to consider which combination of the associated attitudes and mental skills is most desirable. English speakers know that it is possible to have a metaphorical *hot head* or a *cool head* – but rarely a *cold head* or a *warm head*. You can have a *warm heart*, or a *cold heart*,

---

[1] We are grateful to the comments and corrections suggested by two anonymous referees, without which this paper would not be half the paper it is. Any remaining errors and inaccuracies are entirely the authors' responsibility. This study was funded by Maria Koptjevskaja-Tamm's project *Hot or Cold: Universal or Language-Specific?* which is supported by a grant from the Swedish Scientific Council *Vetenskapsrådet* 2009–2011.

Susanne Vejdemo and **Sigi Vandewinkel** (Stockholm university)

but typically not a *hot heart*. Yet in the context above, *cold head* and *hot heart* can be understood for a competent English speaker. The passage above becomes nearly incomprehensible, however, without a thorough unconscious grounding in the way temperature and body parts interact in English metaphors.

This paper will focus on combinations such as *warm heart* and *cold feet*, which we will term "body-related temperature expressions" (henceforth BRTEs). They are interesting from a metaphor studies point of view, because they are in the intersection of two areas, temperature and body-related expressions, that are fundamental to the human experience of the world and provide the source domains for many metaphors in different languages. We will discuss the conceptual, cultural and linguistic motivations for the BRTEs based on a small survey done with speakers of seven languages: English, Ibibio, Japanese, Kannada, Mandarin Chinese, Ojibwe, and Swedish, and we will suggest two conceptual metaphors that underlie conceptualization in all languages involved: these are CONTROL IS COLD/LACK OF CONTROL IS HOT and CARING IS WARM/UNCARING IS COLD. While a great deal of care must be taken with the results of any study done with so few languages, several interesting tendencies can be noted in the data, indicating that this is a promising area for further research. Furthermore, small though this study may be, it also aims at going beyond incidental citations from a handful of languages, striving to present a larger measure of systematic typological support for its claims than has until now been the case.

To be sure, the conceptual metaphors that we propose here are not new to the literature (see Section 9.3). Similar suggestions have been put forward and are well-known in the literature, such as A DROP IN BODY TEMPERATURE STANDS FOR FEAR (Kövecses 2000a: 5; Deignan and Potter 2005: 1241); HOSTILITY IS COLD (Shindo 1998: 41; Shindo 2009: 106); AFFECTION IS WARMTH (Grady 1997: 293; Shindo 1998: 41; Lakoff and Johnson 1999: 50; Rasulić 2015: 272; Shindo 2010: 1); COLD IS EMOTIONALLY UNRESPONSIVE (Grady 2005: 1599; our formulation); INTENSITY OF EMOTION IS HEAT (Kövecses 2000a: 41), to name just a few. Rather, the contribution of this paper is intended to be methodological, i.e. an empirical confirmation of conceptual metaphors suggested in the literature. While previous studies often have focused on one particular emotion (such as ANGER and how this is conveyed in terms of heat) or have drawn their examples from a single language (mainly English) supported by more or less incidental citations from Japanese, Finnish, Spanish or Wolof, this dataset, with its systematic combination of basic temperature items with a body part or body-related item, can offer more robust cross-linguistic support.

While it would certainly be worthwhile to study all expressions using temperature as a source domain, this study is specifically limited to semantically extended uses of temperatures attributed to particular body-related expressions such as *she is a hothead* or *his is a warm smile*. We will present data on the body parts *head, eye, hand, heart* (or heart-like organ), and *liver*. We will also discuss other body-related expressions, such as *voice, smile* and *gaze*. We will limit ourselves to temperature expressions that only express the temperature states (*cold, hot* etc.) and disregard temperature expressions that have additional semantic content (e.g. *boiling, freezing*). In addition, we only investigate temperature expressions that are attributive or predicative of the body-related noun.

We will not discuss whether the non-literal interpretations of BRTEs involve metonymies or metaphors, or indeed metaphtonymies (Geeraerts 2002) or metaphorical metonymies (Kövecses 2000a). We will use metaphor as a cover term and treat it, for the purposes of this paper, as synonymous to the term "semantically extended interpretation."

This paper is structured as follows: The next section (Section 9.2) lists the research questions around which this study is organized. Section 9.3 briefly reviews some of the literature on BRTEs. Specifically, we will consider temperature as an incidental source domain for specific target domains (Section 9.3.2) and as a specific source domain for a variety of target domains (Section 9.3.1). In Section 9.3.3, we address the scalar nature of temperature scales and their projections onto other domains. In Section 9.3.4 we turn to proposed motivations for cross-linguistic similarities and differences.

Section 9.4 introduces the methods and the languages of the study. Section 9.5 presents the results, focusing on BRTEs from several languages which we argue are motivated by the same two conceptual metaphors. We also discuss the potential effects of culture and climate as motivations for BRTEs. Finally, in Section 9.6, we summarize our findings and suggest several directions for future research.

9.2 Hypotheses

We shall be working with four research hypotheses:
1. Metaphorical BRTEs, that is, combinations of a body part (or a body-related expression like *smile*) with a temperature term to convey a non-literal meaning, are common to all human languages;

2. Some body-related expressions will tend to recur as vehicles for temperature-based emotion metaphors while others will be systematically absent or otherwise underrepresented;[2]
3. Certain conceptual metaphors will recur throughout the languages of our study. A corollary to this is that we will expect temperature scales to be translated, in part or *in toto*, to potentially scalar target domains, such as emotions;
4. Where the data cannot be explained by appealing to conceptual metaphors, an explanation can be sought in climate, or some other language- or culturally-specific factor, as an interfering/competing dynamic.

9.3 Background

The metaphors that are most likely to be found cross-linguistically are those whose source domains reflect fundamental and important experiences in human life. Orientational metaphors – where the source domain is spatial – are particularly clear examples of this (Lakoff and Johnson 1980: 15), as are ontological metaphors, where experiences are likened to physical objects (Lakoff and Johnson 1980: 30). Kövecses (2005: 3) talks about primary metaphors: "To learn [...] "primary" metaphors is not a choice for us: It happens unconsciously and automatically. [...] In other words, universal primary experiences produce universal primary metaphors."

It would seem, then, that BRTEs, containing elements of two basic and likely universal semantic domains, provide a fruitful area for further typological and metaphorical research.

9.3.1 Temperature as a source domain

Several researchers have examined temperature as a source domain and investigated which different target domains it can map onto. Lehrer (1970) discusses static and dynamic elements in the semantics of the English terms *hot*, *warm*, *cool* and *cold*. She writes that the field of emotional sensations that these word

---

[2] While we do not assume that the target domains of these combinations always are emotions, we note that emotions have often been brought up in the literature as cross-linguistically appearing results of BRTEs (cf. e.g. Lakoff 1987: 406ff and Kövecses 2000b: 164–166).

can be used for can be subdivided into several categories like anger or excitement, sexual passion and friendliness or cordiality (arguments and discussions.) Another category, which Lehrer (1970: 353) calls a parameter rather than a category, is the association between *hot* and involvement and strong feelings, and *cold* with non-involvement and lack of feeling. This also means that if a feeling is mapped onto a temperature lexeme (e.g. friendliness onto warmth), the antonym of the temperature lexeme can be metaphorically mapped onto the antonym of the temperature lexeme (unfriendliness onto cold).

This line of thought is taken up in Shindo (1998), who presents several conceptual metaphors with temperature as the source domain. A physiology-based metonymy, in which many emotions are associated with a physical increase in body temperature, leads to the conceptual metaphor EMOTIONS ARE HEAT. Realizations of this more general metaphor are ANGER IS HEAT; JEALOUSY IS HEAT; A GREAT IMPRESSION IS HEAT; DESIRE IS HEAT. Another different conceptual metaphor with temperature as source domain that Shindo addresses is POSSESSION IS WARMTH, exemplified in submetaphors like RICHNESS IS WARMTH; AFFECTION IS WARMTH; COMFORT IS WARMTH. This metaphor is also ultimately metonymical since, according to Shindo, retaining body heat means being covered with something and thus possessing it. A third type of extended expressions with temperature as source domain is metonymies based on concrete experiences. Since heat is dangerous to humans, the metonymy HEAT STANDS FOR DANGER is intuitive, and since cooked food is hot, so is the metonymy HEAT STANDS FOR FRESHNESS.

Lehrer thus suggested ANGER/EXCITEMENT, SEXUAL PASSION, and FRIENDLINESS/CORDIALITY as target domains for the temperature source domain in English. Shindo added JEALOUSY and the feeling of (making a) GREAT IMPRESSION. Kövecses added LOVE, CURIOSITY, DESIRE and AMBITION (ambition: *Behind his soft-spoken manner, the fires of ambition burned;* curiosity / desire: *Dan burned to know what the reason could be* etc.), and suggested the conceptual metaphor of A DROP IN BODY TEMPERATURE IS FEAR (*he had cold feet* 'he was afraid') (Kövecses 2000a: 81). For later research into temperature as a source domain, see also Bergström (2010), Juvonen and Nikunlassi (2015) and Rasulić (2015).

9.3.2 Temperature as one of several source domains for a particular target domain

Many of the extant studies on metaphorical interpretations of temperature expressions focus mostly on individual target domains. A particularly productive domain is the emotion of anger. Lakoff and Kövecses (1987: 196–198) write about the cognitive model of anger inherent in American English, discussing such conceptual metaphors as ANGER IS THE HEAT OF A FLUID IN A CONTAINER (*you make my blood boil* 'you make me angry') and the more general conceptual metaphor THE PHYSIOLOGICAL EFFECTS OF AN EMOTION STAND FOR THE EMOTION.

Geeraerts and Grondelaers (1995), however, point out that just because there seems to be an embodied conceptualization – a link between the emotional state and a physiological temperature effect, such as a person feeling warmer when they are angry – that does not necessarily mean that this effect corresponds to a psychological reality. In English, expressions like *to make one's blood boil*, could be taken as evidence that contemporary speakers have a conceptual link between being angry and being hot, but it could also be the case that the boiling blood is instead an obsolete metaphor for the humoral doctrine: a prescientific medical theory that, among other things, linked temperature to certain body parts and certain emotions. Kövecses (1995: 198 ff.) acknowledges this, and uses more cross-linguistic data (from Japanese, Chinese, Hungarian, Tahitian and Wolof) to make the case that, regardless of culture, there is still a widespread tendency to link anger and high temperatures. The conceptualization of anger is not necessarily that of a fluid in a container: in Chickasaw *sa-palli* means 'I am hot' and 'I am angry', to give just a single example (Kövecses 1995: 194).

Several authors continued the discussion of cross-cultural differences and similarities with anger as a target domain – Yu (1995) contrasts English with Chinese, and Matsuki (1995) compares English and Japanese. Both these authors recognize the cross-cultural importance that temperature plays in the conceptualizations of anger, while also pointing out language-specific differences, particularly in which parts of the body anger is situated. Kövecses (2000b:169) continues the discussion, concluding that "anger is both (near) universal and culture-specific." He refers to this as "body-based social constructionism" because it connects both the recognition of universal elements of the body (human physiology) and culture-specific elements of cultural explanation. Apart from the humoral theory, Kövecses addresses several other culturally different takes on anger and temperature, so that while Hungarian and English share the conceptual metaphor ANGER IS FIRE, in Hungarian this is commonly elaborated as the body being a pipe with a burning substance inside (Kövecses 2000b: 216). Following Yu and Matsuki, Kövecses also notes that different cultures locate anger in different body parts: to mention two examples, Japanese associates anger with the belly while Zulu associates it with the heart (Kövecses 2000b: 216).

9.3.3 The scalarity feature of the temperature domain

A scalar correspondence was implied in Lehrer (1970), in which high temperatures map onto high emotions, and low temperatures onto lack of emotions. This is explicitly stated in Shindo (1998), who adds that this is one of the reasons that temperature is such a useful source domain: since temperature expressions originally have a built-in quantitative scales, they can easily reflect several different levels of intensity in an abstract concept (1998: 39). The scalarity feature is also discussed at length in Kövecses (2000: 143 ff.) who suggests such conceptual metaphors as THE HIGHEST DEGREE OF INTENSITY IS THE HIGHEST DEGREE OF HEAT (fire) (as in e.g. *the president launched his anti-drugs campaign in a blaze of publicity)*, and CHANGE OF INTENSITY IS A CHANGE OF HEAT (as in e.g. *he has been advised to take a long family holiday to take the heat off the scandal.*)

Consider the following example:

HAPPY IS WARM/SADNESS IS A LACK OF HEAT
(1) English
That warmed my spirits.
Losing his father put his fire out; he's been depressed for two years.
(Kövecses 2000a: 24–25)

In (1), the antonymic/oppositional target domain of HAPPINESS – SADNESS is structured by a mapping from an equally antonymic WARM – COLD schema. The inherently positive emotion in this target domain in English (i.e. happiness) is associated with warmth, while the inherently negative emotion (i.e. sadness) is associated with coldness (Kövecses 2000a: 44).

Several such scales (warm to cold, hot to cool) may exist alongside one another, all using temperature as a source domain. Certain metaphors may also only activate a sub-stretch of a temperature scale as a source domain (e.g. using only the cooling temperature range), or, indeed, the scale in its entirety (using both cooling and warming ranges). Take for instance the structure of the target domains ANGER and LUST. A great deal of anger and a great deal of lust is seen as hot in English (Kövecses 2000a). A better, more general, metaphor for these target domains could perhaps be said to be VOLATILE DESTRUCTIVE INTENSE FEELING IS HOT (suggested by Shindo 1998) or INTENSE AROUSAL IS HOT. By extension, this sanctions describing the opposites of these intense feelings as *cold*, as in (2) and (3).

LUST IS HEAT/LACK OF LUST IS COLD
(2) English
S/he's got a hot body.
S/he's frigid.
(Introspection)

VOLATIVE ANGER IS HEAT/CALMNESS IS COOL
(3) English
He is a real hothead.
He should keep his head cool.
(Introspection)

But calmness is not the only opposite of volatile anger; another option is non-volative, quiet anger. Thus speakers can also use the following expression:

VOLATIVE ANGER IS HEAT / CALM ANGER IS COLD
(4) English
He was filled with a cold rage.
(Introspection)

A cold rage is a rage which does not lead the person to act out, scream or hit something, which are otherwise actions associated with volative anger.

Note that the two last scales end in different temperature terms – cool and cold respectively. Rasulić (2015) compares English and Serbian temperature metaphors, and notes that the cooling range is used for quantitative aspects of the target domain – different levels of intensity of emotion – while the warming range is not. Rather, warm and hot have qualitative differences, and can indeed be used as endpoints for different kinds of conceptual metaphors; distinctions on the cooling range, by contrast, may be employed to introduce further nuances. An example of this in English is how friendliness can be expressed with *warm* but not *hot* smiles or words; and how a less intense version of a *hot-head* cannot be described as a **warm-head*. By contrast, a cool smile (in a negative sense) and a cold smile show a difference in intensity of unfriendliness.

9.3.4 Motivations for crosslinguistic similarities and differences

We have seen that various authors have found evidence for cross-linguistically recurring conceptual temperature related metaphors. Among others, Yu (1995) has examples from Chinese; Matsuki (1995) and Shindo (1998, 2000) from Japanese; Kövecses (2000a) from Hungarian, Tahitian, Wolof, Chickasaw; Rasulić (2015) from Serbian; Juvonen and Nikunlassi (2015) from Finnish.

A prevalent cross-linguistic tendency is the use of body parts in combination with temperature expressions. Like Shindo (1998) and Kövescses (2000a) we believe that the cross-linguistic similarities found in BRTEs are due to temperature sensations being grounded in shared human physiology, while the differences can be motivated by external factors like maybe culture and climate. It is not so easy to demonstrate a link between perceived bodily temperature and any emotions that could be connected to this, but Zhong and Leonardelli (2008) managed to show, through experiments, a link between the subjective feeling of a drop in body temperature and increased feelings of loneliness. Similarly a subjective experience of an increase of body temperature is associated by participants with inclusion and friendship. Shindo (1998) connects increase in body temperature with feelings of anger, joy and/or love, while a drop in body temperature is connected with fear (see Table 1).

Table 1: Some suggested connections between physiological perceptions and emotions from Shindo (1998) and Zhong and Leonardelli (2008)

Physiological effect	Emotion	Reference
Increase in body temperature	Anger, joy, love	Shindo (1998)
Drop in body temperature	Fear	Shindo (1998)
Subjective feeling of a drop in body temperature	Loneliness	Zhong and Leonarcelli (2008)
Subjective feeling of increase of body temperature	Inclusion, friendship	Zhong and Leonarcelli (2008)

In a recent study, Nummenmaa et al. (2014) ran five experiments with over 700 speakers of Swedish, Finnish, and Taiwanese. Regardless of language family or cultural background, speakers named the same (overlapping) areas of the body as being activated or deactivated when emotional words, stories, movies or facial expressions were encountered. The authors conclude that "emotional feelings are associated with discrete, yet partially overlapping maps of bodily sensations, which could be at the core of the emotional experience" (Nummenmaa et al. 2014: 5) (See also Maalej and Yu [2011] and Sharifian et al. [2008]).

If the perception of an increase or decrease in body temperature when experiencing emotions of anger, loneliness or love is a physiological universal, metaphors based on temperature expressions reflecting this would be likely to appear in many languages.

Kövecses (2000a: 169) mentions the possibility that there is a small chance that similarities found across languages may be due to chance or language contact and not based on shared physiological and physical surroundings. We agree with him that chance and language contact can never be completely excluded as reasons, but that the more we analyze diverse languages, the stronger the argument is for an embodied conceptualized physiology as the reason for the recurring metaphors.

If our shared bodies is a recurrent hypothesis in the literature for the crosslinguistic similarities in metaphorical meanings of BRTEs, then our different cultures have often been suggested as the source for the crosslinguistic differences. Separate cultures have developed distinct ways of talking and thinking about the interplay between temperatures, physiological sensations, and various aspects of the human condition, such as emotions (see e.g. Kövecses 2000b: 167ff). Metaphorically interpreted BRTEs in these communities can be linked to, for instance, cultural perceptions and folk explanations associated with particular emotions, or the locate climate. For instance, Shindo points out that the seat of particular emotions in body parts is most likely culturally determined and thus varies:

> ... heat in some part of the body is often expressed in order to designate an emotion. We can assert that a part of the body represents excitement caused by an emotion. The commonly expressed part which is considered to be the place most easily affected by each emotion is decided by each culture (Shindo 1998: 42).

An example of a language-specific seat of emotion is the Japanese metaphor related to controlling anger: as *hara* 'anger' intensifies, it rises from the stomach to the chest and culminates in the head (as cited in Kövecses 2000b: 163). Some BRTEs will have metaphorical interpretations that are harder to link directly to a physiological reaction, such as the Japanese conceptual metaphor RICHNESS IS WARMTH/POVERTY IS COLD, as in (5) below.

(5) Japanese
Kyou   wa   futokoro   ga   atatakai / samui
Today   TOP   breast   SUBJ   warm   / cold
'Today my breast is warm / cold' (Lit.)
'Today I'm rich / poor' (Metaph.)
(Shindo 1998: 17)

One potential factor for mapping emotions onto temperature terms is folk medicine and received cultural notions about the temperature of body parts (regardless of their empirical-scientific value). Geeraerts and Grondelaers (1995) show that the Hippocratic humoral theory of medicine, which links temperature variation in different body parts with different moods and illnesses, is strongly connected to several west European metaphorical BRTEs. Similar theories have been historically very important globally, and may have influenced BRTEs in English, Swedish, Kannada and Mandarin Chinese – to name just the languages featured in this paper; the system is still actively used, among speakers of Kannada and Chinese.

A second local factor that might be expected to motivate BRTEs is the environment and the prevailing climate. Al-Abed Al-Haq and El-Sharif's (2008) comparative study on metaphors involving happiness and anger in Arabic and English brings up metaphors with temperature as source domain. The authors find evidence for an underlying conceptual metaphor HAPPINESS IS A COLD/FROZEN FLUID IN A CONTAINER. Other metaphors for happiness in Arabic involve rain and clouds – and Al-Abed Al-Haq and El-Sharif (2008) take this to indicate that it is the typical climatic environment that Arabic is spoken in – one where intense heat is a problem and water is scarce – that is the underlying reason for the metaphors: in Arabic the cooling temperature range is sometimes associated with positive emotions. They contrast them with English metaphors, typically (but not exclusively) spoken in much colder climates. Perrin (2015) likewise suggests a connection with the local climate for Wolof (spoken in Senegal where the temperature never sinks below 17 degrees Celsius) and the fact that expressions with cold temperatures are generally positive – the author contrasts this with French (spoken mainly in France where temperatures can go below 0 degrees Celsius) where cold expressions can be perceived as both positive and negative.

Pre-empting our results, we find that the great majority of metaphorically interpreted BRTEs brought up in this paper have emotions as target domains. This lets us use the body-based social constructionism developed by Kövecses (2000a) to reconcile both the potentially universal and language particular metaphorical evidence. The approach acknowledges both the cross-linguistically universal and the culture-specific in emotion language, concluding that "some aspects of emotion language and emotion concepts are universal and clearly related to the physiological functioning of the body. Once the universal aspects [...] are parsed out, the very significant remaining differences in emotion language and concepts can be explained by reference to differences in cultural knowledge." (Kövecses 2000a: 183).

9.4 Data and data collection

This study is based on elicited data from seven languages: English, Ibibio, Japanese, Kannada, Mandarin Chinese, Ojibwe, and Swedish. The details of the elicitation process will be presented in Section 9.4.1. Section 9.4.2 will summarize the relevant data about each language and the informants.

9.4.1 Elicitation

The elicitation was performed in two steps. The first step was to establish a likely list of basic and frequent temperature terms in the source languages. For this a simplified version of the temperature elicitation questionnaire developed by Koptjevskaja-Tamm (2007) was used.

In a second step the names for the various body parts were elicited from the informants, through pointing and naming of the body-related expression by the researchers; these were: head, mind/brain, eye(s), gaze/look, back, spine, breast/torso, hand, finger(s), stomach, nose, mouth, voice, smile, person, liver, heart, leg(s), foot, and toe. Next, using a specially designed questionnaire, each elicited body part was combined with all of the temperature terms (e.g. *head* with *hot*, *head* with *warm* etc.) and speakers were asked if it was possible to talk about this body-related expression being or having the temperature indicated and having the combination mean something more than just this body part being of the specified temperature. To anticipate potential misunderstandings, specific examples from English were provided, such as *warm heart* meaning 'someone who is kind'. The metalanguage throughout was English; all speakers were competent speakers of the metalanguage, and already knew the meanings of the English extended expressions used as examples.

Direct elicitation in this manner was done with speakers of Kannada, Ibibio, Ojibwe, English and Mandarin Chinese. Indirect elicitation, through email, was done for Japanese. The Swedish data was gathered through introspection, since one of the authors is a native speaker of Swedish. The elicitation phase of the project thus involved collecting new data from some languages, viz. Ibibio, Kannada and Ojibwe, which previously have seen very little work done on semantically extended expressions.

It must be mentioned that English, both as a metalanguage and as a language all of the informants spoke with (at least) some fluency, may have influenced our informants' judgments. Furthermore, the Native American language Ojibwe has had a long history of cultural influence from the English- and French-speaking communities in the US and Canada (for more on both the social situation for

Ojibwe speakers and the Ojibwe temperature terminology, see Lockwood and Vejdemo (2015).) We have not pursued these possible confounders any further, since that would require additional experimental setups and a shift of focus that would lead us far outside the scope of our stated goals.

9.4.2 The languages

This study comprises data from seven languages, summarized in Table 2 below.

Table 2: Languages and temperature terms in this study. Japanese is written with Romaji orthography; Chinese in Pinyin orthography; and Ojibwe in the "double vowel" orthography system, or, for elicited material, in IPA[3]

Language [Family]	Temperature terms
English [Germanic]	1. *hot* 2. *warm* 3. *lukewarm* 4. *cool* 5. *cold*
Ibibio [Benue-Congo]	1. *afjup* 'hot' or *ajeye* 'hot' 2. *mmèmé* 'warm' 3. *ndedeŋ* 'cold and damp' or *adeŋe* 'cold'
Japanese [Isolate]	1. *atsui* 'hot' 2. *atatakai* 'warm' 3. *nurui* 'lukewarm' 4. *tsumetai* 'cold [felt with entire body]' or *samui* 'cold [felt with part of the body]'
Kannada [Dravidian]	1. *bisi* 'hot' or *cheke* 'hot' 2. *betʃige* 'warm' 3. *tannege* 'cold' or *cheliaktajde* 'cold'
Mandarin Chinese [Sinitic]	1. *re4* 'hot' 2. *wen1 nuan3* 'warm' or *nuan3 huo5* 'warm' 3. *liang2* 'cool' 4. *leng3* 'cold'

---

[3] The elicitation data for Ojibwe were further supplemented with material from Weshki-ayaad et al. (2009).

Tab. 2 (continued)

Language [Family]	Temperature terms
Eastern Ojibwe (Anishinaabemowin) [Algonquian]	1. *gzh-* 'hot' 2. *gishoo-* 'warm' 3. *dk-* 'cold'[4]
Swedish [Germanic]	1. *het* 'hot' 2. *varm* 'warm' 3. *ljummen* 'lukewarm' 4. *kylig* 'cool' or *sval*[5] 'cool' 5. *kall* 'cold'

The languages are, with the exception of the Germanic languages Swedish and English, from different language families, and they are also spoken in different climates.

There has been some scholarly debate over whether Algonquian languages have metaphors at all. Markey (1985) claims that Algonquian languages in general lack conscious metaphors, and so do several speakers that we have met. This is contested by Rhodes (1985), who acknowledges that the number of metaphors in the Algonquian language Ojibwe is limited but that they do exist. Even in languages with relatively few metaphors, embodied, orientational and perception metaphors show up (Lakoff and Johnson 1980: 15). At any rate, if metaphor-poor Ojibwe is found to feature any extended uses of body part temperature expressions at all we would take this as support for the very basic role that temperature plays in our categorization of the world.

---

[4] There are basic morphosyntactic characteristics which reveal a distinction between tactile temperature terms, which are used for temperatures perceived by a part of the body, and non-tactile temperature terms which are perceived by the whole body. For the purposes of this study we will disregard these differences.

[5] There are some lexical restrictions on which headwords the adjectives *kylig* and *sval* can be used with, but a detailed discussion of this lies outside the scope of this chapter (but see Koptjevskaja-Tamm and Rakhilina 2006).

9.5 Analysis and results

In this section we discuss whether and to what extent our research hypotheses as listed in Section 9.2 are borne out by the data. This will be done in three steps. First, Section 9.5.1 takes up hypothesis three, that certain conceptual metaphors employ temperature scales as proxies for scalar expressions (e.g. emotions). Two such metaphors are shown to be supported by the data: Emotional control vs. lack of emotional control (Section 9.5.1.1); and caring vs. uncaring (Section 9.5.1.2).

Section 9.5.2 takes up hypothesis four, and consider whether at least some portions of the data can be accounted for by three culturally-specific factors, i.e. the humoral folk theory of medicine (9.5.2.1); age and gender (9.5.2.2); and climate[6] (9.5.2.3).

Finally, the other two hypotheses – dealing with the questions of (near-) universality and the cross-linguistic (dis)preference for certain body parts as BRTES – are dealt with in Section 9.6.1: they are more general in nature, and responses to them will only emerge through the discussions of hypotheses three and four.

9.5.1 Scales and conceptual metaphors

The data gathered for this study show support for two cross-linguistically recurring conceptual metaphorical interpretation of BRTES: LACK OF EMOTIONAL CONTROL IS HOT/EMOTIONAL CONTROL IS COLD; and FRIENDLY IS WARM/UNFRIENDLY IS COLD. The languages where the conceptual metaphors were found differ in how much of the scales are used.

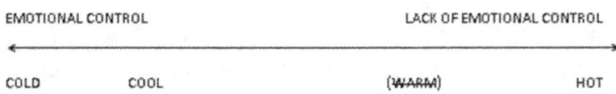

Figure 1: Emotional control and temperature

The first semantically extended temperature scale that our dataset offers empirical support for is one where a temperature scale going from either cold or cool to hot is projected onto the emotional opposites of emotional control versus lack of emotional control (see Figure 1). This temperature scale does not incorporate

---
6 This factor is culturally specific in our dataset, where no clear sets of languages/cultures can be distinguished based on a shared climate.

the temperature state warm. Not all languages exploit the scalarity to contrast the two emotional opposites with the temperature opposites; some only use one end of this scale.

Secondly, we can also provide empirical support for a semantically extended temperature scale going from cold or cool to warm, which is conceptually projected onto the emotional opposites of unfriendly, uncaring and unkind on the one hand, and friendly, caring and kind on the other (see Figure 2). This temperature scale typically does not incorporate hot, a more intense heat than warm. Furthermore, not all languages use the scalarity (i.e. map temperature opposites onto emotional opposites); some only use one end of this scale.

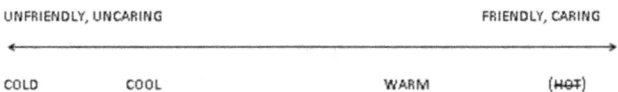

UNFRIENDLY, UNCARING			FRIENDLY, CARING	
COLD	COOL		WARM	(HOT)

Figure 2: (Un)friendliness and temperature

We will now discuss the cross-linguistic data for these scales in more detail.

9.5.1.1 Emotional control and lack of emotional control

It has been suggested (Lakoff 1987) that the lack of control associated with heat can be traced to the lack of control over and the danger of a boiling hot liquid – we see this in the well-known conceptual metaphor ANGER IS THE HEAT OF A FLUID IN A CONTAINER (Geeraerts 2006: 241). But dangerous things besides anger are associated with high temperatures, like stolen goods being described as *hot* in English, and dangerous and threatening circumstances associated with hot in Japanese. Thus it might be useful to posit a higher conceptual metaphor: LACK OF CONTROL IS HOT. The opposite of lack of control, the actual control, is often seen represented by "cool" or "cold".

English as well as Mandarin Chinese and Ibibio project the emotional scale between being in emotional control to lacking emotional control onto a scale going from cold to hot (but not including warm). English and Mandarin Chinese use the body part head, while Ibibio uses heart. Swedish uses only the colder part of the scale together with head to indicate calmness and rationality. In contrast, Kannada uses only the hotter part of the scale together with head to indicate someone being upset and stressed out, but does not use the colder part of the scale. Likewise, Japanese uses the hotter part of the scale for anger (head) and passion (heart).

Illustrative examples for the body parts head and heart, where an opposition in temperature is mapped onto an opposition in emotional control, have been provided in Table 3. For the sake of completeness, the relevant data from all languages have been included: greyed-out cells indicate that we were unable to find any metaphorical interpretation of the particular temperature state + body-related expression at all.

Table 3: Some examples of the mapping of temperature scales onto (lack of) emotional control for *head* and *heart*. n/a indicates that there were no expressions in the language that matched the conceptual metaphor under scrutiny – for example, there is no expression in English where *warm head* or *warm heart* means 'lack of emotional control.'

Head/heart	cooling range		warming range	
	COLD	COOL	WARM	HOT
English	n/a	HEAD: calm	n/a	HEAD: angry
M. Chinese	HEAD: calm	n/a	n/a	HEAD: impulsive
Ibibio	HEART: calm	n/a	n/a	HEART: angry
Swedish	HEAD: rational, composed	n/a	n/a	n/a
Japanese	n/a	n/a	n/a	HEAD: angry / HEART: passionate
Kannada	n/a	n/a	n/a	HEAD: upset, stressed out
Ojibwe	n/a	n/a	n/a	n/a

Head and *heart* were almost the only body parts found in the data with this metaphorical interpretation, and *head* is the more common one; an additional example of the pattern exists for *voice*.

We will now proceed to discuss some individual examples.

The examples in (6) and (7) show that a 'cold/hot head' in Mandarin Chinese is associated with emotional control and impulsiveness, respectively; and the ones in (8) and (9) show that the opposition 'cold/hot heart' in Ibibio corresponds to an opposition in (lack of) emotional control.

(6) Mandarin Chinese
 tou2nao3 leng3 jing4
 head.brain cold quiet
 'Brain is cold and quiet.' (Lit.)
 'To be calm.' (Metaph.)
 (Elicitation)

(7) Mandarin Chinese
 tou2nao3 fa1 re4
 head.brain become hot
 'The head becomes hot.' (Lit.)
 'Become impulsive; you feel regret afterwards.' (Metaph.)
 (Elicitation)

(8) Ibibio
 a-dèŋè ésìt
 3SG-be.cold heart-kidney
 'S/he has a cold heart-kidney.'
 'S/he is a calm person.'
 (Elicitation)

(9) Ibibio
 úfjóp úfjóp ésìt
 be.hot be.hot heart-kidney
 'S/he has a hot heart-kidney.'
 'S/he is easily angered.' (Metaph.)
 (Elicitation)

The combination of hot and head metaphorically stands for anger in Japanese, and for a similar out-of-control negative emotion in Kannada; examples are provided in (10) and (11), respectively.

(10) Japanese
 Atama-ga katto atsuku-na-tta
 Head-NOM flare.up hot-became-PAST
 'My head got hot.' (Lit.)
 'I became angry.' (Metaph.)
 (Kövesces 2000b: 165)

(11) Kannada
 tale   bisi   marko   ta-ne
 Head   hot   doing   something-MASC
 'He is making his head hot.' (Lit.)
 'He is going to work himself up, stress out over something.' (Metaph.)
 (Elicitation)

Japanese has two synonyms for 'heart': *kokoro* and *mune no uchi* (literally 'inside the chest'). While a hot *kokoro* has no extended meaning, a hot *mune no uchi* indicates a very passionate, excited emotion.

(12) Japanese
 Atsui   mune   no   uchi
 Hot   chest   POS   inside
 'A hot heart.' (Lit.)
 'Passionate, excited.' (Metaph.)
 (Elicitation)

It might be worth noting that it seems to be the more severe cooling term that is often chosen to indicate emotional control (*pace* the English *keep a cool head*). In addition to the cases mentioned above, Swedish, which has a term *kylig* for 'cool', instead uses the more severe cooling term *kall* 'cold', as shown in (13). However, for completeness' sake we must also note that, while Mandarin Chinese uses the coldest available term, *lang3* 'cold', instead of *liang2* 'cool', the entire study only contained one semantically extended use of *liang2*.

(13) Swedish
 Ett   kallt   huvud   är   viktigare   än   ett   varmt   hjärta
 A   cold   head   is   important.CMP   than   a   warm   heart
 'A cold head is more important than a warm heart.' (Lit.)
 'It is more important to be rational and composed than to be kind and caring.' (Metaph.)
 (Introspection)

We believe that it is the temperature value (hot, cold etc.) that is more likely to motivate the same cross-linguistic meaning, rather than which body part is used in the expressions. As Shindo (1998) notes, the focus of emotions in the body varies between cultures. This is reinforced by examples such as (14), where a cold voice in Ibibio motivates a reading of calmness. Cold voices in many other languages typically indicate unfriendliness.

(14) Ibibio
    á-dèŋé   úyío
    3SG-be.cold voice
    'S/he has a cold voice.'
    'S/he seems calm.' (Metaph.)
    (Elicitation)

9.5.1.2 Caring and uncaring

A second conceptual metaphor that is readily apparent from the data is the one that projects the warming temperature range onto friendliness or a caring disposition; and an unfriendly or downright hostile attitude is often seen as cold. We, therefore, propose a conceptual metaphor CARING IS WARM; UNCARING IS COLD, because this phenomenon seems to generally include terms for 'warm', and not for 'hot'. In our data, the temperature items are used with several different body-related expressions – examples are given in Table 4 for 'heart' (or heart-like organ, if the language, like Ibibio, does not distinguish the heart from e.g. the kidney), the most common body part used for this purpose.

Table 4: Some examples of the mapping of temperature scales onto (un)caring for 'heart.' n/a means that that expression is not productive for the metaphor under scrutiny: e.g. 'cool' plus 'heart' was not a productive metaphor in Swedish.

Heart				
	cooling range		warming range	
	COLD	COOL	WARM	HOT
Japanese	disinterested, uncaring	n/a	kind	n/a
Swedish	uncaring, unkind	n/a	caring, kind	n/a
English	uncaring, unkind	n/a	caring, kind	n/a
Mandarin Chinese	n/a	n/a	n/a	generous
Ibibio	n/a	n/a	caring, kind	n/a
Ojibwe	uncaring	n/a	n/a	n/a
Kannada	n/a	n/a	n/a	n/a

The Germanic languages (Swedish and English) and Japanese exploit the scale effect and project a scale going from cold to warm – but not hot – onto the emotional opposition between uncaring and caring. This is illustrated in (15) through (19):

(15) Swedish
Han   har   ett   varmt   hjärta
'He   has   a   warm   heart.' (Lit.)
'He is kind and caring.' (Metaph.)
(Introspection)

(16) Swedish
Han   har   ett   kallt   hjärta
'He   has   a   cold   heart.' (Lit.)
'He is uncaring.' (Metaph.)
(Introspection)

(17) English
She has a warm heart (Lit.)
'She is kind and caring.' (Metaph.)
(Elicitation)

(18) English
She has a cold heart. (Lit.)
'She is unfriendly and uncaring.' (Metaph.)
(Elicitation)

(19) Japanese
Tsumetai   kokoro
cold   heart
'Disinterest, uncaring.' (Metaph.)
(Elicitation)

Ibibio and Mandarin Chinese only employ the warming range of the temperature scale when it comes to BRTEs with heart.

In the previous section we saw that a cold heart in Ibibio indicated calmness, following a general LACK OF CONTROL IS HOT metaphor; by contrast, 'warm heart' follows the UNCARING IS COLD metaphor to signify a kind and caring person, as illustrated in (20):

(20) Ibibio
mmèmé   ésìt
warm   heart/kidney
'A warm heart/kidney.' (Lit.)
'A kind and caring person.' (Metaph.)
(Elicitation)

In Mandarin Chinese, it is hot that is combined with heart instead of warm in (21) and (22); the extended meaning is slightly different ('generous, helping' instead of 'friendly, caring'), but similar enough to the use in Swedish, English, Japanese and Ibibio.

(21) Mandarin Chinese
ta1   *hen3*   *re4*   *xin1*
S/he   very   hot   heart
'S/he has a very hot heart.' (Lit.)
'S/he is a good, generous, helping person.' (Metaph.)
(Elicitation)

(22) Mandarin Chinese
ta1   *shi4*   *re4*   *xin1 chang3*
S/he   COP   hot   heart stomach
'S/he has a hot heart.' (Lit.)
'S/he is a good, generous, helping person.' (Metaph.)
(Elicitation)

Since Mandarin Chinese BRTEs tend to use *re4* 'hot' (*wen1 nuan3* 'warm' only occurred once in our elicited material), we do not see this as an invalidation of our earlier statement that, in general, the conceptual metaphor seems mostly focused on the warm, not hot, part of the warming range of the temperature scale.

Metaphor-poor Ojibwe, too, maps the temperature domain onto an emotional domain, but employs only the cooling range of the scale, as in (23):

(23) Ojibwe
Daki-de'e
Cold-heart
'The heart is cold.' (Lit.)
'A person who has this doesn't care about others.' (Metaph.)
(Weshki-ayaad and Gambill 2009, *q.v. dakide'e*, and elicitation)

While 'heart' is the body part that is perhaps most readily associated with emotions, CARING IS WARM; UNCARING IS COLD is associated cross-linguistically with several other body-related expressions. Table 5 below summarizes the occurrence of BRTEs for an additional four body parts and related expressions: 'eyes', 'hand', 'smile' and 'voice'.

Table 5: Some examples of the mapping of temperature scales onto (un)caring for 'eyes', 'smile', 'hand' and 'voice'. For the cooling range, the items aligned left have the extended meaning only with 'cold'; n/a means that that expression is not productive for the metaphor under scrutiny.

Eyes/hand/smile/voice				
	cooling range		warming range	
Language	COLD	COOL	WARM	HOT
Japanese	EYES: unfriendly SMILE: uncaring, hostile		EYES: kind HAND: caring SMILE: affectionate VOICE: encouraging	n/a
Swedish	EYES: uncaring HAND: unhelpful SMILE: uncaring VOICE: unkind		EYES: caring HAND: caring SMILE: affectionate VOICE: kind	n/a
English	EYES: unfriendly SMILE: uncaring, hostile VOICE: unfriendly, unkind		EYES: caring SMILE: affectionate VOICE: friendly	n/a
Mandarin Chinese	EYES: hostile, unfriendly VOICE: hostile, unfriendly		SMILE: affectionate	n/a
Kannada	EYES: miffed, unfriendly		n/a	n/a
Ibibio	n/a n/a		EYES: caring VOICE: peaceable n/a	n/a
Ojibwe	n/a	n/a	n/a	n/a

It is again Swedish, English and Japanese that associate the opposition between warm and cold with an opposition between friendliness and unfriendliness when combined with the body part eye(s); see (24) through (27) for some representative examples. Swedish even uses the scalarity of the cold–cool conceptual relationship: *kyliga ögon* 'cool eyes' is less unfriendly than *kalla ögon* 'cold eyes'.

(24) Swedish
Hon   såg   på   honom   med   kyliga/kalla   ögon
She   looked at   him   with   cool/cold   eyes
'She gave him a cold look.' (Lit.)
'She looked at him in an unfriendly/very unfriendly fashion.' (Metaph.)
(Introspection)

(25) English
She looked at him with warm/cold eyes
'She looked at him in a caring, friendly fashion/an unfriendly fashion.' (Metaph.)
(Elicitation)

(26) Japanese
Atatakai   me
Warm   eye(s)
'Kind.' (Metaph.)
(Elicitation)

(27) Japanese
Tsumetai   me
Cold   eye (s)
'An unfriendly look.' (Metaph.)
(Informant, personal communication)

Kannada and Mandarin Chinese only establish this conceptual metaphor on the cooling range of the spectrum; in Kannada, there is an added nuance of frustration to 'cold eyes', explained by our informant as "being miffed".

(28) Kannada
tanne   noṭa
cold   gaze
'A miffed, upset gaze.' (Metaph.)
(Elicitation)

While a 'cold eye' in Mandarin Chinese means 'hostile, unfriendly' (as in (29)), a 'hot eye' does not mean 'caring'; rather, it means 'jealous', as in (30).

(29) Mandarin Chinese
   leng3   yan3   mian4   dui4
   Cold   eye   look.   at.other
   'Look at someone with a cold eye.' (Lit.)
   'Look at someone in a hostile, not so friendly fashion.' (Metaph.)
   (Elicitation)

(30) Mandarin Chinese
   yan3   re4
   eye   hot
   'Jealous.' (Metaph.)
   (Elicitation)

In Ibibio, the metaphorical extension of BRTEs to emotions 'eye(s)' holds true only for the warming range, as in example (31).

(31) Ibibio
   á-kámá   ánjên   mmèmè   mmèmè
   3SG-hold   eyes   warm   warm
   'To look at someone with very warm eyes.' (Lit.)
   'To look kindly at someone.' (Metaph.)
   (Elicitation)

But with a rephrasing, 'warm eyes' instead indicates being weak, fearful and cowardly, as in (32); while this may be a semantic extension from 'kind', it is clearly a different sense.

(32) Ibibio
   á-mé-mém   ánjèm
   3SG-PRES-warm   eyes
   'To have warm eyes.' (Lit.)
   'To be weak, fearful, cowardly.' (Metaph.)
   (Elicitation)

In Swedish and Japanese 'warm' evokes the same extended meaning of friendliness and kindness when coupled with the body part 'hand', as exemplified in (33) and (34); Swedish again transfers the opposition warm/cold to emotional opposites.

(33) Swedish
Han   tog   emot   dem   med   varm/kall   hand
He   received PART   them   with   warm/cold   hand
'He received them with a warm/cold hand.' (Lit.)
'He received them in a friendly, kind and helpful fashion/an unfriendly fashion.' (Metaph.)
(Introspection)

(34) Japanese
Atatakai   te
Warm   hand
'(To be) kind.' (Metaph.)
(Informant, personal communication)

However, this semantic extension likely relates to another transfer, i.e. the physical sensation of feeling (very) cold when nervous or afraid: a 'cold hand' in Mandarin Chinese can mean that someone becomes nervous.

(35) Mandarin Chinese
shou4[xin1]   fa1   liang2
hand.palm   become   cold
'Become nervous (e.g. actress before entering stage).' (Metaph.)
(Elicitation)

The body part related concepts *smile* and *voice* indicate friendliness and caring in English (36), Swedish (37), Japanese (38) and (39), and Mandarin Chinese (40), (41); Swedish and English transfer both ranges of the temperature scale, as seen in Table 5. The Mandarin Chinese example in (40) is the only instance where *wen1-nuan3* 'warm' and not *re4* 'hot' is used for this kind of metaphor.

(36) English
A warm smile/A cold smile
'An affectionate, caring smile / An uncaring, hostile smile.' (Metaph.)
(Elicitation)

(37) Swedish
Hans　röst　var　varm　/　kylig　/　kall
His　voice　was　warm　/　cool　/　cold
'His voice suggested that he was friendly and kind / unfriendly, disinterested and unkind / very unfriendly and unkind.' (Metaph.)
(Introspection)

(38) Japanese
Atatakai　koe
Warm　voice
'Encouraging, friendly.'
(Elicitation)

(39) Japanese
Atatakai　egao　/　Tsumetai　egao.
Warm　smile　/　Cold　smile
'An affectionate, caring smile / An uncaring, hostile smile.' (Metaph.)
(Informant, personal communication)

(40) Mandarin Chinese
wen1nuan3　[de5]　wei1xiao4
warm　[GEN]　smile
'Warm smile.' (Lit.)
'A kind smile.' (Metaph.)
(Elicitation)

(41) Mandarin Chinese
leng3　yu3 qi4
Cold　voice/tone/manner of speaking
'Cold voice.' (Lit.)
'Unkind.' (Metaph.)
(Elicitation)

In Ibibio we only find 'warm voice', and the meaning is not quite 'friendly' but related: 'peaceable'.

(42) Ibibio
mmèmé úyìo
Warm voice
'A gentle, peaceable and mediating voice.' (Metaph.)
(Elicitation)

Overall, then, it appears that two generalizations can be made for CARING IS WARM; UNCARING IS COLD: for the warming range, the area on the temperature scale corresponding to friendliness clearly tends to be 'warm', and not 'hot'; the counter-examples from Mandarin Chinese are due to a dearth of BRTEs with 'warm' (and have a slightly different meaning as well). For the cooling range, the most common way of expressing unfriendliness is by using 'cold', and not 'cool'; additionally, the Germanic languages can sometimes exploit the scalarity between those two to achieve further nuances.

9.5.2 Cultural effects

In addition to cross-linguistic physicality-based conceptual metaphors, it is likely that some of the data reflect other motivations for the projection of temperatures onto emotional domains. Our hypothesis four (see Section 9.2) speculated whether culturally and geographically specific factors might account for portions of our data. Here we will look at three such factors: the humoral theory of disease (Section 9.5.2.1), age and gender (Section 9.5.2.2), and climate (Section 9.5.2.3).

9.5.2.1 Humoral folk medical theories

In Section 9.3.4 we hypothesized that a discredited but long-dominant folk theory of medicine might account for a portion of the BRTEs in our data. However, we have found no clear effects of this theory for the European languages, which could be expected to have been influenced by it. Most interesting is maybe the fact that our Kannada speaker was explicitly taught the Ayurvedic humoral theory of the four humors and their corresponding temperature properties as a child when she grew up in India, and she also reports that knowledge of the humors is widespread among Kannada speakers. Yet we only found two metaphors involving temperature terms and body parts at all in Kannada, neither of them unambiguously connected with the humoral theory.

One of our Mandarin Chinese informants showed a passing familiarity with humoral folk theory and provided two examples which both indicated (different kinds of) sickness, though she was uncertain as to the difference:

(43) Mandarin Chinese
 wo3 de5 wei4 li3 you3 dian3 re4
 I POS stomach in have a.little heat
 'There is a little heat in my stomach.' (Lit.)
 'I am sick in my stomach.' (Metaph.)
 (Elicitation)

(44) Mandarin Chinese
 wo3 de5 wei4 li3 you3 dian3 liang2
 I POS stomach in have a.little coolness
 'There is a little coolness in my stomach.' (Lit.)
 'I am sick in my stomach.' (Metaph.)
 (Elicitation)

However, there are no attributive or predicative metaphorically interpreted BRTES in our Chinese data that shows clear evidence of humoral theory influence.

It seems clear that just because a society places cultural importance on temperature states of the body, this is not necessarily reflected in the existence of BRTES, at least not in temperature state expressions. It may very well be that more humoral influence is found if the net is thrown more widely, and temperature related expressions such as boiling, fever etc. are included. For now, however, we can conclude no influence of the humoral theory on the distribution of BRTES.

9.5.2.2 Age and gender

In addition to some minor effects of the humoral model, we have found evidence for another culture-specific factor influencing the conceptualization of emotions in terms of BRTES, though the effect in our data appears to be minimal. In Ibibio there is an interesting interplay between age and gender and body part temperature expressions. The same expression, in (45) below, has the literal meaning of 's/he has a hot head' but two different extended interpretations depending on the age of the person referred to.

(45) Ibibio
    á-fjóp   *íwùot*
    3SG-be.hot head
    'S/he has a hot head.' (Lit.)
    'S/he is stubborn and naughty [of a child].' (Metaph.)
    'S/he is daring [of an adult].' (Metaph.)
    (Elicitation)

Similarly there are different interpretations if the term *mmèmé* 'warm, soft' is used for a man or a woman: see (46). For a man, being warm means being unmanly, for a woman, that she is kind.[7]

(46) Ibibio
    mmèmé mmèmé ówò-dèn
    'A warm man.' (Lit.)
    'An unmanly man.' (Metaph.)
    (Elicitation)

(47) Ibibio
    mmèmé mmèmé ówòŋ-wàn
    'A warm woman.' (Lit.)
    'A kind woman.' (Metaph.)
    (Elicitation)

This shows that, as expected, social categories, such as gender and age, can have a (limited) effect on the way the temperature source domain is interpreted in semantically extended expressions.

9.5.2.3 Climate effects

In Section 9.3.4 we mentioned the studies by Al-Abed Al-Haq and El-Sharif (2008) and Perrin (2015) which drew a link between climate temperature and temperature metaphors in Arabic and Wolof, respectively. The authors theorize that languages spoken in warmer climates and colder climates should reflect this in their temperature-related metaphors. In our study we found only one potential

---

[7] The senses 'kind', 'friendly' and 'unmanly' might be closely related, semantically speaking. Our informant couldn't say, and neither can we.

data point which might support this (48), from Ibibio, where to look at someone with cold (and damp) eyes is to look kindly at someone – in contrast to many of the other languages where cold eyes were always linked with uncaring and unfriendly attitudes. Ibibio is spoken in a warmer climate than most of the other languages, where, following the logic in Al-Abed Al-Haq and El-Sharif (2008) and Perrin (2015), coolness might be associated with positive emotions.

(48) Ibibio
 á-kámá ánjén dèdèŋ dèdèŋ
 'S/he looks at someone with cold and damp eyes.' (Lit.)
 'To look kindly at someone, to be attracted to someone.' (Metaph.)
 (Elicitation)

Yet Kannada, spoken in a similarly warm climate to Ibibio, showed no such linking between positive and cool – though, admittedly, Kannada had very few metaphorically interpreted BRTEs at all. We have found nothing that strengthens Al-Abed Al-Haq and El-Sharif's (2008) and Perrin's (2015) hypothesis.

9.5.3 Summary

The body parts mouth, nose, ear, arm, finger, leg and toe were never used in BRTEs with metaphorical interpretations in any of the languages; and breast/torso, stomach and liver were used in only one language each; and 'cold feet' were relevant in Swedish and English only. The expression 'cold spine', meaning 'fearful' was used in four languages, but will not be discussed here.

Those body-related expressions that do occur again and again in the elicited material are primarily the heart and the head. In addition hand, smile, voice, eye (and gaze) often occur in BRTEs. These, then, are candidates for future research to focus on. Strikingly often the BRTEs had similar metaphorical meanings.

9.6 Discussion and conclusion

We will first revisit our research questions, and then discuss some future research that the results of these research questions have brought up.

9.6.1 Answering the research questions

The data presented in Section 9.5 allow us to answer some of the research questions we posed earlier (see Section 9.2) with a fair degree of confidence; others we feel less confident about answering, but the data allow us to provide some pointers as to how a more complete answer may be arrived at.

Hypothesis 1 stated that metaphorical interpretations of BRTEs are common to all human languages. For the seven languages in this sample, none was lacking in metaphorical BRTEs. They abound in some languages (viz. English, Swedish, Japanese, Mandarin Chinese and Ibibio) and were comparatively infrequent in others (Kannada, Ojibwe). Yet the very fact that Ojibwe has one of these metaphors – *daki-de'e* 'cold heart'; 'uncaring' – when the language is known to have very few metaphors in general, is interesting. Of course, this may be due to influence from the surrounding English and French; if so, this could be taken as additional support for the easy transferability of temperature scales onto other domains.

With respect to hypothesis 2, the question of whether certain body-related expressions are likewise cross-linguistically attested as vehicles for the metaphors, we have seen that the heart and the head are body parts that are often used in metaphors involving temperature. It is also very common to speak of temperature together with voice, smile and eyes – but most frequently it is not the eyes themselves that are hot or cold, but rather the gaze, the effect of a look.

Hypothesis 3 consisted of two subclaims. The first was that several of the previously suggested conceptual metaphors using temperature as a source domain would be attested in our language sample, more or less systematically. We have indeed found evidence that points to the existence of a few basic, high-level conceptual metaphors, based on the ideas that CARING IS WARM; UNCARING IS COLD and LACK OF CONTROL IS HOT; CONTROL IS COOL that have a high likelihood of appearing cross-linguistically. In different ways, we have seen BRTEs potentially motivated by these high-level conceptual metaphors in all the studied languages, with the exception of Ojibwe which has only shown evidence for CARING IS WARM; UNCARING IS COLD. Our formulations of these conceptual metaphors are similar to the ones suggested by e.g. Shindo (1998) and Kövescses (2000a), among others.

The second subclaim was that the temperature scales would be translated, in part or *in toto*, to potentially scalar target domains, such as emotions. We have found that some languages, for some conceptual metaphors, will map the entire scalar range of the temperature source domain onto a scalar target domain – but that it is also common for languages to use only one temperature term from a particular range (warming or cooling) to map onto the target domain (e.g. using 'warm' to indicate friendliness does not entail using 'hot' to indicate more intense friendliness). This finding corroborates the results in Rasulić (2015) for Serbian and English data.

Hypothesis 4 stated that exceptions to the high-level conceptual metaphors linking emotional and temperature states could be explained by appealing to culturally specific principles (e.g. humoral theory) or climate-specific effects (perceptions of coldness in desert climes). We were unable to find clear examples of humoral theory effects that could not be traced to (physiologically grounded) clines like CARING IS WARMTH; UNCARING IS COLD. This is particularly interesting for Kannada and Mandarin Chinese, where the speakers claimed to be versed in humoral theory. This illustrates that a strong cultural concept need not be projected into language at all.

Another effect of culture may possibly account for exceptions to the conceptual metaphors in the Ibibio BRTEs where age and gender of the subjects affects how their temperature is valued. But neither age nor gender was systematically a factor in our language data.

As for climate-specific exceptions, we found one possible instance in Ibibio, and none in the other languages.

Temperature is a universal constant to human beings and we use our understanding of this bodily perception to try to understand more complex things, like emotions. Understanding how humans perceive and process temperature information is thus an important key to unlocking the semantically extended nature of human reasoning.

9.6.2 Future research

This study has led us to formulate several hypotheses which we believe are worth investigating in further studies.

First, the frequent cross-linguistic existence of two conceptual metaphors we have illustrated here (and which are familiar from the literature) would be strengthened by more examples in more languages. This study, as are many others, is hampered by having informants who are very good at English, and it cannot be excluded that the existence of these conceptual metaphors is due to semantic calquing.

Like Rasulić (2015) we have noticed that metaphorical BRTEs will tend to leverage the quantitative differences on the cooling range for intensification purposes: e.g, in Swedish *ett kallt leende* 'a cold smile' is more unfriendly than *ett kyligt leende* 'a cool smile'. By contrast, scalarity of the warming range will not be employed in a similar manner. This is a hypothesis that could be verified by more data in more languages.

We also propose that it would be interesting to investigate whether all languages do in fact have metaphorical BRTEs. Even languages with purportedly few metaphors, like Ojibwe, seem to have them – though it cannot be ruled out that this is due to semantic calquing.

While we did not find any clear, obvious links (but some circumstantial evidence) between climate and the metaphorical BRTEs in the languages in this study, it is a hypothesis that should still be falsified or verified by more data.

We would also like to further strengthen our claim that it is a limited set of body parts that show up in metaphorical temperature uses, and seek to understand the motivations behind this.

9.7 References

Al-Abed Al-Haq, Fawwaz and Ahmad Al-Sharif. 2008. A comparative study for the metaphors use in happiness and anger in English and Arabic. *US-China Foreign Language* 6 (11): 5–23.

Bergström, Annika. 2010. *Temperatur i språk och tanke: En jämförande semantisk studie av svenska temperaturadjektiv* [Temperature in language and thought. A comparative semantic study of Swedish temperature adjectives]. Gothenburg: Göteborgs universitet dissertation.

Craig, Philip R. 2003. *Vineyard enigma: A Martha's Vineyard mystery.* New York: Avon Books.

Deignan, Alice and Liz Potter. 2004. A corpus study of metaphors and metonyms in English and Italian. *Journal of Pragmatics* 36: 1231–1252.

Geeraerts, Dirk. 2002. The interaction of metaphor and metonymy in composite expressions. In René Dirven and Ralf Pörings (eds), *Metaphor and metonymy in comparison and contrast*, 435–465. Berlin: Mouton de Gruyter.

Geeraerts, Dirk. 2006. *Words and Other Wonders. Papers on Lexical and Semantic Topics.* Berlin: Mouton de Gruyter.

Geeraerts, Dirk and Stefan Grondelaers. 1995. Looking back at anger: Cultural traditions and metaphorical patterns. In John R. Taylor and Robert E. MacLaury (eds.), *Language and the cognitive construal of the world*, 153-179. Berlin: Mouton de Gruyter.

Grady, Joseph. 1997. *Foundations of meaning: Primary metaphors and primary scenes.* Berkeley: University of California dissertation.

Grady, Joseph. 2005. Primary metaphors as inputs to conceptual integration. *Journal of Pragmatics* 37 (10): 1595–1614.

Juvonen, Päivi and Ahti Nikunlassi. 2015. Temperature terms in Finnish. In Maria Koptjevskaja-Tamm (ed.), *The linguistics of temperature*, 491–536. Amsterdam: John Benjamins.

Koptjevskaja-Tamm, Maria. 2007. Guidelines for collecting linguistic expressions for temperature concepts: Version 1 (December 2007). Unpublished manuscript, available at: www.lingfil.uu.se/afro/turkiskasprak/Temp_guidelines_071214.pdf.

Koptjevskaja-Tamm, Maria and Ekaterina Rakhilina. 2006. "Some like it hot": on semantics of temperature adjectives in Russian and Swedish. [Special issue]. *STUF (Sprachtypologie und Universalienforschung)*, 59-2: 253–269.

Kottek, Markus, Jürgen Grieser, Christoph Beck, Bruno Rudolf, and Franz Rubel. 2006. World Map of the Köppen-Geiger climate classification updated. *Meteorologische Zeitschrift* 15: 259–263.
Kövecses, Zoltán. 1995. Anger: Its language, conceptualization, and physiology in the light of cross-cultural evidence. In John R. Taylor and Robert E. MacLaury (eds.), *Language and the cognitive construal of the world*, 181–196. Berlin: Mouton de Gruyter.
Kövecses, Zoltán. 2000a. *Metaphor and emotion: Language, culture, and body in human feeling*. (Studies in emotion and social interaction.) Cambridge: Cambridge University Press.
Kövecses, Zoltán. 2000b. The concept of anger: Universal or culture specific? *Psychopathology* 2000 (33): 159–170
Kövecses, Zoltán. 2005. *Metaphor in culture: Universality and variation*. Cambridge: Cambridge University Press.
Lakoff, George. 1987. *Women, fire, and dangerous things : What categories reveal about the mind*. Chicago: University of Chicago Press.
Lakoff, George and Mark Johnson. 1980. *Metaphors we live by*. Chicago: University of Chicago Press.
Lakoff, George and Mark Johnson. 1999. Philosophy in the flesh: The embodied mind and its challenge to western thought. New York: Basic books.
Lakoff, George and Zoltán Kövecses. 1987. The cognitive model of anger inherent in American English. In Dorothy C. Holland and Naomi Quinn (eds.), *Cultural models in language and thought*, 195–221. Cambridge: Cambridge University Press
Lehrer, Adrienne. 1970. Static and dynamic elements in semantics hot warm cool cold. *Research on Language & Social Interaction* 3: 349–73.
Lockwood, Hunter and Susanne Vejdemo. 2015. 'There is no thermostat in the forest' – the Ojibwe temperature term system. In Maria Koptjevskaja-Tamm (ed.), *The linguistics of temperature*, 721–741. Amsterdam: John Benjamins Publishing.
Maalej, Zouheir A. and Ning Yu (eds.). 2011. *Embodiment vid body parts. Studies from various languages and cultures*. Amsterdam & Philadelphia: John Benjamins Publishing Company.
Markey, Thomas. 1985. The totemic typology. *I Quaderni di Semantica* 6 (1): 175–194.
Matsuki, Kaiko. 1995. Metaphors of anger in Japanese. In John R. Taylor and Robert E. MacLaury (eds.), *Language and the cognitive construal of the world*, 137–51. Walter de Gruyter.
Nummenmaa, Lauri, Enrico Glerean, Riitta Hari, and Jari K. Hietanen. 2014. Bodily maps of emotions. *Proceedings of the National Academy of Sciences (December 30)*. 111.2: 646–6
Perrin, Loïc-Michel. 2015. Climate, temperature and polysemous patterns in French and Wolof. In Maria Koptjevskaja-Tamm (ed), *The linguistics of temperature*, 151–86. Amsterdam: John Benjamins Publishing Company.
Rasulić, Katarina. 2015. What's hot and what's not in English and Serbian: A contrastive view on the semantic extensions of temperature adjectives. In Maria Koptjevskaja-Tamm (ed.), *The linguistics of temperature*, 254–299. Amsterdam: John Benjamins.
Rhodes, Richard A. 1985. Metaphor and extension in Ojibwa. In William Cowan (ed.), *Papers of the 16th Algonquian Conference*, 161–169. Ottawa: Carleton University.
Sharifian, Farzad, René Dirven, Ning Yu, and Susanne Niemeier (eds.). 2008. *Culture, body and language. Conceptualizations of internal body organs across cultures and languages*. Berlin: Mouton de Gruyter.

Shindo, Mika. 1998. An analysis of metaphorically extended concepts based on bodily experience. A case study of temperature expressions (1). *Papers in Linguistic Science* 4: 29–54.

Shindo, Mika. 2009. *Semantic extension, subjectification, and verbalization.* Lanham: University Press of America.

Shindo, Mika. 2010. Subdivisions of temperature concepts. Paper presented at the Temperature in Language and Cognition Workshop, Stockholm University, March 2010. Available at: http://ling-asv.ling.su.se/mediawiki/images/1/16/Shindo.pdf (20 December 2013).

Soriano, Cristina. 2003. Some anger metaphors in Spanish and English. A contrastive review. *Contrastive Cognitive Linguistics, monograph issue of the International Journal of English Studies*, 3(2): 107–122.

Weshki-ayaad, Charlie Lippert, and Guy T. Gambill. 2009. Freelang Ojibwe-English dictionary. Available at: http://www.freelang.net/dictionary/ojibwe.php (December 16, 2009).

Yu, Ning. 1995. Metaphorical expressions of anger and happiness in English and Chinese. *Metaphor and Symbol* 10: 59–92.

Zhong, Chen-Bo and Geoffrey J. Leonardelli. 2008. Cold and lonely: Does social exclusion literally feel cold? *Psychological Science* 19 (9): 838–842.

Michael Fortescue
10. The semantic domain of emotion in Eskimo and neighbouring languages

Abstract: Eskimo languages display a rich array of emotional 'roots' (bound stems) that constitute a distinct morphological category. It is signalled by their unique (and obligatory) derivational potential and is etymologically largely opaque. One can reconstruct the membership of the category already at the Proto-Eskimo stage as referring to 'emotional states or reactions or emotionally coloured mental attitudes'. There are other words referring to emotions that fall outside the morphologically defined category, but these refer generally to more behaviourally overt manifestations of emotional states. Within the individual Eskimo languages the meanings of the roots concerned have sometimes undergone interesting semantic shifts or extensions and the original meanings become represented by other items. In some cases context-dependent polysemy results. This clearly delimited category (also reflected in neighbouring Chukotian languages) promises to contribute to the debate as to what constitutes a 'basic' emotion in linguistic terms, and how these relate to the five or six 'primary' emotions described by psychologists. The type of semantic shifts displayed often appear to reflect a development from more physical/visceral emotions to more abstract or culturally modulated ones.

10.1 Introduction

The semantic domain of emotion is not inherently an easy one to delimit, since it shades off in various directions, in particular into overt behaviour associated with specific emotions, into purely visceral/somatic reactions, and into mental attitudes with mainly epistemic purport. Eskimo languages may be rather unique in delimiting the extent of this domain by displaying an array of emotional "roots" (bound stems) that constitute a distinct morphological category. This represents a useful starting point for comparing and discussing the expression of emotion in a broader typological perspective. The category – and its core members – can be reconstructed back to (at least) Proto-Eskimo times (some 2,000 years ago), as in the Comparative Eskimo Dictionary (Fortescue, Jacobson, and Kaplan 2010). By

---

Michael Fortescue (Copenhagen University)

focussing on the diachronic perspective the otherwise largely opaque (non-metaphorical) etymology of the roots in the contemporary languages can be elucidated. The semantic shifts undergone by these terms in the individual languages will hopefully contribute to the typology of semantic shifts as in the on-going work by Zalizniak et al. (2012), though space precludes isolating the many diachronic pathways reflected in the data. The present study also casts some light on the cognitive underpinnings of the domain as a whole. There are important caveats, however, chief of which is concern with the English glosses given in Fortescue, Jacobson, and Kaplan (2010) (and the sources this reflects).

The category is signalled by the unique (and obligatory) derivational potential of the roots concerned, namely the necessity of combining with the affixes (or "postbases") *-yug- (Inuit -suk-) for an intransitive state, *-yyag- (Inuit -tsak-, Yupik -yagutə-) for intransitive entering a state, *-nar- (Inuit -naq-, in some Yupik -narqə-) for a stimulus potentially evoking the emotion concerned, and *-kə- (Inuit -gi-) for a transitive emotional state oriented towards its stimulus.[1] This is in fact the definitional criterion for what constitutes an "emotional root" in these languages. All of the affixes concerned can be used individually on other stems – -yug- for example is also 'want' or 'tend to', -kə- is 'have as' (transitive possession) or 'consider to be (of a certain quality)', and -nar- is 'be such as to cause' on other than emotional stems. In Yupik also -tar- 'tend to' belongs to this set (cf. Jacobson 1984: 17).[2] It is the set as a whole that is in theory criterial for membership in the category. A typical example is the Central Alaskan Yupik (CAY) root nakləg- 'feel compassion' (from Proto-Eskimo *naŋɬəg-), which occurs in intransitive forms naklegyug(tuq) 'he feels compassion', and nakləgnarq(uq) 'he or it causes one to feel compassion', nakləgntar(tuq) 'he is compassionate', and transitive naklək(aa) 'he feels compassion towards (her)'.[3]

The derivationally defined category seems (to speakers of European languages) to extend beyond emotion as such to include certain stems of epistemic attitude such as 'suspect' or 'doubt', and certain general perceptual notions such as 'notice'. Some emotional roots no longer occur with all affixes of the set (if they ever did) – typically occurring just with transitive *-kə- since they are exclusively directed towards a stimulus, such as 'respect'. And some stems expressing

---

[1] Note that "r" is a voiced uvular fricative in the Eskimo forms cited, and "g" is a corresponding velar fricative.
[2] This may once have been so in Inuit too, to judge by such forms as WG paqumittar- listed under paqumig(aa) in Petersen (1951) (cf. PE *paqu(mi)- below) and naakkittar- (cf. PI *naatki- below).
[3] Some speakers can also use inchoative -yagutə- with this root, according to Jacobson. It may be transitive or intransitive in Yupik (only intransitive in Inuit), as in takaryagut(aa) 'he has become respectful towards (him)' given by Jacobson (1984: 591), from root takar- 'respectful or shy'.

emotion (as we would see it) do not fall into this pattern at all but act as ordinary (in)transitive verbs, perhaps because they refer primarily to overt behaviour. Nevertheless, if one reconstructs the membership of the category back to the Proto-Eskimo stage it is possible to characterize its semantic range fairly precisely as "emotional states or reactions or emotionally coloured mental attitudes", covering a scale from covert (evident only to the experiencer) to overt (directly deducible from external behaviour). Meanings closer to the covert end of the scale would appear to be more likely candidates to be expressed as emotional roots. This uniquely delimited category in Eskimo promises to contribute to the debate as to what is a "basic" emotion, since it is reasonable to suppose that those emotional roots that are reconstructable for the proto-language are in some sense to be regarded as "basic" – at least within this language family.

There is considerable variation from language to language (and dialect to dialect) within the family, with much overlapping of meanings as individual stems drift apart from their common origins and new items are added to or removed from the category over time. Of course a study like the present one is at the mercy of glosses in dictionaries, which may not always be quite accurate and may be full of lacunae as regards specific derivations, although I have chosen the most reliable, contemporary sources wherever possible. See Dorais (1990: 125–130) for variation in expression of "the same" emotions from dialect to dialect across the Inuit continuum, and, for a complete array of emotional roots for one language see Jacobson (1984: 665–6), who lists 54 of them for CAY.[4] There is a somewhat greater number of complete emotional root sets in Yupik than in Inuit (especially CAY), so the situation there can be taken to reflect the original situation rather well, though not all CAY emotional roots can be reconstructed as such in the proto-language. In Briggs (1970, 1995) we have a case study for one Inuit dialect ("Utku", i.e. Utkuhikhalingmiut, an inland variety of Netsilik Inuit) where we see how emotional roots – and other "ordinary" verbs with emotional connotations – can be contextualized, embedded in actual usage and thereby rendered more culturally specific. McNabb (1989) has further exemplification of the contextualization of emotion words in Alaskan Inupiaq. This is an essential step for a more culturally informed understanding of these terms, a matter I shall return to in section 10.5.

---

4 This list misses out a number of items that either act derivationally as ordinary verbs in the modern language or only occur in a single lexicalized combination with one of the affixes from the set (i.e. do not constitute a fully fledged emotional root according to the derivational definition).

Despite this variety, there is a common core of emotional roots that remains virtually unchanged in all forms of Eskimo. This raises interesting questions: given the tendency of emotion words – at least in Indo-European languages – to derive from more overt meanings of physical actions or states that reflect some inner emotion (cf. Buck [1949] 1988: 1084–1169), is this also true of Eskimo emotional roots? In other words, is their origin usually a matter of metonymy? And does the core set of Eskimo emotional roots reflect a truly universal array of "basic" emotions upon which more complex, culturally specific emotional concepts can be built? The category of "emotional root" has a very close parallel in the neighbouring Chukotian languages of Siberia, but not in any other nearby languages (it would in fact appear to be rare globally to have a morphologically distinct category of emotional roots). Is this due to a common stock of "basic" emotions plus a similar Arctic environment, or is it an areal matter?

Table 1: Emotions expressed by emotional roots in Proto-Eskimo

1. Fear	*ira-, *alikə-, *naŋyar-
2. Loneliness and sad feelings	*aliga-,*ar(ə)yu-,*nəka-
3. Frustration	*capir-
4. Anxiety	*kappəya-
5. Shame	*kayŋu-
6. Timidity	*qikə-, *əgtug-
7. Apprehension	*paqu(mi)-, *kama-
8. Worry	*pəŋəg-
9. Disgust	*maruyug-, *əplər-
10. Not feeling like doing s.th.	*aq(ə)ya-
11. Anger	*nəŋ(ŋ)ar-,*qənər-,*ugumi-
12. Regret	*qivru-
13. Jealousy or envy	*cikna-,*tucu-
14. Anguish or suffering	*ikvig-
15. Happiness	*quvya(yug)-
16. Amusement	*təmci-
(17. Feeling at ease)	
18. Thankfulness	*quya-
19. Lust	*əkli-
20. Longing	*qi(C)əlir-
21. Pity	*naŋłəg-
(22. Feeling protective/loving towards)	
23. Uncertainty	*nəryu(g)-, *ukvər-,*nału-
24. Feeling or noticing (generally)	*əlpəkə-

To address these questions I shall examine relevant entries in Fortescue, Jacobson, and Kaplan (2010), that is the words listed there referring to emotions that occur in more than one language or dialect of the family. I shall attempt to pinpoint the earliest meaning/source attributable to the items concerned, focusing on the most widely attested ones. I exclude words referring to purely physical sensations like hunger or physical pain, modally specific perceptual ones such as seeing or hearing, and will refer only peripherally to purely mental ones like thinking or remembering. Table 1 gives an overview of the categories expressed by emotional roots in Fortescue, Jacobson, and Kaplan (2010) with some examples of Proto-Eskimo (PE) roots indicated, all to be discussed below (categories 17 and 22 are not represented by PE reconstructions).

In the following sections I shall start with words in Fortescue, Jacobson, and Kaplan (2010) for negative emotions (the first 14 on Table 1), since this is the largest set and overlaps of meaning here tend to occur between items within this category rather than across the entire range. I shall then proceed to positive emotions (the next 4), and finally consider others less easy to categorize in these terms, such as those of wanting and desiring. It should be understood that this way of dividing up of types of emotion is for convenience of presentation and is not meant to indicate watertight sub-categories. Thereafter I shall make a briefer examination of Chukotian emotional roots, based principally on the information in Fortescue (2005). In the concluding section I shall discuss the relationship between the "basic" emotions described by psychologists and the emotional roots of the Eskimo (and Chukotian) languages. In Figure 1 can be seen the principal languages and dialects referred to. Note that the bold broken line indicates a boundary between families; other broken lines mark boundaries between branches of families and single languages or dialects. Eskimo (sister as a whole to more remote Aleut) is thus traditionally divided into the four extant Yupik languages and a single dialect continuum for the sole Inuit language. Chukotko-Kamchatkan comprises the four Chukotian languages Chukchi, Koryak, Kerek and Alutor, plus much more remotely related Itelmen.

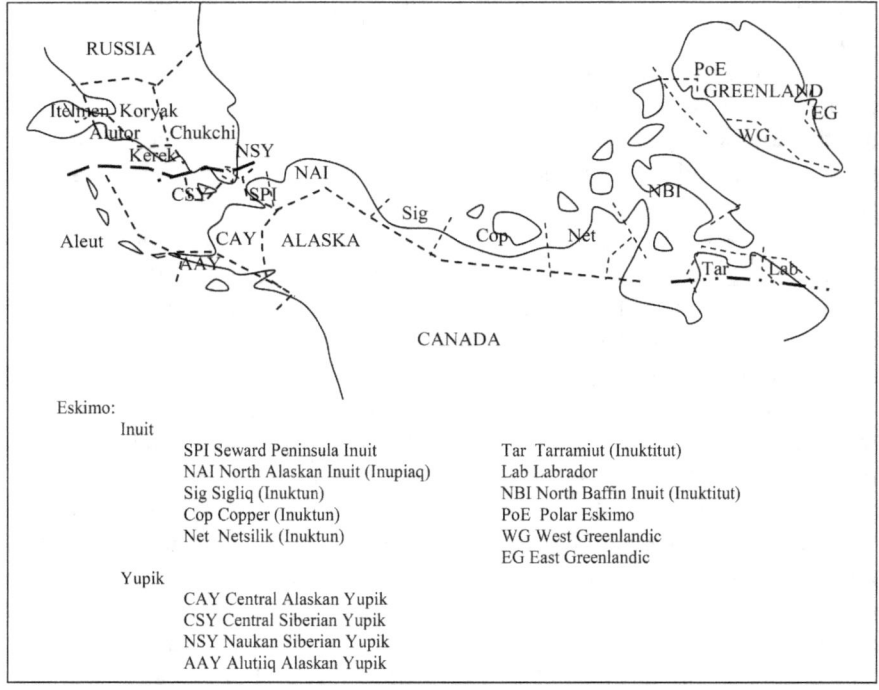

Figure 1: Languages and dialects referred to.

10.2 Negative emotional categories in Eskimo

10.2.1 Fear

A suitable point to start is fear, one of the basic emotions whose physical basis in the human limbic system is rather well understood by neurologists (cf. LeDoux 1998: 113). Fear, for example, crucially involves the participation of the amygdala – though there is of course more to it than that (I shall return to the neurological side of emotion in the concluding section).

There are a number of stems referring to fear that are widespread across the Eskimo-speaking world. One of these, expressing strong fear, is Proto-Yupik emotional root *ira- 'be horrified', which has a direct Eastern Aleut cognate *ira-* 'be afraid' The latter is an important link since it gives an idea of how old the emotional root category might be within Eskimo-Aleut, this being one of the few stems in Aleut where there are clear derivatives exactly parallel with the Eskimo ones, namely *irayu-* 'be respectful, behave well' (with *-yug-*), *irana-* 'be terrible' (with *-nar-*), and transitive *iraXta-* (with innovative *-Xta*) 'be afraid of'. All we have left of the systematic category in Aleut (which has in general undergone much restructuring) is fragments. In Yupik the meaning ranges from 'be afraid' in Alutiiq Alaskan Yupik, 'be amazed' in CAY (as opposed to related *iiXa-* 'be amazed, horrified'), but 'feel aversion or disgust' in Central SiberianYupik. There is a related Proto-Inuit emotional root *iqci-* 'be afraid' (especially of physical injury according to Briggs 1970 as regards Utku).

Perhaps the most common words for fear in Yupik are a cluster of related forms (none forming a complete emotional root set today) related to PE *alikə-* 'be afraid of' (with transitive affix *-kə-*), including Proto-Yupik *alignar-* 'be frightening' (with *-nar-*), as well as non-emotional Proto-Yupik (PY) stems *aliŋə-* be afraid' (probably with affix *-nəg-* of getting) and *aliŋtar-* 'be cowardly'. There is little if any variation in the meaning of these general 'fear' words, although Central Siberian Yupik (CSY), interestingly, has *alignar-* as 'practice shamanism' ('be scary' in Naukanski Siberian Yupik – NSY). They are principally found in the Yupik languages, though there are cognates of *alike-* in West Greenlandic (WG), namely *aligi-* meaning 'consider big', and *alinnar-* 'be big' (Polar Eskimo has *aliŋnak* 'something bad or ugly'). This all suggests an original fully fledged emotional root.

A more specific kind of fear is reflected in PE *naŋyar-* 'be afraid in a precarious place', which seems to have a more general 'be afraid of danger' sense in certain dialects (especially in the high Canadian Arctic – where there are few great heights). In WG it is 'be afraid or giddy in a precarious place, be afraid to go out in one's kayak'. It is a complete emotional root in CAY and CSY, but not fully so elsewhere. Thus the transitive form *naŋiari-* and the *-nar-* form *naŋiarna(q)-* are found in Tarramiut (Schneider 1985) and WG has transitive *naŋiari-* 'afraid of'. In CSY it is 'wince, hesitate, be afraid (of)', which suggests that the original meaning might have been one of physical reaction to danger close to the behavioural end of the scale. The same might be said of WG emotional root *tupi(gi)* 'be surprised at' from PE *tupəkə-*, glossed in Fortescue, Jacobson, and Kaplan (2010) as 'be surprised or excited at'. This is problematical, however, since outside of Greenland it is not an emotional root but is found in an emotional sense in Norton Sound Yupik, where *tupəkə-* means 'be excited to see' (in other, fringe CAY 'agree' and 'take care of'), and in Tarramiut *tupinnaq-* 'be wonderful'. For 'be amazed' in North Alaskan Inuit (NAI), see PE *kama-* below.

On the other hand, PE *ulurya-* 'flinch in fear' is a fully fledged emotional root in most languages where it is attested (it is not found in CSY), despite the overt behavioural reaction element in its meaning – 'wince, afraid of being hit' in

CAY (in Alutiiq Alaskan Yupik – AAY – the meaning is 'dread, be apprehensive' rather). In most languages the *-nar-* form is 'be dangerous or threatening' (but in WG, somewhat more explicitly, 'be such as to make one jump back in fear'), and the transitive equivalent with *-kə-* is 'be apprehensive about' in NAI (in Point Hope 'draw back from') and 'be terrified of' in WG. The *-yug-/-suk-* form is 'flinch' in NAI but 'be terrified' in Copper (which may better reflect the original meaning).

Another Proto-Eskimo stem in Fortescue, Jacobson, and Kaplan (2010) is *tatamə(t)-* 'be startled or terrified'. This ranges in meaning from 'become agitated or nervous' in AAY, through 'be startled' in the other Yupik languages (CAY *tatamə-*), and through various grades of terror to the Greenlandic extreme, where *tatamit-* means 'get violently frightened, die of fright'. Nowhere does it form an emotional root according to the derivational criterion given above, although in Inuit there are isolated forms based on variant root *tatai-* that seem to do so, thus North Alaskan Inuit *tataigi-* 'be fearful of' (in eastern Canadian Tarramiut 'be on the alert because of'), and Copper *tataisuk-* 'tremble with fear', with respectively *-kə-* and *-yug-*. Perhaps the stem focused originally on physical reaction to fearful situations and later became treated as an emotional root in some dialects, but being "borderline" lost some of its derived forms there (more detailed data might reveal their presence nevertheless).

10.2.2 Loneliness or sadness

Possibly remotely (and indirectly) related to *alikə-* above, though representing a very different kind of emotion, is PE *aliga-* 'be lonely', which is derived from a PE stem *ali* 'far away'. There is a wide range of meanings here. The meanings 'lonely, depressed, bored' are retained in all Yupik (note in particular the CSY meaning 'long to go somewhere'). But within the Inuit dialect continuum there is a clear split between those dialects in which the root retains a negative meaning, and those in which the meaning has flip-flopped to a positive one, namely Copper, Netsilik, Tarramiut and Labrador, where *aliasuk-* means 'happy' rather than 'sad' as elsewhere (except North Baffin Inuit and Polar Eskimo where it means 'be afraid' – especially of ghosts in the latter – which reflects the link to *alikə-*). The reason for this surprising turn-about is perhaps to be explained by the derived opposite *aliganarit-* (Inuit *alianait-*), from *aliga-* plus *-nar-* plus negative/caritive *-it-*, which in most dialects means 'be amusing' (also in Alutiiq Yupik), whereas it means 'be boring or unpleasant' in the same dialects that have a negative meaning for *aliasuk-*. The inclusion of the negative morpheme *-it-* in this derivation may have been obscured, leading to the positive interpretation in the latter Canadian dialects – note that Tarramiut, one of these dialects, has the shortened exclamatory form *alianai* 'what fun!' and transitive *alianaigi-* 'find amusing', with the original positive sense. Precisely in these the presence of *-it-* is obscured. But compare also the exclamatory use of words like 'terrific!' in English, which suggests the possibility of a natural semantic flip-flop.

Other roots with a 'lonely' or 'depressed' meaning are PE **nəka-* 'feel inferior or unworthy' and more peripheral PE **ar(ə)yu-* 'be tired or homesick'. **nəka-*, an emotional root, is glossed as 'have hurt feelings' for Kodiak AAY and 'find emotionally painful' in CAY (though an earlier source had 'feel insignificant'). In Inuit, it ranges from 'give s.th. although one feels it is unworthy or inferior' or 'doubt one's ability to do s.th.' (Seward Peninsula Inuit – SPI), through 'be embarrassed, avoid eye contact with another, be silent through lack of confidence' (NAI) to Eastern Canadian Inuktitut intransitive *nika-* 'be bereaved, be sorry for' (transitive *nikagi-* 'not have confidence in, not consider good'). WG has intransitive *nika-* 'be sad, depressed, mourn over', but transitive *nikagi-* 'think s. o./s.th. insignificant, not much' (not oneself!). Note that eastern Canadian Inuit and WG appear to have lost the intransitive *nikasuk-* form, just using the root in the intransitive.

PE **ar(ə)yu-* is in most dialects an "ordinary" stem indicating tiredness (in CSY old age) or in eastern Inuktitut being rejected (in Greenland being tired of s.th.). It forms a complete emotional root set in only one dialect, namely in Prince William Sound Alutiiq, where it means 'be homesick'. Elsewhere within Yupik it is only used in its transitive derived form *aryuqə-* 'be homesick for, be tired of' (but in CAY 'be glad to see someone after a long time'). It is likely that these forms all did once add up to a complete emotional root set indicating something like despondency or frustration.

10.2.3 Frustration

There are two PE stems expressing frustration, namely **capir-* 'block or be blocked' and **capər(nar)-* 'be difficult', both related to **capə-* 'block' (physically – so we are probably dealing with an old metaphor here). The meaning of the first stem (not an emotional root) only has an emotional sense in NSY (*sapirsar-* 'lose the desire to do something, give up') and in Inuit, where it generally means 'feel one cannot do s.th., be discouraged' – in WG 'cannot, not dare' but in Northwest Greenland 'be extremely fond of'.[5] Another related derivative of **capə-* is Pro-

---

[5] Also *sapirnar-* 'be great' in the same area, reminiscent of the kind of exclamatory usage in English 'incredible!', literally 'impossibly hard!'.

to-Inuit (PI) *capiqšaq- 'be inhibited' (cf. the NSY form above), whose meanings range from 'be apprehensive of asking s.th. of s. o.' (SPI), through 'be reserved, shy' (NAI) to 'cannot do or get s.th., be in need' (WG). The second related stem *capər(nar)- is a fully fledged emotional root in CAY – besides capəXnar- 'be difficult' there is capərqə- 'find difficult' and capərsug- 'be hesitant about acting'. Elsewhere only the -nar- form is found, generally in the sense 'be difficult, impossible' (but in CSY 'be very cold', and in Point Hope Inupiaq 'be strong' – cf. the Northwest WG form cited above).

In Inuit there is a similar stem PI *ayuq- 'be unable to do or reach' (in WG and East Greenlandic – EG – also 'be bad'), again not an emotional root as such, but occurring in -nar- extension ayurnaq-'be impossible to do' and transitive -gi- form ayuri- 'cannot do s.th.' (in WG 'not like', i.e. 'consider bad' with the more general sense of *-kə-). This has a probable cognate in Aleut ayqi- as in ayqina- 'be difficult, hard' and ayqiXta- 'find difficult' (both with affixes typical of emotional roots).

10.2.4 Anxiety

Another group of meanings refers to states of anxiety and timidity, overlapping with those for fear discussed above. There are two common related emotional roots of anxiety, one in Yupik, PY *kapəgcug- 'be anxious' and one mainly in Inuit, PE *kappəya- 'feel anxious' (both from *kapət-/kapəg- 'fit tightly'). The former ranges in meaning from 'feel uneasy, restless' (AAY), through 'dread, feel anxiety' (CAY), to 'feel claustrophobic, breathless' in CSY (the glosses perhaps just reflecting different contexts of use but the same underlying emotion). The latter root (mainly Inuit) ranges from NAI 'feel oneself in imminent danger', through 'be anxious' or 'be terrified' in Canada, and 'be worried (e.g. about a sick person)' in WG. There is also a direct Yupik cognate in Hooper Bay/Chevak CAY kapia- 'be in great need, in desperate straits'.

Another emotional root that seems to belong here is PE *atlayug- 'feel strange', derived from *atla 'other' and the intransitive emotional root affix -yug-; it may in most Yupik languages also take transitive *-kə- instead of -yug-. In those Inuit dialects that have retained the combination (in extended form allayuaq-) it is more specifically 'be fearful of strangers' or 'be shy (small child)'. It is difficult to say whether this constitutes an actual emotional root since transitive *-kə- can here be seen in its more general sense of 'consider as (of a quality)' (compare WG allagi- 'find strange') and the transferral of intransitive -yug- to join the transitive derivative could be by analogy with semantically similar genuine emotional roots. The origin of the item is at all events quite transparent.

10.2.5 Shame

The most widespread emotional stem for being 'ashamed' is PE *kayŋu-*. The meaning, with no noticeable variation, is stable across all languages and dialects and is everywhere treated as a fully fledged emotional root, thus for example WG *kaŋŋusug-* 'feel shame', *kaŋŋugi-* 'be ashamed of', *kaŋŋunar-* 'be shameful'.

10.2.6 Timidity

PE *qikə-* 'be shy or respectful' is widely attested (in NAI it is 'feel insecure'), but usually lacks the full complement of affixes associated with emotional roots, although CSY, for example, has a full emotional root in the extended form *qiiksug-* 'feel self-conscious, uneasy due to being watched'. In WG related *qissaar-* 'be shy, embarrassed' is an ordinary stem. Another derivative of *qikə-*, namely *qikcig-* 'look askance at s. o.' has forms in several languages taking transitive affix *-kə-*, as in WG in *qissigi-* 'be shy, afraid of, have caught a glimpse of' (also intransitive *qissigusug-*), and in CAY it forms a fully fledged emotional root *qikcig-* 'feel respectful'. These forms all seem to be related to Prince William Sound AAY *qikirtə-* 'cock head to side', a behavioural stem.

PE *əgtug-* 'be anxious or timid' is only a fully fledged emotional root in CSY and adjacent (now extinct) Sireniki Yupik (glossed as 'be anxious') and in Sigliq Inuit (glossed as 'be timid', transitive 'fear'). WG cognate *ittuur-* is 'be ashamed, shy' and although it does not occur with *-yug-/-suk-*, it is transitivized with *-kə-*, so might once have constituted a full derivational set.

Timidity is also expressed by PE stem *tatur-* 'be intimidated by s. o.'; an emotional root in Yupik with meanings 'be respectful, shy, inhibited' in CAY and 'feel timid, intimidated' in CSY.[6] There are only transitive forms like *taturi-* in the Inuit dialects, ranging in meaning from 'be wary of, fear' (SPI) and 'feel submissive towards, find unapproachable' (NAI), to 'keep back from, dare not approach' (WG). The intransitive forms seem to have been lost.

---

6 AAY, surprisingly, has the meaning, 'want to be in with others' – perhaps understood 'but not dare'.

10.2.7 Apprehension

A widespread stem of apprehension is PE *paqu(mi)- 'dread or be wary', which does not quite constitute a fully fledged emotional root except in WG, but which has forms typical of such roots scattered around in most languages, suggesting its earlier status. In Nunivak CAY *paqumiyug-* is 'be curious' and *paquminarqe-* is 'be such as to make curious', while in CSY *paqumiyug-* is 'be wary of and hesitate to act due to threatening weather'. SPI has *paqquzuk-* 'be cautious', and NAI corresponding transitive *paquri-* 'shun (fearing contamination), regard with fear or caution'. According to Peck (1925) *paqumi(suk)-*, *paqumigi-* is 'meditate (upon)' in Labrador. WG has *paqumisug-*, *paqumigi-* 'be superstitious about s.th., feel disgust for'.[7]

PE *kama- 'be nervously attentive' is an emotional root in most of the languages, and displays a wide range of meanings across the emotional spectrum. Thus within Yupik, *kakmayug-*, *kakmakə-* (an idiosyncratic form, perhaps reflecting earlier *kamag-) is 'feel uneasy, intimidated around people' in Koniak AAY, and CAY *kamayug-* is 'feel suspicious' (transitive *kamakə-* 'suspect') – but in the Nunivak dialect 'feel squeamish'. Within Inuit, where the meanings are more overt and behavioural, *kamanaq-* is 'be great, skillful' in SPI, 'be bossy, strong' in NAI, where *kamasuk-* is 'obey, be amazed' and *kamagi-* 'obey' (the latter 'praise, show respect' in Qawiaraq SPI); in Copper *kamasuk-* is 'pay attention, be afraid, on the alert', *kamanaq-* 'be menacing' and *kamagi-* 'pay attention to, be wary of'; in Tarramiut *kama-* (bare root without *-suk-*) is 'be busy with s.th., meddle with s.th.', the same sense as transitive *kamagi-* (in Labrador the bare stem is 'pay attention to, watch'); within Greenland Polar Eskimo has *kamahuk-* 'be agitated, busy', *kamagi-* 'pay attention to, consider important', but WG and EG *kamag-* 'be angry' (an idiosyncratic form as well as meaning). WG also has, unexpectedly, *kamagi-* 'put up with'. The 'nervously attentive' gloss of the proto-form seems to cover the core meaning here, but there have been some surprising extensions especially in eastern Canada and Greenland.

10.2.8 Worry

The most widespread emotional root of worrying is PE *pəŋəg- 'be worried' (though it is not found in WG). In Inuit it is more specifically 'worry about someone

---

[7] In EG there is *qaqqimi(suC)-* 'follow a taboo, be worried about for cult reasons', but also *paqumigi-* 'be sad about' according to Holm (1888).

absent's safety'. It has an Aleut cognate ŋaag- 'be afraid, apprehensive', transitive ŋaaXta-. Ordinary verbs of thinking may also cover the meaning of 'worry', with or without further derivational affixes. Thus Proto-Yupik *cumər(tə)- 'think or worry' covers 'worry about food and work at providing it' (CAY) and 'think, be sad, bored with, suffer, grieve' (NSY). Proto-Inuit has *icumaaluɣə- 'worry about' from *icuma- 'think' (which may in turn be related to *cumər(tə)-) plus -aluk- 'big' and transitive *-kə-. Neither are emotional roots according to the definition based on derivational potential (though WG has isumaalunnar- with *-nar-). However, Inuit does have forms like Tarramiut isumagi- 'think about' which in WG is 'be worried about', and isumanaq- 'give cause for much thought (a person)', with exactly the same semantic development as in Yupik, but with emotional root affixes *-kə- and *-nar-. I shall return to these 'mental' verbs below.

10.2.9 Disgust

Another of the basic emotional reactions with known underpinnings in the brain is disgust or revulsion (cf. LeDoux 1998: 292). The most general stem here is PE *maruyug- 'feel disgusted' which may be derived from PE *maqə- 'ooze', *maqu- 'suppurate'. It is found throughout the Inuit continuum as 'be disgusted' (in WG also 'be finicky about food') but in Yupik it is only attested in NSY (muryu(g)-). The suffix -yug-, typifying emotional roots, has been thoroughly lexicalized here, so it can hardly be regarded as a fully fledged emotional root today according to the derivational definition, but it can nevertheless combine with further transitive *-kə- in WG maayugi- 'feel loathing for' (added to -yug-, not as normally, replacing it), and in Tarramiut (where the form maquyuk- is 'disdain' in biblical usage, as well as 'be revulsed by') there is also maquyunnaq- 'be disgusting' (WG maayunnar-), with *-nar-. This suggests that there was an original emotional set based on root *maqu- (by metonymy?), of which only the lexicalized combination maruyug- remained at some point, to be re-established later (in part) as the base of a new emotional root. Polar Eskimo cognate mauyuihuk- 'be disgusted' supports this, since -*-yug-/-sug- appears twice in the derivation (lexicalized -yuk-, newer -huk-).

With another stem of revulsion, PE *əplər- 'be revulsed by s.th.' (possibly related to *əpər 'dirt'), we see an interesting cultural extension in the Inuit dialects, away from the original physical meaning as still found throughout Yupik today – 'feel squeamish about something messy and wet' – which combines a specific kind of sensory experience with an emotional reaction to it. In those dialects of Canadian and Greenlandic Inuit that have preserved certain forms of the stem (not the whole set expected of an emotional root), it came to have meanings such as 'be afraid of talking to a relative of one's wife (for cult reasons), be afraid of dealing with s. o. or catching their illness' (Copper *ivliri-* – which in Labrador is 'esteem' according to Peck 1925).[8] In WG *illiri-* is 'value (one's possessions), honour, keep holy', and *illirnar-* 'be valuable' – which in Polar Eskimo is 'be filthy' rather. Fabricius (1804) has the root (*ibler-*) as 'be or keep clean' for WG – compare also EG *ittirta-* 'be clean, tidy'. The common factor here seems to be the breaking of a cult taboo rather than a physical stimulus to the emotional reaction of revulsion; conversely, respecting a taboo is to avoid such an emotion. Respecting a taboo has evidently been transferred in more recent times in Greenland to respecting one's possessions.

Yet another kind of disgust is expressed by PE stem **quginag-* 'be ticklish or squeamish' (an emotional root fully in Yupik and partially in Inuit), but the 'ticklish' meaning may be original here, as it is still the principal one in CSY and most Inuit.[9] Some stems meaning uncontrolled physical reaction (those with strong emotional correlates?) may be treated, it seems, as emotional roots. It has developed the 'squeamish, disgusting' sense in certain (fringe) CAY dialects, in Point Hope Inupiaq (where *quin^{y}ak-* means 'be squeamish, scared of mice', as well as 'tickle'), and in various Canadian dialects – thus Netsilik *quinagi-* 'feel touchy about, be afraid of (esp. insects)', and Polar Eskimo *quinaŋnaq-* 'for s.th. to feel nasty'.

There is also PI **narru-* 'dislike or be disgusted by', which is probably related to PE **narcig-* 'wrinkle nose' ('offended by a strong odour' in AAY) and **narə-* 'smell', and seems to represent the remains of an earlier fully fledged emotional root. Only WG has a complete set of the expected affixal forms attested (with *-sug-*, *-tsag-*, *-nar-* and *-gi-* in Petersen 1951) – most dialects have plain intransitive form *narru-* and transitive *narrugi-* 'reject, disdain' only, but note intransitive Polar Eskimo *narruhuk-* 'be offended, angry' and Tarramiut *narrugusuuti-* 'try to make oneself repulsive' (with reflexive use of applicative *-uti-* after *-gusuk-*).

---

8 Rasmussen (1931) has for Netsilik *ivliriik* 'two that never speak to each other for religious reasons, being named after the same dead person'.
9 In CSY it has apparently separated into two sets: *quigina(yug)-* 'be ticklish', and *quginag(yug)-* 'be terrified (esp. of the supernatural)'. One thinks of small children being terrified – pleasurably? – by a tickling adult, as well as of insects crawling under the skin.

10.2.10 Not feeling like doing s.th.

The basic stem here is PE *əq(ə)ya- 'be lazy', as in CAY qəsa- 'feel lazy, disinclined to act', CSY irsa- 'refuse to do s.th.', reflected in all the Inuit dialects too (intransitive iqiasuk-, etc.). The transitive correlates with *-kə- are more heterogenous in meaning: in CAY it is 'not permit', in CSY 'refuse s. o. or s.th.', but in all Inuit simply 'feel lazy about, not feel like doing s.th.'. This latter meaning is surely the original sense going with the intransitive – not wanting to do something oneself must have been transferred at some point in Yupik to not wanting someone else to do it.

Another word involving rejection or refusal of another kind, PE *qiŋŋar- 'show displeasure', is not a fully fledged emotional root except in certain dialects of CAY, where it can mean 'feel displeasure, be indignant, be annoying, reject (esp. food)', depending on the suffix. Elsewhere it may appear as an ordinary stem meaning 'dislike' – especially foods, but within Inuit NAI has derived form qiŋałuak- 'show displeasure by being sullen', and Sigliq has qiŋaq- 'have a fierce look'. WG has qiŋŋar- 'suffer because one has broken the cultic rules, be irritated' but also transitive qiŋŋari- 'hate' and qiŋŋarnar- 'be infuriating' with *-kə- and *-nar- respectively.

10.2.11 Anger

A further basic kind of emotion word refers to anger. Of these, Eskimo languages have several. Interestingly, few if any of them are actual emotional roots today, probably because this usually overt kind of emotion has such salient behavioural reflexes. Thus PE *nəŋ(ŋ)ar- 'be angry' has this meaning everywhere as an ordinary intransitive verb, with local extensions – e.g. 'sulk angrily' in CAY, 'leave in a huff' in AAY, 'beat one's wife' in Point Hope Inupiaq, 'fight' in Holman Island Copper. In WG it can mean 'be bad-tempered, hysterical (of a child)', and in EG 'be offended'. Only in Tarramiut is the transitive form niŋŋari- 'be angry with' attested, which could be an innovation, replacing the missing form qiŋŋari- under *qiŋŋar- above.

PI *urulu- is rather 'be grumpy, in a bad mood' (in WG 'complain'). The only forms suggesting an earlier emotional root status here are Tarramiut urulugi- 'be in a bad mood because of s. o. or s.th.' (Petersen has a similar form for WG) and urulunaq- 'bothersome'.

There is also a handful of inter-related stems beginning with *qə- (or *əqə-), in particular PE *qəvə(t)- 'go away angrily', and PE *qənər- 'be angry', neither of them emotional roots as such. The former refers primarily to specific angry actions (including running off into the mountains in disappointment or anger in WG, or committing suicide in western Inuktitut – a kind of metonymy?), though it is simply 'be angry' in NSY. Reflexes of *qənər- refer (in Inuit) either to making angry sounds, as in WG qinir- 'growl, grumble' – in Copper specifically of a dog – or (in Yupik) to feeling insulted, as in CSY qənərtə- 'feel slighted'. The meanings in Inuit are predominantly behavioural. The relationship of these words to CAY emotional root əq'u- hate' from PY *əqə- 'angry' (perhaps limited to CAY) is unclear, but there is doubtless a link to Aleut aq(la)- 'be angry' and the stem here probably does represent a very old emotional root.

Another stem of feeling offended, PE *mam(ə)ya-, constitutes an emotional root, at least in some Inuit, as in WG mamia(sug)- 'be offended'. In Yupik it is very fragmentarily attested, principally in AAY papsaa(kə)- 'want to see, be suspicious of.[10] There are also corresponding forms with some of the expected derivational affixes in Canadian and Alaskan dialects, such as NAI mamiagi- 'feel hurt, distressed (by)' (Tarramiut 'detest'), Copper mamianaq- 'be annoying' and mamiasuk- 'be angry'.

Being offended is a more covert form of emotion than anger and thus may be more likely to be expressed by emotional roots. Interestingly, however, a more extreme form of anger, expressed by PE *ugumi- 'be infuriated', is also an emotional root, most fully so in Yupik. It is also interesting as one of the few clear examples of emotional metaphor in Eskimo languages, since it fairly transparently derives from *ugu- 'be heated up', expressions of heat being a well-known source of such verbs across languages. In CSY it is 'feel hatred or frustration' rather than 'be infuriated' (as in CAY), and similar meanings are found across the Inuit dialects, where uuminaq- is often glossed as 'be annoying', and uumigi- as 'hate'. In Tarramiut it is a fully fledged emotional root meaning 'have a grudge against, be angry at'. These seem to reflect a more covert form of anger than the proto-form gloss would suggest.

10.2.12 Regret

There may be a link between *ugu- above and PE *uggur- 'regret', since the WG reflex uxxu(a)r- is 'be angry' (the Tarramiut equivalent is 'regret'). The AAY correlate uurcar- is 'long for s.th. which one might have got but which is now inaccessible', and the CAY equivalent 'regret a loss which might have been prevented'.

---

10 This probably involves contamination with another stem, PE *papði- 'be bothersome', which is an emotional root in Norton Sound Yupik meaning 'find a nuisance'.

The only traces of its probable earlier status as a derivationally defined emotional root are Copper *uggarnaq-* 'causing suffering (e.g. heat, illness)' and WG *uxxu(a)rnar-* 'be annoying', *uxxuri-* 'be annoyed at' (with *-nar-* and *-kə-*).

The usual Yupik stem meaning 'grieve, mourn, regret' is PY **qːvru-* (also found in Point Hope and Nunamiut Inupiaq), which has a transitive form with *-kə-*. There is also PI **qigluk-* 'regret a loss', which in eastern Canada is 'take revenge' and in WG 'be angry because of s.th. lost', but these are not fully fledged emotional roots (today at least), even though WG has transitive *qillugi-* 'not want to lose s.th.', perhaps because they lie close to the overt behavioural pole.

In the meaning 'miss' (e.g. an absent person), PE stem **ivar-* 'look for' is widely used, especially in Yupik, but this appears to be a secondary development (metaphorical?). In Inuit a derived form PI **ivariatci-* has this specific meaning (in NAI and WG and Polar Eskimo), and WG has related *uyariagi-* 'miss s.th. one has been used to' (also *uyarianar-*), but none of these constitutes an emotional root as such. We are reminded that emotional roots may develop in time from non-emotional ones.

10.2.13 Jealousy or envy

Jealousy is a somewhat less "basic" emotion than plain anger, involving an element of cultural overlay. Of the most widespread Eskimo stem here, PE **cikna-* 'be jealous', little need be said, since the meaning is rather homogenous across the languages, combining envy and jealousy (of another's possessions) – though in some Canadian dialects the meaning is 'not want to share, be stingy with' (metonymy?). In CSY it is an emotional root *sikna-* 'feel possessive'. Inuit has developed distinct emotional verbs of sexual jealousy, two in fact for many Canadian and Greenlandic dialects, one for men of a woman, PI **caŋiak-* (which may be related to PE **caŋimmir-* 'want more'), and one for women of a man, **niŋŋaq-* – i.e. PE **nəŋ(ŋ)ar-* 'be angry' discussed above.[11] These are not treated as emotional roots, perhaps because they refer more to overt behaviour of a particular kind.

Another widespread verb of envy is PE **tucu-*, which covers 'desire' and 'admire' as well as 'envy', and does not combine with the full set of emotional derivational affixes either (though Polar Eskimo does have transitive *tuhugi-* 'admire, envy' and Petersen has *tusugi-* for WG). Perhaps the CAY meaning 'want to emulate someone else' is close to the original one.

---

11 This can have the meaning 'be jealous on account of s. o. of the opposite sex' in CAY (either sex, note), as well as 'sulk angrily at not having got one's way'.

It is not certain whether CAY *naŋru(yug)-* 'be critical, find fault with people' from PY **naŋru(r)-* 'criticize' has always been an emotional root or if it is a newer use of the stem by analogy with those referring to envy above. It is attested elsewhere in Yupik in the sense 'curse' (NSY) or 'disapprove' (CSY *naŋru(ri)-*, also *naŋrukə-* 'criticize'), and perhaps also in Tarramiut *narŋa(q)-*, transitive *narŋari-* 'criticize', but nowhere outside of CAY as a fully fledged emotional root allowing the complete set of relevant affixes. It lies at all events close to the overt, behavioural end of the emotional spectrum (even intransitive *naŋruyug-* 'be critical of someone' presupposes at least potential verbal expression aimed at the recipient of this attitude).

Another uncertain case is PE **ucur-* 'praise or envy', which is an emotional root in CAY glossed as 'praise, respect, revere' by Jacobson (1984), reflected in WG *usuri-* 'envy, wish to be in another's place' and *usurnar-* 'be enviable' (parallel forms are found in western Canadian Inuit, but in SPI *uzurnaq-* means 'be great, do a great deed'). Elsewhere (in Yupik and SPI) the transitive meaning 'praise, respect' (with **-kə-*) predominate, though in AAY *ucuryug-* (with *-yug-*) is found, in the meaning 'be astonished'. This all suggests that the item could once have been more widespread as a genuine emotional root. If so, the original meaning might have been 'envy, respect', developing the sense 'praise' by metonymy.

10.2.14 Anguish or suffering

Finally under the rubric of negative emotions, the most general sense of 'suffer' is expressed by PE **ikvig-*, mostly attested in Inuit, where it is a genuine emotional root, though also CSY has *ikfiqə-* 'feel anguish, suffer'. It is not always easy to distinguish this sense from that of PE **atŋir-* 'be in pain', which refers to purely physical pain and therefore can hardly be considered an emotional root (nor does it act like one). NAI has transitive *ikpigi-* 'feel a slight pain from', and Copper *ikpigusuk-*, *ikpigi-* 'suffer, feel pain from' (with extended form *-gusuk-* of **-yug-*).[12] Tarramiut has the equivalents. In WG *ippigi-* is 'find s.th. annoying, unfamiliar or unsuitable' (as also in *ippinnar-*) and intransitive *ippigusug-* or *ippigug-* is 'not feel well'.

---

[12] The *-guk-* reflex of PE **-yug-* is the allomorph found after velar stems in the Inuit dialects. It split off and became a separate affix attached to nominal bases in the sense 'want, thirst for' in Canada and Greenland, but throughout the Inuit dialects it tends to coalesce with the usual verbal reflex *-suk-* as *-gusuk-* or the like (note that syllable-initial */y/ usually becomes /s/ in closed syllables in Inuit).

One other verb of general internal 'hurt' (not an emotional root as such) should be mentioned: PE *ilulngu- 'hurt inside', consisting of nominal stem *ilu- 'inside' and affix *-lŋu- 'hurt in one's –'. It is quite literal in Prince William Sound Alutiiq and SPI Inupiaq, but 'be upset and angry' in CAY. NAI has derivatives meaning 'be sorry for' and 'be emotionally moved' as well as 'hurt inside', while in WG it is 'be moved or sad'. We see here how a derivational affix can have an emotional sense or extension in its own right (precluding the affixes of emotional roots). Besides *-lŋu- note PE *-ŋliqə- 'suffer from lack of –', PI *-ŋr̥iq- 'crave, want', and PE *-ummir- 'suddenly feel –'.

10.3 Positive emotional categories in Eskimo

10.3.1 Happiness

There are fewer items to consider when we turn to positive feelings. (Such is life...) Note that 'love' is not singled out here as its expression is rather heterogeneous – it is treated instead under 10.4.3. and 10.4.4 below. The most widespread "good feeling" emotional root is PE *quvya(yug)- 'be happy', which also has an Aleut cognate, Atkan qumyux(ta)- 'love' (in Attuan 'mourn, miss' rather). Note the -yux- element, i.e. *-yug-, as in the Eskimo cognate. There is little variation in meaning across the Eskimo languages, although CSY has qəsug(yug)- 'be happy, excited' rather (an irregular phonological distortion?), and in WG quia(sug)- is 'be amused' rather, 'be happy' being nuannaar-, a derivation of nuannir- 'be enjoyable'. This latter stem, PE *nunannir-, is also widely attested in this meaning, but it is an ordinary (derived) stem rather than an emotional root. It consists transparently of nominal stem *nuna 'land' plus *-n(n)ir- 'be good to do' (with dissimilation in Inuit), so originally something like 'enjoy being out on the land'. A related stem in Yupik is PY *nunaki- 'be enjoyable'

10.3.2 Amusement

Another widespread positive emotional root is PE *təmci- 'be or find funny', which easily extends to (behavioural) 'laugh (at)', as in transitive SPI tipsii- (with *-kə-) and Polar Eskimo intransitive tissihuk- (Petersen 1951 has all four criterial affixes for WG). The Aleut cognate of this is tumci- 'copulate with (a woman)'. Yupik also has PY *təŋru- 'be enthusiastic, eager', which is attested as a fully fledged emotional root only in CSY (which also has təŋruniqə- 'have fun'), but CAY at least has transitive *təŋrukə-* 'be enthusiastic about'. In AAY *təŋru-/təŋŋu-* is 'be confident, sure of oneself'. This may be related to *təmci-* (compare the suffix in CSY *alaŋru-* below).

10.3.3 Feeling at ease

A less boisterous expression of satisfaction is found in PI **cail(l)i-* 'feel at ease' (NAI 'relax, recover after stress', Tarramiut 'feel at ease', WG 'be at home while others are out'), and related **caima-* 'become calm' (Tarramiut *saimma-* 'be calm, at peace', WG *saama-* 'be kind, mild, satisfied'). In WG *tulluuti-* 'feel satisfied, comforted' is derived from PE **tut-* 'land' plus *-l(l)u(C)ar-* 'well', and words of similar meaning in Yupik – such as CAY *sanqəgtə-* 'be at peace, satisfied' (containing PE **-nqig-* 'be good or well') – are very diverse. None of these are emotional roots as such. CSY does have *itagnaryug-* 'feel satisfied' with *-yug-*, however, and Inuit has *naammagi-* 'be satisfied with' (with *-gi-*) based on *naammag-* 'be enough', which Briggs has as 'feel comfortable or safe' for Utku (besides 'be good, correct').

10.3.4 Thankfulness

The original PE stem for thankfulness, namely PE **quya-* 'be thankful', today means 'be happy' in many dialects. There appears to be entanglement with **quvya(yug)-* 'be happy' above. CAY *quya-* 'be thankful, glad' combines both nuances. The stem is not an emotional root in most dialects according to the derivational crtiterion, but it does display some combinations with **-yug-* and **-kə-*, as in Netsilik *quyahuk-* 'be in a good mood', Tarramiut *quyagi-* 'thank' (also WG), and CAY *quyakə-* 'appreciate'. Beside *quya-* 'thank', WG has derived form *qutsasir-* 'dance around for joy (old woman)'. All the languages use the **-nar-* form as a standard expression of thanks (PE **quyanar*) – although in Tarramiut it means rather 'it doesn't matter, so much the better'. Probably this stem did once form a fully fledged emotional root.

There is another emotional root that covers the sense of gratitude in some languages, namely PE **əlira-/əliŋra-*, glossed in Fortescue, Jacobson, and Kaplan (2010) as 'want to ask for s.th. but not dare'. This is a particularly tricky set to analyse, as it straddles both positive and negative meanings. The languages where it most clearly has a positive meaning are CAY, which has *əliŋra(yug)-* 'be grateful', SPI, which has adverbial expression *iliranamik* 'thank you!', and NAI, which has *iłira(suk)-* 'be grateful, happy', as also in Sigliq. To the east the meaning changes radically to Copper 'want to ask for s.th. but not dare' (taken in Fortescue, Jacobson, and Kaplan [2010] to represent the earliest meaning), also *iliranaq-* 'cause fear (person)', Netsilik 'be afraid, respect' (with overtones of fear of being unkindly treated acc. Briggs 1970: 375 for Utku) and, according to Rasmussen (1931), *iliraŋŋuq-* 'become full of depressing thoughts'. In Tarramiut *ilira(suk)-* is 'fear embarrassment or criticism', and in Aivilik (North Baffin Inuit – NBI) 'be ill at ease'. In WG *ilirasug-* is 'have a bad conscience', *iliranar-* 'be difficult to approach, threatening, taboo', and *iliragi-* 'take care nothing happens to s.th. belonging to another' – also (with a preceding nominalized verbal form) 'not dare'. Finally, back in Yupik territory, CSY *liŋra(yug)-* is 'hesitate to ask (again)', reinforcing the supposed PE meaning. What are we to make of this emotional mishmash? There appears to be some kind of complex metonymy involved: both the deference felt when soliciting something from another (especially someone one respects or looks up to), the fear of it perhaps backfiring, and (potential) gratitude when the outcome is as desired. Different languages have apparently chosen to highlight one aspect or another of the scenario associated with the Proto-Eskimo root. This highlights the complex social or cultural aspects of many emotional expressions, rendering them difficult to translate into English.

10.4 Other Eskimo emotional categories

10.4.1 Lust

Emotional roots that are difficult to categorize as either negative or positive (for reasons other than a historical shift in meaning) include those of wanting or craving. PE **əkli-* 'lust for (sexually)' is a fully fledged emotional stem – the intransitive *-yug-* form is roughly 'have a desire aroused' (this is the gloss given for Kodiag Island AAY). In SPI Inuit the *-suk-* form is glossed as 'flirt' but in NAI as 'be enticed to do s.th.' (*ikl'igusuk-*, with the extended version of *-suk-*); the transitive *-gi-* form is 'desire, covet'. Elsewhere in Canada and Greenland the transitive form with *-gi-* is more common (in the sense 'desire' – usually sexual, but in WG especially of food or drink), although the *-(gu)suk-* intransitive ones also exist. WG *illigug-* is specifically 'one's mouth waters (in expectation of food)'. 'Wanting' is otherwise expressed by affix **-yug-* itself and its derivatives.

There is also PY **ala-* 'desire' (with Aleut cognate *ala-* meaning 'want, need (e.g. food)'), as in CAY *alakə-, alaŋə-* 'be attracted to a member of the opposite sex', which in AAY is an emotional root *ala(yug-)* 'be stingy', and CSY has *alaŋru-* 'miss, be at a loss' – also an emotional root.

10.4.2 Longing

A related but less specific notion is that of longing. There are stems expressing strong desire or longing in the modern languages going back to PE *qi(C)ət- 'be convulsed' and (especially) its derivative PE *qi(C)əlir- 'be worked up (with longing)'. These are ordinary verbal stems, though in CSY *qiliir-* 'covet, desire' is generally treated as an emotional root with intransitive *-yug-* (this is optional). Cognates of the latter in other languages are CAY *qiilərtə-* 'experience and show strong joyful feelings', NAI *qiiligžuk-* 'clench fists and teeth in frustration', Copper *qiilik-* 'have a great desire for, make a grimace when work goes badly', and WG *qiilir-* 'long for s.th.'. The only reflexes of PE *qi(C)ət- itself with these meanings are Tarramiut *qiit-* 'have a great desire for', Labrador 'be parched with thirst', and WG 'long for s.th.', none of them emotional roots. At least some of these meanings belong at the overt behavioural end of the emotional scale.

Note also stem PI *kayuŋŋiq- 'be eager to go', from *kayu- 'strong', which is in most dialects not attested as an emotional root. Tarramiut has *kayuŋiq-* 'be pulling on traces (dog)', and 'be raring to go (person)'. In WG, however, besides *kayuŋir-* 'desire, long for s.th.', there is *kayuŋiri-* 'be attracted by' and *kayuŋirnar-* 'be attractive' with *-kə- and *-nar- respectively, perhaps another example of metaphor.

I treat PE *nəryu(g)- 'eagerly expect, hope' separately under 10.4.5. below.

10.4.3 Pity

Next, there are a number of roots referring to pity. The most important of these is PE *naŋɬəg- 'feel sorry for s. o.', already referred to. Everywhere it has the meaning of feeling pity or compassion – in CAY, for instance, the gloss of *nakɬəqə-* is 'feel compassion towards, be considerate of'. But in some languages and dialects it has a further meaning of 'love, cherish'. This is the case in AAY (*nakɬəkə-*), Canadian Inuktitut (where it is the sole meaning in the eastern dialects), and Polar Eskimo, which has the root in both meanings. EG has *nattii-*'be responsible for, look after affectionately, pity', which suggests a bridge between the two meanings. Some languages have related forms with the meaning 'suffer', e.g. NAI *nagliksaaq-*. In fact there is a probable relationship with PE stem *naŋət- 'finish off, use up', which also means 'suffer' in a number of dialects. Love is evidently not always a purely positive matter: love and suffering on account of love are not incompatible. It is at all events a complex emotion. There is another related stem of suffering, PI *naatki-, which also combines affection and pity, especially in Tarramiut *naakki-* 'be affectionate towards' alongside *naakkigi-* 'have pity on', and compare Copper *naatki-*, WG *naakki(gi)-* 'be sorry for' – but this is not a fully fledged emotional root anywhere today.

Another, less widely attested emotional root of feeling pity for someone is PE **takumcu(g)-*, as in AAY and CAY, where it is glossed 'have pity on, feel compassion towards'. It is based on PE **taku-* 'see or check on' and **-mcug-* 'a little', so the original meaning could have been 'look after, care for', though the contemporary difference between it and *nakłəqə-* in CAY is not clear. Oddly enough, *takumsug-* is glossed as 'go somewhere for pleasure' in St Lawrence Island CSY although mainland Chaplino has *takumsuna-lrii* 'tender' and WG has transitive *takussugi-* 'find ugly to look at' besides *takussunar-* 'look pitiful'.

10.4.4 Feeling protective/loving towards

How do the languages and dialects that don't display the extension of the meaning of **naŋłəg-* from pity to love express the latter emotion? Some Yupik languages use PY stem **piniqə-* 'like, love' (CSY, NSY and Nunivak CAY), which is the transitive version (with **-kə-*) of intransitive *pinir-* 'be good' (so 'consider good').[13] In CSY the intransitive form *piniryug-* (with **-yug-*) means 'be cheerful' and *pinirnar-* is 'be made (to be) pleasing', so this almost makes an emotional root set, though it is likely to be an innovation. The most widespread word for 'love' in CAY is emotional root *kənəg-*, which has no obvious cognates elsewhere, but probably represents the lost stem of PI **əkiŋŋun* 'close friend', as in eastern Canada and Greenlandic *ikiŋŋut*.

The verb for 'love' in contemporary WG and EG *asa-* has an idiosyncratic background, and is not an emotional root at all (it is transitive, requiring antipassive affix *-nnig-* to become intransitive). The complex way this has developed from PI **ažak-* 'be gentle with', involving the definitional intervention of Christian missionaries, is laid out in Fortescue (2001). Suffice it to say that the latter stem is not an emotional one either and that it nowhere else means 'love', although the early missionary Paul Egede has *ašak-* 'look after, treat well' in his dictionary of 1750. Note also Malamiut NAI antipassive *ažaknik-* 'comfort, encourage, soothe s. o.', parallel with the Greenlandic intransitive form *asannig-*. There is a similar kind of stem in CAY that is a fully fledged emotional root, namely *kuzgu-* 'feel compassion towards' (in Hooper Bay/Cevak *kuygur-* 'be protective (bird towards young)'). Despite its very limited distribution this root must be very old, reconstructable as PE **kuðə(g)-*, since it is also found in older WG *kuši-* 'feel pity towards' and

---

[13] CAY (and AAY) also has weaker *asikə-* 'like' from *asir-* 'good' (so also 'consider good').

'become or make better (a sick person)' – in modern WG *kušanar-* is 'be beautiful' and *kušagi-* 'like, think beautiful'. The remaining PI dialects generally use PI **nakuarə-* 'like' (though in Tarramiut *nakuari-* is 'thank, praise for'), a transitive derivation of PI **naku(a)q-* 'be good or strong', parallel with Yupik *piniqə-* above.

10.4.5 Uncertainty

I shall finish this overview with two categories of widely attested emotional roots that seem more emotionally neutral (from a Eurocentric point of view) than those examined so far, close respectively to mental activity or to general perceptual experience. The first category covers PE **əlima-* 'suspect', **nəryu(g)-* 'eagerly expect, hope', **ukvər-* 'believe' and **natu-* 'not know'. Of these, *əlima-* is actually an emotional root only in Inuit – in CAY it is 'be knowledgeable', reflecting its probable source in the combination of *əlit-* 'learn' and stative affix *-(u)ma-*. It is emotionally neutral in modern WG *ilimasug-, ilimagi-* 'expect', but elsewhere has a distinctly negative coloration. Thus in SPI it is 'be suspicious, suspect', in NAI 'be apprehensive, suspect' and in Tarramiut 'be apprehensive, on the look out'. In Polar Eskimo *ilumahuk-, ilumagi-* is 'expect, dread (s.th. bad)'. This is reminiscent of the 'darkening' of the neutral meaning of PY **cumər(tə)-* 'think' in CAY to 'worry' discussed earlier.

There is also a PE stem of expecting s.th. good, namely PE **nəryu(g)-* 'eagerly expect, hope', which everywhere takes the **-kə-* and **-nar-* forms expected of emotional roots (thus in all Inuit *niriugi-* 'hope, expect'), but falls just short of being an emotional root – unless the stem itself contains lexicalized **-yug-* (compare the case of **maruyug-* above).[14]

PE **ukvər-* 'believe' does not quite constitute a fully fledged emotional root in any of the languages – all, even CAY, lack an intransitive *-yug-* form – although the meaning is identical throughout the Eskimo world and all dialects have correlates with **-kə-* ('believe in') and **-nar-* ('believable'). Signs of the set once having been more complete are seen in derivations like CAY *ukvərtar-* 'be gullible' (with the *-tar-* affix that is typical of emotional roots in Yupik). Belief as such (even before any Christian overlay) does have an emotional element ('conviction' or 'wanting to believe') apart from the neutral epistemic stance.

Also the converse of believing, doubting, which is perhaps more obviously emotional, is expressed by an emotional root in Yupik, namely PE **aðgura-*,

---

[14] The apparent source of these forms in Yupik in **nərə-* 'eat' plus **-yug-* 'want to' is probably fortuitous – compare NAI *niriuk-* 'expect, hope' with *nirisuk-* 'want to eat'.

glossed as 'be stubborn or unwilling' in Fortescue, Jacobson, and Kaplan (2010), mainly because of the Inuit cognates, which mean 'be stubborn' (SPI), 'be bold, undaunted' (NAI), or 'be proud' (Copper). In Yupik it is everywhere 'doubt, not believe'. The transitive forms in Inuit (*ažguagi-* in Alaska) mean 'be undaunted by' (NAI) or 'have s.th. against, reprove' (WG *assuari-*), though Qawiaraq also has the meaning 'doubt'. The connection is to be seen in the origin of the set as a derivative of PE **aðgur-* 'go against current or wind' (cognate with Aleut *aðgur-* 'rebuke, forbid'). We are dealing here with a clear case of metaphor – perhaps more than one. The usual Inuit stem for doubting, PI **qulaq-*, is not an emotional root today but could once have been – forms with *-gi-* and *-nar-* are widespread. Both believing and doubting can be grouped under the rubric 'uncertainty', on a scale from fairly certain to fairly uncertain.

We need to consider briefly at this point other epistemic/cognitive verbs in Eskimo, those for knowing, thinking and remembering, since there is evidence that some of these were fully fledged emotional roots in Proto-Eskimo. First, it should be pointed out that the most basic verb of knowing in all forms of Eskimo has the negative meaning 'not know', i.e. PE **natu-*. This takes most of the affixes typifying emotional roots, though not a full set in any one language. Thus CSY has *natukə-* 'not know', *natuyug-* 'be unsure, in doubt' (also transitive equivalent *natuyukə-*) and *natunar-* 'be difficult to know or perceive', and CAY has *natuyug(ci)-* 'feel strange about s.th.' and inchoative *natuyagutə-* 'forget'. So this stem may well have been a fully fledged emotional root in Proto-Eskimo, with the negative ('not-not know', i.e. not be in doubt about) meaning 'know', as in all the contemporary languages. Interestingly, this cannot be said of the other widespread verb of knowing, PE **alicima-* of knowing in the positive sense of being acquainted with (based on **alit-* 'learn').

As suggested in the discussion of PY *cumar(tə)-* in section 10.2.8, verbs of thinking in Eskimo languages display emotional overtones or derivations, particularly of worrying. Another widespread 'mental' verb, PE **ənqa(r)-* 'remember' also displays some forms with typical emotional root affixes, thus CAY transitive *ənqakə-/nəqqakə-*, corresponding to Inuit *itqagi-/iqqagi-* (in Tarramiut = 'be full of attention for' and in WG 'be anxious to get'), and in all Inuit *itqanar-/iqqanar-* (in Tarramiut 'be favoured' but in WG 'look threatening'). WG also has *iqqasug-* 'be worried' with **-yug-* (Berthelsen et al.1997). It is thus likely that this too was once an emotional root, aligning with other verbs involving elements of worry and doubt.

10.4.6 Feeling or noticing (generally)

Of the emotional roots that have a broad perceptual meaning PI *maluɣə- 'notice that s.th. has changed (for the worse)' has a largely negative sense in the west but in Greenland a more emotionally neutral one. In WG *malugi-* is 'notice, discover, feel that', *malunnar-* 'be striking, recognizable', and intransitive *malugusug-* even has a positive sense: 'be happy about a change (or about receiving s.th. one lacked)'. In Alaska *maluknaq-* is 'be different, not as good as before' (SPI) or 'be shameful, seem wrong' (NAI). In Copper *malugi-* is 'not like the way a thing is' and in Tarramiut 'doubt s.th.'s value' – but in Labrador 'notice' (where *malugusuk-* is 'suspect, notice, feel one's drink'). The root appears to have been lost in Yupik.

The case of PE *əlpəkə- is not far removed from that of PI *maluɣə-. It refers to any kind of feeling or sensation, physical or mental. In CSY it is in fact a fully fledged emotional root of being or becoming aware of something (also of 'being edgy'). CAY has the transitive version (*əlpəkə-*) and various other derivations, but not with criterial affix *-yug-. AAY does have the full derivational set, however, and *əlpəgyug-* can be 'have a feeling, sensation or premonition'. In Inuit there is some entanglement between this stem and PE *ikvig- 'suffer', treated above. Distinct from the latter are at least Qawiaraq *ikpii-* 'feel sensation', Netsilik (Spence Bay) *ikpigi-* 'feel (e.g. breeze or pain)', and Labrador *ippigi-* 'be aware of', as also in some other eastern Inuktitut. In all likelihood, then, this was originally an emotional root that has lost its intransitive forms in some of the languages. It is a very general one, however, covering sensations of all kind, purely somatic as well as emotional – note the negative/caritive form *əlpəgitə-* in CAY is 'be numb, insensitive'.

10.5 Summary of the Eskimo data and comparison with Briggs (1970)

In the preceding sections 36 PE emotional roots have been discussed covering the meanings listed in Table 1, with a further 5 that may have been lost from one branch or another of the family (a very conservative estimate). This is not far off the 54 Jacobson (1984: 665–666) lists for contemporary CAY, given that 11 of these are marked as "not strictly roots". The approximate number of roots may thus have remained fairly constant, though many of the specific forms will have become replaced by others or shifted in meaning in individual languages/ dialects.

Although not all emotions are expressed by emotional roots in Eskimo languages, those that are expressed by ordinary verbs seem often to be of a more "overt" nature, directly reflecting behaviour diagnostic for the emotion concerned, for example verbs of anger like PE *nəŋ(ŋ)ar- and *qənər- discussed in section 10.2.11. These will probably always be accompanied by some kind of overt angry behaviour. True emotional roots lie at the other, covert end of the scale, close to words referring to purely internal mental states. Compare PE *mam(ə)ya- 'be offended' which is indeed an emotional root and at the same time represents a more covert emotion than the preceding two items. At all events, the dividing line between the lexicon of emotion and of cognition/perception seems to lie slightly differently in Eskimo languages than in European ones: the meanings presented under 10.4.5. and 10.4.6. above would hardly qualify as "emotional" in English, for example. This may well be an areal phenomenon, as we shall see in comparing the situation in neighbouring Chukotko-Kamchatkan languages.

Before leaving the Eskimo-Aleut family, however, let me make a detour to Briggs' investigation of certain lexical expressions of emotion in Utku, contextualized primarily in domestic situations. Not all of those treated by her (as summarized on p. 375 of her 1970 book) constitute what I would characterize as emotion words as opposed to words with a significant component of accompanying affect. For example her *iva* 'lie next to someone else in bed, with connotations of affectionate cuddling'. This is PE *əva- 'sit on eggs' in Fortescue, Jacobson, and Kaplan (2010), which has been extended to mammals as well as birds in Inupiaq and still further in certain westerly Canadian dialects (metaphorically) to cuddling humans, in the manner depicted by Briggs. In Polar Eskimo it can mean 'warm one's hands on another human body' rather. Of the remaining twenty three terms she lists that display a primary emotional content many correspond to terms I have discussed above – only one important stem in this dialect appears not to be attested outside of Utku, namely *huyuuyaq* 'unhappy because of absence of people', apparently also used to refer to more general situations of discomfort and hostility (compare *aliga- in section 10.2.2). This is probably related to *suyuuŋŋituq* 'there is nothing', which Schneider (1985) marks as "adg", i.e. from west of Hudson Bay. In general, one should be wary of applying the exact meanings Briggs ascribes to the words in Utku directly to other dialects. This is not to deny that they are indeed employed in Utku in emotional contexts of the kind she describes in detail.

The rest of the terms she discusses are as in Table 2, in alphabetical order, cross-referenced to proto-forms in Fortescue, Jacobson, and Kaplan (2010) and the section in which they are discussed above.

Table 2: Emotion words in Briggs (1970)

ayuq	'difficult, unable or impossible' is PI **ayuq-* 'be unable to do or reach' (10.2.3), not an emotional root
hatuq	'grateful, arouse gratitude, kind, helpful' is PI **catuq-* 'take back', nowhere else attested in an emotional sense
huqu	'respond, pay attention to needs of others or disturbing events in own life' is PI **cuqutə(gə)-* 'care about', not an emotional root
ihluaq	'correct, comfortable, safe' is PE **ałurar-* 'be correct or right', not an emotional root
ilira	'fear of being unkindly treated, respectful with overtones of fear' is PE **əlira-* 'want to ask for but not dare (10.3.4)
iqhi	'fear physical injury' is PI **iqci-* 'be afraid' (10.2.1)
kanngu	'wish to avoid displaying oneself before others' is PE **kayŋu-* 'be ashamed' (10.2.5)
kappia	'fear physical injury' is PE **kappəya-* 'feel anxious' (10.2.4)
naamak	'be correct or convenient, feel all right, good, proper, comfortable, safe' is PE **naðama-* 'be enough', not an emotional root
naklik	'feel concern for another's welfare, wish to be with another' is PE **naŋłəg-* 'sorry for' (10.4.3)
ningaq	'feel or express hostility' is PE **nəŋ(ŋ)ar-* 'angry' (10.2.11)
niviuq	'wish to kiss or touch another' is PI **nəviuq-* 'hang around near' (under PE **nəvə-* 'cling to'), not an emotional root
pai	'feel left behind, missing a person who has gone' is PE **pagi-* 'stay at home and look after house', not an emotional root
piyuma	'want s.th., often with connotations of greed, jealousy or envy' is 'empty' stem PE **pi(-)* plus affix PE *-yuguma* 'want to'
qiquq	'clogged with foreign matter, on point of tears, feel hostile' is probably from *qiqur-*'block a fissure in the wall of a snow house', from PE *qiku* 'clay or cement', a metaphorical usage not attested elsewhere
quya	'grateful' is PE **quya-* 'be thankful' (10.3.4)
quvia	'feel happiness' is PE **quvya(yug)-.*'be happy' (10.3.1)
tiphi	'feel like laughing' is PE **təmci-* 'funny' (10.3.2)
tuhuu	'want something belonging to another' is PE **tucu-* 'admire, envy' (10.2.13)
tumak	'withdrawn in unhappiness (especially through absence of others)' is PE **tumag-* 'taste bitter', which does not have an attested emotional sense elsewhere
tupak	'be startled' is PE **tupəkə-* 'surprised, excited' (10.2.1)
unga	'wish to be with another' is PE **uŋa-* 'cling to (child to adult)', not an emotional root
uyyiq	'worry' is PI **užžiq-* 'show what to do (by signs)' (under PE **uðəg-* 'try'), not an emotional root
urulu	'feel or express hostility or annoyance' is PI **urulu-* 'angry, grumpy' (10.2.11)

Although many of the terms she discusses are not expressed as emotional roots (she lists 33 items in all), most of them relate to the proto-language types listed in Table 1. Note that McNabb (1989: 58) believes that *hatuq* is a misinterpretation on Briggs' part. Briggs groups the emotions she discusses into 9 types or "syndromes" corresponding to categories in English (Briggs 1970: 311) – affection, kindness and gratitude, happiness, ill temper and jealousy, humour, fear, anxiety, shyness, and loneliness. Her treatment gives a good idea of the expression in contemporary dialects of such meanings both by original emotional roots (for the more "covert" emotions) and by ordinary stems (sometimes with metaphor involved). Most importantly, her book provides a window into the socio-cultural fine-tuning of emotional expression. Like Briggs, McNabb (1989) in his comparison of Briggs' key terms with cognates in Alaskan Inupiaq, takes the sociologist's position that expressions of affect reveal more about social relations and interaction than about autonomous psychological characteristics.

10.6 The expression of emotional categories in Chukotko-Kamchatkan

The Chukotko-Kamchatkan (C-K) family – at least its major Chukotian branch – is also characterized, quite unlike any other neighbouring languages, by a special category of emotional roots distinguished from ordinary stems by their (obligatory) derivational potential. In the case of Chukotian (i.e. Chukchi, Koryak, Kerek and Alutor) this is a matter of just two forms, one affixal, the other analytic involving an auxiliary verb. Though the means are quite different, the delimitation of this category is remarkably similar to that displayed by Eskimo languages, with extension into certain more or less "neutral" mental states. The affixal means is the addition of the derivational affix *-æt-/-at-* (vowel harmony allomorphs), and sometimes *-æv-/-av-*, both elsewhere general verbalizers of nouns and adjectives, to the root concerned to produce an intransitive verb of feeling. The transitive equivalent is produced by combining auxiliary verb **ləŋ-* 'consider as, acquire as' (Chukchi *ləŋ-/-lyə-*) with the "attributive" case form of the root in *-u/-o*.[15] There is also another auxiliary, **ðəccə-* 'make or turn into' (Chukchi *rətcə-*), which has a resultative or inchoative meaning (much like Eskimo **-yyag-*, but always transitive). The semantics of the first auxiliary is very like that of Eskimo **-kə-*, whose

---

15 The root itself is indeterminate as regards part of speech, but note that (nominal) cases in C-K can be attached to bare verbal bases.

basic function is also one of transitive possession ('have as'). I shall present the forms concerned – taken from my comparative C-K Dictionary (Fortescue 2005) – in the same order as the 24 types of root presented above for Eskimo so as to bring out the close similarity of the two systems. The 24 Proto-Eskimo types of meaning can be seen reflected also in Proto-Chukotian. There are considerably fewer roots to deal with than in the larger Eskimo-Aleut family, and the data from dictionaries is also less complete, so sometimes I need to infer the probable existence of a transitive form with *ləŋ- if only an intransitive one with *-æt- is attested.

10.6.1 Fear

Proto-Chukotian (PC) *cæŋət(t)æt- (with *-æt-) is attested in all the languages as 'be frightened' (Bogoraz 1937 has 'jump with fright'). A similar root is *wit- 'give a jump (of surprise)', which occurs everywhere with affixes *-æt- or *-æv-. Whether they can occur with *ləŋ- is uncertain. However, ləŋ- forms of verbs of fearing certainly do exist: Dunn (1999: 322) gives *ajəly-o ləŋ-* (also with resultative *rətcə-*) 'fear' for Chukchi. Then there is PC *ðiŋtə- 'wonderful or holy', which appears as *jiŋtev-* 'be amazed' in Koryak (according to Kibrik et al. 2000 Alutor cognate *tiŋtə-* is 'able to foresee things'). Compare the CAY meanings of words under PE *ira- in section 10.2.1.

10.6.2 Loneliness and sad feelings

PC *Rælæræ- 'pine away' is in all four languages 'be bored, pine, homesick'. Although it is not attested with *ləŋ-, Koryak has *pawjaqat-* in the same meaning with *-æt- (Žukova 1967). PC *wacq(æv)- 'be bored' occurs with *-æv-. In Chukchi it is 'be disappointed, lose hope', and in Koryak 'be bored, lazy'. PC *yəlo- is 'be sad, bored' in Chukchi (*həlu-* 'sad' in Kerek), but nowhere is an -æt- or ləŋ- form attested. However, another set, PC *pənnə- 'be sad' in Chukchi and Kerek, does have an *-æv- form in Chukchi (*pənnew-* 'get sad, grieve' – Moll et al. 1957), and Koryak has *weŋqat-* 'be sad' that contains *-æt-, and also *emŋol-* in that meaning, which does enter into construction with *ləŋ- (see under 10.6.12 below).

10.6.3 Frustration

PC *pəkav- 'be unable', which is found in this meaning everywhere except Chukchi, contains *-æv-. Koryak also has pəkaw-yəjŋən 'difficulty' – compare PE *capərnar- in section 10.2.3.

10.6.4 Anxiety

PC *pæyciŋæt- 'get agitated' contains *-æt- and occurs everywhere with this sense – in Chukchi also 'curious', and in Koryak 'interested, uneasy, worried'. Dunn has Chukchi peyciŋu ləŋ- 'be curious about' with *ləŋ-, but peycinet- is 'be worried' there too.

10.6.5 Shame

PC *ŋəðkəlat- 'be ashamed' contains *-æt- and is attested in all four languages in this form (e.g. Chukchi ŋərkəlat-). In fact it also appears to have an Itelmen cognate kskozoʔl-kas in the same sense (but without correlates of the typical Chukotian derivational morphemes).[16] The same affix is contained in PC *yæryæt- 'be embarrassed' (Chukchi 'get angry, irritable' rather – apart from in the southern dialect, where it is 'shy, embarrassed'), but no *ləŋ- form is attested for it either.

10.6.6 Timidity

PC *Ræqæliŋ (əlRən) 'cowardly' occurs both with *-æv- (as in Koryak Raqaliŋav- 'be fearful, frightened'), and with *ləŋ- (Chukchi ʔaqaliŋu ləŋ- 'be afraid'). It consists of *Ræqæ- 'bad' and liŋ 'heart' (a rare transparent metaphor or "folk theory"). Koryak also has yiyajat- 'be timid' containing *-æt-.[17]

---

16 Sedanka dialect ŋəskla-laX is borrowed directly from neighbouring Chukotian.
17 Chukchi has yəyar-yəryən 'fear, danger' – the Koryak equivalent is 'carefulness'.

10.6.7 Apprehension

PC *jəmyəmyæt- 'feel dread' ranges from 'feel superstitious dread' in Chukchi to just 'be afraid' in Kerek and Alutor (Muravyova 1979 has root jəmŋə- for the latter). Note related jəmŋev- 'run away, be worried or confused' (with *-æv- rather than *-æt-) in Koryak. PC *æmkumRə- 'careful', found in Koryak, Kerek, Alutor and the Khatyrka dialect of Chukchi, is given by Dunn for Chukchi in the ləŋ- construction: emkumʔu (ləŋ-) 'care about', and refers more to possessions than imagined danger (so perhaps it belongs under 10.6.22 below).

10.6.8 Worry

PC *æŋRæl- 'worry' as in Chukchi eŋʔel- 'worry, get tired, overstrain' occurs both with *-æt- (in the meaning 'be afraid' in Alutor but 'get tired' in Kerek) and with ləŋ- (Koryak eŋRelu ləŋ- 'worry about'). As in Eskimo-Aleut (E-A), worrying is often a connotation of stems meaning 'think'. Thus Koryak ceŋRecen- 'worry' (with reduplication) is probably the "missing" cognate of Chukchi cimyʔu- 'think' (PC *cimŋəRu-, under 10.6.23 below), and Chukchi transitive cimyʔu ləŋ- 'think about' can also be 'worry about, look after' (in Inenlikej 1982).

10.6.9 Disgust

PC *cirmən(æt)- 'feel disgust' occurs also in the transitive ləŋ- construction in Chukchi. The same is true of PC *pajwaq- 'disgust or sorrow', as in Chukchi pajwaqo ləŋ- 'feel disgust at, despise'. Koryak has pawjaq 'sorrow' and pawjaqat- 'pine' – Kamen Koryak has paivaku ləŋ- 'feel aversion, envy' but paivakat- 'feel lonely' according to Bogoraz (1937). Chukchi also has mərkerat- (with *-æt-) 'be disgusted by s.th.' – in the southeast dialect 'be sceptical towards, be occupied with s.th.'.

10.6.10 Not feeling like doing s.th.

PC *Rænq(æt)- 'refuse' also occurs in the ləŋ- construction, 'refuse, dislike' in Chukchi (ʔenqu ləŋ-), but 'dislike' in Koryak, and 'not allow' in Alutor. Note also Chukchi ʔenqew- 'be full, satiated', Koryak RenjqecRet- 'be fed up', and Kerek XanqajRa(a)t- 'not want to'. Also belonging here is perhaps PC *ŋərRæv- (with *-æv-) which is 'refuse to do s.th.' as well as 'get angry' in both Chukchi and Alutor.

10.6.11 Anger

PC *liŋt(æv)- 'get angry' probably contains liŋ 'heart'. It occurs in some dialects with *-æt- rather than *-æv- (thus Palan Alutor liŋtat- 'quarrel'), as also found in Koryak form ŋotav- under PC *ŋot- 'be angry or uncooperative'. In Chukchi and Kerek the latter means rather 'slow moving, not easily manoeuvrable' (a meaning also found in Koryak), so the 'angry, uncooperative' meaning may be a metaphor. A third Chukchi form wicet- 'be annoyed', from PC *vic(æt)- glossed as 'be annoyed', is not so strong in meaning and may lie closer to the overt, behavioural end of the scale (in Koryak it is vicə- 'clumsy, rude', an adjectival form). The only root in this group with attested ləŋ- forms is PC *Ræqu ləŋ- 'hate', based on *Ræqæ- 'bad' (Chukchi also has ʔeqet- 'curse, injure' with *-æt-).

10.6.12 Regret

Another derivative of *Ræqæ- 'bad' has the meaning 'be sorry' in Koryak (also Alutor), namely Reqetetkejug- (literally 'bad think'), although this is not an emotional root (compare PC *təkæj(u)- 'be conscious' in 6.23 below, where there are forms with *-æv- however). There is also PC *emŋol- 'miss', which Moll et al. have in the form emŋolo ləŋ- 'miss s. o.' for Chukchi. In Koryak the root is rather 'sad' (as in Alutor) or 'boring' (a meaning also found in Chukchi and Kerek).[18]

10.6.13 Jealousy or envy

The most widely distributed form for 'envy' is PC *vænnæt-. Moll et al. have transitive form vennu ləŋ- for Chukchi (also found in Koryak). PC *æqənet- 'envy' (also with *-æt-) is limited to Koryak eqənet-, but appears to have been borrowed from there into Itelmen.

10.6.14 Anguish or suffering

Various derivatives of PC *Ræqæ- 'bad' refer to negative emotions, and in Koryak Reqejunet- (with junet- 'live', in turn containing *-æt-) is specifically 'suffer'.

---

18 Note that the Russian gloss *skučat'* can mean either 'be bored' or 'miss (s. o.)'.

Chukchi has nominal *ʔaqa-yəryən* 'misery, misfortune', and (in Moll et al.) *ʔeqecimyʔu-* 'think badly, be upset' (with PC **cimŋeRu-* 'think').

10.6.15 Happiness

The most common root here is PC **kərvi-* 'happy', which in Chukchi is *koryə-*. Dunn has transitive *koryo ləŋ-* 'delight in', and Bogoras has *kərwiw-* 'enjoy oneself' (with **-æv-*, like Kerek *kujyau-* 'be happy'). Another common root is PC **yajma-* 'happy or willing'. In Chukchi there is, beside adverbial form *yajmete* 'amusing', *yajmav-* 'be carried away, fly into a passion', and *yajmo* 'willing, wishing', presumably combinable with **ləŋ-* like Koryak *yajmo ləŋ-* 'want'. Bogoraz has *yaimat-* 'desire' for the southern Chukchi dialect, corresponding to Koryak *yajmat-* 'want'. There are cognates in Itelmen – in particular *kaim* 'merry' in Radlinski (1981–4) for extinct southern Itelmen, but there is also contemporary *xajmaŋto-kas* 'be merry' (Sedanka *vajma* 'happy'), undoubtedly a loan from Chukotian.

10.6.16 Amusement

PC **(cə)yiciv-* 'amusing' is widespread, and found in both **-æt-* form (Chuckchi *yiciwet-* 'amuse oneself, dawdle', with similar forms in Kerek and Koryak) and with **ləŋ-* (Chukchi *yiciwu ləŋ-* 'be amused or entertained by'). There is also *inicyətu ləŋ-* 'be interested in', which may be related. Itelmen *xiɬiva* 'interesting' is probably a loan from Chukotian (Volodin 1976 has *xiɬiwaju eɬe-s* 'mock'). Then there is PC **ataryo ləŋ-* 'laugh at', with corresponding intransiitve **-æt-* forms in Koryak (*acacgat-*) and – probably – Alutor (*sissəŋat-*). Laughter itself is an emotional root in Chukchi and Alutor – in the latter *tanŋav-* 'laugh', *tanŋu ləng-* 'laugh at'. Itelmen has a cognate *łŋeze-kas* 'laugh', and in older sources *tenxšen, txnlyžišcin* 'laugh' and the like, none of them typical emotional root derivations – but note also analytic transitive *łenweju eɬe-s* 'laugh at' given by Georg and Volodin (1999), a more obvious loan from Chukotian.[19]

---

[19] Note that Chukotian/t/is often/ɬ/in Itelmen (next to a sonorant), and that *eɬe-s* is the Itelmen auxiliary corresponding to Chukotian **ləŋ-*.

10.6.17 Feeling at ease

PC *untəm- 'quiet' has the sense 'feel relieved, calm down, be satiated' in Chukchi untəm-ev- with *-æv- (also in Koryak, and borrowed into NSY as untemaawi- 'be calm or indifferent'). Then there is PC *məraj- 'happy', going perhaps with 10.6.15 but attested in the *-æv- form in Chukchi m(ə)raw- 'be content, having received enough' (in Bogoraz 1937), and in the *-æt- form in Alutor mərajat- 'be successful'.

10.6.18 Thankfulness

PC *riRæt- 'be glad', which contains *-æt-, covers the meaning of thankfulness, as in Koryak jiRet- 'be glad, happy, congratulate, thank' and Chukchi adverbial form rʔatetə 'grateful(ly)' (Bogoraz has rʔet- 'be glad'). It is not attested in the ləŋ-construction. This has been borrowed into Itelmen as an ordinary verb, revat-kas 'be happy, glad'.

10.6.19 Lust

PC *yəjin(ðæ)- 'desire' is widely used for any kind of desire, including towards another human being. Thus Chukchi yəjinre- 'strongly desire', but also yiinre- 'stare hungrily or in delight at'. Moll et al. have it in the ləŋ- construction as yiinu ləŋ- 'yearn for'. Koryak has yəjinev- 'be affectionate, happy, caress' (also jinʲŋe- 'want' in 1967) = Alutor yəjinav- 'be affectionate, glad'. Some of the forms given may be due to influence from PC *iyju- 'be childishly affectionate' (itself a childish distortion of the present root?), as in Chukchi tiyjuŋ-, tiyjuŋu ləŋ- 'be childishly affectionate, fondle'.

10.6.20 Longing

PC *tæyjæŋ (tili)- 'strain eagerly forward' does not contain *-æt- but occurs everywhere in the ləŋ- construction, as in Chukchi teyjeŋu ləŋ- 'want' and Kerek tayjaŋu ləŋ- 'desire, love'. There seems to be some entanglement between this stem and the preceding (*yəjin(ðæ)-). Volodin (1976) has Itelmen teyeŋ-kas 'miss (s. o.)'from the Chukotian, but also (p. 206) tesxen-kas 'strain on leash (dog)', which may well be the cognate (both are ordinary stems).[20] If this reflects the original meaning of the stem, we could have here a rare transparent example of metaphor in Chukotko-Kamchatkan.

10.6.21 Pity

PC *jæjwæc- 'feel pity for' occurs with *-æt-/-æv- and ləŋ- everywhere, as in Chukchi *jejwecet-, jejwecu ləŋ-* 'be sorry, feel pity for'. Related to it is PC *jæjwæl 'orphan'. There is also PC *qəlyilu- 'be sorry', which in Chukchi at least can appear in the *ləŋ-* construction, *qəlyilu ləŋ-* 'be sorry for'.

10.6.22 Feeling protective/loving towards

Here belongs the ubiquitous root for 'love' in all Chukotian, namely *(tə)Relŋu (ləŋ-)* (compare the West Greenlandic under PI *ažak-* in section 10.4.4 above). This is principally used in its transitive form with *ləŋ-*, as in Chukchi *ʔəlyu ləŋ-*, but Bogoraz also has it with *-æt-* (and preceding element *tə-) in *qə-tʔəlyəlet-yi* 'love!' (imperative form). The relationship of these forms to Itelmen *lftalate-s* 'love' is obscure – there are some t-initial earlier forms attested, such as *tylxtla-žik* 'love', that are suggestive of a common source. Alutor has, beside Palan *ʔəljŋun* 'love', also *yanjŋu ləŋ-* 'love, esteem, desire' (Kibrik et al. 2000), which is 'sympathize with, favour' in Žukova and Kurebito (2004) – there appears to be some entanglement with PC *yəjin(ðæ)-* 'desire' under 10.6.19. Nagayama (2003) has *yanŋu-* 'love, esteem, desire' and *yanŋu ləŋ-* 'sympathize with'.

10.6.23 Uncertainty

As with Eskimo languages, Chukotian has a number of important verbs treated as emotional roots that from a European perspective are purely epistemic. Thus PC root *(tə)yema-* 'not know' is used in all three 'emotional' forms, the intransitive (Chukchi *yemat-*), the transitive stative (*yemo ləŋ-*), and the transitive resultative (*yemo rətcə-* 'forget'). There is also PC *(tə)yiv-* 'be unknown', as in Chukchi *yiwew-/-tyiwew-* 'become unknown, confused', *yiwu ləŋ-* 'not know'. Alutor has

---

[20] */j/ often goes to/s/in Itelmen, and here there appears to have been metathesis with the */g/ (>/x/).

tyivat- 'forget' and *a-tyiv-ka* 'not knowing'.²¹ Similarly with PC **ləmalav-* 'believe in, trust', as in Chukchi *ləmalaw-*, transitive *ləmalo ləŋ-* 'trust, believe, obey', with equivalents in all the languages – also in Itelmen, which has borrowed it as *ɬmaɬu eɬe-s* 'believe'. PC **mativæt-* 'doubt' also contains **-æt-* (as does PC **ŋiræ(t)-* 'be in doubt or despair').

As for positive 'knowing (s.th.)', this is also expressed by an emotional root construction with **ləŋ-* in all the languages, but the root itself is (exceptionally) an adverb, with cognates in Itelmen, namely PC **ləyi* 'true or known', as in Chukchi *ləyi ləŋ-* 'know' (and resultative *ləyi rətcə-* 'recognize, get to know'). In Koryak the resultative form *ləyi rətcə-* means 'explain'. However, the root is nowhere found in intransitive use, and semantically it overlaps with the territory of 10.6.24 below, i.e. also covers general 'feeling' or 'sensing'. It has apparently been borrowed into Itelmen as *xiq/Xiq eɬe-s* 'know', though this could actually be a cognate (the *-q* is a native adverbial formant).

Also thinking is treated this way (as we saw, this was also possible with Eskimo **icuma-* and **cumer(te)-*). Thus PC **cimŋəru-* 'think' enters into the transitive *ləŋ-* construction, as in Chukchi *cimyʔu ləŋ-*, which, as we have seen under 10.6.8, can mean 'worry about, look after' as well as 'think about'. Koryak has *ceckejuŋ-* 'think' rather, from PC **təkæj(u)-* 'be conscious' (not an emotional root as such – see below under 10.6.24). The plain *-u* form is used as the intransitive stem – but Dunn also gives *cimʔet-* with **-æt-*.

10.6.24 Feeling or noticing (generally)

Koryak *ləyi ləŋ-* can, as mentioned above, mean 'feel, sense' in a rather general sense (Russian *oščutit*). This in turn is related to ordinary stem PC **ləyæl-* 'recognize' (in Chukchi 'recognize, understand', in Koryak and Alutor simply 'recognize'). Chukchi also has *cəkejew-/-tkejew-* in the meaning 'feel, sense' as well as 'be conscious, come to oneself', from PC **təkæj(u)-* 'be(come) conscious' plus the affix **-æv-* found with emotional roots.

The overall parallel between the two families in this area is striking: emotional roots, defined derivationally, cover exactly the same categories in both families, including the "un-European" overlap between emotion and cognition/perception. The question is whether this similarity is due to the universality of "basic" emotions, or to some kind of areal influence. Since the parallel not

---

21 By contrast, 'not know how to do s.th.' is expressed by PC **ælæjti-*, not an emotional root at all.

only covers the expression of emotions as such (seen through European eyes) but also includes, for example, the expression of epistemic uncertainty, it would seem that we are indeed dealing with an areal phenomenon. There is little sign of the emotional root as a morphologically distinct category in Itelmen, where analytic expressions for emotions seem all to be borrowings from Chukotian (I have mentioned the most important ones *en passant*).[22] Thus the parallelism could date back to the period when Chukotians first came into close contact with Eskimos in and around Chukotka, gradually assimilating them and/or pushing them back towards the east (cf. Fortescue 2004 for a more detailed account of the dating and linguistic consequences of the process). Such close contact did not occur with the Kamchatkan Itelmen. If, as I have suggested, the emotional root category goes back to common Eskimo-Aleut times, it would have formed long before it spread into Chukotian (i.e. some time after the breakup of Chukotian and Itelmen). Eskimo wives taken by Chukchi men, having to speak Chukchi (or other Chukotian dialects) to their husbands and children in their own language (the usual situation, continuing into recent times), may have transferred their native linguistic category to the new language, affecting in turn the language of their Chukotian-speaking offspring. Many intransitive verbalizations with *-æt-* and *-æv-* would already have existed in the language to build upon, as would the auxiliary *ləŋ-* construction in the sense 'consider/have as' (perhaps including the precise combination *ləyi ləŋ-* 'know'). The linguistic means offered by Chukotian languages being different from those of Eskimo, it is not surprising that the "same" emerging category should end up being expressed by unrelated morphemes and constructions, yet cover the same semantic ground.

10.7 Emotional categories in Athabaskan and other neighbouring families

There is nothing comparable to the morphologically distinct category of emotional root in E-A and C-K in any other language family of the region. The contrast with the expression of emotion in the Athabaskan languages of Alaska is particularly striking. Basically, this is handled by numerous derivational extensions or "themes" (by prefix string) of a handful of stems, some of them of very general

---

[22] Though Itelmen does have its own transitive auxiliary *eɬe-s* appearing in some of these – including with Russian loans like *žalka eɬe-s* 'pity'. Auxiliary verb constructions as such are a feature of the whole C-K family.

meaning, cross-cutting emotional and physical meanings. The expression of emotion in these languages is, unlike in E-A and C-K, rife with transparent metaphor and morphologically quite unsystematic (see Pasamonik 2012 for emotional body-part metaphors in Beaver Athabaskan). For example, one common stem from which emotional 'themes' are derived is -niic 'move the hand, feel', also classificatory 'handle fabric-like object', as in Ahtna u+n+niic 'love, like' (Kari 1990: 310 – slightly simplified). This is one of the most ubiquitous stems in the language, with many distinct meanings, perhaps originally 'feel s.th. with the hand', made more specific by prefix chains such as the directive sequence u+n- here. So the 'love, like' expression may be metaphorical, from reaching out and touching someone. Some of the other themes formed by this stem and certain preceding prefix strings refer to being happy, being alive, hearing, expecting, knowing and believing.

Another stem of broad meaning with a number of positive emotional themes based on it is -'aa° 'linear object extends', as in the following: su+ko+d+'aa° 'be happy, glad' (Kari 1990: 77), where su is a thematic element ('happiness, enough'). The same stem can also appear in themes with a negative meaning, such as c'+u+d+'aa° 'feel a sharp internal pain' on the same page, with different prefixes.

In other nearby Indian languages of northern America – and in, for example, Nivkh on the Siberian side of the North Pacific – emotional stems are not distinguished morphosyntactically from other kinds of stem.[23] This includes the Wakashan languages, which typologically are otherwise rather like Eskimo-Aleut in being purely suffixing. A dip into the comparative Wakashan dictionary (Fortescue 2007) will show that the stems concerned refer to specific individual emotions (unlike in Athabaskan for the most part). The only notable aspect of the expression of emotional meanings in Wakashan is that there are quite a few bound suffixes which refer to them (this is also true of Eskimo to a lesser degree, as we have seen). Thus there are suffixes meaning 'feel' (*-q'a), 'want or desire' (*-('i:)Xsa(:)), 'liking or longing for' (*-aɬak), 'angry (because of)' (*-aʕ:)yu(k)), 'fearing' (*-i(:)ty'ak), 'expecting or fearing' (*-mi:ʔak), 'troubled by' (*-y'a:), 'fond of (*-bs), and 'inside the body, having emotional quality of' (*-(k)su:qƛ).

---

23 The nearest phenomenon is perhaps the transitive 'final' -êyi(m/hta)- of directed mental action in Cree, which is lexicalized in verbs of feeling/sensation as well as pure cognition (Wolfart 1996: 429).

10.8 Conclusion: the relation of Eskimo emotional roots to 'basic' emotions – polysemy, shift and cognitive motivation

It is tempting to try and equate the 24 categories of emotional root in Eskimo listed on Table 1 directly to what psychologists tell us constitutes the basic array of human emotions, as shown by studies of – amongst other things – universal facial expressions. But deciding what is to count as a "basic" emotion is a controversial matter, since different lists are arrived at depending on one's definition of "emotion", and on what basis they are to be determined (by overt behaviour, by measurable somatic reactions, by verbal report, etc.). Most importantly, the distance between unconscious "emotions" and conscious "feelings", verbally labelled, has somehow to be taken into account. Most of our 24 types can, as a first approximation, be grouped under the six basic emotions described by Johnson-Laird and Oatley (1992). They argue against the compositional theory of emotion that denies the existence of basic emotions altogether and suggest that an examination of the words used by languages to describe emotions should be taken seriously and not rejected as mere folk etymology. Their approach amounts to a kind of prototype perspective on emotion, with the individual emotion words of a given language being "more or less" like the basic, universal set, but subject to culturally specific variation and combination. Their study lies close to the linguistic surface, and is specifically concerned with the emotional reaction to the perception of general categories of event by speakers of English.

I list on Table 3 the categories (of my 24) that seem to fit into their "basic" emotions. The distinction between different emotions within each of these types can be accounted for in terms of different stimulus situations, different strengths of emotion, and specific distinctions of a cultural/social nature.

Table 3: Basic emotions according to Johnson-Laird and Oatley (1992) and corresponding Eskimo emotional root sub-categories

Happiness	Defined as the perception of improving progress towards a goal (15 Happiness, 16 Amusement, 17 Feeling at ease, 18 Thankfulness)
Sadness	When a goal is lost (2 Loneliness and sad feelings, 12 Regret, 14 Anguish or suffering)
Anger	When a plan is blocked (3 Frustration, 11 Anger, 13 Jealousy or envy)
Fear	When a goal conflict or a threat to self-preservation occurs (1 Fear, 4 Anxiety, 6 Timidity, 7, Apprehension, 8 Worry)
Disgust	Of something to reject (5 Shame, 9 Disgust, 10 Not feeling like doing s.th.)
Desire	Of something to approach (19 Lust, 20 Longing, 21 Pity, 22 Feeling protective/ loving towards)

Only categories 23 of epistemic uncertainty and 24 of general sensory registering are difficult to place within the Johnson-Laird and Oatley scheme, since they lie on the borderlines between the purely emotional and, on the one hand, the purely mental/cognitive (**ukvər-*, **aðgura-*), and on the other, generalized sensory perception (**əlpəkə-*, **maluɡə-*). Recall that Eskimo verbs of thinking often display emotionally tinged meanings such as 'worry about' (as with PY **cumər(tə)-* 'think'), and may thus overlap with item 8 on our list. In fact a case could be made for 'worry (about)' being the original meaning of Proto-Eskimo words of thinking, the purely epistemic sense being abstracted later. Also, recall that 'not knowing' seems to be more original as an emotional root than positive 'knowing' in Eskimo. On the other hand, **əlpəkə-* seems to be a hyperonym covering a wide range of feelings and sensations that includes core emotions (as perhaps also the case with **maluɡə-*).

But what is the status of the Johnson-Laird and Oatley list of six "basic" emotions (and similar lists made by other investigators)? Are the six emotions to be taken as "cognitive" (consciously accessible) or as sub-conscious? In other words, are they "declarative" (reportable) or "procedural" (automatic)? LeDoux (1998: 112–114) discusses different approaches to the question, including Johnson-Laird and Oatley's, and notably Ekman's (1984) influential delineation of six basic emotions based on universal facial expressions (with 'surprise' rather than 'desire' as the sixth). His own approach is evolutionary: he argues against those who deny the existence of basic emotions altogether (as opposed to purely social constructs), and describes the function of emotions in terms of unconscious survival strategies with their roots in our pre-human ancestors. The relationship between basic emotions and "feelings" (i.e. consciously accessible emotional experiences) involves a complex interplay between sub-cortical structures such as the amygdala and the long-term memory systems of the neocortex, in which, crucially, bodily reactions are evoked. All these factors converge in (conscious) working memory, which operates at a higher level of symbolic abstraction – and it is here that linguistic labels for experienced emotions are directly relevant.

Cognitive linguists such as Lakoff (1987: 407) have endeavoured to overcome the excessive emphasis on (conscious) cognition in analysing emotion (that LeDoux decries) by taking cognition, as it were, all the way down to the level of bodily emotions in terms of underlying "folk theories" or "cognitive models" of emotion. In the absence of widespread transparent metaphor of emotion in Eskimo languages it is hard to make out any such coherent model apart from the bodily underpinnings of the emotions themselves. But Lakoff is doubtless correct in regarding emotions as events rather than "things", intimately wound up with "prototypical scenarios". Important work has been done in recent years within this general framework, including studies of the expression of various emotions across languages. The studies in Harkins and Wierzbicka (2001), for example, apply the Natural Semantic Metalanguage approach in an attempt to circumvent the problems introduced by relying on English translations for culturally specific categories. This they do by defining contexts of use in terms of a purportedly universal metalanguage. Sceptical about the very notion of "basic emotion" they point out: "Socially acceptable ways of thinking about the kind of events that provoke 'anger', etc. [...] and the kind of behaviour that results from these feelings are integral parts of the emotion itself" (Harkins and Wierzbicka 2001: 7). Certainly many of the Eskimo terms I have discussed above fit poorly within the framework of English emotional categories – *nəryu(g)- 'eagerly expect, hope' in 10.4.5 is a case in point: it covers or combines both 'expect (s.th. good)' and 'hope' in English. For a detailed study of expressions of 'fear' and 'pity' that combines the metaphorical and the metalanguage approaches see Apresjan (1997).

Damasio (2000: 51) makes the further distinction between primary (universal) and secondary or social emotions – and also distinguishes "background" emotions. The latter encompass such internal, visceral or somatic states as fatigue, excitement, sickness, relaxation, stability, and discord. They are "an index of momentary parameters of inner organism state" (Damasio 2000: 286) and are somewhat peripheral to the emotions expressed by emotional roots in E-A and C-K, but can nevertheless be lexically expressed in those languages – usually as ordinary verbal stems (compare for example PI *cail(l)i-* 'feel at ease' under 10.3.3). Apparent exceptions with -*yug*-, CAY *kiir-yug-* and CSY *puqla-yug-* 'feel hot', are not fully fledged emotional roots and may be by analogy with them. Background emotions are certainly ingredient in some of the explicit emotional roots that I have discussed (e.g. PE *ar(ə)yu-* 'be tired or homesick'). Secondary emotions encompass such things as embarrassment, jealousy, guilt and pride, which are subject to socio-cultural variability. Typically they are complex, shame for example involving elements of both (primary) fear (here of social ostracizing or mockery) and disgust (at oneself), also perhaps hope (of getting away with it unnoticed). The development in terms of evolution is, according to Damasio (2000: 342), from background to primary to secondary emotions. Drives and motivations and states of pain or pleasure generally fall outside of these categories (though all have been labelled "emotions" by some investigator or another). The general picture that emerges is of a universal set of subconscious basic emotions, neurologically hard-wired in their own sub-systems and serving evolutionary survival functions, overlaid by a wider array of explicit types of "feelings" coupled to long-term cortical memory and thus available to conscious awareness and assessment. We recognize their applicability to other people by their behaviour, similar to our own when we are subject to situations/contexts of the same type. The meaning of emotion words can be expected to display a degree of social modulation and conventionalization by the very fact of their being labelled lexically.

We can thus say that primary "happiness", for example, lies behind a number of more specific secondary emotions depending on circumstance, for example protective tenderness (towards one's offspring), of love (towards one's mate or a close friend), of amusement (in a convivial situation, e.g. of verbal banter), or thankfulness (for receipt of assistance in attaining some goal). Still more culturally specific uses of words related to this basic emotion may then develop under the aegis of organized religion. Even those roots on our list that lie very close to their "primary" source, such as "disgust" (category 9), refer not just to the basic emotion concerned but to the type of stimulus evoking it, as presented by the particular cultural and physical environment lived in by the Inuit. In fact all emotional roots have a transitive counterpart (with *-kə-) referring to the type of stimulus evoking the feeling concerned. In other words, recognizing the type of stimulus (object or situation) is essential to the feeling, so in this sense it is justified to characterize the emotions referred to by all 24 categories of emotional root as "secondary". Briggs' study of the use of some of these in Utku (until recently one of the least changed communities in the Inuit world) provides us with a glimpse into what these socially determined stimulus types might be.

The divide between these different sub-types of emotion is thus rather diffuse, and indeed the divide between emotion as a whole and cognition (or pure, emotion-neutral thought processes) is fuzzy. What is perhaps special about the Eskimo category of "emotional root" is that it delineates a relatively clearcut semantic domain of concepts felt to be primarily emotional. That the division between emotion and cognition is not made at quite the same place as we in Europe would make it is not so important: the clear-cut opposition of the two in the western world is perhaps due to the long-standing history of dualistic thinking in this domain (I am referring to "folk" as well as philosophical theories).

The 24 types of emotional root unearthed in this paper would thus represent the secondary emotional categories encapsulated in the languages of the Eskimo and Chukotian speaking world. These build upon – but are not limited by – the approximately six primary emotions isolated by psychologists, neurologists and ethologists. By taking a diachronic perspective, reconstructing emotional roots in the proto-languages, we gain a window into an ancient way of categorizing inner emotional experience, one that is becoming less consistently maintained in the individual languages today through lexicalization, loss and replacement. It may fall apart altogether (which seems to have happened already in Aleut) as they adapt to the more complex realities and influences of the contemporary world.

What can the variety of semantic shift and polysemy displayed by our lexical data add to this picture? Although the etymology of emotional roots in Eskimo is largely opaque and it is by no means certain that the semantic "lowest common denominator" chosen in Fortescue, Jacobson, and Kaplan (2010) for the gloss of reconstructed proto-forms is necessarily accurate, the diachronic and comparative data presented above does strongly suggest that the development has always been predominantly from the physical/visceral correlates of emotion to more abstract or general emotion and finally to more culturally determined meanings, i.e. that metonymy coupled with contextual modulation has been the principal driving force. This is not surprising, given that the relationship between an emotion and its outward behavioural manifestation can itself be characterized as "metonymic". A similar point as regards the relationship between emotions and their physiological effects is made by Lakoff (1987: 382) in his analysis of anger.

This development can be exemplified with the first emotional root mentioned in this chapter, Proto-Eskimo *naŋɬəg- 'feel pity for'. The most distant source of the root appears to lie in stem *naŋə- 'be used up', with a transitive derivative meaning 'kill off' or, in some dialects, reflexively, 'suffer'. The emotional root based on this may have been ambiguously 'suffer for another' or 'suffer for oneself', but at all events took on the meaning 'feel pity' with transitive and intransitive forms distinguished by the affixes associated with such roots (*-kə- and *-yug- respectively). In several of the dialects this either developed further into 'love' or that sense became singled out from a more general original meaning. In some of them there is "layering", displaying both the earlier and the later meaning (as is the case with Polar Eskimo *naglii-*). Recall now Briggs' definition of the root in Utku: "feel concern for another's welfare, wish to be with another" (Briggs 1970: 314). This covers both meanings, and provides a broad social context for the use of the root that may have been stable for millennia. The fine-tuning of the meaning would depend on the exact context, in particular towards whom the emotion is directed (e.g. a child or a spouse) and by whom. Only in Greenland is a sharp distinction introduced (probably through outside influence) between the expression of 'pity' and 'love'.

Other examples of development from a more physical to a more abstract emotional meaning can be seen in *tupəkə- 'wince at' and *ulurya- 'flinch' treated above, the first of which developed into 'be surprised' in WG and the second into 'be terrified'. Recall also the relationship between ordinary stem *tatamə(t)- 'be startled or terrified' and emotional root tatai- 'be fearful' mentioned in section 2.1; *ar(ə)yu- 'be tired' (into 'be homesick' or 'be bored' in various dialects); *narru- 'dislike' (ultimately from *narə- 'smell'); *quginag- 'be ticklish or squeamish' (into 'be terrified of s.th. supernatural' in CSY); *maruyug- 'be disgusted' (probably from *maqu- 'suppurate', and developing into WG 'loathe'); *kappəya- and *kapəgcug-, both 'be anxious' (from *kapəg- 'fit tightly', into 'fear physical injury' in Utku and strengthened in some other Canadian dialects into 'be terrified'); *ilulŋu- 'hurt inside' (into 'be upset or angry' in AAY, 'be moved, sorry for' in WG); and *qi(C)əlir- 'be worked up' (into an emotional root meaning 'desire' in CSY).

Less obviously developing from more to less physical is the case of *kama- 'be nervously attentive', which developed into CSY kamayug- 'feel suspicious' but in the Nunivak dialect 'feel squeamish'; in NAI it produced kamasug- 'obey, be amazed at', in Polar Eskimo kamahug- 'be agitated, busy', but in WG both kamag- 'be angry' and – retaining the original meaning somewhat more directly – transitive kamagi- 'put up with'.

The development of more culturally specific meanings we have seen in for example *əplər- 'be revulsed' (related to *əpər 'dirt'), which has developed the meaning 'regard as taboo' and further 'be afraid to talk to s. o. (for cult reasons)', 'be afraid to catch another's illness', and 'respect another's property', so illirnar- is 'be valuable' in WG but 'be filthy' in Polar Eskimo (which better reflects the source of the root). A rather similar cultic meaning has developed from *paqu(mi)- 'dread or be wary' (as in CSY paqumiyug- 'be wary of and hesitate to act due to threatening weather'), which has become 'be superstitious about, feel disgust at' in WG. In the case of *əlira- 'want to ask for s.th. but not dare' discussed in section 10.3.4, we see the fragmentation of what once may have been a unified social context, perhaps best characterized by Briggs' definition for Utku: 'fear of being unkindly treated, respectful with overtones of fear'; by metonymic processes it has been narrowed to 'be grateful', 'be afraid', or 'have a bad conscience' in various dialects.

There are examples of other familiar kinds of semantic shift in the data, such as narrowing and broadening in the case of *naŋyar- 'be afraid in precarious place', which in WG is either 'afraid of heights' or 'afraid of going out on water in kayak' (a matter of context-dependent polysemy), whereas in Tarramiut it has broadened to 'be afraid of danger' in general. Emotional root *əkli- 'lust for' can be applied to both sexual lust and desire for food (with different emphasis in different dialects), but appears to be broadened to the general meaning of 'desire' in some Canadian dialects. This may again be a case of context-dependent polysemy everywhere, however – a Briggsian type investigation is required.

We have also encountered idiosyncratic flip-flops of meaning, as with *aliga- 'be lonely', which has developed a 'happy' meaning in some Canadian dialects. In a few instances the development has been from self-directed to other-directed, as with *əq(ə)ya- 'be lazy, not want to do s.th.', which in Yupik is rather 'not permit, refuse', and *nəka- 'feel inferior or unworthy', which in the transitive WG form nikagi- is 'think s. o./s.th. insignificant or not much'.

Metaphor is also in evidence, but in comparatively few instances, notably with *ugumi- 'be infuriated' (from *ugu- 'be heated up') and *aðgura- 'be stubborn, unwilling' (from *aðgur- 'go against current or wind'). The meaning of the latter ranges from 'doubt' in Yupik to 'be undaunted' in NAI, 'be proud' in Copper and (transitively) 'reprove, have s.th. against' in WG.

I include some examples of these shifts on Figure 2. Many more have been introduced *en passant*.

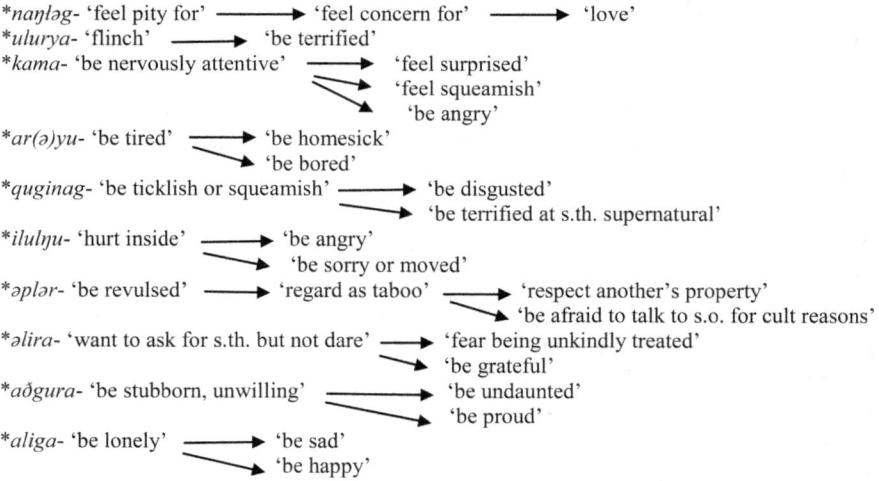

Figure 2: Some semantic shifts from Proto-Eskimo to contemporary dialects

One small group of roots remains more opaque, namely those with an epistemic/cognitive or perceptual sense (and/or source) such as *əlima- 'suspect', *natu- 'not know', *malugə- 'notice', and *ənqar- 'remember'. Note, however, that they have in common with the more obviously "emotional" emotional roots a sense of covert, inward experience, and may have been drawn at an early stage into the morphologically delimited category for that reason. As hinted at above, the division between emotion and mental cognition would appear to be less firmly established in Eskimo and Chukotko-Kamchatkan than in the major European languages.

Perhaps the essence of the category of "emotional root" is then this: although the exact array of items falling within it has fluctuated through time, resulting in synchronic dialect differences, the category itself delineates what the speakers of these languages regard as inward experiences, tinged by emotion but not necessarily expressed in physical manifestation at all (i.e. neither emotions that are always manifest in behaviour of a certain type nor emotionally completely neutral cognition). They can all be experienced inwardly (-*yug-/-suk-*), some thing or event can potentially cause such an experience (-*nar-*), and a particular thing or event can provoke that experience in the experiencer as subject (-*kə-/-gi-*).

10.9 Abbreviations used

AAY Alutiiq Alaskan Yupik
EG   East Greenlandic
C-K Chukotko-Kamchatkan
CSY Central Alaskan Yupik
CSY Central Siberian Yupik
E-A Eskimo-Aleut
EG   East Greenlandic
NAI North Alaskan Inuit
NSY Naukanski Siberian Yupik
PC   Proto-Chukotian
PE   Proto-Eskimo
PI   Proto-Inuit
PY   Proto-Yupik
SPI Seward Peninsula Inuit
WG   West Greenlandic

10.10 References

Apresjan, Valentina Ju. 1997. 'Fear' and 'pity' in Russian and English from a lexicographical perspective. *International Journal of Lexicography* 10 (2): 85–111.
Bergsland, Knut. 1994. *Aleut dictionary*. Fairbanks: Alaska Native Language Center Press, University of Alaska Fairbanks.

Berthelsen, Christian, Birgitte Jacobsen, Robert Petersen, Inge Kleivan, and Jørgen Rischel. 1997. *Oqaatsit. Grønlandsk-dansk ordbog* [Greenlandic-Danish dictionary]. Nuuk: Atuakkiorfik/Ilinniusiorfik.
Bogoraz, Vladimir G. 1937. *Luoravetlansko-russkij slovar'*. Moskva & Leningrad: Gosudarstvennoje učebno- pedagogičeskoje izdatel'stvo.
Briggs, Jean. 1970. *Never in anger. Portrait of an Eskimo family.* Cambridge, Mass.: Harvard University Press.
Briggs, Jean. 1995. The study of Inuit emotions: Lessons from a personal retrospective. In James A. Russell, Jose M. Fernandez-Dols, Anthony Manstead, and Jane C. Wellenkamp (eds.), *Everyday conceptions of emotion*, 203–220. Dordrecht: Kluwer Academic.
Buck, Carl Darling. 1988. *A Dictionary of selected synonyms in the principal Indo-European languages* (1st edition 1949). Chicago: University of Chicago Press.
Damasio, Antonio. 2000. *The feeling of what happens.* London: Vintage.
Dorais, Louis-Jacques. 1990. *1000 Inuit words.* Québec: Association Inuksiutiit Katimajiit, Université Laval.
Dunn, Michael. 1999. *A grammar of Chukchi.* Canberra: Australian National University Ph.D. dissertation.
Egede, Paul. 1750. *Dictionarium Grönlandico-Danico-Latinum* [Greenlandic-Danish-Latin dictionary]. Copenhagen: Havniae.
Ekman, Paul. 1984. Expressions and nature of emotion. In K. Scherer and P. Ekman (eds.), *Approaches to emotion*, 319–43. Hillsdale, N.J.: Erlbaum.
Fabricius, Otto. 1804. *Den grønlandske ordbog forbedret og forøget* [The Greenlandic dictionary improved and augmented]. Copenhagen: C.F. Schubart.
Fortescue, Michael. 2001. Kærlighedens gåde [Love's mystery], *Tidskriftet Grønland* 4–5: 150–158.
Fortescue, Michael. 2004. How far west into Asia have Eskimo languages been spoken, and which ones? *Etudes/Inuit/Studies* 28 (2): 159–183.
Fortescue, Michael. 2005. *Comparative Chukotko-Kamchatkan dictionary.* Berlin: Mouton de Gruyter.
Fortescue, Michael, Steven Jacobson, and Lawrence Kaplan. 2010. *Comparative Eskimo dictionary with Aleut cognates* (2nd edition). Fairbanks: Alaska Native Language Center Press, University of Alaska Fairbanks.
Georg, Stefan and Aleksander P. Volodin. 1999. *Die itelmenische Sprache: Grammatik und Texte* [The Itelmen language: Grammar and texts]. Wiesbaden: Harassowitz Verlag.
Harkins, Jean and Anna Wierzbicka (eds.). 2001. *Emotions in crosslinguistic perspective.* [Cognitive Linguistics Research 17]. Berlin & New York: Mouton de Gruyter.
Holm, Gustav. 1988. *Den østgrønlandske expedition udført i aarene 1883–5* [The East Greenland expedition of 1883–5]. Copenhagen: Meddelelser om Grønland 10.
Inenlikej, Petr I. 1982. *Slovar' čukotsko-russkij i russko-čukotskij* [Chukchi-Russian and Russian-Chukchi dictionary]. Leningrad: Prosveščenie.
Jacobson, Steven. 1984. *Yup'ik Eskimo Dictionary.* Fairbanks: Alaska Native Language Center Press, University of Alaska Fairbanks.
Johnson-Laird, Philip N. and Keith Oatley. 1992. Basic emotions, rationality and folk theory. *Cognition and Emotion* 6: 201–223.
Kari, James. 1990. *Ahtna Athabaskan dictionary.* Fairbanks: Alaska Native Language Center Press, University of Alaska Fairbanks.

Kibrik, Aleksandr E., Sandro V. Kodzasov, and Irina A. Muravyova. 2000. *Jazyk i fol'k!or aljutortsev* [Language and folklore of the Alutor]. Moskva: IMLI RAN Nasledie.
Lakoff, George. 1987. *Women, fire, and dangerous things*. Chicago & London: University of Chicago Press.
LeDoux, Joseph. 1998. *The emotional brain*. London: Weidenfeld and Nicolson.
McNabb, Steven. 1989. Expressive conventions in Inuit society. *Études/Inuit/Studies* 13 (2): 49–67.
Moll, T. A. and P. I. Inenlikej. 1957. *Čukotsko-russkij slovar'* [Chukchi-Russian dictionary] Leningrad: Gosud. Učpedgiz.
Muravyova, Irina A. 1979. Sopostavitel'noje issledovanie morfologii čukotskogo, korjakskogo i aljutorskogo jazykov [Comparative investigation of the morphology of Chukchi, Koryak, and Alutor]. Moscow: Moscow State University PhD dissertation.
Nagayama,Yukari. 2003. *Očerk aljutorskogo jazyka* [Sketch of the Alutor language]. Endangered Languages of the Pacific Rim A2-011, A2-038. Suita: Faculty of Informatics, Osaka Gakuin University.
Pasamonik, Carolina. 2012. "My heart falls out": Conceptualizations of body parts and emotion in Beaver Athabascan. In Anna Idström and Elisabeth Piirainen (eds.), *Endangered metaphors*, 77–102. Amsterdam: John Benjamins
Peck, Edmund J. 1925. *A Dictionary of the Eskimo language*. Hamilton, Ontario: Mission Fund.
Petersen, Jonathan. 1951. *Ordbogêraq* [The little dictionary]. Nuuk: Nûngme ilíniarfigssûp naqitertitai.
Radlinski, I. 1891–4. *Słowniki narzeczny ludów Kamczackich* [Dictionaries of the dialects of Kamchatka] (compiler B. Dybowski). Kraków: Rozprawy Akademii Umiejętności, wydzial filologiczny, 16–18, and 22.
Schneider, Lucien. 1985. *Ulirnaisigutiit, an Inuktitut-English dictionary of Northern Quebec, Labrador and Eastern Arctic dialects* (ed. by D. Collis). Québec: Université Laval Press.
Volodin, Aleksandr P. 1976. *Itel'menskij jazyk* [The Itelmen language]. Leningrad: Nauka.
Wolfart, H. Christoph. 1996. Sketch of Cree, an Algonquian language. In William C. Sturtevant and Ives Goddard (eds.), *Handbook of North American indians, vol. 17: Languages*, 390–439. Washington: Smithsonian Institution.
Zalizniak, Anna A., Maria Bulakh, Dmitrij Ganenkov, Ilya Gruntov, Timur Maisak, and Maxim Rosso. 2012. The catalogue of semantic shifts as a database for lexical semantic typology. In Maria Koptjevskaja-Tamm and Martine Vanhove (eds.), New directions in lexical typology, 633–669. [Special issue] *Linguistics* 50, 3.
Žukova, Alevtina N. 1967. *Russko-korjakskij slovar'* [Russian-Koryak dictionary] Moscow: Sovetskaja entsiklopedija.
Žukova, Alevtina N. and Tokusu Kurebito. 2004. *Bazovyj tematičesky slovar' korjaksko-čukotskix jazykov* [Basic thematic dictionary of the Koryak-Chukchi languages]. Tokyo: Research Institute for Languages and Cultures of Asia and Africa, Tokyo University of Foreign Studies.

Galina Yavorska and Galyna Zymovets
11. Motivational scenarios and semantic frames for social relations in Slavic, Romance and Germanic languages – friends, enemies, and others

Abstract: This paper deals with the terms for social relations in Slavic, Romance and Germanic languages. The words under study represent both interpersonal relationship (FRIEND and ENEMY) and abstract concepts (POWER, CITIZEN, GOVERNOR). The purpose of the paper is to interpret synchronic polysemy patterns in genetically related languages in diachronic terms, i.e. in terms of the 'source – target' model of semantic shifts, and to find out the typologically relevant semantic shifts and the motivational scenarios behind them. The paper focuses on verbal representations of conceptual metonymy and metaphor which exhibit shared and differential properties across languages.

The research demonstrates efficiency of combining diachronic and synchronic approaches in typological analysis of cognate derivatives that exist in genealogically related languages. The etymological data provide evidence for revealing the constituents of concepts that belongs to the social domain. The study has attested a wide range of semantic frames for societal terms in different languages that is to be interpreted as a projection of diversity in human interaction.

11.1 Introduction

Linguistic typology as a research field has demonstrated significant achievements. Considerable progress in this field during the last decades can be attributed to developing new theoretical vistas, particularly the ones in cognitive linguistics, and incorporating new data into the research. Although linguistic typology is concerned with different aspects of language – phonetics, phonology, grammar, and lexical semantics – the latter falls by the wayside of mainstream investigations. Until recently, typological studies of word meanings considered a limited number of lexical fields related to the conceptual domains of particular

---

Galina Yavorska (NIISP, Kyiv) and **Galyna Zymovets** (O.O. Potebnya Institute of Linguistics NASU, Kyiv)

physical objects and sense perception. Among them are the lexical fields of color terms (the most discussed topic), verbs of perception, verbs of motion (Talmy 1985; Maisak and Rakhilina 2007), pain predicates (Britsin et al. 2009) etc. Lexical fields that represent the conceptual domains of mental and societal phenomena tend to remain outside the typological framework, with the exception of mental predicates (Grzegorczykowa and Waszakowa 2003) and kinship terms (Greenberg 1980) which, according to Trubachev (2006), constitute the most stable and archaic segment of the vocabulary. Typological inquiry into the vocabulary of social relations requires further elaboration, since the social domain, along with the physical and mental ones, is a fundamental dimension of human experience.

Diachronically oriented typological studies are even scarcer despite the fact that "typological parallels" constitute an important instrument for verification of etymological reconstructions. Reluctance in diachronic typological studies of word meanings is accounted for by insufficient data as to regular semantic shifts or recurrent models of lexical semantic change in different languages of the world. However, a diachronic perspective has a mighty potential for explaining the current lexical and derivational meanings of cognates. It is demonstrated by the investigation of polysemy developed by societal terms: their semantic evolution results in a synchronic map which registers diachronic changes (Yavorska 1992). Such changes demonstrate numerous metaphoric and metonymic extensions that reflect the previous state of a word's semantic history (Maisak and Rakhilina 2007). These extensions can be described in terms of the contemporary theories of conceptual metaphor and metonymy (Lakoff and Johnson 1980; Panther and Radden 1999), which integrate the findings of traditional linguistics as to semantic shifts grounded on similarity (metaphor) and contiguity (metonymy) between entities (Blank 1999). Therefore, our study relies on both traditional and cognitive linguistic insights.

Linguistic manifestation of concepts that represent social relations in different languages, as well as in one and the same language, varies at different chronological stages. This variability requires a thorough exploration of lexical and grammatical (morphological and syntactic) meanings that expose particular concepts. In this respect, names for the conceptual domain of interpersonal relations are of particular interest, since they both signify social concepts and construe. A quick example is gradation of social distance in different cultures which depends on the degree of intimacy and affection between individuals "within the family, within social or fraternal groups, within neighborhoods, within churches, within schools, within play groups, within transportation groups, within occupational and business groups, within political or national groups" (Bogardus 1933: 266). Gradation of social distance may be demonstrated by the Russian words *друг (drug)* 'friend' and *приятель (priyatel')* 'pal'. *Друг (drug)* is "closer" as compared to *приятель*, i.e. the social distance between *друзья (druz'ya)* 'friends' is shorter than between *приятели (priyateli)* 'pals' (Wierzbicka 1997: 7C). Another important factor is the social rank which is relevant for the "parents" – "children" or "boss" – "subordinate" vertical relations, being less important for horizontal relations between friends, schoolmates, etc.

11.2 Data and methodology

This paper aims to expose diachronic semantic correlations in genetically related languages, and to find out typologically relevant semantic shifts described in terms of "source – target". The data come from monolingual, bilingual and etymological dictionaries of the Slavic, Romance and Germanic languages (BER 1971–2002; Bezlaj 1977–2005; Boryś 2005; Buck 1949; Dauzat 1938; ESBM 1978–1993; ESUM 1982–2012; Fasmer 1964–1973; Kluge 2005; Machek 1968; Skok 1971–1974; Sławski 1952–1982; Walde 1938–1954). We proceed from collecting the data of modern languages to tracking back their initial etymological meanings which construe the analyzed societal concepts the content of which remain typologically opaque. It is presumed that this content results from a number of "left-hand" semantic shifts from the metaphoric or metonymic source concepts to the target concept that belongs to the social domain. Further, this target concept participates in "right-hand" semantic shifts, where it becomes a source concept in conceptual derivation accompanied by derivation of linguistic forms. Therefore, we examine a range of various semantic shifts in cognates across languages. While applying this approach, we presume the hypothetical character of etymological reconstructions, since in some cases establishing the direction of a semantic shift is problematic. So, it should be born in mind that the etymological meanings we work with are rather abstract, i.e. they are rather general and miss subtle semantic and pragmatic properties. The analyzed data expose semantic shifts observed in the senses of polysemous words, and in the derivational meanings which provide complementary information about the further semantic evolution of a created societal term.

Social relations signified with the words under study are primarily various relations between individuals. In this paper, we analyze the terms for both interpersonal social relations (FRIEND and ENEMY) and more general concepts – those of dominance (POWER), community (CITIZEN), and societal roles (GOVERNOR). The subsequent sections examine the meanings of societal terms in the Germanic, Romance and Slavic languages. Capitalized words represent concepts, or meanings that vary in structure and their formal representations across languages. The metalanguage used for describing universal referents for a social domain (e.g. social roles and relations, which are, however, conceptualized differently across languages) is English.

The focus of our attention is the linguistic representations of conceptual metonymy and metaphor which exhibit shared and differential properties across languages. The question which is to be answered in this research resonates with the question posed by Zoltan Kövecses (2005: 131): "*In exactly what ways* does the linguistic expression of shared conceptual metaphors differ or is it similar across languages and, even more importantly, in exactly what ways *can* it differ or be similar and why?"

11.3 The concept POWER

The concept POWER is central for social relations due to its significance in establishing their direction and character. This concept comprises information about an individual or a group of individuals that dominates another individual or a group of individuals thus being eligible to give commands and orders. Our analysis reveals quite different etymological conceptualizations in the considered languages. The Slavic root **vold* means 'to own, rule, lead' (from IE **wold(h)* 'to own',**wold-ti-s* 'power'). There exist several Baltic and Germanic cognates that belong to the same lexical field of executing power: Lithuanian *valdýti, valdaũ* 'to rule, own', *veldéti* 'to inherit'; Lettish *vàldît* 'govern, rule', Gothic *walten* 'manage, rule', German *walten* 'manage, rule', *Gewalt* 'power, violence'. The pro-Romance cognate is Latin *valēre* 'to be strong'. Slavic languages seem to preserve the initial meaning of the IE root. According to Slavic, Baltic and Germanic data, the term for POWER in IE was presumably closely related to the idea of ownership.

The concept OWNERSHIP presents a situation when something belongs to somebody or is in possession of somebody. To own something means to control it and to have it at disposal. In the Slavic languages, the concepts OWNERSHIP and POWER are signified with one and the same root: Serbian *vladati* 'own, have at disposition', Ukrainian *володіти (volodity)* 'to own, control', Russian *владеть (vladet')* 'to own, control', Belarusian *валодаць (valodats')* 'to own', *уладаць (uladats')*'to have at disposition', Polish *włodać* 'to own', Czech *vlastnit* 'to own', Slovak *vládnut', vlastnit'* 'to own', Bulgarian *владея (vladeya)* 'to own, have, dominate'. Development of the form and semantics of societal terms is sufficiently influenced by cultural contacts. For example, the Russian form *владеть (vladet')* 'to own, control' and its derivatives were influenced by the Old Church Slavonic. Numerous derivatives in the Slavic languages reveal the supposed polysemy of the IE root. Most of the Slavic languages formed Nomen Agentis "owner" from the respective verb: Russian *владелец (vladelets)* (imported from Old Church Slavonic), Belarusian *уладальнік (uladal'nik)*, Polish *właściciel*, Czech *vladař, vládce, vlastnik*, Serbian *vlasnik*, Bulgarian *владелец (vladelets), владетел (vladetel)*. Dual access of the linguistic form to the concepts POWER and OWNERSHIP may result from the semantic ambiguity of the initial IE root. Early semantic idiosyncrasy of the root is retained in the contemporary Slavic languages, where POWER is understood as having something under control or owning something.

In the Romance languages, the concept POWER is grounded on the idea of physical strength. French *pouvoir*, Italian *potére*, Spanish *poter* and English *power* (> Anglo-Norman *poer, pouair* etc., Old French *poeir* etc.) are derived from Latin *potentia* (from *potis* 'strong, powerful'). The underlying etymological meaning, which is difficult to precisely define, is however attested in the domain of family relations: Greek ποσις *(posis)* 'spouse', Sanskrit *pátis* 'husband, lord, possessor' (from IE root **poti-* 'powerful, a lord). German conceptualizes POWER differently – as the ability to do something: *Macht* is derived from the Old German verb **mag* 'to be able'. In Czech, understanding of POWER as physical ability is a presumed Germanic influence: *moc* 'strength', 'power over smth'. Germanic and Slavic cognates retain the basic etymological meaning of the IE root **māgh-* 'to be able'.

The concept POWER serves as a base for further semantic shifts, namely the metonymic shift to the meaning of 'authority', which is attested in the Slavic, Germanic and Romance languages: Ukrainian *влада (vlada)*; Russian *власть (vlast')*, Polish *władza*; Belarusian *улада (ulada)*, Czech *vláda*, Slovak *vlada*, German *Macht*, French *pouvoir*. This shift is regular, though not compulsory, since a number of languages employ a different conceptualization of power institutions: Italian *le autorità*, French *autorité*, English *authorities*. The English term is borrowed from French, which shows importance of cultural influence in coining societal terms. The underlying Latin root has the meaning of growing: *auctōritās* < *auctor* 'initiator' < *augeō* 'to grow, multiply'.

The meanings of analyzed forms expose a range of concepts that demonstrate subcategorization in: (a) social relations represented in Nomen Agentis 'governor' in some Slavic languages: Ukrainian *володар (volodar)*, Russian *властелин (vlastelin)*, Polish *włodarz*, Serbian *vlastelin*; (b) territorial units: Russian *волость (volost'), область (oblast')*, Belarussian *воласць (volasts')* 'area', Polish *włość* 'area unit, village', Czech *vlast* 'native country', German *die Macht*, French *domaine*, English *domain* (under French influence), Latin *regiō*, English *region* (from Old French *region* 'land, region, province'). A number of languages demonstrate a semantic shift to the military domain: German *die Macht* 'army' (archaic), *Wehrmacht* (modern), Czech *branná moc* 'army', *námořní moc* 'navy' (this shift is most probably imported to Czech from German). A particular semantic shift inherent in the Germanic languages is from POWER to 'violence': German *Gewalt*, Dutch *geweld*, Danish *vold*, Swedish *våld*, which obviously relates to the mode of power execution. Figure 1 summarizes conceptualization of POWER and its capacity for further semantic development.

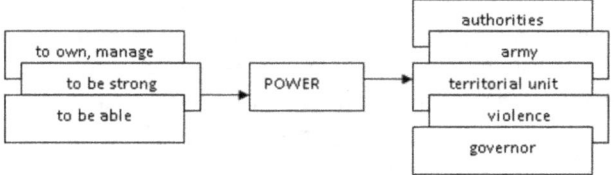

Figure 1: Semantic development of the concept power

11.4 The concept GOVERNOR

Metaphoric and metonymic representations of the GOVERNOR concept differ significantly both across languages and within one and the same language. The concept portrays a person who exercises power, has the authority to give commands and orders, and therefore occupies the highest rank in a social hierarchy. A typical direction of semantic shift is from the physical space domain to the domain of social relations. The space domain is a basic domain that emerges directly from the experience and serves as an important source for further conceptualization (Croft 2006: 272). A shift from the meaning 'a bigger one' to 'governor' is attested in Latin *magister* (the comparative degree of *magnus* 'big', related to Greek μέγας (*megas*) with the same meaning, IE **meg-* 'great') represented afterwards in English *master*, German *Meister* (imported from Latin), French *maître* (continuation of Latin). Another example of a shift from the space domain is German *Herr* (the comparative degree of *hehr* 'elevated'). The Romance languages demonstrate conceptualization of GOVERNOR through the adjective with the meaning 'old-aged' (from Latin *senex* 'old', IE **sen-* 'old'), which is accounted for by significance of the senior social group in the ancient world – Italian *signore*, French *seigneur*, Spanish *señor*. In Latin, GOVERNOR (*dominus*) is conceptualized via a shift from the family domain to the societal domain.

Political constituent of the concept GOVERNOR also employs the shift from spatial relations to the social domain. Etymology of the respective terms in East and South Slavic languages is tracked in the Old Church Slavonic root *правъ (pravŭ)* 'direct, righteous, genuine'. The Old Slavic root *pravъ* < *prō-vos most probably contains the spatial prefix **prō-* ('before, in front of'): Russian/

Ukrainian *правитель (pravitel')* 'governor', Bulgarian *управител (upravitel)* 'manager', Serbian *upravnik* 'manager' (archaic). Another shift is from the meaning of 'leading', i.e. bringing to the direction, steering to the 'governing'. This meaning underpins Greek *κυβερνάω (kybernaō)*, and is further imported to Latin (*gubernare*), and English (*governor*). Some Germanic and Romance terms are derived from Latin *regere* 'direct, guide, rule': English *ruler*, German *Regent*, French *roi, regent*, Italian *reggènte*. The idea of control over direction is also present in Russian/Ukrainian *вождь (vozhd')*, Serbian *vodja*, Polish *wódz*, which are derived from the IE root **uedh-/uodh* 'to lead, bring'. A similar shift is registered in Polish *kierownik*, Ukrainian *керівник (kerivnyk)* 'chief, manager' (from German *kehren* 'to turn, to take a direction'; etymological meaning of the IE root **gei-* is 'to turn around, to bow'). In some languages, the terms for GOVERNOR are motivated by the component 'hand' which is obviously involved in the process of steering and showing direction: Russian *руководитель (rukovoditel')*, Serbian *rukovodilac*, English *manager* (from Italian *maneggiare* derived from Latin *manus*). Conceptualization of governing is also grounded on the initial meaning of putting something in order, with the semantic shift from the domain of direction and space to the domain of social relations: Polish *rządca*, Ukrainian *урядовець (uriadovets')* 'an official' (from Old Slavic **rędъ* 'row, line'). In some Slavic languages the concept GOVERNOR employs the idea of POWER: Czech *vládca*, Serbian *vladar*.

Another constituent of the GOVERNOR concept appears due to the meaning 'placed above' which also belongs to the source domain of physical space: Latin *superānus*, Italian *sovrano*, Spanish *soberano*, French *souverain*. Similar semantic shifts are: from 'person number one' to 'governor' (Latin *prīnceps*, Italian *principe*, French *prince*, German *Fürst*), and from 'the one located at the beginning' to 'a governor, boss' (Greek ἄρχω (arkhō), 'to start/to begin; to govern/rule', Russian *начальник (nachal'nik)* < Old Slavic **po-čъnti* 'to start').

Etymology of some Slavic terms for GOVERNOR – Russian/Serbian/Bulgarian *господин (gospodin)*, Ukrainian *пан (pan)*, Slovak/Polish/Czech *pan* – does not provide sufficient evidence for establishing types of semantic shifts.

The concept GOVERNOR, as a participant of further conceptualizations, is involved in a number of typologically relevant semantic shifts registered in derivatives, such as: Russian *господствовать (gospodstvovat')*, Polish *panować*, Serbian *gospodariti, vladati*, Ukrainian *панувати (panuvaty)*, Belarusian *панаваць (panavats)*, Czech *panovat*, English *dominate, dominance*, German *herrschen, beherrschen, Herrschaft*, French *domination*, Italian *domínio, dominazióne*, Spanish *domination, dominio*. Such derivatives, which exhibit regular transposition between word classes and within one word class, expand the semantic field. Another typologically relevant semantic shift is from 'governor' to 'god': Russian *господь (gospod')*, Ukrainian *господь (hospod')*, Polish *pan*,

pan bóg, Czech *pan, hospodin*, Slovak *hospodin*, Old Church Slavonic Vocative *господи боже (gospodi bozhe)* attested in the Slavic Orthodox cultures, Bulgarian *господ (gospod)*, German *Herr*, English *Lord*. The data also register the semantic shift of GOVERNOR from the domain of interpersonal relations to the domain of economy, which is encountered in several Slavic languages, where the respective term becomes a derivational stem for the Nomen Agentis 'host, landlord': Ukrainian *господар (gospodar)*, Polish *gospodarz*, Slovak *hospodár*, Serbian *gazda* (re-borrowing from Hungarian), Belarusian *гаспадар (gaspadar)*. Further derivatives within the same lexical field are: Ukrainian *господа (hospoda)* 'home', *господарство (hospodarstvo)* 'household', *народне господарство (narodne hospodarstvo)* 'economy', Polish *gospodarka* 'economy', *gospoda* (archaic) 'restaurant, house, household', Belarusian *гаспадарка (gaspadarka)* 'economy', *гаспода (gaspoda)* 'house'. In some languages, the concept GOVERNOR further shifts from the domain of economy to the related domain of politics: Ukrainian *господар (hospodar)*, Russian *господарь (gospodar')* 'ruler of Romania', Bulgarian *господар (gospodar)* (archaic) 'ruler of the state', Polish *państwo* 'state', Latin *dominion* (from *dominus*). The terms for GOVERNOR become derivational stems for nouns with the meaning 'government': Russian *правительство (pravitel'stvo)*, French *gouvernement*, English *government* (borrowed from French), German *Regierung*, Ukrainian *уряд (uriad)*, Czech *vlada*, Serbian *vlada*, Polish *rząd*. Among the typologically relevant cross-linguistic shifts from the GOVERNOR concept is the shift to the polite forms of address: Ukrainian/Belarusian *пан (pan)*, Polish/Czech/Slovak *pan*, Serbian/Bulgarian *господин (gospodin)*; German *Herr*, English *mister*, French *monsieur*, Italian *seignore*. Conceptualization of GOVERNOR and its capacity for further semantic development is shown in Figure 2.

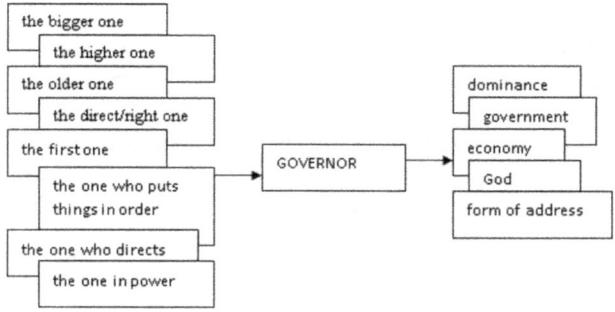

Figure 2: Semantic development of the concept GOVERNOR

11.5 The concept CITIZEN

Being a comparatively new conceptualization, CITIZEN, according to our data, comprises metonymic constituents highlighting the role of power in city communities. The concept provides information about a person who belongs to a particular political and administrative unit constituted by people equal in social rank. The first shift – from a 'a city dweller' to 'citizen' – is attested in Greek πολίτη (*politē*) and in some other European languages influenced by Greek: Russian/Bulgarian гражданин *(grazhdanin)*, German *Burger* (historical), Latin *cīvis*, French *citoyen*, English *citizen*, Italian *cittadino*. Some terms may exhibit a cross-cultural and cross-linguistic impact; e.g. the Russian term is derived from Old Church Slavonic, which is testified by the phonetic form. Conceptualization of CITIZEN emphasizes the historical role of cities in the ancient world and in the medieval Europe. Another semantic shift relevant for construing the concept CITIZEN is from 'community member' to 'citizen': Belarusian грамадзянін *(gramadzianin)*, Ukrainian громадянин *(hromadianyn)* (cf. IE **grem* > ** ger-* 'to collect, put together'). Besides, there is 'a dweller' constituent (Polish *obywatel*) chained with the constituent 'inhabitant of the country'/'subject of the state' (Czech *státní občan*, Serbian *državljanin*, German *Staatsangehöriger*, English *national*). The change of a metonymic source reflects re-arrangement of the concept as a result of re-arranging the societal institutions: a citizen becomes a part of some national community instead of the community of city dwellers. The concept CITIZEN is reluctant to develop further conceptualization. The only derivational meaning is 'being a citizen' inherent in nominalizations – cf. English *citizenship*. Figure 3 summarizes the obtained evidence.

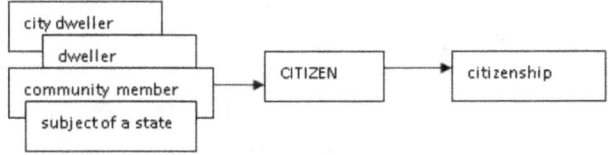

Figure 3: Semantic development of the concept CITIZEN

11.6 The concept COMMUNITY

The concept COMMUNITY represents a group of people who live on the same politically and/or economically homogeneous territory. Conceptualization, mostly metonymic, tends to be grounded on the basic physical space domain. The underlying metonymies are: (1) 'being in one place, being here' (Old Slavic *obĭtjo- 'being around'): Russian *община (obshchina)*, Belarusian *абшына (abshyna)*, Serbian *(opština)*; (2) 'being together': English *community*, German *Gemeinde*, French *commune*, Latin *communita* (both Germanic and Romance names are cognates derived from IE *ko(m)* 'together' and *moin/*mein 'exchange'); (3) 'putting two entities together': Czech *spolek*, Slovak *spolok* (Old Slavic *polŭ* "half" from IE *(s)p(h)el-* 'to split'); (4) 'a group that is put together': Ukrainian *громада (hromada)*.

The terms for COMMUNITY provide derivational stems for the words with the meaning 'society' (Russian/Bulgarian *общество (obshchestvo)*; Czech *společnost*, Slovak *spoločnost*). This meaning is specified in economic and political vocabularies as 'corporation, association' (Czech *spolek, společnost*, Russian *общество (obshchestvo)*, German *Gemeinschaft*, French *communauté, commune*, English *community*). The other typologically relevant conceptual extensions are 'affinity' (Russian *общность (obshchnost')*, German *Gemeinsamkeit*) and 'communication' (Russian *общение (obshcheniye)*, Bulgarian *общуване (obshtuvane)*, French *communication*, English *communication*). Figure 4 displays conceptualization of COMMUNITY and its capacity for further semantic development.

Figure 4: Semantic development of the concept COMMUNITY

11.7 The concepts FRIEND and ENEMY

The concepts FRIEND and ENEMY represent opposite types of interpersonal relations, information about which is construed via different motivators. FRIEND is a person whom you know well and whom you like. It is a person who renders you help and support, and acts for your benefit. ENEMY, conversely, is a person whom you dislike, who acts or speaks against you. Etymological data contributing to these meanings demonstrate several semantic shifts from the domain of physical entities to the social domain (cf. Sakhno and Tersis 2008).

Conceptualization of FRIEND is grounded on the prototypical situation of favorable interaction between two persons, which has names in all Slavic languages: Belarusian/Russian/Ukrainian *друг (drug)*, *приятель (priyatel')*, Russian *товарищ (tovarishch)*, Ukrainian *товариш (tovarysh)*, Polish *kolega*, *przyjaciel* etc. The focus of our research is semantics of the cross-Slavic roots *drug-* and *prijatel-* that yield a number of derivatives. Old Slavic **drugъ* had the meaning 'friend, comrade'. The Baltic languages, closely related to the Slavic group, both genealogically and territorially, have cognate terms, some of which convey the meaning 'togetherness': Lithuanian *draũgas* 'fellow man, comrade', *draũg, draugè* 'together', *sudrùgti* 'to join', Latvian *dràugs* 'comrade, colleague, another member of a pair, another one'. In Prussian, the prefix *draugi-* had the same meaning of 'togetherness, joint existence' (*draugiwaldūnen*, Accusative from 'co-heir'). The origin of the Old Slavic root **drug-* is a problematic issue. Etymological Dictionary of the Ukrainian Language derives this from the IE root **dhrugh-(*dherough-)* 'to be ready, firm, reliable'. However, Trubachev and Martynov argue that *drug* is derived from IE **dhreu-/dhru-* 'firm, reliable, trustworthy'(ESUM 1985, 2; 134). For our research it is important that both interpretations have the seme "firm". It gives grounds to hypothesize that interpersonal relations represented in the FRIEND concept presumed steady and durable support provided by members of a certain community or a group of people.

The root *prijatel-* 'pal' (Old Slavic **prijātelь*) is etymologically linked to the modern Ukrainian сприяти *(spryiaty)* 'to promote, assist'. In Slavic languages, the respective linguistic form prevails over the form *drug-*. Moreover, the form *prijatel-* has cognates in Germanic languages: Gothic *frijōn* 'to love', **frijônds* 'friend', Old German *friunt* 'friend'. The semes shared by these cognates are 'pleasure, satisfaction, love'.

Analysis of etymological sources for *drug-* and *prijatel-* triggers the assumption that Old Slavic registered two types of beneficial interpersonal relations – 'a reliable comrade, fellow soldier', and 'a person whose company is enjoyed", which were respectively named **drug* and **prijātelь*. Synchronic analysis exposes contemporary counterparts of Old Slavic **prijātelь* in several Slavic languages: Ukrainian приятель *(pryiatel')*, Russian приятель *(priyatel')*, Belarusian прыяцель *(pryiatsel')*, Polish *przyjaciel*, Czech *přítel*, Slovak *priateľ*, Bulgarian приятел *(priyatel)*, Slovenian *prijatelj*, Serbian *prijatelj*. Since similar expressions, rooted in IE, are also found in Germanic languages, it is plausible to presume that the concept signified by such cognate forms already existed at the early stages of Old Slavic development, when Slavic and Germanic tribes shared the same territory or were geographical neighbors. The form **drug* has a somewhat different history. In some Slavic languages, its prototypical use became peripheral with the course of time, which could result from substitution of this form in the meaning of 'friend' by some other form. For example, in Polish the forms *drug, druh* are marked as 'obsolete' (Old Polish), in Bulgarian the forms друг *(drug)* and другарин *(drugarin)* are marked as 'archaic, dialectical', and in Czech *druh* is marked as 'archaic'. On the other hand, in all Slavic languages the root *drug-* demonstrated a significant potential for further derivation. In for instance Ukrainian and Russian, which preserve the two Slavic terms – *drug-* and *prijatel-* – for interpersonal relations, these terms are somewhat different in meaning: *друг (drug)* 'friend' and its derivatives *дружба (druzhba)* 'friendship', *дружити / дружить (druzhyty/druzhyt')* 'to be friends' highlight intensity and duration of friendly relations (cf. in collocations: Ukrainian *міцна дружба (mitsna druzhba)* 'firm friendship', Russian *старый друг (staryi drug)* 'old friend'), while the meaning of *приятель (priyatel')* 'pal' does not imply intensity and duration of friendly affection.

Hence, there are two main conceptualizations of FRIEND. The first one employs a metonymic shift from the source domain of affection to the target domain of interpersonal relations, as in cross-Slavic *prijatel-* and Germanic *friend*. This shift is also attested in Greek *φίλος (filos)*, Latin *amicus*, Italian *amico*, Spanish *amigo*, and French *ami*. Another conceptualization, associated with the form *drug-*, makes use of a metonymic shift from the broader source domain of social relations to the narrower target domain of interpersonal relations.

While taking part in further conceptual derivation, the concept FRIEND in all analyzed languages displays a rather conventional shift from 'friend' to 'lover': Slovenian *drug*, Bulgarian *другар (drugar)*, Czech *drug* (archaic), Polish *przyjaciel*, Bulgarian *приятел (priyatel)*, Serbian *prijatelj*, German *Freund, Freundin*, English *friend*, French *mon ami*. A wide range of languages which register this shift testifies to its typological validity. We presume that the semantic shift to 'lover' in the two Slavic forms for the concept FRIEND is explained by its two major semantic constituents – those of 'support' and 'positive emotion'. Meanwhile, the degree of their salience differs across languages. The constituent 'positive emotion' is more salient in the Romance languages where it is overt in motivators retained in the active vocabulary: French *amour*, Italian *amare*. In the Germanic and Slavic terms, which do not have counterpart motivators, the constituent 'positive emotion' is covert and, probably, imported from the Romance languages.

In Slavic languages, the other extensions of the concept FRIEND are registered only through the form *drug-*. Such extensions are founded on the shared idea 'the one who belongs to a group of people with common social interests'. Such interests may concern marriage, economics, politics, and military sphere, thus exhibiting relations within distinct social groups that are contrastive to the relations signified by the Slavic form *prijatel-* which do not imply any social gradation. Some languages demonstrate the semantic shift from 'friend' to 'spouse', which makes salient the idea of the mutual support within a family: Bulgarian and Serbian *друг (drug)* 'partner'. This semantic extension initiates active derivational process in Ukrainian and in Belarusian: Ukrainian *дружина (druzhyna)* 'wife', *дружина (druzhyna)* 'husband' (archaic, poetic), *одружуватися (odru-*

zhuvatysia) ('to get married'), *подружжя (podruzhzia)* ('a married couple'), Belarusian *дружына (druzhyna)* 'wife', *дружына (druzhyna)* 'husband' (archaic, poetic). Similar derived kinship terms and terms of household are attested in other Slavic languages: Slovenian *družina* 'a married couple, a group of relatives, a union', *družinčad* 'servants', Serbian/Croatian *družina* 'entourage, servants'. The form *drug-* is adopted for naming the participants of a wedding ceremony: 'bride's maid' – Ukrainian/Belarusian/Russian *дружка (druzhka)*, Polish *drużka*, Czech *družice*, *družka*, Slovak *družica*; 'best man' – Ukrainian/Russian *дружба (druzhba)*, Polish *drużba*, Czech *družba*, Slovak *družba*.

The form *drug-* is used as a stem in the derivatives that name homogeneous social units. Historically, their first types were represented by various military groups, cf. Old Slavic **druzyna* 'a military unit'. This archaic meaning is also registered in the Germanic languages (Old German *truht* 'community, detachment; Old English *druht* 'guard squadron'). In the East Slavic and West Slavic languages the original meaning 'a military unit' is retained as a peripheral sense of polysemous words: Ukrainian/Russian *дружина (druzhyna)*, Belarusian *дружына (druzhyna)*, Polish *drużyna*, Czech *družyna*. Moreover, this cognate demonstrates a significant potential for development of new meanings. Among non-military social groups conventionally signified with *drug-* derivatives are sport teams: Polish *drużyna* 'sport team'. In Russian and Ukrainian, similar derivatives may denote a non-military group only metaphorically, with metaphors being unconventional.

The meaning of 'a social group' conveyed by the form *drug-* in the South Slavic languages can be further specified as to the members of these groups and their interests: Slovenian *družba* 'society', 'union', 'company', *družen* 'common', *družbenik* 'partner', Bulgarian *дружба (druzhba)* 'fellow countryman society' (archaic), 'professional union' (archaic), Macedonian *друштво (drushtvo)* 'company, organization', Slovenian *družabništvo* 'partners, partnership', *družabniški*, *društvo* 'organized group of people', *društvenik* 'union member' (archaic), Serbian and Croatian *društvo*, 'union, society, group of people', Bulgarian *дружество (druzhestvo)* 'joint stock company, company'. The recent innovation registered in the 20th century and attributed to socialism is the semantic shift from 'a friend' to 'a party comrade': Serbo-Croatian *drug* and Bulgarian *другар (drugar)* served as a word of address; in Polish, *drug* was a word of address applied by pioneers, members of a youth communist organization similar to boy scouts.

To conclude, the two indigenous Slavic forms *drug-* and *prijatel-* that signify the concept FRIEND are presumed to initially differentiate between two kinds of beneficial interpersonal relations. The form *drug-* highlighted a social aspect, and the form *prijatel-* an emotional aspect of interaction. This difference has survived till present, being exposed in a number of semantic shifts that underpin derived words. Figure 5 shows the results of construing the concept friend and its further semantic extensions.

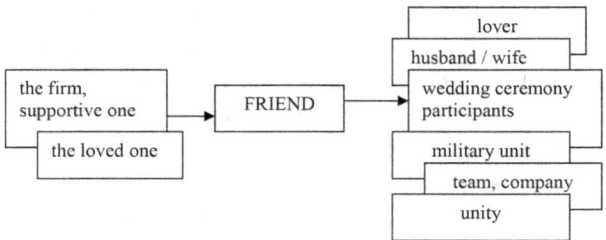

Figure 5: Semantic development of the concept FRIEND

Analysis of the concept ENEMY in Slavic languages testifies to the existence of two semantic motivation models: (1) *prijatelь + a negation suffix creates 'enemy, opponent': Belarusian непрыяцель (nepryiatsel'), Russian неприятель (nepriyatel'), Polish nieprzyjaciel, Czech nepřítel, Slovak nepriatel', Serbian/Croation/Slovenian neprijatelj, Macedonian непријател (nepriyatel); (2) *vorgъ 'enemy, villain' derived from the verb *vъrgati 'to throw': Ukrainian ворог (voroh), Russian враг (vrag) (from Old Church Slavonic), Polish wróg, Czech vrah 'killer', Bulgarian враг (vrag) 'enemy', 'devil', Serbian vrag 'enemy' (archaic), 'devil', Slovenian vrag 'enemy' (archaic), 'devil', 'villain', 'trouble'. The first model accentuates the negative aspect of interpersonal relations, i.e. their emotional constituent opposite to the previously reconstructed positive meaning of the form *prijatelь. In this case interaction is assessed by the individual who has a negative disposition to his/her partner who is not considered to be 'a friend'. Therefore, a person who is not 'my friend' is 'my enemy'. Such a rationale of conceptualization is quite common in Latin and in the Romance languages: Latin inimīcus, French ennemi, Italian nemico, Spanish enemigo, English enemy (borrowed from French).

It should be emphasized that the cross-Slavic opposition is prijatel- vs. neprijatel-, and not drug- vs. vrag-, which may be explained by the more archaic character of the first opposition which represents a purely emotional dimension of interpersonal relations. There are some grounds to assume that the second Slavic term *vorg describes another type of relations. In this case the meaning 'enemy' stems from the meaning of the verb 'to throw away'. According to etymological data, an enemy was 'an outcast, a person forced to leave his/her community', a person 'thrown away' from it. Thus, the term refers not to interpersonal relations per se but to the relations between a community and its member. So, similarly to the root drug-, the focus is not on an individual but on the society to which one belongs.

While analyzing the meaning 'slave, alien' rendered in Indo-European languages, Emile Benveniste (1969: 92–93) suggests an opposite vantage in the semantic development for enemy as 'alien' in Latin *hostis* 'enemy' related to *hospes* 'guest'. 'Alien' (enemy, guest) is an outsider, a person who comes from outside, whereas Slavic **vorgъ* is an outcast, a person who used to be a community member, and then was excluded from it, became 'alien'. Hence, there are opposite directions of ENEMY conceptualization in different languages: (1) an enemy as an alien and possibly an attacker (Latin *hostis*) – in this case an enemy is an individual who challenges and threatens the community, i.e. the agent is an individual, and (2) an enemy as an outcast whom the community opposes and rejects, i.e. the agent is the community (**vorgъ* in Slavic languages).

Another conceptualization of the concept ENEMY is based on the semantic shift from the source domain of physical space to the target domain of social relations: English *opponent*, Italian *avvesario*, Spanish *adversario, contrario*, Russian/Ukrainian/Serbian *противник (protivnik)*. This conceptualization displays understanding of an enemy as an individual or a group placed against you, which implies confrontation.

The semantic extensions of the concept ENEMY signified in the Slavic languages with the forms *neprijatelь-* and **vorgъ* are of different nature. The concept denoted with the form *neprijatelь-* and its derivatives does not display significant semantic shifts, while the concept named with **vorgъ* and its continuants demonstrates a wide range of extensions. The most notable one is the extension demonstrated with the West Slavic from **vorgъ* 'a killer': Czech, Slovak *vrah* 'killer', Czech *vraždit* 'to kill', *vraždivý* (archaic), *vražedný* 'bloody, deadly'(literally 'destructive, slaughtering' – it depicts a regular semantic schema of the person who caused death), *vražda* 'killing', Polish *wrażedlnik* 'killer' (marked as occurring in the Old Testament texts). Another semantic shift is to the meaning 'devil': Old Church Slavonic *врагъ (vragŭ)*, Ukrainian *ворог (voroh)*, Russian/Bulgarian *враг (vrag)*, Slovenian *vrag* 'devil, villain, trouble', Serbian *vrag* 'devil'. Skok (1973: 617) considers this meaning to be a comparatively new one, associated with the advent of Christianity. However, this statement lacks reliable data. The meanings 'enemy' and 'devil' undergo further extension: the continuants of **vorgъ* start to signify a disobedient restless child: Serbian *vrag*, Bulgarian dialectical *враг (vrag)* 'a restless child', with the emphasis not on the physical but mental agility. Russian *чертенок (chertenok)* in the meaning 'prankster, disobedient child' is a semantic analog. Figure 6 demonstrates conceptualization of ENEMY and its capacity for further semantic development.

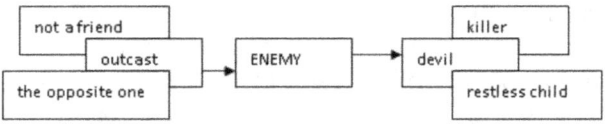

Figure 6: Semantic development of the concept ENEMY

11.8 Summary and conclusions

Our research demonstrates efficiency of combining diachronic (etymological) and synchronic approaches in typological analysis of cognate derivatives that exist in genealogically related languages. The etymological data provide evidence for exposing the constituents of a concept that belongs to the social domain. These constituents are represented in the motivators of linguistic forms that become names of the analyzed concept due to diachronic semantic shifts. The conceptualized entity takes part in further derivational processes, thus demonstrating a range of synchronic semantic shifts. Diachronic and synchronic semantic shifts are mostly metonymic and metaphoric ones. Therefore, the concept signified with a societal term becomes both a target (when it is named) and a source (when it motivates other names). This study shows that some diachronic and synchronic semantic shifts that occur in the Slavic, Romance and Germanic languages have a typological value, whereas other semantic shifts are restricted to one language or a limited number of languages. This research has theoretical implications for developing methodologies applicable in typological inquiries into lexical and derivational semantics.

The results of this study are summarized in the Table 1 below. It shows a wide range of semantic frames for societal terms in different languages that is to be interpreted as a representation of multiplicity of human interaction.

Table 1: Semantic frames for social relations in Slavic, Romance and Germanic languages

Concept	Constituents of conceptualization	Semantic shifts	Derivational potential
POWER	to own to manage to be strong to be able	authorities army	nomen agentis territorial unit violence

Tab. 1 (continued)

Concept	Constituents of conceptualization	Semantic shifts	Derivational potential
GOVERNOR	the higher one the bigger one the older one the direct one the first one the one who directs the one who puts things in order the one who has power	form of address God	dominance government economy
CITIZEN	city dweller dweller state inhabitant community member		abstract noun
COMMUNITY	being here being together put together		society community communication
FRIEND	firm, supportive loving	lover	husband/wife wedding ceremony participants military unit company union
ENEMY	not-friend outcast the opposite one	killer devil restless child	

11.9 References

Benveniste, Emile. 1969. *Le Vocabulaire des institutions indo-européennes. 1. Economie, parenté, société*. Paris: Les Editions de Minuit.

Bezlaj, France. 1977–2005. *Etimološki slovar slovenskega jezika* [Etymological dictionary of the Slovene Language], I–IV. Ljubljana: Mladinska knjiga.

Blank, Andreas. 1999. Why do new meanings occur? A cognitive typology of the motivations for lexical semantic change. In Andreas Blank and Peter Koch (eds), *Historical semantics and cognition*, 61–90. Berlin & New York: Mouton de Gruyter.

Bogardus, Emory S. 1933. A Social Distance Scale. *Sociology and Social Research* 17: 265–271.

BER. 1971–2002. *Balgarski etimologichen rechnik* [Etymological dictionary of the Bulgarian language]. Vol. I–VI. Sofia: BAN.
Boryś, Wiesław. 2005.*Słownik etymologiczny języka polskiego* [Etymological dictionary of the Polish language]. Kraków: Wydawnictwo literackie.
Britsin Viktor, Ekaterina Rakhilina, Tatyana Reznikova, and Galina Yavorska (eds.). 2009. *Kontsept boli v tipologicheskom osveshchenii* [The concept of pain in typological perspective]. Kiev: Dmitry Burago Publishing House.
Brown, Penelope. 2005. *Linguistic politeness*. In Ulrich Ammon, Norbert Dittmar, Klaus J. Mattheier, and Peter Trudgill (eds), *Sociolinguistics / Soziolinguistik*. Vol. 2., 1410–1416. Berlin: Walter de Gruyter.
Buck, Carl D. 1949. *Dictionary of selected synonyms in the principal Indo-European languages: A contribution to the history of ideas*. London & Chicago: University of Chicago Press.
Croft, William. 2006. The role of domains in the interpretation of metaphors and metonymies. In Dirk Geeraerts (ed.), *Cognitive linguistics: Basic readings*, 269–302. Berlin & New York: Mouton de Gruyter.
Dauzat, Albert. 1938. *Dictionaire étymologique de la Langue Française*. Paris: Librairie Larousse.
ESBM. 1978–1993. *Etymalagichny slownik belaruskaj movy* [Etymological dictionary of the Belarusian language]. Vol. I–VIII. Minsk: Nauka i tekhnika.
ESUM. 1982–2012. *Etymologichny slovnyk ukrajinskoji movy* [Etymological dictionary of the Ukrainian language]. Vol. I–VI. Kiev: Naukova dumka.
Fasmer, Maks. 1964–1973. *Etimologicheskij slovar' ruskogo jazyka* [Etymological dictionary of the Russian]. Vol. I–IV. Moscow: Progress.
Geeraerts, Dirk. 2010. *Theories of lexical semantics*. Oxford: Oxford University Press.
Greenberg, Joseph H. 1980. Universals of kinship terminology: their nature and problem of their explanation. In Jacques Maqet (ed), *On linguistic anthropology: Essays in honor of Harry Hojer*, 9–32. Malibu: Udena Publications.
Grzegorczykowa, Renata and Krystyna Waszakowa. 2003. *Studia z semantyki porównawczej. Nazwy barw. Nazwy wymiarów. Predykaty mentalne*, Cz. II. [Studies on comparative semantics. Colors, dimensions, mental predicates. Vol. 2]. Warszawa: Wydawnictwo Uniwersytetu Warszawskiego.
Kluge, Friedrich. 2005. *Etymologisches Wörterbuch der Deutshcen Sprache*. Berlin & New York: Walter de Gruyter.
Koptjevskaya-Tamm, Maria, Martine Vanhove, and Peter Koch. 2007. Typological approaches to lexical semantics. *Linguistic Typology* 11 (1): 159–185.
Kövecses, Zoltán. 2005. *Metaphor in Culture. Universality and Variation*. Cambridge: Cambridge University Press.
Lakoff, George and Mark Johnson. 1980. *Metaphors we live by*. Chicago & London: University of Chicago Press.
Machek, Václav. 1968. *Etymologický slovník jazyka českého* [Etymological dictionary of the Chech language]. Praha: Academia.
Maisak, Timur and Ekaterina Rakhilina (eds.). 2007. *Glagoly dvizheniya v vode: leksicheskaya tipologiya* [Verbs of AQUA motion: lexical typology]. Moscow: Indrik.
Panther, Klaus-Uwe and Günter Radden. 1999. *Metonymy in language and thought*. Amstrdam: Benjamins.
Rakhilina, Ekaterina and Vladimir Plungian. 2007. *O leksiko-semanticheskoy tipologii* [On Lexical Semantic Typology]. In Timur Maisak and Yekaterina Rakhilina (eds.). *Glagoly*

dvizheniya v vode: leksicheskaya tipologiya [Verbs of AQUA motion: lexical typology]. Moscow: Indrik.

Sakhno, Sergey. 2012. *L'image de l'ennemi à travers les termes de différentes langues (données de sémantique historique)*. In Brigitte Krulic, (ed.), *L'ennemi en regard(s). Images, usages et interprétations dans l'histoire et la littérature* (France, Allemagne, Russie, XVIII–XX siècles), 13–30. Bern: Peter Lang.

Sakhno, Sergey and Nicole Tersis. 2008. Is a 'friend' an enemy? Between 'proximity' and 'opposition'. In Martine Vanhove (ed.), *From polysemy to semantic change. Towards a typology of lexical semantic associations*, 317– 339. Amsterdam & Philadelphia: Benjamins.

Skok, Petar. 1971–1974. *Etimologijski rječnik hrvatskoga ili sprskoga jezika* [Etymological dictionary of the Croation or Serbian language]. Vol. I–IV, Zagreb: Akademija znanosti.

Sławski, Franciszek. 1952–1982. *Słownik etymologiczny języka polskiego* [Etymological dictionary of the Polish language]. Vol. I–V. Kraków Towarzystwo miłośników języka polskiego.

Talmy, Leonard. 1985. Lexicalization patterns. In Timothy Shopen (ed.), *Language typology and syntactic description: Grammatical categories and the lexicon*, Vol. 3. 57–149. Cambridge: Cambridge University Press.

Trubachev, Oleg. 2006. *Istoriya slavianskikh terminov rodstva i nekotorykh drevneyshykh terminov obshchestvennogo stroya* [The history of Slavic kinship terms and some ancient social terms]. 2nd. ed. Moscow: KomKniga.

Trubachev, Oleg (ed.). 1974–2013. *Etimologicheskij slovar' slavianskikh jazykov*. [Etymological dictionary of the Slavic languages]. Vol. 1–40. Moskow: Nauka.

Vanhove, Martine (ed.). 2008. *From polysemy to semantic change. Towards a typology of lexical semantic associations*. Amsterdam & Phildelphia: Benjamins.

Walde, Alois. 1938–1954. *Lateinisches Etymologisches Worterbuch* [Etymological dictionary of the Latin language]. Vol. I–II. Heidelberg: Carl Winter.

Wierzbicka, Anna. 1997. *Understanding Cultures through their key words: English, Russian, Polish, German, and Japanese*. Oxford: Oxford University Press.

Yavorska, Galina. 1992. *Leksiko-semanticheskaya tipologiya v sinkhronii i diakhronii* [Lexical semantic typology in synchrony and diachrony]. Kiev: Naukova dumka.

Antoinette Schapper, Lila San Roque and Rachel Hendery
12. *Tree*, *firewood* and *fire* in the languages of Sahul

Abstract: Earlier literature has suggested that colexification of terms for 'tree', 'firewood' and 'fire' may be widespread in Australian and Papuan languages. This feature of Papuan and Australian languages has not yet been considered as a part of a single phenomenon, nor examined in any detail. This paper presents the first in-depth survey of lexical expressions encoding the concepts 'tree', 'firewood' and 'fire'. Looking at 300 languages of Sahul, we plot the frequency and geographical distribution of colexification patterns for the three concepts in individual languages. We include analysis of the relationships between simple and complex terms for these concepts, which further elucidates geographic and genetic patterns of colexification and differentiation. Overall, we find that the most common pattern in the region is to colexify 'firewood' and 'fire', but not 'tree', contra earlier claims. Nevertheless, patterns present in Sahul are rare worldwide, indicating that Sahul is a large diffusion area worthy of further investigation in linguistic studies by Papuanists and Australianists collectively.

12.1 Introduction[1]

Defined as encompassing present-day Australia, New Guinea and surrounding islands, Sahul was first settled with certainty around 45,000 years ago (O'Connell

---

[1] Schapper's research was supported by a Netherlands Organisation for Scientific Research VENI project "The evolution of the lexicon. Explorations in lexical stability, semantic shift and borrowing in a Papuan language family". San Roque's research was supported by the Swedish Research Council project "Complex perspective in epistemic assessment" and the Netherlands Organisation for Scientific Research VENI project "Learning the senses: Perception verbs in child-adult interaction".

Antoinette Schapper (Koninklijk Instituut voor Taal-, Land- en Volkenkunde, Universität zu Köln)
Lila San Roque (Radboud University, Max Planck Institute for Psycholinguistics)
Rachel Hendery (Western Sydney University)

and Allen 2004).[2] It is not only biologically but also linguistically one of the most diverse regions of the world (Gorenflo et al. 2012). The languages of Sahul number many hundreds and form many apparently unrelated families. They are typically characterised as either Papuan or Australian languages: Papuan languages are found in and around the island of New Guinea and are divided into the Trans-New Guinea (TNG) Phylum with more than 300 languages, and around 60 small non-TNG families including a few language isolates (Foley 1986; Ross 2005); Australian languages are found on the Australian continent and divide into the Pama-Nyungan (PN) family with about 180 languages and 27 small non-PN families (Evans 2003; Bowern and Koch 2004). Members of the Austronesian language family that occur in the Sahul area are not included here as "Sahul languages", as – unlike the Papuan and Australian languages which have no known history outside of Sahul – they have their homeland in Formosa (modern-day Taiwan) and spread into Sahul at a relatively late stage in the Holocene (Pawley and Ross 1993; Pawley 2003).

This paper examines colexification patterns in the lexical expressions encoding the concepts for 'tree', 'firewood' and 'fire' in the languages of Sahul. Colexifications of these expressions in the Sahul area have been known in the literature for some time, but remain unexplored in any detail. Preliminary observations are made about their colexification in Papuan languages by Laycock (1986: 4):

> The main conflation to look for here is that of 'tree' and 'fire' – via the intervening concept 'firewood'. It is found in Foe, and is reported to be common in [Trans-New Guinea Phylum] languages.

Similar preliminary observations are made for Australian languages by, among others, Dixon (1980: 103):

> Some – but by no means all – Australian languages take the principle of having a single term to describe some natural object, and also something that can be made from it, to the extreme of having a single lexeme covering both 'tree, wood' and 'fire'.

These Papuanist and Australianist claims are yet to have been connected and considered together as a single phenomenon within a typological area, Sahul. What is more, in each of these works, only a handful of languages displaying

---

[2] Earlier dates of landfalls >50,000 years ago are occasionally found (e.g., in Roberts, Jones, and Smith 1990; Roberts et al. 1994; Thorne, Grun, and Mortimer 1999). However, the validity of these earlier dates is marred by uncertainties about associations between dates and evidence of human activity, about the dates themselves, or both.

the colexification pattern are named; there has been no systematic study of the distribution of this pattern across Sahul. The aim of this paper is to test how accurate these early observations are by extensively surveying the patterns of (non-)colexification of 'tree', 'firewood' and 'fire' terms in both Papuan and Australian languages, classifying the observed patterns, and mapping their geographic distribution. We show that the colexification patterns present in Sahul are rare worldwide, and indicate that Sahul is a large diffusion area worthy of further investigation in linguistic studies by Papuanists and Australianists collectively.

In Section 12.2 we describe our methods of data collection and analysis. We then explore lexification of the three concepts 'tree', 'firewood' and 'fire' with regard to their frequency and geographical distribution, employing a basic classification of the colexification patterns (Section 12.3). The results are contextualised by a survey of the world-wide occurrence of the Sahul colexification patterns in which we find that the Sahul patterns are indeed unusual in the languages of the world (Section 12.4). This is followed by an exploration of complex expressions (e.g., noun + noun combinations) for meanings in the domain and their relationship to simplex expressions (Section 12.5). In Section 12.6 we dub these relationships 'subcolexifications' and use them to bring out areal patterns in the lexification of 'tree', 'firewood' and 'fire' in Sahul. At the same time we present introductory family studies showing the diverse developmental paths of the different colexification patterns within and across Sahul language families. Our conclusions are presented in Section 12.7.

12.2 Data used in the study

12.2.1 Language sampling

This study is based on data from 300 Sahul language varieties: 217 Papuan and 83 Australian.[3] In collecting the data we have sought to sample as widely as possible from these two broad language groups. The languages of Sahul are notoriously

---

[3] This paper reports on the database version of 9 June 2015. Note that, in general, we have not included speech varieties that are generally considered dialects of one language as separate entries in the database. The exception to this is where we found evidence of different colexification patterns within a group, in which case these varieties were recorded as separate "languages". In one case (Kalam Pandanus language) this includes a specialised avoidance variety that has a separate colexification pattern to everyday speech.

un(der)documented and access to materials on them is often difficult (Hammarström and Nordhoff 2012; Nordhoff and Hammarström 2012). As such, our sample is opportunistic rather than balanced. The languages in our survey and the sources we have consulted are given in Appendix I (section 12.9).

Of the 217 Papuan languages in our database, there is a strong skewing towards TNG languages. According to the TNG classification of Pawley and Hammarström (forthcoming) only 86 of the 217 languages sampled come from non-TNG families (including isolates). Table 1 sets out the 26 non-TNG families represented in our sample (often by just a single language), following the groupings of Lewis et al. (2014). Many non-TNG families and isolates are not represented in the sample at all, including many in North-Central New Guinea such as Abinomn, Kwerbic, Left May, Mongol-Langam, Pauwasi Senagi, Yetfa and Yuat-Maramba to name just a few.

Table 1: Sampled non-TNG families (86 languages)

Arafundi (1)	Nimboran (4)
Border (6)	North Bougainville (1)
Central Solomons (3)	North Halmahera (5)
East Bird's Head (2)	Pahoturi River (1)
East New Britain (1)	Ramu-Lower Sepik (2)
Geelvink Bay (1)	Sepik (9)
Hatam-Mansim (1)	Skou-Serra-Piore-I'saka (5)
Kehu (isolate)	South Bougainville (4)
Kuot (isolate)	Tor-Orya (2)
Kwomtari (4)	Toricelli (11)
Lakes Plains (9)	West Papuan (3)
Morehead-Maro (5)	Yawa (1)
Mpur (isolate)	Yele-West New Britain (2)

Within the TNG classification (Table 2), certain families in our sample are over-represented, reflecting the different extents of documentation of TNG groups. For instance, the Timor-Alor-Pantar family, which has around 30 members, is represented in our sample by 14 languages, whereas the Finnisterre-Huon family containing between 60 and 70 members is represented by just 19 languages. Furthermore, within families there is sometimes bias towards one subgroup, such as the low-level Sogeram subgroup which constitutes seven of the 19 languages sampled from the Madang family. Other TNG families go entirely unrepresented. Of the 41 families said by Pawley and Hammarström (forthcoming) to have strong claims to TNG membership, 16 do not appear in our sample (Awin-Pa, Dagan, East Strickland, Inland Gulf, Kamula, Kayagaric, Kiwaian, Kolopom, Kwalean,

Mailuan, Manubaran, Mombum, Somahai, Tirio, Uhunduni and Yareban). Of the 12 families said to have weak claims to TNG membership, 7 do not appear in our sample (Bayono-Awbono, Dem, Mor, Pauwasi, Pawaian, Porome and Sentani).

Table 2: Sampled families of the TNG Phylum (131 languages)

Strong	
Angan (1)	Koiarian (6)
Asmat-Kamoro (4)	Kutubu (2)
Greater Awyu (9)	Madang (19)
Greater Binanderean (3)	Marind (1)
Bosavi (1)	Mek (5)
Chimbu-Wahgi (2)	Moraori (isolate)
Dani (7)	Greater Ok (5)
Duna-Bogaia (1)	Paniai Lakes (2)
Enga-Kewa-Huli (8)	South Bird's Head (2)
Finisterre-Huon (19)	Tanah Merah (isolate)
Gogodala-Suki (2)	West Bomberai (2)
Goilalan (3)	Wiru (isolate)
Kainantu-Goroka (6)	
Weak	
Kaure-Narau (1)	Timor-Alor-Pantar (14)
Mairasi (1)	Turama-Kikiori (1)
Teberan (1)	

The languages of Australia comprise a large family known as Pama-Nyungan, and many smaller families collectively referred to as non-Pama-Nyungan. The non-Pama-Nyungan languages tend to be located in the far north of the country. In this paper, we use the AUSTLANG language name orthographies (Obata 2009) and for Table 3 we use the Walsh and Wurm (1981) tentative classification of Australian language families, with a few updates as described in Koch (2004). Our sample contains 45 Pama-Nyungan languages and 38 non-Pama-Nyungan, so it is skewed towards Pama-Nyungan. Around 75 % of Australian languages belong to the Pama-Nyungan family, so it may be appropriate that this family is heavily represented in our sample in pure numerical terms, though not genetically balanced.

The Paman subfamily is heavily represented here because it is so large. Within the non-Pama-Nyungan languages, our sample contains more languages from the Nyulnyulan family than any other. While Nyulnyulan is one of the larger non-Pama-Nyungan families, there are other large non-Pama-Nyungan families we were not able to sample as thoroughly, as they have not been as well documented.

Overall, it should thus be clear that our data are extensive but not comprehensive, and do not make up a balanced sample that could (for example) be reliably used in statistical analyses. However, they are likely to represent at least some of the trends present in Sahul languages, and point the way towards questions that can be asked both in regard to a more comprehensive sample and within more detailed historical studies of family-level groups.

Table 3: Sampled languages from Australia

Pama-Nyungan sub-families	
Arandic (2)	Paman (13)
Central New South Wales (1)	Rainforest (5)
Kanyara (2)	Thura-Yura (1)
Karnic (3)	Wati (4)
Ngayarta (2)	Yalandjic (2)
Ngumpin-Yapa (3)	Yuin-Kuric (1)
Nyungar (1)	Yuulngu (5)
non-Pama-Nyungan families	
Anson Bay (1)	Limilngan (1)
Bunaban (2)	Mangerrian (3)
Eastern Daly (1)	Maran (2)
Northern Daly (1)	Nyulnyulan (7)
Southern Daly (1)	Tangkic (3)
Western Daly (3)	Tiwian (1)
Gaagadju (1)	Worroran (1)
Gunwingguan (7)	Yiwaidjan (3)

12.2.2 Approach to the data

In collecting data for this study, we sought translations of the English lexical expressions 'tree', 'firewood' and 'fire', or those of other languages in which Sahul language materials occur such as Dutch (*boom, brandhout* and *vuur*) and Indonesian (*pohon, kayu bakar* and *api*). We gathered these terms from dictionaries, wordlists, grammars, and through consultation with scholars who have worked with native speakers of the languages and/or who are themselves native speakers.

In discussing this material, we use the term "colexification", following François (2008), to refer to the situation when the meanings 'tree', 'firewood' and 'fire' are covered in a language by the same lexical item. We do not specify whether the relation between identical translations of our three target senses, 'tree', 'firewood' and 'fire', should be regarded as one of polysemy or semantic vagueness, since that involves a level of lexical semantic analysis that is not available for the majority of the languages in our sample. Thus, we say that in the language Duna, the word *rowa* colexifies 'tree' (1a), 'firewood' (1b) and 'fire' (1c).

Duna [duc][4]

(1) a. *Ayu heka kango=kho hapa **rowa**-ta era-na*
now bird bird_variety=3SG egg rowa-LOC be/put-HAB
ri-tia.
say-PFV.VIS.P
'Now the *kango* bird lays its eggs in **trees**, they say.'
(San Roque 2008: 250)
b. *Nane-na-ka ri-ya, **rowa** ho-ra iri ngoya-wayeni.*
boy-SPEC-CS say-DEP rowa here-CNCL fetch go-WARN
'The boy said, you must not fetch **firewood** from in here.'
(San Roque 2008: 296)
c. ***Rowa**-ka rindi kira-ya...*
rowa-CS land burn-DEP
'The **fire** burned the land...'
(San Roque field recordings)

By contrast, in the language Koromu 'tree' is separately lexified as *tiri* (2a), while 'firewood' (2b) and 'fire' (2c) are colexified as *hekeni*.

---

4 In this paper we include the generally accepted ISO 693-3 code for a language in square brackets after the language name to try and reduce confusion. Languages are given without an ISO 693-3 code in a few instances where it appears from the linguistic literature that a variety constitutes its own language, but has not (yet) been granted an independent ISO 693-3 code. This highlights the importance of recognising that existing ISO 693-3 codes by necessity simplify highly complex linguistic situations, and may be inadequate to reliably describe a particular language variety. Consultation of language- or family-specific sources is recommended for a more complete and nuanced understanding of linguistic nomenclature and identification. Abbreviations in interlinear glosses follow the Leipzig Glossing Rule recommendations, with the following additions: BM, boundary marker; CNCL, concealed location; CS, contrasted subject; DEP, dependent; G/L, goal/locative; S/L, source/locative; SPEC, specific; SR, same reference close succession; VIS.P, visual previous.

Koromo [xes]

(2) a. *I urunu-r-i=uo, **tiri** tai pere-hera=mo.*
 1SG think-PRES-1SG=LNK *tiri* NEG fall-3SG=BM
 'I think, the **tree** will not fall.'
 (Priestley 2009: 380)

b. ***Hekeni** u pa te-pe...*
 hekeni there G/L get-SR
 'We got **firewood** there...'
 (Priestley 2009: 529)

c. ***Hekeni** pate h-amu.*
 hekeni S/L roast-2SG
 'You roast it in the **fire**.'
 (Priestley 2009: 258)

In saying that meanings such as those exemplified in (1a-c) and (2b-c) are colexified, we recognise that they are semantically related to one another in some way, but we do not stipulate the exact nature of the relation.

In using dictionaries and grammars we have, where possible, looked at example sentences showing an in-context use to confirm the lexical expression used for our target meanings. This more extended search was undertaken due to observed discrepancies between the notation of lexical expressions where given as dictionary head words or word list entries, compared to more contextualised uses. A typical example is 'firewood' in the Namia dictionary. Headwords given with the translation 'firewood' are the two complex expressions in (3a). These contrast with examples throughout the dictionary where the simplex expression *mi* appears for 'firewood' (3b to 3e). The dictionary further shows that *mi* colexifies the meanings 'tree' and 'fire'.

Namia [nnm]

(3) a. *par mi, mi tapar* 'firewood'
 b. ***mi** ki nu lwae* 'carried firewood above and below'
 c. *el **mi** panawenprowe* 'the ladies broke firewood'
 d. ***mi** unne powe loko* 'firewood that is completely dry'
 e. ***mi** lope* 'heap firewood'
 (Feldpausch, Feldpausch, and Yalweike 2011)

For a language such as Namia, we take the evidence of examples such as (b-e), together with the examples of *mi* meaning 'tree' or 'fire' as sufficient to indicate a relationship of colexification between 'tree', 'fire' and 'firewood'. However, the distinctive 'firewood' terms as noted in the dictionary entry (*par mi, mi tapar*) are also entered into the database, recognising that alternative patterns are possible (see 12.3.4 for further discussion).

12.2.3 Additional information in the database

Wide-scale data collection that extracts just a few terms cannot, of course, capture the rich lexical and grammatical subtleties that are present in individual languages. While we have restricted our coding and analyses to the relatively cross-linguistically comparable feature of colexification, where possible we also took note of further language-specific information relevant to the semantic domain under study.

For example, in at least three languages in our sample it became apparent that systems of nominal classification contribute to a differentiation of meaning between colexified concepts 'tree', 'firewood', and/or 'fire'. The word *méni* in the Papuan language Kómnzo has different semantics depending on its gender assignment. With feminine agreement, *méni* denotes 'fire' (4a). With masculine agreement *méni* denotes 'firewood' (4b).

Kómnzo [tci]
(2) a.   Zane   keke   zéféth   **méni**   rä.
         DEM   NEG   base   méni   3SG.FEM.COP.NPST
         Zane   katan   **méni**-nzo   rä.
         DEM   small   méni-only   3SG.FEM.COP.NPST
         'This is not the primeval fire. This is just a small fire.'
   b.   Théntös   **méni**   namä   **méni**   yé.
         dried.wood   méni   good   méni   3SG.MASC.COP.NPST
         'The dried wood pieces... It is good firewood.'
         (Christian Döhler, p. c.)

This appears to be part of a larger pattern in Kómnzo whereby gender assignment is used to a limited extent to differentiate a broad set of semantic relationships between nouns similar to mass versus count, albeit with some lexicalisation: for instance, *no* denotes 'water' when feminine and 'rain' when masculine, *thak thak* 'law' (feminine) and 'god' (masculine), *ekri* 'flesh, body' (feminine) and 'meat' (masculine) (Christian Döhler, p. c.). In Bunaq [bfn] gender is similarly exploited to vary the semantics of the lexeme *hotel*. When denoting a tree growing and fixed in the earth, *hotel* is assigned to the animate gender. When denoting dried out, fallen wood such as suitable for use as firewood, *hotel* is assigned to the inanimate gender. This variable gender assignment is used subtly to emphasise different features of the plant referent (Schapper 2009: 186–187), and it may be that this more flexible use of gender assignment precedes the lexicalised pairs seen in languages like Kómnzo.

A rather different strategy for differentiation is found in the Australian language Arrernte [aer], where classificatory posture verbs can be used with the word *ure* to derive the different lexical meanings 'fire' or 'firewood'. *Ure* is used with the 'sit' verb to mean 'fire', but with the 'lie' verb to mean 'firewood' (Wilkins 1989). Lang (1971) similarly notes that in the Papuan language Enga [enq], existence or ownership of a standing tree, *ítá*, is predicated with the existential/posture verb *katengé* (typically used of tall, standing items), whereas existence or ownership of fire, *ítá(té)*[5] is predicated with *síngi* (used of motionless or crawling items); see also Rumsey (2002) for further discussion of the classification of 'tree' and related concepts using posture verbs.

For the purposes of the current survey, we have coded the colexification of a language based solely on the form of a lexical item, as a full treatment of the grammatical behaviour or heterosemy, to use Lichtenberk's (1991) term, of 'tree', 'fire' and 'firewood' items is beyond the scope of this paper. However, languages such as Kómnzo, Bunaq, Arrernte and Enga suggest classification strategies as a topic that is of interest both in relation to the semantic domain currently under study, and in regard to colexification studies more generally.

Where possible, the database also notes other colexifications that are mentioned in the source data with regard to 'tree', 'firewood' and 'fire' terms. An important case in point is lexical expressions for 'wood'. The vast majority of Sahul languages do not have a distinct lexeme for 'wood'; this is colexified with the lexeme used for English 'tree' (cf. the findings of Brown and Witkowski [1983], who argue that generic 'tree' terms typically arise through expansion of an original 'wood' term; however, their sample included only one Australian language and no Papuan languages). In 169 of the Papuan languages surveyed 'tree' and 'wood' were identically colexified (for 37 languages no translation for 'wood' was found in the source used). In only 11 languages were they recorded as non-identical and in three of these there appeared to be a possible derivational relationship between the two lexemes.[6] In the Australian languages only 17 of the 83 languages are

---

5 The Enga dictionary (Lang 1973) lists one term *ítá* as meaning 'tree', 'wood' AND 'fire', with *ítáté* as a variant meaning only 'fire'. However, the discussion in Lang (1971) refers to the relevant terms as *ítá* 'tree, wood' and *ítáté* 'fire'. Thus, the use of classificatory posture verbs in Enga as a potential differentiator between 'tree' and 'fire' meanings needs to be confirmed.

6 Papuan languages for which 'tree' and 'wood' were distinct and there was no discernible relationship between the two forms were: Urim (Torricelli); Kaure (Kaure-Narau); Kalam (Madang); Aisi, Gants, and Manat (Sogeram); Kómnzo (Morehead-Maro) and Mairasi (Mairasi). For all of

recorded as having a word for 'wood' or 'stick' that is different from the word for 'tree' and in all but six of these there exists a colexified word for 'wood'/'tree' as well. In 11 Australian languages no translation for 'wood' or 'stick' was available.

Table 4 shows a few examples of other, in some cases quite unusual, colexifications of 'tree', 'firewood' and/or 'fire' that were not included in our survey in a systematic way, but give insight into the extent of the range of semantic domain(s) and functions that are potentially relevant to this lexical field (see, e.g., Evans (1992) for in-depth discussion of a polysemy 'system network' partially centred around a 'fire'-related term in the language Demiin).[7]

Table 4: Examples of other colexifications with 'tree', 'firewood', 'fire'

Tree/firewood/fire meaning(s)			Other colexification(s) or function	Example language(s)
'tree'	'firewood'	'fire'		
		x	'burn'	Rotokas [roo] (Firchow and Firchow 2008)
		x	'rifle'	Jawoyn [djn] (Merlan and Jacq 2005)
	x		'dry'	Rotokas [roo] (Firchow and Firchow 2008)
	x	x	'camp'	Bandjalang [bdy], Gidabal [gih] (Evans 1992) ‡
x	x		'person who has completed initiation'	Kuuku Ya'u [kuy] (Wilkins 2000)‡

---

these languages there was either colexification or a tentatively possible derivational relationship between the 'wood' term and either 'fire' and/or 'firewood'. A further eight languages were recorded as colexifying 'tree' and 'wood' but also having distinct terms that did not colexify both meanings (e.g., Kiri-kiri *nu* 'tree, wood' versus *mu* 'wood, firewood').

7 Laycock (1986: 4) suggests two (sub)colexifying relationships that we have been unable to confirm on consultation of relevant sources and scholars. First, he writes that "[i]n all Ndu Family languages [...] the word for 'tree' is also specific for 'garamut tree *(Vitex cofassus)*'". We found Proto-Ndu *miy 'tree' (Foley 2005: 129) and its reflexes did not colexify with garamut in Ndu in the manner that Laycock appears to suggest, though garamut terms do involve a 'tree'-like term as follows: Iatmul *miamba*, Manambu *miyemb*, Ngala *ngala namba*, Abelam *miamba*, Yangoru *mtampa* (Coiffier 1996). Second, Laycock writes that in Torricelli languages 'tree' terms 'appear related' to 'sago' terms. We have not found any data to support or refute this suggestion and it remains for future research to pursue further.

Table 4 (continued)

Tree/firewood/fire meaning(s)			Other colexification(s) or function	Example language(s)
'tree'	'firewood'	'fire'		
x	x	x	'matches, lighter'	Duna [duc] (San Roque 2008)
x			'instrument, tool' (e.g., screwdriver, tin opener)	Pintupi [piu] (Hansen and Hansen 1992)
x			noun classifier 'CLF:TREE'	Pamosu [hih] (Tupper 2014)
x			'thing'	Emmi [amy] (Ford 1998) Kayardild [gyd] (Evans 1995)

‡ As we do not have full information for the forms of all three relevant lexemes, Bandjalang, Gidabal and Kuuku Ya'u are not included in maps or frequency counts in the following sections.

Interestingly, as illustrated in the table, several dictionaries and grammars include the information that tree/firewood/fire terms can also be used for introduced items such as matches and other novel tools or products. These examples suggest the 'extendability' of tree/firewood/fire words to other concepts.

The relevant terms may also be used for special semi-grammaticalised functions, for example, Tupper (2014) argues that the generic 'tree' term *na* in Pamosu [hih] is itself used as a noun classifier, combining with more specific tree variety names (e.g. *na mangumbu* 'mangumbu tree'). This pattern of using a generic 'tree' term preceding a more specific tree term is likely present in many other languages of New Guinea, and, as Tupper (2014) discusses in detail, mirrors a generic-specific naming pattern also found in other semantic domains (e.g., in terms for specific animal and bird varieties). Similarly, in the Australian language Murrinpatha the term 'fire' is analysed as having a classifier function (Street 1983); see also Table 12.

12.3 Basic classifications: Frequency and geographic distribution

12.3.1 Overview

In our data, we identify five patterns in the coding of the three terms 'tree', 'firewood' and 'fire', presented in Table 5. The following three letter codes are used in the legends of the maps plotting geographical distributions.

Table 5: Basic patterns of colexification of 'tree', 'firewood' and 'fire'

	Pattern name	Description
abc	full differentiation	three lexical expressions, one for 'tree', one for 'firewood', and one for 'fire'
abb	firewood/fire colexification	two lexical expressions, one for 'tree', and one for 'firewood' and 'fire'
aab	tree/firewood colexification	two lexical expressions, one for 'tree' and 'firewood', and one for 'fire'
aba	firewood differentiation	two lexical expressions, one for 'firewood', and one for 'tree' and 'fire'
aaa	full colexification	one lexical expression for 'tree', 'firewood' and 'fire'

Examples of each type of pattern follow in (5) to (9).

Yimas [yee] {abc}
(5) a. *yan* 'tree'
    b. *ampra* 'firewood'
    c. *awt* 'fire'

Mehek [nux] {abb}
(6) a. *mu* 'tree'
    b. *kiri* 'firewood, fire'

Nasioi [nas] {aab}
(7) a. *koig* 'tree, firewood'
    b. *ntag* 'fire'

Mendi [age] {aba}
(8) a. *ri* 'tree, fire'
    b. *kap* 'firewood'

Guugu Yimithir [kky] {aaa}
(9) *yugu* 'tree, firewood, fire'

In this initial classification we are concerned only with the number of distinct lexical expressions irrespective of their composition and derivation. We do not take into account derivational relationships between the lexical expressions. For instance, under this classification, Daga (terms given in 10) is said to show the firewood differentiation {aba} pattern, even though its 'firewood' term is clearly derived from its 'tree, fire' term.

Daga [dgz]
(10) a. *oma* 'tree, fire'
    b. *oma oaewa* 'dry *oma*' = 'firewood'

Relationships between lexical expressions in this domain are examined in detail in 12.5.

Some languages furthermore show the potential for more than one classification pattern. For the purposes of the main frequency counts and mapping undertaken in this study (12.3.2, 12.3.3), we classify a language that has both colexification and differentiation patterns as the *most* colexified variant. For instance, Sirva (terms given in 11) is primarily classified as having the full colexification {aaa} pattern, as the term *au* covers all three meanings in our domain.

Sirva [sbq]
(11) a. *au* 'tree, firewood, fire'
    b. *asɨk* 'firewood, fire'
    c. *tar* 'tree'

Variant classifications such as found in Sirva are discussed in 12.3.4.

12.3.2 Pattern frequency

Table 6 presents the occurrences of each of the patterns across the Sahul languages we surveyed.

Table 6: Occurrence of patterns in Sahul

		Papuan languages	Australian languages	TOTAL	Percent
abc	full differentiation	92	10	102	34%
abb	firewood/fire colexification	70	64	134	45.5%
aab	tree/firewood colexification	26	0[8]	26	8.5%
aba	firewood differentiation	7	0	7	2%
aaa	full colexification	22	9	31	10%

Using this classification, we find considerably less colexification than we might expect based on prior claims in the literature. Amongst Papuan languages, two patterns dominate: the full differentiation {abc} pattern with 92 languages, and the fire/firewood colexification {abb} pattern with 70 languages. The remaining three other patterns {aab, aba, aaa} all make much less frequent appearances in Papuan languages and together make up less than one quarter of occurrences in our sample (i.e., 65 languages). Amongst Australian languages, the fire/firewood {abb} pattern dominates, with 64 of 83 languages following this pattern. The full colexification {aaa} pattern is found in only nine Australian languages in our sample.

Based on this study, the claims in the literature about colexifications in this domain appear difficult to uphold. Contrary to Laycock (1986), only 10% of Papuan languages surveyed had the colexification of 'tree' and 'fire' (22 of 217). Only three non-TNG languages showed the colexification (Namia [nnm], Western Fas [fqs], and Barupu [wra]), but the colexification can still not be said to be "common" in TNG languages: as we will show below, the colexification is prominent in TNG families in two regions of the central and eastern highlands of New Guinea, but does not feature in the majority of TNG families surveyed. In the Australian literature, too, the full colexification is discussed frequently and in enough detail (O'Grady 1960; O'Grady 1979; Plomley 1976; Hale 1986; Lakoff 1987; Wilkins 2000; Dixon 1980, 2002) to give the impression that it is more common than it really seems to be.

In short, in our data, a dominant pattern throughout Sahul is to colexify 'firewood' and 'fire', and not 'tree'. Full differentiation is also found as a dominant pattern in Papuan languages.

---

8 Bardi and Nunggubuyu have this pattern as an alternative to the {abb} pattern. As neither pattern is more differentiated than the other, it is difficult to know which to count in this table, but we have counted them as {abb}. See section 12.3.4 for further discussion of variant patterns.

12.3.3 Pattern geography

Map 1 plots the distribution of languages according to the five classifications described in Table 1 across the entire Sahul area. This allows us to visualise the possible significance of areal as well as genetic relationships in shared practices of colexification. We look first in more detail at the Papuan languages before discussing the distribution of patterns on the Australian continent.

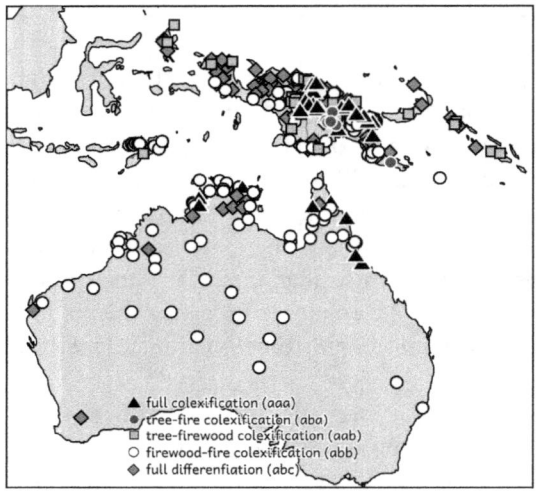

Map 1: Distribution of patterns across Sahul languages

12.3.3.1 The Papuan area

Map 2 shows the distributions of the patterns across the Papuan language area. We see that the three most frequent patterns (full differentiation {abc}, firewood/fire colexification {abb} and tree/firewood colexification {aab}) appear to be found widely across the New Guinea region. The two least frequent patterns, full colexification {aaa} and firewood differentiation {aba}, are much more restricted, being limited to the eastern half of the New Guinea mainland. For the most part, these two patterns are found in languages contiguous with and/or related to one another, suggesting high permeability between these two colexification patterns (see also Map 6 and Map 7).

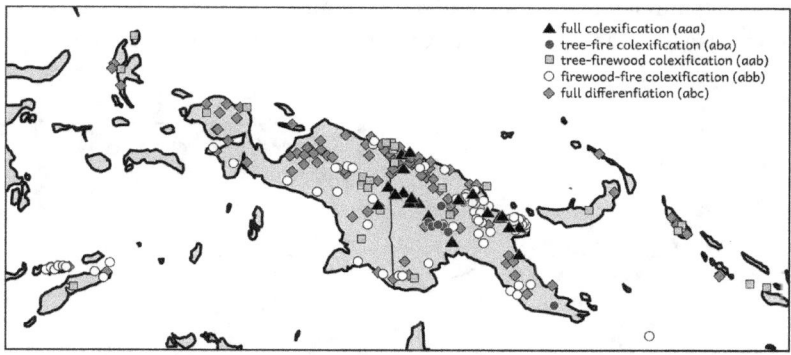

Map 2: Distribution of all patterns across Papuan languages

The full differentiation {abc} pattern dominates across the top of New Guinea to the north of the central cordillera and into the Papuan outlier areas in maritime Oceania (Map 3). This means the pattern is especially common amongst non-TNG languages, but by no means limited to them.

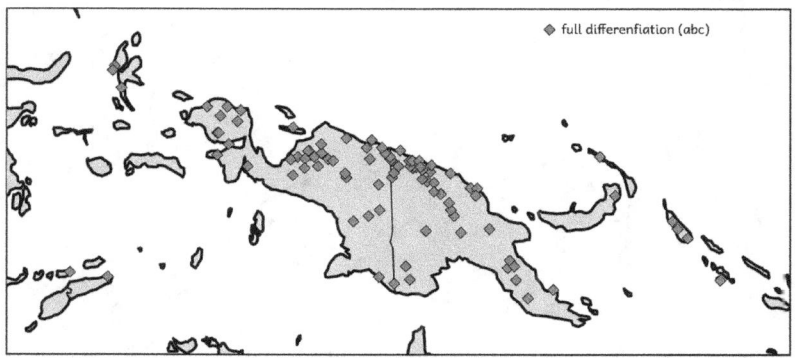

Map 3: Distribution of full differentiation {abc} pattern across Papuan languages

The firewood/fire colexification {abb} pattern (Map 4) is prevalent in the south-western part of the Papuan area, particularly in the Asmat and Dani families of TNG but also including the Papuan outlier area of the Timor-Alor-Pantar family. It also has a strong presence in the adjacent Finnestere-Huon and Madang regions sliding south-east off the back of New Guinea, and makes sporadic appearances in the complex north central New Guinea region and South New Guinea. This distribution suggests that genetic and areal influence may be significant to understanding this pattern. The fact that it is so widespread and appears in many unrelated and non-contiguous families, however, indicates that the pattern is also reasonably likely to exist independently in the various Papuan linguistic groups.

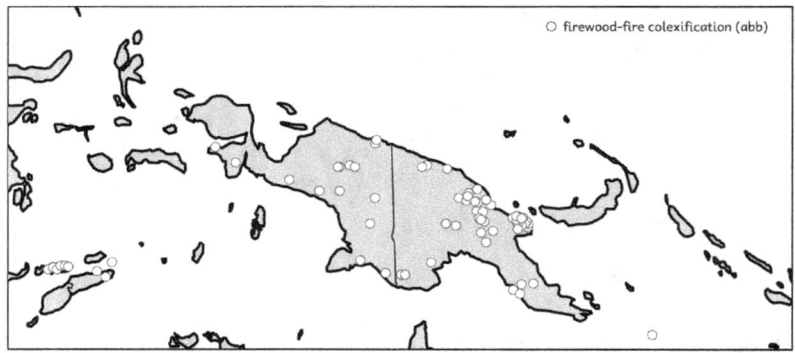

Map 4: Distribution of firewood/fire colexification {abb} pattern across Papuan languages

The tree/firewood colexification {aab} pattern shows no centre but makes appearances in all corners of the Papuan language area (Map 5).

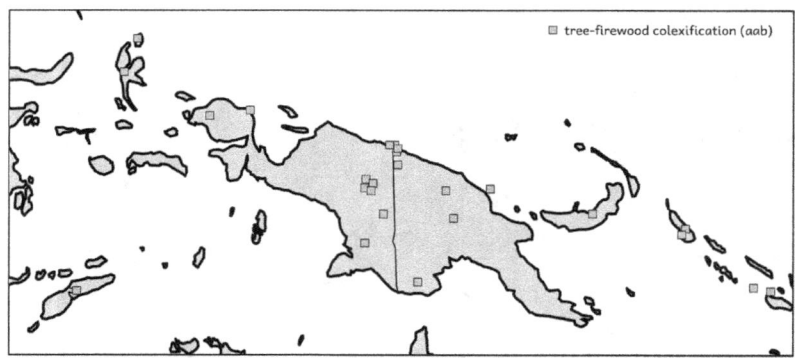

Map 5: Distribution of tree/firewood colexification {aab} pattern across Papuan languages

The full colexification {aaa} pattern (Map 6) is concentrated in two areas: (i) the central highlands, where it spreads across 4 distinct TNG groups, from Huli [hui] in the east through Duna[9] [duc] and the Ok-Okspamin languages into the

---

9 In both Enga (an Engan language) and Bogaia (putatively the only close relative of Duna), 'tree' and 'fire' are colexified, but the terms for 'firewood' are not currently known.

northern-most Awyu-Dumut language, Wambon (Digul variety) [dms]; and (ii) Madang-Finisterre, adjacent language-dense and diversity-rich TNG regions of north-east New Guinea. However, there are also five outliers with the full coflexification {aaa} pattern: two in the north-central area (Barupu [wra] and Western Fas [fqs]), one in the Sepik (Namia [nnm]), one in the Binandere region (Suena [sue]), and one in the Gulf area (Rumu [klq]). This smattering of far-flung languages, including several that are outside the TNG grouping, argues for the possible independent emergence of full colexification, alongside the importance of areal influence. However, six languages with full colexification are noted as having alternative patterns that are more differentiated, for example, 'fire' in the Ok language Bimin [bhl] can be expressed as *ais* 'tree, firewood, fire' or as the alternative term *weing* 'fire'. This suggests that the full colexification pattern may not be a stable state, or that at any rate is likely to co-exist with more specific vocabulary items.

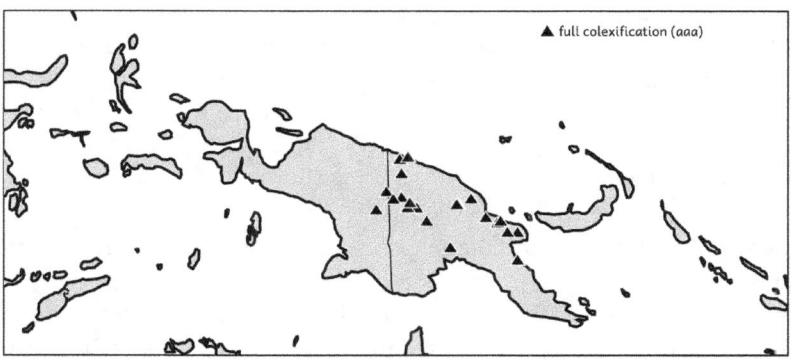

Map 6: Distribution of full colexification {aaa} pattern across Papuan languages

Finally, we turn to the infrequent firewood differentiation {aba} pattern (Map 7). This clusters geographically and or genetically with languages that show full colexification, centering on Engan languages and close neighbours. Within this cluster, there is evidence of inter-family borrowing: the Foe [foi] and Fasu [faa] terms are transparently related to those of Engan languages (see Table 24 in section 12.6.1) for more discussion of this pattern's relation to the full colexification pattern). We also note one outlier in this pattern in the far south-west, Daga [dgz]. Daga is not known to be spoken contiguously with languages that are confirmed as having full colexification, so it seems just possible, albeit somewhat unlikely, that the firewood differentiation pattern exists independently of the presence of a full colexification language.

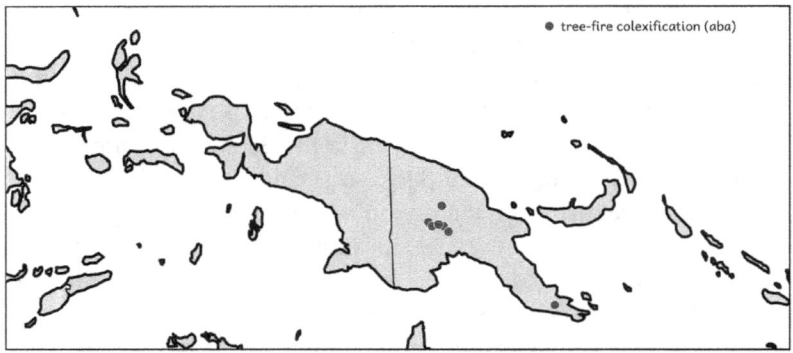

Map 7: Distribution of firewood differentiation {aba} pattern across Papuan languages

In sum, full colexification is most commonly found in TNG languages, but it is not the dominant pattern amongst them, contra Laycock (1986). Much more frequently just 'firewood' and 'fire' are colexified in TNG languages, while no colexification is most common across the full suite of Papuan groups.

12.3.3.2 The Australian area

Map 8 presents the distributions of the colexification patterns across the Australian language area.

We see that the firewood/fire colexification {abb} pattern is so dominant in Australia that it is more difficult to draw geographic conclusions about the distributions of the remaining patterns. It does seem that there is a higher occurrence of other patterns in the north of Australia. As this is also where most non-Pama-Nyungan languages are found, one might expect that this apparent geographical distribution is actually due to these other patterns being more common in non-Pama-Nyungan languages. However, of the 19 languages in our sample that have patterns other than the firewood/fire colexification pattern, nine are non-Pama-Nyungan and ten are Pama-Nyungan. Of the languages with firewood/fire colexification, 24 are non-Pama-Nyungan and 40 are Pama-Nyungan. As such, if there is a difference between the firewood/fire colexifying languages and the rest, it appears to be geographic rather than genetic.

The full colexification {aaa} pattern predominants in two areas, Cape York and the Daly River. Only one language outside these regions, Djinang, has the full colexification {aaa} pattern. Around Cape York it is found in various subgroups of the Pama-Nyungan languages, while around the Daly it occurs in multiple non-Pama-Nyugan families. As we argue in section 12.6.2, the pattern appears to have emerged multiple times in each region presumably under contact effects.

The distribution of the full differentiation {abc} pattern appears more common around the northern edge of Australia than elsewhere. This pattern seems to be more common in non-Pama-Nyungan languages, in particular the Gunwinyguan languages, than in Pama-Nyungan.

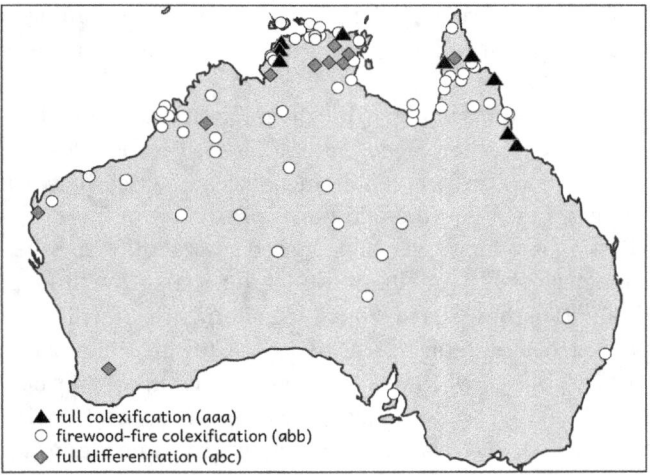

Map 8: Distribution of patterns across Australian languages

A complicating factor in interpreting the Australian data is that the (non-)colexification of lexemes for 'tree', 'firewood' and 'fire', as discussed in the Australianist literature, is sometimes present grammatically, historically or otherwise in more complex ways than mere colexification (see also section 12.2.3). For example, in Dixon's (2002b) extensive discussion of 'tree', 'wood', 'firewood' and 'fire', he lists many regions of Australia where relationships between these terms are found, but on closer examination these regions rarely contain a single language in which the same term is used for all of these meanings. Rather, he refers to regions in which a single term has one or two of the meanings in some languages, and the other meanings in other languages. He notes that this is the case in what he refers to as the North Cape York subgroup, the South-East Cape York Peninsula Group, the Herbert River Group, the Western Yolngu Subgroup, the Mangunj Areal Group, and the Spencer Gulf Basin Areal Group. Some of these groups are considered genetic units by other linguists (cf. Evans 2005; Sutton and Koch 2008). These cases may therefore represent the remnants of earlier colexification in proto-languages, or have resulted from areal transmission.

12.3.4 Languages with variant classifications

As outlined in section 12.3.1, a number of languages are recorded as having more than one possible colexification pattern. For example, in Tiwi [tiw] there is a term *yikwani* which can be used for 'fire' and 'firewood', but there are also terms *wantanga* 'large piece of firewood', *wantangini* 'medium piece of firewood', and *payiwuti* < English *firewood*, which are used only for 'firewood' (Lee 2013). As explained above, in these cases we have classified the language according to the maximum colexification, that is, a language with {abb} and {abc} has been mapped as {abb}.

For the Papuan languages in our sample, 16 languages (from 12 different families) were recorded as having an alternative, more differentiated, lexification. These included 7 firewood/fire colexifying {abb} languages and 3 tree/firewood colexifying {aab} languages which had the additional possibility of full differentiation {abc}, as well as 6 {aaa} languages that showed several different alternative possibilities (2 languages with an alternative {aab} pattern, 2 with {abb} and 2 with {aba}). For half (8) of these 16 languages, the alternative classification arose because of multiple recorded terms for 'firewood'. A further 6 languages had multiple terms for 'fire', one of which was colexified with either 'firewood' and/or 'tree', while the other(s) was not. In most cases, one of the 'fire' or 'firewood' terms was clearly complex and related to the simplex, colexified term (see also 4). Sirva [sbq] was recoded as having distinctive terms for 'tree' (*tar*) and for 'fire, firewood' (*apir*)[10], as well as one word that colexifies all three meanings (*au*), while Kalam [kmh] Pandanus language has two alternatives for 'tree', one of which is colexified with 'fire' and 'firewood' (*sutkeb*) and one of which is not (*tgomeb*).

Of the 83 Australian languages in the database, 19 were recorded as having an alternative classification (8 non-Pama Nyungan and 11 Pama-Nyungan); proportionately considerably higher than for Papuan languages. These included 15 fire/firewood {abb} languages with an alternative full differentiation {abc} pattern, two {abb} languages with alternative {aab}, and two {aaa} languages (alternative {abb}). As with Papuan languages, multiple classifications mostly (but not always) arose through the presence of multiple 'firewood' and/or 'fire' terms. However, for most of the Australian cases there was not a clear derivational relationship discernible between the alternatives (cf. the Tiwi items cited above).

---

10 However, Don Daniels (p.c.) notes that this term is considered archaic.

Table 7 summarises the noted variant classification patterns found in the database.

Table 7: Languages noted to have variant classifications

variant 1	variant 2	Papuan	Australian	TOTAL
abb	abc	7	15	22
abb	aab	0	2	2
aab	abc	3	0	3
aaa	aab	2	0	2
aaa	abb	2	2	4
aaa	aba	2	0	2

The presence of variant (co)lexification possibilities in several of the languages in our database is important for two reasons. First, it serves as a cautionary note that a great many languages have several alternative ways of expressing the same or similar concepts; there is no reason to assume that the languages noted in this section are the only ones that have variant patterns, as in many cases this information appears to go un-noted in the available sources. Second, in further studies these patterns may be able to give us insight into processes of language change and semantic shift in this domain.

12.4 tree/firewood/fire colexification patterns in non-Sahul languages

How peculiar are colexification patterns for the meanings 'tree', 'fire' and 'firewood' that we have identified in Sahul languages? Whilst a full-scale survey is beyond the scope of this paper, in this section we make some preliminary observations about the world-wide occurrence of the Sahul colexification patterns using data from the Automated Similarity Judgement Program (Wichmann et al. 2013), the CLICS Database of Cross-linguistic Colexifications (List et al. 2014)[11], as well as in Urban (2012) and the Proto-Oceanic Lexicon (Ross, Pawley, and Osmond 1998, 2003).

---

[11] CLICS includes the vocabularies that appear in World Loanworld Database (Haspelmath and Tadmore 2009).

Notably, the full Sahul colexification pattern of 'tree', 'firewood' and 'fire' is not recorded in any of the typological databases or overviews that we examined.[12] The nearest to this pattern amongst non-Sahul languages is tree/fire colexification, since we see that in Sahul where 'tree' and 'firewood' were colexified 'firewood' is never completely separately lexified (i.e, at least sub-colexified with 'tree' and 'fire', see section 12.5). Even so, tree/fire colexification is remarkably limited: List et al. (2014) and Urban (2012) do not record any languages colexifying 'tree' and 'fire', while of the 6,895 languages in Wichmann et al. (2013), only 64 language varieties colexified 'tree' and 'fire'. Of these, only 12 were non-Sahul languages; they are presented in Table 8 and Map 9.[13]

Table 8: Non-Sahul languages with 'tree' and 'fire' colexification (Wichmann et al. 2013)†

	'tree'	'fire'	Classification
Cuicatec [cux]	ya7a*	ya7a*	Oto-Manguean, Mixtecan
Bushong [buf]	tey	tey	Niger-Congo, Bantoid
Edo [bin]	era*	era*	Niger-Congo, Edoid
Engenni [enn]	atai	atai	Niger-Congo, Edoid
Epie [epi]	itan	itan	Niger-Congo, Edoid
Wuming Yongbei Zhuang [zyb]	fai	fai	Tai-Kadai
Manobo Dibabawon [mbd]	kayu	kayu	Austronesian
Are [mwc]	keama	keama	Austronesian, Oceanic
Buhutu [bxh]	oyagi	oyagi	Austronesian, Oceanic
Bunama [bdd]	7aiwe	7aiwe	Austronesian, Oceanic
Molima [mox]	aiwe	aiwe	Austronesian, Oceanic
Gedaged [gdd]	ja	ja	Austronesian, Oceanic

† In the table we present the data in the simplified ASJP transcription system, problematic as it is.

---

12 Note the lack of overlap between the languages worldwide that show firewood/fire colexification and tree/firewood colexification in Tables 9 and 10.
13 Thanks to Robert Östling for pointing out this data source and sharing his findings with us, see Östling (this volume).

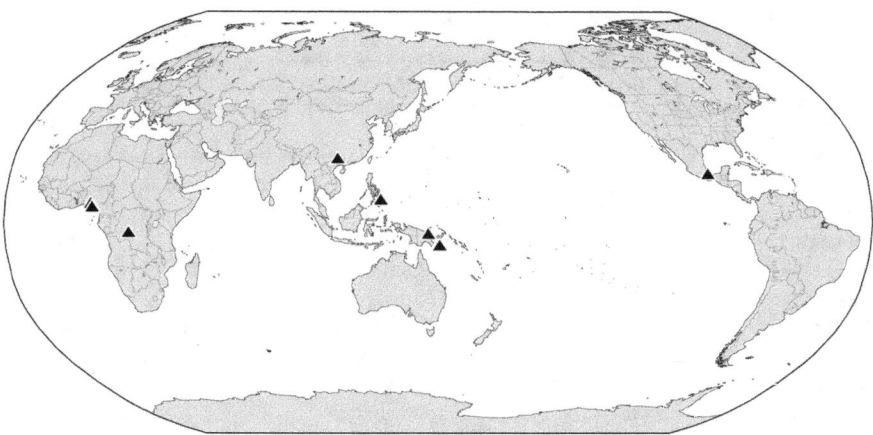

Map 9: Non-Sahul languages with 'tree' and 'fire' colexification

Most striking is that of the 12 non-Sahul languages with tree/fire colexification, five were Austronesian languages of the Oceanic subgroup within the Sahul area, either on New Guinea or in very close proximity to it. Since their ancestral language, Proto-Oceanic, did not colexify these meanings (POc *api 'fire', POc *kaiu 'tree, wood, stick'), the appearance of the colexification pattern amongst these languages is highly suggestive of diffusion from Sahul languages. Are, Buhutu, Bunama and Molima are spoken in a circumscribed region at the tail of New Guinea (appearing as a single symbol on Map 9) and belong to the low-level North Papuan Mainland-D'Entrecasteaux subgroup of the Papuan Tip Linkage, while Gedaged is spoken on the north coast of New Guinea and is in the North New Guinea Linkage. The variety of appearances of the pattern in Oceanic languages means that the colexification of 'tree' and 'fire' has emerged independently at least twice in these languages. The varied forms for 'tree, fire' amongst the North Papuan Mainland-D'Entrecasteaux suggest that the colexification may not be ancestral in the group, but rather innovated multiple times in them following the Sahul pattern.

Firewood/fire colexification is also evidenced elsewhere in the world. Wichmann et al. (2013) does not include 'firewood' and so yields no information on this colexification pattern. However, List et al. (2014) lists ten non-Sahul languages colexifying 'fire' and 'firewood', while Urban (2012) gives a further four and the Proto-Oceanic Lexicon notes two (Ross, Pawley, and Osmond 2007). Table 9 sets out the languages with the colexification and their forms, while Map 10 shows their distribution around the world.

Table 9: Non-Sahul languages with 'firewood' and 'fire' colexification

	'firewood'	'fire'	Classification	Source
Qawasqar [alc]	afcʔar	afcʔar	isolate	List et al. (2014)
Araona [aro]	kʷati	kʷati	Pano–Tacanan	List et al. (2014)
Tsimané [cas]	ǰcih	ǰcih	Moseten–Chonan	List et al. (2014)
Itonama [ito]	ubari	ubari	isolate	List et al. (2014)
Kaingang [kgp]	pĩ	pĩ	Macro-Gê	List et al. (2014)
E'ñapa Woromaipu [pbh]	wahto	wahto	Cariban	List et al. (2014)
Wayuu [guc]	siki	siki	Arawakan	List et al. (2014)
Yavitero [yvt]	kaḽi	kaḽi	Arawakan	List et al. (2014)
Piro [pib]	tši	tši	Arawakan	Urban (2012)
Jarawara [jaa]	yifo	yifo	Arawan	Urban (2012)
Miskito [miq]	pauta	pauta	Misumalpan	Urban (2012)
White Hmong [mww]	taws	taws	Hmong–Mien	List et al. (2014)
Ceq Wong [cwg]	ʔɔs	ʔɔs	Austroasiatic, Aslian	List et al. (2014)
Fijian [fij]	buka	buka	Austronesian, Oceanic	Urban (2012)
Tolomako [tlm]	ɣapu	ɣapu	Austronesian, Oceanic	Ross, Pawley, and Osmond (2003)
Sesake [llp]	(na)kapu	(na)kapu	Austronesian, Oceanic	Ross, Pawley, and Osmond (2003)

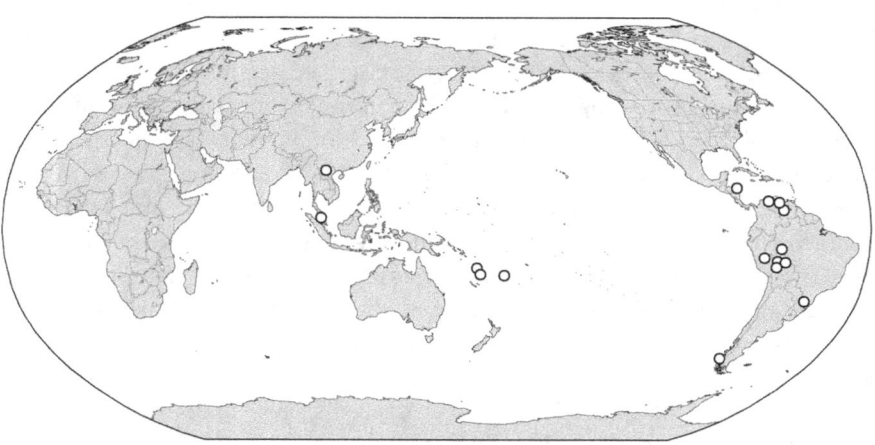

Map 10: Non-Sahul languages with 'firewood' and 'fire' colexification

Apart from two mainland South-East Asian outliers (White Hmong and Ceq Wong), colexification of 'firewood' and 'fire' occurs in the southern Americas and in Oceania.

The South American languages with colexification of 'firewood' and 'fire' are largely focussed in two areas, first in amongst the Amazonian Basin area where Brazil borders with Bolivia and Peru and second in Venezuela. A perfunctory search of the literature revealed several more instances of this colexification (e.g., Apurina [apu] *xamuna* 'fire, firewood' Facundes 2000; Baniwa [bwi] *tidze* 'fire, firewood' Ramirez 2001; Paumari [pad] *siho* 'fire, firewood' Aikhenvald 2010b[14]). Genetics appears to play a role with firewood/fire colexification being particularly common amongst Arawakan and Arawan languages and even reconstructed for Proto-Arawan (*jipho 'fire, firewood', Dixon 2004). A full study of South America is needed to determine the prevalence of firewood/fire colexification across and within families, but this initial look suggests that the pattern may be as widespread there as amongst Sahul languages.

In Oceania, firewood/fire colexification initially appears to have but a few limited instances amongst Austronesian languages of the Oceanic subgroup. However, on closer inspection the colexification pattern occurs frequently. In addition to the Vanuatu languages Tolomako and Sesake in our survey, Alexandre François (p. c.) writes that colexification of 'firewood' and 'fire' is in fact common across Vanuatu being observed "in a large, central region running from Central Maewo [mwo] all the way south to Efate [llp, erk]". Sporadic instances of firewood/fire colexification among Austronesian languages on New Guinea are also found in the literature (e.g., Iamalele [yml] *'ai* 'firewood, fire', Beaumont and Beaumont 1988). Again here the appearance of the colexification pattern amongst these non-Sahul languages is highly suggestive of diffusion from Sahul languages where firewood/fire colexification is widely present. We note, however, that the extent of the diffusion is much wider, with Fiji and Vanuatu, whilst adjacent to it, not typically seen as part of the Sahul area. However, influence from Sahul languages is not to be excluded; the unusual properties of many languages in Vanuatu have been speculated to be the result of Papuan speaker migrations into the region (Blust 2008).

Finally, tree/firewood colexification appears in 12 non-Sahul languages colexifying 'tree' and 'firewood' in List et al. (2014). Table 10 sets out the languages with the colexification and their forms, while Map 11 presents them in visual form. We see from this data that tree/firewood colexification shows no particular areal or genetic skewing, but rather appears to have emerged independently many times the world over, probably via the intervening concept 'wood'.

---

14 These could be considered derivations of one another, since there is a gender difference between the two meanings, one belonging to the *ka*-class, the other the non-*ka* class (Aikhenvald 2010b).

Table 10: Non-Sahul languages with 'tree' and 'firewood' colexification (List et al. 2014)

	'tree'	'firewood'	Classification
Mapudungun [arn]	mamïlʸ	mamïlʸ	Araucanian
Nahuatl, Highland Puebla [azz]	kʷowit	kʷowit	Uto-Aztecan
Mocoví [moc]	ḳoʔpaḳ	ḳoʔpaḳ	Mataco-Guaicuru
Movima [mzp]	koʔo	koʔo	isolate
Oroqen [orh]	mɔː	mɔː	Altaic
Otomi, Mezquital [ote]	zaa	zaa	Oto-Manguean
Puelche [pue]	ipuk	ipuk	isolate
Romani, Vlax [rmy]	kaš	kaš	Indo-European
Selkup [sel]	po	po	Uralic
Saami, Kildin [sjd]	mūrr	mūrr	Uralic
Kathu [ykt]	mas	mas	Sino-Tibetan
Takia [tbc]	ai	ai	Austronesian

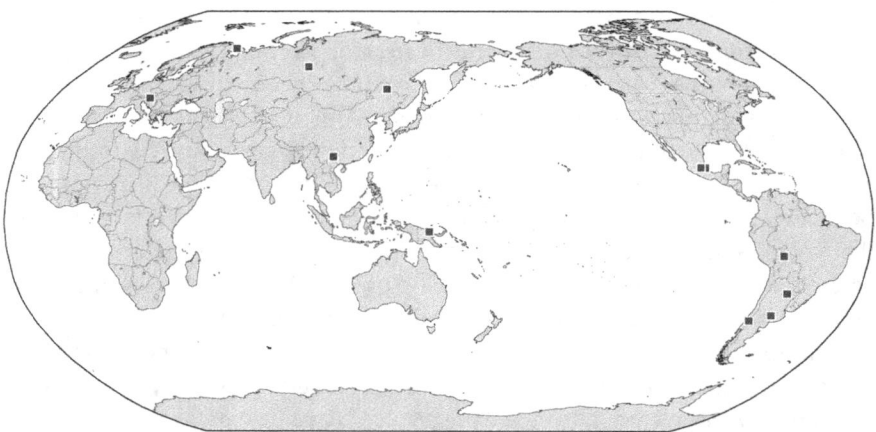

Map 11: Non-Sahul languages with 'tree' and 'firewood' colexification

In sum, worldwide, the colexification of 'tree' and 'fire' (and the related three-way colexification of 'tree', 'firewood' and 'fire') is a phenomenon almost entirely peculiar to Sahul languages. The dominant Sahul pattern of colexifying 'firewood' and 'fire' is unusual crosslinguistically but may also be prevalent in the South American linguistic area, a hypothesis that remains to be tested. The conspicuous areality of the tree/fire and fire/firewood colexification patterns in Sahul is reinforced by their sporadic appearance in the genetically unrelated but areally connected Austronesian languages of the Oceanic subgroup.

12.5 Complex lexical expressions

Studies in lexical semantic typology have increasingly realised that complex lexical expressions constitute semantic extensions of simplex lexical expressions in a similar way as additional meanings of those simplex items (Apresjan 1974: 17; Willems 1983: 426, Evans 1992: 478; Ungerer 2007: 652, Urban 2012: 55–63). Thus far we have considered patterns of colexification only where there is complete identity between the lexical expressions for 'tree', 'firewood' and 'fire' without looking at their constituency in any way. In this section, we look at the makeup of complex lexical expressions for our three concepts, tracing connections between the meanings of the unmarked (simplex) term and the marked (complex) term.

In 49 Papuan languages and five Australian languages in our sample, lexical expressions for 'firewood' (12.5.1) and 'fire' (12.5.2) appear to be complex, built from simplex lexical expressions that denote 'tree', 'fire' and/or (less frequently) 'firewood'. In our data, there are no instances of a lexical expression for 'tree' being complex, and no complex terms for any items that are themselves colexified. That is to say, all complex expressions that we have noted pick out a *single* meaning from the 'tree', 'fire' and 'firewood' domain.

12.5.1 Overt marking of *firewood*

In our data 'firewood' is the most common of the three meanings under consideration to be encoded with a complex expression. In 38 Papuan languages and five Australian languages we find a complex expression that is formed by overtly marking a simplex lexeme denoting 'tree' and/or 'fire'. Thus, the types of complex 'firewood' expression found are either: based on a simple colexified 'tree/fire' term (Table 11); formed from a combination of distinct 'tree' and 'fire' terms (Table 12); based on a distinct 'tree' term (Table 13); or based on a distinct 'fire' term (Table 14).

In ten Papuan languages, 'tree' and 'fire' are colexified as simplex expressions while 'firewood' is lexified with a complex expression (Table 11). Among these, overt markers denoting 'dry' are most common (five languages). Southern Kewa has an unusual overt marker not found elsewhere in *anda* 'house', perhaps a reference to firewood being essentially a domestic item. In Rumu and Namia 'firewood' can be colexified with 'tree, fire', but in each case may be optionally marked with a verb of burning/ignition. In Foe the entire complex 'firewood' term appears to be borrowed from the Engan languages; we do not know if the term *gabu* can also be used independently in Foe to mean 'dry' (see also Table 24).

Table 11: Complex expressions for 'firewood' based on 'tree/fire'

	'tree, fire'	'firewood'
Daga [dgz]	oma	oma oaewa 'dry oma'
Kewapi	repona	repona kapu 'dry repona'
Mendi [age]	ri	ri kap 'dry ri'
Sau [sxx]	ti	ti hapu 'dry ti'
Fasu [faa]	irá	irá póra † 'dry irá'
Foe [foi]	ira	iragabu ‡ '? ira'
Southern Kewa [kjy]	tepana	tepana anda 'house tepana'
Telefol [tlf]	at	at, dugúm át '? at'
Rumu [klw]	ĩ	ĩ, yeikâ-ĩ ‼ 'burning ĩ'
Namia [nnm]	mi	mi, par mi 'making fire mi', mi tapar 'mi for making fire' ¦

† The form appears reduced; pórasa is given as 'dry' in May and Loeweke (1981).
‡ gabu appears to be a borrowing from Engan langauges. In Rule's (1993) Foe dictionary the sequence gabu occurs in nami-gabu 'piebald pig' and gabu bui 'cassowary headdress', neither of which show an immediately obvious connection to firewood.
‼ yeikâ is a transitive verb meaning 'to feed a fire; burn as fuel' (Petterson 1989).
¦ par is a verb meaning 'make fire', ta- is a verbal mood prefix indicating intention (Feldpausch, Feldpausch, and Yalweike 2011).

In seven Papuan languages and two Australian languages, 'tree' and 'fire' are distinct simplex lexical expressions, while 'firewood' is a complex expression based on 'tree' and 'fire' together (Table 12). In Kanum and Ku Waru, 'fire' and 'firewood' are colexified, but 'firewood' can be optionally overtly marked with 'tree' to make it distinct. In Ketengban, a separate lexical expression *ato co* exists alongside the 'fire-tree' compound to denote firewood.

Table 12: Complex expressions for 'firewood' based on 'tree' and 'fire'

	'tree'	'fire'	'firewood'
Abau [aau]	now	yia	now yia 'tree fire'
Berik [bkl]	ti	tokwa	ti tokwa 'tree fire'
Orya [ury]	te	syauk	te syauk 'tree fire'
Kombai [tyn]	dodo	e	ewodo † 'fire tree'
Ketengban [xte]	co	oukke	oukke co 'fire tree', ato co '? tree'
Kanum [khd]	pr	mens	mens, mens pr 'fire tree'
Ku Waru (Bo-Ung) [mux]	uj	tepi	uj, tepi uj 'fire tree'
Noongar [nys]	boorn	karl	karl boorn 'fire tree'
Murrinh-Patha [mwf]	thay	thungku	thungku thay ‡ 'fire tree'

† We analyse -wodo in this expression as a form of dodo.
‡ Harvey and Reid (1997: 20) analyse this not as a compound, but a classifier construction in which the "fire classifier" thungku modifies thay 'tree, wood' to denote 'firewood'.

In ten Papuan languages, 'tree' and 'fire' are distinct simplex lexical expressions, while 'firewood' is a complex expression based on 'tree' (Table 13). Again, the overt markers that are used to create the complex expressions for 'firewood' are 'dry' and 'burn, set alight, cook, roast', all meanings which are frequently colexified in Papuan languages. In Kilmeri 'tree' and 'firewood' are colexified, but 'firewood' is only optionally overtly marked with 'dry' to make it distinct.

Table 13: Complex expressions for 'firewood' based on 'tree'

	'tree'	'fire'	'firewood'
Moskona [mtj]	merga	merah	merga efej 'tree dry'
Meyah [mej]	mega	mah	megej (< mega efej) 'tree dry'
Abun [kgr]	kwe	bot	kwe-gu 'tree dry'
Kilmeri [kih]	ri	sʊ	ri, ri sali 'tree dry'
Melpa [med]	de	dip	ködl de 'set alight/cook tree'
Ekari [ekg]	pija	bodija	jou-pija 'burn/cook tree'
Moni [mnz]	bo	usa	dagindata bo 'burn tree', dapua bo 'burn tree' †
Maybrat [ayz]	ara	tafoh	arko 'tree roast'
Sahu [saj]	ate	uʔu	ate tauʔu 'tree burn' ‡
Mbahám [bdw]	adok	jambu	adok jambu mbembe 'tree burn (in) fire'

† The root for 'burn' is da, with -gindata and -pua, both representing TAM inflections whose meaning is not well understood (see Drabbe 1959: 14, 26).
‡ The verb tauʔu 'burn' is derived from uʔu 'fire' by means of the verbalising prefix ta-.

In 11 Papuan languages and three Australian languages, 'tree' and 'fire' are distinct simplex lexical expressions, while 'firewood' is a complex expression based on 'fire' (Table 14). Overt markers for these complex expressions are varied. In Buin, Pisa, Weri, Bosavi and Nen, the overt markers, despite their variety, similarly pick out the shape or condition of the firewood as in thin lengths of split sticks, perhaps bundled. Warta Thuntai has multiple terms for 'firewood' based on *men* 'fire' depending on its size and intended use. Similarly, Wik Mungkan has a seemingly generic firewood expression formed with *uth* 'really/very', and a more specific one with *yoompan* where a particular kind of plant is used. In Fataluku the complex 'firewood' expression exists alongside a simplex expression that has no relationship to either 'tree' or 'fire' and denotes specifically wood that is dried for burning. In Weri, Klon, Girawa, and Oykangand 'fire' and 'firewood' are colexified, but 'firewood' can be optionally overtly marked to make it distinct.

Table 14: Complex expressions for 'firewood' based on 'fire'

	'tree'	'fire'	'firewood'
Buin [buo]	*kui*	*oguai*	*oguaingke* 'fire finger'
Pisa [psa]	*kasero*	*yī*	*yi kadɛ* 'fire thin'
Weri [wer]	*kʷera*	*es*	*es, esut* † 'fire bundle'
Bosavi [bco]	*i*	*de*	*dehi* ‡ 'fire split_wood'
Nen [ngn]	*wén*	*bnz*	*bnz dng* 'fire piece/length of wood'
Warta Thuntai [gnt]	*per*	*men*	*men tenk* 'fire big', *men sesagwi* 'fire small', *men raropai* 'fire ko._fish'
Wersing [kvw]	*bong*	*ada*	*ada us* 'fire charcoal'
Fataluku [ddg]	*ete*	*aca*	*aca-tananu* 'fire burn', *raka*
Klon [kyo]	*ɛtɛʔ*	*adaʔ*	*adaʔ, adakoʔ* 'fire ?', *adawel* 'fire ?'
Girawa [bbr]	*am*	*ep*	*ep, epin* 'fire ?'
Payungu [bxj]	*jurla, ngambu*	*garla, bir(r)iri*	*garlarnilbuga* ‼ 'fire ?'
Wik Mungkan [wim]	*yuk*	*thum*	*thum uth* 'fire very', *thum yoompan* 'fire ko_wood'
Oykangand [kjn]	*uk*	*alh, ub* ⊣	*alh, alh ub, uk ub*
Tobelo [tlb]	*gòta*	*uku*	*gòta, o uku ma dino* 'ART fire REL burn', 'that which fire burns'

† Weri *ut* has multiple senses: it is a verb meaning 'hang' or 'swing' and a noun meaning 'bundle' (Boxwell and Boxwell 1985).
‡ *Hi* is the past tense of the verb *hima* 'split wood' (Schieffelin and Feld 1998; Schieffelin p.c.)
‼ We also note that 'firewood' might contain *garlarni* 'burn', but this appears to be derived from *garla* 'fire'.
ⱡ The different 'firewood' terms have slightly different denotations: *thum uth* is 'firewood ready to use', *thum yoompan* is 'firewood, firestick' (with *yoompan* by itself listed as 'wood that is good for firewood').
⊣ *Ub* aside from being a lexeme denoting 'fire' is also the "fire" classifier.

12.5.2 Overt marking of *fire*

Overt marking of 'fire' alone to derive it from 'tree' and/or 'firewood' is much less frequent than for 'firewood'. There are a total of seven languages (all of them Papuan) that have complex lexical expressions for fire in our data.

Five of the languages – three belonging to the Awyu-Dumut family – colexify 'tree' and 'firewood', and then use that lexeme in a complex expression for 'fire' (Table 15). None of the overt markers used in these complex 'fire' expressions are known from the sources to have any other independent meanings and they do not appear in any expressions outside the 'fire' term. In Barupu, *âi* can colexify 'fire' as well as 'tree' and 'firewood'. However, there is also the option of overtly marking *âi* with *kéra* or simply using *kéra* on its own to denote 'fire'.

Table 15: Complex expressions for 'fire' based on 'tree, firewood'

	'tree, firewood'	'fire'
Shiaxa [awy]	*yi*	*yi ndo* 'yi ?'
Yenimu [aws]	*yi*	*yi do* 'yi ?'
Mandobo [aax]	*in*	*in ndumbut* 'in ?'
Waskia [wsk]	*tam*	*tama* 'tam-?'
Barupu [wra]	*âi*	*âi, âi kéra* 'âi ?', *kéra*

Two languages in our data have a simplex 'firewood' term on which a complex expression for 'fire' is based, while 'tree' is distinct (Table 16). None of the overt markers used in these 'fire' expressions are known from the sources to have any meaning outside the 'firewood' term. In Mekwei, for which we only have basic wordlist materials, *kei* can colexify 'fire' as well as 'firewood', though it is also possible to overtly mark *kei* with what is given as *ini* in one wordlist and *sini* in another to denote 'firewood'.

Table 16: Complex expressions for 'fire' based on 'firewood'

	'tree'	'firewood'	'fire'
Suki [sui]	*riku*	*ara*	*araka* 'fire ?'
Mekwei [msf]	*kinuk, di*	*kei*	*kei, kei (s)ini* 'fire ?'

12.5.3 Overt marking of *fire* and *firewood*

Overt marking of the lexeme 'tree' to create lexical expressions for 'firewood' and 'fire' is found in five languages (Table 17).

Table 17: Complex expressions for 'firewood' and 'fire' based on 'tree'

	'tree'	'firewood'	'fire'
Kayaka [kyc]	*isa*	*isa waisi* 'tree chopped'	*isare* 'tree-source_of'
Lembena [leq]	*isa*	*isa kapunge* † 'tree dry'	*isate* 'tree-source_of'
Kewa (West) [kew]	*repena*	*repena kaapu* 'tree dry'	*repena egaa* 'tree ember/ hot coal'
Wambon (Yonggom) [wms]	*enop*	*enop kok* 'tree red'	*enop-tenop* 'tree ?'
Guhu-Samane [ghs]	*ee*	*ee ngoru* 'tree dry'	*ee pa* 'tree ?'

† *kapunge* is not found independently in Lembena, but it is cognate with 'dry' in other Engan languages (Franklin p.c.).

12.5.4 Summary of overt marking patterns

In our data, complex lexical expressions are by far the most common for 'firewood', occurring in 48 languages. Only 12 complex expressions for 'fire' are found in our data and none for 'tree'. Complex 'firewood' expressions are about as equally likely to be derived from 'tree' as from 'fire'. However, complex expressions based on 'fire' are typically more opaque than those based on 'tree'. Complex expressions for 'fire' are even less analysable. Where complex expressions for 'firewood' are analysable, we observe commonalities in their overt markers regardless of whether they are derived from 'tree' or 'fire': words for burn(t/ing), ignition, or roasting, words for dry(ing) or dying, and classifier-types word indicating the shape/size of the wood. Overall, complex expressions do not themselves show further colexification.

12.6 Reclassifications and family histories

As shown in the previous section, nearly a fifth of the languages in our sample included a complex 'firewood' or 'fire' term that was based on a simplex 'tree', 'fire' and/or 'firewood' term. In recognition of the relationship between complex and simplex lexical expressions, in this section we map colexification patterns based on the "primary lexifier" as it appears in complex expressions, rather than based on each expression as a whole. We name the relationship between a simplex lexical expression and a complex lexical expression, where the primary lexifier is the same, as "subcolexification". So, in Daga [dgz], for example, *oma* colexifies 'tree' and 'fire', while *oma oaewa* subcolexifies 'firewood', because it shares the primary lexifier *oma*.

Table 18 overviews the classification of languages in our sample on the basis of subcolexifications. The right-most column gives the patterns of subcolexification that are found alongside "complete" colexifications. An uppercase letter represents an overtly marked expression that is subcolexified with the lowercase letter with the same value. For example, Daga has the subcolexification pattern 'aAa'.

Table 18: Reclassification of languages on the basis of subcolexifications

		Papuan languages	Australian languages	Patterns of sub-colexification
abc	full differentiation	66	6	--
abb	firewood/fire colexification	80	68	aBb, abB
aab	tree/firewood colexification	33	0	aAb
aaa	full colexification	38	9	aAa, aAA, aaA

A comparison of Table 18 with Table 6 in section 12.3.1 (which is based on full colexification only) shows some striking differences, for example, the much higher number of languages with full colexification (i.e., those that share a primary lexifier across all three terms). The inclusion of subcolexified items gives us a more complete picture of the distribution and possible histories of certain patterns, which we now discuss in relation to the Papuan (section 12.6.1) and and Australian (section 12.6.2) areas.

12.6.1 The Papuan area

Firstly, patterns revealed by subcolexifications suggest the importance of geographic location for 'strict' full differentiation {abc}, that is, for differentiation where no subcolexification of the three terms was observed (Map 12), and for tree/firewood (sub)colexification {aab, aAb} (Map 13). Both of these patterns are especially prominent in non-TNG languages, especially in the North New Guinea and maritime Melanesian regions.

Map 12 presents the distribution of languages with the full differentiation pattern where there is *no* readily-discernible relationship of subcolexification between 'tree', 'firewood' and 'fire' terms. There is a concentration of this pattern in non-TNG languages, especially along the north coast of New Guinea and into Island Melanesia.

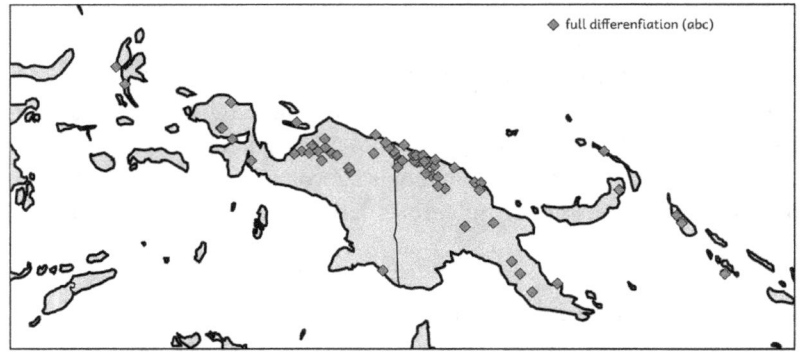

Map 12: Full differentiation {abc} minus subcolexifying languages

Tree/firewood (sub)colexification (Map 13) is found most commonly in the west. The lack of data from the north coast of New Guinea may account for the sketchiness and infrequency of the pattern here; greater sampling from this region could show the pattern to be more widespread than this survey suggests. For example, it is possible that Mek, the one TNG family which consistently displays {aab} and which is adjacent to the north coast New Guinea area may have acquired the tree/firewood colexification pattern through contact with non-TNG neighbours.

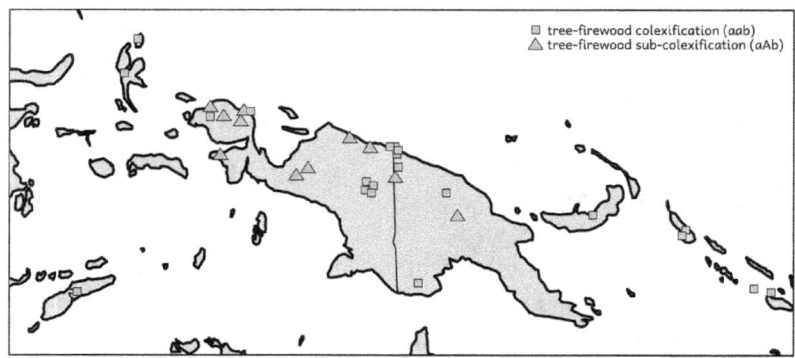

Map 13: Papuan tree/firewood colexification including subcolexifying languages {aab, aAb}

Our initial classification suggested that firewood/fire colexification {abb} was prominent throughout the Papuan area. Analysis of subcolexification confirms the dominance of this pattern (Map 14). Again, both genetic and areal influences appear to be at play.

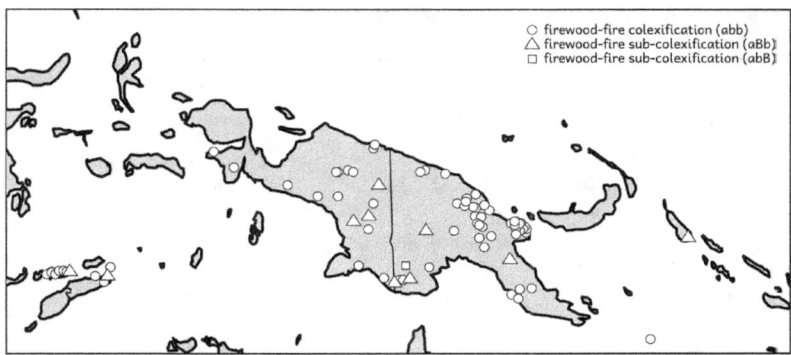

Map 14: Papuan firewood/fire colexification with subcolexifying languages {abb, aBb, abB}

In New Guinea, the dominance of firewood/fire (sub)colexification becomes clearer in southern New Guinea and amongst western TNG families. But areality doesn't appear to be the only determining factor. The firewood/fire (sub)colexification pattern is clearly inherited in some TNG families. For instance, the Asmat languages have not only the same colexification pattern but also consistently cognate terminology (Table 19).

Table 19: 'tree', 'firewood' and 'fire' in the Asmat family

	'tree'	'firewood'	'fire'
Asmat [asc]	os	yis	yis
Sempan [xse]	oho	yuha	yuha
Kamoro [kgq]	ote	uta	uta
Sabakor [asi]	ora	usara	usara

The distant Timor-Alor-Pantar family also reconstructs firewood/fire colexification (reconstructions from Schapper, Huber, and van Engelenhoven (2014)). The inherited pattern persists in all but one known daughter in the family and in most languages with the cognate terminology (Table 20),[15] suggesting that the firewood/fire (sub)colexification pattern is very stable.

---

[15] Bunaq has the divergent tree/firewood colexification pattern. It is likely to be connected with the unique development of gender in the language, a category which plays a role in distinguishing some of the meanings under discussion in this paper. See section 12.2.3.

Table 20: 'tree', 'firewood' and 'fire' in the Timor-Alor-Pantar family †

	'tree'	'firewood'	'fire'
Proto-Timor-Alor-Pantar	*hate	*hada	*hada
Proto-Timor	*hate	*haTa	*haTa
Makasae [mkz]	ate	ata	ata
Makalero	ate	ata	ata
Fataluku [ddg]	ete	aca(-tananu), (raka)	aca
Oirata [kvw]	ete	aṭa	aṭa
Proto-Alor-Pantar	*tei	*hada	*hada
Teiwa [twe]	tei	ħar	ħar
Kaera	tei	ad	ad
WPantar [lev]	yattu	ra	ra
Blagar [beu]	te	ad	ad
Klon [kyo]	ɛtɛʔ	adaʔ, ada(koʔ), ada(wel)	adaʔ
Abui [abz]	(bataa)	ara	ara
Kamang [woi]	(bong)	ati	ati
Kula [tpg]	(asáka)	adá	adá
Wersing [kvw]	(bong)	ada (us)	ada

† Round brackets indicate non-etymological items.

In the Dani family, however, firewood/fire colexification does not seem to be ancestral, but to have emerged twice in the family. In Table 21, we see three sets of cognates (indicated by different shading) that lexically distinguish the meanings 'tree', 'fire' and 'firewood' from one another. In the languages (Wano, Walak and Lower Grand Valley Dani), reflecting all three lexemes, we find the full differentiation pattern. By contrast, the firewood/fire colexification pattern appears to have been created by extending the 'firewood' lexeme to the meaning 'fire' in Nggem, Western Dani and Western Lani, and by extending 'fire' to 'firewood' in Yali.

Table 21: 'tree', 'firewood' and 'fire' in the Dani family

	'tree'	'firewood'	'fire'
Nggem [nbq]	yo	káli	káli
Western Dani [dnw]	eyo	kani	kani
Western Lani	i	kani	kani
Wano [wno]	e	kane	indu
Walak [wlw]	o	kali	indu
Lower GV Dani [dnt]	o	haly	hettouk
Yali [nlk]	e	hondok	hondok

Finally, once subcolexification is taken into account, we see an almost doubled count of languages with full colexification. The firewood differentiation {aba} pattern has in fact disappeared, as in all cases this represents subcolexification {aAa}. Similarly, subcolexification analysis of all languages with overt marking of both 'firewood' and 'fire' {aAA} or just of 'fire' {aaA} results in redistribution of these into a subtype of full colexification. This also results in a more striking geographical distribution of this pattern (Map 15).

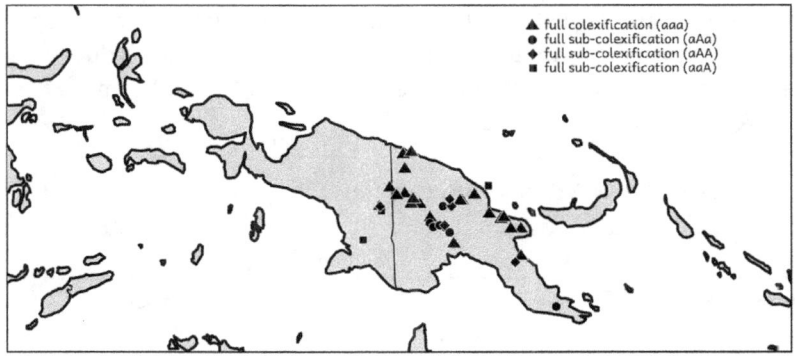

Map 15: Full colexification pattern including subcolexifying languages

We see in Map 15 that, whilst the outliers discussed in section 12.3.3.1 remain, the full (sub)colexification pattern is now distributed across the eastern highlands in a clear line that joins adjacent TNG families with the pattern. The progression runs as follows: starting from the Awyu-Dumut family in the west, the greatest concentration is found in the neighbouring region around the Ok-Oksamin family, Duna, Foe, Fasu and the Engan family in central PNG, from where it leaks into the Madang family and then the Finnestre-Huon family before petering out in the Greater Binanderean family. This analysis, then, confirms Laycock's (1986) suggestion that the colexification of the meanings is particularly strong amongst TNG languages. In fact, in several TNG families, colexification is most likely inherited. For instance, in the Ok-Oksapmin family the expressions colexifying 'tree', 'firewood' and 'fire are clearly related (Table 22), thus indicating that the colexification traces back to their common ancestor.

Table 22: 'tree', 'firewood' and 'fire' in the Ok-Oksapmin family †

	'tree'	'firewood'	'fire'
Bimin [bhl]	*ais*	*ais*	*ais, weing*
Mian [mpt]	*as*	*as*	*as*
Telefol [tlf]	*at*	*at, dugúm át*	*at*
Tifal [tif]	*às*	*às*	*às*
Oksapmin [opm]	*lat*	*lat*	*lat*

† These items have not been reconstructed in the family, but do appear cognate. Many such sets of monosyllabic words with sound correspondences not fitting those found in polysyllabic words are found in the Ok data (Robyn Loughnane p. c.).

Similarly, the Awyu-Dumut proto-language and the proto-languages of its primary subgroups are reconstructed with the complete colexification, despite modern languages having a complex set of subcolexification patterns due to different uses of overt marking. Table 23 presents the Awyu-Dumut language data alongside Wester's (2014) reconstructions.

Table 23: 'tree', 'firewood' and 'fire' in the Awyu-Dumut family †

	'tree'	'firewood'	'fire'
pAwyu-Dumut	**yen[op]*	**yen[op]*	**yen[op]*
pAwyu	**yi*	**yi*	**yi*
Shiaxa [awy]	*yi*	*yi*	*yi (ndo)*
Yenimu [aws]	*yi*	*yi*	*yi (do)*
Pisa [psa]	*(kasero)*	*yi (kadɛ)*	*yī*
Aghu [ahh]	*(kesaxe)*	*yā*	*yā*
pDumut	**en[op]*	**en[op]*	**en[op]*
Mandobo [aax]	*in*	*in*	*in (ndumbut)*
Wambon (Yonggom) [wms]	*enop*	*enop (kok)*	*enop (tenop)*
Wambon (Digul) [wms]	*enop*	*enop*	*enop*
Kombai [tyn]	*(dodo)*	*e(wodo)*	*e*

† Round brackets indicate non-etymological items.

However, the restriction to eastern TNG families makes the pattern as much an areal one as a genetic one. The importance of areality is particularly apparent looking at languages centring on the Engan family. Within this cluster, there is evidence of borrowing across family lines: the terms in Foe and Fasu[16] are transparently related to those of the neighbouring Engan languages Huli and Kewapi (Table 24). An Engan-derived form something lika *ira* (cognate with a 'tree, fire(wood)' term in more distant Engan varieties such as Enga, Kayaka and Lembena) is present throughout the lexical set for both Foe and Fasu. Furthermore, the Foe 'firewood' term incorporates the sequence *gabu*, which is almost certainly derived from a (proto-)Engan word 'dry' (e.g., as found in Kewapi *repona-kapu* 'firewood', Yarapea 2006).

Table 24: Related terms in Foe, Fasu, and nearby Engan languages (Huli, Kewapi)

	'tree'	'firewood'	'fire'
Huli [hui]	*ira*	*ira*	*ira*
Kewapi	*repona*	*repona-kapu*	*repona*
Fasu [faa]	*irá*	*irá póra*	*ira*
Foe [foi]	*ira*	*iragabu*	*ira*

Laycock (1986) (see section 12.1) suggests that 'firewood' is an important bridging concept in the colexification of 'tree' and 'fire' terms. This implies that the firewood differentiation pattern {aba} would most likely not occur. Overall, the low frequency of {aba} patterning and the strong relationship such languages tend to have with {aaa} languages suggest that Laycock's theory concerning the key nature of 'firewood' as a link between 'tree' and 'fire' terms may be substantially correct. Interestingly, the areal pattern also agrees with a hypothesis that firewood differentiation can be a first step *away* from full colexification. Under this scenario, the emergence of a more specific and differentiated 'firewood' term burns the bridge between 'tree' and 'fire', creating conditions conducive to further change.

---

16 The relationships of Foe and Fasu to each other and to Engan languages have been reclassified several times, but no definitive picture of their place(s) within a larger grouping has yet emerged (see Franklin 2001; Franklin 2012; San Roque and Loughnane 2012).

12.6.2 The Australian area

In Australia, the subcolexification analysis illuminates a relationship between 'fire' and 'firewood' terms in "fringe" languages that did not appear to show firewood/fire colexification in the first instance. As a consequence, we see in Map 16 that the vast sweep of Australia covered by Pama-Nyungan languages is entirely given over to the firewood/fire (sub)colexification pattern, whilst other patterns are completely restricted to the north. The difference seems to be areal more than genetic. Both Pama-Nyungan and non-Pama-Nyungan languages most frequently display the {abb} pattern, and the variant patterns {aaa} and {abc} are each found in both Pama-Nyungan and non-Pama-Nyungan languages.

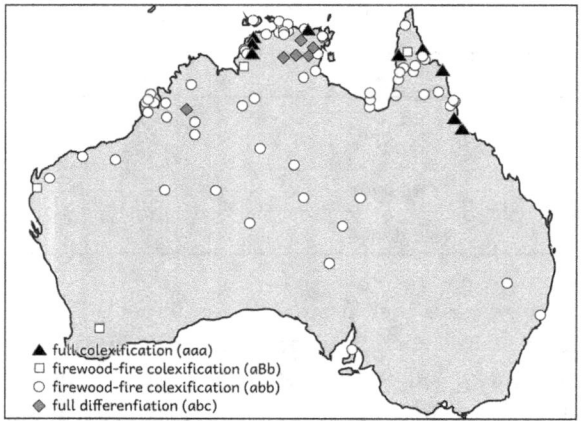

Map 16: Colexification patterns in Australia including subcolexifying languages†
†: a white circle represents a "complete" colexifying language {abb}; a white square represents a language in which 'firewood' is subcolexified with 'fire' {aBb}.

After subcolexification is taken into account, the full differentiation {abc} pattern is areal, being limited to the Top End region. It is chiefly found in the Gunwinyguan family (Table 25), with four of the six languages showing the pattern coming from that family. The lack of clearly cognate terms throughout this domain means that the full differentiation {abc} pattern cannot with any certainty be said to be inherited in the family. The appearance of full differentiation {abc} in the Yolngu language, Ritharrngu, is likely a result of contact: Ritharrngu *bäl* 'firewood' looks to be a borrowing of Ngandi/Rembarrnga *bal* 'firewood'. In Bunuba, the only other language with full differentiation, however, the {abc} pattern is unexplained.

Table 25: 'tree', 'firewood' and 'fire' in the Gunwinyguan languages

	'tree'	'firewood'	'fire'
Nunggubuyu [nuy]	ṟangag	nguṟa, -lhaj-, ṟangag, nguṟa	nguṟa, -yiga, wurg, anig
Bininj Gun-wok [gup]	kun-miluru	kun-rak	kun-rak, kun-mimal
Dalabon [ngk]	duhl	dah-no	mimal, nguy
Jawoyn [djn]	layn	ngan-jangalk, ngan-yam	nguyamo, wuurk
Ngandi [nid]	ḏanda?	bal	ḏaṇič, wurk
Rembarrnga [rmb]	borloh	bal	ngurah, wurrk

On Cape York Peninsula and immediately to its south, full colexification {aaa} appears repeatedly in languages with different subgrouping affiliations. It cannot be reconstructed and has emerged along different pathways of semantic extension in the different languages. For instance, when we compare the two Paman languages with the full colexification against proto-Paman (Table 26), we see that Wik Ngathan has extended the original 'firewood/fire' term to the concept of 'tree', while Guugu Yimidhirr has extended the original 'tree' term to the concepts of 'firewood' and 'fire'.[17]

---

[17] The Automated Similarity Judgment Program Database gives Gugu-Bujun as having tree/fire colexification (no firewood term recorded), but inspection of the source (Holmer 1988) reveals that the language with the pattern is in fact Guugu Yimithirr (referred to by Holmer as Gugu Yimidir).

Table 26: 'tree', 'firewood' and 'fire' in the Paman subgroup †

		'tree'	'firewood'	'fire'
	proto-Paman‡	*yuku	*cuma	*cuma
Umbindhamuic	Umbindhamu	yuku	yuma	yuma
Middle Pama	Ayabadhu	yuku	thuma	thuma
	Pakanh	yuku	thuma	thuma
	Wik Mungkan	yuk	thum (uth), thum (yoompan)	thum
	Wik Ngathan	thuma	thuma	thuma
Northern Pama	Uradhi	yuku	uma	uma
SW Pama	Yir Yiront	yoq	thum	thum
	Kok-Kaper	yok	per	per
	Kuuk Thaayorre	yuk	paath	paath
	Oykangand	uk	alh, alh ub, uk ub	alh, ub
Lamalamic	Morrobalama	orrang	aθa	aθa
Norman Pama	Kurtjar	luaanh	weerd	weerd
Yimidhirr-Yalan-ji-Yidinic	Guugu Yimithirr	yugu	yugu	yugu
	Kuku-Yalanji	juku	baya	baya, kunjin, ngalku
	Yidiny	jugi	buri	buri
	Gunggay	dandu	buri	buri

† Round brackets indicate non-etymological items in complex expressions. Unshaded cells indicate items not reflecting proto-terms.
‡ Proto-Paman reconstructions are taken from Bowern (2015) and ultimately derive from an unpublished manuscript by Kenneth Hale. The reconstruction *cuma is only given with the meaning 'fire'. Given that all Paman languages in our database which have a reflex of *cuma for 'fire' also use that term for 'firewood', we infer the proto-Paman *cuma also meant 'firewood'. Hale also gives the alternative reconstruction *piri ~*puri for 'fire' (and presumably also 'firewood').

Similarly, when compared to Dyirbal and Mamu, the Girramay dialect appears to have extended the original 'tree' term to 'firewood' and 'fire' (Table 27). The other two Herbert River languages with full colexification, Nyawaygi and Wargamay, however, have apparently innovated their own terms in this domain.

Table 27: 'tree', 'firewood' and 'fire' in the Herbert River region languages[18]

	'tree'	'firewood'	'fire'
Dyirbal [dbl]	*yugu*	*buni*	*buni*
Mamu [dbl] †	*yugu*	--	*buni*
Giramay [dbl] †	*yugu*	--	*yugu*
Nyawaygi [nyt]	*dyanu*	*dyanu*	*dyanu*
Wargamay [wgy]	*wagun*	*wagun*	*wagun*

† These two Dyirbalic dialects are not included in the preceding maps or frequency counts as we don't have 'firewood' terms for either. The dialectal information comes from Dixon (1972:40).

In the region of Daly River, we also find multiple instances of full colexification (Table 28). It appears to be very much an areal feature, though noticeably absent from the Western Daly, being found in at least three families: Eastern Daly (Matngele), Anson Bay (Wadyiginy) and Northern Daly (Malak Malak). Full colexification was likely to have been present in more languages. At least four other languages in the Daly region are recorded as having tree/fire colexification. We saw in the previous section that all Papuan languages which (sub)colexify 'tree' and 'fire' also (sub)colexify 'firewood'. We take it to be likely, therefore, that these Daly languages also colexified 'firewood' in this way, or had a complex, subcolexified 'firewood' term such as in the Southern Daly language, Murrinh-Patha.

---

[18] Herbert River is thought by some to constitute a subgroup of Pama-Nyungan. We use it here merely as a cover label for this set of languages and do not take them to be a subgroup.

Table 28: 'tree', 'firewood' and 'fire' in the Daly region languages

		'tree'	'firewood'	'fire'
Western Daly	Marrithiyel [mfr]	*thawurr*	*sjánjsji*	*sjánjsji*
	Maranunggu [zmr]	*tawar*	*yimny*	*yimny*
	Emmi [amy]	*thawarr*	*nyiminy*	*nyiminy*
Eastern Daly	Kamor † [xmu]	*dala, yim*	--‡	*yim*
	Matngele [zml]	*yim*	*yim*	*yim*
Anson Bay	Wadyiginy [wdj]	*winy*	*winy*	*winy*
Northern Daly	Malak Malak [mpb]	*tyung*	*tyung*	*tyung*
	Kuwema [woa]	*tyuŋu*	--‡	*tyuŋu*
Kungarakany	Kungarakany [ggk]	*pɔŋɔ*	--‡	*pɔŋɔ*
Marrku-Wurrugu	Marrgu [mhg]	*Tuna*	--‡	*Tuna*
Southern Daly	Murrinh-Patha [mwf]	*thay*	*thungku thay*	*thungku*

† Kamor sources differ as to the lexification patterns in this domain: Tryon (1974) has *yim* for both 'fire' and 'tree', while Mark Harvey (p. c.) gives *dala* as a distinct 'tree' term.
‡ Due to the lack of a 'firewood' term in the available documentation, these languages are not included in the preceding maps or frequency counts. They are included here for the fact that they show colexification of 'tree' and 'fire'. Data for these languages derives from Tryon (1970, 1974) and Mark Harvey (p. c.).

The final instance of the full colexification {aaa} pattern is in the Yolngu language, Djinang. Djinang appears to have developed the pattern independently. As we see from Table 29, Djinang uses the term *junggi* for all three concepts in this domain, while in the closely related Murrungan dialect this term is only used for 'fire'. In any case full colexification should not be reconstructed to Proto-Yolngu, as the Southern Yolngu languages all have an {abb} or {abc} pattern. The wide variety of actual terms, however, make any reconstruction of the 'tree', 'firewood', 'fire' set in this family difficult. It is striking that the term *dyung(u)* is also found for the full colexification in the Northern Daly languages. (Note that the orthographic conventions of *dy* in the Northern Daly languages and *j* in Djinang denote the same sound). The Daly languages are not directly adjacent to Yolngu, but it is possible the term exists in other languages of this region for which we have no available data.

Table 29: 'tree', 'firewood' and 'fire' in the Yolŋu languages (data from Bowern 2015)

		'tree'	'firewood'	'fire'
Southern	Dhuwal [duj]	gäyu, darpa	wunakina	ŋorrtja, wunakina
	Djapu [duj]	dharpa	buyuka	buyuka
	Gupapuyngu [guf]	gäyu	gurtha, däl	gurtha
	Ritharrngu [rit]	raŋa', mapudumun, dharpa	bäl	dhaŋutha
Western	Djinang [dji]	*junggi*	*junggi*	*junggi*
	Murrungan [dji]	*gurrchi*	--†	*junggi* *ngurrgirning*
	Wurlaki [dji]	*gurrchi*	--†	*ngirrchnyirakirni*
	Marrangu [dji]	*gurrchi*	--†	*milgirning*

† Due to the lack of a 'firewood' term in the available documentation, these languages are not included in the preceding maps or frequency counts. They are included here as comparison with Djinang, of which they are usually considered dialects. The difference in 'fire' terms is therefore interesting.

In sum, full colexification and full differentiation are comparatively rare in Australia. Each pattern has emerged multiple times with some areal influences and genetic effects observable. Firewood/fire colexification remains a largely stable, and likely inherited, pattern across much of the Australian language area, supported by the meanings attributed to various proto-Pama-Nyungen reconstructions (Alpher 2004 cited from Bowern 2015): Proto-Pama-Nyungan *kUnV 'fire, firewood', *wIkVn 'fire, firewood, hot, warm', *wA(r)lu 'fire, heat, firewood, angry, fighter, day, sun, cook'.

12.7 Conclusion

This paper has looked at lexical expressions for the meanings 'tree', 'firewood' and 'fire' in 300 language varieties in Sahul, and examined the relationships between simple and complex expressions for these concepts in individual languages. In examining the relationships we differentiated between "(full) colexification" where there is complete identity between the lexical expressions used for the meanings and "subcolexification" where there is a relationship between a simplex lexical expression and a complex lexical expression by way of a shared primary lexifier. This analysis proved a useful tool in bringing out areal patterns in the lexification of 'tree', 'firewood' and 'fire' in Sahul.

In the first place, our survey reveals that the most common (sub)colexification pattern for the three meanings amongst Sahul languages is to colexify 'firewood' and 'fire', but not 'tree'. This finding contradicts long-standing claims made in the Papuanist and Australianist literature of a widespread colexification of all three meanings. Instead, the full colexification pattern appears in a more restricted set of languages in eastern New Guinea and northern Australia, while firewood/fire colexification appears across the Sahul area, though with a skewing towards TNG languages (outside of the eastern highlands) and towards southern New Guinea. We also find that two other patterns, the tree/firewood colexification pattern and the full differentiation pattern, are by no means marginal amongst Papuan languages. What is more, they are concentrated across the north of New Guinea and into Island Melanesia. This distribution is especially striking once subcolexification is also taken into account, and is highly reminiscent of Nichols' (1997) North-West Coastal population which she identifies on the basis of a study a morpho-syntactic features across the Sahul area. If there is a link, this would mean that tree/firewood colexification and full differentiation represent newer patterns in the Sahul area which have replaced the southern and highland patterns of firewood/fire colexification in the first instance and full colexification in the second, patterns coinciding with Nichols' earlier South-East Interior population.

A preliminary world-wide survey of lexification of 'tree', 'firewood' and 'fire' further revealed that the full colexification pattern and the firewood/fire colexification patterns are rare worldwide. Full colexification (including the closely related tree/fire colexification pattern) is almost entirely absent elsewhere, while firewood/fire colexification showed some areality in South America alone. Cross-linguistically, both patterns show a strong areal skewing towards Sahul. An important piece of evidence for the areality of these two colexification patterns is their appearance in genetically unrelated but areally connected languages that are not Sahul languages, in particular Austronesian languages of the Oceanic subgroup. Yet, even English-based creole languages in the Sahul area show similar areally "adjusted" patterns. In the Australian contact-language Kriol, for example, *baya, faiya,* or *paiya* < *fire* can be used for 'fire', or 'firewood'. Both the word *wadi* < *wood* and the word *stik* < *stick* can be used for 'tree' or 'wood' (Lee 2014). In this way, speakers have recreated the regionally most common pattern with the lexical resources of an unrelated language that did not originally follow that pattern. Similarly, while standard Tok Pisin shows the full differentiation (Mihalic 1971), regional varieties of this lingua franca may reflect colexifications that are present in local indigenous languages (Don Daniels p. c.). In these cases we can be certain of areal transmission, and therefore it is reasonable to suspect it in other cases where the details of the contact history are not as well documented.

Throughout the paper we have made preliminary observations on not only the areality of the patterns we observe but also their distribution over families. We observe in particular in the cases of firewood/fire colexification and full colexification that they appear to have a range of histories. That is, in some families it is clear that these two patterns are inherited from the family's proto-language. In others, analysis of the lexical expressions used indicates the patterns were innovated at a low level within the family, sometimes on multiple occasions and seemingly via different pathways, while still others have borrowed the lexemes and patterns from other families. A fuller study of the diachrony of these patterns in Sahul is needed to understand the developmental paths of the different colexifications. Future work will examine whether it is possible to set up implicational hierarchies that predict in which order specific colexified meanings appear across languages and, conversely, which specific colexified meanings are first to get distinguished, either by overt marking or relexification.

The study of colexification patterns provides a resource for studies of language contact and typology in general that has so far scarcely been exploited (Koptjevskaja-Tamm and Liljegren forthcoming). Cross-linguistically, there are few colexifications that are extremely common, while there are many that are found in relatively few languages only. Without the access to large amounts of lexical data and the ease of digital sorting, filtering and mapping that we benefit from today, it has previously been difficult to test intuitions and assertions about the pervasiveness of a given semantic association with any degree of certainty. Individual features such as the colexification of 'tree', 'firewood' and 'fire' have therefore enjoyed a prominence in the literature that perhaps corresponds better to their striking nature rather than to their ubiquity. Still, our study shows that, semantically, Papuan and Australian languages have rare typological patterns in common, highlighting the need for a resetting of sights to span across the Torres Straits and connect New Guinea and Australia in a new field of Sahul areal linguistics.

12.8 Acknowledgements

This study would not have been possible without the generous support of many people who contributed data (see Appendix 1), and in many cases helped us not only in regard to their own languages of expertise but also in getting in touch with other relevant researchers. We would particularly like to thank the following individuals for their help with understanding the data from "their" languages: Claire Bowern, Mark Harvey, Paul Black, Maïa Ponsonnet, Jennifer Wilson, Karl Franklin, Edgar Suter, Don Daniels, Tom Honeyman and Lise Dobrin. Harald Hammarström also gave invaluable assistance in granting us access to all manner of obscure and ortherwise unobtainable materials , and we likewise thank SIL-PNG for working hard to make so much of their collection freely available online. This paper would not have come into existence without the patience and encouragement of Maria Koptjevskaja Tamm. It was further improved by the input of two anomymous reviewers, and of Alex François and Robert Östling, not to mention the thoughtful editing of Päivi Juvonen. Any remaining errors are our own responsibility.

12.9 Appendix: Languages included in the counts and maps presented in this paper

Abau [aau]	(Lock 2011)
Abui [abz]	Kratochvíl and Delpada (2008)
Abun [kgr]	(Berry and Berry 1999)
Aghu [ahh]	(Wester 2014)
Agi [aif]	(Jennifer Wilson p.c.)
Aisi Musak [mmq]	(Don Daniels p.c.)
Alamblak [amp]	(Bruce 1984)
Alawa [alh]	(Heath 1980)
Alekano Gahuku [gah]	(Deibler 2008)
Ambulas [abt]	(Kambu and Kerry 1992)
Amele [aey]	(Roberts 1987)
Amurdak [amg]	(Robert Mailhammer p.c.)
Angave [--]	(Speece 2006)
Aomie Managalasi [aom]	(Parlier and Parlier n.d.)
Arabana [ard]	(Luise Hercus p.c.)
Arandai Sebyar [jbj]	(Voorhoeve 1985)
Arandai Werigar [jbj]	(Voorhoeve 1985)
Arrernte [aer]	(Henderson and Dobson 1994)
Asmat [asc]	(Barclay 2008)
Au [avt]	(Jennifer Wilson p.c.; Scorza 1985)
Awiakay [--]	(Darja Hoenigman p.c.)
Ayabadhu [ayd]	(Verstraete 2015)
Baibai [--]	(Baron 1983; Tom Honeyman p.c.)
Baniata Touo [tqu]	(Frahm 1999)
Barai [bbb]	(Olson 1975)
Bardi [bcj]	(Bowern 2015; Bowern 2012)
Barupu [wra]	(Corris 2005)

Bauzi [bvz]	(David Briley p.c.)
Benabena [bef]	(Young and Young 1975)
Berik [bkl]	(Westrum, Westrum, Songkilawan, and Sowenso 1986)
Biaka (Nai) [bio]	(Hamlin 1998)
Bilinarra [nbj]	(Meakins 2013)
Bimin [bhl]	(Healey 1964; Weber 1997; Thomas Weber p.c.)
Bininj Gun-wok [gup]	(Garde 2009)
Biritai [bqq]	(Clouse 1997)
Blagar [beu]	(Hein Steinhauer p.c.)
Borong (Kosorong) [ksr]	(Edgar Suter p.c.)
Bosavi (Kaluli) [bco]	(Schieffelin and Feld 1998)
Buin [buo]	(Laycock 2003)
Bunuba [bck]	(Bowern 2015)
Bunaq [bfn]	(Schapper 2009)
Burarra [bvr]	(Glasgow 1994)
Cemaun Arapesh [ape]	(Lise Dobrin p.c.)
Dadibi [mps]	(Whitby, Sisinama, and Aseana 1990)
Daga [dgz]	(Murane 1963)
Dalabon [ngk]	(Maïa Ponsonnet p.c.)
Darkinyung [xda]	(Jones 2008)
Dedua [ded]	(Edgar Suter p.c.)
Deirate [--]	(Clouse 1997)
Demta [dmy]	(Smits and Voorhoeve 1994)
Djapu [duj]	(Dixon and Blake 1983)
Djinang [dji]	(Waters 1989)
Dhuwal [duj]	(Claire Bowern p.c.)
Dyirbal [dbl]	(Dixon 1972)
Doutai [tds]	(Clouse 1997)
Duna [duc]	(San Roque 2008)
Edopi [dbf]	(Clouse 1997)
Eipomek [eip]	(Volker Heeschen p.c.)
Ekari [ekg]	(Steltenpool 1969)
Emmi [amy]	(Ford 1998)
Erre [err]	(Bruce Birch p.c.)
Fasu [faa]	(Loeweke and May 1981)
Fataluku [ddg]	(Aone van Engelenhoven p.c.)
Fayu [fau]	(Clouse 1997)
Foe [foi]	(Rule 1993)
Fore [for]	(Scott 1980)
Fuyug [fuy]	(Bradshaw 2007)
Gaagudju [gbu]	(Mark Harvey p.c.)
Gadsup [gaj]	(Frantz and Frantz 1962)
Galela [gbi]	(Wattimury, Tetelepta, and Kakerissa 1992)
Gamilaraay [kld]	(Austin and Nathan 1998)
Ganggalida [gcd]	(Nancarrow 2014)
Gants [gao] [gao]	(Don Daniels p.c.)

Gathang [kda]	(Lissarrague 2010)
Girawa [bbr]	(Lillie 1999)
Gogodala [ggw]	(Charlotte van Tongeren p.c.)
Gooniyandi [gni]	(Bowern 2015)
Gresi [grs]	(Purba, Paidi, and Karoba 2002)
Guhu-Samane [ghs]	(Hoopusu and Richert 2002)
Gunggay [yii]	(Dixon 1991)
Gupapuyngu [guf]	(Claire Bowern p.c.)
Gurindji [gue]	(Meakins, McConvell, Charola, McNair, et al. 2013)
Guugu Yimithirr [kky]	(Wilkins 2000)
Halu [--]	(Jennifer Wilson p.c.)
Hatam [had]	(Reesink 1999)
Huli [hui]	(Lomas 1989)
Iatmul [ian]	(Jendraschek 2012)
Iau [tmu]	(Janet Bateman p.c.)
Idi [idi]	(Volker Gast p.c.)
Iha [ihp]	(Flassy 1993)
Imonda [imn]	(Seiler 1985)
I'saka (Krisa) [ksi]	(Donohue and San Roque 2004)
Iwaidja [ibd]	(Pym and Larrimore 2011)
Jabirrjabirr [dyb]	(Bowern 2015)
Jawoyn [djn]	(Merlan and Jacq 2005)
Kaera [---]	(Klamer n.d.)
Kalam G [kmh]	(Pawley 2012)
Kalam K [kmh]	(Pawley 2012)
Kalam PL [kmh]	(Pawley 2012)
Kamang [woi]	(Schapper and Manimau 2011)
Kamano [kbq]	(Banala, Drew, Mattocks, Mattocks, et al. 2007)
Kamasau [kms]	(Sanders and Sanders 1996)
Kamoro [kgq]	(Bert Voorhoeve p.c.)
Kanum [khd]	(Matthew Carroll p.c.)
Kâte [kmg]	(Edgar Suter p.c.)
Kaure [bpp]	(Dommel and Dommel 1991)
Kayaka [kyc]	(Karl Franklin p.c.)
Kayardild [gyd]	(Evans 1995)
Kayetetye [gbb]	(Harold Koch p.c.)
Kehu [khh]	(Kamholz 2012)
Kesawai (Koromu) [xes]	(Priestley 2009)
Ketengban [xte]	(Sims 1990)
Kewa South (Erave/Pole) [kjy]	(Rule 1977)
Kewa West [kew]	(Franklin 1978)
Kewapi	(Yarapea 2006)
Kilmeri [kih]	(Gerstner-Link 2012)
Kinalaknga [--]	(Edgar Suter p.c.)
Kiri-Kiri [kiy]	(Isolde Kappus p.c.)
Klon [kyo]	(Louise Baird p.c.)
Kobon [kpw]	(John Davies p.c.)

Koiari [kbk]	(Dutton 2003)
Koita [kqi]	(Dutton 2010)
Koko-Bera [kkp]	(Paul Black p.c.)
Komba [kpf]	(Edgar Suter p.c.)
Kombai [tyn]	(Wester 2014)
Kómnzo (Wara) [tci]	(Christian Döhler p.c.)
Korafe-Yegha [kpr]	(Farr and Farr 2008)
Korowai [khe]	(Wester 2014)
Korupun (Kimyal) [kpq]	(Volker Heeschen p.c.)
Kriol [gvn]	(Lee 2014)
Ku Waru (Bo-Ung) [mux]	(Alan Rumsey p.c.)
Kuku-Yalanji [gvn]	(Oates 1992)
Kula [tpg]	(Nicholas Williams p.c.)
Kumukio [kuo]	(Edgar Suter p.c.)
Kunimaipa [kup]	(Geary 1977)
Kuot [kto]	(Lindström 2002)
Kurtjar [gdj]	(Paul Black p.c.)
Kuuk Thaayorre [thd]	(Gaby 2006)
Kwoma (Waskuk) [kmo]	(Bowden 1997)
Kwomtari [kwo]	(Honsberger, Honsberger, and Tupper 2008)
Lardil [lbz]	(Leman 1997)
Lavukaleve [lvk]	(Angela Terrill p.c.)
Lembena [leq]	(Karl Franklin p.c.)
Limilngan [lmc]	(Mark Harvey p.c.)
Lower Grand Valley Dani [dni]	(Bromley 1981)
Maia [sks]	(Hardin, Loeweke, May, Price, et al. 2007)
Mairasi [zrs]	(Peckham 1991)
Makalero [---]	(Huber 2011)
Makasae [mkz]	(Huber 2008; Juliette Huber p.c.)
Malak Malak [mpb]	(Dorothea Hoffmann p.c.)
Mali Baining [gcc]	(Stebbins 2012)
Manambu [mle]	(Aikhenvald 2010a)
Manat [pmr]	(Don Daniels p.c.)
Mand [ate]	(Don Daniels p.c.)
Mandobo [aax]	(Wester 2014)
Maranunggu [zmr]	(Tryon 1970)
Marind [zrs]	(Drabbe 1955)
Marra [mec]	(Greg Dickson p.c.)
Marrithiyel [mfr]	(Green 1989)
Martu Wangka [mpj]	(Marsh 1992)
Matngele [zml]	(Dorothea Hoffmann p.c.)
Mauwake [mhl]	(Järvinen and Kwan 1990)
Mawng [mph]	(Hewett, Dineen, Stainsby, and Field 2013)
Maybrat [ayz]	(Dol 2007)
Mbahám [bdw]	(Fanny Cottet p.c.)
Mehek [nux]	(Adam Hatfield p.c.)
Mekwei [msf]	(Smits and Voorhoeve 1994)

Melpa [med]	(Stewart and Strathern n.d.)
Mende [sim]	(Nozawa 2006)
Mendi (Angal) [age]	(Karl Franklin p.c.)
Mengerrdji [zme]	(Bruce Birch p.c.)
Meyah [mej]	(Gravelle 2004)
Mian [mpt]	(Fedden 2007)
Migabac [mpp]	(Edgar Suter p.c.)
Mongi (Kube) [kgf]	(Edgar Suter p.c.)
Mnanki [--]	(San Roque n.d.)
Moni [mnz]	(Drabbe 1959)
Moraori [mok]	(Wayan Arka p.c.)
Morrobalama [umg]	(Verstraete and Rigsby 2015)
Moskona [mtj]	(Gravelle 2010)
Motuna [siw]	(Masa Onishi p.c.)
Mountain Koiari [kpx]	(Garland and Garland 1983)
Mpur [akc]	(Odé 2002)
Murik [mtf]	(Foley 1991; William Foley p.c.)
Murrinh-Patha [mwf] [--]	(Street 1983)
Nabak [naf]	(Smits and Voorhoeve 1998)
Nafri [nxx]	(Smits and Voorhoeve 1998)
Nama [nmx]	(Jeff Siegel p.c.)
Namia [nnm]	(Feldpausch, Feldpausch, and Yalweike 2011)
Narungga [nnr]	(Narungga Aboriginal Progress Association 2006)
Nasioi [nas]	(Hurd and Hurd n.d.)
Nen [ngn]	(Nicholas Evans p.c.)
Ngandi [nid]	(Heath 1978)
Ngarluma [nrl]	(Hall and Von Brandenstein 1971)
Nggem [nbq]	(Etherington 2002)
Nimanburru [nmp]	(Bowern 2015)
Nipsan [nps]	(Volker Heeschen p.c.)
Nomu [noh]	(Edgar Suter p.c.)
Noongar [nys]	(Whitehurst 1997)
Nunggubuyu [nuy]	(Heath 1982)
Nyamal [nly]	(Burgman 2007a)
Nyawaygi [nyt]	(Wilkins 2000)
Nyikina [nyh]	(Bowern 2015)
Nyulnyul [nyv]	(McGregor 1996)
Oirata [kvw]	(Josselin de Jong 1937)
Oksapmin [opm]	(Loughnane 2009)
Olo [ong]	(Staley 1994)
One [aun]	(Sikale, Crowther, and Donohue 2001)
Ono [ons]	(Edgar Suter p.c.)
Orya [ury]	(Clouse 1997)
Oykangand [kjn]	(Hamilton 1997)
Pakanh [pkn]	(Hamilton 1997)
Pamosu [hih]	(Tupper 2014)
Payungu [bxj]	(Burgman 2007b)

Pele-ata [ata]	(Hashimoto 1996)
Pintupi [piu]	(Hansen and Hansen 1992)
Pisa [psa]	(Wester 2014)
Pitjantjatjara [pjt]	(Goddard 1992)
Poko-Rawo [rwa]	(Matthew Dryer p.c.)
Rawa [rwo]	(Edgar Suter p.c.)
Rembarrnga [rmb]	(Saulwick 2003)
Ritharrngu [rit]	(Claire Bowern p.c.)
Rotokas [roo]	(Firchow and Firchow 2008)
Rumu [klq]	(Petterson 1989)
Sabakor [asi]	(Bert Voorhoeve p.c.)
Sahu [saj]	(Visser and Voorhoeve 1987)
Sau (Samberigi) [ssx]	(Karl Franklin p.c.)
Sehudate	(Clouse 1997)
Selepet [spl]	(Edgar Suter p.c.)
Sempan [xse]	(Burung 2007)
Sene [sej]	(Edgar Suter p.c.)
Shiaxa [awy]	(Wester 2014)
Sibe (Nagovisi) [nco]	(Kazuya Inagaki p.c.)
Simog (Auwe) [smf]	(Seiler 1985)
Siroi [ssd]	(van Kleef 2007)
Sirva (Sileibi) [sbq]	(Don Daniels p.c.)
Skou [skv]	(Donohue 2004)
Somba (Burum) [bmu]	(Olkkonen and Olkkonen 1990)
Srenge Aruop [lsr]	(Matthew Dryer p.c.; Lea Brown p.c.)
Suena [sue]	(Wilson and Wilson 2008)
Suki [sui]	(Charlotte van Tongeren p.c.)
Taikat (Arso) [aos]	(Stokhof 1983)
Tanahmerah [tcm]	(Smits and Voorhoeve 1998)
Tause [tad]	(Song Kim p.c.)
Tauya [tya]	(Lorna MacDonald p.c.)
Tehit [kps]	(Flassy 1991)
Teiwa [twe]	(Klamer and Sir 2012)
Telefol [tlf]	(Healey 1966; Healey and Healey 1977; Healey 1981)
Ternate [tft]	(Hayami-Allen 2001)
Thalanyji [dhl]	(Austin 1992)
Tidore [tvo]	(Staden 2000)
Tifal [tif]	(Healey and Steinkraus 1972)
Timbe [tim]	(Edgar Suter p.c.)
Tiwi [tiw]	(Lee 2013)
Tobelo [tlb]	(Hueting 1908)
Tobo [tbv]	(Edgar Suter p.c.)
Umbindhamu [umd]	(Clair Hill p.c.)
Umpila [ump]	(Clair Hill p.c.)
Una (Larye) [mtg]	(Volker Heeschen p.c.)
Ungarinyin [ung]	(Rumsey 1982)
Uradhi [urf]	(Dixon and Blake 1983)

Urim [uri]	(Hemmilä and Luoma 1987)
Urningangk [urc]	(Bruce Birch p.c.)
Usan [wnu]	(Ger Reesink p.c.)
Walman [van]	(Matthew Dryer p.c.; Lea Brown p.c.)
Wadyiginy [wdj]	(Ford 1990)
Waffa [waj]	(Hotz and Stringer 1979)
Wajarri	(Wilkins 2000)
Walak [wlw]	(Apriani Arilaha p.c.)
Walmajarri [wmt]	(Hudson 1978)
Wambon Digul [wms]	(de Vries and de Vries-Wiersma 1992)
Wambon Yonggom [wms]	(Wester 2014)
Wanggamala [wnm]	(Luise Hercus p.c.)
Wangkangurru [tiw]	(Luise Hercus p.c.)
Wano [wno]	(Wiem Burung p.c.)
Wantoat [wnc]	(Edgar Suter p.c.)
Waris (Walsa) [wrs]	(Brown 2007)
Warlpiri [wbp]	(Swartz 2012)
Warrgamay [wgy]	(Wilkins 2000)
Warrwa [wwr]	(Bowern 2015)
Warta Thuntai (Guntai) [gnt]	(Kyla Quinn p.c.)
Waskia [wsk]	(Barker and Lee 1985)
Weri [wer]	(Boxwell and Boxwell 1985)
Wersing [kvw]	(Schapper and Hendery 2014)
Western Dani [dnw]	(Barclay 2008)
Western Fas [fqs]	(Tom Honeyman p.c.)
Western Lani	(Apriani Arilaha p.c.)
Wik Mungkan [wim]	(Kilham, Pamulkan, Pootchemunka, and Wolmby 2011)
Wik Ngathan [wig]	(Clair Hill p.c.)
Wiru [wiu]	(Kerr 1966)
Western Pantar [lev]	(Holton and Koly 2008)
Wutung [wut]	(Doug Marmion p.c.)
Yali [nlk]	(Sonja Riesberg p.c.)
Yawa [yva]	(Jones, Paai, and Paai 1989)
Yawuru [ywr]	(Bowern 2015)
Yele [yle]	(Henderson 1974; Stephen Levinson p.c.)
Yenimu [aws]	(Wester 2014)
Yeri [yev]	(Jennifer Wilson p.c.)
Yidiny [yii]	(Wilkins 2000)
Yimas [yee]	(Foley 1991; William Foley p.c.)
Yinhawangka [wgg]	(no author 2008)
Yir-Yiront [yiy]	(Alpher 1991)
Yopno [yut]	(Edgar Suter p.c.)

12.10 References

Aikhenvald, Alexandra Y. 2010a. *A grammar of Manambu*. Oxford: Oxford University Press.
Aikhenvald, Alexandra Y. 2010b. Gender, noun class and language obsolescence: The case of Paumarí. In Eithne B Carlin and Simon van de Kerke (eds.), *Linguistics and archeology in the Americas: The historization of language and society*, 235–252. Leiden: Brill.
Alpher, Barry. 1991. *Yir-Yoront lexicon: Sketch and dictionary of an Australian language*. Trends in Linguistics, Documentation 6. Berlin: Mouton de Gruyter.
Alpher, Barry. 2004. Pama-Nyungan: Phonological reconstruction and status as a phylogenetic group. In Claire Bowern and Harold Koch (eds.), *Australian languages: Classification and the comparative method*, 93–126. Current Issues in Linguistic Theory 249. Amsterdam & Philadelphia: John Benjamins.
Apresjan, Jurij D. 1974. *Leksičeskaja semantika: Sinonimičeskije sredstva jazyka*. Moscow: Nauka.
Austin, P. and D. Nathan. 1998. *Kamilaroi/Gamilaraay web dictionary*. Canberra: AIATSIS. http://www1.aiatsis.gov.au/aseda/WWWVLPages/AborigPages/LANG/GAMDICT/GAMDICT.HTM, accessed October 16, 2014.
Austin, Peter. 1992. *A dictionary of Thalanyji, Western Australia*. Bundoora: La Trobe University Department of Linguistics.
Banala, Nelson, Dorothy E. Drew, Joyce Mattocks, Rich Mattocks, and Audrey Payne. 2007. Kamano-Kafeʔ Kemofo Agafaʔe dictionary for Kamano-Kafeʔ English Tok Pisin. Manuscript. http://www.sil.org/pacific/png/abstract.asp?id=48956.
Barclay, Peter. 2008. *A grammar of Western Dani*. Munich: LINCOM.
Barker, Fay and Janet Lee. 1985. *Waskia diksenari: Waskia, Tok Pisin, English*. Ukarumpa: Summer Institute of Linguistics.
Baron, Wietze. 1983. Kwomtari survey. Manuscript. http://www.sil.org/pacific/png/abstract.asp?id=928474550873
Beaumont, John R. and Margaret Beaumont. 1988. Iamalele-English dictionary. Manuscript. http://www.sil.org/pacific/png/abstract.asp?id=48957.
Berry, Keither and Christine Berry. 1999. *A description of Abun: A West Papuan language of Irian Jaya*. Canberra: Pacific Linguistics.
Blust, Robert A. 2008. Remote Melanesia: One history or two? An addendum to Donohue and Denham. *Oceanic Linguistics* 47(2): 445–459.
Bowden, Ross. 1997. *A dictionary of Kwoma: A Papuan language of North-East New Guinea*. Canberra: Pacific Linguistics.
Bowern, Claire. 2012. *A grammar of Bardi*. Berlin:Mouton de Gruyter.
Bowern, Claire. 2015. Australian lexical database. Yale University.
Bowern, Claire and Harold Koch, eds. 2004. *Australian languages: Classification and the comparative method*. Amsterdam: John Benjamins.
Boxwell, Maurice and Helen Boxwell. 1985. Weri dictionary. Manuscript.
Bradshaw, Robert L. 2007. *Fuyug grammar sketch*. Data Papers on Papua New Guinea Languages 53. Ukarumpa, Papua New Guinea: SIL-PNG Academic Publications. http://www-01.sil.org/pacific/png/pubs/928474523773/Fuyug_ Grammar_sketch.pdf.
Bromley, H. Myron. 1981. *A grammar of Lower Valley Dani*. Canberra: Pacific Linguistics.

Brown, Bob. 2007. Diksenari: Walsana Moa, Pisinna Moa, Englisna Moa: A short dictionary of the Walsa (Waris) language, Tok Pisin and English. Manuscript. http://www.sil.org/pacific/png/abstract.asp?id=48988.

Brown, Cecil H. and Stanley R. Witkowski. 1983. Polysemy, lexical change and cultural importance. *Man* 18: 72–89.

Bruce, Leslie. 1984. *The Alamblak language of Papua New Guinea (East Sepik)*. Canberra: Pacific Linguistics.

Burgman, Albert (ed.). 2007a. *Nyamal dictionary: English-Nyamal finderlist and topical wordlist*. *Wangka Maya*. South Hedland: Wangka Maya.

Burgman, Albert (ed.). 2007b. *Bayungu dictionary English – Bayungu wordlist and thematic wordlist*. South Hedland: Wangka Maya.

Burung, Willem. 2007. The phonology of Wano. *SIL Electronic Working Papers* 2007–003. http://www-01.sil.org/silewp/2007/silewp2007-003.pdf.

Clouse, Duane A. 1997. Toward a reconstruction and reclassification of the Lakes Plain languages of Irian Jaya. In Karl J. Franklin (ed.), *Papers in Papuan Linguistics 2*, 133–236. Canberra: Pacific Linguistics.

Coiffier, Christian. 1996. Vegetal names in the Ndu languages. *The Mon-Khmer Studies Journal* 25: 109–124.

Corris, Miriam. 2005. *A grammar of Barupu: A language of Papua New Guinea*. Sydney: University of Sydney PhD thesis.

Deibler, Ellis W. (Jr). 2008. Dictionaries of Alekano – English and English – Alekano. Manuscript. http://www.sil.org/pacific/png/abstract.asp?id=51218.

Dixon, Robert M. W. 1972. *The Dyirbal language of North Queensland*. Cambridge: Cambridge University Press.

Dixon, Robert M. W. 1980. *The Languages of Australia*. Cambridge: Cambridge University Press.

Dixon, Robert M. W. 2002. *The Australian languages: Their nature and development*. Cambridge: Cambridge University Press.

Dixon, Robert M. W. 2004. Proto-Arawá phonology. *Anthropological Linguistics* 46: 1–83.

Dixon, Robert M. W. and Barry J. Blake. 1983. *Handbook of Australian Languages Vol. 3*. Canberra: Australian National University Press.

Dixon, Robert M. W. and Tony Irvine. 1991. *Words of our country: Stories, place names, and vocabulary in Yidiny, the Aboriginal language of the Cairns-Yarrabah region*. St Lucia: University of Queensland Press.

Dol, Philomena. 2007. *A grammar of Maybrat: A language of the Bird's Head Peninsula, Papua Province, Indonesia*. Canberra: Pacific Linguistics.

Dommel, Peter and Gudrun E. Dommel. 1991. *Aki Tlaplik Soltok = Perbendaharaan kata bahasa Kaure = Kaure vocabulary*. Jayapura: Universitas Cenderawasih and Summer Institute of Linguistics.

Donohue, Mark. 2004. A grammar of the Skou language of New Guinea. Manuscript. http://hdl.handle.net/11858/00-001M-0000-0012-7AAC-9.

Donohue, Mark and Lila San Roque. 2004. *I'saka: A Sketch Grammar of a Language of North-Central New Guinea*. Canberra: Pacific Linguistics.

Drabbe, Peter. 1955. *Spraakkunst van Het Marind: Zuidkust Nederlands Nieuw-Guinea*. *Studia Instituti Anthropos*. Wien-Mödling: Drukkerij van het Missiehuis St.Gabriël.

Drabbe, Peter. 1959. *Spraakkunst Der Moni-Taal*. Hollandia.

Draper, Norm and Sheila Draper. 2002. *Dictionary of Kyaka Enga: Papua New Guinea*. Canberra: Pacific Linguistics.

Dutton, Tom. 2003. *A dictionary of Koiari, Papua New Guinea*. Canberra: Pacific Linguistics.
Dutton, Tom. 2010. *Reconstructing proto Koiarian : The history of a Papuan language family*. Canberra: Pacific Linguistics.
Etherington, Paul Anthony. 2002. *Nggem morphology and syntax*. Northern Territory University, MA Thesis.
Evans, Nicholas. 1992. Multiple semiotic systems, hyperpolysemy and the reconstruction of semantic change in Australian languages. In Guenter Kellermann and Michael D. Morrissey (eds.), *Diachrony within synchrony: Language history and cognition*, 475–508. *Duisburger Arbeiten Zur Sprach- Und Kulturwissenschaft / Duisburg Papers on Research in Language and Culture 14*. Frankfurt: Peter Lang.
Evans, Nicholas. 1995. *A grammar of Kayardild: With historical-comparative notes on Tangkic*. Berlin: Mouton de Gruyter.
Evans, Nicholas. 2003. *The Non-Pama–Nyungan Languages of Northern Australia. Comparative studies of the continent's most linguistically complex region*. Canberra: Pacific Linguistics.
Evans, Nicholas. 2005. Australian languages reconsidered: A review of Dixon (2002). *Oceanic Linguistics* 44: 242–286.
Facundes, Sidney da Silva. 2000. *The language of the Apurinã people of Brazil (Maipure/ Arawak)*. Buffalo, NY: University at Buffalo, SUNY PhD thesis.
Farr, James and Cynthia Farr. 2008. *Korafe-Yegha da dikiseneri: The Korafe-Yegha dictionary*. Manuscript. http://www.sil.org/pacific/png/abstract.asp?id=50567.
Fedden, Sebastian. 2007. *A grammar of Mian*. Melbourne: University of Melbourne PhD thesis.
Feldpausch, Thomas and Becky Feldpausch. 2011. Namia dictionary. Manuscript. http://www-01.sil.org/acpub/repository/Namia_dict_2011.pdf.
Firchow, Irwin B. and Jacqueline Firchow. 2008. Rotokas-English dictionary. Manuscript. http://www.sil.org/pacific/png/abstract.asp?id=49879.
Flassy, Don AL. 1991. *A grammar sketch of Tehit, a Toror language the West Doberai Peninsula, New Guinea (Irian Jaya)*. Leiden: Leiden University PhD thesis.
Flassy, Don AL. 1993. *Struktur bahasa Iha*. Pusat Pembinaan dan Pengembangan Bahasa: Departemen Pendidikan dan Kebudayaan.
Foley, William A. 1986. *The Papuan languages of New Guinea*. Cambridge: Cambridge University Press.
Foley, William A. 1991. *The Yimas language of New Guinea*. Stanford: Stanford University Press.
Foley, William A. 2005. Linguistic prehistory in the Sepik-Ramu basin. In Andrew Pawley, Robert Attenborough, Jack Golson and Robin Hide (eds.), *Papuan pasts: Cultural, linguistic and biological histories of Papuan-speaking peoples*, 109–144. Canberra: Pacific Linguistics.
Ford, Lysbeth. 1990. *The phonology and morphology of Bachamal (Wogait)*. Canberra: The Australian National University MA thesis.
Ford, Lysbeth. 1998. *A description of the Emmi language of the Northern Territory of Australia*. Canberra: The Australian National University PhD thesis.
Frahm, Roxanne Margaret. 1999. *Baniata serial verb constructions*. Auckland: University of Auckland MA thesis.
François, Alexandre. 2008. Semantic maps and the typology of colexification: Intertwining polysemous networks across languages. In Martine Vanhove (ed.), *From polysemy to semantic change: Towards a typology of lexical semantic associations*, 163–215. Amsterdam: John Benjamins.
Franklin, Karl J. 1978. *A Kewa dictionary: With supplementary grammatical and anthropological materials*. Canberra: Pacific Linguistics.

Franklin, Karl J. 2001. Kutubuan (Foe and Fasu) and Proto Engan. In Malcolm Ross and Darrell Tryon (eds.), *The boy from Bundaberg: Studies in Melanesian linguistics in honour of Tom Dutton*, 143–154. Canberra: Pacific Linguistics.

Franklin, Karl J. 2012. Counting systems in Engan and Proto-Engan. *Language and Linguistics in Melanesia* 30: 32–64.

Frantz, Chester and Marjorie Frantz. 1962. Gadsup Dictionary. Manuscript. http://www.sil.org/pacific/png/abstract.asp?id=49638.

Garde, Murray. 2009. The language of fire: Seasonality, resources and landscape burning on the Arnhem Land Plateau. In Jeremy Russell-Smith, Peter J. Whitehead, and Peter M. Cooke, (eds.), *Culture, ecology and economy of fire management in North Australian savannas: Rekindling the Wurrk tradition*, 85–164. CSIRO Publishing.

Garland, Roger and Susan Garland. 1983. Mountain Koiali-English dictionary, English-Mountain Koiali dictionary. Manuscript. http://www-01.sil.org/pacific/png/pubs/928474531068/Mtn_Koiali_Dict.pdf.

Geary, Elaine. 1977. *Kunimaipa grammar: Morphophonemics to discourse*. Workpapers in Papua New Guinea Languages 23. Ukarumpa: Summer Institute of Linguistics.

Gerstner-Link, Claudia. 2012. *A grammar of Kilmeri*. Munich: Ludwig-Maximilians-University Habilitation thesis.

Glasgow, K. 1994. *Burarra-Gun-Nartpa dictionary with English finder list*. Darwin: Summer Institute of Linguistics.

Goddard, C. 1992. *Pitjantjatjara/Yankunytjatjara to English dictionary*. 2nd edition. Alice Springs: IAD Press.

Gorenflo, L. J., Suzanne Romaine, Russell A. Mittermeier, and Kristen Walker-Painemilla. 2012. Co-occurrence of linguistic and biological diversity in biodiversity hotspots and high biodiversity wilderness areas. *Proceedings of the National Academy of Sciences* 109(21): 8032–8037.

Gravelle, Gilles Gerard. 2004. *Meyah: An East Bird's Head language of Papua, Indonesia*. Amsterdam: Amsterdam University PhD thesis.

Gravelle, Gloria. 2010. *A grammar of Moskona: An East Bird's Head language of West Papua, Indonesia*. Amsterdam: Vrije Universiteit PhD Thesis.

Green, Ian. 1989. *Marrithiel: A language of the Daly River region of Australia's Northern Territory*. Canberra: The Australian National University PhD thesis.

Hale, Kenneth. 1986. Notes on world view and semantic categories: Some Warlpiri examples. *Features and Projections* 25: 233–254.

Hall, Harold. A. and C. G. von Brandenstein. 1971. *A partial Vocabulary of the Ngalooma Aboriginal tribe*. Canberra: Australian Institute of Aboriginal Studies.

Hamilton, Philip. 1997. Uw Oykangand and Uw Olkola multimedia dictionary. Kowanyama Land and Natural Resources Management Office. http://www.oocities.org/athens/delphi/2970/

Hamlin, Newton Burgess. 1998. *Nai verb morphology*. Columbia: University of South Carolina MA thesis.

Hammarström, Harald and Sebastian Nordhoff. 2012. The languages of Melanesia: Quantifying the level of coverage. In Nicholas Evans and Marian Klamer (eds.), *Melanesian languages on the edge of Asia: Challenges for the 21st Century*, 13–33. Honolulu: University of Hawai'i Press.

Hansen, Ken C. and Lesley E. Hansen. 1992. *Pintupi/Luritja dictionary*. 2nd edition. Alice Springs: IAD Press.

Hardin, Barbara, Eunice Loeweke, Jean May, Mavis Price, Edwin Richardson, Susan Richardson, and Linda Weisenburger. 2007. Maia-English-Tok Pisin dictionary: English-Maia dictionary: Tok Pisin-Maia dictionary. Manuscript. http://www.sil.org/pacific/png/abstract.asp?id=50696.

Harvey, Mark and Nicholas Reid. 1997. *Nominal classification in Aboriginal Australia*. Amsterdam & Philadelphia: John Benjamins.

Hashimoto, Kazuo. 1996. Ata-English dictionary with English-Ata finderlist. Manuscript. http://www-01.sil.org/pacific/png/show_work.asp?id=928474531097.

Haspelmath, Martin and Uri Tadmor. 2009. World loanword database. Leipzig: Max Planck Institute for Evolutionary Anthropology. http://wold.clld.org/.

Hayami-Allen, Rika. 2001. *A descriptive study of the language of Ternate, the northern Moluccas, Indonesia*. Pittsburgh: University of Pittsburgh PhD thesis.

Healey, Alan. 1964. *The Ok language family in New Guinea*. Canberra: The Australian National University PhD thesis.

Healey, Alan. 1981. Telefol medical vocabulary. Manuscript. http://www.sil.org/pacific/png/abstract.asp?id=52247.

Healey, Phyllis M. 1966. *Levels and chaining in Telefol sentences*. Canberra: Pacific Linguistics.

Healey, Phyllis M. and Alan Healey. 1977. *Telefol dictionary*. Canberra: Pacific Linguistics.

Healey, Phyllis M. and Walter Steinkraus. 1972. *A preliminary grammar of Tifal, with grammar notes*. Santa Ana, California: SIL.

Heath, Jeffrey. 1978. *Ngandi grammar, texts, and dictionary*. Canberra: Australian Instititute of Aboriginal Studies.

Heath, Jeffrey. 1980. *Basic materials in Warndarang: Grammar, texts and dictionary*. Canberra: Pacific Linguistics.

Heath, Jeffrey. 1982. *Nunggubuyu dictionary*. Canberra: AIATSIS.

Hemmilä, Ritva and Pirkko Luoma. 1987. Urim grammar. Manuscript. http://www.sil.org/pacific/png/abstract.asp?id=52255.

Henderson, James E. 1974. Rossel Island (Yeletnye). In Kenneth A. McElhanon (ed.), *Legends from Papua New Guinea*, 156–160. Ukarumpa: Summer Institute of Linguistics.

Henderson, John and Veronica Dobson. 1994. *Eastern and Central Arrernte to English dictionary*. Alice Springs N.T.: Institute for Aboriginal Development.

Hewett, Heather, Anne Dineen, David Stainsby, and Robin Field. 2013. *Maung-English interactive dictionary*. AuSIL Interactive Dictionary Series A–8: AuSIL. http://ausil.org/Dictionary/Maung/preindex.htm.

Holmer, Nils M. 1988. *Notes on some Queensland languages*. Pacific Linguistics D–79. Canberra: Pacific Linguistics.

Holton, Gary and Mahalalel Lamma Koly. 2008. *Kamus Pengantar Bahasa Pantar Barat: Tubbe-Mauta-Lamma*. Kupang, Indonesia: UBB-GMIT.

Honsberger, Murray, Carol Honsberger, and Ian Tupper (eds). 2008. *Kwomtari phonology and grammar essentials*. Data papers on Papua New Guinea languages 55. Ukarumpa: SIL-PNG Academic Publications.

Hoopusu, Ttopoqogo and Ernest L. Richert. 2002. Noo Supu: A Triglot dictionary. Manuscript. http://www.sil.org/pacific/png/abstract.asp?id=48989.

Hotz, Joyce M. and Mary D. Stringer. 1979. Waffa, Tok Pisin, English. Manuscript. http://www.sil.org/pacific/png/abstract.asp?id=48857.

Huber, Juliette. 2008. *First steps towards a grammar of Makasae: A language of East Timor*. Munich: LINCOM.

Huber, Juliette. 2011. *A grammar of Makalero: A Papuan language of East Timor*. Leiden: University of Leiden PhD thesis.
Hudson, Joyce. 1978. *The core of Walmatjari grammar*. Canberra: Australian Institute of Aboriginal Studies.
Hueting, A. 1908. *Tobèloreesch-Hollandsch woordenboek met Hollandsch-Tobèloreesche inhoudsopgave*. 's-Gravenhage: Nijhoff.
Hurd, Conrad and Phyllis W Hurd. N.d. *Nasioi language course*. Port Moresby: Department of Information and Extension Services.
Järvinen, Liisa and Poh San Kwan. 1990. Mauwake lexicon. Manuscript. http://www.sil.org/pacific/png/abstract.asp?id=49080.
Jendraschek, Gerd. 2012. *A grammar of Iatmul*. University of Regensburg. *Habilitation thesis*.
Jones, Caroline. 2008. *Darkinyung grammar and dictionary: Revitalising a language from historical sources*. Nambucca Heads NSW: Muurrbay Aboriginal Language and Cultural Cooperative.
Jones, Linda, Zeth Paai, and Yohanes Paai. 1989. *Ayao Yawa Mo Mona Nanentabo Ranugan = Perbendaharaan Kata Bahasa Yawa = Yawa Vocabulary*. Irian Jaya: Program Kerjasama UNCEN-SIL, Universitas Cendarawasih: Summer Institute of Linguistics.
Josselin de Jong and Jan Petrus Benjamin. 1937. *Oirata, a Timorese settlement on Kisar*. Amsterdam: Noord-Hollandsche Uitgevers-Maatschappij.
Kambu, Anton, Andrew Kerry, and Nix Yuanigi (compilers); Wilson, Patricia R. (ed.). 1992. Ambulas-Wingei dictionary. Manuscript. http://www.sil.org/pacific/png/abstract.asp?id=50686.
Kamholz, David. 2012. The Keuw isolate: Preliminary materials and classification. [Special issue] *Language & Linguistics in Melanesia*, 243–268.
Kerr, Harland. 1966. *A preliminary statement of Witu grammar*. Honolulu: University of Hawai'i MA thesis. http://www.sil.org/resources/archives/9516.
Kilham, Christine, Mabel Pamulkan, Jennifer Pootchemunka, and Topsy Wolmby. 2011. *Wik Mungkan-English interactive dictionary*. AuSIL Interactive Dictionary Series A–6: AuSIL. http://ausil.org/Dictionary/Wik-Mungkan/lexicon/mainintro.htm.
Klamer, Marian and Amos Sir. 2012. *Kosa Kata Bahasa Teiwa-Indonesia-Inggris (Teiwa-Indonesian-English Glossary)*. Kupang: Unit Bahasa dan Budaya.
Klamer, Marian. 2015. Kaera. In Antoinette Schapper (ed.), *The Papuan languages of Timor, Alor and Pantar: Sketch grammars. Vol. 1*, 97–146. Berlin: Mouton de Gruyter.
Koptjevskaja-Tamm, Maria and Henrik Liljegren. Forthcoming. Semantic patterns from an areal perspective. In Raymond Hickey (ed.). *The handbook of areal linguistics*. Cambridge: Cambridge University Press.
Kratochvíl, František and Benidiktus Delpada. 2008. *Kamus Pengantar Bahasa Abui*. Kupang, Indonesia: UBB-GMIT.
Van Kleef, Sjak. 2007. Siroi-English dictionary: English-Siroi dictionary. Manuscript. http://www.sil.org/pacific/png/abstract.asp?id=49128.
Koch, Harold. 2004. A methodological history of Australian linguistic classification. In Claire Bowern and Harold Koch (eds.), *Australian languages: Classification and the comparative method*, 17–60. [Current Issues in Linguistic Theory 249]. Amsterdam & Philadelphia: John Benjamins.
Lakoff, George. 1987. *Women, fire and dangerous things*. Chicago: Chicago University Press.
Lang, Adrianne. 1971. *Nouns and classificatory verbs in Enga (New Guinea): A semantic study*. Canberra: Australian National University PhD thesis.

Lang, Adrianne. 1973. *Enga dictionary with English index*. Canberra: Pacific Linguistics.
Laycock, Don C. 1986. Papuan languages and the possibility of semantic classification. In Donald C. Laycock, Walter Seiler, Les Bruce, M.A. Chlenov, R. Daniel Shaw, Susanne Holzknecht, Graham Scott, Otto Nekitel, S.A. Wurm, L.R. Goldman, and J.S. Fingleton, J. (eds), *Papers in New Guinea Linguistics* No. 24. A-70:1-10. Canberra: Pacific Linguistics, The Australian National University.
Laycock, Donald C. 2003. *A dictionary of Buin: A language of Bougainville*. Canberra: Pacific Linguistics.
Lee, Jason (ed.). 2014. *Kriol-English interactive dictionary*. AuSIL Interactive Dictionary Series A–9: AuSIL. http://ausil.org/Dictionary/Kriol/index-en.htm.
Lee, Jenny. 2013. *Tiwi-English interactive dictionary*. In Maarten LeCompte (ed.). 2nd edn. AuSIL Interactive Dictionary Series A–4: AuSIL. http://ausil.org/Dictionary/Tiwi/intro.htm.
Leman, N. K. 1997. *Lardil dictionary*. Queensland, Australia: Mornington Shire Council. Gununa: Mornington Shire Council.
Lewis, M. Paul, Gary F. Simons, and Charles D. Fennig. 2014. *Ethnologue: Languages of the world*. 17th edn. Dallas, Texas: SIL. http://www.ethnologue.com.
Lichtenberk, Frank. 1991. Semantic change and heterosemy in grammaticalization. *Language* 67(3): 475–509.
Lillie, Patricia. 1999. Girawa dictionary. Manuscript. http://www.sil.org/pacific/png/abstract.asp?id=47685.
Lindström, Eva. 2002. *Topics in the grammar of Kuot*. Stockholm: Stockholm University PhD thesis.
Lissarrague, Amanda. 2010. *A grammar and dictionary of Gathang: The language of the Birrbay, Guringay and Warrimay Nambucca Heads: Muurrbay*. Nambucca Heads: Muurrbay Aboriginal Language & Culture Co-operative.
List, Johann-Mattis, Thomas Mayer, Anselm Terhalle, and Matthias Urban. 2014. CLICS: Database of cross-linguistic colexifications. http://clics.lingpy.org.
Lock, Arnold Hugo. 2011. *Abau grammar*. Data Papers on Papua New Guinea Languages, 57. Ukarumpa, Papua New Guinea: SIL-PNG Academic Publications. http://www.sil.org/pacific/png/abstract.asp?id=928474542179.
Loeweke, Eunice and Jean May. 1981. Fasu Namo Me dictionary. Manuscript. http://www.sil.org/pacific/png/abstract.asp?id=48460.
Lomas, Gabriel Charles Jacques. 1989. *The Huli language of Papua New Guinea*. Sydney: Macquarie University PhD thesis.
Loughnane, Robyn. 2009. *A grammar of Oksapmin*. Melbourne: University of Melbourne PhD thesis.
Marsh, James. 1992. *Martu Wangka-English dictionary*. Berrima, N.T.: Summer Institute of Linguistics.
May, Jean and Eunice Loeweke. 1981. Fasu (Námo Mē)-English dictionary. Manuscript. http://www.sil.org/pacific/png/abstract.asp?id=48460.
McGregor, William B. 1996. *Nyulnyul*. Munich: LINCOM.
Meakins, Felicity, (ed.). 2013. *Bilinarra multimedia database*. Darwin: AuSIL. http://ausil.org/Lexicons/Bilinarra/index.htm.
Meakins, Felicity, Patrick McConvell, Erika Charola, Norm McNair, Helen McNair and Lauren Campbell (eds.). 2013. *Gurindji Multimedia dictionary*. AuSIL. http://ausil.org/Dictionary/Gurindji/, accessed October 16, 2014.

Merlan, Francesca, and Jacques Pascale. 2005. *Jawoyn-English dictionary and English finder list*. Katherine, N.T.: Diwurruwurru-jaru Aboriginal Corporation.
Mihalic, Frank. 1971. *The Jacaranda dictionary and grammar of Melanesian Pidgin*. Milton, Queensland: Jacaranda.
Murane, Elizabeth. 1963. Daga-English dictionary. Manuscript. http://www.sil.org/pacific/png/abstract.asp?id=49559.
Nancarrow, Cassy. 2014. *Gangalidda to English dictionary*. Cairns: Carpentaria Land Council Aboriginal Corporation.
Narungga Aboriginal Progress Association, ed. 2006. *Nharangga Warra: Narungga dictionary*. Maitland: Wakefield Press.
Nichols, Johanna. 1997. Sprung from two common sources: Sahul as a linguistic area. In Patrick McConvell and Nicholas Evans (eds.), *Archaeology and linguistics: Aboriginal Australia in global perspective*,135–168. Melbourne: Oxford University Press.
No author. 2008. *Yinhawangka: Yinhawangka dictionary, English-Yinhawangka wordlist and topical wordlists*. Port Hedland.
Nordhoff, Sebastian and Harald Hammarström. 2012. Glottolog/Langdoc: Increasing the visibility of grey literature for low-density languages. In Nicoletta Calzolari (ed.), *Proceedings of the 8th International Conference on Language Resources and Evaluation [LREC 2012], May 23–25*, 3289–3294. Paris: ELRA.
Nozawa, Michiyo (compiler); Apinqua, Clement, David Apinqua, Francis Levermbu, and Peter Wanewain, (eds.). 2006. Mende triglot dictionary. Manuscript. http://www.sil.org/pacific/png/abstract.asp?id=48461.
O'Connell, James F. and Jim Allen. 2004. Dating the colonization of Sahul (Pleistocene Australia-New Guinea): A review of recent research. *Journal of Archaeological Science* 31: 835–853.
O'Grady, Geoffrey N. 1979. Preliminaries to a proto nuclear Pama-Nyungan stem list. In Stephen A. Wurm (ed.), *Australian Linguistic Studies*. 107–139. Canberra: Pacific Linguistics. Australian National University.
O'Grady, Geoffrey N. 1960. More on lexicostatistics: Comments. *Current Anthropology* 1: 338–339.
Oates, Lynette F. 1992. *Kuku-Yalanji dictionary*. Barnawartha: L. Oates.
Obata, Kazuko. 2009. AUSTLANG-Online Australian Indigenous Languages Database. *Incite* 30(4).
Odé, Cecilia. 2002. A sketch of Mpur. In Ger P Reesink (ed.), *Languages of the Eastern Bird's Head*, 45–107. Canberra: Pacific Linguistics.
Olkkonen, Kaija and Soini Olkkonen. 1990. Somba-Siawari (Burum Mindik)–English dictionary. Manuscript. http://www.sil.org/pacific/png/abstract.asp?id=48953.
Olson, Michael L. 1975. Barai grammar highlights. In Tom E Dutton (ed.), *Studies in languages of Central and South-East Papua*, 471–512. Canberra: Australian National University. http://www.sil.org/resources/archives/22976. (Accessed 2 December, 2014.)
Parlier, Jim and Jaki Parlier. N.d. *Dictionaries of Papua New Guinea Vol 4: Managalasi language*. Ukarumpa: Summer Institite of Linguistics. http://www-01.sil.org/pacific/png/pubs/928474523074/Managalasi_Dictionary.pdf.
Pawley, Andrew. 2003. Grammatical categories and grammaticisation in the Oceanic verb Complex. *Cornell Working Papers in Linguistics* 19(Spring): 149–172.
Pawley, Andrew. 2012. On the argument structure of complex predicates in Kalam, a language of the Trans New Guinea family. In Zhenya Antic, Charles B. Chang, Clare S. Sandy, and

Maziar Toosarvandani (eds.), *The Thirty-Second Annual Meeting of the Berkeley Linguistics Society*, 83–108. Berkeley: University of California at Berkley.

Pawley, Andrew and Harald Hammarström. Forthcoming.The Trans New Guinea family. In Bill Palmer (ed.), *Papuan Languages and Linguistics*. Berlin: Mouton de Gruyter.

Pawley, Andrew and Malcolm Ross. 1993. Austronesian historical linguistics and culture history. *Annual Review of Anthropology* 22: 425–459.

Peckham, Nancy. 1991. *Farir Mairas Na'atuei: Perbendaharaan kata bahasa Mairasi*. Ukarumpa: University of Cenderawasih and Summer Institute of Linguistics.

Petterson, Robert G. 1989. Rumu lexicon. Manuscript. http://www.sil.org/pacific/png/abstract.asp?id=48967.

Plomley, Norman. JB. 1976. *A word-list of the Tasmanian Aboriginal languages*. Launceston: Government of Tasmania.

Priestley, Carol. 2009. *A grammar of Koromu (Kesawai), a Trans New Guinea language*. Canberra: The Australian National University PhD thesis.

Purba, Theodorus T., Yacobus Paidi, and Semuin Karoba. 2002. *Sintaksis bahasa Gresi*. Jakarta: Pusat Bahasa, Departmen Pendidikan Nasional.

Pym, Noreen and Bonnie Larrimore. 2011. *Iwaidja-English interactive dictionary*. Charles E. Grimes (ed.), AuSIL Interactive Dictionary Series A–2: AuSIL. http://ausil.org/Dictionary/Iwaidja/lexicon/mainintro.htm.

Ramirez, Henri. 2001. *Dicionário Baniwa–Português*. Manaus: Editora da Universidade do Amazonas.

Reesink, Ger P. 1999. *A grammar of Hatam: Bird's Head Peninsula, Irian Jaya*. Canberra: Pacific Linguistics.

Roberts, John. 1987. *Amele*. London: Croom Helm.

Roberts, Richard G., Rhys Jones, and M. A. Smith. 1990. Thermoluminescence dating of a 50,000-year-old human occupation site in northern Australia. *Nature* 345, 153–156.

Roberts, Richard G., Rhys Jones, Nigel A. Spooner, Andrew S. Murray, and M. J. Head. 1994. The human colonization of Australia: optical dates of 53,000 and 60,000 bracket human arrival at Deaf Adder Gorge, Northern Territory. *Quaternary Science Reviews* 13: 575–183.

Ross, Malcolm D. 2005. Pronouns as a preliminary diagnostic for grouping Papuan languages. In Andrew Pawley, Robert Attenborough, Robin Hide, and Jack Golson (eds.), *Papuan pasts: Cultural, linguistic and biological histories of Papuan-speaking peoples*, 15–66. Canberra: Pacific Linguistics.

Ross, Malcolm D., Andrew Pawley, and Meredith Osmond. 1998. *The lexicon of Proto-Oceanic: Volume 1, Material culture*. Canberra: Australian National University.

Ross, Malcolm D., Andrew Pawley, and Meredith Osmond. 2003. *The lexicon of Proto-Oceanic, Volume 2, the Physical Environment*. Canberra: The Australian National University.

Ross, Malcolm D., Andrew Pawley, and Meredith Osmond. 2007. *The lexicon of Proto-Oceanic*. Canberra: ANU Press. http://press.anu.edu.au?p=29541.

Rule, Murray W. 1977. *A comparative study of the Foe, Huli, and Pole languages of Papua New Guinea*. Sydney: University of Sydney PhD thesis.

Rule, Murray W. 1993. *The culture and language of the Foe: The people of Lake Kutubu, Southern Highlands Province, Papua New Guinea*. Port Moresby: Chevron Niugini.

Rumsey, Alan. 1982. *An intra-sentence grammar of Ungarinjin, North-Western Australia*. Canberra: Pacific Linguistics.

Rumsey, Alan. 2002. On the grammaticalization of posture verbs in Papuan languages, its bodily basis and cultural correlates. In John Newman (ed.), *The linguistics of sitting, standing and lying*, 179–211. Amsterdam: John Benjamin.

San Roque, Lila. n.d. Mnanki fieldnotes.

San Roque, Lila. 2008. *An introduction to Duna grammar*. Canberra: The Australian National University PhD thesis.

San Roque, Lila and Robyn Loughnane. 2012. Inheritance, contact and change in the New Guinea Highlands evidentiality area. *Language and Linguistics in Melanesia*. Part II, 397–427.

Sanders, Arden and Joy Sanders. 1996. *Wand Tuan Wand Puate: Yumbo Yumbo Buagi Raqe Wund: As tok bilong Tok Ples Wand Tuan: Kamasau practical tri-glot dictionary*. Ukarumpa: SIL. http://www-01.sil.org/pacific/png/pubs/928474533781/Kamasau_Dictionary.pdf.

Saulwick, Adam. 2003. *A first dictionary of Rembarrnga: Compiled by Adam Saulwick; Incorporating material recorded by Carolyn Coleman and Graham McKay*. Maningrida: Maningrida Arts and Culture.

Schapper, Antoinette. 2009. *Bunaq: A Papuan language of central Timor*. Canberra: Australian National University PhD thesis.

Schapper, Antoinette and Rachel Hendery. 2014. Wersing. In Antoinette Schapper (ed.), *The Papuan languages of Timor, Alor and Pantar. Sketch grammars. Volume I*, 339–390. Berlin: Mouton de Gruyter.

Schapper, Antoinette, Juliette Huber, and Aone van Engelenhoven. 2014. The relatedness of Timor-Kisar and Alor-Pantar languages: A preliminary demonstration. In Marian Klamer (ed.), *Alor-Pantar Languages: History and Typology*, 99–154. Berlin: Language Science Press.

Schapper, Antoinette and Marten Manimau. 2011. *Kamus pengantar bahasa Kamang-Indonesia-Inggris*. Kupang: Unit Bahasa dan Budaya.

Schieffelin, Bambi B. and Steven Feld. 1998. *Bosavi-English-Tok Pisin dictionary (Papua New Guinea): Bosabi Towo: Liya: Ingilis Towo: Liya: Pisin Towo: Liya: Bugo:= Tok Ples Bosavi, Tok Inglis, Na Tok Pisin*. Canberra: Pacific Linguistics.

Scorza, David. 1985. *A sketch of Au morphology and syntax*. Canberra: Pacific Linguistics.

Scott, Graham. 1980. *Fore dictionary*. Canberra: Pacific Linguistics.

Seiler, Walter. 1985. *Imonda, a Papuan language*. Canberra: Pacific Linguistics.

Sikale, John, Melissa Crowther, and Mark Donohue. 2001. *Silla Palla One Miri: One dictionary*. Sydney: Department of Education, Sandaun Province and Department of Linguistics, University of Sydney.

Sims, Andrew. 1990. *Deiyo upu = Perbendaharaan kata bahasa Ketengban = Ketengban vocabulary*. Jayapura: Universitas Cenderawasih: Summer Institute of Linguistics.

Smits, Leo and C. L. Voorhoeve. 1994. *The J. C. Anceaux collection of wordlists of Irian Jaya languages B: Non-Austronesian (Papuan) languages (Part I)*. (Irian Jaya Source Material No. 9 Series B, 3.) Leiden-Jakarta: DSALCUL/IRIS.

Smits, Leo and C. L. Voorhoeve. 1998. *The J. C. Anceaux collection of wordlists of Irian Jaya languages B: Non-Austronesian (Papuan) languages (Part II)*. (Irian Jaya Source Material No. 10 Series B, 4.) Leiden-Jakarta: DSALCUL/IRIS.

Speece, Richard F. 2006. Angave dictionary. Manuscript. http://www.sil.org/pacific/png/abstract.asp?id=48458

Staden, Miriam van. 2000. *Tidore: A linguistic description of a language of the North Moluccas*. Leiden: Leiden University PhD thesis.

Staley, William. 1994. Theoretical implications of Olo verb reduplication. *Language and Linguistics in Melanesia* 25, 185–190.

Stebbins, Tonya. 2012. *Mali (Baining) dictionary Mali-Baining Amēthamon Angētha Thēvaik.* Canberra: Pacific Linguistics.

Steltenpool, J. 1969. *Ekagi-Dutch-English-Indonesian dictionary.* The Hague: Martinus Nijhoff.

Stokhof, W. A. L. (ed.). 1983. *Holle lists: Vocabularies in languages of Indonesia, Vol.5/2: Irian Jaya: Papuan languages, Northern languages, Central Highlands languages.* Canberra: Pacific Linguistics.

Street, Chester S. 1983. *English-Murrinh-Patha, Murrinh-Patha dictionary.* Wadeye: Wadeye Press.

Sutton, Peter and Harold Koch. 2008. Australian languages: A singular vision (Review article on R.M.W. Dixon 2002, Australian languages: Their nature and development). *Journal of Linguistics* 44: 471–504.

Swartz, Stephen M. 2012. *Warlpiri interactive dictionary.* AuSIL Interactive Dictionary Series B-3: AuSIL. http://ausil.org/Dictionary/Warlpiri/aboutwarlpiri.htm. (Accessed 17 October, 2014.)

Stewart, Pamela J. and Andrew J. Strathern. N.d. Melpa – German – English dictionary. The Pamela J. Stewart and Andrew J. Strathern Archive Pittsburgh: University of Pittsburgh, Digital Research Library. http://www.stewartstrathern.pitt.edu.

Thorne, Alan, Rainer Grün, Graham Mortimer, Nigel A. Spooner, John J. Simpson, Malcolm McCulloch, Lois Taylor, and Darren Curnoe. 1999. Australia's oldest human remains: Age of the Lake Mungo 3 skeleton. *Journal of Human Evolution* 36, 591–612.

Tryon, Darrell. 1970. *An introduction to Maranungku (northern Australia).* Canberra: Pacific Linguistics.

Tryon, Darrell. 1974. *Daly family languages, Australia.* Canberra: Pacific Linguistics.

Tupper, Ian. 2014. *A grammar of Pamosu.* Melbourne: LaTrobe University PhD thesis.

Ungerer, Friedrich. 2007. Derivational morphology and word-formation. In Dirk Geeraerts and Hubert Cuyckens (eds.): *The Oxford handbook of Cognitive Linguistics*, 991–1025. Oxford: Oxford University Press.

Urban, Matthias. 2012. *Analyzability and semantic associations in referring expressions: A study in comparative lexicology.* Leiden: Leiden University PhD thesis.

Verstraete, Jean-Christophe and Bruce Rigsby. *A grammar and lexicon of Yintyingka.* Pacific Linguistics 648. Berlin: De Gruyter Mouton.

Visser, Leontien E. and Clemens L. Voorhoeve. 1987. *Sahu-Indonesian-English dictionary and Sahu grammar sketch.* Dordrecht: Foris.

Voorhoeve, Clemens L. 1985. Some notes on the Arandai language, South Bird's Head, Irian Jaya. *Irian* 13, 3–40.

De Vries, Lourens J. and Robinia de Vries-Wiersma. 1992. *The morphology of Wambon of the Irian Jaya Upper-Digul area: With an introduction to its phonology.* The Hague: Martinus Nijhoff.

Walsh, Michael J. and Stephen A. Wurm. 1981. Maps of Australia and Tasmania. In S. A. Wurm and S. Hattori (eds.), *Language atlas of the Pacific area. Part 1: New Guinea area, Oceania, Australia.* Maps 20–23. Canberra: Australian Academy of the Humanities.

Waters, Bruce E. 1989. *Djinang and Djinpa: A grammatical and historical perspective.* Canberra: Pacific Linguistics.

Wattimury, E., J. Tetelepta, and O. Kakerissa. 1992. *Morfologi dan sintaksis bahasa Galela.* Jakarta: Departemen Pendidikan dan Kebudayaan.

Weber, Thomas. 1997. Bimin grammar essentials. Manuscript. http://www.sil.org/pacific/png/abstract.asp?id=928474543843.

Wester, Ruth. 2014. *A linguistic history of Awyu-Dumut: Morphological study and reconstruction of a Papuan language family*. Amsterdam: Vrije Universiteit PhD thesis.

Westrum, Peter N., Susan Westrum, Deetje Songkilawan, and Paulus Sowenso. 1986. *Ol Unggwanfer Berik olem/Perbendaharaan kata bahasa Berik/Berik vocabulary*. Jayapura: Universitas Cenderawasih and Summer Institute of Linguistics.

Whitby, Clyde, Po Sisinama, and Aseani. 1990. Dadibi, Tok Pisin, English, Po Dage Dabe. Manuscript. http://www-01.sil.org/pacific/png/pubs/928474531100/Dadibi_Dictionary.pdf.

Whitehurst, Rose. 1997. *Noongar dictionary: Noongar to English and English to Noongar*. 2nd edition. Carey Park: Noongar Language and Culture Centre.

Wichmann, Søren, André Müller, Annkathrin Wett, Viveka Velupillai, Julia Bischoffberger, Cecil H. Brown, Eric W. Holman, Sebastian Sauppe, Zarina Molochieva, Pamela Brown, Harald Hammarström, Oleg Belyaev, Johann-Mattis List, Dik Bakker, Dmitry Egorov, Matthias Urban, Robert Mailhammer, Agustina Carrizo, Matthew S. Dryer, Evgenia Korovina, David Beck, Helen Geyer, Patience Epps, Anthony Grant, and Pilar Valenzuela. 2013. The Automated Similarity Judgment Program Database (version 16). Leipzig.

Wilkins, David P. 1989. *Mparntwe Arrernte: Studies in the structure and semantics of grammar*. Canberra: Australian National University PhD thesis.

Wilkins, David P. 2000. Ants, ancestors and medicine: A semantic and pragmatic account of classifier constructions in Arrernte (Central Australia). In Gunter Senft (ed.), *Systems of nominal classification*, 147–216. Language, culture and cognition. Cambridge: Cambridge University Press.

Willems, Dominique. 1983. Syntax and semantics: On the search of constants in verbal polysemy. In Shiro Hattori and Kazuko Inoue (eds.): *Proceedings of the XIIIth International Congress of Linguists*, August 29 – September 4 1982, 425–429. Tokyo: CIPL.

Wilson, Darryl and Lael Wilson. 2008. Suena – English dictionary and English – Suena dictionary. Manuscript. http://www.sil.org/pacific/png/abstract.asp?id=50697.

Yarapea, Apoi Mason. 2006. *Morphosyntax of Kewapi*. Canberra: Australian National University PhD thesis.

Young, Robert A. and Rosemary Young. 1975. Benabena dictionary. Manuscript. http://www.sil.org/pacific/png/abstract.asp?id=48459.

Daniela Marzo and Birgit Umbreit
13. Investigating lexical motivation in French and Italian

Abstract: This chapter deals with a specific aspect of lexical motivation, viz. *motivatability*. Using a newly developed questionnaire method we test four cognitively founded hypotheses concerning the motivational preferences of native speakers of French and Italian. We show that *motivatability* depends on factors such as the *frequency of a stimulus* (hypothesis 1), the *salience of its meaning* (hypothesis 2) and the *conceptual relation* between the stimulus and other lexical units (hypotheses 3 and 4).

Additionally, our results show that these factors interact under certain circumstances: For example, the degree of salience of a given meaning can overrule the factor of frequency and can itself be overruled by the directional preferences of certain conceptual relations (e.g. metaphorical similarity). As expected, the stimuli display all in all a fairly similar distribution of underlying conceptual relations in both languages. Contrary to our assumptions, however, metaphorical similarity and not conceptual contiguity is the prevailing conceptual relation in our metalinguistic *motivatability* task, whereas the dominance of conceptual contiguity seems to be confined to unconscious motivation phenomena.

13.1 Introduction

This paper is concerned with one of the central aspects of lexical semantics: lexical motivation. More precisely, we test four cognitively founded hypotheses on *motivatability*, i.e. one particular facet of lexical motivation with a questionnaire study. Our assumptions concern motivational preferences of native speakers that are hypothesized to depend on factors such as the frequency of a stimulus (hypothesis 1), the salience of its meaning (hypothesis 2) as well as the conceptual relation between the stimulus and other lexical units (hypotheses 3 and 4).

Daniela Marzo (LMU Munich) and **Birgit Umbreit** (University of Tübingen)

The results of our study on the motivatability of 100 French and 100 Italian lexical units strongly speak in favor of an interaction of these factors.[1]

The structure of the paper is as follows: After clarifying our understanding of lexical motivation (section 13.2), we present, in section 13.3, our cognitively and typologically founded hypotheses on fundamental operating principles of lexical motivation (hypotheses 1 and 2) and motivational preferences of the French and the Italian lexicon (hypotheses 3 and 4). After a short presentation of the linguistic material that is used (section 13.4), we introduce a new method to investigate lexical motivation (section 13.5). Section 13.6 presents the results of our questionnaire study, which are discussed from a cognitive perspective in section 13.7. Section 13.8 finally summarizes the findings of this paper.

13.2 Lexical motivation from the native-speaker's perspective

Lexical motivation concerns either the relation between the form of a linguistic sign and its meaning, as e.g. in the case of onomatopoetic signs, or the relation between two different signs. In this contribution we concentrate on the latter perspective. More precisely, we understand the term of lexical motivation in the sense of Koch (2001a: 1156). That is, "a lexical item L_1 (lexeme, word, idiom) expressing a concept C_1, is motivated with respect to a lexical item L_2 expressing a concept C_2, if there is a cognitively relevant relation between C_1 and C_2, paralleled by a recognizable formal relation between the *signifiants* of L_1 and L_2 [...]." The English L_1 *banker* is thus motivated with respect to the L_2 *bank*, because English native speakers perceive a *formal* relation between the forms as well as a cognitively relevant relation between the concepts (henceforth *conceptual* relation) of the two lexical units, i.e. units consisting of a lexical form and a single sense, cf. Cruse (1986: 77, 80). While in the case of L_1 *banker* and L_2 *bank* the formal relation corresponds to suffixation (cf. *bank-er* ← *bank*), the conceptual relation is based on proximity or contact between the two concepts (INSTITUTION and PERSON INVOLVED IN INSTITUTION), i.e. on a contiguity relation.

---

[1] The study we present is joint work with Peter Koch (†) and Verena Rube that was realized within the DFG-granted project *Lexical Motivation in French, Italian and German* headed by Peter Koch (SFB 441/B6, 2005–2008). We thank Peter Koch, Verena Rube as well as the anonymous reviewers for their collaboration and helpful comments. All errors remain ours.

The notions of "cognitively relevant" conceptual and "recognizable formal" relation in Koch's definition, i.e. the notion of a *perceived* motivational relation, needs to be explained in more detail. If we say that a motivational relation between two lexical units is perceived by native speakers, this means that these units (henceforth *motivational partners*[2]) are not motivated *per se*: L_1 *banker* can be considered as motivated only because native speakers relate it upon active reflection to its motivational partner L_2 *bank*. On these grounds, Rettig (1981: 75–76) speaks of motivatability rather than of motivation. L_1 *banker* is thus motivatable.

In Koch's model, the possible combinations of formal and conceptual relations are represented in a bidimensional grid, which is given in a simplified version in Table 1.

In this table, the horizontal axis comprises the universal and closed inventory of cognitively relevant, i.e. conceptual relations (for a more detailed description of these relations cf. Koch 2001a: 1158–1160 and Koch and Marzo 2007). The vertical axis displays the language-specific open inventory of formal relations.

In Koch's original model, the list of formal relations comprises not only word-formation devices (cf. *banker* above), but also idioms and formal identity/polysemy, i.e. lexeme-formation devices in a broad sense. Since polysemy combines formal identity of two lexical units with a conceptual relation resulting from a semantic shift, it can contribute to lexical motivation, too (for a detailed discussion of this issue cf. Marzo 2011: 254–255, 2008 and 2013). Italian *cuore* 'centre' is thus motivated with respect to Italian *cuore* 'the organ heart', because they are related not only by formal identity (i.e. polysemy), but also semantically: *cuore* 'centre' is a metaphor, as e.g. *il cuore della città* 'the centre of the city' is not really a heart, but has a similar position and function with respect to the city as *cuore* 'heart' has with respect to the human body (both are more or less in the centre and both are in a way the pulsating element). Thus, the underlying conceptual relation is metaphorical similarity.

---

[2] We speak of *motivational partners* rather than of a *motivated form* and its *motivational base*, because the latter terminology implies a unidirectional understanding of lexical motivation according to which the formally or semantically more complex form is as a matter of principle motivated via a less complex form, the motivational base (cf. Iacobini 2000). However, we think that in certain cases the lexical units can, in principle, motivate each other (cf. Umbreit 2010 and 2015).

Table 1: Simplified bidimensional grid (adapted from Koch and Marzo 2007: 268, originally Koch 2001a: 1160)

	motivation							
	cognitively relevant conceptual relations							
absence of motivation	formal relations	conceptual identity	conceptual contiguity	metaphorical similarity	cotaxonomic similarity	taxonomic superordination	taxonomic subordination	conceptual contrast
	formal identity/ polysemy							
	word class alternation							
	suffixation							
	prefixation							
	composition							
	lexicalized syntagma							
	idiom							
	...	...	...	...	...	...	...	...

Traditionally, the decision about which words of a given language are motivated has primarily been based on the introspection of the linguist conducting the respective study (for some exceptions cf. 13.5.1). This does not only hold for the pioneering studies by Saussure ([1916] 1972), Ullmann (1957, 1962) and Gauger (1971) who defined and refined the term motivation, but also for studies that analyze the motivation of representative parts of a language's lexicon (e.g. Rufener 1971; Shaw 1979; and Sanchez 2008 on English and German, Scheidegger 1981 on French and German).

However, establishing motivation by the linguist's introspection can be problematic in various respects. Marzo and Rube (2006: 154) and Marzo (2013: 76–79) claim that motivational partners and relations established by a linguist probably do not correspond to the average linguistic consciousness of native speakers: the linguist has special knowledge about etymology and/or word-formation rules that lead to a higher percentage of motivated words than ordinary native speakers would find in the same sample despite their capability of establishing synchronic formal and semantic relations between words and of explaining these relations formally and semantically (a phenomenon called "synchronic etymological competence" by Augst 1975). As the aforementioned authors further argue, another disadvantage of the linguist's introspection is that many words can be motivated in different ways (e.g. via a formally related word form or via another meaning of the same word form). A single person (in the case of linguists, not always native) cannot decide on objective grounds which motivational relation has to be considered as the most salient one, whereas asking a group of native speakers will reveal a (stronger or weaker) preference for one of the candidates (cf. Umbreit 2010, 2011). Thus, using the judgments of non-linguists has not only the advantage of better reflecting the linguistic consciousness of a speech community, but also of indicating the ease of perceptibility (cf. 13.7.3) of different motivational relations.

A new method that has been developed on the fundament of previous native speaker-based studies on lexical motivation is introduced in 13.5.2.

13.3 Hypotheses

13.3.1 Hypotheses concerning the elicitation of motivational partners

According to our definition of lexical motivation (cf. 13.2.), lexical units can in principle be motivated via any motivational partner as long as the latter is connected to the former through a formal and a conceptual relation. However, previous lexicological and psycholinguistic work has revealed that factors such as the formal complexity of the stimulus, the frequency of its form as well as the salience of its meaning and the conceptual relations to its potential motivational partners might directly influence the choice of the actual motivational partner(s). The main purpose of this section is to present our hypotheses on the impact of these factors on lexical motivation.

It is obvious, for example, that the majority of motivational processes correspond to the direction "more complex unit motivated via less complex unit" (cf. Umbreit 2010, 2011 and 2015), as the more complex forms often already "contain" the most obvious motivational partner, i.e. the less complex motivational base, in their form: While formally simple words consist of one lexeme that does not bear any additional word-formation affix, complex words are recognizable products of affixation or compounding. Now, if subjects are presented with formally complex stimuli, they generally prefer to motivate these stimuli via less complex forms. This tendency conforms to the traditional conception of lexical motivation as unidirectional, that considers only formally (and in a compositional perspective semantically) complex words as motivatable (cf. e.g. Saussure [1916] 1972; Ullmann 1957, 1962; Gauger 1971).

In addition to formal complexity of a word form, its frequency (understood as frequency of occurrence in a particular corpus) can safely be assumed to play a role in lexical motivation. For example, it has been observed by numerous authors (e.g. Bybee 1988: 131; Plag 2003: 49; Schmid 2007: 118–119, 125–126; Caron 2008: 62) that frequent words are more salient than infrequent words, i.e. that they can be accessed faster and more easily. If we transfer this observation to the task of motivating words, this means that more frequent motivational partners should be found more easily than less frequent ones, i.e. that it is easier to motivate given stimuli via more frequent word forms[3] than via less frequent ones. Accordingly, the less frequent a stimulus is, the more easily it can be motivated, because, likewise, the number of more frequent formally and semantically related lexical units, which constitute easily accessible potential motivational partners, is higher. Of course, this assumption only holds if a word form is not that infrequent that the speakers don't know it and lack any intuition about its connections to other words. High frequency forms, on the contrary, should generally be more difficult to motivate, because all available motivational partners are less frequent and therefore harder to access.

However, the factors *formal complexity* and *frequency* are not to be seen as independent phenomena: It has repeatedly been observed that complex forms are normally derived from more frequent base forms (Marchand 1964: 13; Bybee 1985: 57; Plag 2003: 111, 176). Thus, there certainly is a correlation between less complex and more frequent on the one hand and between more complex and less frequent on the other hand, which will be discussed in more detail below (cf. 13.6.1.1.2).

Against the background of these observations, we can safely formulate the following hypothesis:

(1) Low frequency [LF] word forms are motivated more easily than high frequency [HF] word forms.

Although more frequent word forms are hypothesized to be motivated less easily than less frequent word forms we do not believe that they are, in principle,

---

[3] We speak of word forms here because frequency counts normally take only forms but not meanings into account and thus do not apply to lexical units or to lexemes.

altogether opaque. An observation concerning the relation between differently salient meanings of polysemous stimuli seems of particular relevance in this context. Cognitive salience according to Schmid (2007: 119) is the ease of activation of "concepts in actual speech events", as revealed for example in sentence production tasks (see below). As has been confirmed by different semantic tests (cf. Perfetti and Lindsay 1974; Durkin and Manning 1989; Williams 1992), it is usually easier for informants to find a more salient meaning for a lexical unit that is presented in a less salient meaning than vice versa. If we transfer this observation to the task of motivating a formally simple lexical unit, we might expect that informants motivate it via another, more salient meaning of the same lexeme, if such a meaning is available. We thus assume a salience effect that is parallel to the frequency effect which emerges for the retrieval of formally different motivational partners. In conformity with the considerations exposed above we expect the following hypothesis to hold:

(2) If a lexical unit is motivated via a formally identical lexical unit, the second most salient meaning is motivated via the most salient meaning but not vice versa.

Since LF forms are supposedly motivated primarily via formally less complex words of the same word family (cf. hypothesis 1), we think that this tendency holds especially for HF forms.

13.3.2 Hypotheses concerning the conceptual relation between two motivational partners

Different language types are generally expected to manifest different exploitations of the inventories of formal and cognitively relevant conceptual relations (cf. Table 1; Koch 2001a: 1166–1167; Koch and Marzo 2007: 273–274), though there are undeniable universal preferences. Additionally, there is also room for language- (and culture-)specific exploitations (Steinberg 2014: 340). This means that, with regard to the cognitive dimension, the most frequently underlying conceptual relation can vary from language to language. Yet, as French and Italian represent a closely related pair of languages and show rather similar lexical and semantic structures (Koch 2001a: 1164),[4] we expect that there are no strong differ-

---

[4] But cf. Koptjevskaja-Tamm, Vanhove, and Koch (2007: 181) for the view that "even closely related languages can manifest striking differences in their lexical organization".

ences between the two languages as far as the proportions of the seven conceptual relations are concerned:

(3) The distribution of conceptual relations in French and Italian is fairly similar because of the close relation between the languages.

In this respect, the underlying relation that according to previous lexicological studies prevails in both the synchrony and the diachrony of Romance and other languages, is conceptual contiguity as opposed to the other cognitively relevant relations exposed in Table 1.[5] Therefore, we hypothesize that conceptual contiguity is also the dominant relation found in speaker judgments on lexical motivation:

(4) Conceptual contiguity is the prevailing conceptual relation that underlies lexical motivation in French and Italian.

13.4 Tested linguistic material

In order to verify the hypotheses presented in section 3 in a comparative way, we used 100 French and 100 Italian lexical units, that we had previously chosen according to their frequency (high vs. low) and to the salience of their meanings (most salient vs. second most salient meaning):[6]

Table 2: Distribution of the 100 stimuli per language according to frequency and salience

50 high frequency [HF] word forms		50 low frequency [LF] word forms	
25 word forms with most salient meaning [S1]	25 word forms with second most salient meaning [S2]	25 word forms with most salient meaning [S1]	25 word forms with second most salient meaning [S2]

---

[5] For Romance languages cf. Waltereit (1998), Koch (2004: 49), Koch and Marzo (2007: 280–281); for typologically different languages and the conceptual field HEAD Steinberg (2014: 339); but see Blank (1997: 253, 269) and Marzo (2013) for the view that metaphorical similarity and conceptual contiguity are equally important.

[6] The complete stimulus lists for both languages can be obtained from the authors of this chapter.

As can be seen from Table 2, each word form, belonging to either the HF or the LF group, was investigated in two different meanings; the most salient [S1] and the second most salient [S2]. For example, the LF stimulus It. *indirettamente* was presented to the informants with either the meaning 'through other channels or persons' [S1] or with the meaning 'in an non-explicit way' [S2], cf. also Fig. 1 in 5.2.1. The HF word forms in each language correspond to the 25 most frequent nouns, verbs, adjectives, and action-modifying adverbs listed in the frequency dictionaries by Juilland, Brodin, and Davidovitch (1970) for French and Juilland and Traversa (1973) for Italian. The LF word forms were randomly chosen out of the frequency range 10 (French) and 10 to 9 (Italian).

The saliences of the meanings are based on a previously realized Sentence Generation and Definition Task (SG&DT). In this questionnaire, the native informants were simply presented with word forms and had to create an example sentence for as many different meanings of the word form they could think of, as well as provide a definition, i.e. a paraphrase or synonym, of each exemplified meaning. The standardization and clustering of the meanings by the investigators led to a list of meanings with different frequencies of occurrence. It was supposed that the more frequently a meaning is exemplified, the more salient it is.[7] Accordingly, the meaning referred to as "most salient" is the one with the highest number of occurrences in the SG&DT, the meaning referred to as "second most salient" corresponds to the second most frequently given meaning in the SG&DT and so on.[8]

The main criteria for the stimulus selection being frequency and salience, the stimuli were not matched for formal complexity, which thus constitutes a random variable. Yet, a survey of the stimuli sample shows that there is, as expected (cf. 13.3.1 and 13.6.1.1.2), a correlation of formal complexity and frequency, HF forms mostly being formally simple.[9]

---

7 For a detailed justification of the presumed correspondence of frequency and salience as well as for a more detailed presentation of the SG&DT cf. Marzo, Rube, and Umbreit (2007); Marzo (2013: 121–126).
8 The SG&DT was realized for a total of 400 French and 400 Italian word forms covering different frequency ranges. More precisely, we investigated the first 100 lexical words every 1000 words in Juilland, Brodin, and Davidovitch (1970) for French and Juilland and Traversa (1973) for Italian.
9 In the HF group, all but one French stimulus (*monsieur* 'man' [S1] and 'gentleman' [S2], which can be decomposed into *mon* and *sieur*; *sieur* being relatable to *sire* and *seigneur* was also seen by 60% of the informants) are formally simple. The LF group, on the contrary, comprises an almost equal number of formally complex and formally simple word forms in both languages: 12 complex forms vs. 13 simple forms in French and 13 complex forms vs. 12 simple forms in Italian,

13.5 Method

13.5.1 Methods used in previous native speaker-based studies on lexical motivation

There are a few investigations that make use of speaker judgments in order to study lexical motivation or related phenomena (e.g. Berko 1958; Augst 1975; Derwing 1976; Fill 1980a, 1980b), but these studies are unsatisfactory in various respects and therefore cannot be used as a model for our purpose.

Berko (1958) as well as Derwing (1976: 46–48 replicating Berko's study) presented their informants with questions of the type "Why is an X called an X?" (e.g. "Why is a blackboard called a blackboard?") in order to assess the degree of consciousness about complexity of words of the subjects (in Berko's case children). Some of the answers did indeed indicate a motivational partner as well as a hint to its conceptual relation to the stimulus. For example, in "a blackboard is called a blackboard, because it is a board and because it is (sometimes) black" (Berko 1958: 157), both the stimulus *blackboard* and its motivational partners *board* and *black* are mentioned. In addition, the causal relation can easily be interpreted as a contiguity relation. Still, this kind of question is in general too open as to uniformly elicit motivational partners matching our definition of motivation (cf. 2.): Informants often gave answers based on *identity* ("a blackboard is a blackboard because it is a blackboard") or *functional* responses ("a blackboard is a blackboard because you write on it").

Augst (1975), Derwing (1976: 50–54) and Fill (1980a, 1980b) presented their informants with a potential motivational pair and let them decide on the degree of relatedness of the two motivational partners on predefined scales. With that, they strongly biased their subjects, as these might have thought of a totally different motivational partner if one stimulus had been presented alone. Besides, it is much easier to perceive a motivational relation if the motivational partner is already given. Another shortcoming of the approaches discussed so far is that they either do not indicate the conceptual relation between the stimuli at all (Augst 1975) or that the responses they elicit do not allow for an unequivocal decision about the nature of the conceptual relation (Berko 1958; Derwing 1976; Fill 1980a, 1980b).

---

with products of conversion (e.g. Fr. *ruiner* 'to ruin' from *ruine* 'ruin') being counted as formally simple.

13.5.2 The Tübingen Two-Step Method

Despite their various shortcomings, the predecessor studies described in 13.5.1 can be used as a basis for developing a new method for investigating lexical motivation in accordance with our definition (cf. 13.2.). Since our study is supposed to reveal both the formal and the conceptual dimension of lexical motivation, one of the central and innovative characteristics of the method used in our research project is its division into two steps: the first step in which for each stimulus a formally related motivational partner is identified and the second step, in which the conceptual relation between the stimulus and its most frequently given motivational partner is determined.[10] Both steps were carried out via the www. The following subsections present step 1 and step 2 separately.

13.5.2.1 The questionnaire on motivational partners (step 1)

In order to elicit the most salient motivational partners of French and Italian words (for the material cf. 13.4.) without biasing the subjects, only the stimulus itself is presented, together with a definition and an example sentence (cf. Figure 1). We use a modified version of Berko's test (Berko 1958), making reference to the particular meaning in which the stimulus is presented. By this means polysemy, i.e. formal identity (cf. 13.2.), can be integrated as a motivational device. Thus, after reading a detailed introduction to the task in which the notion of *word family* was explained, the informants have to answer the following question for each stimulus: "Why, in your opinion, can the given word be used in the given meaning?" What follows is a small multiple-choice part comprising four response options that are here translated into English (for the French version of the questionnaire cf. Figure 1):

---

10 Pilot studies had revealed several advantages of two separate questionnaires in comparison to a single questionnaire covering both the formal and the conceptual relation: First of all, the task was much easier for the informants as they had to deal with only one aspect of motivational relations. Furthermore, the investigators were able to analyze the results of step 1 before starting with step 2, which allowed them to conduct the second step only with the stimulus and its most frequently indicated motivational partner. Additionally, incomprehensible or ill-expressed paraphrases given by the informants could be replaced by better formulations, which guaranteed unequivocal definitions in step 2 (cf. also Marzo 2013: 97).

1. The word is related to another word in the same word family.
2. The word is composed of other words.
3. The meaning is related to another meaning of the same word.
4. There isn't any relation to another word or to another meaning.

As can be easily understood, response option 1 accounts for words related to the stimulus via derivation, whereas option 2 refers to compounds. Option 3 is meant to account for polysemy, and option 4 can be chosen for opaque stimuli, i.e. stimuli the respondents are not able to motivate. The multiple-choice part allows for an observance of our definition of lexical motivation, as it does not leave space for free associations or for answers of the identity or functional kind that Berko (1958) received (cf. 13.5.1), but guarantees a formal relation to the stimulus. In case the informants vote for one of the first three response options, they are asked to provide and define the word(s) and/or the meaning(s) they are thinking of (cf. Figure 1 for an example of response type 3). The answers of 30 respondents are clustered by the investigators in order to find the most frequently given (i.e. most salient) motivational partner for each stimulus (for the results cf. 13.6). Only the latter is used to build a motivational pair with the original stimulus. The conceptual relations between the original stimuli and the majoritarian motivational partners are then investigated in step 2, the questionnaire on conceptual relations that is presented in the next section. The results are described in 13.6.2.

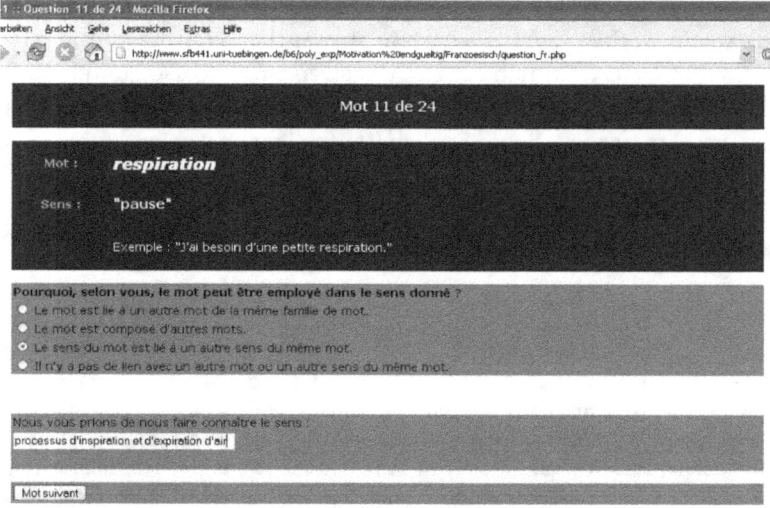

Figure 1: French questionnaire for step 1 with the stimulus *respiration* 'break', for which another meaning of the same word is given here.

13.5.2.2 The questionnaire on conceptual relations (step 2)

The second step of the Tübingen Method consists of a questionnaire meant to elicit the conceptual relations between the two constituents of a given motivational pair, both provided with definitions and example sentences. The testing of several versions of open and closed questionnaire types (cf. Marzo, Rube, and Umbreit 2006) had revealed a semi-closed questionnaire as the most suitable one. It consists of nine response options, seven of which are paraphrases for the conceptual relations on which motivation can be grounded (cf. 13.2.). The remaining two response options allow informants to describe other relations (in case they consider the given options as inappropriate) or to deny a relation between the stimuli (in case they think there is none). The respective word forms and meanings appear as variables in the paraphrases. For almost all response options (except for options 5 and 9 in Table 3) respondents are asked to give an explanation for their choice in a text field. In the case of option 5, which stands for cotaxonomic similarity, the hyperonym of the two stimuli has to be inserted. No explanation is necessary in case the subjects do not see any semantic relation between the stimulus and the motivational partner (cf. option 9). Table 3 shows the paraphrases translated into English, together with the respective conceptual relation for the French motivational pair *pension* 'internat' (En. 'boarding school') and *pension* 'allocation' (En. 'pension, annuity'), i.e. for a case of polysemy.

Table 3: Paraphrases used in questionnaire 2 standing for the seven conceptual relations distinguished by Koch (2001a: 1159–1160)

1	'internat' is the same as 'allocation', because _____	conceptual identity
2	'internat' and 'allocation' have nothing to do with each other although you can perceive a certain similarity between them insofar as _____	metaphorical similarity
3	'internat' and 'allocation' are generally closely related to each other in space and/or in time insofar as _____	conceptual contiguity
4	'internat' is the opposite of 'allocation' insofar as_____	contrast
5	'internat' and 'allocation' are both types of _____	cotaxonomic similarity
6	'internat' is a type of 'allocation', because _____	taxonomic subordination
7	There are different types of 'internat' and one of them is 'allocation', because _____	taxonomic superordination

Tab. 3 (continued)

8	'internat' and 'allocation' are not related in one of the ways proposed above, but _____	relation to formulate by participants
9	I do not see any relation between 'internat' and 'allocation'.	semantically opaque

In the course of data analysis, the investigators compare the conceptual relation chosen by the informants to the justification of their choice. If both parts correspond to each other, the chosen relation is confirmed; if not, the response is either assigned to another relation (if the explanatory statement is unequivocal enough[11]), or labelled as "not interpretable". Generally, greater importance is attached to the freely formulated relation.

13.6 Results

13.6.1 Results concerning hypotheses (1) and (2) tested in step 1 of the questionnaire study

13.6.1.1 Motivational partners: hypothesis (1)

According to hypothesis (1) (cf. 13.3.1) LF word forms can be motivated more easily than HF word forms. In this section we will present the results concerning hypothesis (1) first from the quantitative perspective of how many stimuli were considered as motivated at all by the informants (cf. 13.6.1.1.1) and second from the qualitative perspective of to what extent these results show an interaction between frequency and formal complexity on the one and motivatability on the other hand (cf. 13.6.1.1.2).

---

[11] For the motivational pair exemplified in Table 3, one of the informants chose response option 2, i.e. metaphorical similarity. In his/her explanatory statement, however, the informant says: "on paie une pension pour l'internat...c'est peut-être pour cela que l'on a nommé ainsi cette institution. " (En. "you pay a pension [i.e. fees] for a boarding school... this is perhaps why this institution has been named alike"). Here, it is clearly a relation of contiguity that is described. We therefore chose conceptual contiguity as the outcome of the informants' answer despite his/her original choice.

13.6.1.1.1 Motivation and opacity

Figure 2 indicates the proportion of motivated and *opaque* (i.e. not motivated) lexical units for both French and Italian as a result of step 1 of the questionnaire study (cf. 13.5.2.1). Stimuli were counted as motivated only if a relative majority of informants named the same motivational partner. This rather strict criterion is probably the reason why in both languages a slight majority of the stimuli (53 % in French and 66 % in Italian, cf. Figure 2) has to be considered as opaque. In fact, only for one French stimulus (viz. *falloir* in its S1 meaning 'to be necessary') no motivational partner at all was found, while all other stimuli in French and in Italian yielded at least one motivational partner, the majority (55 % of the Italian and 57 % of the French stimuli) having 5 or more and some of them even more than 10 different motivational partners (such as e.g. 12 motivational partners for It. *sconvolgere* 'to shock someone emotionally').

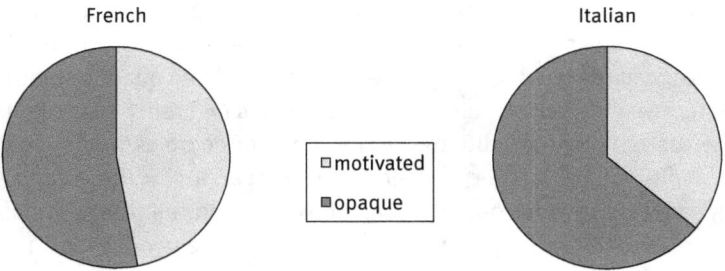

Figure 2: Percentages of motivated and opaque words in French (47 % of motivated stimuli vs. 53 % of opaque stimuli) and in Italian (34 % of motivated words vs. 66 % of opaque stimuli).

This large variety of motivational partners explains, at least in part, why in some cases the opacity option (option 4 in the multiple choice part in step 1; cf. 13.5.2.1) was majoritarian. In fact, in several cases such as Fr. *pouvoir* [S1] ('to be capable of doing something') or It. *palco* [S2] ('privileged place in a theatre = balcony') the opacity option constitutes the relative majority (37 % and 44 % respectively), if we count each type of motivational partner separately. However, the opacity option constitutes only a minority, if we add up the percentages of all types of motivational partners (63 % in the case of *pouvoir* S1 and 56 % in the case of It. *palco* S2). In some cases we do not even need to add up all motivational partners to get a relative majority over the opacity option (44 %, cf. above): in the case of It. *palco* S2, 46 % of the subjects motivated this stimulus via a variety of formally identical lexical units alone. Given the omnipresence of polysemy (cf. e.g. Victorri and Fuchs 1996: 13) and its special importance for HF vocabulary (Zipf 1949: 19–31; Krott, Schreuder, and Baayen 1999: 917; cf. also Marzo 2013: 132–133), it is obvious, that the total number of *potential* motivational partners is relatively high in this group.[12] In view of such an abundant choice of potential motivational partners, it is no surprise that different informants pick different potential motivational partners as *actual* motivational partners. As a consequence, the relative majority of the opacity option does not necessarily reflect absolute opacity in the sense of total lack of motivation, but rather indicates, in many cases, divergence of motivational partners across subjects. Hence, this disagreement hints, in a way, at different degrees of opacity and motivation.

13.6.1.1.2 The interaction of frequency and formal complexity with motivatability

In order to study the interaction between the factors frequency and formal complexity on the one and motivatability on the other hand, we divided the two frequency-based conditions of each language into two subconditions, viz. simple and complex forms. By means of this cross-classification, we obtained four conditions. We then assigned the results of step 1, i.e. all motivated and opaque stimuli (cf. 13.6.1.1.1) to these conditions. Figure 3 shows the results for French in percent.

Please note that as there are different proportions of complex and simple forms in our sample, the explanatory power of the comparison of these conditions is slightly reduced. In addition, we have to bear in mind that the stimulus set is comparatively small (for both aspects cf. 13.4.). For these two reasons, the results presented in the following sections are to be considered as first tendencies that have to be confirmed by a larger data sample.

---

[12] In principle, all lexical units that have a perceivable formal and conceptual relation to the stimulus unit are potential motivational partners. This means that at least all lexical units from the stimulus' word family and from the same word form are potential motivational partners (but cf. Marzo, Rube, and Umbreit 2011 for further cases, Umbreit 2010 and 2015 for restrictions on the direction of motivation as well as Marzo 2013 for restrictions on the types of motivational partner).

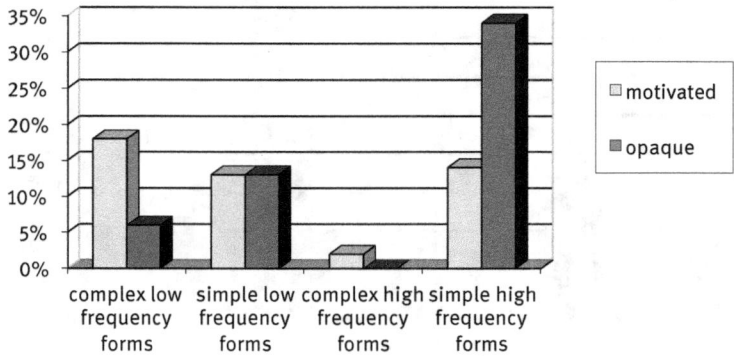

Figure 3: Percentages of motivated and opaque words in French in relation to frequency and formal complexity.

As expected, the biggest part of the opaque stimuli, 34 %, consists of simple HF forms. Within the latter condition, the relation between motivated and opaque stimuli is 29 % to 71 %. In contrast, in the formally complex HF group, none of the stimuli is opaque, i.e. the motivatability amounts to 100 %. However, this condition consists of only two stimuli, namely *monsieur* (cf. also note 9) with its most salient and second most salient meanings. On the contrary, the formally simple LF group has an equal number of motivated and opaque stimuli (13 % each, out of 100 stimuli). Still in concordance with hypothesis (1), in the formally complex LF condition only six stimuli (i.e. 25 % within this group) are considered opaque by the informants, which corresponds to 75 % of motivated stimuli within this condition.

If we compare the different conditions with regard to motivated stimuli (in sum 47 %), 18 % pertain to the complex LF group, 13 % to the simple LF group, 2 % to the complex HF group and 14 % to the simple HF group. The fact that the percentages of motivated stimuli in the simple conditions are almost equal to the percentage of motivated stimuli in the complex LF condition seems, at first sight, to falsify hypothesis (1). That this is not true, but due to an interaction between hypotheses (1) and (2) will be shown in 13.7.2.

Thus, the results for French clearly confirm hypothesis (1): With 62 % of motivated stimuli (= 31 out of 50 lexical units), the tendency towards motivatability of the LF forms is nearly twice as strong as for the HF forms, which, in turn, manifest a motivatability degree of only 32 % (= 16 motivated lexical units out of 50). That frequency correlates with formal complexity in that especially HF forms are formally simple has already been shown in section 4 above (cf. especially note 9).

As Figure 4 shows, the speakers' intuitions for Italian lead to similar results.

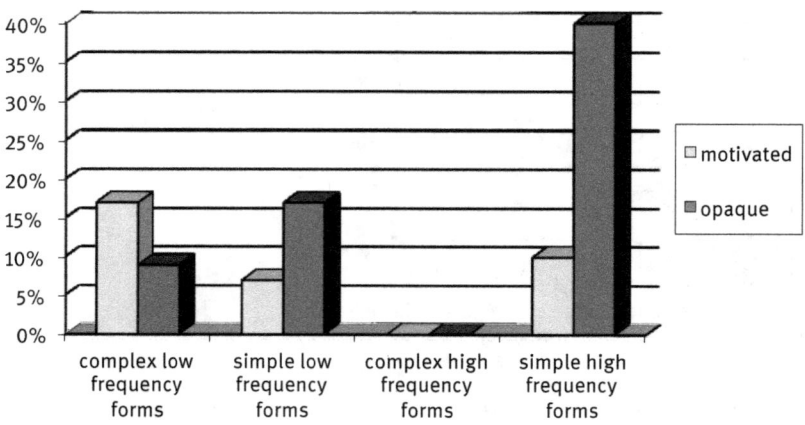

Figure 4: Percentages of motivated and opaque words in Italian in relation to frequency and formal complexity.

Unlike in the corresponding French condition, there are no HF forms which are complex in our Italian sample, so that the Italian stimuli were actually assigned to only three different conditions. Again confirming hypothesis (1), the biggest part of the opaque stimuli, 40%, consists of simple HF forms. More precisely, within the simple HF condition, only 20% of the stimuli were motivated by native speakers, while 80% are opaque. In contrast, 65% of the complex LF forms were motivated (17% out of the total number of stimuli), which is a bit less than in French (75%), but still confirms hypothesis (1). Another difference in comparison to French is that in the simple LF condition the relation between motivated and opaque stimuli is 29% to 71%, whereas in French the distribution between motivatability and opacity in this group was absolutely equal, i.e. 50% each. Yet, the results for Italian confirm hypothesis (1), too, as they show that it seems to be more difficult to motivate formally simple stimuli (that are, in general, more frequent) than formally complex ones (that are, in general, less frequent). From the point of view of the total percentage of motivated stimuli (34%), the repartition is somewhat less balanced than in French (cf. above and the discussion in 13.7.), with 17% belonging to the complex LF condition, 7% to the simple LF condition and 10% to the simple HF condition. Despite these minor differences, the results of the Italian questionnaire study confirm hypothesis (1) even more clearly than French: With 48% (i.e. 24 out of 50 lexical units) of motivated stimuli, the tendency towards motivatability within the LF forms is more than twice as strong as for the HF forms, which manifest only 20% of motivated stimuli (i.e. 10 out of 50 lexical units) within their group. Thus, in Italian, too, a correlation of frequency and formal complexity is to be found (cf. 13.3.1. and 13.4., note 9).

13.6.1.2 Salience and motivatability: hypothesis (2)

With respect to the motivation of our stimuli via other meanings of the same word form, the aim of our study was to take a closer look at the relation between the most salient and second most salient meanings of our stimuli. On the basis of previous studies concerning this question, we expected that the S2 meanings of the lexical units are motivated via the S1 meanings but not vice versa (hypothesis 2). In Figures 5 and 6, the different types of motivational partners for each language are illustrated.[13]

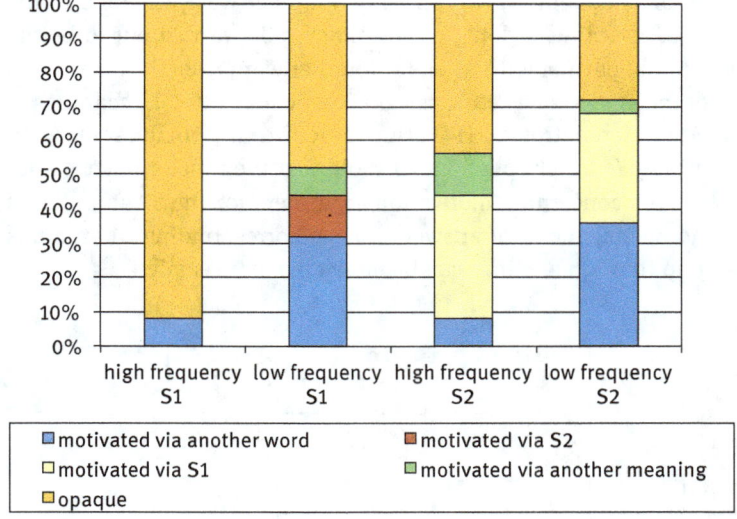

Figure 5: The nature of the motivational partners in French.

These results confirm hypothesis (2) insofar as the HF forms presented in their S2 meaning are indeed predominantly motivated via S1, provided that they are not considered opaque. Hypothesis (2) seems to partly hold for the LF forms presented in S2, too, although – as expected – the proportion of motivation via other words from the same word family is slightly higher. HF forms presented in S1, on the contrary, are – again as expected – not motivated at all via their S2 meaning.

---

13 In both figures we distinguish opacity, motivation via S1 or S2 of the same word form (where S1 corresponds to the most salient, S2 to the second most salient meaning) and motivation via another word from the same word family. "Motivated via another meaning" stands for motivation via meanings of the same word form that correspond neither to S1 nor to S2.

Admittedly though, the majority of the stimuli from this condition was not motivated at all (92% opacity). This confirms again both hypothesis (1) and (2) (cf. 13.3.1 and 13.6.1.1.2). In the LF S1 group, however, three stimuli were motivated via their S2 meaning, although the majority of the stimuli, just like in the LF S2 condition, were motivated via formally different word family members (cf. the discussion of this phenomenon in 13.7.2).

The following example will illustrate this result: The LF word Fr. *pilier* in its S2 meaning 'supporting person, sponsor', was with 77 % mainly motivated via the S1 meaning of the same word form, viz. 'pylon', whereas only 6 % of the answers referred to other words from the same word family and 17 % of the subjects considered the stimulus as opaque. However, when Fr. *pilier* was presented to the informants in the S1 meaning 'pylon', Fr. *pile* 'stack, pile' turned out to be the prevailing motivational partner with 33 %, i.e. another word from the same word family. The rest of the answers has to be assigned to opacity (30 %), meanings of the same word form different from S2 (14 %) and other words from the same word family different from *pile* 'stack, pile' (23 %). Note that the much higher homogeneity of the answers concerning motivational partners for the S2 stimulus in comparison to the heterogeneity of answers for the corresponding S1 stimulus confirms once again that S2 meanings can be motivated more easily.

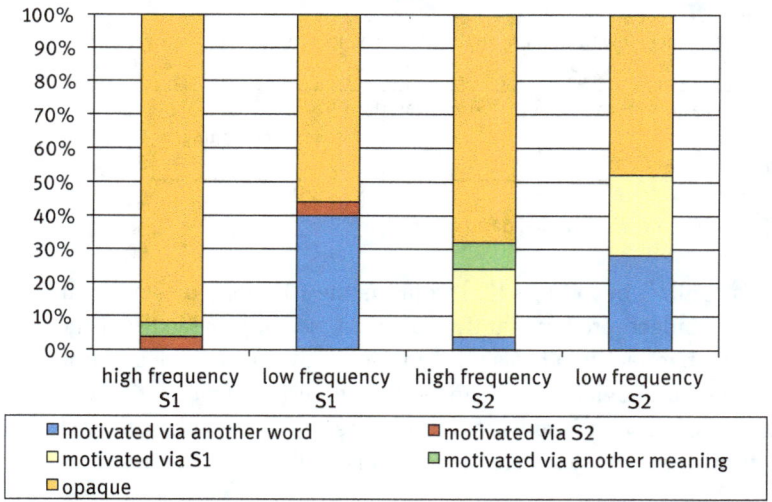

Figure 6: The nature of the motivational partners in Italian.

Figure 6 shows that for Italian hypothesis (2) is also confirmed for the HF S2 forms, where S1 meanings of the same stimulus constitute the second most frequent motivational partner after opacity. As in French, hypothesis (2) holds partly for the S2 LF group, too, motivations via S1 being here again the second most frequent strategy after motivations via formally different words from the same family. In contrast, in both S1 groups, only one out of 25 stimuli is motivated via the S2 meaning (cf. the discussion in 13.7.2). This finding again corroborates hypothesis (2). In Italian, too, the HF S1 group mainly consists of opaque stimuli (92%), but the LF S1 condition has motivation via other words from the same word family as its dominating motivational strategy and, with that, conforms not only to the LF S2 group, but also to the results for the equivalent subgroups in French. Summing up these findings, hypothesis (2) is confirmed both for French and Italian.

13.6.2 Results concerning hypotheses (3) and (4) tested in step 2 of the questionnaire study

If the original stimulus is judged as opaque by a majority of informants in step 1, it is not further investigated in step 2. This is why in step 2 the number of investigated stimuli is smaller than in step 1 and differs between the two languages. More precisely, in step 2 two questionnaires per language are employed. The French questionnaires contain 23 stimuli pairs each and the Italian ones 18 stimuli pairs each. In this step as well, the answers of 30 informants per questionnaire are evaluated. For the presentation of the results of step 2, only the dominant conceptual relation of each of the motivational pairs is considered.[14] Figures 7 and 8 give the sum of the dominant relations per motivational pair in percent for French and Italian respectively, with the most frequently represented relation in bold.

---

[14] For this reason, stimuli that are motivated in step 1 have to be considered semantically opaque in step 2 in cases where a majority of informants does not see a conceptual relation.

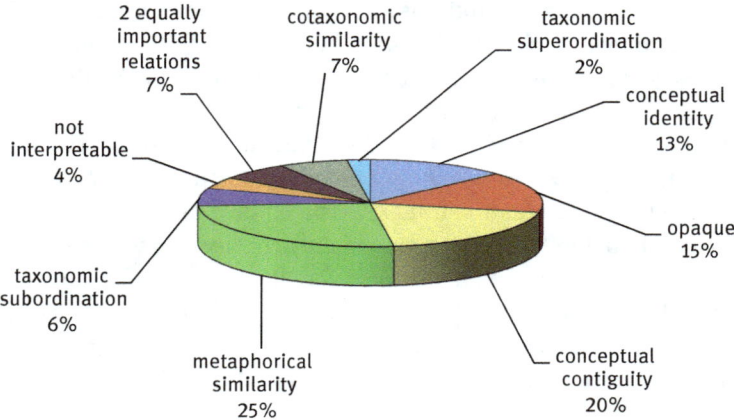

Figure 7: The distribution of conceptual relations for the French stimuli.[15]

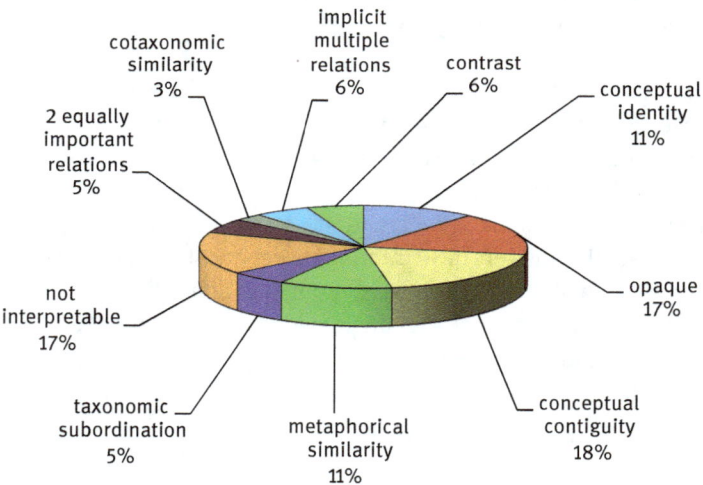

Figure 8: The distribution of conceptual relations for the Italian stimuli.[16]

---

15 Apart from the conceptual relations that are taken from Koch's 2 ventory (cf. 13.2. and the labels "semantically opaque" and "not interpretable" (cf. 13.5.2.2), one additional category was necessary for the classification of the informants' answers: All cases in which two different conceptual relations were equally strong are subsumed under "2 equally important relations".

16 In Italian, another additional category occurs that had to be introduced during the data analysis: "Implicit multiple relations" means that the respondents connected the given motivational partners implicitly via more than one conceptual relation. As an example, for the Italian motiva-

Our expectations concerning the conceptual relations between the stimuli and their most frequent motivational partner, namely a similar distribution of the different relations in French and in Italian (hypothesis 3), with a predominance of conceptual contiguity in both languages (hypothesis 4), were only partly met, as can be seen from Figures 7 and 8. As far as the distribution of the relations is concerned, hypothesis (3) is for the most part confirmed, in that in both languages the most important conceptual relations are conceptual contiguity, metaphorical similarity and conceptual identity, whereas the other relations are fairly less frequent. There are even no cases at all of conceptual contrast as a dominating relation in French and of taxonomic superordination in Italian. Although the absence of these relations is of course partly due to the restricted stimuli material, these conceptual relations constitute undoubtedly marginal ones in French and Italian word-formation. However, hypothesis (4), saying that conceptual contiguity would be the prevailing relation is only true for Italian while in French metaphorical similarity is stronger (for a discussion of this unexpected result cf. 13.7.3).

An interesting outcome of step 2 that was neither predicted by hypothesis (3) nor by hypothesis (4) is that there seems to be a correlation between the type of perceived conceptual relation (i.e. contiguity, metaphorical similarity, conceptual contrast etc., cf. Table 1) between the stimulus and the majoritarian motivational partner on the one hand and the number of subjects that motivated the stimulus via the respective majoritarian motivational partners on the other. In other words, certain conceptual relations tend to get positive answers by more subjects than others do (though this cannot be said to be a rule without exceptions and has to be tested systematically with more data). This is, for example, the case for metaphorical similarity that is, in general, picked by more than 50 % of the subjects, as in the case of French *pilier* 'supporting person' [S2] that was related to French *pilier* 'pillar, column' by 23 out of 30 subjects (i.e. by 77 %). This conceptual relation seems to be, in a way, easier to find and thus lead to a higher degree of semantic transparency than others do (if semantic transparency is defined as the number of agreeing subjects). The same might hold for conceptual contrast,

---

tional pair *santuario* 'very important place for a certain sector' – *santo* 'person worshipped for his or her piety', one of the informants chose metaphorical similarity as the underlying relation and said in his/her justification: "il termine santuario nella sua accezione originaria è il luogo in cui si venerano i santi" (En. 'the term santuario in its original meaning is the place where saints are worshipped'). This answer not only explains the metaphorical similarity perceived between the stimulus meaning of *santuario* and the one specified by the informant, but also hints to a contiguity relation between *santuario* 'place where saints are worshipped' and *scnto* 'saint'. Thus, the relation between the given motivational partners as described by the informant is twofold: metaphorical similarity + conceptual contiguity.

although there is only one case in our data sample. For Italian *indirettamente* 'in a non-explicit way' [S2] the relation of conceptual contrast was very clear in the sense that 30 out of 30 subjects, i.e. all of them, agreed on it and motivated it by Italian *direttamente* 'in an explicit way'.

In contrast, examples of conceptual relations that are obviously harder to find are cotaxonomic similarity and conceptual contiguity. French *croire* 'to trust someone, to count on someone' [S2] was connected to its majoritarian motivational partner French *croire* 'to think something' via cotaxomic similarity by a relative majority of only 7 out of 30 informants (i.e. 23 %). A similar phenomenon can be observed for Italian *vedere* 'to understand (intuitively)' [S1], that was connected to its motivational partner *vedere* 'to see with one's eyes' via conceptual contiguity by only 8 out of 30 subjects (i.e. 27 %). The potential significance of these results for a theory of lexical motivation will be discussed in 13.7.3.

13.7 Discussion

As has been shown in 6., hypotheses (1), (2) and (3) are confirmed, while hypothesis (4) seems to be falsified by the French data. In this section, we will discuss those results of the previous sections in more detail that were either not fully predicted by the hypotheses or seem, at first sight, to contradict them.

13.7.1 Interaction between hypotheses (1) and (2)

In 13.6.1.1.2. we have shown that 18 % of the motivated French stimuli pertain to the complex LF condition, 13 % to the simple LF condition and 14 % to the simple HF condition. In Italian, the distribution has been revealed to be more or less similar, with 17 % (complex LF forms), 7 % (simple LF forms) and 10 % (simple HF forms).

While the results for the complex LF conditions perfectly match the assumption of hypothesis (1), the almost equal percentages of motivated stimuli in the simple groups in French, and to a slightly lesser extent in Italian, seem, at first sight, to challenge it. Upon closer inspection, however, the nearly equal percentages are due to the interaction of the effects predicted by hypotheses (1) and (2). The frequency (plus complexity) effect assumed by hypothesis (1) interacts with the salience effect predicted by hypothesis (2) insofar as stimuli in their S2 meaning are generally motivated more easily than stimuli in their S1 meaning, even if they are highly frequent and formally simple. This leads to a certain balancing between opaque and motivated stimuli in each of the stimuli groups. Recall that all stimuli, irrespective of their frequency range and degree of complexity, were investigated in their most salient and in their second most salient meaning.

13.7.2 Motivation of S1 via S2: Directional preferences

In 13.6.1.2. we have stated for French that in the LF S1 group, three stimuli (namely French *poli* 'polite', *raide* 'steep' and *vaisseau* 'blood vessel') were motivated via their S2 meaning, although the majority of the stimuli, just like in the LF S2 group, was motivated via formally different word family members (as predicted by hypothesis 1). In the Italian LF S1 group, one stimulus, namely *ricoprire* 'to have a certain function' was also motivated via S2 *ricoprire* 'to cover something (physically)'. In contrast to French, in Italian even one stimulus of the HF S1 condition was motivated via S2: *trovare* 'to discover something (immaterial)' [S1] was motivated via *trovare* 'to discover something (material)' [S2] by 16 out of 30 subjects (i.e. 53 %). As these cases contradict hypothesis (2) at first sight, they deserve a more detailed discussion.

With the background of conceptual metaphor theory, it is quite safe to assume that the reason for S1 being motivated via S2 in the case of LF French *poli*, *raide* and *vaisseau* as well as Italian *ricoprire* can be found in the semantic shifts by which these stimuli are concerned: S1 is actually a metaphorical extension of S2 in all four cases. As metaphors generally are unidirectional (cf. e.g. Lakoff 1993: 216–218; see also the literature quoted and the questionnaire data presented in Marzo 2013: 131–132 and Umbreit 2015: 35–37, 114–115, 200–285, in contrast to other conceptual relations, it is no surprise that subjects motivate the target concept (in our cases S1) via the source concept (in our cases S2) and not, as predicted by hypothesis (2), the other way around. The salience-of-meaning-effect is, in general, a very robust effect, which can even, in some cases, overrule the frequency-of-form-effect (cf. 13.7.1.). However, it is, in turn, susceptible to be overruled by directional preferences of certain conceptual relations, in our case metaphorical similarity.

This is confirmed by step 2 of our questionnaire study. Recall that in step 2 of this study, subjects had to specify the conceptual relation between the stimulus and its major motivational partner that had been elicited in step 1. For French *poli* 'polite' 23 out of 30 participants (i.e. 77 %) perceived a relation of metaphorical similarity to *poli* 'polished/rubbed' (in the sense that a polite person is a person whose manners have been cleaned of anything rude). French *vaisseau* 'blood vessel' and its major motivational partner *vaisseau* 'vessel, ship' were connected by 15 out of 30 subjects (i.e. 50%) also through metaphorical similarity, because they perceived a functional similarity between the two concepts: the blood vessel is similar to a ship insofar as it transports something (blood) just like the latter does (merchandise, people, etc.). Although French *raide* 'steep' was motivated via the S2 unit *raide* 'rigid, physically inflexible' in step 1 of the questionnaire study by 14 out of 30 subjects (i.e. 47%), the relation between these two units was considered as semantically opaque by a relative majority of subjects (43%, i.e. 13 subjects) in step 2. Still, the second most frequent answer in step 2 was the connection of the S1 and S2 lexical units via metaphorical similarity by 9 out of 30 participants (i.e. 33%). Similarly to French *raide*, Italian *ricoprire* 'to have a certain function' was considered as motivated via S2 *ricoprire* 'to cover something (physically)' by 10 out of 30 subjects in step 1 (i.e. by 33%), whereas it was considered as semantically opaque in step 2 by 15 informants (i.e. 50%). Again, the second most frequent interpretable answer type was metaphorical similarity that was chosen by 13% of the subjects (i.e. 4 informants out of 30). In sum, in all four cases the motivational direction from S1 to S2 is guided by the unidirectionality of the corresponding metaphor. The principle of unidirectionality of metaphors seems to interact with the salience principle, insofar as the former overrules the latter. Thus, the validity of the suggested extension of hypothesis (2) to the LF condition is not contradicted by this finding, but has to be modified as in (2)':

(2)' If a lexical unit is motivated via a formally identical lexical unit, the second most salient meaning is motivated via the most salient meaning but not vice versa, except in the case of metaphorical similarity, whose unidirectionality overrules the salience effect.

The results for Italian *trovare* in step 1 are slightly different, but do also fit hypothesis (2)'. In contrast to step 1, in which 'to discover something (immaterial)' [S1] was motivated via *trovare* 'to discover something (material)' [S2], a relative majority of the participants of step 2 (i.e. 37%) considered the relation between these two lexical units as semantically opaque. The second most frequent result for this stimulus pair in step 2 is the category "not interpretable" (23%), which consists of answers that could not be assigned to a conceptual relation in an unequivocal manner.[17] Only the third most frequent answer was clearly a specific conceptual relation, more precisely cotaxonomic similarity (20%). Though in this case the

---

17 Interestingly, the reason for which our research team could not assign 23% of the answers unequivocally to any of the answer types of the questionnaire is that many subjects chose the "free formulation option" (no. 8 in the questionnaire of step 2, cf. Table 3). Most of them actually

motivation of a S1 unit via a S2 unit is not guided by the directionality of metaphorical similarity, we still can make an important observation on directional preferences overruling the salience effect: the concrete-over-abstract-principle (Blank 1997: 173–178, 378; Radden and Kövecses 1999: 45–46): From a cognitive perspective we seem to prefer understanding abstract concepts by the help of concrete concepts rather than vice versa. Applied to our motivational issues, this means that irrespective of the kind of similarity by which the two lexical units *trovare* S1 and S2 can actually be connected, S1 is more abstract than S2 insofar as the second argument of the verb denotes an immaterial entity in the former, but a material object in the latter case. This might be the reason for *trovare* S1 being motivated via *trovare* S2. This is also true in the case of the metaphors Fr. *poli* S1 'polite' and It. *ricoprire* [S1] 'to have a certain function', because S1 is not only the metaphorical meaning, but also the more abstract meaning.

13.7.3 Reflections on hypotheses (3) and (4): methodological issues

In the light of the results presented in 13.6.2 it looks, at first sight, as if hypotheses (3) and (4) are disconfirmed: conceptual contiguity is only the most important conceptual relation in the Italian, but not in the French data, where metaphorical similarity prevails. What is of particular importance in this context is that, in addition to the diverging importance of conceptual contiguity in the two languages, the number of not interpretable results differs rather strongly: 17 % in Italian vs. 4 % in French. In view of the genetic closeness and general typological similarity of French and Italian (cf. Koch 2001a: 1164), it is quite safe to assume that a higher percentage of interpretable answers in Italian would have led to the same result as in French, with metaphorical similarity being the most frequent conceptual relation. Even if this is a valid reason not to abandon hypothesis (3), it still looks, at first sight, as if such a result would completely disconfirm hypothesis (4). It will now be shown that in spite of these data a predominant role of conceptual contiguity does not have to be abandoned completely, if we consider it from a slightly different view on lexical motivation. In section 13.6.2 we showed that there is a correlation between the type of perceived conceptual relation between the stimulus and the motivational partner on the one hand and the number of subjects that motivated the stimuli via the respective motivational

---

described a similarity relation, but their answers were not unambiguous enough as for assigning them to metaphorical or cotaxonomic similarity.

partner on the other hand. From the perspective of this result, it looks as if some conceptual relations, such as e.g. metaphorical similarity, can be used for motivational purposes more easily than others.

One plausible reason for this phenomenon has already been discussed in another context in 13.7.2: the directionality of certain conceptual relations such as metaphorical similarity. As a matter of fact, this (in a certain sense more obvious) conceptual relation is also the one for which a preferred direction of motivation can be stated. In other words, it is easier to establish a (functional) similarity between French *pilier* 'supporting person' and *pilier* 'pillar, column' (cf. 13.6.2.) than the other way around, because metaphors are usually unidirectional (cf. 13.7.2.). In a similar way, we might assume that the relation of conceptual contrast can be established more easily from Italian *indirettamente* 'in a non-explicit way' to *direttamente* 'in an explicit way' than the other way around, 'in an explicit way' being the less marked concept (cf. e.g. Mayerthaler 1981: 15 on markedness of negative expressions). In contrast to conceptual relations that tend to be unidirectional, those that have no preferred direction (as e.g. contiguity, cf. Radden and Kövecses 1999: 22) tend also to be harder to name and to describe for our subjects, which leads to a lesser degree of transparency (in the above-mentioned sense), though there might be differences as for subtypes of these relations (e.g. in the case of different contiguity types, cf. Marzo 2013: 180–183 and Umbreit 2015: 219–226).

Another reason, for which some conceptual relations play a more important role in our questionnaire study than others do, is their ease of perceptibility. Even if this reason is undoubtedly connected to the directionality issue mentioned above – insofar as the ease of perceptibility of an established relation between two lexical units L_1 and L_2 is greater from L_1 to L_2 than from L_2 to L_1 if L_1 is, e.g. a metaphorical extension of L_2 – it will be discussed separately here, because it has important methodological implications. In a cognitive and psycholinguistic perspective, the understanding of similarity-based metaphors can be said to require a bigger cognitive effort than the understanding of contiguity-based metonymies (cf. Marzo 2013: 118–119 and the literature quoted therein), most certainly because conceptual metaphors generally associate two different frames, whereas metonymies typically work within one and the same frame (see e.g. Koch 1999: 145–148, 2001b: 202). As a consequence of this cognitive effort, metaphors are "more noticeable" (Fauconnier and Turner 2003: 70) than other conceptual relations are. We are, in this sense, more consciously aware of metaphorical extensions than of metonymical extensions. In contrast, metonymical shifts (and thus conceptual contiguity) are more natural (e.g. Croft 2003: 87) and therefore go unnoticed more easily.

If we transfer this greater ease of perceptibility of metaphorical similarity with respect to conceptual contiguity to our motivatability issues, it is then no surprise that if a motivational partner is connected to a stimulus mainly via metaphorical similarity, this connection is explicated by more informants than in the case of motivational partners being connected to their stimulus via conceptual contiguity. Still, this does not mean that conceptual contiguity is, in general, less important than metaphorical similarity. It might just be less important in our data, because the Tübingen Two-Step Method we deliberately used (cf. 13.5.2.) inquires motivatability, which is a conscious phenomenon (cf. 13.2.), and not unconscious motivatedness (cf. Rettig 1981 in general; Marzo 2013: 45–48 and Umbreit 2015: 187–193, 195–198 on conscious and unconscious aspects of lexical motivation). If we want to study unconscious aspects of lexical motivation, we should complement our offline-data with psycholinguistic online-data (cf. Marzo and Rube 2006: 159) in the future, collected e.g. in priming experiments like those presented by Klepousniotou (2002) who showed that we need more time to process metaphors than to process metonymies. However, even if such priming experiments are prone to show that contiguity-based metonymies are processed significantly faster than similarity-based metaphors this does not contradict our offline-data, but complements them: it is only natural that conceptual relations that are more noticeable (because they demand a greater cognitive effort) are more important in metalinguistic offline-studies that require active reflection, whereas they are processed more slowly in online-studies (still because they are cognitively more costly) in which the subjects are not even aware of the research question.

Summing up these reflections on the results of our questionnaire study from the perspective of hypotheses (3) and (4), we have, however, to say that in order to completely confirm or disconfirm these hypotheses, we should (i) corroborate our results by checking more data for both languages (as well as for other language types) and (ii) complement our offline-results by online-results. The discussion of the potential reasons for the unexpected results have rather shown that especially hypothesis (4) should be reformulated as in (4)', because (4)' captures all aspects of lexical motivation and because it is more plausible from a cognitive and psycholinguistic perspective.

(4') a. Conceptual contiguity is the most easily processed conceptual relation that underlies lexical motivatedness, most probably also in French and Italian.
b. Conceptual contiguity is not the prevailing conceptual relation underlying lexical motivatability in any language because of its limited ease of perceptibility. Lexical motivatability is more likely to be driven by more noticeable conceptual relations, such as e.g. metaphorical similarity.

13.8 Conclusion

The preceding sections have shown that a native speaker-based approach to lexical motivation, together with the innovative Tübingen Two-Step Method for gathering judgments of native speakers, leads to new insights with respect to lexical motivation. Our hypotheses (1) and (2) have been confirmed in that the degree of motivatability of lexical units in French and in Italian is influenced by factors such as the frequency of the word form (interacting with formal complexity) as well as the salience of the respective meaning. Additionally, it has turned out that the degree of salience of a given meaning can, on the one hand, overrule both the factors of frequency and formal complexity, and is, on the other hand, susceptible to be itself overruled by the directional preferences of conceptual relations such as metaphorical similarity. As far as the conceptual relations are concerned, the French and Italian stimuli show, as expected, a fairly similar distribution (hypothesis 3). However, our original hypothesis (4) on the dominance of conceptual contiguity in French and Italian had to be modified insofar as conceptual contiguity is most certainly of importance in unconscious motivatedness, but not in metalinguistic motivatability, where metaphorical similarity has turned out to be much more important.

As a consequence of this finding, future studies on lexical motivation should not only extend the investigated linguistic material and languages, but also complement the above-presented approach by taking into account the unconscious mental operations native speakers perform when confronted with relations between words. These amplifications will allow us to tackle more typologically oriented aspects of lexical motivation, such as possible combinations of formal and semantic devices, universal and language type-specific preferences, etc. – in short to establish cross-linguistically comparable motivational profiles of various languages and language types, which at the moment constitute rather a desideratum than a result of lexical semantic typology (cf. Koch and Marzo 2007: 273; Koptjevskaja-Tamm, Vanhove, and Koch 2007: 168).

13.9 References

Augst, Gerhard. 1975. *Untersuchungen zum Morpheminventar der deutschen Gegenwartssprache*. Tübingen: Narr.
Berko, Jean. 1958. The child's learning of English morphology. *Word* 14: 150–177.
Blank, Andreas. 1997. *Prinzipien des lexikalischen Bedeutungswandels am Beispiel der romanischen Sprachen*. Tübingen: Niemeyer.

Bybee, Joan. 1985. *Morphology. A study of the relation between meaning and form.* Amsterdam/ Philadelphia: Benjamins.

Bybee, Joan. 1988. Morphology as Lexical Organization. In Michael Hammond, and Michael Noonan (eds.), *Theoretical morphology. Approaches in modern linguistics,* 119–141. San Diego etc.: Academic Press.

Caron, Jean. 2008. *Précis de psycholinguistique.* 2nd edn. Paris: Quadrige/PUF.

Croft, William. 2003. Il ruolo dei domini semantici nell'interpretazione di metafore e metonimie. In Livio Gaeta and Silvia Luraghi (eds.), *Introduzione alla linguistica cognitiva,* 77–100. Rome: Carocci.

Cruse, David A. 1986. *Lexical semantics.* Cambridge: Cambridge University Press.

Derwing, Bruce L. 1976. Morpheme recognition and the learning of rules for derivational morphology. *The Canadian Journal of Linguistics* 21 (1): 38–66.

Durkin, Kevin and Jocelyn Manning. 1989. Polysemy and the subjective lexicon: semantic relatedness and the salience of intraword senses. *Journal of Psycholinguistic Research* 18 (6): 577–612.

Fauconnier, Gilles and Mark Turner. 2003. Polysemy and conceptual blending. In Brigitte Nerlich, Zazie Todd, Vimala Herman, and David D. Clarke (eds.), *Flexible patterns of meaning in mind and language,* 79–94. Berlin & New York: Mouton de Gruyter.

Fill, Alwin. 1980a. Durchsichtige Wörter im Englischen: Betrachtungsweisen und Forschungsansätze. *Arbeiten aus Anglistik und Amerikanistik* 5 (1): 13–35.

Fill, Alwin. 1980b. *Wortdurchsichtigkeit im Englischen. Eine nicht-generative Studie morphosemantischer Strukturen. Mit einer kontrastiven Untersuchung der Rolle durchsichtiger Wörter im Englischen und Deutschen der Gegenwart.* Innsbruck: Institut für Sprachwissenschaft, Universität Innsbruck.

Gauger, Hans-Martin. 1971. *Durchsichtige Wörter. Zur Theorie der Wortbildung.* Heidelberg: Winter.

Iacobini, Claudio. 2000. Base and direction of derivation. In Geert Booij, Christian Lehmann, and Joachim Mugdan (eds.), *Morphology/Morphologie. An international handbook on inflection and derivation/Ein internationales Handbuch zur Flexion und Wortbildung,* 865–876. Vol. 1, Berlin & New York: Mouton de Gruyter.

Juilland, Alphonse, Dorothy Brodin, and Catherine Davidovitch. 1970. *Frequency Dictionary of French Words.* Den Haag & Paris: Mouton de Gruyter.

Juilland, Alphonse and Vincenzo Traversa. 1973. *Frequency dictionary of Italian words.* Den Haag/Paris: Mouton de Gruyter.

Klepousniotou, Ekaterini. 2002. The processing of lexical ambiguity: Homonymy and polysemy in the mental lexicon. *Brain and Language* 81: 205–223.

Koch, Peter. 1999. Frame and contiguity: On the cognitive basis of metonymy and certain types of word formation. In Klaus-Uwe Panther and Günter Radden (eds.), *Metonymy in language and thought,* 139–165. Amsterdam & Philadelphia: Benjamins.

Koch, Peter. 2001a. Lexical typology from a cognitive and linguistic point of view. In Martin Haspelmath, Ekkehard König, Wulf Oesterreicher, and Wolfgang Raible (eds.), *Language typology and language universals. An international handbook,* 1142–1178. Vol. 2. Berlin & New York: Mouton de Gruyter.

Koch, Peter. 2001b. Metonymy. Unity in diversity. *Journal of Historical Pragmatics* 2 (2): 201–244.

Koch, Peter. 2004. Metonymy between pragmatics, reference, and diachrony. *metaphorik.de* 7: 6–54.

Koch, Peter and Daniela Marzo. 2007. A two-dimensional approach to the study of motivation in lexical typology and its first application to French high-frequency vocabulary. *Studies in Language* 31 (2): 259–291.

Krott, Andrea, Rob Schreuder, and Harald Baayen. 1999. Complex words in complex words. *Linguistics* 37 (5): 905–926.

Koptjevskaja-Tamm, Maria, Martine Vanhove, and Peter Koch. 2007. Typological approaches to lexical semantics. *Linguistic Typology* 11: 159–185.

Lakoff, George. 1993. The contemporary theory of metaphor. In Andrew Ortony (ed.), *Metaphor and thought*, 202–251. 2nd edn. Cambridge: Cambridge University Press.

Marchand, Hans. 1964. A set of criteria of derivational relationship between words unmarkes by derivational morphemes. *Indogermanische Forschungen* 68: 170–175.

Marzo, Daniela. 2013. *Polysemie als Verfahren lexikalischer Motivation. Theorie und Empirie am Beispiel von Metonymie und Metapher im Französischen und Italienischen.* Tübingen: Narr.

Marzo, Daniela. 2011. Intrinsic or extrinsic motivation? The implications of metaphor- and metonymy-based polysemy for transparency in the lexicon. In Klaus-Uwe Panther, and Günter Radden (eds.), *Motivation in grammar and the lexicon*, 251–267. Amsterdam & Philadelphia: Benjamins.

Marzo, Daniela. 2008. What is iconic about polysemy? A contribution to research on diagrammatic transparency. In Ludovic De Cuypere and Klaas Willems (eds.), *Naturalness and iconicity in linguistics*, 167–187. Amstderdam & Philadelphia: Benjamins.

Marzo, Daniela and Verena Rube. 2006. What do you think where words come from? Investigating lexical motivation empirically. In Valery Solovyev, Vera Goldberg, and Vladimir Polyakov (eds.), *The VIIIth International Conference Cognitive Modelling in Linguistics. Proceedings*, 152–161. Vol.1. Moskau, Kazan State University.

Marzo, Daniela, Verena Rube, and Birgit Umbreit. 2006. Lexical motivation and speaker judgements. Poster, *Linguistic Evidence II*, Tübingen, 2.–4.2.2006.

Marzo, Daniela, Verena Rube, and Birgit Umbreit. 2007. Salience and frequency of meanings: A comparison of corpus and experimental data on polysemy: 42–53. Submission #205, *Corpus Linguistics 2007 Pre-Conference Proceedings*.

Marzo, Daniela, Verena Rube, and Birgit Umbreit. 2011. Similarité sans contiguïté – la dimension formelle de la motivation lexicale dans la perspective des locuteurs. In Sarah Dessì Schmid, Ulrich Detges, Paul Gévaudan, Wiltrud Mihatsch, and Richard Waltereit (eds.), *Rahmen des Sprechens. Beiträge zu Valenztheorie, Varietätenlinguistik, Kreolistik, Kognitiver und Historischer Semantik*, 367–378. Tübingen: Narr.

Marzo, Daniela and Birgit Umbreit. 2008. How to choose stimuli for experiments on lexical ambiguity? A comparison of data sources for psycholinguistic experiments. Poster, *Linguistic Evidence III*, Tübingen, 31.1.–2.2.2008.

Mayerthaler, Willi. 1981. *Morphologische Natürlichkeit*. Wiesbaden: Athenaion.

Perfetti, Charles A. and Robert Lindsey. 1974. Polysemy and memory. *Journal of Psycholinguistic Research* 3 (1): 75–89.

Plag, Ingo. 2003. *Word-formation in English*. Cambridge: Cambridge University Press.

Radden, Günter and Zoltán Kövecses. 1999. Towards a theory of metonymy. In Klaus-Uwe Panther and Günter Radden (eds.), *Metonymy in language and thought*, 17–59. Amsterdam & Philadelphia: Benjamins.

Rettig, Wolfgang. 1981. *Sprachliche Motivation. Zeichenrelationen von Lautform und Bedeutung am Beispiel französischer Lexikoneinheiten*. Frankfurt am Main & Bern: Lang.

Rufener, John. 1971. *Studies in the motivation of English and German compounds*. Zürich: Juris.

Sanchez, Christina. 2008. *Consociation and dissociation. An empirical study of word-family integration in English and German*. Tübingen: Narr.
Saussure, Ferdinand. [1916] 1972. Reprint. *Cours de linguistique générale*. Paris: Payot.
Scheidegger, Jean. 1981. *Arbitraire et motivation en français et en allemand. Examen critique des thèses de Charles Bally*. Bern: Francke.
Schmid, Hans-Jörg. 2007. Entrenchment, salience, and basic levels. In Dirk Geeraerts and Hubert Cuyckens (eds.), *The Oxford handbook of cognitive linguistics*, 117–138. Oxford: Oxford University Press.
Shaw, James H. 1979. *Motivierte Komposita in der deutschen und englischen Gegenwartssprache*. Tübingen: Narr.
Steinberg, Reinhild. 2014. *Lexikalischer Wandel und Polygenese: der Konzeptbereich Kopf*. Tübingen: Stauffenburg.
Ullmann, Stephen. 1957. *The principles of semantics*. 2d edn. Oxford: Blackwell.
Ullmann, Stephen. 1962. *Semantics. An introduction to the science of meaning*. Oxford: Blackwell.
Umbreit, Birgit. 2010. Does love come from to love or to love from love? Why lexical motivation has to be regarded as bidirectional. In Sascha Michel and Alexander Onysko (eds.), *Cognitive approaches to word-formation*, 301–333. Berlin & New York: Mouton de Gruyter.
Umbreit, Birgit. 2011. Why multiple motivation is a cognitively justified phenomenon. In Klaus-Uwe Panther and Günter Radden (eds.), *Motivation in grammar and the lexicon*, 269–286. Amsterdam & Philadelphia: Benjamins.
Umbreit, Birgit. 2015. *Zur Direktionalität der lexikalischen Motivation. Motiviertheit und Gerichtetheit von französischen und italienischen Wortpaaren auf der Basis von Sprecherbefragungen*. Tübingen: Narr.
Victorri, Bernard and Catherine Fuchs. 1996. *La polysémie. Construction dynamique du sens*. Paris: Hermes.
Waltereit, Richard. 1998. *Metonymie und Grammatik. Kontiguitätsphänomene in der französischen Satzsemantik*. Tübingen: Niemeyer.
Williams, John N. 1992. Processing polysemous words in context: Evidence for interrelated meanings. *Journal of Psycholinguistic Research* 21 (3): 193–218.
Zipf, George K. 1949. *Human behaviour and the principle of least effort: An introduction to human ecology*. New York: Hafner.

Wiltrud Mihatsch
14. Types of motivation in folk plant taxonomies

Abstract: Hyponymic hierarchies are frequently considered the most important structure of the noun lexicon. However, elaborate lexical hierarchies are quite rare in everyday language, where usually very few levels of generalization can be observed and where hyponymy is not the most important principle of organization. Much more important for the lexical organization is the prominent status of the basic level. As shown by cognitive psychologists and cognitive linguists such as Eleanor Rosch, this is the level where the most salient concepts of a hierarchy can be found. Most importantly, the basic level is the most general level where concrete concepts can still be represented by a global image. In this contribution I will analyze semantic and morphological motivation relations such as polysemy patterns and word formation processes in several Romance taxonomies of plant names, which show very different motivation patterns above and below basic level and which thus reveal the cognitive set-up of lexical taxonomies. These will be shown to be largely determined by basic-level imagery, which is refined below basic level and which helps to form composite collective concepts that underly the superordinate level.

14.1 Introduction[1]

The study of cross-linguistic motivation relations in the lexicon is a central issue in the relatively new field of lexical typology (cf. Koptjevskaja-Tamm, Vanhove, and Koch 2007). So far, studies focus on cross-linguistic semantic and motivational patterns in particular conceptual domains (Koptjevskaja-Tamm, Vanhove, and

---

[1] I would like to thank the editors for their helpful comments on an earlier version of this paper as well as the useful remarks and suggestions provided by two anonymous reviewers. One reviewer suggests a wealth of data from other Indo-European and Non-Indoeuropean languages which support my analysis and which might easily provide the basis for another paper on this topic. In this paper I refer to these additional data in a very condensed way. I am also grateful to Joshua Bebout for the stylistic revision of this paper.

Wiltrud Mihatsch (University of Tübingen)

Koch 2007: 161), which reveal general as well as language-particular patterns. In some cases we even find typological patterns revealing common lexical patterns in genealogically unrelated languages, as Talmy (1985) has shown for motion verbs.[2] However, such an approach, restricted to specific conceptual domains, does not usually lead to possible generalizations across particular domains. As a matter of fact, one of the main methodological problems pertains to finding "a reasonable level of abstraction" in the choice of the phenomenon to be investigated (Koptjevskaja-Tamm, Vanhove, and Koch 2007: 178).

One such reasonable level of abstraction might be the analysis of lexical configurations (Cruse 1986: 112) such as hierarchies based on *hyponymy*, which may reveal general domain independent patterns of the lexicon, an approach adopted in Mihatsch (2006). Of course, if very general cross-domain patterns are investigated, the number of lexical items to be analysed is very high. This might explain why such an approach has hardly ever been chosen and this is also why this contribution may only be the starting point for true typological studies in this domain.

In this study, I will show clearly differing lexical properties according to the level of taxonomic generalisation, tendencies shared by several Romance and Germanic languages, which may be explained as a consequence of common cognitive and communicative properties of lexical items and concepts on different taxonomic levels.

Why *taxonomies*? Taxonomic structures such as *thing – living thing –plant – tree – birch – silver birch* are frequently considered the most important structure of the noun lexicon (cf. Miller 1998: 24). However, such well-ordered multilevel taxonomies seem to be closely related to the development of Western science, while elaborate lexical hierarchies are quite rare in everyday language. Here, usually very few levels of generalization can be observed and hyponymy is not the only principle of organization in these hierarchies (Mihatsch 2006: 1–4, 153–161). Everyday language hierarchical structures are anchored in the *basic level*, which cognitive psychology and prototype semantics have shown to be the level where we find the most salient, i.e. most frequent and most easily recalled and accessed, concepts of a hierarchy of concrete nouns such as *tree*. The basic level is defined as the most general level where concepts can plausibly still be represented by a global image (Rosch et al. 1976: 398–405). On the linguistic level, this is reflected by the fact that basic-level lexemes (which may shift, to some extent at

---

[2] In some cases patterns of semantic change seem to be related to grammatical phenomena, for instance, the obligatoriness or lack of plural marking on the noun may bias categorization processes underlying semantic change as shown in Mihatsch (2005).

least, to the subordinate level, depending on the domain and the language), are usually simplex nouns. On that level, semantic representations based on images are more convincing than verbal definitions according to the experimental data presented in Rosch et al. (1976) and similar studies. On the superordinate level, the representation and conceptualization rather corresponds to a combination of several basic-level concepts in a kind of collective concept, while subordinate levels are refined basic-level concepts.

In Mihatsch (2006) I analysed lexical (folk) taxonomies of concrete nouns, namely plants, animals and a selection of artefacts in French and Spanish, along with the consideration of other languages, in order to arrive at cross-domain generalizations.

The underlying structuring principles do not seem to vary a lot cross-linguistically, however, I am able to show that the motivation types are determined by the word-formation types a particular language prefers.

The aim of this contribution is to present and analyse motivation relations in several *Romance noun taxonomies* in the domain of plants. I will also point out relevant observations for other languages and take into account the results obtained from the other domains analysed in Mihatsch (2006, 2007a, 2007b, 2008a, 2008b) and Mihatsch and Steinberg (2011), which revealed the same patterns. I will discuss how far underlying cognitive principles may show in the morphological and semantic dimension of motivation[3], in correlation with the level of generalization and (proto-) typicality.

The data underlying this paper are mainly taken from lexicographical sources, contemporary dictionaries as well as historical and etymological dictionaries. I try to cover as much ground as possible, with a focus on French and Spanish. While this analysis is certainly not exhaustive, I hope to have captured the most important tendencies of motivation in lexical hierarchies, since all the observations made for plant taxonomies also apply to artifacts (cf. Mihatsch 2006). Here I have excluded motivation patterns which transcend hierarchical relations, such as metaphorical or metonymically motivated relations.

In my survey of semantic and morphological motivation patterns I will show very diverging structures above and below the basic level, which reveal the cognitive set-up of lexical taxonomies, an aspect of motivation in the lexicon which hasn't yet been addressed systematically and globally in lexical typology.

I will first present a short introduction into the cognitive foundations of hierarchical levels and the notion of basic level in prototype semantics. I will then

---

[3] Circularity is avoided by referring to results from cognitive psychology, as done in Mihatsch (2006).

show and explain three types of motivation types: purely semantic motivation, compounding and derivational patterns, which all point to a highly salient basic level, but also show some interesting differences in the nature of the motivation relations. I will try and establish links between linguistic patterns of motivation and representational properties of the different hierarchical levels which have been investigated in psycholinguistics and which will be presented very briefly in the following section.

14.2 Cognitive and communicative foundations of lexical taxonomies

Lexicographic definitions which classically rely on the genus proximum and differentiae specificae often appear redundant, pedantical or just banal with the most common concrete nouns such as *tree*, *cat* or *table*. This suggests that such lexicographic strategies do not plausibly reflect the semantics of these nouns as stored in our mental lexicon. The communicative salience, i.e. preferential use, of the basic level, on which these nouns are situated, was detected by Brown (1958). Anthropologists and ethnobiologists (cf. Berlin 1972, 1992) discovered the basic nature of the intermediate level in folk taxonomies. Berlin distinguishes five main hierarchical levels, of which the middle level, the so-called generic level (partly corresponding to "basic level" in other works, cf. below), where nouns such as *dog*, *birch* or *oak* can be found, is most salient and phylogenetically primary. Here, lexemes tend to be morphologically opaque. Rosch et al. (1976) confirmed this observation from a psycholinguistic experimental perspective. Their experiments suggest that the concepts on what they call the basic level are the most general ones which can still be represented by a global shape (Rosch et al. 1976: 398–405), an aspect that has been confirmed since then (Barsalou 1992: 183). The cognitive advantage shows in as diverse aspects as picture naming tasks and ontogenesis Rosch et al. (1976: 417) show that basic-level nouns are acquired very early. Since Rosch et al.'s (1976) fundamental study, the phenomenon of the basic level has been extensively studied from a psycholinguistic point of view (a good overview can be found in Murphy 2002: chapter 7). The following table illustrates the similarities and differences between Rosch et al's psycholinguistic and cognitive-perceptual study and Berlin's ethnobiological analysis (based on linguistic properties of Mayan expressions on different levels of generalization):

Table 1: Salience and levels of generalization in two approaches

Rosch et al. 1976	Berlin 1972, 1992
	Unique beginner: *plant*
Superordinate level: *plant*	Life form: *tree*
Basic level: *tree / oak*	Generic level: *oak*
Subordinate level: *live oak*	Specific level: *live oak*
	Varietal level: *southern live oak*

According to Rosch et al. (1976: 388) concepts such as HAMMER, TROUSERS, TABLE and CAR as well as MAPLE, BIRCH are basic-level concepts. However, the latter seem to be intuitively more specific than the artefacts. Rosch et al. (1976) detect that not only the generic level concepts observed by ethnobiologists, but also the more general biological life-form level concepts TREE, FISH and BIRD behave like basic-level concepts (Rosch et al. 1976: 392–392) although the level below may be linguistically more salient due to the expertise of the linguistic community (Berlin 1992: chapter 2).

Thus there seems to be a certain flexibility as to basicness. More specifically, the criterion of a global shape defines an upper limit of generalization, which still may have basic-level properties, while expertise may render any subordinate-level item more salient. In this case the motivation relations typical for the relation between the basic level and the subordinate level can be found on more specific levels, but never above the life-form level. This is true for nouns designating human beings, here we observe a dramatic shift of salience to the perceptual subordinate level since the individual human being is socially highly salient and it is nearly impossible for us to abstract from differences between the sexes (Mihatsch 2015b).

Apart from the ontogenetic and psycholinguistic consequences (see Rosch et al. 1976) basic-level nouns show a series of linguistic properties which distinguish them from the lexical units above and below, such as high token frequency (Mihatsch 2006: 48; Geeraerts, Grondelaers, and Bakema 1994: 36–37), their morphological opacity versus the greater transparency above and below the basic level (Berlin 1992: 15–17, 29–34). Furthermore basic-level items seem to be far more productive than nouns of other levels of generalization (Schmid 1996: 1). Related to these properties is their higher age, a property mentioned in ethnobiological studies (Anderson 1986: 200; Berlin 1992: 275). All in all the notion of basic level seems to be a fundamental one for the organization of concepts underlying concrete nouns and it is one of the key concepts of cognitive linguistics and in particular prototype semantics (cf. Kleiber 1990). It is also accorded a prominent position in all the more recent introductions to cognitive linguistics, such as Evans and Green (2006) and Schmid (2007). The psychological and linguistic evidence for the basic level is very robust, while the more widely studied prototypicality is much more problematic since it may arise due to quite heterogeneous factors (cf. Löbner 2003: 276 for a lucid discussion). Nevertheless, to this day, hardly any systematic lexicological studies have been dedicated to the basic level apart from the important studies by Geeraerts, Grondelaers, and Bakema (1994), Schmid (see for instance Schmid 1996) and Ungerer (such as 1994) focussing on English, as well as my own analyses of Romance data (Mihatsch 2004, 2006, 2007a, 2007b, 2008a, 2008b).

If basic-level nouns can be represented by global maximally simple visual gestalts the question is how the subordinate and superordinate level are represented. In the case of subordinates, experiments suggest that subordinate concepts refine the basic-level gestalt by adding usually perceptual properties (Gauthier et al. 2000: 144). However, familiarity on subordinate level may lead to a holistic representation of subordinate nouns. Before industrialization the botanical expertise of the average speaker was very high, which explains the many short opaque nouns on generic level – the most salient level of folk taxonomies according to Berlin (1972, 1992), which, however, corresponds to the perceptually defined subordinate level according to Rosch et al. (1976) possibly reflecting a holistic visual representation, as in the case of Sp. *pino* 'pine', *roble* 'oak', *haya* 'beech', or Fr. *hêtre* 'beech', *chêne* 'oak', *pin* 'pine' (Gougenheim 1975, 3: 45–46; Guyot and Gibassier 1960: 20–36). Regardless of expertise and greater salience of subordinates, basic-level items maintain their cognitive properties (Tanaka and Taylor 1991: 475), although the rather infrequent use of some basic-level nouns may lead to lexical gaps on this level (Berlin 1992: 188–190) – this is certainly true for the cohyponyms of tree, namely 'herbaceous plant', but not for the very salient basic-level life form nouns meaning 'tree'.

An important phenomenon contributing to the hierarchical make-up of nouns on the subordinate level is prototypicality, a notion far more studied than the basic level itself. *Prototypes* are typical members of a basic-level category (see Koch 1996; Löbner 2003: 276 for a critical evaluation). Here I will assume the position of standard theory according to which prototypes are subordinate schematic concepts (Kleiber 1993: 29–33, 40–42), which may underly lexical units and which may optimize and thus represent the whole basic-level category and lead to the distinction between marginal and more central items (cf. Kleiber 1993: 34).

While on the basic level and below concepts underlying count nouns may be represented globally by more or less specific shapes, the organization must be qualitatively different above the basic level, since by definition, no global shape is possible here. When asked to define superordinates, i.e. nouns above the basic level, subjects usually give only single, mainly functional attributes or several hyponyms on the basic level (Wisniewski and Murphy 1989: 256). This suggests that here the representation may rely on verbal definitions or the combination of several basic-level gestalts. Thus not only subordinates but also superordinates conceptually derive from basic-level concepts. Ontogenetically the differentiation below the basic level precedes the generalization above the basic level, which seems to be linked to scientific classifications (cf. Berlin 1972: 59) and which is cognitively more complex than specification. The lack of information above the basic level as well as the role of learned categorization explains why in many languages and many domains there are lexical gaps on the superordinate level (see Mihatsch 2006: 92 for an overview over relevant crosslinguistic observations), which is also the case in the plant domain, where many languages do not have nouns meaning 'plant' (Berlin 1972: 78–80, 1992: 190). As Berlin (1972: 78) writes,

> "[w]hile man has no doubt tacitly recognized the world of plants as a conceptual category since earliest times, it does not appear to have been essential to provide the concept with a distinctive label until quite recently".

However, superordinate categories might implicitly appear as grammatical categories such as classifiers and derivational suffixes – if superordinates are lexically expressed they tend to be learned expressions or collective nouns reflecting the conceptually composite structure (Mihatsch 2006: 92 f. and chapter 4).

Starting out from these observations we might expect to find the following motivational patterns:
- a strong bidirectional motivational link between nouns designating the prototype on subordinate level and nouns on the basic level
- a strong unidirectional link between the basic level and subordinate nouns derived from or depending on the basic level
- a strong unidirectional link between the basic level and superordinate nouns, also semantically depending on or derived from the basic level.

14.3 Motivation patterns in lexical hierarchies

It is a very ambitious aim to determine motivation patterns in lexical taxonomies, since lexical units may have many different sources, not necessarily related to other nouns in the same hierarchy, such as metaphors and metonymy (which are not considered here, but see Koch 2005). Furthermore, lexicalization processes tend to render obscure motivation patterns that may have existed at some stage.

This means that when trying to find systematic patterns reflecting hierarchical relations one has to take into account motivation patterns at different periods. The data presented in this paper are taken from my own studies and complemented by other sources where necessary. The focus will be on Romance languages, with additional data from Germanic and in some cases from Non-Indo-European languages. I will study semantic motivation without morphological motivation, i.e. semantic change and the resulting polysemic structures as well as compounding, derivation, grammatical gender patterns and cases of remotivation.

14.3.1 Semantic change and semantic motivation

14.3.1.1 Specialization and generalization

Semantic change within a hyponymic hierarchy can be of three kinds: specialization, generalization as well as cohyponymic shifts, while the more frequent types of semantic change, metonymy and metaphor, transcend hierarchical relations. Semantic change involving generalization or specialization leads to what Gévaudan (1997) calls vertical polysemy. In principle, these kinds of change may affect all hierarchical levels in all directions. However, a closer look reveals clear preferences and different causes of change depending on the hierarchical level with regard to the basic level and the influence of prototypes.

14.3.1.1.1 Specialization of basic-level nouns
The close conceptual link between prototype and basic-level concept often surfaces in a shared lexical expression.[4] The semantic motivation may here arise as a consequence of specialization of basic-level terms to a prototype. This type of change is quite straightforward from a communicative point of view. Frequent uses of the basic-level lexeme when referring to more specific prototypes may lead to an entrenchment and subsequent conventionalization of this more specific use, as shown in Mihatsch (2006: 61). The use of a hyperonym instead of a hyponym is logically always correct and therefore very inconspicuous. Thus specialization typically starts out from the basic level and acquires a prototype reading, which can also be seen in the case of Ancient Greek δρῦς (drûs) 'tree'

---

[4] This, however, is particularly problematic in scientific contexts, where prototypes tend to get marked by adjectives such as German *echt* or reduplications as in the case of the Latin biological term *Rosa rosa*.

acquiring the meaning 'oak' (Guyot and Gibassier 1960: 18). However, in other cases not the attraction of a prototype, but the occurrence in certain frames may lead to specialization, for instance in the frame of farming (also see Blank 1997: 205) as in German *Kraut* 'herbaceous plant' to Southern German 'cabbage' (Kluge 1999). A further indirect cause for the specialization of basic-level nouns is the entrenchment and growing salience of rather but not exclusively atypical subordinate nouns, which may lose their conceptual (and in some cases morphological) dependency on the basic level and cognitively acquire basic-level properties themselves (Rosch et al. 1976: 434; Barsalou 1992: 183–184). In this case the basic-level noun and the salient subordinate noun may become cohyponyms and the former hyperonym may thus acquire a more specific reading, as in the case of the now cohyponymous *trousers* and *jeans*. While originally *trousers* is the hyperonym of *jeans*, it eventually led to a reinterpretation of the basic-level noun *trousers* to the subordinate meaning 'traditional trousers, excluding jeans'. (cf. Cruse 2000: 183). The same phenomenon can be observed in other languages, such as Spanish *pantalon* and *vaqueros*, the latter being an ellipsis of *pantalón(es) vaquero(s)* 'jeans', literally 'cowboys trousers'.

14.3.1.1.2 Generalization of subordinate nouns

Although basic-level nouns tend to be the most ancient and stable ones diachronically, there are cases where the basic-level noun is derived from other nouns, even sub- and superordinate ones (Mihatsch 2006: 61–62, 147–148, 186–190). Subordinate-level nouns may acquire basic-level meaning via generalization. Semantically, generalization is more complex than specialization, since this innovation leads to uses violating the original sense when referents may be referred to by a former cohyponym. However, the close link between a prototype and the basic level explains why the nouns designating a prototype may easily generalize and thus become a basic-level noun, all the more so as prototypes or at least very familiar nouns may serve as an optimization of the basic-level category as in the case of Western Apache *t'iis* 'cottonwood (tree)' acquiring a more general meaning *t'iis* 'tree' (see the remarks in Berlin 1972: 68), or Lat. *baca* 'laurel berry' to Fr. *baie* 'berry' (Rey 1998). An anonymous reviewer has pointed out that the same case can be observed in some Turkic languages, which have a noun meaning 'tree' related to a protoform *derek*, probably meaning 'poplar/tree' (Tenishev and Dydo [eds.] 2006: 423). Generalization may also be caused by frames in which one subordinate of a basic category prevails, in which case the referents of the subordinate more or less cover the whole basic-level category within that specific frame. For instance, the Saami noun *rassi* 'herbaceous plant' was borrowed from

Norwegian *gress* 'grass' (Anderson 1986: 212) in an environment like the Arctic tundra where herbaceous plants other than grass are scarce.

The existence of compounds or syntagms originally corresponding to compounds or syntagms with a subordinate noun, but which designate a cohyponym of the subordinate as in *roble australiano* 'Grevillea robusta' vs. *roble* 'Quercus robur', may also lead to the generalization of the originally subordinate head component, in this case *roble*, a case discussed below. The process of generalization proceeds very slowly and may vary according to the degree of entrenchment of the different vertical senses (cf. Langacker 1987, 1: 373–376). For instance the superordinate *cow* (not specified for sex) is less established than the sex-indifferent *dog*, as opposed to *dog* meaning 'male dog' as Lyons (1977, 1: 309) shows in the different acceptability of ?*That cow is a bull* and *that dog is a bitch*.

These cases of generalization and specialization between the basic level and the subordinate level, often involving prototypes, are cases of natural semantic change not triggered by external conscious attempts to establish new terms. The results are concrete nouns representing good simple gestalts, in particular specialization representing a case of lexicalization comparable to the concretization of abstract nouns, an equally frequent type of lexicalization far more systematically studied than the taxonomic changes described here (cf. Mihatsch 2006: 16–23, 2009).

14.3.1.1.3 Generalization of basic-level nouns

Cases of *generalization* above the basic level are less straightforward, since here the good gestalt of the basic level is given up and the composite character of superordinates combining several basic-level concepts is not morphologically reflected in the emerging lexical unit. In many of these cases of generalization above the basic level learned influence is very probable (cf. Berlin 1992: 194–195; Berlin 1972: 59), as with the recent Quechua (Cochabamba) noun *sach'a* 'plant' from *sach'a* 'tree' (Lefebvre 1972: 50, cited in Berlin 1992: 195) or Saami *rassi* 'herbaceous plant' (< Norwegian *gress* 'grass') sometimes used as a more general noun meaning 'plant' (Anderson 1986: 212), or in Kirwinian and Hanunóo, where nouns designating trees are in some contexts used with the meaning 'plant' (Conklin 1954 and Malinowski 1935, cited in Berlin 1972: 78). Similarly, in Europe, Albertus Magnus became aware of the kingdom Plantae and created the new meaning of the Latin noun *planta*, which originally meant 'sapling' (Glare 1968–1982), since Latin did not have a noun meaning 'plant'. This is the source of the learned noun Fr. *plante* 'plant' borrowed in the 16th century (Rey 1998) and the semilearned Spanish noun *planta*, attested since the 15th century (Corominas and Pascual 1980–1991). The French learned synonym *végétal* appears around 1600, the Spanish equivalent is regularly documented in the 15th century, after a short appearance as hapax legomenon (Corominas and Pascual 1980–1991 ; Rey 1998). Learned influence can also be observed in other domains on superordinate level, for processes involved in the creation of terminology and the vernacularization of these terms see Mihatsch (2004, 2006: chapter 4).

Another rather colloquial type of semantic generalization of basic-level nouns involves frames. One basic-level concept may in some specific cases represent all possible concepts of the frame, a case of pars pro toto. For instance in the frame 'washing up' the Sp. *plato* 'dish' in *platos* 'dirty dishes' (note the parallel development in English and Spanish) may be used as a collective superordinate, thus involving a process of generalization from plate to tableware as well as a process of semantic enrichment in the context of the frame 'washing up'. Since in this frame visual differences need not be taken into account, one exemplary element is enough to present the whole category within this frame.

14.3.1.1.4 Specialization of superordinate-level nouns

As shown above, although basic-level nouns are cognitively primary, they may be linguistically derived. They may not only be derived from concepts outside the hierarchy or subordinates, but also from superordinates. The process leading from the emergence of a superordinate term to its specialization as a basic-level term is very intricate and follows a typical cross-linguistically observable sequence of semantic changes.

In many cases superordinates start out as learned terms. However, superordinates may also arise in everyday language, first as functional or abstract nouns without a semantic relation with basic-level nouns such as 'mouvable property' and become collectives such as *furniture* in the course of lexicalization. As shown in Mihatsch (2006: 115–127, 2007a) there is a general path from such abstract nouns to group collectives (following Leisi's terminology [1971: 31–32], see Mihatsch [2015a] for morphological and semantic properties of collectives). Group collectives are based on contiguity relations as in 'furniture/equipment of a flat', which may become further lexicalized to what Leisi calls "generic nouns", or, more recently, object mass nouns, i.e. mass nouns referring to objects (see Chierchia 1998, Rothstein 2010), rather based on similarity relations such as *cattle* as opposed to *herd* or *furniture* as in *furniture shop*, not requiring a frame any longer, but referring to more homogeneous items and not necessarily, but preferentially, to a plurality of referents. At that stage we often observe the emergence of pluraliatantum as in *clothes* which reflect the preferential reference to a plurality of items and the conjunction of several basic-level items (thus corresponding to a sort plural), which in turn may lead to count hyperonyms in a few cases as with

Fr. *meuble*, which started as a noun meaning 'movable property' and now means 'piece of furniture' (Rey 1998). Again, the steps from functional nouns to group collectives and from group collectives to generic nouns are cases of lexicalization leading to simpler more stable concrete gestalts. However, the last step leading from a generic noun to a count hyperonym is highly marked and in my opinion triggered by the grammatical system, i.e. the prevailing count nouns designating simple objects, and the Western model of strict taxonomic organization based on logical inclusion via learned influence. The directionality of these processes is suspended when the emerging count hyperonyms disappear or are replaced by pluraliatantum. This rather seems to be a natural semantic change whereby a simpler gestalt asserts itself again, since the plural form reflects the composite conceptual representation combining several basic-level concepts. Therefore, as shown in Mihatsch (2006: 136–148) superordinate count nouns are diachronically very unstable and tend to disappear. However, not only the remotivation via plural forms, but also specialization may again lead to cognitively more basic lexical units by reducing the complex conceptual make-up to one simple gestalt, as in the case of Vulgar Latin *vĭrdĭa* 'greenery' to Sp. *berza* 'cabbage' (Corominas and Pascual 1980–1991), or Eng. *garment* 'piece of clothing' to *garment* 'coat' (Simpson and Weiner [eds.] 2000). Both processes of lexicalization, pluralization and specialization, lead to simpler conceptual representations. They affect everyday collective superordinates as well as originally learned collective or singular count nouns. This explains why Fr. *plante*, Sp. *planta*, Ger. *Pflanze* and Eng. *plant* tend to designate herbaceous plants in everyday language (Wartburg 1922; Moliner 1998; Rey-Debove and Rey [eds.] 1993), corresponding to a life form, i.e. a basic-level concept. The reason why superordinates polygenetically tend to specialize in this way is probably due to the fact that all the analysed languages already had well entrenched nouns for the other important and certainly visually more salient life form 'tree'. Interestingly, in Argentinian Spanish *planta* colloquially designates the basic-level concept tree (Corominas and Pascual 1980–1991), possibly influenced by Italian *pianta* 'tree', as in *pianta di ciliegio* 'Kirschbaum' (Wartburg 1922 sub voce *planta* and *plantare*; Maddalon 1998: 461). The more recent learned terms Sp. *vegetal* and Fr. *végétal* 'plant', which are not yet part of everyday language, do not show such entrenched specialized uses, although some uses point to similar developments (Mihatsch 2006: 187–189). Here we can observe a tendency to be used as cohyponyms of nouns meaning 'tree' even in formal settings as in: *La réglementation en vigueur concernant les arbres et végétaux*. 'The effective regulation concerning trees and plants' (http://plantencyclo.free.fr/sp/nmauric_plantation_reglementation.htm, page last consulted on the 6th of November 2012). The equivalent English *vegetable* was first used in the learned sense of 'plant' in the 16th century and is now used in the specialized meaning 'edible plant' (Simpson and Weiner [eds.] 2000).

All in all semantic motivation founded on vertical polysemy can be diachronically very stable, for instance Latin *herba* was already polysemous, meaning 'grass' and, very commonly 'herbaceous plant' as a cohyponym of *arbor* 'tree' and (more marginally) meaning 'plant' (Glare 1968–1982). This polysemy persists in French *herbe* and Spanish *hierba* (Walde and Hofmann 1938–1965 sub voce *herba*; Moliner 1998; Rey-Debove and Rey [eds.] 1993).

Specialization as a natural lexical change leading to a conceptual simplification to basic-level concepts is often accompanied by sound changes indicating integration into the everyday language. Thus we tend to find parallels between a vernacular semantics reflecting basic-level preference and vernacular phonology. Latin *planta* 'sapling' enters as a botanical term meaning 'plant' in Medieval Latin, preserved in this sense in Sp. *planta* and Fr. *plante* or It. *pianta*, while the everyday nouns Sp. *llanta* 'cabbage', Venetian *piantela*, *pianton* 'poplar or willow seedling', Lombardian *pianta* 'tree' (also in Standard Italian!) and other dialectal variants (Wartburg 1922 sub voce *planta* and *plantare*; Maddalon 1998: 461) show semantic specialization and a greater degree of phonological adaptation to the respective vernacular. All in all we can see two opposed tendencies, generalization above the basic level triggered by learned influence and the need to create superordinate terms and specialization to the basic level triggered by integration into the vernacular lexicon and the cognitive attraction of the basic level.

14.3.1.2 Horizontal shifts

Within taxonomies, horizontal relations are just as important for the speakers as vertical ones, as different cohyponymic motivation relations show. They may even be more important than is typically suspected. Logically, *cohyponymy* is more complex than hyponymy, since cohyponyms possess differing traits on top of common traits corresponding to their hyperonym, while hyponymy shows logically straightforward intensional and extensional inclusion relations. Thus in order to detect cohyponymy, at least according to feature-based approaches, speakers would first determine a common superordinate, then the differing traits. From this perspective cohyponymy appears to be a relation derived from hyponymy, a by-product, so to speak, and this maybe explains why it is less studied and generally underestimated in lexicology. From a cognitive perspective (in particular prototype semantics) the picture is quite different. As I have shown, basic-level imagery determines the conceptual representation of the different levels of generalization. From this perspective cohyponymy is a similarity relation within one domain and is therefore less complex than vertical relations, at least on the basic level and below. Here, the similarity is directly established on the basis of a global (visual) comparison of two or more gestalts. This explains why, unlike hyponymy, cohyponymy is more robust in word association tests, slips of the tongue, and errors due to aphasia (Aitchison 2003: 86–99; Leuninger 1986: 231–232, 237; Miller and Johnson-Laird 1976: 248–249). Children tend to reinterpret hyponymy as cohyponymy (Markman, Horton, and McLanahan 1980: 229). From a diachronic perspective cohyponymic shifts and the emerging semantic motivation relations seem to occur mainly between relatively similar subordinate items, while shifts transcending a basic-level domain have to be interpreted as metaphors. Cohyponymic shifts may derive less central nouns from cohyponymic prototypes. However, according to Blank (1997: 207) cohyponymic meaning change is not very frequent, which is certainly due to the fact that such shifts and the resulting polysemy may cause communication problems (Blank 1997: 207, 217). However, shifts on these levels do appear when nouns are applied to referents in new environments, which does not lead to the mentioned communication problem as in the case of Peninsular Spanish *alerce* 'larch' acquiring the New World meaning 'Fitzroya patagonica', a Southern Chilean cypress species (Seibert 1996: 219) or *roble* 'oak' with the New World meaning 'Nothofagus obliqua' (Seibert 1996: 211). Similar processes of cohyponymic shifts in combination with frame shifts can be observed with many other nouns on genus level such as English *oak* (Simpson and Weiner [eds.] 2000). Many such cohyponymic shifts are also attested for Indo-European, for instance Doric Greek *phagós* 'oak', Old Russian *buz* 'elder', Latin *fagus* 'beech' and many others, all supposedly cognates related to ie. *$bh\bar{a}gó$-s*, probably 'beech' (Kronasser 1952: 106, cited in Blank 1997: 212). An anonymous reviewer very generously points out a wealth of analogous examples from Indo-European languages (Buck 1949: 529–530) as well as Turkic languages (Tenishev and Dydo [eds.] 2006: 40–425), interestingly, the shifts are always within one domain, for instance in the domain of fruit trees or shrubs or trees which do not produce edible fruit (Tenishev and Dydo [eds.] 2006: 413).

To conclude this section, semantic motivation arising from semantic change reveals conceptual links within lexical hierarchies which point to a highly salient basic level, which mainly shows in processes of generalization and specialization resulting in vertical polysemy, in some cases cohyponymic shifts. Both subordinate and superordinate-level nouns conceptually depend on basic-level concepts.

14.3.2 Morphological motivation

As I have argued so far, semantic motivation shows in many cases motivation relations triggered by semantic change within taxonomies, which are all closely linked to the basic level and the prototype. However, perhaps more wide-spread is taxonomy-internal motivation which also reflects in morphological relations. This may be related to the avoidance of communication problems by the more explicit word-formation products and the avoidance of semantic violations in the course of change. Perhaps more importantly, pure semantic change may usually only produce one derived expression within a taxonomy, while word formation may produce many formally different expressions without leading to communication problems.

14.3.2.1 Endocentric compounds and the strange case of cohyponymic intrusion

Morphological complexity tends to signal greater semantic complexity, this is the case with compound subordinate terms in comparison with simplex basic-level terms. The derivation of subordinate nouns from basic-level nouns seems particularly straightforward. However, again the picture is more complex than it seems at first glance and several sub-cases have to be distinguished, first of all, the degree of (proto-)typicality of the subordinates. While prototypes are often linked to the basic level via polysemy and semantic change (shown in Mihatsch 2006: 61–63), very atypical marginal items do not seem to be morphologically and semantically closely linked to basic-level nouns. It is interesting to note that Hoffmann and Kämpf (1985) observe that both highly typical and very atypical referents of a basic concept tend to be designated by subordinate terms, while more central, but not prototypical items (for instance referents cognitively similar to the prototype but less commonly experienced) tend to be referred to by basic-level nouns, particularly in tasks under time pressure (Hoffmann and Kämpf 1985: 225). Further studies will have to show in how far the preference for subordinate naming of typical referents may lead to the independent naming of prototypes, or, if this is not the case, why not.

This might explain why we find endocentric compounds or lexicalized syntagms, usually with life-form or salient genus level nouns (according to Berlin 1992) or basic-level nouns (according to Rosch at al. 1976) as heads (Mihatsch 2006: 63), with "exotic" overseas plants which are visually rather prototypical such as Fr. *arbre à pain* 'Artocarpus altilis' (Rey-Debove and Rey [eds.] 1993 sub voce *arbre*), or Sp. *árbol de la canela* 'Cinnamomum zeylanicum' (Moliner 1998 sub voce *árbol*) and many others (see the lists in http://fr.wikipedia.org/wiki/ Liste_des_plantes_appel%C3%A9es_arbres, and Sánchez de Lorenzo-Cáceres). In American Spanish we find syntagms with Am. Sp. *palo* 'pole/tree/shrub' (Moliner 1998 sub voce *palo*), as in *palo santo* 'Bulnesia sarmientoi', literally 'holy stick/tree' (Seibert 1996: 96–99), occasionally also occurring in isolation with the meaning 'tree'. Morphological motivation here serves as a memory aid for rather unfamiliar words. Chaffin (1997) shows that the linguistic form is particularly important for the activation of new or unfamiliar words, while familiar words are rather activated via their semantics.

Basic-level life-form nouns meaning 'herbaceous plant' such as Sp. *hierba* or Ger. *Kraut* also appear in many compounds and lexicalized syntagms designating common European plants such as Sp. *hierbabuena* 'mint' (literally 'good herb') (also see Moliner 1998 sub voce *hierba* for a long list of further lexicalized syntagms). In German we find many compounds such as *Heidekraut* 'Erica' or *Scharbockskraut* 'Ficaria verna'. The colloquial more specific meaning of the originally learned Ger. *Pflanze*, Eng. *plant*, Fr. *plante* and Sp. *planta* as in *eggplant* or Sp. *planta de Navidad* 'Euphorbia pulcherrima' seem to appear more often with overseas plants, certainly related to the learned origins of these heads and the relative recency of these compounds – just like the syntagms based on nouns meaning 'tree', while the more familiar European tree nouns are rather derivations, as shown below. Endocentric compounds with superordinates above the basic level are restricted to vernacularized scientific terms as in *Samenpflanze(n)* or *seed plants*.

Since in biological taxonomies expertise can render subordinate levels more salient and cognitively holistic, such endocentric compounds or syntagms can also be found below the life-form level. While Latin had simplex nouns for different deciduous or evergreen oak species, such as *īlex* 'Quercus ilex', *sūber* 'Quercus suber', in French there are many lexicalized syntagms containing *chêne*, such as *chêne vert* (beside the simplex *yeuse*) 'Quercus ilex', (*chêne*) *rouvre* 'Quercus petraea', *chêne-liège* 'Quercus suber' (Rey-Debove and Rey [eds.] 1993 sub voce *chêne*). The corresponding Spanish *roble* is more specific, since it is restricted to the deciduous species of the genus Quercus as in Sp. *roble albar* 'Quercus petraea' (Moliner 1998 sub voce *roble*), while the evergreen oaks, which are more widespread in Spain than in France, have opaque nouns such as *encina*, *carrasca* 'Quercus ilex', *quejigo* 'Quercus faginea', *coscoja*, *chaparro*, 'Quercus coccifera', *alcornoque* 'Quercus suber'.

As in the case of the purely semantic motivation relations discussed above, cohyponymic relations accompanied by morphological motivation do exist, although they tend to get overlooked in the literature on compounding. In these cases the compounds are not endocentric since what appears to be the head is really a cohyponym of the whole complex expression. It is not always easy to distinguish between strictly endocentric compounds and cohyponymic motivation, the closer to the prototype the derived concept is the more plausible is a cohyponymic motivation relation. The fact that many cases seem to be ambiguous between a hyponymic and a cohyponymic motivation relation is due to the tendency of meaning generalization of the head within such complex nouns. This may lead to implicit hyperonyms (cf. Langacker 1987: 373–376) and a resulting vertical polysemy, semantically arising from the creation of a more general category comprising the base category and the cohyponymic category designated by the compound. Such hyperonyms often only exist in the complex nouns, but not in isolation. When wheat and sorghum were introduced in Tzeltal the noun meaning 'wheat' was derived from *?išim* 'corn' namely *kašlan ?išim* 'Castilian corn', similarly Sorghum *móro ?išim* 'Moors corn'. As a consequence *?išim*, originally meaning 'corn' underwent meaning generalization to 'cereal' (Berlin 1972: 74–75). Thus when new cohyponyms are derived from a prototype or a more familiar cohyponym the noun designating the prototype may thus get semantically "stretched". This effect may also be related to the strong tendency to interpret such compounds as endocentric compounds, probably due to our Western taxonomic bias, which explains why the coordination *coats and macs*, but not **coats and raincoats* is acceptable, at least according to Rohdenburg (1988: 295).

One might also argue that the above examples with French *chêne* are such cohyponymic compounds, since the simplex *chêne* is also used with the meaning 'decidous species of the genus Quercus' as in *Les forêts sont de chênes et yeuses* (Christophe de Villeneuve 1821: 149, also see Simpson and Weiner [eds.] 2000 sub voce *oak*, see the first sense [a] for a similar pattern). More obvious cases with 'oak' are cohyponymic compounds transcending the genus Quercus such as Sp. *roble australiano* or Fr. *chêne d'Australie* 'Grevillea robusta' (literally 'Australian oak').

Typically, learned vernacular botanical plant names are based on such cohyponymic nominal elements, combined with modifiers overtly expressing a deviation. Thus *acebo* 'Ilex aquifolium' and *falso acebo* (or *acebo chino*) 'Osmanthus heterophyllus' belong to different families (Sánchez de Lorenzo-Cáceres). Often we find motivation pairs of wild and domesticated species as in Sp. *higo* 'fig tree' and *cabrahígo* 'wild fig tree'. Sometimes the originally more familiar base is modified in analogy with the derived expressions as in *higo común* 'common fig tree'.

Such cohyponymic morphological motivation relations are more common than might be expected, not only in Romance and Germanic languages (see Mihatsch 2006: 69–70 for more cases and more detailed analyses).

14.3.2.2 Co-compounds

Direct morphological motivation relations between superordinate and basic-level lexemes are harder to find, at least in Germanic and Romance languages. While superordinates tend to be morphologically more complex than basic-level lexemes "[t]he linguistic features of the higher level terms are somewhat more difficult to explain in iconic terms" (Croft 2003: 220). As shown above many superordinates are morphologically complex function nouns, without a morphological relation within the hierarchy. In fact, we would expect links with basic-level nouns, in which superordinates are conceptually anchored according to the psycholinguictic studies presented above. However, we do find occasional syntagms consisting of two representative basic-level items in Romance and Germanic languages, thus reflecting the composite nature of everyday superordinates as in Latin *arbor et herba* 'tree and grass/herbaceous plant' (Wartburg 1922 sub voce *planta*; Ullmann 1963: 181, cited in Berlin 1992: 195). In everyday language such expressions are often preferred to simplex superordinates (Aitchison 2003: 96). However in certain languages a special type of compound reflects exactly this motivation relation, namely co-ordinative compounds, rather rare in Indo-European languages, widespread in East and Southeast Asia (Wälchli 2005: 191) and other languages. In many domains, both artefacts and biological entities superordinates are expressed by this specific type of compound. In the plant domain life form nouns are combined:

(1) Mandarin *huā-mù* flower+tree ='vegetation'
    (Li and Thompson 1981: 50)

(2) Tzeltal *te'ak'* tree+vine ='vegetation'
    (Berlin 1992: 195)

(3) Vietnamese *cây-cỏ* tree-plant/grass ='vegetation'
    (Thompson 1965: 129)

Such collectives in a wider sense can be both group collectives or generic nouns/object mass nouns (cf. Wälchli 2005: 139) and show a similar preference for plural reference as the collective superordinates discussed above (Wälchli 2005: 152). Thus the type of semantic hierarchical motivation seems to be universal or at least cross-linguistically very wide spread, while the formal type of motivation relation depends on the morphological means of each particular language.

Again, motivation relations show the conceptual make-up of lexical hierarchies. Like in the case of purely semantic motivation compounding shows strong dependency relations between basic-level and both subordinate and superordinate-level nouns. However, here, morphological relations make these links more explicit, which is particularly striking in the case of co-compounds. Furthermore, endocentric compounds seem to specialize in the lexicalization of not too common and neither prototypical nor marginal subordinate concepts, thus serving as a memory aid.

14.3.2.3 Derivational motivation relations in lexical hierarchies

As we have seen compounding reflects perceptual cognitive semantic motivation relations in a far more complex and intriguing way than might be expected. One might therefore ask how far derivation processes may show similar motivation relations, despite the formal and semantic differences between typical cases of compounding and typical cases of derivation. While compounds and lexicalized syntagms inherit rather specific lexical semantic information from their components, derivational affixes are much more general in meaning. However, even semantically very general affixes may again become anchored in more specific domains, when series of derived expressions cluster in one domain and get lexicalized to some extent in lexicalization patterns (Laca 2001: 1222), this is the case of Fr. *-ier* and Sp. *-al*, *-o* for designations of trees. Such patterns represent an intermediate step between the more abstract word formation meaning and the meaning of the individual derived expression and may then reflect relations between the basic level and other levels, as will be discussed in the following section.

14.3.2.3.1 Vertical derivation relations and special function of grammatical gender

The correlation between derivational morphology and the role of the basic level in lexical taxonomies has hardly been studied. The following quote still seems to be true except for my own studies, on which this section is founded, and several papers by Hans-Jörg Schmid and Friedrich Ungerer on the relation between word formation and the basic level:

> The theory of categorisation developed in prototype semantics distinguishes three levels of categorisation [...]. Although there is probably some relevant correlation between derivational expression and the non-basic-level status of a category, no studies seem to have been devoted to this question. (Laca 2001: 1224)

As shown above, in English and German many nouns designating trees are endocentric compounds with a head component meaning 'tree', i.e. typically, subordinate nouns are compounds containing basic-level nouns. In the Romance languages nouns designating fruit trees are usually derived from the noun designating the fruit, such as *pommier* 'apple tree' from Fr. *pomme* 'apple', Sp. *manzano* 'apple tree' from *manzana* 'apple' (cf. Koch 1999). Many of these "tree"-suffixes, such as Spanish *-al, -ero* (Rainer 1993: 194, 197, 398, 479, 488–489), French *-ier*, Portuguese *-eira, -eiro* originally served to derive relational adjectives (Pharies 2002: 229–231; also see Rainer 1993: 194, 398, 677). This specialization seems to be a case of a derivational lexicalization pattern, perhaps via a series of syntagms consisting of a relational adjective and a nominal head meaning 'tree' (cf. Pharies 2002: 229–231; Stempel 1959: 262). Interestingly the lexicalization pattern leads to a basic-level affix meaning 'tree/shrub' as with Sp. *-al* as in *almendral* 'almond tree' (Rainer 1993: 398), *-ero* as in *albaricoquero* 'apricot tree' (Rainer 1993: 488), *-o* as in *castaño* 'chestnut tree', (Rainer 1993: 622), fr. *-ier* as in *cérisier* 'cherry tree', Portuguese *-eira* y *-eiro* as in *pereira* 'pear tree' or *medronheiro* 'Arbutus unedo'. A closer look reveals a close relation between the *grammatical gender* of the lifeform nouns and the derivational products in the modern Romance languages, with an interesting diachronic trajectory. The oldest means of deriving tree nouns in Romance languages seems to be gender inversion (Roché 2002: 290) based on the usually feminine nouns designating fruits. This process can still be seen in pairs such as Spanish *manzana* 'apple'/*manzano* 'apple tree', while in Sardinian fruit and tree are designated by the same noun, for instance *pira* 'pear'/'pear tree' (Koch 1999: 342). A trace of gender inversion might also be seen in the masculine French suffix *-ier* for deriving tree nouns, since the prevailingly feminine bases for the derivation of fruit trees have lead to a majority of masculine tree nouns. According to Roché (2002: 289) the masculine suffix is not plausibly due to the masculine gender of French *arbre*, since Latin *arbor* was still feminine when the derivation pattern emerged. In Portuguese we find both feminine and masculine affixes *-eira* and *-eiro* with tree derivations. Here we might have a case of gender preservation of the lexical base as in *medronheiro* 'Arbutus unedo (strawberry tree)' from *medronho* 'the fruit of the strawberry tree' or *ameixieira* 'plum tree' from *ameixa* 'plum', even in the case of more recent formations such as *bananeira* 'banana tree' from *banana* 'banana', or *coqueiro* 'coconut tree' from *coco* 'coconut' (Stempel 1959: 235–236), also with herbaceous plants such as *morangueiro* 'strawberry (plant)' from *morango* 'strawberry (fruit)' (Stempel 1959: 240).

In Spanish the situation seems to be more complex, since both *-ero* and *-era* appear in derived nouns designating plants. A closer look reveals a semantic pattern (cf. Mihatsch 2006: 81, 2008a) as can be shown in the following table from Mihatsch (2008a). The table collects Rainer's examples (Rainer 1993: 476–

480, 485–492), complemented by all the derivations found in Amador (2009), whose data are from dictionary of the Real Academia Española (he consulted the 21st edition from 2001). I have also added derivations found in the database by José Manuel Sánchez de Lorenzo-Cáceres, a selection reflecting Peninsular Spanish derivational products. The base usually designates the fruit or edible part, however, in some cases the base may designate the characteristic shape of the flowers (as in *trompetero* from *trompeta* 'trumpet') and other aspects, usually reflecting contiguity relations (also see Koch 2005: 168, 180–182). In some cases, there are competing derivations, in particular the one in *-o*. I have decided to count those plants which visually resemble trees in size or shape, as trees, including, for instance, the banana tree, which is botanically a herbaceous plant.

Shrubs and herbaceous plants seem to belong to one category according to the derivational pattern reflected by *-ero* and *-era*:

Table 2: Grammatical gender in Spanish plant names containing *-era/-ero*

	Masculine product of derivation	Feminine product of derivation
Tree names derived from a masculine base	*aguacatero* 'avocado tree' *albaricoquero* 'apricot tree' *alberchiguero* 'apricot tree' *alcanforero* 'camphor tree' *asarero* 'cherry laurel' *avuguero* 'pear tree' *bananero* 'banana' *cafetero* 'coffee' *caquilero* 'kaki' *clavero* 'clove tree' *cocotero* 'coconut palm/tree' *duraznero* 'peach tree' *jabonero* 'golden-rain tree' *jazminero* 'jasmine' *jinjolero* 'jujuba' *melocotonero* 'peach tree' *membrillero* 'quince' *nisperero* 'kumquat' *nispolero* 'medlar' *pistachero* 'pistacio tree' *platanero* 'banana tree' *tulipero* 'tulip tree'	*datilera* 'date palm' *higuera* 'fig tree' *pelambrera de Florida* 'Florida Thatch Palm' (< *pelambre* m./f.)

Table 2 (continued)

	Masculine product of derivation	Feminine product of derivation
Shrub or herbaceous plant names der. from a masc. base	*algodonero* 'cotton' *ajonjero* 'atractylis/thistle'	*ajonjera* 'atractylis/thistle' *berrera* 'cutleaf water parsnip' *cambutera* 'cardinal vine' *coguilera* '(lardi-)zabala tree' *chayotera* 'chayote' *cheflera* 'umbrella tree' *chumbera* 'prickly pear' *esparraguera* 'aparagus' *platanera* 'banana' *tomatera* 'tomato'
Tree names derived from a fem. base	*algarrobero* 'locust tree' *almendrero* 'almond tree' *azamboero* 'quince' *bananero* 'banana plant' *canelero* 'cinnamon tree' *cascarillero* 'cascarilla' *castañero* 'chesnut' *ciruelero* 'plum tree' *garrofer* 'carob tree' *guayabero* 'guava' *limero* 'lime tree' *manzanero* 'apple tree' *naranjero* 'orange tree' *papayero* 'papaya' *trompetero* 'angle's trumpet'	*almendrera* 'almond tree' *brevera* 'fig tree' *cidrera* 'citron' *manzanera* 'apple tree' *morera* 'mulberry tree' *noguera* 'walnut tree' *pelambrera* de *Florida* 'Florida Thatch Palm' (< *pelambre* m./f.)
Shrub or herbaceous plant names der. from a masc. base	*grosellero* 'currant bush' *pimentero* 'pepper (plant)'	*alcachofera* 'artichoke' *alcaparrera* 'caper' *algarrobera* 'locust tree' *arvejera* 'vetch' *avellanera* 'hazel' *calabacera* 'pumpkin' *estrelladera* '(tree) pellitory' *fresera* 'wild strawberry' *tunera* 'prickly pear'

As can be seen in the table above neither gender inversion nor gender preservation prevail. However, if we look at the distribution of the two columns we can detect a certain tendency: The feminine suffix *-era* produces mostly nouns which designate herbaceous plants[5] and shrubs, while -*ero* produces nouns designating trees or plants resembling trees. In other words, everyday language does not make discrete botanical distinctions, here rough perceptual information determines categorization. Some exceptions may be vestiges of an older system, for instance *higuera* 'fig tree' probably from Lat. *ficaria arbor,* 'fig.ADJ.FEM tree', which incidentally often resembles a shrub or small tree (analogously, *brevera*, a fig variety), as well as *noguera* from *nucaria arbor* 'nut.ADJ.FEM tree' (Moliner 1998; cf. Stempel 1959: 263). In the case of *datilera* 'date palm' the feminine gender might be based on the hyperonym *palmera*, a rather atypical tree (cf. English *date-palm*), in an analogous fashion *pelambrera de Florida* 'Thrinax floridana' (also meaning 'mop of hair', which may point to an alternative explanation of the feminine gender via metaphor), a kind of palm tree. In the case of *cidrera* 'Aloysa riphylla' the fact that it grows as a shrub might contribute to the adoption of the feminine gender. Nouns ending in -*ero* in table 1 designate trees, except for *algodonero* 'cotton/Gossypium' and *grosellero* 'Ribes rubrum', which are shrubs (Kunkel 1984: 171) and *pimentero* 'Piper', which is a large climber (Kunkel 1984: 279). *Bananero* and *platanero* 'banana tree' designate a herbaceous plant, but one resembling trees in shape and height, this conceptualization also shows in *banana-tree* (cf. Simpson and Weiner [eds.] 2000, sub voce *tree*). *Ajonjero* is probably an ellipsis of *cardo ajonjero*, designating several kinds of thistle. The older feminine derivation *olivera* 'olive tree' has now been replaced by the masculine *olivo* (Pharies 2002: 229–231). *Morera* 'mulberry tree' grows as small trees or shrubs (Kunkel 1984: 239), which might explain the feminine gender.

All in all the choice of the formation type prevailing in different Romance languages seems to show a correlation between the grammatical gender of the noun designating the life form tree and the grammatical gender of the derivational products. In Latin *arbor* 'tree' was a feminine noun, as it still is in Portuguese and in Sardinian (in Puddu 2000–2012, sub voce *àlbere*, both genders are mentioned). Portuguese derives tree nouns with both -*eira* and -*eiro* via gender preservation. Since fruit nouns are often feminine, the resulting tree nouns are often feminine, too, thus reflecting the link to feminine *árvore* 'tree' (also see Geiger 1966: 178 who assumes a direct link). This is also true for Sardinian, which also has gender preservation as in *pira* 'pear, pear tree' combined with conversion and a feminine[6] noun meaning tree (Geiger 1966: 180; Koch 1999: 342; Roché 2002: 284).

---

5 It is not always possible to distinguish between suffixation and ellipses as in (*hierba*) *jabonera* 'Saponaria officinalis', which might trigger the entrenchment of this pattern (also see Diccionario Manual e Ilustrado de la Lengua Española 1989, s.v. *hierba*).
6 According to the DLS both genders are possible.

Spanish *árbol* 'tree' as well as Fr. *arbre* 'tree' and It. *albero* are masculine, as in most other Romance languages, although feminine forms are still attested in the Middle Ages and some time beyond (Pötters 1970: 211; Roché 1997: 275). As shown in table 2, Spanish tends to derive fruit-tree nouns on the basis of the masculine suffix *–ero*. French has opted for the masculine suffix *-ier*. Italian has gender inversion with mostly masculine derivations (*pera* 'pear' > *pero* 'pear tree'),

This confirms Zubin and Köpcke's (1986) observation that on the basic level, gender serves to differentiate nouns (Zubin and Köpcke 1986: 148, 173), while basic-level and subordinate-level nouns often share the grammatical gender (cf. Zubin and Köpcke 1986: 158). Thus we observe a motivation relation indirectly reflecting the hyponymic relation between the basic and the subordinate level via derivational series of cohyponyms and a common gender.

14.3.2.3.2 Cohyponymic derivation

As I have shown above, vertical relations may indirectly be seen in derivation and gender patterns, although not via a direct motivational link between the basic-level noun and its subordinate nouns. Perhaps less frequent but also reflecting motivation relations are derivation relations leading to direct motivation between cohyponyms, which may also be witnessed on seemingly endocentric compounds, as discussed above. Here we might also expect strong links between prototype and less prototypical or central members on subordinate level. Certain suffixes seem to be specialized in such similarity relations (or rather deviation relations) meaning "no real X" (Delhay (1996: 199) as is the case of French *-ass*), as in *cognasse* 'wild quince' (from *coing* 'quince') (Delhay 1996: 349), but we also find diminutive suffixes or functionally equivalent adjectives such as Fr. *petit* 'small' as in *petit if/ivette* 'Ajuga chamaepitys', literally 'small yew', (Delhay 1996: 181). Since diminutives are based on comparisons, the base and its product are automatically on the same level of generalization.[7] Such suffixes are most productive on the subordinate level.

---

[7] An anonymous reviewer suggests the diminutive *arbolito* 'fresh water plant Ammania' for a case of specialization based on the diminutive (Zaragoza Larios, 5). I would rather classify this case as a metaphor, although one within the plant taxonomy, since the water plant is herbaceous, but resembles a tree in its shape.

14.3.3 Remotivation

Motivation relations can also emerge independently of the formation of new words – as cases of *remotivation* (see Harnisch 2010; Seebold 1999). Remotivation or secondary motivation (Fill 2004: 1618) does not produce new lexical units with a new meaning derived from the meaning of its components, but rather leads to an explicitation of an existing simplex. It is thus opposed to the common fate of morphologically transparent units, i.e. lexicalization (see Mihatsch 2006: 16–23, 2009), which leads to the loss of morphological compositionality. The best known and most frequently analysed type of remotivation is folk etymology (see Bernhard 2004). In the case of folk etymology a generally opaque lexeme is analysed as a morphologically complex form. Here some cases of anchoring in the basic level are attested, as in *Trampeltier* (<*Dromedar* 'dromedary'), or *Murmeltier* 'marmot' (< *murmuntin* < Lat. *murem montis* 'mountain mouse'), in both cases the last syllable is remotivated as *Tier* in the life form sense of 'mammal'. Lexical units that can be affected by folk etymology are usually not morphologically transparent for the average speaker, are phonologically complex and long enough to be analysed and they need segments that are phonologically and semantically similar to existing lexical units, although the semantic similarity can be quite far-fetched in many cases. The result is either a formal and/or a semantic remotivation (Harnisch 2010: 7; Fill 2004: 1617). All in all folk etymology is strongly restricted due to the formal and semantic conditions that have to be fulfilled and seems to be a consequence of language comprehension processes of unfamiliar lexical items, which, by decomposition, can be linked to known familiar elements and thus help memorization (Bernhard 2004: 93). Results from comprehension tasks show that, for instance, morphological segmentation is triggered by any input, even non words, if the segments superficially resemble inflection morphemes (Marslen-Wilson 2007: 180, 184–185).

Far more frequent although less studied is morphological remotivation by addition of segments (see the classifications in Harnisch 2010: 19; Fill 2004: 1618). Such cases used to be somewhat hidden in works on word formation, linguistic change and, from a normative perspective, in style manuals (see Mihatsch and Steinberg 2011: 411 for an overview). Only recently has there been a systematic interest in such cases (see Harnisch 2010 for a representative up-to-date collection of papers on remotivation in the lexicon and in grammar). Mihatsch and Steinberg (2011) show morphological remotivation in the domain of body parts, for instance compounds such as *eyebrow* that are synonymous with one of their components, in this case *brow*, showing the strong underlying part-whole and part-part relations in the domain of body parts. In domains with a stronger hierarchical organization such as the domains of plants and animals remotivation rather reflects taxonomic relations. Corbin and Corbin (1991: 62) call this effect "paradigmatic integration", a phenomenon already noted by Hermann Paul:

> Die Tendenz, isoliert stehende und darum fremdartige Wörter an geläufige Sprachelemente anzuknüpfen, zeigt sich auch darin, dass dieselben häufig gestützt werden durch Zusammensetzung mit einer allgemeinen Gattungsbezeichnung... (Paul [1880] 1995: 222)

Again the basic level determines these relations. Remotivation produces parallel effects to the ones discussed in the preceding sections, since in most cases the added "redundant" hyperonyms are basic-level terms, i.e. terms on the level of life form as in English *oak tree, birch tree, elm tree, palm tree, beech tree* (Simpson and Weiner [eds.] 2000; Faiss 1978: 42) as well as German *Lorbaum* 'laurel tree', *Buchsbaum* 'box tree' (Paul [1880] 1995: 222), but also with an added noun *Kraut* meaning 'herbaceous plant' as in *Bilsenkraut* 'Hyoscyamus', *Farnkraut* 'fern' among others (Paul [1880] 1995: 222). Below the life form level we find *chesne yeuse*, literally 'holm-oak oak' (attested in 1564, cf. Rey 1998). Such patterns are also very common with loanwords and may be more or less entrenched. Ad-hoc uses reflecting this pattern are not hard to come by, even in specialized texts, see, for instance the Mapudungun loan *ñire* remotivated as *árbol de ñire* 'Nothofagus antarctica' on a governmental website (http://www2.medioambiente.gov.ar/sian/scruz/flora/enfermed.htm, page last consulted on the 7th of November 2012).

It is hardly surprising that secondary motivation is not restricted to compounding. The tree affixes discussed above also appear as signs of secondary motivation as in Fr. *palmier* 'palm tree' (< *palme* 'palm tree'), in an analogous fashion Sp. *palmera*, in Fr. *peuplier* 'poplar'[8], *robinier* 'Robinia tree' (Rey 1998), Sp. *membrillero* 'quince tree' (Stempel 1959: 248), Port. *pinheiro* 'pine tree', *salgueiro* 'willow tree' and *ulmeiro* 'elm tree' (Pötters 1970: 217–218).

The lexicalization pattern of Spanish *-ero* in tree names and *-era* in names of shrub and herbaceous plants also shows in remotivated formations, thus *-era* redundantly appears with herbaceous plants (Rainer 1993: 479) such as *brecolera* 'Broccoli', *cambronera* 'Lycium barbarum', *candilera* 'Phlomis lychnitis', *junquera* 'Juncus', *mimbrera* 'willow tree' (often cultivated as a shrub, which may explain the feminine form). Further examples can be easily found with loanwords in the case of *jambolero* 'Eugenia jambos' (Sánchez de Lorenzo-Cáceres) and many other tree nouns (Corbin and Corbin 1991: 62; Laca 2001: 1217, 1221; Rainer 1993: 479; Mihatsch 2007b, 2008a for more cases).

---

8 Eng. *poplar* tree is historically doubly remotivated, it is a loan of the remotivated Old French noun *poplier* with an additional redundant head *tree* (OED).

Loanwords or exocentric compounds may also be hierarchically integrated by adopting the grammatical gender of the basic-level hyperonym (Rainer and Varela 1992: 123), Ambadiang (1999: 4853) assumes that the stronger the hyponymic link the clearer the semantic gender assignment. This can be seen in particular with new world trees named on the basis of loans from indigenous languages, usually masculine in Spanish such as Sp. *ñire* 'Nothofagus antarctica', *raulí* 'Nothofagus procera', *ñapindá* 'Acacia tucumanensis', (Moliner 1998; Seibert 1996: 211), or in the case of an exocentric compound such as Sp. *quebracho* 'Schinopsis' (< *quebra* + *hacha* 'break + axe'), which unlike some other exocentric compounds does not adopt the feminine gender of the nominal element *hacha*. The gender adaptation can also be observed with learned botanical terms from Latin as they are integrated into everyday language, such as Fr. *conifère* 'conifer', originally a feminine botanical term, now masculine in everyday language (cf. Grevisse and Goosse 1993: 733), while German *Konifere* is feminine although *Baum* 'tree' is masculine. Here the salient subordinates, namely forest trees, which tend to be feminine such as *Kiefer* 'pine tree' and *Tanne* 'fir tree', may explain this tendency. Similar cases of genus adaptation can be observed with herbaceous plants, as predicted by Zubin and Köpcke (1986) with a grammatical gender contrasting with the other important life form *tree*, at least in Spanish, French and Italian. The life form nouns are feminine in the case of Sp. *hierba* and *planta* (in the colloquial sense) as well as Fr. *herbe* and *plante* (in the colloquial sense), sometimes also in uses of the feminine nouns Fr. *fleur*, Sp. *flor* or Ger. *Blume* 'flower'. Many exocentric formations in this domain are also feminine, such as *pegamoscas* 'Ononis natrix', literally 'sticks flies' and many others (Bustos Gisbert 1986: 241; Rainer 1993: 263). The same is true for loans designating herbaceous plants such as Fr. *anémone* 'anemone' (Roché 1997: 36–37, 93, 114). Plausibly, the gender of the life form noun meaning 'tree' might also be influenced by the equally salient genus level, thus the motivation relation may be bidirectional. In Spanish the feminine Latin tree names ending in *-us*, an otherwise typically masculine ending, became masculine, as in *fresno* 'ash', *higo* 'fig', *pino* 'pine' and *tejo* 'yew' (Menéndez Pidal 1925: 178). This also seems to be the case in French with *frêne* 'ash' or *pin* 'pine', (Nyrop 1908: 338) which in turn seem to have influenced cohyponyms of Celtic or Germanic origin such as Fr. *aune* 'alder', *charme* 'hornbeam', *coudre* 'hazel', *saule*, *saus*, 'willow' und *verne* 'alder', which often were still feminine in Old French (Roché 1997: 124). Plausibly the life form nouns Sp. *árbol* and Fr. *arbre* may have adopted the masculine gender under the influence of a whole series of salient hyponyms on genus level and not only due the masculine looking ending *-or* as assumed in Rey 1998 (sub voce *arbre*).

Remotivation is the strongest case in point when it comes to motivation showing conceptual structures, since remotivation serves no other purpose (such as the creation of new lexical items) than reflecting conceptual and lexical relations on the formal level.

14.4 Conclusion

Although this study is based on restricted data – mainly Romance and Germanic languages – and concentrates on one domain, namely plants, it is backed up by analyses of further domains (Mihatsch 2006) and observations from other languages. My analysis may thus point to cross-linguistic cross-domain motivation relations which reveal the conceptual structures underlying folk taxonomies, in particular the importance of the basic level. As the semantic and morphological (re-)motivation relations – comprising semantic change, compounding, derivation, gender patterns – show, the relations are highly complex. The following table gives a summary of the observed motivational patterns within the lexical plant hierarchies analysed above:

Table 3: Overview over conceptual links within plant hierarchies and the relations with motivation types according to my data

	Semantic motivation	Morphological motivation by compounding	Morphological motivation by derivation
cohyponymic shifts between subordinate nouns) (14.3.1.2)	yes ie. *bhāgó-s, 'beech' >> Doric Greek *phagós* 'oak	yes seemingly endocentric compounds *chêne* 'decidous species of the genus Quercus' >> *chêne vert* 'Quercus ilex'	yes Fr. *coing* 'quince' >> *cognasse* 'wild quince'

Table 3 (continued)

	Semantic motivation	Morphological motivation by compounding	Morphological motivation by derivation
Prototype > basic level (14.3.1.1.2)	yes Norwegian *gress* 'grass >> Saami *rassi* 'herbaceous plant'	no	derivational patterns tend to indirectly reflect a maximally schematic implicit basic-level concept (see table 2)
Basic level > prototype (within a frame or in general) (14.3.1.1.1)	yes German *Kraut* 'herbaceous plant' >> Southern German 'cabbage'	no	
Basic level > non-marginal non-prototypical concept (14.3.1.1.1)	no	yes Sp. *árbol* 'tree' >> *árbol de la canela* 'Cinnamomum zeylanicum'	
Basic level > perceptually marginal subordinate concept (14.3.1.1.1)	no	no	
Basic level > superordinate level (14.3.1.1.3)	yes – but related to learned contexts Quechua (Cochabamba) *sach'a* 'tree' >> *sach'a* 'plant'	co-compounds combining two basic-level nouns Tzeltal *te'ak'* tree+vine ='vegetation'	
Superordinate level > basic level (14.3.1.1.4)	yes Fr. *plante* 'plant>> 'herbaceous plants'	no	

This overview shows quite clearly that there are strong bidirectional semantic motivation relations between nouns designating prototypes and the basic level, while relations between the basic level and non-prototypical nouns tend to be morphologically motivated. Motivation seems to be generally non-existent or marginal between the basic level and marginal subordinates.

The motivation relations between the basic level and the superordinate level show interesting restrictions. As for semantic motivation relations, generalization transcending the basic level is restricted to learned contexts and rather conscious creations of scientific terms, while the basic level is an important centre of attraction for specialization in everyday language. However, co-compounds combining several basic-level items are well established in languages with this type of compounding, which perfectly reflects the conceptual dependency of the superordinate level on the basic level. Endocentric compounds for non-prototypical subordinate nouns with basic-level nouns as heads are well established, but not at all with superordinate heads. Perhaps rather unexpectedly, cohyponymic links surface in both semantic and morphological motivation relations.

All in all the salience of the basic level and the prototype are seen very clearly in the motivation relations. However, the picture is indeed much more complex. This complexity is due to several factors. First of all, the basic level is both the center of attraction and expansion, secondly, subordinate levels may acquire cognitive basic-level status, which may lead to vertical shifts below the basic level, while the conceptualization is qualitatively completely different on the superordinate level, which leads to the asymmetries described above. Furthermore, cohyponymic motivation relations turn out to be more important than expected and may lead to subsequent "vertical" shifts. Finally, motivation relations may either be due to natural lexical change or to learned influence, which semantically differ quite significantly. When we study motivation, it is therefore crucial to look at the nature, the directionality and the causes of these relations.

14.5 References

Aitchison, Jean. 2003. *Words in the mind: An introduction to the mental lexicon*, 3rd edn. Oxford: Blackwell.

Amador Rodríguez and Luis Alexis. 2009. *La derivación nominal en español: Nombres de agente, instrumento, lugar y acción*. Frankfurt am Main & Berlin & Bern & Bruxelles & New York & Oxford & Wien: Lang.

Ambadiang, Théophile. 1999. La flexión nominal. Género y número. In Bosque Muñoz, Ignacio and Violeta Demonte (eds.), *Gramática descriptiva de la lengua española*. Vol. 3, I, 4843–4913. Madrid: Espasa Calpe.

Anderson, Myrdene. 1986. Folk natural history: Crossroads of language, culture, and environment. In Peter C. Bjarkman and Victor Raskin (eds.), *The real-world linguist. Linguistic applications in the 1980s*, 185–217. Norwood, New Jersey: ABLEX.

Barsalou, Lawrence W. 1992. *Cognitive psychology. An overview for cognitive scientists.* Hillsdale, New Jersey & Hove: Lawrence Erlbaum.

Berlin, Brent. 1972. Speculations on the growth of ethnobotanical nomenclature. *Language in Society* 1: 51–86.

Berlin, Brent. 1992. *Ethnobiological classification: Principles of categorization of plants and animals in traditional society.* Princeton, New Jersey: Princeton University Press.

Bernhard, Gerald. 2004. Schwierige Wörter, Motivierung und Volksetymologie. In Franz Lebsanft and Martin-Dietrich Gleßgen (eds.) *Historische Semantik in den romanischen Sprachen*, 91–101. Tübingen: Niemeyer.
Blank, Andreas. 1997. *Prinzipien des lexikalischen Bedeutungswandels am Beispiel der romanischen Sprachen*. Tübingen: Niemeyer.
Brown, Roger. 1958. How shall a thing be called? *Psychological Review* 65: 14–21.
Buck, Carl D. 1949. *A Dictionary of selected synonyms in the principal Indo-European languages. A contribution to the history of ideas*. Chicago: University of Chicago Press.
Bustos Gisbert, Eugenio de. 1986. *La composición nominal en español*. Salamanca: Universidad de Salamanca.
Chaffin, Roger. 1997. Associations to unfamiliar words: Learning the meanings of new words. *Memory and Cognition* 25 (2): 203–226.
Chierchia, Gennaro. 1998. Reference to kinds across languages. *Natural Language Semantics* 6: 339–405.
Corbin, Danielle and Pierre Corbin. 1991. Un traitement unifié du suffixe -ier(e). In Danielle Corbin (ed.), *La formation des mots: Structures et interpretations*, 61–145. (Lexique 10.) Lille: Presses universitaires de Lille.
Corominas, Juan and José A. Pascual. 1980–1991. *Diccionario crítico etimológico castellano e hispánico*. 6 Vols. Madrid: Gredos.
Croft, William. 2003. *Typology and universals*, 2nd edn. Cambridge: Cambridge University Press.
Cruse, David Alan. 1986. *Lexical semantics*. Cambridge: Cambridge University Press.
Cruse, David Alan. 2000. *Meaning in language*. Oxford: Oxford University Press (Oxford textbooks in linguistics).
Delhay, Corinne. 1996. *Il était un petit x: Pour une approche nouvelle de la catégorisation dite diminutive*. Paris: Larousse.
Evans, Vyvyan and Melanie Green. 2006. *Cognitive linguistics: An introduction*. Edinburgh: Edinburgh University Press.
Faiss, Klaus. 1978. *Verdunkelte Compounds im Englischen*. Tübingen: Narr.
Fill, Alwin. 2004. Remotivation and reinterpretation. In Geert Booij, Christian Lehmann, Joachim Mudgan, and Stavros Skopeteas (eds.), *Morphology: An international handbook on inflection and word-formation*, 1615–1625. Berlin & New York: Mouton de Gruyter.
Gauthier, Isabel, Michael J. Tarr, Jill Moylan, Adam W. Anderson, Pawel Skudlarski, and John C. Gore. 2000. Does visual subordinate-level categorisation engage the functionally defined fusiform face area? *Cognitive Neuropsychology* 17: 143–163.
Geeraerts, Dirk, Stefan Grondelaers, and Peter Bakema. 1994. *The structure of lexical variation meaning, naming and context*. Berlin & New York: Mouton de Gruyter.
Geiger, Walter E. 1966. 'Fruit', 'fruit tree', and 'grove' in Spanish: A study in derivational patterning. *Romance Philology* 20: 176–186.
Gévaudan, Paul. 1997. La polysémie verticale: Hypothèses, analyses et interprétations. *PhiN* 2: 1–22 (http://www.fu-berlin.de/phin/phin2/p2t1.htm).
Glare, Peter Geoffrey William. 1968–1982. *Oxford Latin dictionary*. Oxford: Clarendon.
Gougenheim, Georges. 1975. *Les mots français dans l'histoire et dans la vie*. Vol. 3. Paris: Picard.
Grevisse Maurice and André Goosse. 1993. *Le bon usage: Grammaire française*, 13th edn. Paris & Louvain-La-Neuve: Duculot.

Guyot, Lucien and Pierre Gibassier. 1960. *Les noms des arbres*. Paris: Presses Universitaires de France.
Harnisch, Rüdiger. 2010. Zu einer Typologie sprachlicher Verstärkungsprozesse. In Rüdiger Harnisch (ed.), *Prozesse sprachlicher Verstärkung: Typen formaler Resegmentierung und semantischer Remotivierung*, 2–23. Berlin & New York: Mouton de Gruyter.
Hoffmann, Joachim and Uwe Kämpf. 1985. Mechanismen der Objektbenennung: Parallele Verarbeitungskaskaden. *Sprache und Kognition* 4: 217–230.
Kleiber, Georges. 1990. *La sémantique du prototype*. Paris: Presses Universitaires de France.
Kluge, Friedrich. 1999. *Kluge Etymologisches Wörterbuch der deutschen Sprache*, 23rd edn. Bearbeitet von Elmar Seebold. Berlin & New York: Mouton de Gruyter.
Koch, Peter. 1996. Le prototype entre signifié, désigné et référent. In Hiltrud Dupuy-Engelhardt (ed.), *Questions de méthode et de délimitation en sémantique lexicale: Actes d'EUROSEM 1994*, 113–135. Reims: Presses Universitaires de Reims.
Koch, Peter. 1999. Tree and fruit: A cognitive-onomasiological approach. *Studi Italiani di Linguistica Teorica ed Applicata* 28 (2): 331–347.
Koch, Peter. 2005. Taxinomie et relations associatives. In Adolfo Murguía (ed.), *Sens et références. Mélanges Georges Kleiber*, 159–191. Tübingen: Narr.
Koptjevskaja-Tamm, Maria, Martine Vanhove, and Peter Koch. 2007. Typological approaches to lexical semantics. *Linguistic Typology* 11: 159–185.
Kunkel, Günther. 1984. *Plants for human consumption*. Königstein: Koeltz.
Laca, Brenda. 2001. Derivation. In Martin Haspelmath, Ekkehard König, Wulf Oesterreicher, and Wolfgang Raible (eds.), *Language typology and language universals: An international handbook*. Vol. 2, 1214–1227. Berlin & New York: Mouton de Gruyter.
Langacker, Ronald W. 1987. *Foundations of cognitive grammar*. Vol. 1: Theoretical prerequisites. Stanford: Stanford University Press.
Leisi, Ernst. 1971. *Der Wortinhalt: Seine Struktur im Deutschen und im Englischen*, 4th edn. Heidelberg: Quelle & Meyer.
Leuninger, Helen. 1986. Mentales Lexikon, Basiskonzepte, Wahrnehmungsalternativen: Neuro- und psycholinguistische Überlegungen. *Linguistische Berichte* 103: 224–251.
Li, Charles N. and Sandra A. Thompson. 1981. *Mandarin Chinese: A functional reference grammar*. Berkeley: University of California Press.
Löbner, Sebastian. 2003. *Semantik: Eine Einführung*. Berlin: Mouton de Gruyter.
Lyons, John. 1977. *Semantics*. Vol. 1. Cambridge & New York & Melbourne: Cambridge University Press.
Maddalon, Marta. 1998. Biotassonomie e categorie cognitive. Proposte di analisi lessicale per il repertorio fitonimico. In Giovanni Ruffino (ed.), *Atti del XXI Congresso Internazionale di Linguistica e Filologia Romanza, Palermo 18–24 settembre 1995, Vol. III: Lessicología e semantica delle lingue romanze*, 459–469. Tübingen: Niemeyer.
Markman, Ellen M., Marjorie S. Horton, and Alexander G. McLanahan. 1980. Classes and collections: principles of organization in the learning of hierarchical relations. *Cognition* 8: 227–241.
Marslen-Wilson, William D. 2007. Morphological processes in language comprehension. In Gareth Gaskell (ed.), *Oxford handbook of psycholinguistics*, 175–193. Oxford: Oxford University Press.
Menéndez Pidal, Ramón. 1925. *Manual de gramática histórica Española*, 5th edn. Madrid: Librería general de Victoriano Suárez.

Mihatsch, Wiltrud. 2004. Labile Hyperonyme. In Franz Lebsanft and Martin-Dietrich Gleßgen (eds.), *Historische Semantik in den romanischen Sprachen*, 43–54. Tübingen: Niemeyer.
Mihatsch, Wiltrud. 2005. Experimental data vs. diachronic typological data: Two types of evidence for Linguistic Relativity. In Stephan Kepser and Marga Reis (eds.), [Studies in Generative Grammar; 85] *Linguistic evidence – Empirical, theoretical, and computational perspectives*, 371–392. Berlin: Mouton de Gruyter.
Mihatsch, Wiltrud. 2006. *Kognitive Grundlagen lexikalischer Hierarchien untersucht am Beispiel des Französischen und Spanischen*. Tübingen: Niemeyer.
Mihatsch, Wiltrud. 2007a. Taxonomic and meronomic superordinates with nominal coding. In Zaefferer, Dietmar and Andrea Schalley (eds.), *Ontolinguistics: How ontological status shapes the linguistic coding of concepts*, 359–378. Berlin: Mouton de Gruyter.
Mihatsch, Wiltrud. 2007b. How the basic level restricts hyponymy: Trees and other plants. In Ibarretxe-Antuñano, Iraide, Carlos Inchaurralde, and Jesús M. Sánchez-García (eds.), *Language, mind, and the lexicon*, 165–191. Frankfurt am Main: Lang.
Mihatsch, Wiltrud. 2008a. Patrones de lexicalización y sufijos derivativos: el caso de -era/-ero. In Lisyová, Olga (ed.), *Actas del I Seminario Internacional de Hispanística, 7–9 septiembre 2006, Prešov*, 143–159. Prešov: Prešov university.
Mihatsch, Wiltrud. 2008b. Spatiale Aspekte lexikalischer Taxonomien: Italienische Substantive oberhalb der Basisebene. In Gerald Bernhard and Heidi Siller-Runggaldier (eds.), *Sprache im Raum – Raum in der Sprache*, 188–209. Frankfurt: Lang.
Mihatsch, Wiltrud. 2009. Nouns are things: Evidence for a grammatical metaphor. In Antonio Barcelona, Günter Radden, Klaus-Uwe Panther, and Linda L. Thornburg (eds.), *Metonymy and metaphor in grammar*, 75–97. Amsterdam & Philadelphia: Benjamins.
Mihatsch, Wiltrud. 2015a. Collectives. In Müller, Peter O., Ingeborg Ohnheiser, Susan Olsen, and Franz Rainer (eds.), *HSK word-formation. An international handbook of the languages of Europe*, 1183–1195. Berlin: Mouton De Gruyter.
Mihatsch, Wiltrud. 2015b. La position taxinomique et les réseaux méronymiques des noms généraux 'être humain' français et allemands. In Mihatsch, Wiltrud and Catherine Schnedecker (eds.), *Les noms d'humains: une catégorie à part?*, 85–113. (Zeitschrift für französische Sprache und Literatur – Beihefte, Neue Folge ZFSL-B). Stuttgart: Steiner.
Mihatsch, Wiltrud and Reinhild Steinberg. 2011. Redundant compounds. In Dessì Schmid, Sarah, Ulrich Detges, Paul Gévaudan, Wiltrud Mihatsch, and Richard Waltereit (eds.), *Rahmen des Sprechens. Beiträge zu Valenztheorie, Varietätenlinguistik, Kreolistik, Kognitiver und Historischer Semantik. Peter Koch zum 60. Geburtstag*, 411–424. Tübingen: Narr.
Miller, George A. and Philip N. Johnson-Laird. 1976. *Language and perception*. Cambridge & London & Melbourne: Cambridge University Press.
Miller, George A. 1998. Nouns in WordNet. In Christiane Fellbaum (ed.), *WordNet: An electronic lexical database*, 23–46. Cambridge, Massachusetts/London: The MIT Press.
Moliner, Maria. 1998. *Diccionario de uso del español*, 2nd edn. 2 Vols. Madrid: Gredos.
Murphy, Gregory L. 2002. *The big book of concepts*. Cambridge, Massachusetts: The MIT Press.
Nyrop, Kristoffer. 1908. *Grammaire historique de la langue française*. Vol. 3. Kopenhagen: Gyldendal.
Paul, Hermann. [1880] 1995. *Prinzipien der Sprachgeschichte*, 10th edn. [Konzepte der Sprach- und Literaturwissenschaft 6.] Tübingen: Niemeyer.
Pharies, David. 2002. *Diccionario etimológico de los sufijos españoles*. [Biblioteca Románica Hispánica, V, Diccionarios 25]. Madrid: Gredos.

Puddu, Mario. 2000–2012 *Ditzionàriu de sa limba sarda* (http://www.ditzionariu.org). Cagliari: Edizioni Condaghes.
Pötters, Wilhelm. 1970. *Unterschiede im Wortschatz der iberoromanischen Sprachen. Beitrag zu einer vergleichenden spanisch-portugiesischen Semantik*. Cologne: University of Cologne PhD-thesis.
Rainer, Franz and Soledad Varela. 1992. Compounding in Spanish. *Rivista di Linguistica* 4: 117–142.
Rainer, Franz. 1993. *Spanische Wortbildungslehre*. Tübingen: Niemeyer.
Real Academia Española. 1989. *Diccionario manual e ilustrado de la lengua española*, 4th edn. Madrid: Espasa Calpe.
Rey, Alain (ed.). 1998. *Dictionnaire historique de la langue française*, 2nd edn. 3 Vols. Paris: Dictionnaires Le Robert.
Rey-Debove, Josette and Alain Rey (eds.). 1993. *Le Nouveau Petit Robert. Dictionnaire alphabétique et analogique de la langue française*. Paris: Dictionnaires Le Robert.
Roché, Michel. 1997. *La variation non flexionnelle du genre des noms. Diachronie, diatopie, diastratie*. (Cahiers d'Etudes Romanes) Toulouse: Université de Toulouse II Le Mirail Centre de Linguistique et de Dialectologie.
Roché, Michel. 2002. Gender inversion in Romance derivatives with -arius. In Sarah Bendjaballah, Wolfgang U. Dressler, Oskar E. Pfeiffer, and Maria D. Voeikova (eds.), *Morphology 2000: Selected papers from the 9th Morphology meeting, Vienna, 24–28 February 2000*, 283–291. Amsterdam & Philadelphia: Benjamins.
Rohdenburg, Günter. 1988. Problems of hierarchical organization and lexical specificity involving compounds and their equivalents in English and German. In Josef Klegraf and Dietrich Nehls (eds.), *Essays on the English language and applied linguistics on the occasion of Gerhard Nickel's 60th birthday*, 284–299. Heidelberg: Groos.
Rosch, Eleanor, Carolyn B. Mervis, Wayne D. Gray, David M. Johnson, and Penny Boyes-Bream. 1976. Basic objects in natural categories. *Cognitive Psychology* 8: 382–439.
Rothstein, Susan. 2010. Counting and the mass-count distinction. *Journal of Semantics* 27(3): 343–397.
Sánchez de Lorenzo-Cáceres, José Manuel. Árboles ornamentales (http://www.arbolesornamentales.es/, page last consulted on the 5th of November 2012).
Schmid, Hans-Jörg. 1996. Basic-level categories as basic cognitive and linguistic building blocks. In Edda Weigand and Franz Hundsnurscher (eds.), *Lexical structure and language use: Proceedings of the International Conference on Lexicology and Lexical Semantics, Münster, September 13–15, 1994, Vol. I*, 285–295. Tübingen: Niemeyer.
Schmid, Hans-Jörg. 2007. Entrenchment, salience and basic levels. In Dirk Geeraerts and Hubert Cuyckens (eds.), *The Oxford handbook of cognitive linguistics*, 117–138. Oxford: Oxford University Press.
Seebold, Elmar. 1999. Lexikalisierung und Verdeutlichung. In Wolfgang Falkner and Hans-Jörg Schmid (eds.), *Words, lexemes, concepts. Approaches to the lexicon: Studies in honour of Leonard Lipka*, 63–67. Tübingen: Narr.
Seibert, Paul. 1996. *Farbatlas Südamerika: Landschaften und Vegetation*. Stuttgart: Ulmer.
Simpson, John and Edmund Weiner (eds.). 2000. *Oxford English dictionary*, 3rd edn. Oxford: Oxford University Press (http://dictionary.oed.com).
Stempel, Wolf-Dieter. 1959. Zur Frage des Geschlechts der romanischen Obstbaumnamen auf -arius. *Zeitschrift für romanische Philologie* 75: 234–268.

Talmy, Leonard. 1985. Lexicalization patterns: Semantic structure in lexical forms. In Timothy Shopen (Ed.), *Language typology and syntactic description: Vol. 3. Grammatical categories and the lexicon*, 36–149. Cambridge: Cambridge University Press.

Tanaka, James W. and Marjorie Taylor. 1991. Object categories and expertise: Is the basic level in the eye of the beholder? *Cognitive Psychology* 23: 457–482.

Tenishev Edhyam R. and Anna V. Dydo (eds.). 2006. *Sravnitelno-istoricheskaya grammatika tyurkskih yazykov. Pratyurkskij yazyk-osnova. Kartina mira pratyurkskogo etnosa po dannym yazyka* [Comparative grammar of Turkic languages. The Proto-Turkic basic language. The Word Picture of the Proto-Turkic ethnos (by language data)]. Moscow: Nauka.

Thompson, Laurence C. 1965. *A Vietnamese grammar*. Seattle: University of Washington Press.

Ungerer, Friedrich. 1994. Basic level concepts and parasitic categorization: A cognitive alternative to conventional semantic hierarchies. *Zeitschrift für Anglistik und Amerikanistik* 42: 148–162.

Villeneuve, Christophe de. 1821. *Statistique du département des Bouches-du-Rhône: avec atlas, dédiée au roi*. Volume I. Marseille: Ricard.

Walde, Alois and Johann Baptist Hofmann. 1938–1965. *Lateinisches etymologisches Wörterbuch*, 3rd edn. 3 Vols. Heidelberg: Winter.

Wartburg, Walther von. 1922. *Französisches etymologisches Wörterbuch: Eine Darstellung des galloromanischen Sprachschatzes*. 25 Vols. Ed. by Otto Jänicke (1972–1987) and Carl Theodor Gossen (1979–1983). Basel: Zbinden.

Wisniewski, Edward J. and Gregory L. Murphy. 1989. Superordinate and basic category names in discourse: A textual analysis. *Discourse Processes* 12 (2): 245–261.

Wälchli, Bernhard. 2005. *Co-compounds and natural coordination*. Oxford: Oxford University Press.

Zaragoza Larios, Carlos. 2013. Nombres comunes de plantas arvenses en Aragón (http://www.aragon.es/estaticos/GobiernoAragon/Departamentos/ AgriculturaGanaderia.M.edioAmbiente/AgriculturaGanaderia/Areas/03_Sanidad_ Vegetal/01_Protecci%C3%B3n_Vegetal/cpv_ana/NOMBRES_COMUNES%20.pdf, page last consulted on the 16th of December 2015).

Zubin, David A. and Klaus-Michael Köpcke. 1986. Gender and folk taxonomy: The indexical relation between grammatical and lexical categorization. In Colette G. Craig (ed.), *Noun Classes and Categorization*, 139–180. Amsterdam & Philadelphia: Benjamins.

Maksim Russo
15. Differences and interactions between scientific and folk biological taxonomy

Abstract: This paper deals with the semantic shifts relevant for animal and plant names collected in connection with the project "Catalogue of semantic shifts in the languages of the world" (cf. Zalizniak et al. 2012). The recurrent motivational patterns behind these shifts are used as a means for understanding the cross-linguistically recurrent regularities in the interrelations between the scientific and the pre-scientific, folk ("naïve") taxonomies in the domain of biology. The paper also considers how the different models of the world (the naïve and the scientific one) have influenced each other and compares the scientific understanding of type specimen, type species, type genera etc., with the prototype-based description of the folk biological items in cognitive psychology and linguistics. Finally it pays attention to the traces of the scientific biology in the folk biology by examining the cases of the penetration of the scientific biological terminology into common language and the accompanying semantic shifts.

This paper deals with semantic shifts relevant to animal and plant names. The recurrent motivational patterns behind these shifts have been collected in connection with the project *Catalogue of semantic shifts in the languages of the world*. These are used as a means for understanding the cross-linguistically recurrent regularities in the interrelations between scientific and pre-scientific, folk ("naïve") taxonomies in the domain of biology. For example, in some shifts the difference between folk and scientific taxonomy is especially evident, as in the treatment of snakes, serpent-like fish (eels, loaches), caterpillars and worms that often have related names and are therefore "naïvely" conceived of as belonging to the same taxon. Particularly interesting and revealing cases arise due to a widespread method of lexical adaptation for naming new species of animals and plants encountered as a result of culture contact. The method consists of constructing a compound including the name of something like the typical species complemented by a qualifying epithet. The paper will also consider how these different models (naïve and scientific) of the world have influenced each other and compare the scientific understanding of type specimen, type species, type genera etc., on the one hand, and the prototype-based description of folk biologi-

---

Maksim Russo (Moscow, news site Polit.ru)

cal items in cognitive psychology and linguistics, on the other. We will finally pay attention to the traces of scientific biology in folk biology. We examine cases of the penetration of scientific biological terminology into common language and the accompanying semantic shifts[1].

15.1 Some characteristics of folk biology nomenclature

Over the centuries of its history, scientific biology has developed fairly accurate principles to classify the organic world. Over the past 50 years, scientific biology has replaced eco-morphological characteristics (behaviour and organism structure) by classifications based on molecular genetic data and cell organelle structure. Creation of zoological and botanic nomenclature – species and higher taxa names – follows strict rules (McNeill et al. [eds.] 2006; Ride et al. [eds.] 2001; Kluge 2000: 42–67).

Classification of animals and plants implicitly presented in natural languages (folk biology, ethnobiology) differs from scientific classification by a number of indicators. Our purpose is to review how the formation of scientific biological categories has interacted with folk biology principles.

15.1.1 Folk species

As Berlin and Brown established in their works (Berlin 1992; Berlin, Breedlove, and Raven 1973; Brown 1977; Brown 1979), a traditional culture usually marks out about 600 folk species of plants and slightly fewer species of animals. Those "species" normally correspond not to scientifically classified species, but to higher taxa, such as genera and sometimes even larger units, such as orders or

---

[1] The paper was prepared is a part of the work on the "Catalogue of semantic shifts in the languages of the world" at the Institute of Linguistics, Russian Academy of Sciences, Moscow (Anna A. Zalizniak, Maria Bulakh, Dmitrij Ganenkov, Ilya Gruntov, Timur Maisak, Maxim Russo). In 2006–2009 the project of the Catalogue was part of the international project "Core vocabulary in a typological perspective: semantic shifts and form/meaning correlations" supported by an INTAS (grant #05-1000008-7917). In 2010–2012 the Catalogue was supported by the Russian Foundation for Humanities, grant #10-04-00156a. I am grateful to Alexandra Bruter, Ivan Semushin, Anna Sakoyan, Vera Tsukanova and Idelia Ayzjatulova for inestimable help in the preparation of this paper.

families. Atran (1990) suggested a special term "generic-species" for such units of folk taxonomy.

Although the works by Berlin and Brown mainly drew on the material of nonliterate Oceanic and South American languages, their principal results are true for other languages too, including those with a long literary tradition and elaborated scientific terminology. Marking out "generic-species" can be easily observed in the "folk biology" of Russian urbanites as well. As surveys among Russian speakers show, they normally differentiate *vorobej* 'sparrow' from other birds, being unaware of the fact that in central Russia there are two species of Passer genus, English sparrow (Passer domesticus) and tree of sparrow (Passer montanus) (Dement'ev 1968: 588, 591). Among acaudate amphibians Russians usually recognize two folk species *ljaguška* and *žaba*. Biologists find in this region six species associated with *ljaguška* (European fire-bellied toad [Bombina bombina]), common frog (Rana temporaria), garlic toad (Pelobates fuscus), marsh frog (Rana ridibunda), pool frog (Rana esculenta), and moor frog (Rana terrestris), and two species associated with *žaba*: green toad (Bufo viridis) and common toad (Bufo bufo) (Bannikov 1971: 45–58, 61–73). Extention of taxa in folk taxonomy is clearly shown within the world of insects. Thus, among folk taxonomic group *komary* (Culicidae, Emoididae and Tipulidae families in scientific taxonomy) Russian folk biology marks out probably only *komary* sensu stricto 'gnats', *senokoscy* 'crane gnats' and *tolkunčiki* 'dagger flies' (sometimes from a school biology course respondents might also know *maljarijnyj komar* 'anopheles mosquitoes', although many people use this term for crane flies). Meanwhile, entomologists count 86 species of Culicidae family and about 1000 (!) species of crane flies across the former USSR territory (Mazoxin-Poršnjakov 1970: 304: 308). French ornitonim *chevalier* lit. 'cavalier' designates to several sandpipers from the genus *Tringa* (Russian *ulit*): spotted redshank, common redshank, marsh sandpiper, common greenshank, green sandpiper, wood sandpiper (Fridman and Koblik 2006: 38), but in bilingual French-Russian dictionaries *chevalier* more often is translated as *ulit* 'Tringa'.

Such a typical feature of folk biology as equivalence of basic names to genus occurs not only in everyday language but also where scienctific terminology could be expected. We are referring to such spheres as floriculture, amateur gardening, and food commerce. As an example, we provide the usage of different fishes names in Russian on price tags in various fish stores (according to our own observations and the guidebook [Lajus et al. 2009]). As can be seen, one trade name corresponds to several species, frequently of one genus but sometimes of various genera. For example, the Russian term *zubatka* refers to four species from genus Anarhichas (A. lupus, A. orientalis, A. minor, A. latifrons). Russian *kambala* describes eight species from six genera (Pleuronectes platessa, Limanda aspera, Platichthys flesus, Platichthys stellatus, Hippoglossoides platessoides, Solea solea, Psetta maxima, Psetta maeotica). English common names of these fishes are broken down into four folk-species: *plaice* (Pleuronectes platessa, Hippoglossoides platessoides), *sole* (Limanda aspera, Solea solea), *flounder* (Platichthys flesus, Platichthys stellatus), and *turbot* (Psetta maxima, Psetta maeotica).

The central nature of the genus (generic-species) category for folk taxonomy is confirmed by research (Atran 1990). Typically, in the world's languages one-word names are only used to designate generic-species categories. In the process of language acquisition by children, plant names are learnt, as a rule, at a genus level, and "then children work up the generalizing hierarchy, and down the specializing hierarchy" (Lakoff 1987: 55–56). It is also interesting that folk taxonomy categories have more adequate correspondence to biological systematic taxa exactly at genus level, and there is a growing number of mismatches at other levels (Lakoff 1987).

It is important to notice the absence of one-to-one correspondence between the species of plants and animals and their names in traditional cultures. One plant, which has a set of characteristics (the color of the petals, smell, taste, location of growth, flowering time, toxicity, use in household or folk medicine), can have a variety of names, each of which represents one of these characteristics. Thus, common chicory (Cichorium intybus) in different Russian dialects is known as *lugovnik* (from *lug* 'meadow', since it grows in the meadows), *pridorožnik* (from *pri doroge* 'near road', as growing on roadsides), *sinecvetka* (*sinij* 'blue' + *cvesti* 'to blossom', because of the petals' color), *ščerbak* (from *ščerbatyj* 'chipped', due to the jagged leaves), *zarniki* (*zarja* 'dawn, sunrise', since the flowers open at 4–5 a.m.) and *petrov batog* (literally 'Peter's stick', since flowering begins in mid-summer, around the day of St. Peter and Paul as celebrated in the Russian Orthodox Church, Kolosova, 2009: 229–231). As another example, the name of dandelion (Taraxacum officinale) in Finnish dialects (Koppaleva 2007: 180–182): *keltakukka* 'yellow flower', *voikukka* 'butter-flower' (due to the color of the petals), *puuhukukkane* 'fluffy flower', *pöl(l)ykukkane* 'dusty flower' (due to external appearance and method of seed dispersal), *lamppu* 'lamp' (due to the appearance of the plant once the seeds are lost), *maitoheinä* 'milk herb' (because of the latex produced by the plant), *karkijakukka* 'bitter flower' (due to taste), *tšikorheinä* 'chicory-grass' (dried and roasted dandelion roots are used for a coffee substitute instead of chicory) and *otrakukka* 'barley-flower' (due to the time of flowering, coinciding with the period of barley seeding or also because of the usage as coffee substitute).

In contrast, plants that in scientific biology may relate not only to different species, but to different genera or even families, in common language have the same name because of conjoint characteristic. Thus, Russian *moločaj* (from *moloko* 'milk') in certain dialects can refer to several plants that discharge latex when broken: Chelidonium majus, Tragopogon pratensis, Sonchus oleraceus, Lactuca scariola, Taraxacum (several species), Euphorbia (several species) (Kolosova, 2009: 10–15, Merkulova 1967: 99–100, Annenkov 1878: 139), while in Russian scientific terminology *moločaj* referred only to genus *Euphorbia*. Russian *pervocvet* (from *pervyj* 'first' + *cvesti* 'to blossom') in some dialects meant early flowering plants: Primula (several species), Pulmonaria officinalis (Annenkov 1878: 272, 279), whereas in scientific terminology *pervocvet* corresponds only to genus Primula. Finnish *vilukukka* means 'common hepatica (Hepatica nobilis)', 'yellow anemone (Anemone nemorosa)', 'wood anemone (Anemone ranunculoides)', literally 'cold flower', due to early flowering of these plants.

It should be noted that in folk taxonomy "hybrid species" that combine features of different groups can be found. In Slavic folk culture such types include *laska* 'least weasel (Mustela nivalis)' (features of mammals and birds are combined) and *letučaja myš* 'bat' (features of lower animals and birds are combined) (Gura 1997: 603–604). Weasel in Slavic culture tends to be close to swallow. Both weasel and swallow are considered patrons of livestock: a weasel running under a cow, or a swallow flying over one are said to provide a large yield of milk (Gura 1997: 227–228, 231, 631–632). In Slavic legends, riddles and songs, weasel and swallow are united by a spinning and weaving motif (Gura 1997: 218–220). This is reflected in polysemy: Ancient Russian *lastočka*, *lastovica*, *lastica* mean 'swallow' and 'weasel'. In modern literary Russian words *laska* 'least weasel' and *lastočka* 'swallow' are monosemantic but in dialects they can have both meanings 'least weasel' and 'swallow' (Filin and Sorokoletov [eds.] 1980: 274).

Snake-like animals such as worms, caterpillars, loaches, lampreys, eels, and legless lizards are often related to snakes in folk culture. Integration of all these creatures in one folk taxonomic group is shown in a number of semantic shifts mentioned in the *Catalogue of semantic shifts in the languages of the world*: 'snake' – 'caterpillar', 'snake' – 'eel', 'snake' – 'loach (fish)', 'snake' – 'lamprey', 'snake' – 'worm'. Snake-like fishes themselves are also often confused in popular culture (Tolstoj [ed.] 1995: 479): Russian, Ukrainian, Belarusan *v'jun* 'loach, Misgurnus', Polish *wijun* 'lamprey', Russian *ugor'* 'eel', dial. *ugor'* 'loach', Polish *węgor* 'loach', Czech *piskoř*, Polish *piskorz* 'loach', Slovenian *piskor* 'lamprey', Serbian *piskor* 'moray' and Ukrainian *veretilnicja* 'lamprey', 'loach'.

Some species are represented in folk taxonomy as particularly close and connected to each other. In the Russian naïve biology *vorona* 'crow (Corvus cornix)' and *voron* 'raven (Corvus corax)' are presented as male and female versions of one species, whereas in terms of scientific biology they are representatives of two different species. The cuckoo in Russian traditional culture was associated with a hawk. As noted in (Dobrovol'skij 1894: 89, op. cited by Gura 1997: 21): "people think that [...] one bird could turn at will into a cuckoo or into a hawk".

15.1.2 Folk life-forms

It is important for our subsequent purposes to consider apart a folk life-form, or group, of animals which is frequently marked in traditional cultures. This group comprises insects, arachnoids, snakes, frogs, lizards, worms, and mice (Žuravlev 2005: 611–612, 647–650) and can be referred to as "lower animals". It is similar to what has been marked out by Brown as the 'wug' group (see subsection 15.1.3), but unlike the latter, it frequently includes snakes.

In folk lexica one general term for the creatures in this group is often used. For example, Slavic *gadŭ identifies snakes, lizards, frogs, toads, turtles and fishes (mostly serpent-like), some mammals (rats and mice in the first place) as well as insects, particularly the stinging ones, and parasites (Trubačev [ed.] 1979: 81–82, Gura 1997: 274–275; Gura 1995: 491–493). Compare Russian *gad* 'serpent' (North-West dialects) (Filin and Sorokoletov [eds.] 1970: 89) and *gadina* generalized 'mice or rats' (Vologda) (Filin and Sorokoletov [eds.] 1970: 91).

Lower animals are often united not only by objective characteristics (small size, multiplicity, proximity to ground) but also with negative appraisal from speakers: Russian obsolete and colloquial *gady* 'amphibian or reptiles' and *gad* 'a man who made something repulsive, disgusting', *gadkij* 'abhorrent; bad, loathsome, nasty, vile' (Efremova 2006). This fact is also displayed in pre-Slavic *gnusŭ derivatives, the basic meaning of which is associated with a feeling of disgust (Russian *gnusnyj* 'disgusting, repulsive', Bulgarian dial. *gnus* 'disgust', Macedonian *gnas* 'disgust', Czech *hnus* 'disgust, muck, vile' (Trubačev [ed.] 1979: 183). This root also appears in following names of animals: *gnus* 'collective name of harmful insects; biting insects (midges, gnats, gadflies and other)' (Siberia), 'midges, mosquito, ticks' (Amur region, Chelyabinsk, Perm, Ural, Nord of European Russia), 'gadlies, gnats' (Arkhangelsk), 'insects demolishing grain crops' (Vyatka, Krasnoyarsk, Tobolsk), 'locusts' (Yenisei), 'insects living in the house (fleas, cockroaches, spiders, etc.)' (Tobolsk, Tomsk, Siberia), 'flies, beetles, worms and other small creatures returning to life as it becomes warmer in spring' (Perm) (Filin and Sorokoletov [eds.] 1970: 248–249), *gnusa* 'small biting insects (gnats, mosquito, gadflies, flies)' (Olonets) (Filin and Sorokoletov [eds.] 1970: 249), *gnusina* (Amur region), *gnusota* 'midges, gnats, gadflies' (Nord of European Russia, Siberia, Tomsk) (Filin and Sorokoletov [eds.] 1970: 250–251) and *gnuska*, *gnusna* 'midges, gnats, gadflies' (Gecova [ed.] 1980: 163).

Krivoščapova (2007: 25-26) mentions that derivatives of this root in Russian dialects can indicate quite diverse animals, to which speakers ascribe various harmful actions. In this way the word demonstrates a flexibility of class limits that is typical of folk taxonomy: *gnus* 'animals demolishing grain crops or causing damage to house (mainly rodents)' (Vyatka), 'mice' (Olonets, Pechora) 'hamsters', 'field mice', 'hares' (Tobolsk), 'carnivorous mammals, dangerous for man and livestock' (Tobolsk, Irkutsk), 'bears' (Tobolsk), 'birds (Siberian jay, European jay) eating Siberian pine nut' (Tobolsk) and 'worms supposedly living in the human body in the case of various diseases, especially venereal' (North and East of European part of Russia, Siberia) (Filin and Sorokoletov [eds.] 1970: 248-249).

As another root, which attributes the idea of disgust to "lower creatures", Krivoščapova (2007: 26) demonstrates **kast'*: Russian dial. *kast'* 'damage caused to a field by grazing cattle; prank, dirty trick', 'faeces, excrement', 'rat or mouse', 'rubbish, disgusting thing', 'curse, swearword' (Trubačev [ed.] 1983: 157), 'collective name harmful animals' (Filin and Sorokoletov [eds.] 1977: 118) and *kastit'* 'leave droppings (about insects)' (Sverdlovsk region).

Outside the Slavic languages, Arabic *hāmmat-* (olρö) has similar semantics: "Any venomous creeping thing or reptile or the like, that is allowed to be killed; such as scorpion, serpent, or louse; that has deadly venom, like the scorpion; and sometimes, that is noxious; any reptile or the like, from louse to serpent" (Lane 1955: 3045), "bete qui rampe, qui se traine par terre, surtout reptile malfaisant (comme le scorpion, etc.)" 'crawling creature that crawls on the ground, especially harmful reptile (like scorpion, etc.)' (Biberstein-Kazimirski 1860, 2: 1443). In Muqaddimat al-Adab, the dictionary by al-Zamakhshari: "Word hawāmm- usage (plural from hāmat-) [...] shows that it meant not insects in modern sense, but all 'creepings', with subdivision to 'large' (snakes, lizards, scorpions, rats) and 'small': [...]: ants, lice, worms, dung beetles, locusts, wasps, butterflies, flies, gadflies, and mosquitoes" (Bertel's 1982: 58).

Among the data collected by Brown (1984: 226-267), we can find a wide range of such groups: Nuaulu *tekene* 'snake, worm, centipede, giant giant millipede, eel', Dugum Dani *wato* 'insect, reptile, amphibian', Kyaka Enga *kau* 'snake, lizard, caterpillar, grub, worm, scorpion, reptile-like insect, fish', Kayan *telusung* 'insect, spider, maggot', Kayapo *maja* 'insect, scorpion, spidet, tick, crayfish, pseudoscorpion', Kugu-Nganhchara *yuky* 'insect, insect larva, leech, jellyfish, other', Mandarin Chinese *chúng* 'insect, worm, nonsnake reptile', Navaho *ch'osh*[2]

---

[2] In modern literal Navajo *ch'osh* became a term designating invertebrate animals. In idiomatic descriptive expressions *ch'osh* designates various groups of invertebrates: *ch'osh bijááď hastání* 'insect' from *ch'osh* + *bijááď* 'his legs' + *hastą́ą́* 'six', *ch'osh bikágá ntł'izí* 'crab', *ch'osh ch'ééh*

'insect, spider, scorpion, snake, nonsnake reptile', Patep *myel* 'snake, worm, lizard, centipede', Azande *agbiro* 'insect, small nonsnake reptile, toad, tortoise', Classical Nahuatl *tlalapan nemi* 'insect, worm, snake', Fore *kabágina* 'insect, spider, worm', Hill Pandaram *puchi* 'insect, crustacean, small nonsnake reptile, amphibian', Japanese *mushi* 'bug, worm, snail', Kilangi *makoki* 'insect, spider, tick, mite, worm, snake, nonsnake reptile, frog, toad, centipede, slug, snail, leech', Mataco *wo* 'insect, spider, worm', Minnesota Ojibwa *manido.šlag* 'insect, snake, toad', and Siane *hanu* 'insect, spider, frog'.

15.1.3 The folk kingdoms

At the top levels of folk taxonomy separation into plants and animals is universal (Atran 1990: 211–213). The terms *unique beginners* (Berlin, Breedlove, and Raven 1973; Urban 2010) or *folk kingdoms* (Berlin 1992) are used to designate these groups in folk classification. Anthropologists researching folk classifications of animals and plants noticed long ago that in many languages common names for animals or plants are absent (Berlin, Breedlove, and Raven 1973: 215). Lexical designations in such languages appear only on the next level of classification – folk life-forms: tree, vine, herbaceous plant, bird, wug (made from *worm + bug*, offered in Brown 1984: 16), fish, snake and others (Berlin, Breedlove, and Raven 1973: 266–267; Berlin 1992: 161)[3]. According to the data of Urban, who made a sampling of 129 languages, there are no common terms for animals in 29 of them (Urban 2010: 206).

Some ethnobiologists suggest that the absence of specific labels for folk kingdoms in a language means the absence of these categories in a respective culture (Brown 1974). Others (Berlin 1974; Berlin 1992: 190) do not share that point of view. In order to prove the universality of such categories as "animals" and "plants", they provide both purely ethnographic reasons – such as results of

---

dighánii 'gastropods', *ch'osh bits'a'ígíí* 'bivalves', *ch'osh bikǫ'í* 'firefly' from *ch'osh + bi-* 'its' + *kǫ'* 'fire' + *-í* 'nominalizer', *ch'osh bíláshgaantsohí* 'lobster', *ch'osh bits'a' doolk'oolígíí* 'clam', *ch'osh ditł'ooí* 'caterpillar' from *ch'osh + ditł'ooí* 'the hairy one' (< *ditł'o* 'it is hairy, hirsute') + *-í* 'nominalizer', *ch'osh doo yit'íníí* 'microorganism' from *ch'osh + doo* 'not' + *yit'į́* 'it is visible' + *-ii* 'nominalizer', *łeeyi' ch'osh* 'earthworm', *ch'osh bijáád neeznánígíí* 'ten-legged crustaceans', *táłtł'ááh ch'osh daadánígíí* 'shrimp', 'Caridea'.

3 The folk life-form level is universal, but boundaries of folk life-forms in different languages may vary. For example in Igbira bushes with grass and herbs are the part of life-form *avį́* (vs. *ǫchį́* 'trees') and in Gouin bushes are united with trees in the folk life-form *tííbìŋgu* (vs. *hĩẽŋgù* 'grass, herb') (Brown 1984: 138–139).

classification tests for native speakers where creatures are normally grouped into animal and plant classes (Berlin, Breedlove, and Raven 1968; Hays 1976) – and linguistic, such as the limited co-occurrence of animals' and plants' names and the attribution of these names to different nominal classes. For example, Berlin (1992: 191–193) provides such linguistic illustrations to support the position that in Tzeltal ethnobiological classification folk kingdoms are separated. First of all, the verbal base *-ti'* 'eat (meat)' is used in Tzeltal only in relation to animals along with mushrooms and chilli. Tzeltal people call mushrooms 'earth's meat' (*lumilal ti'bal*). According to Tzeltal faiths, chili peppers in distant past were birds. Second, different number suffixes, *-tejk* for plants and *-kojt* for animals, are used in the Tzeltal language.

The need for common terms for animals and plants emerges as a given society obtains writing culture, science and regular education. And even in such conditions these terms may not be developed simultaneously. While Ancient Greek φυτόν (*phytón*) 'plant' and ζῷον (*zôon*) 'animal' serve this purpose in Aristotle's and Theophrastus's writings, Latin *planta* became such a term no sooner than in the 13th century, and its derivatives in English and French started to play this role even later – in or after the 17th century (Kuprijanov 2005: 14). Slaughter (1982) supposes that the emergence of such terms is connected, first and foremost, with the development of script. This scenario of generating common terms was repeated in non-literate languages during the 19th and 20th centuries during the process of forming a script and literary norm and putting formal education into operation.

No wonder that foreign loanwords are more frequently used as names of folk kingdoms. The best known are Latin *planta* 'plant' and *animal* 'animal', widely spread in European languages. But also loanwords as names of folk kingdoms are used in Thai *sàt* 'animal' (< Sanskrit *sattva*, Morev 1964: 761), Hausa *dàbbàa* 'animal' (< arab.), Vietnamese *động mật* 'animal' (< Chinese), Indonesian *héwan* 'animal' (< Arabic), Rifian *nnəwwā* 'plant' (< Arabic), Lower Sorbian *flanca* 'plant' (< German *Pflanze*), Kildin Saami *rāss'* 'plant' (< Swedish *gräs*), Manange *rop* 'plant' (< Nepali) and Thai *puīt* 'plant' (< Sanskrit *bīja*) (Haspelmath and Tadmor [eds.] 2009). We can see that sources of adoption are lexemes from languages that in particular societies were perceived as languages of culture, science and education.

The other method of creating terms for folk kingdoms is compounding. In this way Mansi *uj-hul* 'animal', literally 'beast' + 'fish' (Balandin and Vaxruševa 1958), Tzeltal *te'ak'* 'plant' (literally 'tree' + 'liane') (Berlin 1992: 195), Sentani *obojoku* 'animal' (literally 'pig' + 'dog') and Takia *borgun* 'animal' (literally 'pig' + 'dog') emerged (Urban 2010: 212). Such denotations can preserve their original appearance in languages for a long time: as an example, in the classical Latin expression *arbor et herba* with the meaning 'plants in general'. In classical Chinese literature plants as a whole were named *cǎoshù* (草树) or *cǎomù* (草木) literally 'herbs and trees' (Ošanin [ed.] 1983, 2: 810), e.g., in the title *Cao mu qi* '[Treatise of] Teacher of herbs and trees' by the Chinese author Ye Ziqi (1327–1390) (Titarenko [ed.] 2009, 5: 392).

During the creation of terminology a name for one of the folk life-forms belonging to the kingdom was customarily used for the name of the whole folk kingdom. For example "mammals" for animals and "grass" for plants. For languages which got their writing systems recently, dictionaries are mostly created by lexicographers whose native language is different. These lexicographers sometimes intentionally, sometimes unconsciously, extend or narrow the meaning of a word of the language being described, transforming these words into analogues of the terms of their native language. One can trace it, comparing the translations of the words in the dictionaries designed for translating from language being described to one of the European languages, and usage of these words in the dictionaries designed for translating from one of the European languages to the language being described. Later, if national biological terminology appears, these words take corresponding place in it. Evenki *bəjŋə̄* (from *bəj-* 'to hunt') in descriptive dictionaries gets the meaning 'beast (except cloven-hoofed)', 'wolf' (Vasilevič 1958: 74), 'fur-bearing animal' (Vasilevič 1934: 19), 'beast, animal' (Boldyrev 2000, 1: 90 provides examples illustrating that the word is only used to describe wild animals, game). And in *Russian-Evenki vocabulary* (Vasilevič 2005, 1: 130), the function of which is designated as "a handbook for 5–9 grade", the proposed translation for this word is a general term 'animal'. In Verner's *Ket-Russian and Russian-Ket dictionary* (Verner 2002) for junior school students the Ket word *assel'* (from *es'da se'*, *es'sel'* 'wild deer') has 'beast' as the first meaning, and 'animal' as the second (Verner 2002: 17). In the Russian-Ket part of the dictionary this word is proposed as the translation for the Russian *životnoe* 'animal' unreservedly (Verner 2002: 152).

Turning to dictionaries of African languages, we find the same pattern. In Kirundi and Kinyarwanda dictionaries made by the Methodist Church missionary Betty Cox and her colleagues, in the English-Kirundi/Kinyarwanda components of the dictionaries, we see monosemic translations of the words *plant* – Kirundi, Kinyarwanda *imbuto* (Cox 1969b: 102; Cox, Adamson, and Teusink 1969: 100) and *animal* – Kinyarwanda *inyamaswa*, *igisīmba* (Cox, Adamson, and Teusink 1969: 62), whereas in Kirindi/Kinyarwanda-English components we found that *inyamaswa* means 'wild animal' and *igisīmba* means 'animal (especially little, biting)', 'insect' (Cox 1969: 48), while in both languages *imbuto* means not only 'plant', but also 'seed, fruit' (Cox, Adamson, and Teusink 1969: 6; Cox 1969b: 19).

When such dictionaries start being employed in school education they unavoidably influence the usage of native language words, and in languages that have no common names for animals and plants such names appear, which consequently leads to corresponding modification of folk taxonomy. As a result there appears polysemy, wherein a word is used as in habitual sense of life-form ('mammal' or 'grass') as in wide sense ('animal' or 'plant').

It is incorrect to think that such occurrences can be found only in languages which recently started to build their script and scientific terminology. In common Russian we can easily find examples where birds, fishes and insects are not attributed to the animals category, as well as trees that are not considered plants. Russian speakers find expressions like *životnye i pticy* lit. 'animals and birds' or *rastenija i derev'ja* 'plants and trees' to be normal, but they would categorize as abnormal expressions like **životnye i lošadi* 'animals and horses', **rastenija i travy* 'plants and herbs', because horse is included into the folk life-form animals and herbs are included into plants. Sometimes such un-terminological use of the words "plants" and "animals" can occur in (other than biological) scientific literature. For example, in the title of a dictionary (Konovalova 2000), the word *rastenija* 'plants' is used, although in fact this dictionary contains only the names of herbacious plants, not trees.

Standard Russian language dictionaries do not reflect the difference between terminological and common word usage. Plants (*rastenija*) in such dictionaries are defined in accordance with their scientific definition, frequently with elements of encyclopedic explanation: "organism that feeds on air by photosynthesis and from soil (rarely – from other nutrient solution) to which it is attached" (Švedova et.al. 2009: 816); "organism, generally growing standstill and feeding on non-organic substances of soil and air. Higher plants commonly include three main members: fixed in soil root, above-ground caulis and leaves. Fungi, lichens, rockweeds and bacteria belong to inferior plants" (Ušakov [ed.] 1935–1940); "organism, generally growing standstill and feeding (unlike animals) on air (by photosynthesis) and soil"(Kuznetsov [ed.] 2006: 305), "organism, feeding on non-organic substances of air and soil, commonly fixed on its inhabitation" (Lopatin and Lopatina 1997: 584); "growing standstill organism, representing one of the life-forms on the Earth and forming wildlife together with animal organisms" (Černyšëv [ed.], XII: 886).

For the word *životnoe* 'animal' major Russian dictionaries also do not separately mention the meaning of "above-ground quadruped, mostly mammals", comprising by their definitions all the kingdom of animals: "living body, creature, that have the ability to move and feed, unlike most plants, on ready-made organic substances" (Švedova et al. 2009: 234); "living creature, capable of feeling and moving" (Ušakov [ed.] 1935–1940); "any living body, except for plant" (Černyšëv [ed.], IV: 125; Kuznetsov [ed.] 2006: 1100; Lopatin and Lopatina 1997: 152). The majority of dictionaries make only one concession to folk biology, acknowledging a second meaning of the word *životnoe*, excluding humans from other animals (Švedova et al. 2009; Ušakov [ed.] 1935–1940; Ožegov and Švedova 1991: 664; Kuznetsov [ed.] 2006: 1100).

In quite a similar way, the English words *animal* and *plant* are used in non-special texts. The word *plant* in everyday language is mostly applied to small herbal plants and not to trees and bushes (Buck 1988: 521), while *animal* is applied to mammals (Rosch Heider 1973: 113, 315; Brown 2002: 474–475). English-language lexicography reflects such a phenomenon, including for *animal*, as well as the meanings 'animals on the whole' and 'animals, except human', also the meaning 'a mammal, as opposed to a bird, reptile, fish, or insect' (Soanes and Stevenson [eds.] 2005). Some dictionaries even consider such a meaning first (Sinclair [ed.] 2008). For the word *plant* Soanes and Stevenson (2005) include the sub-meaning 'a small plant, as distinct from a shrub or tree'.

A list of similar examples can be easily compiled for other languages. In Romanian non-specialized texts using Internet search engines, we find abundant expressions: *plante și copaci* 'plants and trees', *plante și arbori* 'plants and trees', *animale și insecte* 'animals and insects', *animale și pești* 'animals and fishes' and *animale și păsări* 'animals and birds', in Modern Greek texts – ζώα και έντομα 'animals and insects', ζώα και ψάρια 'animals and fish', ζώα και φίδια 'animals and snakes', ζώα και πτηνά 'animals and birds' and δέντρα και φυτά 'trees and plants'.

Rosch Heider (1973) and Lakoff (1973: 458–459) suggest describing such cases through the use of a prototype notion determining the hierarchy of belonging to animal or plant categories. Wierzbicka solves the problem of describing such categories by introducing additional conditions like "people can say something like that about creatures like that" and "some creatures of that kind do not have a characteristic.., but, if people want to imagine such creatures, they would imagine someone who has feathers" (Wierzbicka 1990: 361–362), defining the category "bird".

In any case, while describing the usage of words like Russian *životnoe* or English *animal*, we should acknowledge they are double-valued: $životnoe_1$ correlates with all species of the animal kingdom, and $životnoe_2$ correlates with the basic life-form – above-ground quadrupeds, firstly mammals. That double value is the result of interaction between scientific and everyday worldviews, and scientific terminology with common language.

Herein the interaction takes place in two directions. On the one hand, folk life-form names, becoming biological terms, expand their denotation and convert into a common designation of plants or animals, and later terminological usage of those words becomes part of the common language whereby the above-mentioned type of polysemy appears (e.g., the case of Hungarian *állat* 'livestock, cattle' and 'animal').

On the other hand, a synthetically made or naturalized scientific term, found in everyday speech, gains features that are indicative of folk biology terms and starts being used with regard to more narrow denotation – the basic folk lifeform. This is the case, for example, for Latin *animal* and *plant*, which were naturalized in many languages.

As a model of situation where adopted from scientific terminology get additional meanings typical of the folk worldview, we can examine loanwords from the lexifier in a Creole language. In Tok Pisin the word *abus* represents an earlier loanword from English *animal* (with vocalization l, falling of unstressed syllable and m > b) (Romaine 1992: 158)[4]. Transferring into Tok Pisin, this word also gained a meaning 'meat' (Volker et al. 2008: 1), which is not one of the English word meanings. Until the 1960-s the word *abus* was the common term for terraneous animals, but is now rivalled by the *animal* (Romaine 1992: 161) that was borrowed from the English later.

Urban (2010) concludes that there is an interconnection between the existence of lexical descriptions of folk kingdoms and mode of subsistence. According to Urban's observations, in small societies of hunters and gatherers it is most likely that there are no names for folk kingdoms. Societies practicing advanced agriculture are the most likely to have folk kingdom terms not characterized by polysemy (Urban 2010: 214–216). Admitting the correctness of his conclusion, we consider it necessary to underline the fact that in languages of advanced agricultural and literate societies the terms for folk kingdoms, as used in everyday life, semantically act like terms from "traditional societies". Such folk kingdom terms become polysemic and can mean both folk kingdom and basic life-form. In this regard, the mutual influence of terminological lexis and folk worldview vocabulary comes to be a point of extra interest.

Despite the vast amount of collected data, the work (Urban 2010) was not aimed at composing the most complete list of semantic shifts that show the genesis of the common term for plants in the languages of the world. So we have made an attempt to consider Urban's materials and add data from the *Catalogue of semantic shifts in the languages of the world*. The same work has been done for semantic shifts that provide the genesis of the common term for animals.

---

4 We must mention the alternative etymology comparing Tok Pisin *abus* with the words of Austronesian languages of New Britain and New Ireland (Kove *basi* 'small animal', Nakanai *basibasi* 'small game', *pasi* 'big game', Mamusi *posi* 'meat') (Romaine 1992: 158).

15.1.3.1 Semantic shifts for 'animal'

Sources of animal folk kingdom names are divided into four main groups. The first group includes meanings relating to the most general characteristics of a typical animal. The animal lives, exists, breaths and moves. The second group of sources refers to the uses of animals by humans. The animal is hunted and eaten. The third group includes animal properties that emphasize the difference between animals and humans. The animal cannot speak, usually is covered in fur and has four legs. And the fourth group of semantic shifts is enlargement of folk life-forms (mammal > animal, fish > animal, livestock > animal etc.).

The most frequent semantic shift in the first group is 'to live' > 'animal'. It is attested in Old Church Slavonic *životŭ* 'life', *životĭno* 'animal' (Cejtlin, Večerka, and Blagova [eds.] 1994: 217–218).This word is also common in other Slavic languages: Russian *životnoe*, Bulgarian *životno*, Croatian *živòtinja* et al. In addition to the Slavic the same Indo-European roots underlie Lithuanian *gyvolis*, Lettish *dzīvnieks* (Buck [1949] 1988: 138). Romanian *jivină* 'live creature; wild animal, mammal' also has a Slavic origin (Ciorănescu 2007: 446; Coteanu, Seche, and Seche 1998; Borş [ed.]) 2005, 1: 1187). This semantic shift we can find in a languages all over the word, for example in Ancient Greek ζῶ (*zõ*) 'to live' > ζῷον (*zõon*) 'animal' (Liddell et al. 1996: 758, 760), Mongolian *am^j* 'life' > *am^{j}tan* 'animal, live creature', Chuvash *čĕr* 'live, animate', *čĕrčun* 'animal' (Fedotov 1996, 2: 414), Irish *bēo* 'to live' > *beatha* 'life' (gen. *beathaidh*) > *beathaidheach* 'animal' (Buck [1949] 1988: 138), Arabian حياة (*ḥayāt*) 'life' > حيوان (*ḥaywān*) 'animal' (Biberstein-Kazimirski 1860, 2: 523–524), Seri *ziix ccam* 'animal (general term)', lit. 'thing that is alive'[5] (Felger and Moser 1985, 56–60), Central Alaskan Yup'ik *ungungva* 'to be alive', *ungungsiiq* 'animal' (Fortescue, Jacobson, and Kaplan 1994: 376), Northern Saami *eallit* 'to live', *ealli* 'animal' (Mäkäräinen 2007: 40), Lenakel *nar amíuh* 'animal' ('thing' + 'alive'), Nez Perce *waq'íswit* 'life', *waq'íswitin* 'animal' and Kiliwa *-ipaa-* 'to be alive', *tkwipaay* 'animal' (Urban 2010: 212). Sometimes target meaning includes both animals and humans as in Romanian *vietate* and *viețuitoare* 'live creature' from *viu* 'live' (Coteanu, Seche, and Seche 1998).

The semantic shift 'to move' > 'animal' is typical for two language areas: East and South-East Asia, and North America. It is represented in Mohave *ipay=k* 'to move', *'ichipay* 'insect', 'animal' (in compounds) (Munro, Brown, and Crawford 1992: 40, 99), Blackfoot *iksowa'pomaahkaa* 'animal', lit. 'at.ground.level-about-move.along.on.foot' (Urban 2010: 212), and Hawaiian *holoholo* 'to go for a walk,

---

5 It may be that in Seri the semantic shift 'fish' > 'animal' occured, cf. the general term for fish, *zixcamáa*, lit. 'true animal' (Felger and Moser 1985, 56–60).

ride, or sail' > *holoholona* 'animal' (Pukui and Elbert 1992: 28). In Hani *nivzeig* 'animal' is formed from *niv-* 'to move' with an unclear second element (Urban 2010: 212). Mandarin Chinese *dòng* (動, in compounds 动) 'to move' (Ošanin [ed.] 1983, 3: 553) is used in *dòngwù* (动物) 'animal' lit. 'moving thing'. The Chinese name is a loan translation in several East Asian languages, for example Japanese *dō-butsu* (動物) lit. 'moving thing' (Konrad [ed.] 1970, 1: 209). Dakota *śkaŋ* 'to move' (Riggs 1992: 445) gives *wamakaśkaŋ* 'creeping creature, worm', dial. 'game animals, especially bisons' (Riggs 1992: 518), 'animals' (Williamson 1992: 7). Missionary Williamson mentioned that this word was a common name for animals as creatures that locomote along the ground (Riggs 1992: 518).

Notably, the shift 'to breathe' > 'animal' is attested only in the Indo-European languages. This shift is bounded up with shifts 'to breathe' > 'soul', 'to breathe' > 'man', 'to breathe' > 'life', 'wind' > 'soul'. Here we do not separate close shifts 'soul' > 'animal' and 'to breathe' > 'animal' that are individually represented in the *Catalogue of semantic shifts in the languages of the world*. Old Church Slavonic *dyhati* 'to breathe' is kindred with Gothic *dius* 'animal'. The same Indo-European root generated Old Norse *dȳr*, Old English *dēor*, Old High German *tior*, Danish *dyr*, Dutch *dier* etc. In English, the word's meaning was narrowed to 'deer' (Lehmann 1986: 92–93; Buck [1949] 1988: 138). Latin *anima* 'soul' > *animal* 'mammal', later 'animal'. Also from Latin *anima* Old Irish *anim* was borrowed alongside derivatives of Old Irish *anmanda* and Modern Irish *ainmhidhe* 'animal' (Buck [1949] 1988: 137–138). In Sanskrit, there are words *prāṇa-* 'breathing'and *prāṇin-* 'live creature' (MacDonell 1893: 185). In Romanian, there are two non basic terms for animals, *dihanie* (< Slavic *dyhanie* 'breathing') and *suflare* (Romanian *a sufla* 'to breathe', Latin *sufflare* 'to blow') (Ciorănescu 2007: 292, 758; Coteanu, Seche, and Seche 1998).

There are two meanings that more often became sources of the meaning 'live creature', but are also attested as shifting meaning to 'animal'. The first is 'to be', the second is 'to create'. Thai *sàt* 'animal' was borrowed from Sanskrit *sattvá* 'being, existence', 'live creature' (Morev 1964: 761; MacDonell 1893: 330). In many languages such names serve as non-basic designations for animals or as hyperonyms for all living creatures. Such terms can be verbal nouns, participles (Russian *suščestvo*, Romanian *fiinţă*, English *being*, Hungarian *lény*) or lexicalized infinitives (Spanish *ser*, Italian *essere*, French *être*, German *Wesen*). The semantic shift 'to create' > 'animal' is found in Ukrainian *tvoryty* 'to create' > *tvaryna* 'animal' (URS, VI, 18). This verb's derivatives can denote living beings in many Slavic languages (Russian *tvar'*, Serbo-Croatian *tvar*, Polish *twór* and Belorussian *stvarennja*), but only in Ukrainian did the word become not only a folk kingdom name, but also a biological term: *u mori živut' rizni mors'ki tvaryny* 'there are many different marine animals in the sea', *teplokrovni tvaryny* 'hot-blooded animals', *gubky* – *typ prymityvnyh bagatoklitynnyh tvaryn, jaki vedut' prykriplenyj sposib žyttja* 'sponge is a phylum of multicellular animals which are sessile'. As well as derivatives of verb 'to be, exist', these terms are frequently used as hyperonyms for living beings: Russian *sozdanie*, Latin *creatura*, Romanian *făptură* (< Latin *factura*), Romanian *săzdanie* (< Slavic), Romanian *zidire*, *ziditură* (< *a zidi* 'to build', originally a Slavism [Coteanu, Seche, and Seche 1998; Ciorănescu 2005: 854]) and Turkish *yaratmak* 'to create' > *yaratık* 'creature'.

The second group of semantic shifts reflects regarding animals as food. Therefore the most frequent semantic shift is 'meat' > 'animal': Esimbi *ɛnyimi* 'meat', 'animal' (Coleman), Lingala *nyama* 'meat', 'animal' (Divuilu [ed.] 2005: 45, 75), Hausa *nama* 'meat', 'animal' (Urban 2010: 211), in Robinson (1913: 274–275) the second meaning is recorded only for the expression *nama daji* 'wild animal', lit. 'forest meat', Swahili *nyama* 'meat', *mnyama* 'animal' (Polikanov 1997; Rechenbach 1967: 340, 410), Yoruba *ẹran* 'meat', *ẹran, ẹranko* 'animal' (Laptuhin et al. 1987: 94, 154), Kewa *ari* 'meat', *ari yeanu* 'meat', 'animal', *arimu* 'animals (Franklin 2007: 11–12). Koreguaje *va'i* 'meat', 'animals' (Cook and Gralow 2009: 123), Ngambay *da*, Yir-Yoront *minh*, Sora *jelu:n*, Yanomami *yaro*, Efik *unam* 'meat', 'animal' (Urban 2010: 211), Saramaccan *mbéti* 'meat', 'animal' (< English *meat*), Miriwung *ngarin*, and Gajirrabeng *ngardin* 'meat', 'animal'. The Miriwung word was borrowed by Gurindji (Haspelmath and Tadmor [eds.] 2009). The interesting example form colloquial African French is given in (Bagana and Langner 2014: 97). In Republic of the Congo *animal* has both meaning 'animal' and 'meat'. We suppose second meaning arose under the influence of African languages.

Tok Pisin *abus* means 'meat' (*kakaruk na pik, em on gutpela abus long kaikai* 'chicken and pig are good meat to eat') and 'animal' (*i gat planti kain kain abus long bikbus* 'there are many kinds of animals in the deep jungle') (Volker et al. 2008: 1), about terrestrial animals, see Romaine (1992: 161).

Also in the second group we can find the semantic shifts 'to eat' > 'animal' and 'to hunt' > 'animal'. The first is present in Yuki *lik'* 'to swallow' > *he'lik'ke* 'animal' (Urban 2010: 214) and in Yana *moo-yau(na)* 'animal' from *moo-* 'to eat' with a nominalizer. The word *moo-yau(na)* can be understood as 'living thing which eats' and as 'living thing which is eaten' (Urban 2010: 213). The semantic shift 'to hunt/to kill ' > 'animal' is found in North America languages: Quileute *ʔixʷá·tso* 'animal', *ʔixʷá·t̓sil* 'to hunt'. The direction of derivation is unclear (Urban 2010: 214), Haida *gina ti7araa* 'animal', lit. 'creature/thing-be killed' (Urban 2010: 212), Oneida -*lyo*- 'to kill' > *kutilyoʔshúha* 'animals' (Urban 2010: 212).

In the third group three semantic shifts are united: 'dumb' > 'animal', 'quadrupedal' > 'animal' and 'fur' > 'animal'. The meaning 'dumb' is a source for the basic animal term in Classical Arabic *bahīmat-* (بهيمة) 'animal' from *ʔabham-* (أبهم) 'qui ne sait ou ne peut pas parler' ('which does not know how to or is unable to speak')> (Biberstein-Kazimirski 1860, 2: 174). Also Romanian *necuvântător* (literally 'non-speaking') means 'animal',but it is not a basic term (Coteanu, Seche, and Seche 1998). Compare also domestic animals "which has a mouth that does not speak", characteristic in Hittite texts and Georgian descriptive designations of heavy beasts *p'ir-ut'q'v-i* literally 'not-speaking-mouth' (Gamkrelidze and Ivanov 1984, 2: 471–472). We assume that the shift 'dark' > 'animal' in Komi *pemid* 'dark' > *pemös* 'animal' (Lytkin and Guljaev 1970: 219) is related to 'dumb' > 'animal'. Probably the semantic evolution in this case followed a path like 'dark' > 'foolish' > 'unreasonable' > 'animal' or 'dark' > 'dumb' > 'animal'.

The shift 'fur' > 'animal' is observed in Japanese *ke* (毛) 'hair, fur', *kedamono* (獣) 'animal' (lit. 'hair thing') (Konrad [ed.] 1970, 1: 532–533) and in Anggor *ninehondi* 'animal' which is derived from 'fur' + 'mother' (Urban 2010: 213).

The semantic shift 'quadrupedal' > 'animal' is present in Nuuchahnulth *sa-štuup, sa-xtuup* 'animal', lit. 'crawl.on.all.fours.creature' (Urban 2010: 213). Hausa *dábbàa*, and Kanuri *dábbà* 'animal' were borrowed from Arabic *dābba* (دابّة) 'four-legged' (Haspelmath and Tadmor [eds.] 2009). Chukchi *yánnik* 'animal' and Koryak *yájnik* 'animal', *təyəjniŋək* 'to hunt' are probably etymologically linked with *ŋərá-q* 'four' (Fortescue 2006).

Cf. also Cahuilla *ʔíʔihiŋaviš* 'animal' – from *ʔí* 'legs' (the second element is unclear (Urban 2010: 214)), Alabama *iyyi* 'feet', *óstàaka* 'four', *nàasi iyyi óstàaka* 'animal', lit. 'creature with four feet' (Sylestine, Hardy, and Montler 1993). The name "quadrupedal" was widespread in ancient Indo-European languages as a descriptive denotation of animals (mostly in opposition to human, "bipedal"): Sanskrit *cátuṣpad-*, Mycenaean Greek *qe-te-ro-pi*, Ancient Greek τετράπους *tetrápous*, Umbrian *petur-pursus* and Latin *quadrupes* (Gamkrelidze and Ivanov 1984, 2: 474).

The most frequent cases are when folk lifeforms became the source for animal in general. We do not dwell here on the widespread cases of European languages in which the prototype 'mammal' is singled out from words with the meaning 'animal' (see section 15.1.3). This semantic shift can also be found outside Europe, for example in Tzeltal, a dialect of Tenejapa *čanbalam* 'mammal (except human, bats and armadillos)', 'animal' (Hunn 1975: 310; Hunn 1975a: 21–22).

In several languages such categories as 'domestic animals' and 'wild animals' become folk life-forms. Both can later transform into a general term for animals. The shift 'livestock, domestic animal' > 'animal' is found in Khoekhoe (Nama) *ûitsama*, Rendille *náf*, Basque *amere* 'livestock', 'animal' (Urban 2010: 211), Nahuatl *yolca* 'domestic animal' in the dialects of the municipalities Mecayapan y Tatahuicapan in the state of Veracruz (Walters et al. 2002, 208, 215) and *yōlcatl* 'animal' literary language, Aymara *uywa* 'livestock. cattle' (Bacarreza 2000: 239), but in general meaning 'animals' in Aymara Wikipedia[6], cf. also (Urban 2010: 207, 211). Hungarian *állat* 'animal' (*emlős állat* 'mammal', *állattan* 'zoology'), 'domestic animal, cattle' (Gáldi 1987: 34), 'livestock' (Hadrovics and Gáldi 1986). The Hungarian word was borrowed by Selice Romani *áloto* 'animal', 'livestock' (Haspelmath and Tadmor [eds.] 2009).

The shift 'wild animal' > 'animal' is attested in So *emtos* 'wild animal' > 'animal' (Heine and Carlin 2010: 15) and Kinyarwanda *inyamaswa* 'wild animal' (Cox, Adamson, and Teusink 1969: 34), 'animal' (Cox, Adamson, and Teusink 1969: 62).

A remarkable case is Romanian *lighioană* '(wild) animal' > 'animal (mainly domestic)', which supposedly came from an interim meaning 'evil spirit'. Etymologically, the Romanian word comes from the Church Slavonic *legewnŭ* 'legion' from the utterance by the demon in the country of the Gerasenes (Mark 5:9): *legewnŭ imę mně* 'My name is Legion' (Ciorănescu 2007: 468).

We would like to discuss particularly three semantic shifts with folk lifeforms as their source. The first is 'fish' > 'animal'. This semantic shift is found in two languages spoken on islands. The Eninhdhilyakwa tribe lives on Groote Island in the Gulf of Carpentaria, speakers of Rapa Nui live on Easter Island. Eninhdhilyakwa *akwalaya* 'sea animals', 'fishes' > 'animals' (Waddy 1988: 70), Rapa Nui *îka* 'fish' > 'animal', for example, *îka ariga koreha* 'horse', lit. 'animal with the face of a koreva fish' (Englert 1977).

The semantic shift 'bird' > 'animal' is a case specific to Polynesian languages. In accordance with the fact that Polynesian fauna was fairly poor, historically these languages have no common term even for the folk life-form "mammal". Naturalized species (like rats and domestic animals) were often included into a wider class that united all nonmarine animals. Later reflexes of Proto-Polynesian *manu* 'bird' (Brown 1981: 103) were used for mammals. In Tahitian *manu* is used in two meanings: a more general – 'ground animals' (as opposed to *i'a* 'marine animals') and narrower – 'birds and flying insects' (Lemaître 1995: 70). In Rapanui *manu* is applied only to birds and insects, but when sheep were first brought to Easter Island, islanders called them *manu va'e e-há*, that literally means 'four-legged bird' (Englert 1977). A combination of reflexes of **manu* meanings 'ground animal' and 'bird' is also mentioned for Mangarevian (Tregear 1899: 46), Samoan (Pratt 1896: 208), Tongan, Anuta, Tikopia, and Tuamotu (Brown 1981: 95). In some other Polynesian languages **manu* reflexes lost the meaning 'bird' and are used only for ground animals. In these languages birds are usually designated by a combination of a reflex of *manu with the word 'to fly': Niuean *manu lele*, West Uvean *manu lele*, Rennellese (Munggava-Mungiki) *manu gege*, Nukuoro *manu lele*

---

6 http://ay.wikipedia.org/wiki/

and Cook Island Māori (Rarotongan) *manu-rere* (Brown 1981: 90, 95). In modern Fijian the reduplicated form *manumanu* became a general term for animals, and birds are referred to with the expression *manumanu vuka*, where *vuka* means 'to fly' (Geraghty 1994: 140, 142).

Outside the Polynesian languages we find just two examples of this semantic shift. In Tok Pisin the term *pisin*, loanworded from English *pigeon*, has the meaning 'bird'. Up until the 1920-s *pisin* was used in compound constructions as a common term for mammals, birds and even fish: *pisin i kalap antap* 'bird', literally 'animal that moves above', *pisin i save subim wara* 'fish', literally 'animal that moves around in water' (Romaine 1992: 161–162). Later the words *abus* and *animal* began being used as common names for animals. A modern Tok Pisin dictionary (Volker et al. 2008: 67) does not attribute the meaning 'animal' to *pisin*, but we can count the sense 'tribe, totem' as a trace of such a meaning (*yu bilong wanem pisin?* 'what clan do you belong to?'). The word *pisin* preserved the meaning 'bird', and fish became denoted by the word *pis* < English *fish* (Volker et al. 2008: 212). In Gawwada (Afro-Asiatic, Eastern Cushitic language spoken in southern Ethiopia) *ʔaake* means both 'animal' and 'bird' (Haspelmath and Tadmor [eds.] 2009). The direction of this shift in Gawwada is unclear.

It is difficult to explain the shift 'wug' > 'animal'. It can be assumed that the source of the meaning 'animal' is a combined life-form 'wug-mammal'. This folk life-form is attested by Brown in Koiwai, Mokilese and Tzotzil (Zinacantan), Daga and Southern Paiute (Chemehuevi dialect) (Brown 1984: 30–31). The existence of such forms might be explained by the fact that birds, fish and snakes are in the most marked zone of the zoological life-form sequence (Brown 1984: 24). The term for 'wug' or for 'mammal' in language implies terms for 'bird', 'fish' and 'snake' but not vice versa. Mammals and wugs in such languages can receive one general label. This path of semantic development, in our opinion, explains the semantic shift 'wug' > 'animal' in Mohave and Nivkh: Mohave *'ichipay* 'insect', 'animal' (in compounds), for example *ichipay iihukwakyuly* 'elephant' (lit. 'animal with long nose') (Munro et al. 1992: 40), Nivkh *ŋa* 'animal, mammal', 'insect' *ŋχi ŋa* 'wild animal', *tol ŋa* 'sea animal', *pirifiri ŋa* 'harmful insect' and *mat' ŋa* 'small bug' (Savel'eva and Taksami 1970: 222).

In Kildin Saami perhaps the polysemy 'insect, bug' and 'animal' arose originally in an ironic use of the word. Stinging insects were described as mammals (animals): Kildin Saami *žēva* 'insect, bug' (*ēmm'ne oavvtej pējves't, jugke žēva ëadtej* 'Earth warmed by the sun and each insect came to life'), 'animal' (*kuedt' žēva* 'domestic animals', *pāmm' žēva* 'carnivorous animals') (Kuruč [ed.] 1985: 88). It may be that such polysemy appeared in Russian dialects which were a source for Saami *žēva*, cp. Russian *živnost'* 'lice' (Saratov) (Filin and Sorokoletov [eds.] 1972: 152), *živod'* 'parasitic insect' (Vologda) (Filin and Sorokoletov [eds.]

1972: 154) and *život* 'horseflies, gnats, gadflies etc.' (Pskov) (Filin and Sorokoletov [eds.] 1972: 158).

It should be noted in Hiligaynon there is a lexeme *sápat* 'animal', 'beast' and *sápat-sápat* 'vermin, insect, parasite, or the like' (Kaufmann 1934) and Kinyarwanda *igisīmba* 'animal (especially small and biting)', 'insect' (Cox et al. 1969, 48). In Seychellois Creole *bebet* 'animal', 'insect', 'rude man' is borrowed from French *bébête* 'animal' (Haspelmath and Tadmor [eds.] 2009).

15.1.3.2 Semantic shifts for 'plant'

The most frequent semantic source of 'plant', according to the collected material, is the meaning 'to grow'. The semantic shift 'to grow' > 'plant' can be found in at least seven Indo-European roots: Ancient Greek φύω (*phýō*) 'to grow' > φυτόν (*phytón*) 'plant' (Liddell et al. 1996: 1966), Lithuanian *áugti* 'to grow' > *áugalas* 'plant' (Liberis 1988: 95–96), Common Slavic *rasti* > Russian *rastenie*, Belorussian *raslina*, Czech *roslina*, Polish *roślina* 'plant' and other Slavic, Sanskrit *viruh-* 'to sprout, to produce shoots, to develop (about plant)' > *vīrúdh* 'plant (grass, bush)' (MacDonell 1893: 294), German *wachsen* 'to grow' > *Gewächs* 'plant', Swedish *växa* 'to grow' > *växt* 'plant' (Berglund [ed.] 2007: 893–894) and Ossetic *zajyn* 'to grow' > *zajægoj* 'plant' (Abaev 1989: 284). Outside of the Indo-European languages, we see more then ten examples of this semantic shift: Alutiiq *nau-* 'to grow (of plant)' > *nauq* 'plant' (Fortescue, Jacobson, and Kaplan 1994: 207), Chaplino Yupik *pītaquq* 'to sprout' > *pītun* 'plant' (Fortescue, Jacobson, and Kaplan 1994: 261), Chukchi *tŋé-, -nŋe-* 'to grow', *tŋé-cʔə-n* 'plant, flower', Koryak *táŋe-, -nŋe-* 'to grow', *təŋé-chə-n* 'plant', Tatar *ys-* 'to grow' > *ysemlek* 'plant' from the common Turkic root meaning 'to grow, to rise' (Sevortjan 1974: 552–553), Turkish *bit-* 'to grow' > *bitki* 'plant' from another Turkic root with the same meaning (Sevortjan 1978: 154–155), Japanese *shokubutsu* (植物) 'plant, vegetable world, flora', lit. 'growing thing' (Konrad [ed.] 1970, 2: 54), Finnish *kasvaa* 'to grow' > *kasvi* 'plant' (Vahros and Ščerbakov 2007: 203–204), Komi *bidmini* 'to grow' > *bidmög* 'plant' (Beznosikova, Ajbabina, and Kosnyreva 2000: 68), Hungarian *növekedni* 'to grow' > *növény* 'plant' (Gáldi 1987: 566), Indonesian *tumbuh* 'to grow' > *tumbuhan* 'plant' (Korigodskij, Kondraškin, and Zinov'ev 1961: 1010) and Hawaiian *ulu* 'to grow', *mea ulu* 'plant' ('thing' + 'to grow') (Pukui and Elbert 1992: 139).

Some other semantic shifts that give rise to a general term for 'plant' are connected to terms for folk life-forms (tree, grass), parts of plants (stem, fruit, flower), and with the verb meaning 'to plant'. The shift 'herb, grass' > 'plant' is present in Swedish *gräs* 'grass' > Kildin Saami *rāss'* 'plant' (Kuruč [ed.] 1985: 288), Dakota *wato* 'grass' (Riggs 1992: 539) > 'plant' (Williamson 1992: 141), Eninhdhilyakwa *amarda* 'herbaceous plant' > 'plants' (Waddy 1988: 70) and Serbo-Croatian *biljka* 'plant' (Tolstoj 1957: 39), cf. in the sense of the biological kingdom: *botanika e grana biologie koja se bavi naučnim pročavanem biljaka* 'botany is a branch of biology that deals with the scientific study of plants'. The shift 'tree' > 'plant' occurs in languages of South and Central America and Africa: Seri *hehe* 'wood, log, stick, branch, tree, pole' > 'any plant, regardless of size' (Felder and Moser 1985: 56–60), Manga-Kanuri *kə̀ská* 'tree', 'bush', 'wood', 'plant', for example, *kə̀ská mánà kámúyé* 'a kind of water lily' (Jarret 2007: 84), Seychellois Creole *pye* 'tree', 'plant' (< French *pied* 'foot') (Haspelmath and Tadmor [eds.] 2009; Chaudenson 1974: 842–843) and Quechua *sach'a* 'tree' > 'plant'. To describe trees strictly Quechua uses expression *sach'a pura* lit. 'true tree' (Berlin 1992: 195).

Parts of plants do not often play this role. The semantic shift 'caulis, stem, stalk' > 'plant' can be observed in Evenki *orōkto* 'grass (withered), hay, straw; culm' (Boldyrev 2000, 2: 474), Aldan dialect 'plant' (Myreeva 2001: 65), also in the Russian-Evenki dictionary (Vasilevič 2005, 2: 148), Swahili *mmea* 'shoot, sprout', 'plant', 'agricultural crop', 'vegetation, verdure' (Polikanov 1997; Rechenbach 1967: 337) and Yukuna *ínaji* 'bush', 'plant', 'stem, stalk, shoot' with an unclear direction of shift (Shauer et al. 2005, 47: 228). The shift 'seed, fruit' > 'plant' is represented in Kinyarwanda, Kirundi *imbuto* 'seed, fruit', 'plant' (Cox, Adamson, and Teusink 1969: 6; Cox 1969b: 19). Thai *puīt* 'seed, seedlings', 'plant' (*puīt yuīn tòn* 'perennial plant') is a loanword from Sanskrit *bīja* 'seed, grain' (Haspelmath and Tadmor [eds.] 2009; MacDonell 1893: 196; Morev 1964: 527). And the shift 'flower' > 'plant' is attested in Otomi *doni* 'flower', 'plant' (Haspelmath and Tadmor [eds.] 2009). Tarifiyt Berber (Rifian) *nnəwwā* 'plant' is a loan from Arabic (Moroccan) رون (*nəwwar'*) 'flower', Classic Written Arabic رَّاون (*nuwwār*) 'blossom, flower' (Haspelmath and Tadmor [eds.] 2009).

The verbal meaning 'to plant' as a source for folk kingdom terms leads us to believe that the appearance of the term coincides with the era of agriculture. This semantic shift is widespread geographically: Ge'ez *takala* 'to put into, to put in, to stick in, to place; to plant' > *takl* 'plant' (Dillmann 1955: 563–564), Old Church Slavonic *saditi* 'to plant' > *sadŭ* 'plant'[7], Mandarin Chinese *zhìwù* (植) 'to plant, to cultivate' *zhìwù* (植物) 'plant; vegetation, flora' (Ošanin [ed.] 1983, 3: 307), Kaingang *ēkrãn* 'to plant', *ēkré* 'plant' (Wiesemann 2002: 10) and Hausa *shúukàa* 'to sow, to plant', 'plant' (Haspelmath and Tadmor [eds.] 2009), in Robinson (1913: 333, 335) only the verbal meaning and derivative *shipka* 'small plants' are found.

---

7 This word is used in Codex Suprasliensis and Codex Zographensis as a translation of Ancient Greek φυτόν *phytón* (Cejtlin et al. [eds.] 1994: 590).

We have also found one case when the meaning 'green' is the source of a term 'plant'. In Selice Romani *zelen* 'green' > *zelenipe* 'plant' is borrowed from Slovak *zelená* 'green' (Haspelmath and Tadmor [eds.] 2009). Apart from folk kingdom terms, however, this semantic shift is also observed in Russian *zelen'* 'greenery, verdure', Lezgian *q:az* 'green colour', 'young green corn shoots' (Talibov and Gadžiev 1966: 175), Mongolian *nogoon* 'green', 'greenery, verdure', English *greens* 'greenery, vegetables', French *verdure* 'greenery, verdure, grass, leaves, vegetables', Lettish *zàḷš* 'green', *zāla* 'grass' (Andronov 2002: 217) and from the same Indo-European root Lithuanian *žolė* 'grass' (Buck [1949] 1988: 522; Liberis 1988: 920).

15.1.4 Specifying epithets

Usually generic species name consist of one primary lexeme (simple unitary word). If generic species contain several taxa of a lower rank (folk varietas), the most typical representative is denoted by one-word term and the others are described with specifying epithets (e.g. *fox* 'Vulpes vulpes' and swift fox 'Vulpes velox', arctic fox 'Vulpes lagopus'). If in traditional culture it is necessary to give a name to a new species of plants or animals, the name is normally given by comparison with better-known species. A name of a new species in such cases is often a phrase or a compound. The compound includes a typical species name complemented by a qualifying epithet. Frequently this epithet means 'foreign, overseas', 'strange'.

We can find many similar examples in languages from different regions: Athapaskan *tli čo?ʰ*'horse', lit. 'dog big' (Witkowski and Brown 1983: 569), Tzotzil *castillan ʔixim* 'wheat', lit. 'Castilian maize', Zoque *castellan-tunuc* 'chicken', lit. 'Castilian turkey' (Brown 1999: 27), Dakota *omnicagmigmi* 'pear', lit. 'beans round', Cheyenne *meovemaxemeu* 'peach', lit. 'fuzzy apple' (Brown 1999: 28), Bachajón Tzeltal *tumin cčix* 'sheep', lit. 'cotton deer', Chuvash *şĕr ulmi* 'potato', lit. 'earth apple' (Degtjarev 2002: 51–52), Mongolian *dalajn nohoj* 'seal', lit. 'sea dog', Spanish *trigo sarraceno* 'buckwheat', lit. 'Saracen wheat', Welsh *gwenith Indian* 'maize', lit. 'Indian wheat', Chechen *lättkomur* 'raspberry', lit. 'earth mulberry' (Hazbulatov 2004: 69), Avar *tsorosortl* 'maize', lit. 'wheat from Tsoro[8]' (Hazbulatov 2004: 98), Tigrinya *mašäla baḥri* 'maize, lit. foreign sorghum' (Kane 2000: 1103), Harari *bäḥar zāf* 'eucalyptus' (Leslau 1963: 40), Zway *barzaf* 'eucalyptus'

---

8 The region of Tsoro is now Zaqatala and Balakan districts of northwestern Azerbaijan.

(Leslau 1979: 135) and Gogot *bähar zaf* 'eucalyptus', lit. 'foreign tree' (Leslau 1979: 135).

This particular mechanism in the formation of folk nomenclature will be important for further consideration of the influence of "naïve biology" on the scientific taxonomy (section 15.2.1).

15.2 Interaction between scientific and folk biological taxonomies

15.2.1 Influence of a "naïve" model of the world on scientific concepts

First of all, it is worth noting that as "naïve" biology in many ways reflects human views preceding the emergence of science or at an early stage of its formation, the history of biological science, when viewed from the perspective of a linguist who studies a linguistic model of the world, may look like a process of overcoming of the concepts "inherited" from "naïve biology". An important example of how scientific biology in its development at first used the heritage of "naïve" biology and then overcame it is the modern taxonomy of the organic world and the establishment of binomial (binary) nomenclature.

Descriptions of flora and fauna in works by ancient authors – Pliny the Elder, Dioscorides, Theophrastus, Aristotle – primarily covered flora and fauna of the eastern Mediterranean. With the further development of biology (especially actively since the 16th century), new species were described by scientists from countries further to the north (Germany, England, France). Names of new species were formed based on the names of Mediterranean species with the help of the mechanism of folk biology that has been described above.

Let us see how plant names were formed in the first printed "herbals" by German authors. The first three of these works' authors are: Otto Brunfels (1488–1534), Hieronymus Bock (alias Tragus, 1498–1554), and Leonhart Fuchs (1501–1566) (Arber 1912: 47–63). The method for adding new species to the terminology in these herbals was the same as the mechanism in naïve biological nomenclature. Brunfels' herbal describes mallow, known from antiquity, and calls it *Malva*, whereas local German species is marked as 'horse mallow' (*Malva equina*). Bock mentions ancient melissa (*Mütterkraut*) and German 'common melissa' (*Gemein Mütterkraut*). Fuchs calls ancient melissa "true" (*Melissophylon verum*), while referring to common Melissa with the epithet "bastard" (*Melissophylon vulgaris vel adulterinus*) (Atran 1990: 131–132).

At the end of the 17th century, the principle of "one genus – one name" was formulated in biology (Kupriyanov 2005). Names of all species belonging to one genus should begin with the same word or set expression – the name of a genus. Names of species should be formed by adding more or less verbose differences of species (so called *differenitae specificae*) to the genus name. Linnaeus made this principle universal and subjected the description of differences between species to strict rules. According to Linnaeus' estimates, the length of the differentiation should not be more than 12 words (Linnaeus 1751: 228). Using verbose names in practice has been associated with certain difficulties. First, they were long, and second, they can be changed: after addition of new species into a genus, *differenitae specificae* should be revised.

In the mid 1740s Linnaeus and his students began experimenting with the use of so called trivial names (Latin *nomina trivialia*). Trivial names were limited by only two rules: they should not be repeated within the genus and should not change after the addition of a new species. In contrast with *differentiae specifica*, *nomina trivialia* were given to plants and animals even of genera consisting of a single species (Linnaeus 1758). Thus the basis for modern binomial nomenclature of plants and animals –consisting of genus and species name (the latter is former nomen trivile) (Jeffrey 1977) – was laid down and it is easy to see specifying epithets in this nomenclature.

Another example of "naïve biology" heritage that has long existed in scientific model of the world is the preservation of aggregate categories corresponding to "lower" animals in naïve nomenclature. Isolation of special groups of "lower" animals remained in scientific biological taxonomy for a long time (Kuprijanov 2005: 19–20). Vertebrata (fishes, amphibians, reptiles) have been separated of this aggregate category relatively early. However, even after this separation there still remained aggregate groups within verberates, like Latin *Amphibia* – according to 18th–19th century classifications they were a group covering all terrestrial vertebrates except birds and mammals. By the end of the 19th century, the name *Amphibia* (in Russian academic literature *gady*) was assigned to amphibians, but gradually fell out of scientific use. Invertebrates remained an undivided group for a longer period. The regular study of "lower animals" began only after Carl Linnaeus, who was the first to distinguish *Insecta* "insects" from *Vermes* "worms" (Linnaeus 1758).

Other "folk life-forms" of animals and plants also remained for a rather long time. In earlier experiments of classification, the construction of folk life-forms prevailed, and later, with the development of science, the number of folk life-forms decreased. In the first European classification of plants by Theophrastus

(I.III.1 quoted by Theopheastus 1916: 22–23) tree (δένδρον déndron), shrub (θάμνος thámnos), subshrub or suffrutex (φρύγανον phrýganon) and herb (πόα póa) were marked out.

The first attempt at scientific classification of plants in China was made by Lĭ Shízhēn (1518–1598). In his work, he divided plants into herbs (cao), crops (gu), vegetables (cai), fruit trees (guo) and trees (mu) (Titarenko [ed.] 2009, 5: 388) – typical example of folk life-forms, only in the specific details do they differ from the division in European cultures. In Pierre Belon's work about birds (1555), he also examined bats, and in his book about fish (1551), also crocodiles, whales, turtles, otters and some marine invertebrates were described (Kuprijanov 2005: 59). A similar example is found in the field of botany– a long-time division of plants into two main groups, "trees" and "grass", complied with "naïve biology", whereas in modern scientific botany it is recognized, for example, that the herb alchemilla is more congeneric to apple and cherry (Rosaceae family), and wheat to bamboo (Gramineae family) than alchemilla and wheat are to each other.

Scientific biological classification seeks to reflect the evolutionary history of taxa. All species, dating back to the same ancestor (and only these) are combined into one genus; genera, in their turn, into one family and so on. Strictly following this principle in the 1960s became known as phylogenetic systematics (Hennig 1966; Wiley 1981; Kljuge 2000: 25–28). It admits the existence of only monophyletic systematic groups in classification (derived from common ancestor). Monophyletic groups are opposed to polyphyletic, in which their constituent subgroups are more closely related to other groups not included in this particular one. Isolation of a polyphyletic group is usually based on passing resemblance.

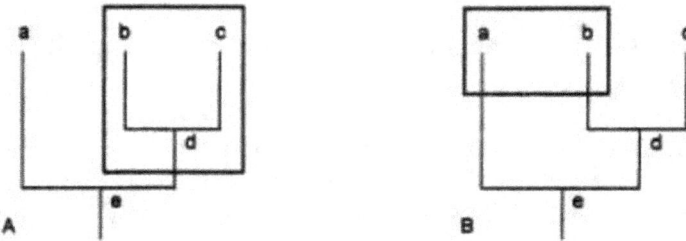

Figure 1: Monophyletic (A) and polyphyletic (B) groups.

An example of monophyletic group, comprising types b, c and their common ancestral species d is marked with a dark outline is shown on the left. The polyphyletic group which includes types a and b but not includes type c that diverged from the same ancestor (d) with b is shown on the right (Kljuge 2000).

An example of a polyphyletic group could be *pinnipeds* (Latin Pinnipedia), considered as an order of mammals. In fact, one of pinnipeds subgroups (walruses and eared seals [Otariidae]), is akin to the bear family (*Ursidae*), and the other (earless seals) to the weasel family (Mustelidae). The pinnipeds have no common ancestor. As a result, in modern taxonomy former pinnipeds have been divided into two separate families within the order of predators (Tedford 1976). This is therefore an example of how modern approach to biological classification (known as «cladistics») does not accept some of the larger aggregated groups inherited from «naïve biology Finally, another very characteristic feature of "naïve biology" should also be mentioned here. With a necessary correction, it is used in scientific biology too, and the rejection of it in science would clearly be inappropriate. "Naïve biology" objects are often successfully described using the concept of a "prototype", which is known from cognitive psychology and linguistic semantics. In different cultures, we can allocate more or less prototypical plant and animal species to such concepts as birds, trees, etc. These prototypes have direct correspondence within scientific biology, where each species has mandatory set type specimen (stored in a museum or herbarium), for species there is a type specimen, for family – a type genus, and so on (Kljuge 2000: 51). Such an approach based on type taxa selection was reflected in the proposals to reform biological nomenclature, taking type species names for the names of taxa. In this case, for example, angiosperms (Angiospermae) will be called *Magnolia*. In the last update of the *International code of botanical nomenclature* the term Magnoliophyta is given as the main term for angiosperms, but Angiospermae is also admissible. (McNeill et al. 2006, article 16.1).

15.2.2 The opposite influence: traces of scientific biology in folk biology

Certainly, for today's Europeans who have received an education in schools and colleges, the naïve model of the world has already been transformed under the influence of science. This applies not only to the area of "naïve biology". According to Jakovleva, "in modern human world model the border between naïve and scientific worldviews has become less distinct" (Jakovleva 1994: 10). So it is possible that the "naïve zoology" of a modern Russian citizen no longer contains the idea that whales and dolphins are fish. Instead there is an understanding that they belong to the class of mammals, but are often mistakenly classified as fish (information about this mistake has almost become "commonplace"). Similar cases of the penetration of scientific concepts and terms into the realm of folk conceptions was typical before the 20th century.

For example, the word *nasekomoe* 'insect' in the Russian language was initially a scientific term only. It appeared in the 18th century and was first recorded in a dictionary in 1731. According to the origin, this word is morpheme-by-morpheme calque of Lat. *insectum* (Černyx 1993, 1: 560; Fasmer 1989, 3: 47), but already in the first half of the 19th century it came into common use in the standard language (it occurs in poems by Pushkin and Fet, as well as prose by Gogol and Turgenev), and the term *nasekomoe* has taken its place in the Russian language model of the world. However, according to Krivoščapova (2007: 23), the word *nasekomoe* is almost entirely absent from dialects even in the 21st century, and the lexemes *gnus, drjan', bukaški, moškara* ('gnats, trash, insects, midges') and others are used instead of it.

In the very rare cases when this word was recorded by dialectologists it often changes meaning, shifting from a scientific term into a naïve biology concept. In the Tomsk region: *volosec, ili volos – takaja nasekomaja, pakost', kak volos, tol'ko živoj* 'volosets or a hair – such insect, filth, just like a hair but alive', (Filin and Sorokoletov [eds.] 1985: 157). "Live hair" is a standard term for the Russian folk culture description of the freshwater horsehair worm (Russian *volosatik*, Latin *Nematomorpha*). In the Novosibirsk region, recorded in 1970: *nasekomaja* 'amphibian or reptile' – *Zmeja, jaščerica ili ljaguška – eto nasekomaja* 'Snake, lizard or frog are *nasekomaja*' (Filin and Sorokoletov [eds.] 1985: 157). And in Russian generally, in colloquial speech, the semantics of the word *nasekomoe* is far from the strictly delimited meaning of a biological term. For example, spiders and mites, which in zoology refers to a different class – Arachnids – are considered to be insects. The fact that in Russian folk nomenclature spiders are counted as insects explains the semantics of the word *pauk* 'spider' in Russian dialects: *pauk* 'gadfly' in Perm region, recorded in 1914 (Sorokoletov [ed.] 1990: 238), *pauki* 'gadflies, horseflies' in Sverdlovsk region (Krivoščapova 2007: 22).

We believe that the influence of scientific taxonomy on folk taxonomy explains the unusual property of the British ornithonyms system noted in Fridman and Koblik (2006). In English, birds' species are differentiated very subtly by use of composite terms: *swinhoe's white-throated rock thrush* (Petrophila gularis), *red-throated diver* (Gavia stellata), *ruddy Shelduck* (Tadorna ferruginea), *yellow-legged buttonqual* (Turnix tanki), *parrot crossbill* (Loxia pytyopsittacus).

These names recall scientific nomenclature, but they are not calques of Latin terms. At the same time, one-word names of birds in English show a correspondence to genera or even larger groups that is typical of folk taxonomy: large groups of passerine united under the names *finch* and *sparrow*, most whitethroats, chiffchaffs, millerbirds and other similar species are united by the ornithonym *warbler*.

The boundaries between science and naïve models of the world in biology are perhaps more blurred than in other areas. So, beyond all doubt, Australian plant *Melaleuca alternifolia*, or the Philippine fish *Pandaka pygmaea* are not included in Russian "naïve biology": they are known only to professional botanists (and pharmacologists), and ichthyologists, while, quite the contrary, plantain or bass are included. But if you take the guppy fish (Lebistes reticulatus), which became a popular aquarium object in Russia in the second half of the 20th century, it is difficult to provide a clear answer to the question of whether it belongs to "naïve biology". These questions are partially reflected in socio-linguistic research on the interaction between professional jargon and sublanguages with the literary language.

Of course, "naïve biology" in the minds of people in rural areas and especially representatives of "traditional cultures", who live close to nature, is richer and more developed than that of urban citizens. However, they can find fairly specific things such as "naïve genetics", often within discussions surrounding genetically modified organisms. Such facts should rather be an object of interest not to linguistics but for other disciplines studying social consciousness, collective myths in modern society, etc.

15.3 Conclusion

Folk systematics is a stable knowledge system reflected in the language, which is reproduced not only in archaic societies but even in written cultures up to the 21st century. Depending on the genre of speech different transitional forms can be found from systems that are completely based on folk taxonomy through to systems with few folk elements. A focus on the reader's interests leads authors to use more illustrative and familiar categories of the folk systematic, rather than classifications corresponding to cutting-edge science (Pavlinov and Ljubarskij 2011: 24–27). Folk classifications is easy to understand and to learn as a result of a predominant use of external features and utilitarian properties in comparison with scientific systematics, which tends to create a classification reflecting the genesis of organisms.

In particular cases, researchers note the significant correspondence between species in folk systematics and species described by professional zoologists. There is a widely known example of bird-of-paradise species in New Guinea folk systematics (Mayr 1957; 1988). However, this happens only when the species, identified by zoologists, have easily distinguishable externals. There are many examples in which folk systematics unites different biological species into one (see section 15.1.3). There are also cases when folk species are more nuanced than biological. Folk systematics identifies as separate species larvae and adult forms, males and females when sexual dimorphism is strong, colour variations, summer and winter appearances, varieties of cultivated plants, breeds of animals. All these cases show that "folk systematicians" do not distinguish species according to a modern scientific understanding, but just determine some classification which is meaningful and "obvious" for them (Pavlinov and Ljubarskij 2011: 29).

There are rare cases when a distinction between particular species in folk classification, at first rejected by biologists, later becomes scientifically acknowledged. The species of tapir from the Brazilian forest, described at the end of 2013 (Tapirus kabomani) was well-known by the Karitiâna people living near its habitat (Cozzuol et al. 2013). Moreover, a specimen of this animal was obtained as early as 1913 by Theodore Roosevelt and Cândido Rondon Scientific Expedition. Local hunters assured the expedition members that it was a separate species of a tapir, but the specialists from American Museum of Natural History identified it as the well-known lowland tapir (Tapirus terrestris). Such occasions, however, do not demonstrate the real existence of "folk species" in general. They merely remind us that scientists should not totally ignore local inhabitants' knowledge of the nature of the region.

Biology normally creates scientific terms based on the ordinary lexical items that in one or another way reflect folk biology The development of scientific systematics largely consists in the overcoming of the "heritage" of folk systematics. This development is gradual. One of the early stages can be the genesis of folk kingdoms (see section 15.1.3). During the first stages of the formation of scientific systematics, methods for the alignment of species was not yet developed, so high-level taxa were distinguished on the ground of external resemblance. This is why until the middle of the 19th century high-level taxa were substantially folk biological life-forms, while such taxa as genus and species had already been built on the genealogical principle. The boundary lay approximately at the level of family and order (Pavlinov and Ljubarskij 2011: 489). Consistent rejection of the classification based on life-forms in favor of taxa with common ancestry took place only in the 1960–s when phylogenetic systematics appeared.

It is significant that when eco-morphological classification, which does not claim to reflect the organisms' genealogic history, appeared in the 19th century, the groups discriminated by this approach coincided with the high-level taxa of folk systematics. The first attempt at eco-morphological classification was the work of Alexander von Humboldt (Humboldt 1806), where "the basic forms of life" were determined. Subsequently the concept of the life-form was developed in such works as Warming (1884, 1895); Aleev (1986); Usteri (1941) and others and became a specific approach in the study of biodiversity, which was named ecomorphology or biomorphology (Pavlinov 2007; Ljubarskij 1992).

Folk taxonomy has a number of linguistic characteristics which are present in all or in most languages of the world. Taxa of the highest rank (folk kingdoms, if they are present in a given language, and folk life-forms) have names which consist of one word. Also, generic species are labeled with one word. Folk varietas if necessary are described with folk species names and specifying epithets, but the most typical representative is denoted by a one-word term. When members of the culture come across plants or animals that are exotic for them, these species become associated with the most similar local taxa. Names for new species are formed with the names of familiar species and specifying epithets (section 15.1.4). This last feature was inherited by Linnean binary nomenclature from folk systematics (section 15.2.1). The fact of special interest is that scientific biological terms which have become popular in everyday language obtain semantic features which are characteristic for terms of folk biology.

The practical significance of studying folk biological nomenclature and correlating it with scientific terminology has substantially increased lately, because of the active participation of local inhabitants of Africa, South America and Southeast Asia in the field of biological research (Araya, Schmiedel, and von Witt 2009; Basset et al. 2000, 2004; Janzen 1993; Janzen and Hallwachs 1992, 2011). Local people participating in such studies are sometimes called para-ecologists para-taxonomists or biodiversity facilitators. Before starting work, they receive special initial biological training. In order to organize such training, it is important to understand the structure of the biological lexicon of their language and to teach them to use scientific terms correctly.

15.4 References

Abaev, Vasilij I. 1989. *Istoriko-etimologičeskij slovar' osetinskogo jazyka*. [Historical and etymological dictionary of Ossetic]. Vol. IV. Leningrad: Nauka.
Aleev, Jurij G. 1986. *Èkomorfologija* [Ecomorphology]. Kiev: Naukova dumka.
Andronov, Aleksej V. 2002. *Materialy dlja latyšsko-russkogo slovarja*. [Materials for Lettish-Russian dictionary]. Saint Petersburg: Saint Petersburg State University. Faculty of Philology.
Annenkov, Nikolaj I. 1878. *Botaničeskij slovar'*. [Botanical dictionary]. Saint Petersburg: The Imperial Saint Petersburg Academy of Sciences.
Araya Yoseph N., Ute Schmiedel, and Caitlin von Witt. 2009. Linking 'citizen scientists' to professionals in ecological research, examples from Namibia and South Africa. *Conservation Evidence* 6: 11–17.

Arber, Agnes. 1912. *Herbals, their origin and evolution, a chapter in the history of botany 1470–1670*. Cambridge: Cambridge University Press.
Atran, Scott. 1990. *Cognitive foundations of natural history: towards an anthropology of science*. Cambridge: Cambridge University Press.
Bacarreza, Donato G. 2000. *Diccionario basico del idioma aymara*. La Paz: Instituto de Estudios Bolivianos.
Bagana, Gerome and Aleksandr N. Langner. 2014. *The fate of the French in Africa*. Moscow: INFRA-M.
Balandin, Aleksej N. and Matrëna P. Vaxrusheva. 1958. *Mansijsko-russkij slovar' s leksičeskimi paralleljami iz južno-mansijskogo (kondinskogo) dialekta*. [Mansi-Russian dictionary with lexical from South Mansi (Konda) Dialect]. Leningrad: Učpedgiz.
Bannikov, Andrej G. 1971. *Zemnovodnye i presmykajuščiesja SSSR*. [Amphibians and reptiles of the USSR]. Moscow: Mysl'.
Basset, Yves, Vojtech Novotny, Scott E. Miller, and Richard Pyle. 2000. Quantifying biodiversity: Experience with parataxonomists and digital photography in Papua New Guinea and Guyana. *BioScience* 50, No. 10: 899–908.
Basset, Yves, Vojtech Novotny, Scott E. Miller, George D. Weiblen, Olivier Missa, and Alan J. A. Stewart. 2004. Conservation and biological monitoring of tropical forests: the role of parataxonomists. *Journal of Applied Ecology* 41: 163–174.
Berglund, Britt-Marie (ed.). 2007. *Novyj bol'šoj švedsko-russkij slovar'*. [New comprehensive Swedish-Russian dictionary]. Moscow: Živoj jazyk.
Berlin, Brent. 1992. *Ethnobiological classification: principles of categorization of plants and animals in traditional societies*. Princeton, NJ: Princeton University Press.
Berlin, Brent. 1994. The relation of folk systematics to biological systematics and nomenclature. *Annual Review of Systematics and Ecology* 17: 259–271.
Berlin, Brent, Dennis E. Breedlove, and Peter H. Raven. 1968. Covert categories and folk taxonomies. *American Anthropologist*, New Series, Vol. 70: 290–299.
Berlin, Brent, Dennis E. Breedlove, and Peter H. Raven. 1973. General principles of classification and nomenclature in folk biology. *American Anthropologist*, New Series, 75(1): 214–242.
Bertel's, A. E. 1982. Razdely slovarja, semantičeskie polja i tematičeskie gruppy slov [Lexicon units, semantic fields and topical lexical groups]. *Voprosy jazykoznanija* 4: 52–64.
Beznosikova, Lucija M., Evgenija A. Ajbabina, and Raisa I. Kosnyreva. 2000. *Komi-russkij slovar'*. [Komi-Russian dictionary]. Syktyvkar: Insitiute of language, literature and history. Komi Scientific Centre. Ural Department of the Russian Academy of Sciences.
Biberstein-Kazimirski, Albin de. 1860. *Dictionnaire arabe-français*. 2 vols., Paris: Editions G.-P. Maisonneuve.
Boldyrev, Boris V. 2000. *Èvenkijsko-russkij slovar' v 2 tomax*. [Evenki-Russian dictionary in 2 vol.]. Novosibirsk: Nauka.
Borş, Anton (ed.). 2005. *Dicţionar român-rus sinonimizat*. [Romanian-Russian dictionary with synonyms]. Vol. 1. Chişinău: Ştiinţa. Prup Intarnaţional.
Brown, Cecil. H. 1974. Unique beginners and covert categories in folk biological taxonomies. *American Anthropologist*, New Series 76: 325–327.
Brown, Cecil. H. 1977. Folk botanical life-forms: their universality and growth. *American Anthropologist*, New Series 79. 317–342.
Brown, Cecil. H. 1979. Folk zoological life-forms: their universality and growth. *American Anthropologist*, New Series 81. 791–817.

Brown, Cecil. H. 1981. Growth and development of folk zoological life-forms in Polynesian languages. *The Journal of the Polynesian Society*. 90, 1: 83–110.
Brown, Cecil. H. 1984. *Language and living things*. New Brunswick: Rutgers University Press.
Brown, Cecil. H. 1999. *Lexical acculturation in native American languages*. New York & Oxford: Oxford University Press
Brown, Cecil. H. 2002. Paradigmatic relations of inclusion and identity I: Hyponymy. In Alan Cruse, Franz Hundsnurscher, Michael Job and Peter Rolf Lutzeier (eds.), *Lexicologie/ Lexicology*, Vol. 1, 472–480. Berlin & New York.: Mouton de Gruyter
Buck, Carl D. 1988. Reprint. *A Dictionary of selected synonyms in the principal indo-european languages. A contribution to the history of ideas*. Chicago & London: University of Chicago Press.
Cejtlin, Ral'a M., Radoslav Večerka, and Emilija Blagova (eds.). 1994. *Staroslavjanskij slovar' (po rukopisjam X – XI vekov)*. [Old Church Slavonic dictionary (based on X – XI centuries manuscripts)]. Moscow: Russkij jazyk.
Černyx, Pavel. 1993. *Istoriko-ètimologičeskij slovar' sovremennogo russkogo jazyka v dvux tomax*. [Historical and etymological dictionary of modern Russian language in 2 vol.]. Moscow: Russkij jazyk.
Černyšëv, Vasilij I. (ed.). 1948. *Slovar' sovremennogo russkogo literaturnogo jazyka v 17 tomax* [Modern Russian literary language dictionary in 17 vol.]. Moscow & Leningrad: Izdatel'stvo Akademii nauk SSSR.
Ciorănescu, Aleksandru. 2005. *Dicţionarul etimologic al limbii române*. [Romanian etymological dictionary]. Bucureşti: Editira SAECULUM I. O.
Chaudenson, Robert. 1974. *Le lexique du parler créole de la Réunion*, 2 vols, Paris: Honoré Champion.
Coleman, Arnold D. Esimbi dictionary On-line http://www.rogerblench.info/Language/ Niger-Congo/Bantoid/Tivoid/Esimbi/Esimbi%20dictionary.pdf (accessed 7 February 2012).
Cook, Dorothy M. and Frances L. Gralow. 2001. *Diccionario bilingüe koreguaje–español, español–koreguaje*. Bogotá: Editorial Alberto Lleras Camargo. On-line www.sil.org/americas/colombia/pubs/DiccKoreguaje_41797.pdf (accessed 7 February 2012).
Coteanu Ion, Luiza Seche, and Mircea Seche. 1998. *Dicţionarul explicativ al limbii române*. [Romanian explanatory dictionary]. Bucureşti: Academia Română, Institutul de Lingvistică "Iorgu Iordan", Editura Univers Enciclopedic. On-line http://dictionare.edu.ro (accessed 7 February 2012).
Cox, Betty E. 1969a. *English – Kirundi dictionary*. Winona Lake: General Missionaty Board of the Free Methodist Church.
Cox, Betty E. 1969b. *Kirundi – English dictionary*. Winona Lake: General Missionaty Board of the Free Methodist Church.
Cox Betty E., Myra Adamson, and Mariel Teusink. 1969. *Dictionary Kinyarwanda – English English – Kinyarwanda*. Winona Lake: General Missionaty Board of the Free Methodist Church.
Cozzuol Mario A., Camila L. Clozato, Elizete C. Holanda, Flávio H. G. Rodrigues, Samuel Nienow, Benoit de Thoisy, Rodrigo A. F. Redondo, and Fabrício R. Santos. 2013. A new species of tapir from the Amazon. In *Journal of Mammalogy*, 94(6): 1331–1345.
Degtjarev, Gennadij A. 2002. *Chuvašskaja narodnaja agrobotaničeskaja terminologija*. [Chuvash folk agrobotanical terminology]. Čeboksary: Chuvash State Institute of the Humanities.
Dement'ev, Georgij P. 1968. *Pticy SSSR*. [Birds of USSR]. Moscow: Mysl'.

Dillmann, August. 1955. *Lexicon linguae aethiopicae cum indice latino*. [Geez dictionary with Latin index]. New York: Friedrich Ungar.
Divuilu, Felix (ed.). 2005. *English – Lingala / Lingala – English dictionary*. Croydon: Congolese Voluntary Organisation.
Dobrovol'skij, Vladimir N. 1894. Zvukopodražanija v narodnom jazyke i poèzii [Onomatopoeia in folk language and poetry]. *Ètnografičeskoe obozrenie* [Ethnographical review]. 3: 81–96
Efremova, Tat'jana F. 2006. *Sovremennyj tolkovyj slovar' russkogo jazyka*. [Modern explanatory dictionary of the Russian language]. Moscow: AST, Astrel', Harvest.
Englert, Sebastián. 1977. *Diccionario Rapanui-Espanol, redactado en la Isla de Pascua*. New York: AMS Press.
Fasmer, Max. 1987. *Ètimologičeskij slovar' russkogo jazyka*. [Etymological dictionary of the Russian language]. Moscow: Progress.
Fedotov, Mihail R. 1996. *Etimologičeskij slovar' čuvašskogo jazyka v dvux tomax*. [Etymological dictionary of the Chuvash language]. Čeboksary: Chuvash State Institute of the Humanities.
Felger, Richard S. and Mary B. Moser. 1985. *People of the desert and sea: Ethnobotany of the Seri indians*. Tuscon: University of Arizona Press
Filin, Fedot P. and Fedot P. Sorokoletov (eds.). 1970. *Slovar' russkix narodnyx govorov. Tom VI*. [Dictionary of Russian dialects. Volume VI]. Moscow, Leningrad (Saint-Petersburg): Nauka.
Filin, Fedot P. and Fedot P. Sorokoletov (eds.). 1972. *Slovar' russkix narodnyx govorov. Tom IX*. [Dictionary of Russian dialects. Volume IX]. Moscow, Leningrad (Saint-Petersburg): Nauka.
Filin, Fedot P. and Fedot P. Sorokoletov (eds.). 1977. *Slovar' russkix narodnyx govorov. Tom XIII*. [Dictionary of Russian dialects. Volume XIII]. Moscow, Leningrad (Saint-Petersburg): Nauka.
Filin, Fedot P. and Fedot P. Sorokoletov (eds.). 1980. *Slovar' russkix narodnyx govorov. Tom XVI*. [Dictionary of Russian dialects. Volume XVI]. Moscow, Leningrad (Saint-Petersburg): Nauka.
Filin, Fedot P. and Fedot P. Sorokoletov (eds.). 1985. *Slovar' russkix narodnyx govorov. Tom XX*. [Dictionary of Russian dialects. Volume XX]. Moscow, Leningrad (Saint-Petersburg): Nauka.
Fortescue, Michael D. 2006. *Comparative Chukotko-Kamtchatkan dictionary*. Berlin & New York: Mouton de Gruyter.
Fortescue, Michael D., Steven A. Jacobson, and Lawrence D. Kaplan. 1994. *Comparative Eskimo dictionary: with Aleut cognates*. Fairbanks: Alaska Native Language Center, University of Alaska.
Franklin, Karl. 2007. *Kewa – English Dictionary*. On-line www.sil.org/pacific/png/pubs/0000515/Kewa_English_dict.pdf (accessed 7 February 2012)
Fridman, Jurij S. and Evgenij A. Koblik. 2006. O nazvanijax ptic v doslovnom perevode s evropejskih jazykov [About bird names in literal translation from European languages]. *Mir ptic* [World of birds] 1(34): 33–39.
Gáldi, László. 1987. *Vengersko-russkij slovar'*. [Hungarian-Russian dictionary]. Moscow, Budapest: Russkij jazyk, Magyar Tudományos Akadémia.
Gamkrelidze, Tamaz V. and Vjačeslav V. Ivanov. 1984. *Indoevropejskij jazyk i indoevropejcy. Rekonstrrukcija i istoriko-tipologičeskij analiz prajazyka i protokultury*. [Indo-European and the Indo-Europeans: A reconstruction and historical analysis of a proto-language and a proto-culture]. Tbilisi: Publishing house of the Tbilisi state university.
Gecova, Ol'ga G. (ed). 1980. *Arxangelskij oblastnoj slovar'* [Arkhangels region dictionary]. Moscow: Nauka.

Gura, Aleksandr V. 1995. Gady. In Nikita I. Tolstoj, (ed.) *Slavjanskie drevnosti. Ètnolingviskičeskij slovar'* [Slavic antiquities. Ethnolinguistic dictionary]. Vol. 1, 546–548. Moscow: Meždunarodnyje otnoshenija: 491–493.

Gura, Aleksandr V. 1997. *Simvolika životnyx v slavjanskoj narodnoj tradicii* [Animal symbolism in Slavic folk tradition]. Moscow: Indrik.

Hadrovics, László and László Gáldi. 1986. Magyar-orosz szotar / *Vengersko-russkij slovar' v dvuh tomah.* [Hungarian-russian language in 2 vol.]. Budapest: Terra.

Haspelmath Martin and Uri Tadmor (eds.). 2009. *World loanword database.* Munich. Max Planck Digital Library. On-line: http://wold.livingsources.org/ (accessed 7 February 2012).

Hays, Terence E. 1976. An empirical method for the identification of covert categories in ethnobiology. *American Ethnologist.* 3: 489–507.

Hazbulatov, Bekhan A. 2004. *Fitonimy v čečenskom jazyke: sinxronno-diaxronnyj analiz.* [Phytonyms in Chechen. Synchronic and diachronic analysis]. Groznyj: Chechen state pedagogical institute Ph. D. dissertation.

Heine, Bernd and Eithne Carlin. 2010. *A dictionary of So, a Nilo-Saharan language of NE Uganda.* Cambridge. Roger Blench, Kay Williamson Educational Foundation. On-line http://www.rogerblench.info/Language/Nilo-Saharan/Kuliak/So%20dictionary.pdf (accessed 7 February 2012).

Hennig, Willi. 1966. *Phylogenetic systematics.* Urbana: The University of Illinios Press.

Humboldt, Alexander von. 1806. *Ideen zur einer physiognomic der gewachse.* Tübingen: Cotta.

Hunn, Eugene S. 1975a. A Measure of the degree of correspondence of folk to scientific biological classification. *American Ethnologist.* 2: 309–327.

Hunn, Eugene S. 1975b. The Tenejapa Tzeltal version of the animal kingdom. [Special issue] *Anthropological Quarterly*, Vol. 48, No. 1, Cognitive Studies in Mesoamerica 14–30.

Jakovleva, Ekaterina S. 1994. *Fragmenty russkoj jazykovoj kartiny mira (modeli prostranstva, vremeni, vosprijatija)* [Fragments of the Russian languge model of the world (models of space, time and peception)]. Moscow: Gnozis.

Janzen Daniel H. and Winifred Hallwachs. 1992. *Training parataxonomists for Costa Rica's national biodiversity inventory: the experiences of the first predominantly female course.* Unpublished Report. On-line http://www.paraecologist.org/images/9/9c/Janzen-Hallwachs_1992_female_parataxonomists.pdf (accessed 14 June 2014).

Janzen Daniel H. and Winifred Hallwachs. 2011. Joining Inventory by parataxonomists with DNA barcoding of a large complex tropical conserved wildland in Northwestern Costa Rica. *PLoS ONE* 6 (8): e18123. On-line http://www.plosone.org/article/info%3Adoi%2F10.1371%2Fjournal.pone.0018123 (accessed 14 June 2014).

Janzen Daniel H., Winifred Hallwachs, Jorge Jimenez, and Rodrigo Gámez. 1993. The role of the parataxonomists, inventory managers and taxonomists in Costa Rica's national biodiversity inventory. In Walter V. Reid, Sarah A. Laird, Carrie A. Meyer, Rodrigo Gámez, Ana Sittenfeld, Daniel H. Janzen, Michael A. Gollin, and Calestous Juma (eds.), *Biodiversity prospecting*, 223–254. Washington, D.C.: World Resources Institute.

Jarrett, Kevin. 2007. *A dictionary of Manga, a Kanuri language of Eastern Niger and NE Nigeria.* Cambrige: Roger Blench, Kay Williamson Educational Foundation & Mallam Dendo Ltd. On-line http://www.rogerblench.info/Language%20data/Nilo-Saharan/Saharan/Manga%20dictionary%20Unicode.pdf (accessed 7 February 2012).

Jeffrey, Charles. 1977. *Biological nomenclature.* London: Edward Arnold.

Kane, Thomas L. 2000. *Tigrinya-English dictionary.* I, II. Springfield: Dunwoody Press.

Kaufmann, John. 1934. *Visayan – English dictionary (Kapulúñgan Binisayá – Ininglís)*. Iloilo. La Editoral. On-line http://www.bohol.ph/diksyunaryo.php (accessed 7 February 2012).
Kiričenko, Ilja M. (ed.). 1963. *Ukrainsko-russkij slovar'. Tom VI*. [Ukrainian-Russian cictionary. Volume VI]. Kiev: Izdatel'stvo Akademii Nauk Ukrainskoj SSR.
Kljuge, Nikita Ju. 2000. *Sovremennaja sistematika nasekomyx. Principy sistematiki živyx organizmov I obščaja sistema nasekomyx s klassifikaciej pervičnobeskrylyx i drevnekrylyx*. [Modern systematics of insects. Principles of systematics of living organisms and general system of insects with classification of Apterygota and Palaeoptera]. Saint Petersburg: Saint Petersburg State University.
Kolosova, Valerija B. 2009. *Leksika i simvolika slavjanskoj narodnoj botaniki*. [Lexis and symbolism of the Slavic folkbotany]. Moscow: Indrik.
Konovalova, Nadežda I. 2000. *Slovar' narodnyx nazvanij rastenij Urala*. [Folk plantnames dictionary of Ural]. Ekaterinburg: Ural State Pedagogical University.
Konrad, Nikolaj I. (ed.). 1970. *Bol'šoj japonsko-russkij slovar'*. [The comprehensive Japanese-Russian dictionary] Moscow: Sovetskaja enciklopedija.
Koppaleva, Julija E. 2007. *Finskaja leksika flory (stanovlenie I funkcionirovanie)*. [Finnish floral vocabulary (formation and development)]. Petrozavodsk: Karelian research centre of Russian Academy of Sciences.
Korigodskij, Robert N., Oleg N. Kondraškin, and Boris I. Zinov'ev. 1961. *Indonezijsko-russkij slovar'*. [Indonesian-Russian dictionary]. Moscow: Gosudarstvennoe izdatel'stvo inostrannyx i nacional'nyx slovarej.
Krivoščapova Julija A. 2007. *Russkaja entomologičeskaja leksika v ètnolingvističeskom osveščenii*. [Russian entomoloical vocabulary from the ethnolinguistic point of view]. Ekaterinburg: Ural State University Ph. D. dissertation.
Kupriyanov, Aleksej V. 2005. *Predystorija biologičeskoj sistematiki* [Prehistory of the biological taxonomy]. Saint-Petersburg: European University at Saint-Petersburg.
Kuruč, Rimma D. (ed.). 1985. *Saamsko-russkij slovar'*. [Saami-Russian dictionary]. Moscow: Russkij jazyk.
Kuznecov, Sergej A. (ed.). 2006. *Bol'šo tolkovyj slovar' russkogo jazyka* [Comprehensive explanatory dictionary of the Russian language]. Saint Petersburg: Norint.
Lajus, Dmitrij L., Julija A. Lajus, Konstantin A. Zgurovsij, Vasilij A. Spiridonov, and Tat'jana Čužekova. 2009. *A vy znaete, čto pokupaete?* [Do you know what you buy?]. Moscow: WWF Russia.
Lakoff, George. 1973. Hedges: A study in meaning criteria and the logic of fuzzy concepts. *Journal of Philosophical Logic*, 2: 458–508.
Lakoff, George. 1987. *Women, fire and dangerous things: What categories reveal about the mind*. Chicago & London: University of Chicago Press.
Lane, Edward W. 1955. *Arabic-English lexicon*. New York.: Ungar.
Laptuhin, Viktor V., Valentina A. Majanc, Ekaterina I. Kedajtene, and Valentina I. Mitrohina. 1987. *Učebnyj russko-xausa-joruba slovar'*. [The learners Russian-Hausa-Yoruba dictionary]. Moscow: Russkij jazyk.
Lehmann, Winfred P. 1986. *A Gothic etymological dictonary*. Based on 3 ed. of Vergleichendes Woerterbuch der Gotiscen Sprache b S. Feist. Leiden.:Brill.
Leslau, Wolf. 1963. *Etymological dictionary of Harari*. Berkely. Los Angeles & Berkeley: University of California Press 1963.
Leslau, Wolf. 1979. *Etymological dictionary of Gurage (Ethiopic)*. Vol. I: Individual dictionaries. Wiesbaden: Otto Harrassowitz.

Liberis, Anatas. 1988. *Litovsko-russkij slovar'*. [Lithuanian-Russian dictionary]. Vilnius: Mokslas.
Liddell, Henry G., Robert Scott, Henry S. Jones, and Roderick McKenzie. 1996. *Greek-English Lexicon*.Oxford: Oxford University Press.
Linnaeus, Carolus. 1751. *Philosophia botanica in qva explicantur fundamenta botanica cum definitionibus partium, exemplis terminorum, observationibus rariorum, adjectis figuris aeneis*. Stockholmiæ [Stockholm]: Apud Godofr. Kiesewetter.
Linnaeus, Carolus. 1758. *Systema naturae per regna tria naturae :secundum classes, ordines, genera, species, cum characteribus, differentiis, synonymis, locis* (10th edn.). Stockholmiæ [Stockholm]: Laurentius Salvius. On-line http://www.biodiversitylibrary.org/item/10277#page/3/mode/1up (accessed 14 June 2014)
Ljubarskij Georgij Ju. 1992. Biostilistika i problema klassifikacii žiznennyx form [Biostylistics and the problem of classifying life-forms]. *Biology Bulletin Reviews*. Vol. 53, 5: 649–661.
Lopatin, Vladimir V. and Ljudmila E. Lopatina. 1997. *Russkij tolkovyj slovar'*. [Russian explanatory dictionary]. Moscow: Russkij jazyk.
Lytkin, Vasilij I. and Evgenij S. Guljaev. 1970. *Kratkij ètimologičeskij slovar' komi jazyka*. [Concise etymological Komi dictionary]. Moscow: Nauka.
MacDonell, Arthur A. 1893. *A Sanskrit-English dictionary*. London & New York: Logmans, Green and Co.
Mazoxin-Poršnjakov, Georgij A. 1970. *Nasekomye SSSR*. [Insects of USSR]. Moscow: Mysl'.
Mayr, Ernst W. 1957. Species concepts and definitions. In Ernst W. Mayr (ed.) *The Species Problem*. Washington (D.C.): AAAS.
Mayr, Ernst W. 1988. *Toward a new philosophy of biology*. New York: Cambrige university press.
McNeill, John, Fred R. Barrie, Hervé M. Burdet, Vincent Demoulin, David L. Hawksworth, Karol Marhold, Dan H. Nicolson, Jefferson Prado, Paul C. Silva, Judith E. Skog, John H. Wiersema, and Nick J. Turland (eds.). 2006. *International code of botanical nomenclature (Vienna Code) adopted by the seventeenth International Botanical Congress, Vienna, Austria, July 2005* (electronic ed.), Vienna: International Association for Plant Taxonomy, http://ibot.sav.sk/icbn/main.htm (accessed 7 February 2012).
Merkulova, Valentina A. 1967. *Očerki po russkoj narodnoj nomenklature rastenij* [Studies of Russian folk nomenclature of plants]. Moscow: Nauka.
Morev, Lev N. 1964. *Tajsko-russkij slovar'* [Thai-Russian Dictionary]. Moscow. Sovetskaja Enciklopedija.
Munro, Pamela, Nellie Brown, and Judith G. Crawford. 1992. *A Mojave dictionary*. Los Angeles: UCLA Occasional Papers in Linguistics 10.
Myreeva, Anna N. 2001. *Leksika èvenkijskogo jazyka. Rastitel'nyj i životnyj mir*. [Evenki vocabulary. Flora and fauna]. Novosibirsk: Nauka.
Ošanin, Il'ja M. (ed.). 1983. *Bol'šoj kitajsko-russkij slovar'*. [Comprehensive Chinese-Russian dictionary]. Moscow: Nauka.
Ožegov, Sergej I. and Natalija Ju. Švedova. 1991. *Tolkovyj slovar' russkogo jazyka*. [The explanatoty dictionary of the Russian language]. Moscow: Russkij jazyk.
Pavlinov, Igor'. 2007. On the structure of biodiversity: some metaphysical essaya. In Schwartz Jan (ed.) *Focus on biodiversity research*, 101–104. New York: Nova Sci. Publ.
Pavlinov, Igor' and Georgij Ljubarskij. 2011. *Biologičeskaja sistematika (Èvoljucija idej)* [Biological systematics: evolution of ideas]. Moscow: KMK Scientific Press Ltd.
Polikanov, Dmitrij V. 1997. *Swahili-Russian dictionary*. Moscow. On-line http://www.kamusiproject.org/en/russian (accessed 7 February 2012).

Pukui, Mart K. and Samuel H. Elbert. 1992. *New pocket Hawaiian dictionary*. Honolulu: University of Hawaii Press.
Rechenbach, Charles W. 1967. *Swahili – English dictionary*. Washington: The Catholic University of America Press.
Ride, William D.L., Harold G. Cogger, Claude Dupuis, Otto Kraus, Alessandro Minelli, F. Christian Thompson, and Philip K. Tubbs. 2001. *International code of zoological nomenclature*. Fourth Edition. (electronic ed.) London. The International Trust for Zoological Nomenclature. http://www.nhm.ac.uk/hosted-sites/iczn/code/index.jsp?booksection=preface&nfv= (accessed 7 February 2012).
Riggs, Stephen R. 1992. *A Dakota – English dictionary*. St. Paul: Minnesota Historical Society Press.
Robinson, Charles H. 1913. *Dictionary of the Hausa language*. Vol. I. Hausa – English. London: Cambrige University Press.
Romaine, Suzanne. 1992. *Language, education, and development: urban and rural Tok Pisin in Papua New Guinea*. Oxford: Oxford University Press.
Rosch Heider, Eleanor. 1973. Natural categories. *Cognitive Psychology* 4: 328–350.
Schauer, Junia G., Stanley Schauer, Eladio Yucuna, and Walter Yucuna. 2005. *Diccionario bilingüe yukuna-español, español-yukuna*. Bogotá: Editorial Fundación para el Desarollo de los Pueblos Marginados.
Savel'eva, V. N. and Čuner M. Taksami. 1970. *Nivxsko-russkij slovar'*. [Nivkh-Russian dictionary]. Leningrad: Prosceščenie.
Sevortjan, Ervand V. 1974. *Ètimologičeskij slovar' tjurkskix jazykov: Obščetjurkskie i meztjurkskie osnovy na glasnye*. [Turkic etymologucal dictionary. Comon Turkic stems on vowels]. Moscow: Nauka.
Sevortjan, Ervand V. 1978. *Ètimologičeskij slovar' tjurkskix jazykov:Obščetjurkskie i meztjurkskie osnovy na bukvu "B"*. [Turkic etymologucal dictionary. Comon Turkic stems on B]. Moscow: Nauka.
Sinclair, John (ed.). 2008. *Collins COBUILD advanced learner's English dictionary*, 6th edn. London: HarperCollins.
Slaughter, Mary M. 1982. *Universal languages and scientific taxonomy in the seventeenth century*. Cambridge: Cambrige University Press.
Soanes, Catherine and Angus Stevenson. 2005. *Oxford dictionary of English*. Revised Edition. Oxford: Oxford University Press.
Sorokoletov, Fedot P. (ed.). 1990. *Slovar' russkix narodnyx govorov. Tom XXV*. [Dictionary of Russian dialects. Volume XXV]. Moscow & Leningrad (Saint-Petersburg): Nauka.
Švedova, Natalija Ju., Ljubov' V. Kurkina, and Leonid P. Krysin. 2009. *Tolkovyj slovar' russkogo jazyka s vključeniem svedenij o proishoždenii slov*. [The explanatory dictionary of Russian with the addition of information on the origin of the words]. Moscow: Azbukovnik.
Sylestine, Cora, Heather K. Hardy, and Timothy Montler. 1993. *Dictionary of the Alabama language*. Austin: University of Texas Press. On-line http://www.lingtechcomm.unt.edu//~montler/Alabama/Dictionary/(accessed 7 February 2012).
Talibov, Bukar V. and Magomed M. Gadžiev. 1966. *Lezginsko-russkij slovar'*. [Lezgian-Russian dictionary]. Moscow: Sovetskaja enciklopedija.
Tedford, Richard H. 1976. Relationship of pinnipeds to other carnivores (Mammalia). *Systematic Zoology*. 25 (4): 363–374.

Theopheastus. 1916. *Enquiry into plants and minor works on odours and weather signs with an english translation by sir Arthur Hort, Bart., M.A. formerly fellow of Trinity college, Cambridge in two volumes.* London & New York: William Heinemann, G. P. Putnam's sons.
Titarenko, Mihail L. (ed.). 2009. *Duxovnaja kul'tura Kitaja. Ènciklopedija v pjati tomax.* [Chinese spiritual culture. Encyclopaedia in 5 vol.]. Moscow: Vostočnaja literatura.
Tolstoj, Nikita I. 1957. *Serboxorvatsko-russkij slovar'.* [Serbo-Croatian-Russian dictionary]. Moscow: Gosudarstvennoe izdatel'stvo inostrannyx i nacional'nyx slovarej.
Tolstoj, Nikita I. (ed.). 1995. *Slavjanskie drevnosti. Ètnolingviskičeskij slovar'* [Slavic antiquities. Ethnolinguistic dictionary]. Vol. 1. Moscow: Meždunarodnyje otnošenija.
Trubačev, Oleg N (ed.). 1979. *Ètimologičeskij slovar' slavjanskix jazykov Tom VI.* [Etymological dictionaty of Slavic languages]. Moscow: Nauka.
Trubačev, Oleg N (ed.). 1983. *Ètimologičeskij slovar' slavjanskix jazykov. Tom IX.* [Etymological dictionaty of Slavic languages. Volume IX]. Moscow: Nauka.
Urban, Matthias. 2010. Terms for the unique beginner: Cross-linguistic and cross-cultural perspectives. *Journal of Ethnobiology*, 30(2): 203–230.
Ušakov, Dmitrij N. (ed.). 1935–1940. *Tolkovyj slovar' russkogo jazyka v 4 tomax.* [Russian explanatory dictionary in 4 vol.]. Moscow: Gosudarstvennyj institut "Sovetskaja Entsiklodedija", OGIZ, Gosudarstvennoe izdatel'stvo inostrannyx I natsionalnyx slovarej. On-line http://feb-web.ru/feb/ushakov/ush-abc/default.asp (accessed 27 December 2015).
Usteri, Alfred. 1941. *Die Pflanzen-Wesen.* Zürich: R. Geering Verlag.
Vahros, Igor' and Antti Ščerbakov. 2007. *Bol'šoj finsko-russkij slovar'.* [Comprehensive Finnish-Russian dictionary]. Moscow: Živoj jazyk.
Vasilevič, Glafira M. 1934. *Èvenkijsko-russkij (tungussko-russkij) slovar') dialektologičeskij slovar'.* [Evenki-Russian (Tungus-Russian) dialectological dictionary]. Leningrad: Učpedgiz.
Vasilevič, Glafira M. 1958. *Èvenkijsko-russkij slovar'.* [Evenki-Russian dictionary]. Moscow: Gosudarstvennoe izdatel'stvo inostrannyh i nacional'nyh slovarej.
Vasilevič, Glafira M. 2005. *Russko-evenkijskij slovar' v dvux častjax.* [Russian-Evenki dictionary in 2 vol.]. Saint Petersburg: Prosveščenie.
Verner, Geinrih K. 2002. *Slovar' ketsko-russkij i russko-ketskij.* [Ket-Russian and Russian-Ket dictionary]. Saint Petersburg: Drofa.
Volker, Craig A., Susan Baing, Brian Deutrom, and Russel Jackson. 2008. *Papua New Guinea Tok Pisin English dictionary.* Oxford: Oxford University Press.
Waddy, Julie A. 1988. *Classification of plants and animals from Groote Eylandt aboriginal point of view* (2 vols.). Darwin: Australian National University, North Australia Research Unit.
Walters, Joseph C. W., Marilyn Minter de Wolgemuth, Plácido Pérez Ernandes, Esteban Pérez Ramírez, and Christofer H. Upton. 2002. *Diccionario de Náhuatl de los municipios Mecayapan y Tatahuicapan de Juárez, Veracruz.* México: Instituto Lingüístico de Verano.
Warming, Eugen. 1884. Über perenne Gewächse. *Botanisches Centralblatt*, Bd. 18. H 19: 16–22.
Warming, Eugen. 1885. *Plantesamfund – Grundtræk af den økologiske plantegeografi.* Kjøbenhavn: P.G. Philipsens Forlag.
Wierzbicka, Anna. 1990. Prototypes saves: on the uses and abuses of the notion of prototype in linguistics and related fields. In Tsohatsidis, Savas L. (ed.) *Meanings and prototypes: Studies in linguistic categorization,* 347–367. London & New York: Routledge.
Wiesemann, Ursula Gojtéj. 2002. *Dicionário bilingüe Kaingang – Português.* [Bilingual Kaingang Portugal dictionary] Curitiba: Editora Evangélica Esperança.

Wiley, E. O. 1981. *Phylogenetics: The theory and practice of phylogenetic systematics*. New York: Wiley Interscience.
Williamson, John P. 1992. *An English – Dakota dictionary*. St. Paul: Minnesota Historical Society Press.
Witkowski, Stanley and Cecil H. Brown. 1983. Marking-reversals and cultural importance. *Language*. Vol. 59, 3: 569–582.
Žuravlev, Anatolij F. 2005. *Jazyk i mif. Lingviskičeskij kommentarij k trudu A. N. Afanasieva "Poètičeskie vozzrenija slavjan na prirodu"*. [Language and myth. Linguistic commentary to A. N. Afanasiev's book "The poetic outlook on nature by the Slavs"]. Moscow: Indrik.

Markus Ising
16. Holistic motivation: Systematization and application to the COOKING domain

Abstract: This chapter introduces the term *holistic motivation* in order to account for expressions such as English *redskin* or *lady's slipper*. In these cases, we can posit a target concept (NATIVE AMERICAN or the specific PLANT) that is associated with a source concept (a Native American supposedly has RED SKIN, and the plant's flower looks like a SHOE FOR WOMEN) and is therefore expressed with the term literally denoting this source concept. The chapter shows how this widespread phenomenon can be integrated in the traditional theory of linguistic motivation. It also reports on a typological case study that systematically searched 75 languages for holistic motivation in the target domain of COOKING. In this domain, we find contiguous, metaphorical, taxonomic and mixed relations between the target concepts TO COOK / THE COOK and the respective source concepts. Interestingly, taxonomic relations are by far the most frequent type of holistic motivation – a fact that has not yet been observed in studies restricted to Indo-European languages.

16.1 What is linguistic motivation? Definition and outline of the chapter

A definition of linguistic motivation can borrow much from psychology. For example, we know that a person's behaviour such as smiling or whistling can be motivated by a certain state of mind (e.g. the happiness of having submitted your PhD thesis) because there is a CAUSE-EFFECT contiguity between state of mind and behaviour. More abstractly speaking, we could identify the behaviour with the motivated *target* (since it is affected by motivation). The state of mind is then the motivating *source* which determines the motivation on the basis of an essential *factor* (here: the CAUSE-EFFECT contiguity). This analogy from psychological to linguistic motivation has been established in recent Cognitive Linguistics (see Radden and Panther 2004: 4; Panther and Radden 2011: 9), leading to the definition in (1).

Markus Ising (University of Tübingen)

(1) A linguistic unit (target) is motivated if some of its properties are shaped by a linguistic or non-linguistic source and language-independent factors (adapted from Radden and Panther 2004: 4).

Following this definition, we can expect that a speaker of English recognizes the linguistic form *cock-a-doodle-doo* (= target) as standing for the COCK'S CROW (= non-linguistic source) because there is an iconic relation between form and content (= language-independent factor). In a similar vein, a linguistic target unit like Hungarian *körtefa* 'pear tree' is expected to be motivated since the language-user can easily discern the lexical units *körte* 'pear' and *fa* 'tree' (= linguistic sources) and describe which language-independent relations exist between them and the whole compound. For example, the speaker could motivate *körtefa* by saying that it is composed of *körte* and *fa* and justify this compounding conceptually ("A pear tree is a subtype of a tree"/"Pears are the characteristic fruit of a pear tree" etc.).

Once the basic definition of linguistic motivation is clear, there is still a wide range of phenomena that linguists have subsumed under this term. In order to make clear what I understand by *holistic motivation* and how this type relates to the other phenomena, I will briefly introduce a typology of linguistic motivation in 16.2. In 16.3., I will describe the formation of the language sample that I searched for holistic motivation in the COOKING domain. The qualitative and quantitative presentation of the data on COOKING will be done in 16.4., leading to more general concluding remarks on holistic motivation as such (16.5.).

16.2 A typology of linguistic motivation

For the discussion of the phenomena associated with motivation in linguistics, I propose the systematization illustrated in Figure 1.

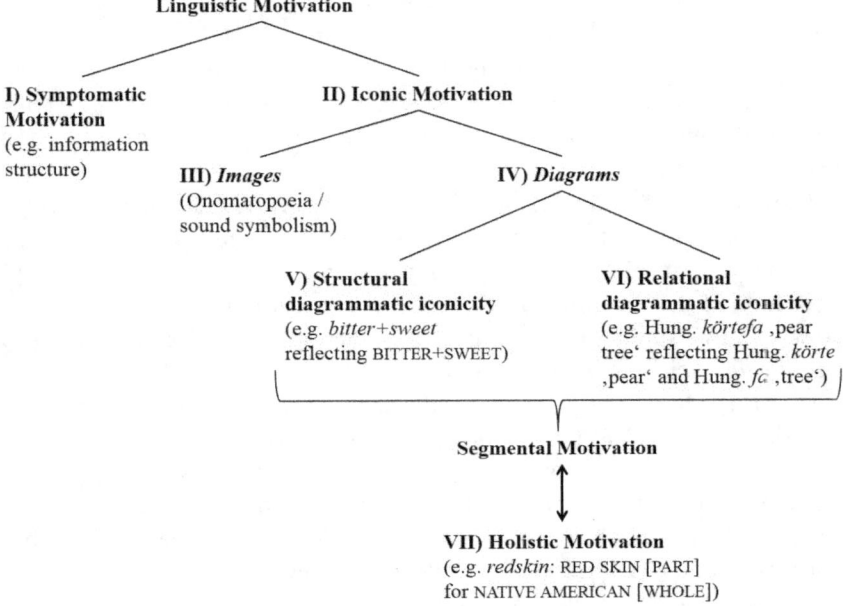

Figure 1: A typology of linguistic motivation

The split between I and II stands for a quite elementary distinction concerning Panther's and Radden's definition: can the motivating source be identified with the speaker (I) or with the subject he communicates (II)? Example (2) illustrates the former, (3) the latter.

(2) a. *Peter told his teacher an amazing story yesterday.*
 b. *It is **Peter** who told his teacher an amazing story yesterday.*
 c *It is **his teacher** whom Peter told an amazing story to yesterday.*
 d. *It is **yesterday** that Peter told his teacher an amazing story.*

(3) *cock-a-doodle-doo, to snore,* German *piepsen* 'to pipe' etc.

The syntactic targets (2a–d) vary because the speaker highlights different parts of his message. Following a universal cognitive principle that can be called "attend first to the most urgent task" (Givón 1994: section 2 and Lehmann 2007: 118), he begins the sentence with the semantic role he wants to underline. In this sense, the varying information structure in (2) is a symptom of the speaker's varying attitude.

As we have seen in the previous section, onomatopoeia such as *cock-a-doodle-doo* belong to type II because their form is iconically shaped by the subject denoted (here: the COCK'S CROW). Together with sound symbolism (e.g. *to snore* and *piepsen* which include sounds that resemble the respective action), Peirce (1960) called them images (III) because they represent the closest content > form motivation: the form physically imitates its content.

Diagrams (IV), by contrast, display a more abstract relation between source and target. Structural diagrams (V) such as *bitter-sweet* are iconic because the formal composition of the two lexemes *bitter* and *sweet* reflects the conceptual addition of the compound's sense (= a TASTE that precisely combines BITTER+SWEET). In a similar vein, number inflections such as German *der Junge-Ø* 'the boy' – *die Junge-n* 'the boys' can be described as structural diagrams: the plural form is phonically and graphically longer than the singular and thus reflects the fact that the former refers to more boys (= content) than the latter.

Finally, the discussion of relational diagrams (VI) brings us back to the example of Hungarian *körtefa* 'pear tree'. As mentioned in 16.1., the speaker is expected to "look through" the target compound *körtefa* 'pear tree' at related linguistic source units (e.g. its modifier *körte* 'pear') when he motivates the former with the latter. Koch's motivational square in Figure 2 illustrates how such relational motivation between lexical form/concept pairs can be modelled.

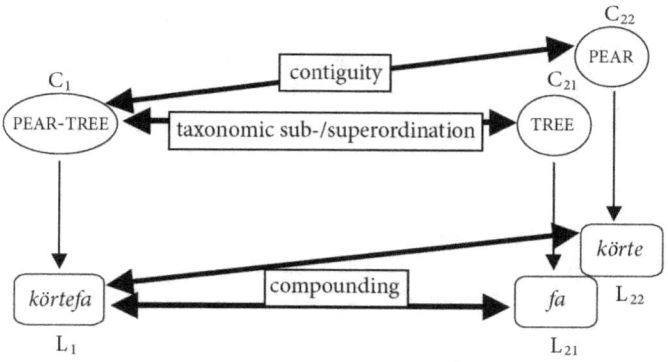

Figure 2: Motivational square for compounding, example Hungarian *körtefa* < *körte* and *fa* (see Koch and Marzo 2007: 266).

In this square, L_1, L_{21} and L_{22} represent the forms ("Lexical items") expressing their respective concepts C_1, C_{21} and C_{22}. What is important here is the horizontal dimension which links the possibly motivated lexical unit L_1/C_1 to its motivating lexical units L_{21}/C_{21} and L_{22}/C_{22}. While both *körte* and *fa* are obviously related to *körtefa* via compounding, the conceptual relations accompanying this compounding process diverge: head and modifier show different associations with respect to the whole compound. *Körtefa* represents a hyponym of its head *fa*, since a PEAR TREE is a subtype of a TREE. This is why the relation between C_{21} and C_1 is a case of taxonomy. Thus, if the speaker motivates *körtefa* by stating that a pear tree is a sort of a tree, he conceptually highlights the taxonomic subordination C_{21} (ANY) TREE > C_1 PEAR TREE in Figure 2. Alternatively, the speaker can conceptually highlight the modifier-compound relation, saying that pears are the characteristic fruit of a pear tree. This C_{22}-C_1 relation is not of a taxonomic nature (PEARS are neither a sort of a PEAR TREE nor the other way round), but a case of conceptual contiguity: FRUIT and TREE are two concepts closely related by our world knowledge.[1]

Now, when we look back at structural and relational diagrams, they can both be described as cases of segmental motivation. This is because the question of V and VI was always why and how the speaker may motivate a compound (e.g. *bitter-sweet* or Hungarian *körtefa*) with respect to contained lexemes, and why he does or does not add inflectional morphemes (German *Junge-Ø / Junge-n*). The last motivation type VII differs from them all in so far as the conceptual behaviour of a whole linguistic expression is analyzed. An example is English *redskin* for NATIVE AMERICAN as indicated in Figure 3.

---

[1] In the last decades, this rather intuitive definition of contiguity as the link between two "closely related" concepts has been discussed on all levels of abstraction. When we return to our example *körtefa*, its contiguous modifier-compound relation can be described in the most concrete way as FRUIT-TREE or more abstractly as a case of PRODUCT-PRODUCER contiguity. Even more abstractly, the relation between the two concepts can be grasped as spatial CONTACT between bounded (i.e. countable) entities (see Peirsman and Geeraerts 2006: 310). Blank's (1997: 249–253) conception of contiguity as either CO-PRESENCE or SUCCESSION of concepts is definitely the most abstract approach – here, our relation between a fruit and its tree would obviously be subsumed under CO-PRESENCE. Note that all current theories of contiguity consider meronymies, that is part-whole relations, as a subtype or even as the most central type of contiguity (see again Peirsman and Geeraerts 2006). I adhere to this view in the presentation of my data (see especially Daba *ka ta wili* in 16.4.1).

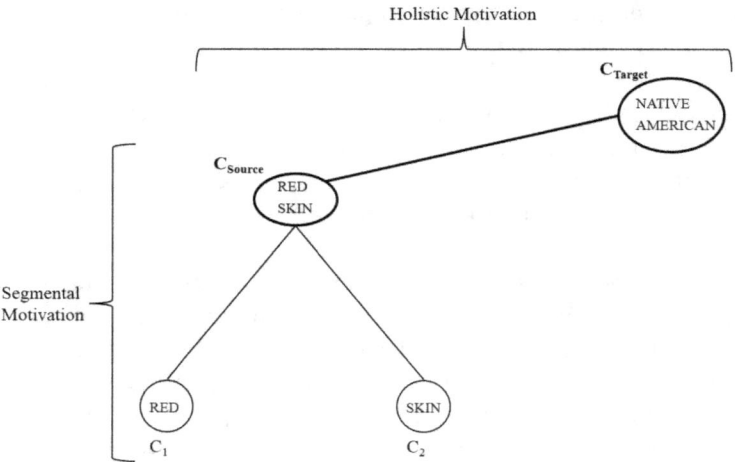

Figure 3: Segmental and holistic motivation, English *redskin* (inspired by Geeraerts 2002: 456).

As Figure 3 shows, research on holistic motivation begins where segmental motivation ends. This is because in contrast to the motivation of relational diagrams such as *körtefa*, the relation between the literal concept C_{Source} and its conceptual parts C_1 and C_2 is not central for the motivation of English *redskin*. In other words: the speaker won't say that English *redskin* stands for a sort of SKIN that is RED, but that it refers to a NATIVE AMERICAN because he is supposed to have RED SKIN. We thus have to ask what makes the speaker use a complex expression like *redskin* not literally (in the sense of C_{Source}), but referring to C_{Target}. In the present case, the answer is obviously a whole < part shift: the PERSON is conceptualized by means of his supposedly RED SKIN. In other cases such as English *lady's slipper*, we encounter a holistic metaphor C_{Target} PLANT < C_{Source} WOMAN'S SHOE.

More generally speaking, holistic motivation is a borderline case of (1) in so far as the essential target-source relation is conceptual in nature: the formal target *redskin* is (segmentally) shaped by C_{Source} RED SKIN, but the essential process for explaining the motivation here is the association of a conceptual target NATIVE AMERICAN with precisely this conceptual source RED SKIN on the basis of conceptual relations such as contiguity and metaphorical similarity (= language-independent factors). As a consequence, the form literally standing for C_{Source} is used to express C_{Target}.

So defined, the motivation type VII explains phenomena that have been discussed in neighbouring linguistic disciplines such as word formation. For example, the Sanskrit grammar knew *bahuvrihi*, also called possessive compounds which express the possessor (C_{Target}) via his possession (C_{Source}): our

16. Holistic motivation: Systematization and application to the Cooking domain

REDSKIN supposedly has RED SKIN as well as a REDBREAST has a RED BREAST, and *blue helmet* refers to a SOLDIER that has a BLUE HELMET on his head.[2]

Possessive compounds only grasp those cases of holistic motivation that are contiguity-based. Later lexicological research included metaphorical similarity, too: Blank (1998: 22) distinguishes integral metonymies such as the Italian version of Figure 3 (*pellerossa* 'Native American', literally 'red skin') and integral metaphors like Italian *lingua di gatto*, which is conceptually identical to French/English *langue de chat* (C_{Target} CHOCOLATE BISCUIT < C_{Source} CAT'S TONGUE). Finally, Gévaudan (1999: 21–23) considers both as a sort of *verschachtelte Ableitungen* ('nested derivations') since *redskin, langue de chat* etc. lend themselves to a combined, segmental and holistic analysis.

As Fill (1980: 22), Gévaudan (1999: 23) and Geeraerts (2002: 455–461) point out, holistic motivation can involve several conceptual steps. Figure 4 below illustrates how Dutch *badmuts* is not only used to denote the C_{Source} SWIMMING CAP, but jocularly refers to the C_{Target} BALD PERSON as well. An explanation of this holistic shift $C_{Target} < C_{Source}$ has to draw on an additional bridging concept PERSON WEARING A SWIMMING CAP that I call C_{Bridge}. The holistic motivation, then, is the combined effect of metaphorical similarity (C_{Target} – C_{Bridge}) and contact contiguity (C_{Bridge} – C_{Source}): "A bald person looks like a person wearing a swimming cap, so let's denote him with this object", a language-conscious speaker of Dutch might say.

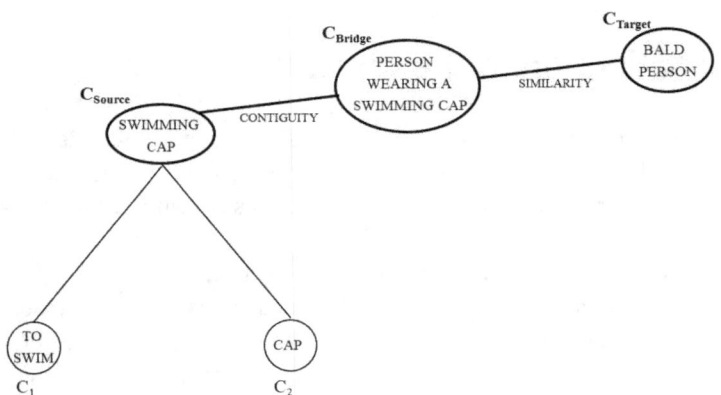

Figure 4: Two-stage holistic motivation, Dutch *badmuts*

---

[2] For a recent overview of how possessive compounds have been systematized within other types of compounding see Scalise and Bisetto (2009).

Holistic motivation is a widespread phenomenon. So far, holistic shifts have been mentioned here and there in the literature for conceptual target domains such as PERSON (e.g. English *redskin, white coat, addlebrain*; German *Blauhelm* 'blue helmet'; Italian *gattamorta* 'yes-man', literally 'dead cat'), LOCATION (e.g. French *pied-à-terre* 'secondary residence', literally 'foot-to-ground'), PLANT (German *Löwenmaul* 'snapdragon', literally 'lion's mouth', *Frauenschuh* 'lady's slipper'; K'iche' *saq wach* 'potato', literally 'white face') and various cases of OBJECT (English *paperback, cupboard*; French *dent-de-loup* 'barb', literally 'tooth of wolf').[3] However, research in holistic motivation is still incomplete in various respects. First, no target domain has yet been searched systematically for holistic motivation. As a consequence, we do not know whether contiguity and metaphorical similarity are the only conceptual relations – as Blank's distinction between integral metonymy and integral metaphor suggests – or whether e.g. taxonomic holistic shifts occur as well (think of a hypothetical C_{Target} TO COOK < C_{Source} TO DO THE HOUSEWORK where the source concept is clearly more general and thus a hypernym of the target concept). Secondly, we lack quantitative studies in holistic motivation.

The empirical pilot study described hereafter tries to give a first answer to these questions. It consists in a qualitative and quantitative investigation of holistic motivation in the target domain of COOKING. Before the results are presented in 16.4., I will describe my method of data gathering in 16.3.

16.3 Data collection in the COOKING domain

Adequate language sampling in linguistic typology is anything but simple. It is frequently said that the more genetic, geographical and typological variance the sample displays, the more general can be the conclusions drawn (cf. for different weighting of such sampling parameters Bell (1978: 129–135) or Perkins (2001: 431–433)). Unfortunately, it is one thing to design a perfect sample, but it is quite another to get relevant linguistic data out of it. This is particularly true in lexical typology: if at all dictionaries of every sample language exist, their presentation of a given linguistic form may not be sufficient for the intended research. For example, a dictionary may give an expression equivalent to English *to cook*, but

---

[3] These nominal examples are taken from Blank (1998, 2001), Fill (1980) and Gévaudan (1999). For Dutch examples from verbal target domains (e.g. *met spek schieten* 'to boast', literally 'to shoot with bacon') see Geeraerts (2002: esp. 439–453).

it need not necessarily indicate if this expression is a derivation, a compound or another complex lexical unit and what the respective parts of the expression stand for.

Thus, if the lexical typologist does not want to restrict his investigation to languages he or his colleagues personally know, he can systematically increase scientific collaboration: "We think that successful lexical-typological research can only rarely be a 'one researcher's job' but should in most cases build on collaborative work involving language experts, semanticists, typologists [...]" (Koptjevskaja-Tamm, Vanhove, and Koch et al. 2007: 177). This is the way I pursued for my typological exploration into the COOKING domain. In order to cover the widest possible range of language types, I decided to send a questionnaire to 310 members of SIL International, i.e. missionaries in the field as well as language consultants, Bible translators and typologists. Their feedback from all continents led to a sample of 75 languages from 31 language families, with Austronesian (12), Niger-Congo (11) and Trans-New Guinea languages (8) forming the biggest genetic blocks.

Since I was not only interested in holistic motivation (VII) but in all types of diagrammatic iconicity (see IV in Figure 1), I asked my informants most generally for complex expressions of TO COOK and THE COOK ("Is the formation of the words that express the idea of TO COOK and/or of the person doing it, THE COOK, transparent in a language you know, i.e. are they composed of various parts?") as well as for the relation between the verbal and the nominal expression ("Do you know one or more language(s) with a particular formal relationship between the words for the activity TO COOK and the person THE COOK (in case they both exist)?"). I illustrated both questions with invented examples, and the experts were asked to insert their expressions in glossed sentences.

As the questions show, I was interested in the most generic cooking conceptualizations corresponding to the ones expressed by English *to cook / the cook*. I left aside cooking subtypes such as TO FRY, TO BROIL, TO STEAM, TO BOIL etc. where the problem of language-specific quantity and structure of cooking types arises (see e.g. Lehrer 1974: 155–167). This means that my questionnaire defined the target concepts TO COOK and THE COOK very generally: in the verbal domain, it did not matter whether the cooking process is conceptualized from the starting point, i.e. from the INGREDIENTS ('to prepare food [= ingredients] by applying heat') or from the end point, i.e. the DISH ('to prepare food [= dish] by mixing, combining, and heating the ingredients').[4] In the nominal domain, I did not specify whether the expression of THE COOK should refer to 'a person who has cooked (a particu-

---

4 These and the following definitions are taken from *Frame Net* (https://framenet.icsi.berkeley.edu/fndrupal/IntroPage; April 15th, 2016). Obviously, English *to cook* satisfies both definitions

lar meal) or who cooks (in general)' or rather to 'a person who prepares food as a means of employment'. However, in languages where the occasional and the professional cook are expressed differently, I only took the expression for the former.

16.4 Holistic motivation in the target domain of COOKING: Qualitative and quantitative analysis

16.4.1 Holistic contiguity

What types of holistic motivation did the questionnaire study outlined in 16.3. reveal? First of all, in the case of the verbal target concept TO COOK, we find contiguity-based holistic shifts such as (4) from Daba:[5]

(4)   ka   ta   wili
       INF   prepare   sauce
       'to   prepare   sauce'
       'to   cook'

When C_{Target} TO COOK is conceptualized as C_{Source} TO PREPARE SAUCE, it can be classified as a whole < part contiguity analogous to the NATIVE AMERICAN < RED SKIN contiguity in Figure 3. The description of TO PREPARE SAUCE as a partial process of TO COOK is supported by the fact that unlike cooking-subtypes such as TO BOIL, TO STEAM, TO GRILL etc., preparing sauce does not represent a cooking event on its own: the sauce as its product is not usually eaten alone.[6] In the case of Daba, this holistic whole < part shift results in *ka ta wili* denominating TO COOK, see Figure 5:

---

since its patient role can be the INGREDIENT (*Cook the rice over a medium heat for 15 minutes*) as well as the DISH (*This year's celebration banquet was cooked by Pierre Tourgis from Paris*).
5 I am grateful to Ruth Lienhard who provided these data for me. According to her, the *ka* prefix can be equivalent to the English infinitive markter *to*. Beyond that, *ka* is one of a few quite polyfunctional Daba prefixes, see for details Mouchet (1966: 67–69).
6 More precisely, the crucial difference is that taxonomic subtypes rather occasionally constitute parts of a hypernym concept, think of several dishes of one and the same cooking event that are boiled, steamed or grilled respectively, or even the use of several consecutive cooking subtypes for one dish. Meronyms like the source concept of (4), on the contrary, always are part of such a bigger whole.

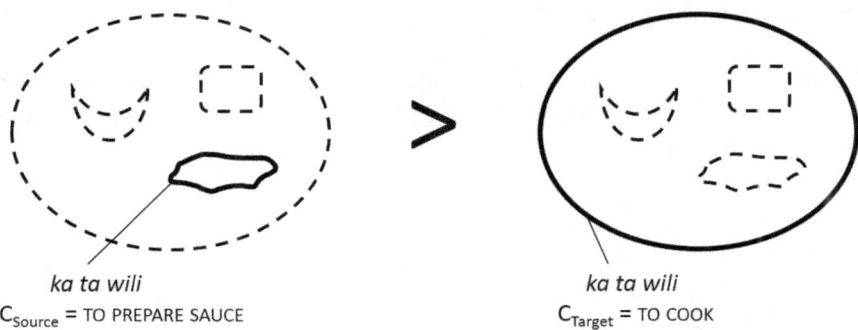

Figure 5: Holistic (part-whole) contiguity: Daba *ka ta wili* TO COOK

In the graphic above, the symbols within the frames represent several possible partial processes of TO COOK. Why has just the partial process TO PREPARE SAUCE been selected for this shift? In fact, the SAUCE is a constitutive part of Daba MEALS, and consequently the same can be said about their procedural equivalents TO PREPARE SAUCE and TO COOK. Above all, this is confirmed by ethnologic research: in his Daba dictionary, Mouchet (1966: 160) translates *wuli* [sic] with "sauce (accompagnant le millas)" ['sauce (accompanying millet)'], both ingredients being dominant in their culture.[7] Given this cultural background, it is not surprising that the Daba expressions for a (female) COOK and the KITCHEN are based on the same source concept TO PREPARE SAUCE:[8]

(5a) (*hidi*) *ma ta wili* (5b) *jik tu wuli*
 (person) REL prepare sauce   hut prepare sauce
 'the one who prepares sauce'   'hut of sauce preparing'
 'cook (f.)'   'kitchen'

---

[7] See Lienhard and Giger (1975: 42). Converging evidence for this agricultural region comes from Kera: there, too, a variety of millet and sauce types are set items for lunch and dinner (cf. Ebert 1976: 174–175). Not surprisingly, individual Kera expressions for these recurrent cooking processes exist, too: *wédé sò* 'to make boule (=hardened millet paste)' and *dèfé k'əsáw* 'to prepare sauce' (Mary Pearce, personal communication).

[8] For pointers to (5a), I am again grateful to Ruth Lienhard (personal communication). She gave me the complete expression including *hidi* 'person' which according to Mouchet (1966: 183) may be omitted: *ma* alone can function as a subject relative marker used to express the agent (see Mouchet 1966: 134). Concerning (5b), I follow the spelling of Mouchet (1966: 182) who always lists *wuli* instead of *wili*. *Wuli* entails the vocalic assimilation *ta > tu* of the preceding element (see Mouchet 1966: 51–52).

16.4.2 Holistic metaphor

Holistic shifts based on metaphorical similarity can be found in the target domain of COOKING, too. Consider the lexical unit for TO COOK in Sakha (also known as Yakut):[9]

(6) *buhar-*
 buh-ar
 ripen-CAUS
 'to make ripe'
 'to cook'

Semantically, the source concept (TO RIPEN) is in no way logically related to its target concept (TO COOK). While the former can be described as part of the frame NATURE, the latter is a human action and thus conceivable as a part of the frame HUMANITY (see Figure 6 below). Thus, using the expression of TO RIPEN for TO COOK represents a case of domain mapping which has generally been seen as the definitional trait of metaphor at least since Croft (1993).

A metaphorical relation between a source and a target concept usually displays a concrete analogy that can be meta-linguistically described. To give an example, English *heart* may be used in *heart of a person* as well as in *heart of the city* because in both the literal and the metaphorical sense the entity designated is conceptualized as BEING IN THE MIDDLE of something. The analogous link between TO RIPEN and TO COOK consists in similar external conditions which cause the processes of ripening and cooking: in both cases, THE EFFECT OF HEAT transforms the respective RAW MATERIAL (illustrated by the rectangles in Figure 6) into a (BETTER) EDIBLE MATERIAL (the triangles in Figure 6).

---

[9] I have adapted this gloss from Pakendorf and Novgorodov (2009), compare the World Loanword Database (http://wold.clld.org/word/71312353604912655). I am very grateful to Brigitte Pakendorf for discussing in depth the Sakha data with me.

16. Holistic motivation: Systematization and application to the Cooking domain — 545

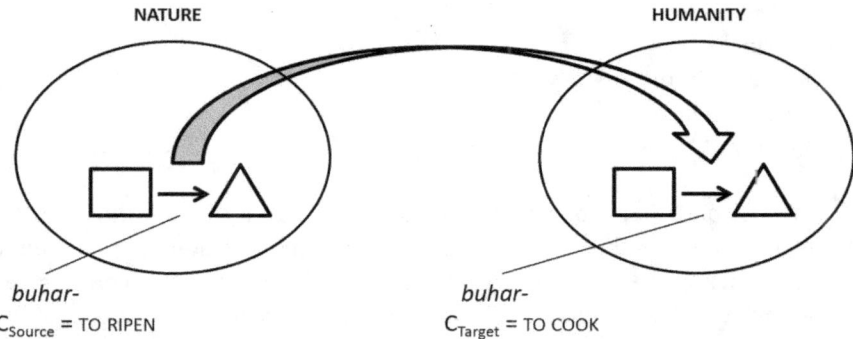

Figure 6: Holistic metaphor: Sakha *buhar-* TO COOK

In contrast to Daba, the expression of THE COOK is not based on the verbal one. In Sakha, we instead encounter an agentive nominalization based on *as* 'food', compare (7).

(7) *aschyt*
    as-chyt
    food-AGENT.NOMINALIZER
    'food maker'
    'cook (n.)'

Here, too, we can posit a holistic shift. If C_{Target} THE COOK is conceptualized as C_{Source} FOOD MAKER, the relation between them is taxonomic in nature. The C_{Source} literally is a hypernym of the C_{Target} since MAKING FOOD is less specific than MAKING FOOD BY ADDUCING HEAT (= COOKING). Such taxonomic shifts as a third type of holistic motivation are discussed more detailed in the next section.

16.4.3 Holistic taxonomic subordination

As the discussion of (7) has already indicated, my sample also contains cooking expressions whose holistic $C_{Source} > C_{Target}$ shifts go beyond contiguity and metaphorical similarity. The expression for THE COOK from Sumerian can serve as another example of holistic taxonomy.

(8) *endib*[10]
   en-dib
   master-to.burn
   'master of burning'
   'cook (n.)'

C_{Target} THE COOK is here conceptualized as C_{Source} MASTER OF BURNING. Figure 7 shows how I analyze this $C_{Source} > C_{Target}$ shift as a result of taxonomic subordination. A priori, a MASTER OF BURNING is not necessarily a COOK. It is a more abstract concept which is easily imaginable in other target domains than COOKING that deal with BURNING, too. As the broken circles in Figure 7 show, a MASTER OF BURNING could also be a person ingeniously using fire for HEATING, LAND CLEARANCE, POTTERY, WARFARE etc. But COOKING is certainly the most obvious conceptual frame of BURNING: cooking is a highly relevant target domain in everyday life, and cooking with fire is the most traditional way of preparing food by adducing heat.[11] This daily relevance of burning for cooking, I argue, results in THE COOK being the most obvious MASTER OF BURNING (cf. the bold line and elements in Figure 7), pulling consequently *endib* down on the lower level as an expression of THE COOK.

---

10 I am very grateful to Thomas Goldammer for his pointers to these Sumerian data. He rightly stresses that *endib* is attested once in a lexical list that opposes Sumerian and Akkadian words, but not in the Sumerian texts that have survived. This list clearly associates *endib* with Akkadian *nuḫatimmu* 'cook (n.)'.
11 Compare Lévi-Strauss (1965: 21) who speaks of an evolutionary "antériorité du rôti sur le bouilli" [precedence of the roasted on the boiled].

16. Holistic motivation: Systematization and application to the Cooking domain —— **547**

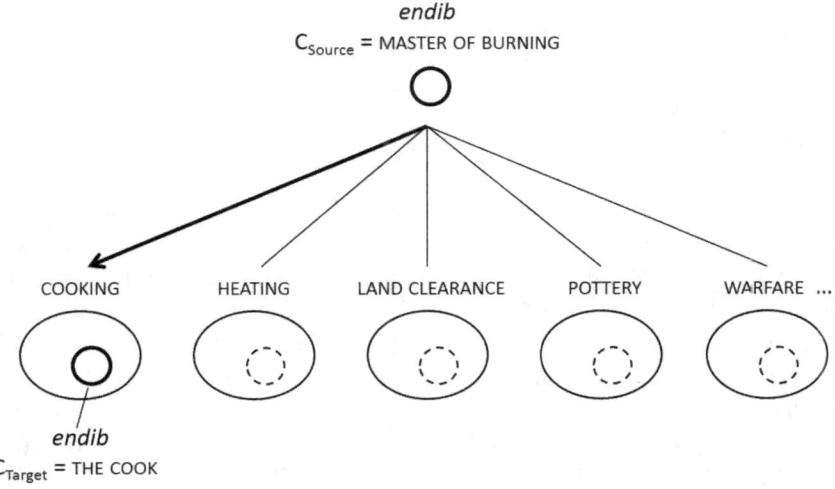

Figure 7: Holistic taxonomic subordination: Sumerian *endib* THE COOK

As in the case of Sakha *buhar-/aschyt*, the expression of TO COOK in Sumerian shares no lexeme with the expression of THE COOK. But just like the nominal *endib*, its verbal counterpart is a result of taxonomic subordination. In fact, Sumerian *šeĝ₆* is a very general lexeme whose basic sense is C_{Source} TO MAKE HOT. Depending on the context, it refers to three subtypes of making hot: the $C_{Target\,1}$ TO DRY, the $C_{Target\,2}$ TO FIRE (CLAY) or in fact the $C_{Target\,3}$ TO COOK. Thus, while *endib* is restricted to one taxonomic subordination (MASTER OF BURNING > THE COOK), *šeĝ₆* can be described as economically serving three such taxonomic subordinations.

16.4.4 Holistic taxonomic superordination combined with holistic contiguity

Finally, there is one case of holistic motivation in my sample that implies two consecutive holistic shifts (similar to Dutch *badmuts* in Figure 4). While not having any expression for THE COOK, the language community of Lakota conceptualizes TO COOK as TO SOFTEN, see (9):[12]

---

[12] I express my thanks to Regina Pustet who drew my attention to Lakota and willingly discussed details of (9).

(9) lol'íx'ą
 loló-íx'ą
 soft-do
 'to make soft'
 'to cook'

Again, we have to ask what motivates the speaker to associate the C_{Target} TO COOK with the C_{Source} TO SOFTEN. A first step is certainly the repeated experience that many types of cooking lead from rather hard ingredients to softer food (see the bold procedural abstraction of SOFTENING in each of the frames on the lower level of Figure 8). For example, whether you boil peas, carrots, rice or noodles, whether you braise meat or steam fish, the result is always softer that the raw ingredient (eggs being an exception). Grilling and frying are less clear in this respect: they lead to a contradictory transformation – think of a roast becoming soft, but its crackling hard. At best, they could be associated with softening because even grilling and frying make the product tender and thus better chewable. But they are certainly more peripheral to the softening association than boiling, steaming or braising.

My claim is that the majority of cooking subtypes do include softening and that this frequent contiguity of SOFTENING on the lower level of Figure 8 makes this concept appear as a collateral effect of COOKING in general. Cognitively speaking, such a generalization is equivalent to the taxonomic superordination C_{Source} TO SOFTEN (BY BOILING / BY STEAMING / BY BRAISING...) > C_{Bridge} TO SOFTEN (BY COOKING), illustrated by step 1 in Figure 8.

16. Holistic motivation: Systematization and application to the Cooking domain — 549

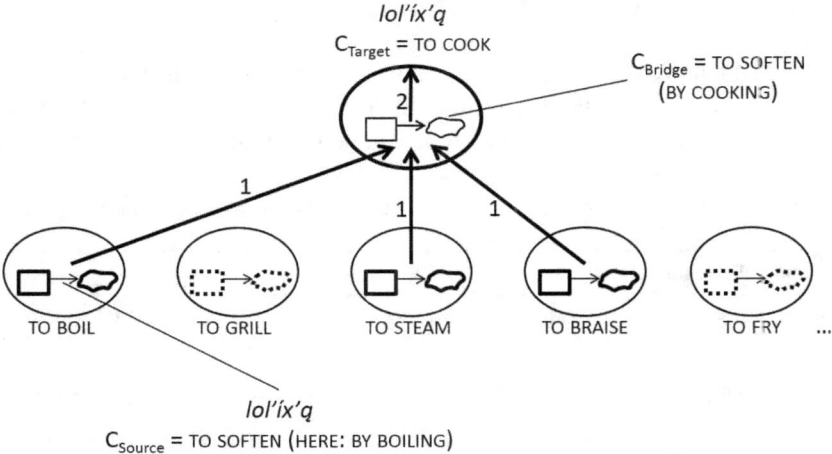

Figure 8: Holistic taxonomic superordination + holistic contiguity: Lakota *lol'íx'q* TO COOK

The conceptual shift of *lol'íx'q* does not stop at this stage. This is because *lol'íx'q* does not denote collateral SOFTENING, but the C_{Target} TO COOK itself. Since C_{Bridge} TO SOFTEN (BY COOKING) is one of many processes that occur during a typical cooking event, I describe this $C_{Bridge} - C_{Target}$ contiguity as a part-whole relationship. In sum, then, the $C_{Source} > C_{Target}$ shift involves taxonomic superordination $C_{Source} > C_{Bridge}$ as well as a contiguous shift from the partial process C_{Bridge} to the whole cooking action C_{Target} (= step 2 in Figure 8). Figure 9 summarizes this instance of holistic motivation on the basis of the *badmuts* illustration above.

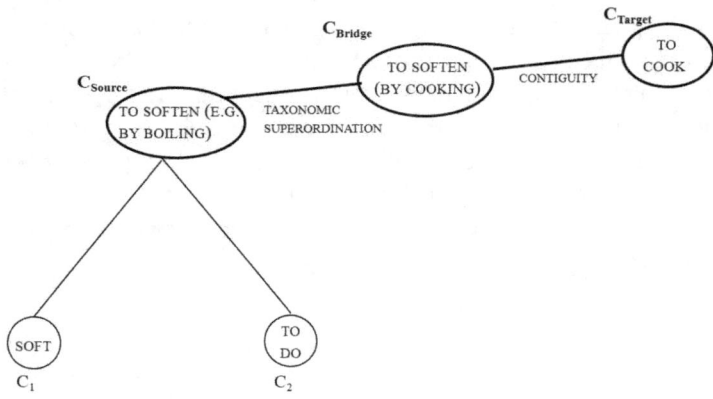

Figure 9: Two-stage holistic motivation, Lakota *lol'íx'q*

16.4.5 The quantitative dimension

Sections 16.4.1. to 16.4.4. have shown that holistic motivation in the target domain of COOKING includes contiguity, metaphorical similarity and taxonomic shifts alike. Table 1 illustrates the quantitative side of holistic motivation in my sample.

Table 1: Quantitative analysis of holistic motivation in the target domain of COOKING[13]

Relation of holistic shift	Frequency	Examples
Contiguity	2 (14 %)	See (4) above; Flathead *k'wl'sncut* C_{Target} TO COOK < C_{Source} TO MAKE FIRE
Metaphorical similarity	2 (14 %)	See (6) above; Agta *luto* C_{Target} TO COOK < C_{Source} TO RIPEN
Taxonomic subordination	8 (57 %)	See (7) and (8) above; Japanese *ryôri (suru)* C_{Target} TO COOK < C_{Source} TO SETTLE, ARRANGE; Pacoh *taʔ karreːŋ* C_{Target} TO COOK < C_{Source} TO DO WOMAN'S WORK
Taxonomic superordination	1 (7 %)	Ngäbere *ungwe rien* C_{Target} TO COOK < C_{Source} TO ROAST IN A POT
Mixed relations	1 (7 %)	See (9) above

Overall, 14 of the 75 languages contained in my sample display holistic motivation in the COOKING domain. Holistic motivation is much more frequent for TO COOK than for THE COOK. This is partly because I did not count a noun when it is based on a holistically motivated verb. An example is Flathead *sxwk'wl'sncu* C_{Target} THE COOK < C_{Source} FIRE MAKER: in isolation, it could be described as holistic taxonomic subordination (theoretically, a FIRE MAKER could make fire for other purposes than cooking and thus is a more abstract concept than THE COOK). But *sxwk'wl'sncu* is a secondary formation based on the verb *k'wl'sncut* C_{Target} TO COOK < C_{Source} TO MAKE FIRE in Table 1. In such cases, I considered that the speaker does not undertake the verbal and the nominal conceptual shift separately but only the verbal shift and, in a second step, simply derives the agentive noun from the semantically shifted verb.

---

[13] I am very grateful to the following language experts for their pointers to the data in Table 1: Sally Thomason, Thomas Headland, Martina Ebi, Dick Watson and Bill Bivin.

16.5 Concluding remarks

In 16.2., the paper discussed motivation of linguistic units containing several lexemes and/or morphemes (inflected forms, word formation, syntax). I then focused on complex units of the lexicon in order to introduce holistic motivation (VII) as an approach completing the segmental types V and VI. After the description of my data gathering in 16.3., I presented in detail the qualitative and quantitative dimension of holistic motivation in the target domain of COOKING (16.4.).

As Table 1 summarizes, there are two main results. Qualitatively, the holistic shifts from the respective source concept to the target concept TO COOK or THE COOK are not only based on contiguity and metaphorical similarity (remember already Blank's distinction between integral metonymy and integral metaphor), but are also taxonomic in nature: we find source concepts that are either hypernyms or hyponyms of TO COOK/THE COOK. What is more, the quantitative analysis revealed that holistic taxonomy and especially taxonomic subordination is by far the most frequent type of holistic motivation: no less than 57 percent of the target concepts originate in a more general source concept. When we add the cases of taxonomic superordination and mixed relations, a total of 71% of holistic shifts involve taxonomy.

A final remark concerns the status of holistic motivation with respect to the language system. I would distinguish three types:

a) The holistic shift has a purely explanatory value when the expression has been created to directly denote the C_{Target}. Think of English *redskin*, Italian *gattamorta* or French *dent-de-loup* which – as compounds – never had the literal meaning 'red skin', 'dead cat' or 'tooth of a wolf'. From the start of their lexical existence, their only raison d'être was to creatively express the conceptual targets NATIVE AMERICAN, YES-MAN and BARB. This is why cases like *gattamorta* or *dent-de-loup* have been called "originäre metaphorische Wortbildungen" ['genuine metaphorical word formations'] (Blank 1998: 22) whose literal source concept is merely a "virtuelle [...] Zwischenbedeutung" ['virtual [...] intermediate meaning'] (Gévaudan 1999: 28).

b) The second type is represented by Dutch *badmuts* (cf. Figure 4 above) which motivates the C_{Target} BALD PERSON on the basis of the C_{Source} SWIMMING CAP. This type is comparable to type a) to the extent that C_{Source} and C_{Target} do not coexist as meanings in the lexicon of the respective language. But here, it is C_{Source} which represents the lexical meaning, while C_{Target} and thus the holistic motivation as such is a pure discourse effect.

c) The third type differs from types a) and b) precisely because both the C_{Source} and the C_{Target} are part of the lexicon, be it simultaneously (e.g. as polysemous meanings) or consecutively (in the sense of old vs. new meaning). An example for the latter is English *cupboard* which has undergone semantic change from the literal C_Source BOARD FOR CUPS AND OTHER VESSELS, via a first target concept CABINET WITH SHELVES, FOR KEEPING CUPS, DISHES to the current, more general second target concept CABINET WITH ANY SORT OF CONTENT (see OED, s.v. *cupboard, n.*). Over time, changes in pronunciation and/or spelling may make it difficult for native speakers to retrace this diachronic holistic motivation ([ˈkʌpbɔː(r)d] > [ˈkʌbəd]; see also English *holiday* [ˈhʊlədeɪ] C_Target TIME OFF FROM WORK / VACATION < Middle Engl. *holy day* [həʊliˈdeɪ] C_Source RELIGIOUS FEAST). With Blank (2001: 1600), such a loss of transparency can indeed be called demotivation.

It is difficult to decide to which of these types each holistic shift detected in the COOKING domain belongs. Again, this is primarily because not all languages presented in 16.4. are lexicologically described. And even if they were, a classification as type a), b) or c) would still require diachronic data as well as synchronic judgements of native speakers. At best, the existing diachronic lexicography of Sakha could support a classification of *buhar-* as polysemous type c): in the last fifty years, virtually every Sakha dictionary lists both the C_Source TO RIPEN and the C_Target TO COOK as the two principal meanings of *buhar-* (or of its non-causative variant *bus-*).[14] Such reflections, however, go beyond the scope of this article: research on holistic motivation – which investigates conceptual paths in the mind of the speaker – does not depend on the lexical status of the involved conceptualizations.

16.6 References

Bell, Alan. 1978. Language samples. In Joseph H. Greenberg (ed.), *Universals of human language. 1. Method and theory*, 123–156. Stanford: Stanford University Press.
Blank, Andreas. 1997. *Prinzipien des Lexikalischen Bedeutungswandels am Beispiel der Romanischen Sprachen*. Tübingen: Niemeyer.
Blank, Andreas. 1998. Kognitive italienische Wortbildungslehre. *Italienische Studien* 19: 5–27.
Blank, Andreas. 2001. Pathways of lexicalization. In Martin Haspelmath, Ekkehard König, Wulf Oesterreicher, and Wolfgang Raible (eds.), *Language typology and language universals: An international handbook*, 1596–1608. Berlin: De Gruyter.
Croft, William. 1993. The role of domains in the interpretation of metaphors and metonymies. *Cognitive Linguistics* 44: 335–370.

---

[14] Cf. Krueger (1962); Sleptsov (2005); Monastyrjew (2006); Straughn (2006).

Geeraerts, Dirk. 2002. The interaction of metaphor and metonymy in composite expressions. In René Dirven and Ralf Pörings (eds.), *Metaphor and metonymy in comparison and contrast*, 435–465. Berlin: De Gruyter.

Gévaudan, Paul. 1999. Semantische Relationen in nominalen und adjektivischen Kompositionen und Syntagmen. *PhiN. Philologie im Netz 9*: 11–34.

Givón, Talmy. 1994. Isomorphism in the grammatical code. Cognitive and biological considerations. In Raffaele Simone (ed.), *Iconicity in Language*, 47–76. Amsterdam & Philadelphia: Benjamins.

Koch, Peter and Daniela Marzo. 2007. A two-dimensional approach to the study of motivation in lexical typology and its first application to French high-frequency vocabulary. *Studies in Language* 31 (2): 259–291.

Koptjevskaja-Tamm, Maria, Martine Vanhove, and Peter Koch. 2007. Typological approaches to lexical semantics. *Linguistic Typology* 11, 159–185.

Krueger, John R. 1962. *Yakut Manual*. Bloomington: Indiana University Press.

Lehmann, Christian. 2007. Motivation in language. Attempt at a systematization. In Peter Gallmann, Christian Lehmann, and Rosemarie Lühr (eds.), *Sprachliche Motivation: zur Interdependenz von Inhalt und Ausdruck*, 105–140. Tübingen: Narr.

Lehrer, Adrienne. 1974. *Semantic fields and lexical structure*. Amsterdam: North-Holland Publishing Company.

Lévi-Strauss, Claude. 1965. Le cercle culinaire. *L'Arc* 26: 19–29.

Lienhard, Ruth and Martha Giger. 1975. *Daba (Parler de Pologozom): Description Phonologique*. Yaoundé: Société Internationale de Linguistique.

Monastyrjew, Wladimir. 2006. *Jakutisch: Kleines erklärendes Wörterbuch des Jakutischen (Sacha – Deutsch)*. Wiesbaden: Harrassowitz.

Mouchet, Jean. 1966. *Le Parler Daba: Esquisse Grammaticale ; précédée d'une Note sur l'Ethnie Daba ; suivie de Lexiques Daba – Français et Français – Daba*. Yaoundé.

OED = *Oxford English Dictionary* (http://www.oed.com).

Pakendorf, Brigitte, and Innokentij Novgorodov. 2009. Sakha vocabulary. In Martin Haspelmath and Uri Tadmor (eds.), *World loanword database*, 1588 entries. Leipzig: Max Planck Institute for Evolutionary Anthropology. http://wold.clld.org/vocabulary/19.

Panther, Klaus-Uwe and Günter Radden (eds.). 2011. *Motivation in grammar and the lexicon*. Amsterdam & Philadelphia: Benjamins.

Peirce, Charles Sanders. 1960. *Collected papers*. Vol. 2, Cambridge: Harvard University Press.

Peirsman, Yves, and Dirk Geeraerts. 2006. Metonymy as a prototypical category. *Cognitive Linguistics* 17 (3): 269–316.

Perkins, Revere D. 2001. Sampling procedures and statistical methods. In Martin Haspelmath, Ekkehard König, Wulf Oesterreicher, and Wolfgang Raible (eds.), *Language typology and language universals: an international handbook*, 419–434. Berlin: De Gruyter.

Radden, Günter and Klaus-Uwe Panther (eds.). 2004. *Studies in linguistic motivation*. Berlin & New York: Mouton de Gruyter.

Scalise, Sergio and Antonietta Bisetto. 2009. The classification of compounds. In Rochelle Lieber and Pavol Štekauer (eds.), *The Oxford handbook of compounding*, 34–53. Oxford: Oxford University Press.

Sleptsov, Petr Alekseevic (ed.). 2005. *Explanatory dictionary of the Yakut language. Vol. 2 (letter B)*. Novosibirsk: Nauka.

Matthias Urban
17. Motivation by formally analyzable terms in a typological perspective: An assessment of the variation and steps towards explanation

Abstract: This article tackles a question raised by one of the founding figures of lexical typology, Stephen Ullmann: to what degree do languages differ in the extent to which they resort to morphologically analyzable lexical items? Drawing on a worldwide sample of 78 languages for which a standard set of 160 mostly nominal meanings is investigated, the article demonstrates that variability in this area is indeed profound. Correlations between the relative prevalence of analyzable items in a language with the size of its consonant inventory, the complexity of its syllable structure, and the length of its nominal roots suggest that, typologically, languages with a simple phonological structure are those in which analyzability in the lexicon is most profound. Possible explanations for this observation in terms of the avoidance of homonymy and pressure exerted by different linguistic subsystems on each other are discussed.

17.1 Introduction

Following current definitions (Koch 2001; Koch and Marzo 2007), lexical motivation is a property of a lexical item which shows a formal relation to one or more other lexical items that mirrors a conceptual relation between the concepts that they respectively denote. Word-formation is an important motivational device. The French *poirier* 'pear tree', for example, is motivated by the formal and semantic relation to *poire* 'pear', from which it is derived. But lexical motivation also includes other kinds of complex items which establish this double relation, as well as the extreme case of polysemy, in which the formal relation is one of complete identity. Both aspects of lexical motivation – the formal and the conceptual – are worthwhile topics for cross-linguistic research.

Regarding the former, the question of differences between languages in the *quantity* of motivated items in their lexicon has been a major concern of research

---
Matthias Urban (Leiden University)

in what is coming to be called lexical typology. Saussure ([1916] 1967) raised this question early on (he introduced, alongside the famous notion of the arbitrariness of the linguistic sign also that of relative motivation), as did Ullmann (1962, 1966) later. Much more recently, Koch and Marzo (2007: 273) ask, but do not answer the question "are there more or less formally transparent languages"? The issue concerned still earlier writers as well, see Urban (2012: chapter 2) for review.

Ullmann (1962: 105) was aware of the difficulties in unambiguously identifying and quantifying polysemy, and suggested restricting oneself to motivation by morphological analyzability in a quantitative study, as in the case of French *poirier*:

> With morphological motivation one is on firmer ground: it is the most clear-cut and least subjective of the three types, and certain broad tendencies stand out very clearly...

Later on, Ullmann made some casual methodological suggestions for such an investigation (1966: 223):

> It might be possible to devise some statistical test for these relative frequencies. Such a test might be based on samples from dictionaries, on a representative selection of texts, or on both.

Scattered statements in the literature suggest that cross-linguistic variability in the prevalence of motivated analyzable terms in the lexicon is indeed profound. It is thus a typological variable of great interest which has not yet been investigated systematically in spite of suggestions such as Ullmann's. For instance, Seiler (1976: 6) says about Cahuilla that "[t]he analysability and morphological transparency of a considerable portion of all nominal expressions [...] is immediately recognisable", and O'Meara and Bohnemeyer (2008: 332–333) even state for Seri that "[c]omplex expressions [...] are in fact pervasive in the Seri nominal lexicon" and that the rarity of unanalyzable terms is a "general typological characteristic of the nominal lexicon of Seri".

This paper reports on an investigation very similar to that suggested by Ullmann. It was carried out applying methods of modern linguistic typology, a discipline that has grown immensely since Ullmann's times. As Ullmann suggested, it is restricted to lexical motivation by morphological analyzability, excluding polysemy. Details of the approach and a first description of the cross-linguistic variation in the domain of analyzability in the lexicon follow in section 17.2. However, even more interesting than assessing the mere distribution of the differential degrees of analyzable terms in the languages of the world is to ask why this distribution is as it is, i.e. to try to understand why lexical motivation is present to a smaller or larger degree in different languages. Section 17.3

describes a number of factors which appear to be relevant, and a final discussion appears in section 17.4.

17.2 Approach and data

The present approach makes use of a list of 160 mostly perceptually apprehensible "nominal" concepts (see Appendix A), where it is assumed that they possess properties (most prominently, stability of meaning independent of contextual factors) that make them easier to compare across languages than event-denoting "verby" expressions (cf. Cruse 1986: 152; Foley 1997: 35). The concepts are organized into four semantic domains: terms for natural kinds, artifacts, body-parts and body-liquids, and terms for phases of the day plus a few miscellanea. There is no direct predecessor to the list, though it was partly inspired by works such as Buck (1949) in the domain of nature-related terms and Brown (1999) in that of artifacts. Here, the latter include both items of some antiquity in most cultures (e.g. 'knife') as well as more recent items of acculturation (e.g. 'car') to also take into account the behaviour of languages when it comes to denominating new stimuli. Regarding body-part terms, which have been rather well studied from a cross-linguistic point of view, care was taken that parts are included that have hitherto received relatively little attention. Terms for the meanings were gathered from extant sources and/or were provided by experts for seventy-eight languages (see Appendix B), each of which belongs to a different language family recognized in Dryer (2005). For each language, the criterion for inclusion was that counterparts for more than 104, or 65%, of the meanings on the list were available.[1] The assumption is that the mapping from meaning to form is many-to-many (cf. Haspelmath and Tadmor 2009): there may be several unrelated items in a given language corresponding to a single meaning (synonymy or, more commonly, near-synonymy), and, conversely, there may be a single equivalent covering the range of two or more of the meanings on the list (polysemy, vagueness, homonymy, or, to use a deliberately ambiguous term with respect to this distinction for the application in cross-linguistic studies coined by François 2008, 'colexification'). Rather than trying to single out the "best" equivalent, several

---

[1] This procedure leads to a strong representation of languages of the Americas. As Dahl (2008) suggests that they have been underrepresented in many previous typological samples, this is in principle desirable; nevertheless, it may be the case that they are in fact overrepresented in the present sample. Since the sample was not manipulated in hindsight, this should be borne in mind when contemplating the evidence presented here.

corresponding terms were accepted per language for a given referent. Since these may, of course, have differing formal properties (one may be analyzable, another morphologically simple), this entails, perhaps paradoxically at first sight, that in the present analysis a language may transpire to have 0.5, 0.33, etc. analyzable terms for a given meaning. The sum of these values for individual meanings in one language yields the absolute analyzability score. Observe that "analyzability" in this sense neither presupposes nor necessarily implies ability on behalf of native speakers to decompose the terms into their parts, although it would be worthwhile or even preferable to take speaker judgments into account. Further, since equivalents for all meanings could not be retrieved for all sampled languages, the resulting figure was divided by the number of meanings for which data are available. This, finally, yields the relative analyzability score for each of the sampled languages, and this is the variable which is discussed in the following sections. However, alongside merely being registered, analyzable terms were also classified into three broad types, illustrated here with some Bezhta examples from Comrie and Khalilov (2009): (i) the lexical type, which involves more than one lexical root (e.g. that for *häyš ƛ'äq'e* 'eyelid', which consists of the word for 'eye' in the genitive case and 'roof'); (ii) the derived type, characterized by presence of a single lexical root (e.g. *ƛišiyo* 'waterfall', which is in fact the past participle of a verb meaning 'to become entangled'); and (iii) the rare alternating type, in which senses are distinguished by some kind of grammatical alternation (e.g. *häydä* 'glasses', the plural of 'eye'). Not taken into account were analyzable terms composed of morphology that does not have a motivating force and semi-analyzable terms.

17.3 The cross-linguistic variation in analyzability

Purely descriptively, the investigation confirms the initial conjecture as to the cross-linguistic variability in the relative number of analyzable items: the range of their number is from very few analyzable terms for the investigated concepts, as in Aymara, which receives a relative analyzability score of 4.9%, to as large a score as 50.2% for Kiliwa.[2] Thus, Kiliwa has *ha?kw?nymarkwiy* 'cloud voice' where English, for example, has the unanalyzable *thunder*, *wa?hkapu?* 'house

---

[2] What is of interest are probably not the absolute percentages, since these depend to some degree on the concepts one investigates, but rather the fact that there is variability when semantics, by way of using a standardized list of concepts, is kept constant.

opener' where English has *key*, *nymayuyuw* 'breast eye' where English has *nipple*, *khwathyuul* 'flowing blood' where English has *vein*, and so on (Kiliwa data and literal translations from Mixco 1985). The map in Figure 1 plots the result for the investigated languages onto a map of the world. Each dot represents a sampled language, and the size of the dot corresponds to the relative analyzability score: the larger the dot, the higher the score, the smaller the dot, the lower the score.

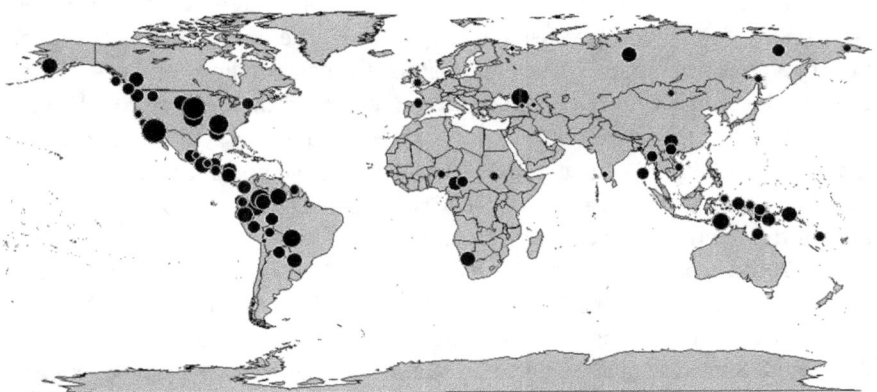

Figure 1: Differential degree of analyzability in the sampled languages

From eyeballing the map, one can identify some geographical hotspots in which languages with a high number of analyzable terms are frequent, such as Eastern North America and the lowlands of South America. However, simple visual inspection of distributions on maps is an unreliable technique for assessing areality (Cysouw 2005, among others). Using a standard breakdown of the world into six macro-areas (Africa, Australia-New Guinea, Eurasia, Oceania, North America, South America, from Dryer 1992), there is some evidence for areality, but no clearly statistically detectable difference between the areas ($p = .0712$ by a Kruskal-Wallis rank sum test, $\chi^2 = 10.1461$, df = 5). Given that areal convergence thus does not appear to be a decisive factor in governing the behaviour of individual languages, the question that immediately emerges is: what is? Possible factors are carved out in the following section.

17.4 In search of conditioning factors

17.4.1 Rationale

A priori, the question is entirely open, but also lends itself to empirical investigation. Prevalence of analyzability in the lexicon as a typological trait is a variable that has not been addressed previously in a systematic fashion, and hence there is no literature on which to base new hypotheses. Therefore, a series of preliminary hypothesis-generating statistical tests on the basis of the entire set of 142 features in the *World Atlas of Language Structures* (Haspelmath et al. 2005), which deal with a diverse range of phonological, morphological, syntactic and lexical topics, was run in the statistics environment R (R development core team 2009). This test series suggested an influence of two of the features dealing with phonology on the relative analyzability score, namely consonant inventory size (Maddieson 2005a) and syllable structure (Maddieson 2005b), among other features. More precisely, as consonant inventories became larger and syllable structures more complex, the number of analyzable terms among the meanings investigated decreased. Since the overlap between Maddieson's and the present sample was quite small, additional data from published sources were gathered for the languages of the present sample in order to assess whether the dependency could be substantiated, while maintaining Maddieson's general coding schemes. Because of errors in Maddieson's (2005a) data, they were later updated taking into account changes effectuated in Maddieson (2013).[3]

Moreover, for the final analysis, it is not only important to have as complete datasets as possible, but also to control for areal factors, as usual in modern typology. For the present topic, this is even more imperative since there clearly are some areal differences in analyzability (although insignificant), but also because, as noted by Maddieson (2005a, b), the cross-linguistic distribution of the phonological features is highly skewed (for the sake of illustration, one can think of the large consonant inventories of languages in the American Northwest transcending genealogical boundaries, Mithun 1999: 314–315). In order to ascertain whether the significance of the preliminary tests is spurious because of areal

---

[3] Languages for which values have been changed are Arabela (from moderately large to small), Guaraní (from average to moderately small), and Great Andamanese (from small to average). The erroneous value for Oneida in Maddieson (2005) had already been noted and corrected in Urban (2012). In addition, the value for Kildin Saami was changed from moderately large to large (as per Riessler and Wilbur 2007: 74) and that for Bezhta from large to moderately large (as per Zaira Khalilova p.c.).

influences, generalized linear mixed models were built in R for the two candidate factors. This type of statistical analysis is increasingly used in a variety of disciplines, including psycholinguistics, where it is important to generalize over different participants in order to rule out that the results of an experiment are biased or even spurious due to the unusual behaviour of (few) individual test subjects. For this purpose, mixed models include two basic types of variables: so-called fixed effects, which are generally those variables of interest, over which the experimenter typically has control, and which s/he hypothesizes to be relevant for the behaviour of the response variable, and random effects, over which the experimenter has no control and for which generalizations are not of interest generally (such as the individual subjects participating in an experimental study, the particular animals a biologist observes to make generalizations about the species, etc.).

Just as in an experimental test setting one wants to generalize over the behaviour of different participants, in typology one wants to generalize over the behaviour of languages in different linguistic areas. Hence, mixed models were constructed with the relative analyzability score as the response, the phonological features of interest included as fixed effects and linguistic macro-area (in the breakdown of Dryer 1992) as a random effect (see also Cysouw 2010 for an approach to typology and the question of controlling for area using generalized linear mixed models).[4] Code by Baayen (2009) and Bates and Maechler (2009) was used for the analysis. Initially, models involving both a random intercept (meaning, in this case, that the relative degree of analyzability is allowed to vary from area to area) and random slopes components (meaning that the impact of the phonological properties may vary from area to area as well, being stronger in some regions of the world and weaker or even nonexistent in others) were built. On the basis of these models, assumptions of mixed models (normality and homogeneity of residuals) were checked by visual inspection of histograms of the residuals and plots of fitted and residual values. When visual inspection left doubts as to whether the assumptions are fulfilled, an additional Shapiro-Wilk test for normality of the residuals and a correlation test between fitted vs. residual values

---

4 An issue with this statistical technique, powerful as it is, is that it is not well suited for the classical task of linguistic typology of making inferences about all possible human languages, including all those spoken in the past but vanished today. This is because the linguistic diversity encountered today represents only a small fraction of what may be possible due to historical contingencies, and any statistical inference is thus necessarily based on this fraction alone. For this reason, all generalizations arrived at in this article pertain to the present-day linguistic diversity, but not to all possible human languages (cf. Cysouw 2010: 258fn5 for similar cautionary remarks).

were carried out. To simplify model structure, the random slopes component was subsequently removed if a likelihood ratio test comparing the full model with a reduced model only involving random intercepts indicated that random slopes are not required. This was the case for all models. Finally, further likelihood ratio tests were carried out to compare the resulting simplified models including the fixed effects with reduced models only including the random effect.

Given that the preliminary test battery on the WALS data consisted of 142 tests, one would expect the emergence of spurious significance simply by chance at an α-level of .05 in the case of 142 × .05 ≈ 7 of the tests. Therefore, a smaller validation sample using additional data in Urban (2012) was constructed to assess whether the result can be replicated using the same mixed model design.

17.4.2 Consonant inventory

Figure 2 is a boxplot[5] showing the effect of the size of the consonant inventory on the relative analyzability score (not simultaneously visualizing areal effects to maintain easy readability).

---

[5] Boxplots are a useful visualization technique for statistical distributions. Here, the y-axis shows the relative number of analyzable items, and each of the boxes corresponds to one of the levels of the phonological features, as coded by Maddieson (2005a, c). The thick black line within each group represents the median for the relative analyzability score within that group, and the size of the boxes and the dashed lines (the so-called whiskers) indicate the variance around that mean: the smaller the boxes and whiskers, the smaller the variance around the mean, the larger, the greater the variance. Generally, 50% of datapoints in each group fall into the box. Individual dots above or below the boxes represent outliers, that is, individual languages which are very far removed from the median of the group they belong to. Finally, the width of the boxes gives an idea of the number of observations within each group: the narrower the box, the smaller the number of observations (that is, languages in the sample having a particular phonological property such as an average-sized consonant inventory), the wider the box, the larger the number of observations.

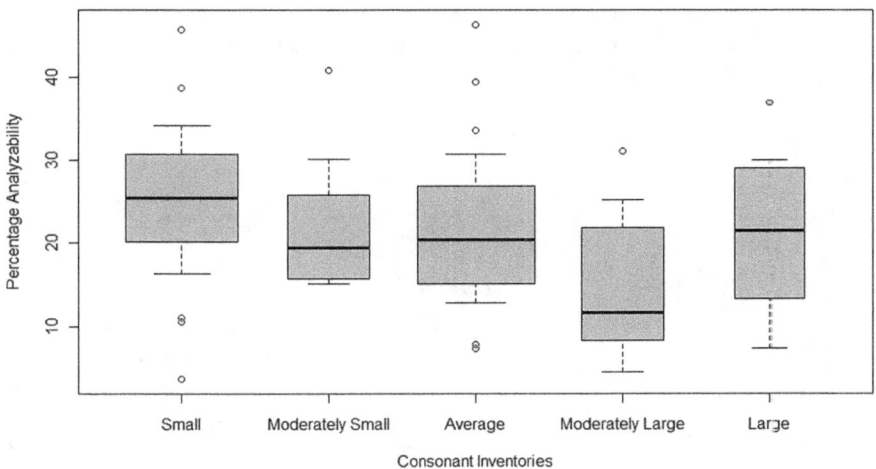

Figure 2: Relative degree of analyzability depending on size of the consonant inventory. Box width indicates number of data points within a category.

As the figure shows, there is a downward trend in the relative analyzability score as consonant inventories become larger, though this effect is somewhat uneven between groups and, surprisingly, the languages with the largest consonant inventories behave in an unexpected way. In the mixed model design, the size of a consonant inventory is relevant as a factor and the p-value (estimated by Markov Chain Monte Carlo (MCMC) simulation with 100,000 replicates) associated with the predictor itself is weakly significant at .04727.

In the validation sample, it was also the case that the relative analyzability score was lower for languages with large consonant inventories compared to those with small ones, but the impact of consonant inventories as a predictor was less clear. Together with the only weak significance of the main model, it transpires that the connection needs further attention to be fully accepted as valid, and hence its identification as a relevant factor here is preliminary only.

17.4.3 Syllable structure

Figure 3 is a boxplot showing the relative degree of analyzability depending on complexity in syllable structure. There is a very similar dependency here: languages with simple syllable structure (i.e. no consonant clusters and no consonants in coda position) tend to have a higher value for the relative analyzability score than do those with moderately complex syllable structure (allowing a consonant in coda position, and initial clusters of consonant plus glide), which in turn tend to score higher than those with complex syllable structure (i.e. allowing for more elaborate clusters).

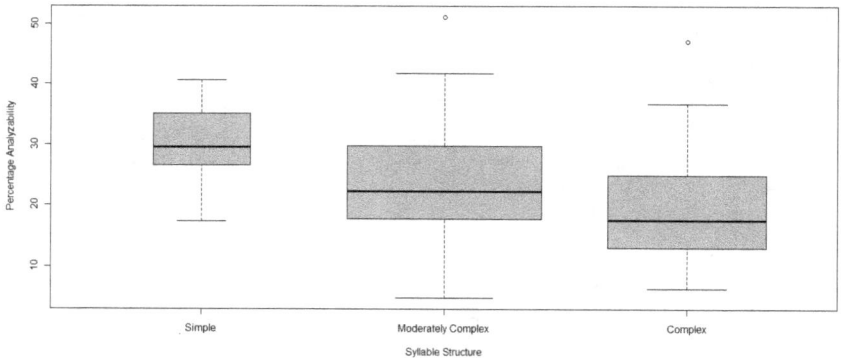

Figure 3: Relative degree of analyzability depending on complexity of syllable structure. Box width indicates number of data points within a category.

As for consonant inventories, the impact of the differences in syllable structure is significant (MCMC-estimated p-value = .0102), and the effect could be replicated on the basis of other data in the validation sample.

These two pieces of evidence, taken together, are able to account for the behaviour of many individual languages and areal differences:[6] the difference between Western and Eastern North America mentioned above corresponds to a basic asymmetry in phonological complexity, in particular pertaining to size of the consonant inventory between these two parts of the continent (Sherzer 1973). This also may correlate with the fact that Polynesian languages, famous for their small number of consonants (and having a simple (C)V syllable structure), have

---

[6] Given that these two factors are relevant, it is natural to wonder whether the other major variable in complexity of phonological systems, namely the size of the vowel inventory, has an impact as well. Therefore, data from Maddieson (2005c) were amended for the languages of the present sample as well. In fact, when plotting the relation, the result looks very similar: as vowel inventories become smaller, mean values of the relative analyzability score rise. However, when taking into account areal factors by including area as a random effect in a mixed model design, there is no appreciable difference made by the factor vowel inventory (p = .5896), indicating that areal skewings play, unlike the other two investigated factors, a major role here. This, of course, underlines the need to control for areal influence in typology to rule out spurious results.

on average a higher number of analyzable lexical items when compared with their Austronesian kin.

17.4.4 Root structure

However, there is residual variation in the degree of analyzability that remains puzzling: for instance, all indigenous language families of the Caucasus sampled, namely Northwest Caucasian (represented by Abzakh Adyghe), Kartvelian (represented by Laz), and Nakh-Daghestanian (represented by Bezhta) are well-known for having a large number of distinctive consonants, and also allow for complex syllables. Yet, Abzakh Adyghe scores very high with respect to the analyzability score (in fact, it has the highest value for Eurasia as a whole), while Laz and Bezhta receive very low scores, which is all the more puzzling since Northwest Caucasian consonant inventories are typically even larger when compared to those from the other two Caucasian families. So, if anything, one would expect the situation with regard to analyzability to be the other way around in light of the global dependencies identified by statistical analysis. This suggests that there is at least one further, as yet undetected, factor at work so far. Comparative discussion of the structure of lexical items in Caucasian languages in Rayfield (2002: 1041) provides a clue as to what that factor may be for the variation encountered in the Caucasus specifically. Unlike Kartvelian (at least in the nominal domain) and Nakh-Daghestanian,

> Abkhaz and Circassian [=Adygheian, MU] contrast a prodigious wealth of consonants with a paucity of vowels and strict limits on permissible syllable structure. Roots tend to be monosyllabic, sometimes mono-consonantal, consequently with many homophones. Consonants in initial position rarely occur in clusters of more than two, and there are a very limited number of such clusters... As in, say, Chinese, the number of acceptable syllables that can constitute a root morpheme in N.W. Caucasian roots is so small that, in order to express a wide number of concepts or to name, say, flora and fauna, specific lexemes have to be constructed by recombining two or more other lexemes, or otherwise monosyllabic lexemes are polysemantic.

Note that root structure is a different variable than syllable structure: as the Northwest Caucasian case shows, allowing for complex syllables does not necessarily mean that they occur with high frequency in the lexicon, and conversely, simple syllable structure does not correspond directly to short roots, as they may be made up of several syllables. There are further statements on languages with a relatively high degree of analyzable lexical items which corroborate the suspicion that the typical phonological structure of the lexical root is another relevant factor, not only in shaping diversity in the Caucasus, but also operating more generally. Werner (1997: 46) and Watkins (1984: 75) state for Ket and Kiowa respectively that roots are typically monosyllabic, with the disyllabic roots attested usually being identifiable as old lexicalized compounds.

Unfortunately, this emerging hypothesis is not easily testable, because for the majority of sampled languages no explicit discussion of typical root structure shapes is available in the literature. Consequently, the following provisional method was used: the number of syllables was counted for each of the unanalyzable lexical items in the data for the present study, and subsequently, the weighted mean was calculated to give an idea of the average structure of the lexical word generally. This is not always easy, since the data at hand are represented orthographically, requiring one to often infer phonology from orthography. A particular issue in this respect is the question as to whether sequences of vowels should be treated as diphthongs or be syllabified as nuclei of separate syllables, since this may heavily influence the resulting figures regarding the number of syllables. For instance, in Toaripi, sequences of up to five vowels are frequent, and any arbitrary decision as to their phonological status would greatly influence results in one way or another. Luckily, for this task in general, as well as for the problem of syllabification of vowel sequences, primary descriptions of the languages are often of help. However for nine sampled languages: Mali, Rotokas, the aforementioned Toaripi, Kildin Saami, Cheyenne, Arabela, Cayapa, Chayahuita, and Cubeo, sequences of orthographic vowels are highly frequent, and their proper interpretation remains unclear; hence, for this specific task, they were excluded from analysis entirely.[7]

Of course, the lexicon is vast, and the typical structure of the root is assessed only on the basis of a very small subset here; however, where statements on the typical root structure are made in the literature on the languages, the figures obtained for the present study are typically in agreement.

The resulting weighted means for the remaining sixty-nine languages were then included in a mixed model design as a fixed effect, area as a random effect, and the relative analyzability score as the response to be modelled. Root Structure had an impact on this response to a significant degree (MCMC-estimated p-value = .0355). This impact on the degree of analyzability is plotted in figure 4. For the purpose of visualization, root length in terms of syllables was divided into four

---

[7] For other languages where orthographic vowel sequences exist but are less frequent, they were treated in a way that biases against the hypothesis: for languages where the analyzability score is below the cross-linguistic mean of 22.81 % they were analyzed as diphthongs, and for languages above the mean as sequences.

groups: short, moderately short, moderately long, and long (but for modelling, the actual, more informative values were used).

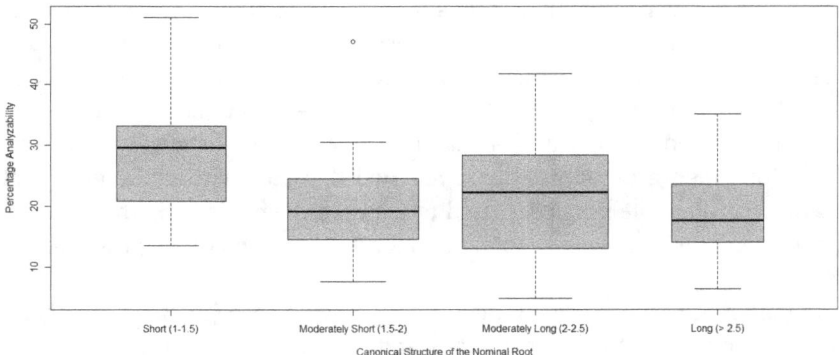

Figure 4: Relative degree of analyzability depending on length of nominal roots. Box width indicates number of data points within a category.

17.4.5 Summary

Thus, the answer to Koch and Marzo's (and Ullmann's) question seems to be: yes, there are languages with a high degree of formal transparency, that is a high relative analyzability score. These languages tend to possess simple phonological systems with regard to their syllable structure and – tentatively – consonant inventories as well as comparably short lexical roots. This by no means excludes the possibility that there can be further factors at play, such as large-scale contact-induced lexical replacement which enriches the lexicon with unanalyzable loanwords (see Urban 2012 for discussion of possible further factors). Nevertheless, phonological restrictions do seem to exert some structural pressure on the lexicon, causing it to adapt by an increased number of analyzable lexical items. Ross (1980) is a revealing case study on a language outside the present sample showing this pressure: the phonological system of Vanimo allows for the generation of as few as 960 distinct morphemes, and this is counterbalanced by the ample use of complex expressions making up for the paucity of possible phonologically distinct morphemes.

17.5 Discussion

It is important to realize that significant correlations are not explanantia in themselves, but rather explananda, and thus the question that one needs to pose is: why are the correlations there in the first place? By addressing this question, one enters the final stage in the explanation of interdependencies between typological variables in terms of Bybee (1988): empirical generalizations were made concerning an apparent influence of (at least) three factors on the degree of relative analyzability, then a principle was formulated that summarizes the empirical generalizations (simple phonology and root structure entails high analyzability in the lexicon), and finally, an explanation for the operation of the principle has to be identified.

A number of recent works in linguistic typology, Bybee (1988) among them, emphasize that typological distributions and universal tendencies in language structure have to be understood from the historical factors that bring them about.

Rayfield (2002: 1041), as quoted above, comments on the high incidence of homophony in Northwest Caucasian, caused by the severe restriction of possible root shapes. In fact, there is a venerable, although not unproblematic, principle in historical linguistics dating back to Gilliéron and Rocques (1912): homonymy avoidance. According to this principle languages (or rather, their speakers) take countermeasures against the possibility of detrimental effects of homonymy or near-homonymy to successful communication by ousting certain cases of homonymy from the lexicon. Case studies include, but are by no means limited to Williams (1944), Campbell (1975), and Dworkin (1993), see Urban (2012) for more thorough review.[8] Malkiel (1979: 2–3; 7) provides a typology of the potential outcome of homonymic clashes: next to simple "peaceful" continued coexistence, one homonym may oust another, they may merge, or differentiate in form and possibly in meaning.

While there is ample literature on lexical loss or irregular sound change due to putative homonymy avoidance, empirical evidence for coining neologisms for this purpose, which would be needed to make a convincing case for homonymy avoidance as an operative factor, is quite sparse in the literature, although not nonexistent. Shi (2002: 76) states that, as the phonological system of Chinese simplified considerably over the past 1,000 years or so, one way to bring about the disyllabification of the lexicon well-known to Sinologists is the replacement of inherited terms by two-syllable (and hence, morpheme) compounds. Coates

---

[8] And note that quite to the contrary there may also be language change that creates rather than wards off additional homonymy, see e.g. Dixon (2004: 71) on Jarawara.

(1968) is a case-study from Germanic that demonstrates how later phonological collapse of erstwhile distinct Proto-Germanic *pīhstila 'thistle,' *pinhslā 'pole, beam, tongue' and *pehsalōn 'adze' (an old tool for wood processing) caused replacement of one or another inherited term by a newly coined compound in some daughter languages.

In addition, there are theoretical concerns regarding homonymy avoidance as a functional principle in diachrony. Some elaborations suffer from an undue personalization of language as a deliberately acting agent, neglecting the role of speakers as instigators of innovations. But even if a decisive role of the speaker in language change is acknowledged, it remains questionable whether such speakers actually produce innovations (such as complex neologisms) with the explicit goal of changing their language. Their motives for innovation may well be very different. Once such innovations have occurred, however, it is still arguable that because of certain properties which some innovations possess they may have an advantage leading to their propagation across a speech community (cf. Koch 2005: 233–236; 238–242 and references therein; for the distinction between innovation and propagation in language change see also Croft 2000: 4–5). Enhanced distinctiveness vis-à-vis a possibly confusable homonym or near-homonym may well be such an advantage.

Thus, without postulating a principle stating that languages generally abhor homonymy, a possible avenue of explanation is to assume that in languages with simple syllable and root structure and perhaps small consonant inventories, these bring about restrictions on the possible number of phonologically distinct lexical roots causing lexical homonymy at a rate high enough to lead to possible confusion in communication.

However, issues remain: first, as noted by most authors writing on the topic, for homonymy avoidance to be a plausible explanatory factor for diachronic changes, the relevant lexical items need to be in danger of co-occuring in the same stretch of discourse. Otherwise, there is no actual danger of confusion in communicative events. Second, its pervasiveness as a principle in historical linguistics generally is disputed.

Therefore, also in light of the sparse evidence in the literature for coinage of complex terms for the purpose of homonymy avoidance, it seems worthwhile to consider taking a broader perspective. To reiterate, the evidence resulting from the present study suggests an influence by syllable and root structure on the overall linguistic system causing it to exploit word-formation devices to a larger extent than those with ample phonological resources. A more abstract line of reasoning would therefore be to hypothesize that as the number of actually lexically exploited morpheme shapes approaches that of the possible shapes that can be generated by the phonological system (see Krupa 1966 for a quantitative study on Maori), there is pressure on the linguistic system to counter the limited expressive possibilities, either by the introduction of phonemic tone (Matisoff 1973; see Urban 2012 for discussion of tone as a relevant factor), the introduction of analyzable lexical items for an increased range of concepts, a combination of these, or yet another strategy. In fact, Nettle (1995, 1998) makes quite similar observations, although his datasets are either much smaller (Nettle 1995) or more geographically restricted (Nettle 1998). While not concerned with morphological analyzability, but rather with word length in terms of segments, he establishes a similar inverse relationship with phonological complexity: languages with many phonemes have shorter words than those with few (though note again that in the present study the influence of the size of the consonant inventory is not straightforward). Obviously, complex terms terms are longer segmentally than the elements they consist of, so the two results are fully compatible with one another. Furthermore, the concluding discussion in Nettle (1998: 244) similarly suggests that "lexical expansion" by the coinage of complex terms is responsible for the correlations observed. Nettle (1999: 144) summarizes:

> as a result [of speakers' tendency to underarticulate driven by economy, MU], sets of words that were previously distinct become homophones. When words have become homophones, speakers may have to compensate by some kind of lexical strategy, such as coining a new word or paraphrase. ... Discrimination failure leads to smaller inventories, and the lexical strategies by which meaning is maintained tend to produce longer word forms. The pressure on the language from discrimination failure thus precisely balances that due to articulatory economy. The actual system of any given language emerges from a dynamic equilibrium between these two factors.

In this sense, the present evidence can be read as a variation on the old theme of speakers being suspended between the drive towards economical linguistic behaviour on the one hand and the necessity to attain communicative efficiency on the other, present from pre-Structuralist thinking (e.g. Gabelentz 1901), through French structuralism (e.g. Martinet 1952), up to present-day linguistic theorizing (e.g. Haspelmath 1999).

Whichever explanation one prefers, the evidence presented here may provide an implication for current linguistic theory: if one is willing to view analyzability in the lexicon, that is morphological complexity in lexical items, as a type of linguistic complexity as much discussed recently (Miestamo, Sinnemäki, and Karlsson 2008; Sampson et al. 2008), this can be construed as evidence for a tradeoff between complexity in linguistic subsystems (compare the 'equi-complexity axiom'): phonological simplicity tends to go hand in hand with complexity in lexical items and vice versa (although "complexity" in this sense is subject to differing definitions and not an entirely clear-cut concept, see Miestamo 2008 for an overview of different approaches).[9]

17.6 Acknowledgments

My sincere thanks go to Johanna Mattissen for providing lexical data for Laz, to Tonya Stebbins and Julius Tayul for making available a pre-print version of their Mali dictionary, and to Joseph Atoyebi, Ekaterina Gruzdeva, Andrej Nevedov, Pamela Munro with Catherine Willmond, and Frank Seifart for checking and amending the Yoruba, Nivkh, Ket, Chickasaw, and Bora data respectively. Further, I thank Bodo Winter for first drawing my attention to mixed models, and am indebted to him, Michael Cysouw, and Roger Mundry for continued advice on statistical matters. I also wish to thank the reviewers for this paper and the editors of the present volume for their input and suggestions, as well as Kate Bellamy for proofreading. Responsibility for shortcomings rests entirely with me.

17.7 Appendix A: list of meanings

I. Nature-Related and topological concepts: 1. Animal, 2. Ashes, 3. Bark, 4. Bay, 5. Beak, 6. Bird, 7. Bloom (blossom, flower), 8. Branch, 9. Bud, 10. Cave, 11. Clearing, 12. Cloud, 13. Coal, 14. Coast, 15. Dew, 16. Dust, 17. Eclipse, 18. Egg, 19. Embers, 20. Estuary, 21. Feather, 22. Flame, 23. Flood, 24. Foam, 25. Fog/Mist, 26. Forest, 27. Gold, 28. Grass, 29. Headland, 30. Honey, 31. Horizon, 32. Horn, 33. Lagoon, 34. Lake, 35. Lightning, 36. Meteoroid (shooting/shining star), 37. Milk, 38. Milky Way, 39. Moon, 40. Mountain, 41. Mushroom (fungus), 42. Nest, 43. Plant, 44. Puddle, 45. Rain, 46. Rainbow, 47. Resin, 48. River/stream, 49. river bed, 50. Root, 51. Seed, 52. Shadow, 53. Sky, 54. Smoke, 55. Soil, 56. Spark, 57. Spring/Well, 58. Star, 59. Steam, 60. Straw, 61. Sun, 62. Swamp, 63. Tail, 64. Thorn, 65. Thunder, 66. Tree, 67. Valley, 68. Volcano, 69. Waterfall, 70. Wave, 71. Wax, 72. Whirlpool
II. Artifacts, 1. Airplane, 2. Ball, 3. Bed, 4. Belt, 5. Boat, 6. Car, 7. Chair, 8. Clock, 9. Glasses, 10. House, 11. Key, 12. Knife, 13. Ladder, 14. Mirror, 15. Needle, 16. Paper, 17. Pen, 18. Rope, 19. Scissors, 20. Shoe, 21. Road/Street/Way, 22. Table, 23. Toilet, 24. Train, 25. Weapon, 26. Window

---

9 There is neuropsychological evidence summarized in Libben (2006) that in the processing of compounds, both constituent parts are neurally activated, even if the semantic relation between their meaning and the compound meaning is non-transparent. This indicates that, indeed, their cognitive representation is more "complex" than that of simplex lexical items.

III. Body Parts and Body Fluids: 1. Adam's apple, 2. Ankle, 3. Beard, 4. Belly/Stomach, 5. Bladder, 6. Blood, 7. Bone, 8. Brain, 9. Breast, 10. Buttocks, 11. Calf, 12. Cheek, 13. Chin, 14. Eyeball, 15. Eyebrow, 16. Eyelash, 17. Eyelid, 18. Finger, 19. Fingernail, 20. Guts, 21. Heart, 22. Jaw, 23. Kidney, 24. Lip, 25. Liver, 26. Lungs, 27. Mouth, 28. Mucus, 29. Navel, 30. Neck, 31. Nipple, 32. Nostrils, 33. Pupil, 34. Pus, 35. Rib, 36. saliva/spittle, 37. Scar, 38. Skin, 39. Snot, 40. Semen, 41. Sweat, 42. Tear, 43. Tendon/Sinew, 44. Testicle, 45. Tongue, 46. Tooth, 47. Urine, 48. Uvula, 49. Vein, 50. Womb, 51. Wrinkle

IV. Basic Temporal Concepts and Miscellanea, 1. Dawn, 2. Day, 3. Dusk, 4. Night, 5. Noon, 6. Sunrise, 7. Sunset, 1. Man (human being), 2. Saturday, 3. Virgin, 4. Widow

17.8 Appendix B: Sample Languages, ordered by macroarea

Note: Full references as well as data on phonological features is in Urban (2012).

I. Africa: 1. Hausa (Afro-Asiatic), 2. Katcha (Kadugli), 3. Khoekhoe (Khoisan), 4. Mbum (Niger-Congo), 5. Ngambay (Nilo-Saharan)

II. Australia-New Guinea: 1. Baruya (Trans-New-Guinea), 2. Berik (Tor), 3. Buin (East Bougainville), 4. Kaluli (Bosavi), 5. Kwoma (Sepik), 6. Mali (Baining-Taulil), 7. Meyah (East Bird's Head), 8. Rotokas (West Bougainville), 9. Sahu (East Papuan), 10. Toaripi (Eleman), 11. Yir Yoront (Australian)

III. Eurasia: 1. Abzkah Adyghe (Northwest Caucasian), 2. Badaga (Dravidian), 3. Basque (Basque), 4. Bezhta (Nakh-Daghestanian), 5. Chukchi (Chukotko-Kamchatkan), 6. Ket (Yeniseian), 7. Khalkha (Altaic), 8. Laz (Kartvelian), 9. Nivkh (Nivkh), 10. Kildin Saami (Uralic), 11. Welsh (Indo-European), 12. Kolyma Yukaghir (Yukaghir)

IV. North America: 1. Biloxi (Siouan), 2. Carrier (Na-Dene), 3. Upper Chehalis (Salishan), 4. Cheyenne (Algic), 5. Chickasaw (Muskogean), 6. Highland Chontal (Tequistlatecan), 7. Ineseño Chumash (Chumashan), 8. Haida (Haida), 9. Itzaj (Mayan), 10. Kiliwa (Hokan), 11. Kiowa (Kiowa-Tanoan), 12. Nez Perce (Penutian), 13. Nuuchahnulth (Wakashan), 14. Oneida (Iroquoian), 15. Santiago Mexquititlan Otomí (Oto-Manguean), 16. Pawnee (Caddoan), 17. Pipil (Uto-Aztecan), 18. Xicotepec de Juárez Totonac (Totonacan), 19. Wappo (Wappo-Yukian), 20. Central Yup'ik (Eskimo-Aleut), 21. Copainalá Zoque (Mixe-Zoque), 22. San Mateo del Mar Huave (Huavean)

IV. South America: 1. Aguaruna (Jivaroan), 2. Arabela (Zaparoan), 3. Aymara (Aymaran), 4. Bora (Huitotoan), 5. Bororo (Macro-Gê), 6. Carib (Cariban), 7. Cashinahua (Panoan), 8. Cavineña (Tacanan), 9. Cayapa (Barbacoan), 10. Chayahuita (Cahuapanan), 11. Cubeo (Tucanoan), 12. Embera (Choco), 13. Guaraní (Tupian), 14. Hupda (Vaupés-Japurá), 15. Jarawara (Arauan), 16. Miskito (Misumalpan), 17. Piro (Arawakan), 18. Imbabura Quechua (Quechuan), 19. Rama (Chibchan), 20. Wichí (Matacoan), 21. Yanomámi (Yanomam)

IV. Southeast Asia & Oceania: 1. Great Andamanese (Andamanese), 2. Bwe Karen (Sino-Tibetan), 3. White Hmong (Hmong-Mien), 4. Sedang (Austro-Asiatic), 5. Tetun (Austronesian), 6. Yay (Tai-Kadai), 7. Bislama (Creole)

17.9 References

Baayen, R. Harald. 2009. *languageR: data sets and functions with 'analyzing linguistic data: a practical introduction to statistics'*. R package version 0.955.
Bates, Douglas and Martin Maechler. 2009. *lme4: linear mixed-effects models using S4 classes*. R package version 0.999375-32.
Bybee, Joan. 1988. The diachronic dimension in explanation. In John A. Hawkins (ed.), *Explaining language universals*, 350-379. Oxford: Blackwell.
Brown, Cecil H. 1999. *Lexical acculturation in Native American languages*. Oxford: Oxford University Press.
Buck, Carl Darling. 1949. *A dictionary of selected synonyms in the principal Indo-European languages*. Chicago & London: The University of Chicago Press.
Campbell, Lyle. 1975. Constraints on sound change. In Karl-Hampus Dahlstedt (ed.), *The Nordic languages and modern linguistics* 2, 388-406. Stockholm: Almqvist & Wiksell.
Coates, William Ames. 1968. Near-homonymy as a factor in language change. *Language* 44 (3): 467-479.
Comrie, Bernard, and Madzhid Khalilov. 2009. Bezhta vocabulary. In Martin Haspelmath and Uri Tadmor (eds.), *World Loanword Database*. Leipzig: Max Planck Institute for Evolutionary Anthropology. http://wold.livingsources.org/vocabulary/15.
Croft, William. 2000. *Explaining language change: an evolutionary approach*. Harlow: Longman.
Cruse, D. Alan. 1986. *Lexical semantics*. Cambridge: Cambridge University Press.
Cysouw, Michael. 2005. Quantitative methods in typology. In Gabriel Altmann, Reinhard Köhler, and Rajmond G. Piotrowski (eds.), *Quantitative linguistics: an international handbook*, 554-578. Berlin & New York: Mouton de Gruyter.
Cysouw, Michael. 2010. Dealing with diversity: towards an explanation of NP-internal word order frequencies. *Linguistic Typology* 14 (2/3): 253-286.
Dahl, Östen. 2008. An exercise in a posteriori language sampling. *Sprachtypologie und Universalienforschung* 61 (3): 208-220.
Dixon, Robert M.W. 2004. *The Jarawara language of Southern Amazonia*. Oxford: Oxford University Press.
Dryer, Matthew S. 1992. The Greenbergian word order correlations. *Language* 68 (1): 81-138.
Dryer, Matthew S. 2005. Genealogical language list. In Martin Haspelmath, Matthew S. Dryer, David Gil, and Bernard Comrie (eds.), *The world atlas of language structures*, 584-644. Oxford: Oxford University Press.
Dworkin, Steven N. 1993. Near-homonymy, semantic overlap and lexical loss in Medieval Spanish: three case studies. *Romanistisches Jahrbuch* 44: 271-281.
Foley, William A. 1997. *Anthropological linguistics*. Oxford: Blackwell.
François, Alexandre. 2008. Semantic maps and the typology of colexification: intertwining polysemous networks across languages. In Martine Vanhove (ed.), *From polysemy to semantic change*, 163-215. Amsterdam & Philadelphia: John Benjamins.
Gabelentz, Georg von der. 1901. *Die Sprachwissenschaft. Ihre Aufgaben, Methoden, und bisherigen Ergebnisse*. Second Edition. Leipzig: Tauchnitz.
Gilliéron, J. and M. Roques. 1912. *Études de géographie linguistique*. Paris: Champion.
Haspelmath, Martin. 1999. Optimality and diachronic adaptation. *Zeitschrift für Sprachwissenschaft* 18 (2): 180-205.

Haspelmath, Martin, Matthew S. Dryer, David Gil, and Bernard Comrie (eds.). 2005. *The world atlas of language structures*. Oxford: Oxford University Press.
Haspelmath, Martin and Uri Tadmor. 2009. The loanword typology project and the world loanword database. In Martin Haspelmath and Uri Tadmor (eds.), *Loanwords in the world's languages: a comparative handbook*, 1–34. Berlin & New York: Mouton de Gruyter.
Koch, Peter. 2001. Lexical typology from a cognitive and linguistic point of view. In Martin Haspelmath, Ekkehard König, Wulf Oesterreicher, and Wolfgang Raible (eds.), *Language typology and language universals*, 1142–1178. Berlin & New York: Mouton de Gruyter.
Koch, Peter. 2005. Sprachwandel und Sprachvariation. In Angela Schrott and Harald Völker (eds.), *Historische Pragmatik und historische Varietätenlinguistik in den romanischen Sprachen*, 229–254. Göttingen: Universitätsverlag Göttingen.
Koch, Peter and Daniela Marzo. 2007. A two-dimensional approach to the study of motivation in lexical typology and its first application to French high-frequency vocabulary. *Studies in Language* 31 (2): 259–291.
Krupa, Viktor. 1966. *Morpheme and word in Maori*. The Hague: Mouton.
Libben, Gary. 2006. Why study compound processing? An overview of the issues. In Gary Libben and Gonia Jarema (eds.), *The representation and processing of compound words*, 1–23. Oxford: Oxford University Press.
Maddieson, Ian. 2005a. Consonant inventories. In Martin Haspelmath, Matthew S. Dryer, David Gil, and Bernard Comrie (eds.), *The world atlas of language structures*, 10–13. Oxford: Oxford University Press.
Maddieson, Ian. 2005b. Syllable structure. In Martin Haspelmath, Matthew S. Dryer, David Gil, and Bernard Comrie (eds.), *The world atlas of language structures*, 54–57. Oxford: Oxford University Press.
Maddieson, Ian. 2005c. Vowel quality inventories. In Martin Haspelmath, Matthew S. Dryer, David Gil, and Bernard Comrie (eds.), *The world atlas of language structures*, 14–17. Oxford: Oxford University Press.
Maddieson, Ian. 2013. Consonant inventories. In Matthew S. Dryer and Martin Haspelmath (eds.).*The World Atlas of Language Structures Online*, Leipzig: Max Planck Institute for Evolutionary Anthropology, http://wals.info/chapter/1.
Malkiel, Yakov. 1979. Problems in the diachronic differentiation of near-homophones. *Language* 55 (1): 1–36.
Martinet, André. 1952. Function, structure, and sound change. *Word* 8 (1): 1–32.
Matisoff, James A. 1973. Tonogenesis in Southeast Asia. *Southern California Occasional Papers in Linguistics* 1: 71–95.
Miestamo, Matti. 2008. Grammatical complexity in a cross-linguistic perspective. In Matti Miestamo, Kaius Sinnemäki, and Fred Karlsson (eds.), *Language complexity: Typology, contact, change,* 23–41. Amsterdam/Philadelphia: John Benjamins.
Miestamo, Matti, Kaius Sinnemäki, and Fred Karlsson (eds.). 2008. *Language complexity: Typology, contact, change.* Amsterdam & Philadelphia: John Benjamins.
Mithun, Marianne. 1999. *The languages of Native North America*. Cambridge: Cambridge University Press.
Mixco, Mauricio J. 1985. *Kiliwa dictionary*. Salt Lake City: University of Utah Press.
Nettle, Daniel. 1995. Segmental inventory size, word length, and communicative efficiency. *Linguistics* 33 (2): 359–367.
Nettle, Daniel. 1998. Coevolution of phonology and the lexicon in twelve languages of West Africa. *Journal of Quantitative Linguistics* 5 (3): 240–245.

Nettle, Daniel. 1999. *Linguistic diversity.* Oxford: Oxford University Press.
O'Meara, Carolyn and Jürgen Bohnemeyer. 2008. Complex landscape terms in Seri. *Language Sciences* 30 (2/3): 316–339.
R Development Core Team. 2009. *R: A language and environment for statistical computing, version 2.9.2.* Vienna: R Foundation for Statistical Computing.
Rayfield, Donald. 2002. Some distinctive characteristics of the vocabulary of Caucasian languages. In D. Alan Cruse, Franz Hundsnurscher, Michael Job, and Peter Rolf Lutzeier (eds.), *Lexikologie/Lexicology*, 1039–1042. Berlin & New York: Mouton De Gruyter.
Riessler, Michael and Joshua Wilbur. 2007. Documenting the endangered Kola Saami languages. In Tove Bull, Jurij Kusmenko, and Michael Rießler (eds.), Språk og språkforhold i Sápmi, 39–82. Berlin: Nordeuropa-Institut der Humboldt-Universität.
Ross, Malcolm D. 1980. Some elements of Vanimo, a New Guinea tone language. *Papers in New Guinea Linguistics* 20, 77–109.
Sampson, Geoffrey, David Gil, and Peter Trudgill (eds.). 2008. *Language complexity as an evolving variable.* Oxford: Oxford University Press.
Saussure, Ferdinand de. 1967 [1916]. *Cours de linguistique générale.* Paris: Payot.
Seiler, Hansjakob. 1976. *Introductory notes to a grammar of Cahuilla.* Cologne: Arbeiten des Kölner Universalien-Projekts (akup) 20.
Sherzer, Joel. 1973. Areal linguistics in North America. In Thomas A. Sebeok (ed.), *Current trends in linguistics. Vol. 10.2: Linguistics in North America*, 749–795. The Hague: Mouton.
Shi, Yuzhi. 2002. *The establishment of modern Chinese grammar. The formation of the resultative construction and its effects.* Amsterdam & Philadelphia: John Benjamins.
Ullmann, Stephen. 1962. *Semantics. An introduction to the science of meaning.* Oxford: Blackwell.
Ullmann, Stephen. 1966. Semantic universals. In Joseph H. Greenberg (ed.), *Universals of Language. Report of a Conference held at Dobbs Ferry, New York, April 13–15, 1961*, 217–262. Cambridge, Mass. & London: MIT Press.
Urban, Matthias. 2012. *Analyzability and semantic associations in referring expressions. A study in comparative lexicology.* Leiden: Max Planck Institute for Evolutionary Anthropology and Universiteit Leiden PhD Dissertation.
Watkins, Laurel J. 1984. *A grammar of Kiowa.* Lincoln: University of Nebraska Press.
Werner, Heinrich. 1997. *Die Ketische Sprache.* Wiesbaden: Harrassowitz.
Williams, Edna Rees. 1944. *The conflict of homonyms in English.* New Haven: Yale University Press.

Subject index

A

Analyzability 14, 555–570
Animate, animacy (see also Inanimate) 100, 102, 103, 116, 136, 363, 506
Annotation transfer 165–166
Antonym(y) 7, 9, 52, 57, 67, 68, 78, 86, 100, 131–152, 253
– Canonical antonym(s) 131, 133, 134, 139–142, 147
Areal(ity) 3, 5, 6, 10, 12, 101, 157, 158, 169, 229, 244, 288, 311, 321, 322, 357, 370, 371, 373, 375, 381, 382, 390, 391, 395, 396, 399, 401–403, 559, 560, 562, 564
Automated Similarity Judgement Program, ASJP 159, 161, 168, 169, 171, 377

B

Basic level 13, 33, 457–466, 469–472, 475, 480–486
Biological classification 13, 517, 518
Biological terminology 493, 494, 502
Blending 50, 53
Body-related temperature expressions, BRTE 249–282
Borrowing 21, 37, 54, 56, 59, 77, 158, 226, 230, 342, 355, 373, 395, 397

C

Causative 54, 225–228, 230, 235–237, 245, 552
Classifier 366, 388
CLICS database 160
Climate 249, 251, 252, 257–259, 263, 276, 278, 279, 281, 282
Cognate 188, 190, 198, 208–210, 290, 294, 295, 297, 303, 305, 309, 314–316, 318, 320, 321, 335, 338, 345, 347, 350, 391, 392, 395, 397
Cognition 7, 67, 68, 99, 131–134, 178, 237, 311, 321, 323, 326, 327, 331
Cognitive Linguistics 3, 15, 132, 133, 135, 136, 144, 228, 335, 462, 533
Cohyponymy 469, 470

Colexification 5, 6, 10, 12, 13, 137, 157–161, 168, 170–173, 224, 355–357, 360, 362, 363–365, 367–383, 388–403, 557
Color terms 96, 160, 336
Complex expressions 357, 362–388, 401, 541, 567
Compound 171, 205, 384, 471, 473, 474, 483, 493, 511, 514, 534, 536, 537, 541, 569, 571
Concept, conceptual 2, 3, 4, 6, 8, 11–14, 23, 28, 30–41, 43, 46–51, 53, 55–59, 95, 106, 133, 135–144, 161, 167, 168, 172, 173, 203, 204, 214, 218, 249–256, 258, 259, 263–265, 268, 270–272, 276, 280, 281, 335–350, 356, 381, 395, 397, 423–425, 427, 429, 430, 432–436, 438, 443–452, 457–459, 463–471, 473, 474, 483, 484, 486, 518, 519, 521, 533, 536–540, 542–544, 546, 548–552, 555, 571
– contiguity (see also Contiguity) 423, 426, 435, 444–452, 537
– metaphors (see also Metaphor) 3, 4, 11, 12, 48, , 49, 249–256 258, 259, 263–265, 268, 270, 272, 280, 281, 336, 338, 447, 450
– relation 2, 13, 31, 57–59, 142, 271, 423–427, 429, 430, 432–436, 438, 443–452, 537, 538, 540, 555
Construction 8, 22, 24, 59, 99, 106, 118, 120, 135, 143, 144, 150, 161, 181, 192, 196, 205, 223 228, 230, 231, 233, 235–241, 243–245, 314, 316, 319–322, 516
Continuous construction 9, 131, 144
Discontinuous construction 131, 135, 144
Contact induced language change 230
Contiguity (see also Conceptual contiguity) 2, 35, 36, 38, 40, 41, 43–46, 48, 49, 54, 59, 76, 78, 90, 119, 239, 244, 336, 424, 430, 432, 436, 445, 450, 451, 467, 477, 533, 537–540, 542, 543, 545, 547– 551
Contiguous 40, 43, 44, 55, 78, 80, 90, 370, 371, 533, 537, 549

Co-occurrence 9, 131, 140–142, 144, 147, 152, 162, 501

D
Derivation 55, 95, 292, 297, 303, 308, 337, 346, 368, 434, 464, 471, 475, 476, 479, 480, 484, 508, 541
Differentiation 13, 36, 45, 48, 355, 363, 364, 368–371, 373–376, 389, 390, 392, 393, 395–397, 401, 402, 463, 516
Diffusion 13, 84, 355, 357, 379, 381
Dimension 36, 51, 52, 59, 133–135, 137, 140, 142, 144, 336, 348, 429, 433, 459, 536, 550, 551
Discourse frames (see also Frame, Micro-frame) 148, 150, 151, 152
Dominant pattern 369, 374

E
Emotions 4, 10–12, 80, 90, 97, 119, 236, 237, 249, 250, 252–259, 263, 266, 267, 271, 273, 277, 279, 280, 281, 285–290, 292, 294, 298–302, 306, 307, 311–313, 317, 321–328, 331, 346
Enantiosemy 7, 52, 67–91
Etymology 55, 57, 58, 286, 324, 328, 340, 341, 426, 481, 505
Evaluation 7, 67, 68, 70–72, 80, 166, 202, 462

F
Fire 10, 12, 13, 41, 71, 119, 157, 160, 161, 168–171, 173, 179, 238, 254, 255, 355–403, 495, 500, 546, 547, 550
Firewood 10, 12, 13, 160, 355–403
Folk biology 493–495, 504, 505, 515, 518, 521, 522
Folk kingdom 502, 505–507, 513, 514
Folk life-form 498, 500, 503–505, 510, 511
Folk species 494, 495, 521, 522
Folk taxonomy 495–497, 499, 500, 503, 519, 520, 522
Formal relation 2, 424, 425, 434, 555
Frame (see also Discourse frame, Micro-frame) 7–9, 11, 33–37, 39–43, 45, 46, 48, 49, 53, 56, 57, 67, 95, 97, 98, 105–108, 110, 111, 113, 115–117, 119, 121, 131, 134, 145–152, 228, 239, 240, 244, 335, 350, 450, 465, 467, 470, 485, 541, 543, 544, 546, 548
Frame-based approach 8, 95, 98
Frame method 7, 8, 97

G
Gender 2, 140, 229, 263, 276–278, 281, 363, 364, 381, 392, 464, 475–480, 483, 484
Generalization 21, 26, 27, 31–34, 36, 38, 43, 44, 53, 54, 57, 58, 457–461, 463–467, 469, 470, 473, 480, 485, 548
Geographic(al) distribution 12, 159, 232, 238, 243, 355, 357, 366, 370, 371, 393
Gibbs sampling 162–164
Goal-directed action sequence 186, 202, 203
Grammaticalization 5, 21, 118, 120, 185, 223, 224, 226, 228, 231, 243–245

H
Hand action 11, 177, 182, 184, 195, 196, 202, 203, 205, 207, 208, 210, 211, 213, 217
Homonymy 555, 557, 568, 569
Homonymy avoidance 568, 569
Humoral theory 249, 254, 259, 276, 277, 281
Hyponymy 457–470

I
Idiomatic expressions 83, 223, 224, 244
Inanimate (see also Animate) 102, 103, 188, 217, 363
Interpersonal relations (see also Social relations) 236, 238–240, 336, 342, 344–348
Irony 7, 52, 67–70, 89

L
Language contact 13, 34, 56, 223, 230, 231, 258, 403
Lexical change 23, 34, 44, 54, 59, 469, 486
Light verb construction 11, 182, 223, 224, 226–228, 230, 231, 233, 234, 236–239, 241, 243–245

M
Mapping 48–50, 115, 119, 135, 255, 258, 265, 268, 271, 357, 368, 403, 544, 557

Meaning change 7, 21–32, 34, 36–38, 43, 47, 50–59, 227, 470
– hearer-induced meaning change 21, 29, 30
– innovative meaning change 24, 25–27, 29, 58
– reductive meaning change 26, 29, 37, 57, 58
– speaker-induced meaning change 30
Meaning potential 136, 216, 218, 219
Metaphor(see also Conceptual metaphor) 3, 4, 7, 8, 11, 12, 22, 27, 29, 39, 47–53, 57, 58, 68, 80, 90, 113–115, 117, 119, 120, 178, 179, 193, 197, 215, 244, 249–259, 262–265, 268–272, 274, 276, 278, 280–282, 293, 300, 306, 309, 313, 315, 317, 320, 323, 326, 330, 335, 336, 338, 425, 447–451, 463, 464, 470, 479, 480, 538–540, 544, 545, 551
Metaphorical application 179, 180, 216, 227, 241, 245
Metaphorical similarity 2, 423, 425, 430, 436, 445, 447–452, 538–540, 544, 545, 550, 551
Metonymy 3, 7, 11, 22, 27, 28, 38–40, 42–49, 51–58, 67, 68, 76, 78, 79, 90, 113, 115–117, 119, 120, 178–180, 190, 194, 196, 200, 201, 227, 228, 236–240, 253, 288, 297, 300–302, 305, 328, 335, 336, 338, 463, 464, 540, 551
– constituent metonymy 179, 190, 194, 227
– context metonymy 179, 190, 227, 228, 239, 240
– effect metonymy 179, 190, 196, 200, 227, 228, 237, 238
– end-point metonymy 116
Micro-frame (see also Frame) 106, 107
Moscow semantic school 8, 97–99, 103
Motivatability 13, 244, 423–425, 436, 438–441, 451, 452
Motivatedness 244, 451, 452
Motivation 1–3, 13, 14, 55–57, 188, 216, 231, 324, 348, 423–428, 430, 432–435, 437, 438, 441, 443, 446, 447, 449–452, 457, 459–461, 463, 464, 469–475, 480–486, 533–542, 545, 547, 549–552, 555, 556
– holistic motivation 13, 14, 533–550

– lexical motivation 2, 423–428, 430, 432–434, 446, 449, 451, 452, 555, 556
– relative motivation 556
– segmental motivation 537, 538
Multifunctionality 228, 229

N
Natural Semantic Metalanguage(see also NSM) 8, 326
Negation 67–69, 74, 75, 78, 79, 82–86, 89, 90, 136, 348
New Testament 9, 157, 161, 165–170, 173
Nominal classification 363
NSM (see also Natural Semantic Metalanguage) 96, 97, 106

O
Opposition 7, 32, 42, 50, 68, 70, 72, 75, 76, 81, 88, 90, 100, 108, 131, 133–137, 143, 152, 265, 269, 271, 273, 327, 348, 509
Overt marking 383, 386–388, 393, 394, 403

P
Pain 4, 8, 89, 95, 97, 102, 114, 119, 120, 150, 192, 203, 289, 302, 310, 323, 327, 336, 471
Phylogenetic systematics 517, 521
Pidgin languages 11, 223–245
Plant names 13, 457, 473, 477, 493, 496, 515
Polyphyletic groups 517, 518
Polysemy 1–3, 5, 7–14, 24–29, 36, 37, 40, 56, 58, 67, 97, 115, 116, 133, 137, 144, 157, 170, 177, 178, 179, 181, 185, 188, 216, 223, 224, 227–229, 243, 245, 285, 324, 328–330, 335, 336, 338, 361, 365, 425, 433–435, 437, 457, 464, 469–471, 473, 497, 503, 505, 511, 555–557
Primary lexifier 388, 389, 402
Prototype 11, 32, 33, 34, 177, 182, 183, 188, 190, 196, 199, 200, 202, 206, 214, 217, 218, 324, 458, 459, 462–465, 469, 471, 473, 475, 480, 486, 493, 504, 509, 518

Q
Qualia roles 213
Questionnaire study 423, 424, 436, 437, 440, 443, 447, 448, 450, 451, 542

R
Rebranding 120
Register variation 177, 204
Root structure 565, 566, 568, 569

S
Scalarity 255, 264, 271, 276, 281
Semantic field 100, 104, 107, 114, 121, 177, 178, 216, 218, 342
Semantic map 8, 9, 95, 107–112, 117
Semantic primes 96, 121
Semantic shift 1–3, 5–15, 21, 26, 27, 67–69, 88, 89, 95, 97, 98, 113, 114, 117–120, 177 –179, 184, 199, 216–218, 223, 226, 227, 236, 243–245, 285, 286, 328–330, 335–337, 339–344, 346–350, 355, 377, 425, 447, 493, 494, 497, 505–514
– substantive semantic shifts 178, 179, 216, 217
Social relations (see also Interpersonal relations) 10, 12, 313, 335–341, 346, 349, 350
Sound 30, 95, 104, 105, 107, 114, 115, 199, 200, 209, 216, 219, 240, 291, 293, 295, 300, 303, 400, 469, 536, 568
Species 31, 42, 43, 470, 472, 473, 493–497, 504, 510, 514–522, 561
Specification 72, 463
Subjectification 28, 45, 46
Syllable structure 14, 555, 560, 563–567
Synonym(y) 97–100, 137, 140–142, 167, 170, 267, 431, 466, 557

T
Taxonomy 34, 471, 480, 493, 495–497, 499, 500, 503, 515, 516, 518–520, 522, 537, 545, 551

Temperature 4, 10–12, 84, 134, 137, 249, 250–282
Tübingen Two-Step Method 433, 451, 452
Typology 1, 3, 4, 6–9, 13–15, 58, 59, 69, 95–102, 106, 107, 111–114, 116, 118, 120, 121, 133, 135, 136, 151, 152, 157, 158, 172, 286, 335, 383, 403, 452, 457, 459, 534, 535, 540, 555, 556, 560, 561, 564, 568
– grammatical typology 97–102, 106, 107, 112, 136
– lexical typology 1, 3, 4, 7–9, 14, 95–99, 101, 102, 106, 107, 111, 113, 114, 116, 118, 120, 121, 133, 135, 136, 151, 152, 157, 158, 172, 457, 459, 540, 555, 556

U
Unidirectional(ity) 425, 428, 447, 450, 463

V
Verbs
– cooking 14, 104, 233, 238, 533, 534, 540–533
– cutting and breaking 95, 96, 103, 105, 200
– eating and drinking 4, 96, 103
– falling 101, 115, 118, 331, 505
– flying 102, 104, 107, 497, 510
– hitting 177–219
– jumping 115, 118
– oscillation 105, 117
– posture 364
– rotation 8, 95, 102, 103, 104, 117
– swimming and floating 102, 105, 110 –113, 117

W
Word alignment 161, 162, 165, 166, 168 –170
Word length 57, 570

Language index

A

Abau [aau] 384, 404
Abinomn [bsa] 358
Abui [avz] 392, 404
Abun [kgr] 385, 404
Adyghe [ady] 565, 572
Aghu [ahh] 394, 404
Aghul [agx] 114
Agi [aif] 404
Agta, Casiguran Dumagat [dgc] 550
Aguaruna [agr] 572
Ahtna [aht] 323
Aisi Musak [mmq] 404
Akkadian [akk] 546
Alabama [akz] 509
Alamblak [amp] 404
Alawa [alh] 404
Alekano Gahuku [gah] 404
Alutiiq [ems] 291–293, 303, 512
Alutor [alr] 289, 313, 314, 316–321
Ambulas [abt] 404
Amele [aey] 404
Amurdak [amg] 404
Ancient Greek [grc] 464, 501, 506, 509, 512, 513
Andamanese (see Mixed Great Andamanese)
Angave [aak] 404
Anggor [agg] 509
Anglo-Norman [xno] 339
Anuta [aud] 510
Aomie Managalasi [aom] 404
Apache (see Western Apache)
Apurina [apu] 381
Arabana [ard] 404
Arabela [arl] 560, 566, 572
Arabic [ara] 233, 259, 278, 499, 501, 508, 509, 513
Arabic, Gulf [afb] 224, 234
Arandai Sebyar [jbj] 404
Araona [aro] 380
Arapesh (see Cemaun Arapesh)
Are [mwc] 379
Armenian [hye] 110, 114, 115
Arrernte, Eastern Arrente [aer] 364, 404
Asmat [asc] 371, 391, 404
Athabaskan languages [ath] 322, 323
Au [avt] 404
Australian languages [aus] 5, 160, 177, 180, 227, 228, 355–357, 359, 364, 365, 369, 375, 376, 383–385, 403
Austronesian languages [map] 230, 256, 378–382, 402, 505, 541, 572
Avar [ava] 514
Awiakay [---] 404
Ayabadhu [ayd] 398, 404
Aymara [aym] 509, 510, 558, 572
Azande [zne] 500

B

Bachajón Tzeltal (see also Tzeltal) [tzh] 514
Badaga [bfq] 572
Baibai [bbf] 404
Bandjalang [bdy] 365, 366
Baniata Touo [tqu] 404
Baniwa [bwi] 381
Barai [bbb] 404
Bardi [bcj] 369, 404
Barupu [wra] 369, 373, 386, 387, 404
Baruya [byr] 572
Basque [eus] 509, 572
Bauzi [bvz] 404
Bazaar Malay [---] 232–234, 236–238, 242, 244
Beaver [bea] 323
Belarusian [bel] 338, 339, 341–345, 347, 348
Benabena [bef] 404
Berber (see Tarifiyt Berber)
Berik [bkl] 384, 405, 572
Bezhta [kap] 558, 560, 565, 572
Biaka Nai [bio] 405
Bilinarra [nbj] 405
Biloxi [bll] 572
Bimin [bhl] 373, 394, 405
Bininj Gun-wok [gup] 397, 405
Biritai [bqq] 405
Bislama [bis] 138, 230, 232, 234, 237–240, 242–245, 572
Blackfoot [bla] 506
Blagar [beu] 392, 405

Bora [boa] 571, 572
Borong (Kosorong) [ksr] 405
Borôro (*Bororo) [bor] 572
Bosavi (see also Kaluli) [bco] 359, 385, 386, 405
Bouyei (*Yay) [pcc] 572
Buhutu [bxh] 378, 379
Buin (see also Terei) [buo] 385, 386, 405, 572
Bulgarian [bul] 79, 87, 89, 91, 115, 338, 339, 341–349, 498, 506
Bunama [bdd] 378, 379
Bunaq [bfn] 363, 364, 392, 405
Bunuba [bck] 397, 405
Burarra [bvr] 405
Burum (see Somba)
Bushong [buf] 378
Bwe Karen [bwe] 572

C

Cahuilla [chl] 509, 556
Cape Pidgin Dutch [---] 232, 234, 237, 242
Carib (see Galibi)
Carrier [crx] 572
Cashinahua [cbs] 572
Catalan [cat] 138
Cavineña [cav] 572
Cayapa (see Chachi)
Cemaun Arapesh [ape] 405
Central Alaskan Yupik [esu] 286, 287, 291–310, 314, 326
Central Maewo [mwo] 381
Central Siberian Yupik [ess] 291–296, 298–307, 309, 310, 326, 329,
Central Yupik (*Central Yup'ik) [esu] 572
Ceq Wong [cwg] 380
Chachi (*Cayapa) [cbi] 566, 572
Chaplino Yupik [ess] 512
Chayahuita [cbt] 566, 572
Chehalis (see Upper Chehalis)
Cheyenne [chy] 514, 566, 572
Chickasaw [cic] 254, 257, 571, 572
Chinese [zho] 108, 109, 116, 117, 144, 181–183, 254, 257, 501, 502, 565, 568
Chinese Pidgin English [cpi] 232, 234, 236, 242
Chinook [chh] 234
Chinook Jargon [chn] 229, 232–242, 244, 245

Chontal (see Highland Chontal)
Chukchi (see also Chukot) [cke] 289, 313–322, 509, 512, 572
Chukot (see also *Chukchi) [ckt] 289, 313–322, 509, 512, 572
Chukotko-Kamchatkan languages [---] 12, 289, 311, 313, 320, 331,
Chumash (see Ineseño)
Church Slavonic [chu] 70, 71, 79, 88, 91, 338–340, 342, 343, 348, 349, 506, 507, 510, 513
Chuvash [chv] 506, 514
Classical Nahuatl [nci] 500
Cook Island Māori (Rarotongan) [rar] 511
Copainalá Zoque [zoc] 572
Copper (Inuktun) [---] 292, 296, 298–302, 304, 306, 307, 309, 310, 330
Crimean Tatar [crh] 114
Croatian [hrv] 347, 506
Cubeo [cub] 566, 572
Czech [ces] 7, 68, 80, 87, 91, 338–349, 497, 498, 512

D

Daba [dbq] 537, 542, 543, 545
Dadibi [mps] 405
Daga [dgz] 358, 368, 373, 384, 388, 389, 405, 511
Dakota [dak] 507, 512, 514
Dalabon [ngk] 397, 405
Dani (see Dugum Dani, Grand Valley Dani and Western Dani)
Danish [dan] 214, 340, 507
Darkinyung [xda] 405
Deirate [---] 405
Demiin [---] 365
Demta [dmy] 405
Dhuwal [duj] 401, 405
Djapu [duj] 401, 405
Djinang [dji] 374, 400, 401, 405
Doutai [tds] 405
Dugum Dani [dnw] 499
Duna [duc] 361, 366, 372, 394, 405
Dutch [nld] 9, 133, 139, 234, 340, 360, 507, 539, 540, 547, 551
Dyirbal [dbl] 398, 399, 405

E

E'ñapa Woromaipu [pbh] 380
East Greenlandic [kal] 294
Eastern Ojibwe [ojg] 262
Edo [bin] 378
Edopi [dbf] 405
Efate [llp, erk] 381
Efik [efi] 508
Eipomek [eip] 405
Ekari [ekg] 385, 405
Embera (see Northern Emberá)
Emmi [amy] 366, 400, 405
Engenni [enn] 378
English [eng] (see also Old English) 1, 2, 9, 11, 13, 23, 25, 26, 36, 44, 46, 49, 50, 52, 54, 55, 70–75, 77–79, 81–83, 85, 87–89, 91, 103, 114, 116–119, 132–134, 136, 138–149, 152, 162–168, 171, 173, 179, 185, 186, 188–190, 193, 199, 200, 207, 209–211, 214, 215, 224, 227, 229, 230, 232, 234, 235, 249, 250, 252–256, 259–262, 264, 265, 267–272, 274, 279–281, 286, 293, 305, 311, 313, 324, 326, 338–344, 346–349, 360, 364, 376, 402, 424, 426, 433, 435, 462, 467, 468, 470, 476, 479, 482, 495, 496, 501, 502, 504, 505, 507, 508, 511, 514, 519, 533, 534, 537–542, 544, 551, 552, 558, 559
Eninhdhilyakwa [aoi] 510, 512–513
Epie [epi] 378
Erave (see Kewa)
Erre [err] 405
Erzya [myv] 114
Esimbi [ags] 508
Eskimo [iku] 12, 234, 285–292, 296–301, 303, 305, 306, 308–311, 313, 314, 316, 320–331, 572
Eskimo-Aleut languages [---] 290, 311, 314, 316, 323, 572
Evenki [evn] 502, 513

F

Fas (see Western Fas)
Fasu [faa] 373, 384, 394, 395, 405
Fataluku [ddg] 385, 386, 392, 405
Fayu [fau] 405

Fiji Pidgin Hindustani [---] 232, 234, 236, 240, 242
Fijian [fij] 380, 511
Finnish [fin] 185, 186, 188, 189, 209, 210, 215, 250, 257, 496, 497, 512
Flathead / Salish [sal] 550
Foe [foi] 356, 373, 383, 394, 395, 405
Fore [for] 405, 500
Français-Tirailleur [---] 232, 234, 237–241, 244, 245
French [fra] (see also Old French) 1, 2, 13, 26, 28, 32, 33, 37, 49, 50, 55, 73, 77, 79, 85, 91, 185, 186, 188, 189, 207, 209, 210, 215, 225, 234, 235, 244, 259, 260, 280, 339, 340–344, 346, 348, 423, 424, 426, 429–431, 433–435, 437–441, 443–452, 459, 466, 469, 472, 473, 476, 480, 482, 483, 495, 501, 507, 508, 512–514, 539, 540, 551, 555, 556, 570
Fuyug [fuy] 405

G

Gaagudju [gbu] 405
Gadsup [gaj] 405
Gajirrabeng [gdh] 508
Galela [gbi] 405
Galibi Carib (*Carib) [car] 572
Gamilaraay [kld] 405
Ganggalida [gcd] 405
Gants [gao] 365, 405
Gathang [kda] 405
Gawwada [gwd] 511
Ge'ez [gez] 513
Gedaged [gdd] 378, 379
German [deu] (see also Old High German) 15, 21, 114, 116, 162–165, 185, 186, 188, 189, 207–211, 215, 338–347, 424, 426, 464, 465, 472, 476, 482, 483, 485, 501, 507, 512, 515, 535–537, 540
Gilyak (see also *Nivkh) [niv] 323, 511, 571, 572
Giramay [dbl] 399
Girawa [bbr] 385, 386, 405
Gogodala [ggw] 359, 406
Gogot [gru] 515
Gooniyandi [gni] 406
Gothic [got] 338, 345, 507

Govorka [---] 232, 234, 236, 239, 242
Greek [grk] (see also Ancient Greek and Mycenaean Greek) 71, 339–341, 343, 346, 464, 470, 501, 504, 506, 509, 512, 513
Greenlandic (see East Greenlandic and West Greenlandic)
Gresi [grs] 406
Guarani (*Guaraní) [grn] 560, 572
Guhu-Samane [ghs] 388, 406
Gulf Pidgin Arabic [---] 224, 232, 234, 236–240, 242, 244, 245
Gunggay [yii] 398, 406
Gupapuyngu [guf] 401, 406
Gurindji [gue] 508
Guugu Yimithirr [kky] 367, 397, 398

H
Haida [hai] 508, 572
Halh Mongolian (*Khalkha, see also Mongolian) [khk] 572
Halu [---] 406
Hani [hni] 507
Hanunóo [hnn] 466
Harari [har] 514
Hatam [had] 358, 406
Hausa [hau] 501, 508, 509, 513, 572
Hawaiian [haw] 234, 506, 512
Hawaiian Pidgin English [hwc] 224, 232, 234, 237, 238, 240, 242
Herschel Island Pidgin Eskimo [---] 232, 234, 239, 242, 243, 244
Highland Chontal [chd] 572
Hiligaynon [hil] 512
Hill Pandaram [mjp] 500
Hindi [hin] 111, 117
Hindustani [hif] 234
Hiri Motu [hmo] 232, 233
Hittite [hit] 509
Hmong/Hmong Daw (see also *White Hmong) [mww] 380, 572
Huave (see San Mateo del Mar Huave)
Huli [hui] 372, 395
Hungarian [hun] 254, 257, 342, 505, 507, 510, 512, 534, 536, 537
Hupdë (*Hupda) [jup] 572

I
Iamalele [yml] 381
Iatmul [ian] 365
Iau [tmu] 406
Ibibio [ibb] 11, 249, 250, 260, 261, 264–271, 273, 275–281
Idi [idi] 406
Iha [ihp] 406
Imonda [imn] 406
Indonesian [ind] 116, 360, 501, 512
Ineseño (*Ineseño Chumash) [inz] 572
Inuit (see Seward Peninsula Inuit)
Inuktitut (see North Baffin Inuit and Tarramiut)
Inuktun (see Copper and Sigliq)
Inupiaq (see North Alaskan Inuit)
Irish [gle] (see also Old Irish) 506, 507
I'saka Krisa [ksi] 406
Italian [ita] 2, 13, 28, 46, 51, 79, 88, 91, 116, 138, 244, 339–343, 346, 348, 349, 423–425, 429, 430, 431, 433, 437, 439, 440, 442–452, 468, 469, 480, 483, 507, 539, 540, 551
Itelmen [itl] 289, 315, 317–322
Itonama [ito] 380
Itzá (*Itzaj) [itz] 572
Iwaidja [ibd] 406

J
Jabirrjabirr [dyb] 406
Jamamadí (see *Jarawara) [jaa] 380, 568, 572
Jaminjung [djd] 10, 180–182
Japanese [jpn] 9, 11, 116, 117, 119, 120, 133, 139, 144, 145, 148, 233, 249, 250, 254, 257, 258, 260, 261, 264–275, 280, 500, 507, 509, 512, 550
Jarawara (see Jamamadí)
Jarawara [jaa] 380, 568, 572
Jawoyn [djn] 365, 397, 406
Juba Arabic [---] 232, 233

K
K'iche' [quc] 540
Kaera [---] 392, 406
Kaingang [kgp] 380, 513
Kalam [kmh] 364, 376
Kaluli (see also Bosavi) [bco] 572
Kamang [woi] 392, 406

Language index — 585

Kamano [kbq] 406
Kamasau [kms] 406
Kamor [xmu] 400
Kamoro [kgq] 391, 406
Kannada [kan] 11, 249, 250, 259–261, 264–268, 271, 272, 276, 279–281
Kanum [khd] 384
Kanuri [kau] 509, 513
Karachay-Balkar [krc] 117
Katcha-Kadugli-Miri (*Katcha) [xtc] 572
Kathu [ykt] 382
Kaure [bpp] 364
Kayaka [kyc] 388, 395
Kayan [pdu] 499
Kayapo [txu] 499
Kayardild [gyd] 366, 406
Kayetetye [gbb] 406
Kehu [khh] 358, 406
Kera [ker] 543
Kerek [krk] 289, 313, 314, 316–319
Kesawai Koromu [xes] 406
Ket [ket] 502, 566, 571, 572
Ketengban [xte] 384, 406
Kewa South Erave/Pole [kjy] 383, 384, 406
Kewa, Kewa West [kew] 388, 406, 508
Kewapi [---] 384, 395
Khakas [kjh] 111, 116
Khalkha (see Halh also)
Khoekhoe (see also Nama) [naq] 509, 572
Kilangi [laj] 500
Kiliwa [klb] 506, 558, 559, 572
Kilmeri [kih] 385
Kinyarwanda [kin] 502, 510, 512, 513
Kiowa [kio] 566, 572
Kiri-Kiri [kiy] 365, 406
Kirundi [run] 502, 513
Kirwinian [kij] 466
Klon [kyo] 385, 386, 392
Kobon [kpw] 406
Koiari [kbk] 406
Koita [kqi] 406
Koiwai [kwh] 511
Kok-Kaper [kkp] 398
Kolyma Yukaghir (see Southern Yukaghir)
Kombai [tyn] 384, 395, 407
Komi [kom] 102, 104, 105, 113, 509, 512
Kómnzo Wara [tci] 407

Korafe-Yegha [kpr] 407
Korean [kor] 110, 111
Koreguaje [coe] 508
Koromu (see Kesawai) 361
Korowai [khe] 407
Korupun =Kimyal [kpq] 407
Koryak [kpy] 103, 289, 313–319, 321, 509, 512
Kove [kvc] 505
Kriol [rop] 402
Kugu-Nganhchara [wua] 499
Kuku-Yalanji [gvn] 398, 407
Kula [tpg] 392, 407
Kungarakany [ggk] 400
Kunimaipa [kup] 407
Kuot [kto] 358, 407
Kurtjar [gdj] 398, 407
Kuuk Thaayorre [thd] 398, 407
Kuuku-Ya'u [kuy] 366
Kuwema [woa] 400
Kwoma (Waskuk) [kmo] 572
Kwomtari [kwo] 358, 407
Kyaka Enga [kyc] 499

L

Labrador [---] 292, 296, 298, 306, 310
Lakota [lkt] 547, 549
Lani (see Western Lani)
Lardil [lbz] 407
Latin [lat] (see also Vulgar Latin) 1, 2, 30, 32, 33, 36, 37, 45, 51, 338–344, 346, 348, 349, 464, 466, 468–470, 472, 474, 476, 479, 483, 501, 505, 507–509, 516, 518, 519
Latvian [lav] 118, 345
Lavukaleve [lvk] 407
Laz [lzz] 565, 571, 572
Lembena [leq] 388, 395
Lenakel [tnl] 506
Limilngan [lmc] 360, 407
Lingala [lin] 508
Língua do Preto [---] 232, 233, 234, 237, 242
Lithuanian [lit] 116, 118, 338, 345, 506, 512, 514
Lombardian [lmo] 469

Lower Grand Valley Dani [dni] 359, 371, 392, 393, 499
Lower Sorbian [dsb] 501

M
Maewo (see Central Maewo)
Maia [sks] 407
Mairasi [zrs] 359, 365
Makalero [---] 392, 407
Maksae [mkz] 407
Malak Malak [mpb] 399, 400
Malay [msa] 234
Mali, Mali Baining [gcc] 566, 571, 572
Mamu [dbl] 398, 399
Mamusi [kdf] 505
Manambu [mle] 160, 365
Manange [nmm] 501
Manat [pmr] 365
Mand [ate] 407
Mandarin (Chinese) [cmn] 10, 11, 166–168, 249, 250, 259–261, 264–277, 280, 281, 474, 499, 507, 513
Mandobo [aax] 387, 394, 407
Manga-Kanuri [kby] 513
Mangarevian [mrv] 510
Manobo Dibabawon [mbd] 378
Mansi [mns] 501
Manyika [mxc] 103
Mapudungun [arn] 382, 482
Maranunggu [zmr] 400, 407
Marind [mrz] 359, 407
Marra [mec] 407
Marrangu [dji] 401
Marrgu [mhg] 400
Marrithiyel [mfr] 400, 407
Martu Wangka [mpj] 407
Mataco [mzh] 500
Matngele [zml] 399, 400
Mauwake [mhl] 407
Mawng [mph] 407
Maybrat [ayz] 385, 407
Mbahám [bdw] 385, 407
Mbum [mdd] 572
Mehek [nux] 367
Mejah, Meyah [mej] 385, 408, 572
Melanesian [---] 230
Melanesian Pidgin English [---] 230

Melpa [med] 385, 407
Mende [sim] 407
Mendi Angal [age] 367, 384, 408
Mengerrdji [zme] 408
Mian [mpt] 394, 408
Minnesota Ojibwa [ciw] 500
Miriwung [mep] 508
Mískito (*Miskito) [miq] 380, 572
Mixed Great Andamanese (*Great Andamanese) [gac] 560, 572
Mnanki [---] 408
Mocoví [moc] 382
Mohave [mov] 506, 511
Mokilese [mkj] 511
Molima [mox] 378, 379
Mongolian (see Halh Mongolian) [khk] 506, 514
Moni [mnz] 385, 408
Moraori [mok] 359, 408
Morrobalama [umg] 398, 408
Motu [meu] 233
Motuna [siw] 408
Mountain [kpx] 571
Movima [mzp] 382
Mpur [akc] 358, 408
Murik [mtf] 408
Murrinh-Patha [mwf] 384, 399, 400
Murrungan [dji] 400, 401
Mwotlap [mlv] 138
Mycenaean Greek [gmy] 509

N
Nahuatl, Highland Puebla [azz] (see also Classical Nahuatl) 382, 500, 509
Nakanai [nak] 505
Nama (see also KhoeKhoe) [nmx] 509
Namia [nnm] 362, 369, 373, 383, 384
Narungga [nnr] 408
Nasioi [nas] 367
Naukan Siberian Yupik [---] 291
Navaho [nav] 241, 499
Ndyuka [djk] 233
Ndyuka-Trio Pidgin [njt] 232, 233, 243
Nen [ngn] 385, 386
Nepali [nep] 501
New Caledonian Pidgin French [---] 232, 233

New South Wales Pidgin English [---] 232, 234, 236–240, 244, 245
Nez Perce [nez] 506, 572
Ngäbere [gym] 550
Ngambay [sba] 508, 572
Ngandi [nid] 397
Ngarluma [nrl] 408
Ngbandi [ngb] 234
Nggem [nbq] 392, 393
Nimanburru [nmp] 408
Nipsan [nps] 408
Niuean [niu] 510
Nivkh (see also Gilyak) [niv] 323, 511, 571, 572
Noongar [nys] 384, 408
North Alaskan Inuit (Inupiaq) [ipk]/[esi] 287, 291, 292, 294, 298, 299, 301, 303, 311, 313
North Baffin Inuit (Inuktitut) [ike] 292, 293, 300, 305, 306, 310
Northern Emberá (*Embera) [emp] 572
Norwegian [nor] 214, 466, 485
Nuaulu [nxl]/[nni] 499
Nukuoro [nkr] 510
Nunggubuyu [nuy] 369, 397
Nuuchahnulth [nuk] 509, 572
Nyamal [nly] 408
Nyawaygi [nyt] 398, 399
Nyikina [nyh] 408
Nyulnyul [nyv] 359, 360, 408

O

Ojibwa (see Minnesota Ojibwa)
Ojibwe (see Eastern Ojibwe)
Oksapmin [opm] 394
Old (High) German [goh] 339, 345, 347, 507
Old English [ang] 23, 25, 26, 347, 507
Old French [fro] 25, 51, 55, 339, 482, 483
Old Irish [sga] 507
Old Norse [non] 507
Old Russian [orv] 470
Olo [ong] 408
One [aun] 408
Oneida [one] 508, 560, 572
Oroqen [orh] 382
Orya [ury] 384, 408
Ossetic [oss] 512

Otomi, Estado de México (also *Santiago Mexquititlan Otomî) [ots] 572
Otomi [---] 513
Otomi, Mezquital [ote] 382
Oykangand [kjn] 385, 386, 398

P

Pacoh [pac] 550
Paiute (see Southern Paiute)
Pakanh [pkn] 398, 408
Pamosu [hih] 366
Pandaram (see Hill Pandaram)
Pantar (see Western Pantar)
Patep [ptp] 500
Paumari [pad] 381
Pawnee [paw] 572
Payungu [bxi] 386, 408
Pele-ata [ata] 408
Persian [fas]/[pes] 10, 103, 111, 115, 116, 181, 182, 218, 224, 228
Pidgin Delaware [dep] 232, 234, 238, 242
Pidgin Madame [---] 232, 233
Pintupi [piu] 366, 408
Pipil [ppl] 572
Piro [pie] 380, 572
Pisa [psa] 385, 386, 394 409
Pitjantjatjara [pjt] 409
Pitkern-Norf'k [pih] 229
Plains Indian Sign [psd] 232, 234, 236–238, 240–242, 244, 245
Poko-Rawo [rwa] 409
Polar Eskimo [---] 291, 292, 296, 297, 298, 301, 303, 306, 308, 311, 328, 329
Pole (see Kewa)
Polish [pol] 70, 79, 80, 87, 91, 101–103, 116, 118, 338, 339, 341–343, 345–349, 497, 507, 512
Portuguese [por] 234, 476, 479
Prussian [prg] 345
Puelche [pue] 382

Q

Qawasqar [alc] 380
Quechua, Cochabamba [que] 466, 485, 513, 572
Quechua, Cusco [quz] 100

Quichua, Imbabura Highland (*Imbabura Quechua) [qvi] 572
Queensland Pidgin English [---] 232, 234, 236, 238–240
Quileute [qui] 508

R
Rama [rma] 572
Rapa Nui [rap] 510
Rarotongan (see Cook Island Māori)
Rembarrnga [rmb] 397, 409
Rendille [rel] 509
Rennellese (Munggava-Mungiki) [mnv] 510
Rifian [---] 501, 513
Ritharrngu [rit] 397, 401, 409
Romani (see also Selice Romani)
Romani, Vlax [rmy] 382
Romanian [ron] 32, 504, 506–510
Romanian Pidgin Arabic [rms] 232, 233
Roquetas Pidgin Spanish [---] 232, 233
Rotokas [roo] 365, 409, 566, 572
Rumu [klq] 373, 383, 384, 409
Russian [rus] (see also Old Russian) 2, 7, 9, 67–73, 75–81, 84–89, 91, 98, 100–103, 108, 109, 114, 116–120, 133, 139, 234, 317, 321, 322, 336, 338, 339, 341–349, 470, 494–499, 502–504, 506–508, 511–514, 516, 518–520
Rutul [rut] 118

S
Saami, Kildin [sjd] 382, 501, 511, 512, 560, 566, 572
Saami, Northern Saami [sme] 465, 466, 485, 506, 511
Sahu [saj] 385, 409, 572
Sakha / Yakut [sah] 544, 545, 547, 552
Salish (see Flathead)
Samoan [smo] 510
San Mateo del Mar Huave [huv] 572
Sango [sag] 232, 234, 237–239, 242
Sanskrit [san] 87, 115, 339, 501, 507, 509, 512, 513, 538
Santiago Mexquititlan Otomí (see Estado de México Otomi)
Saramaccan [srm] 508
Sardinian [srd] 2, 476, 479

Sedang [sed] 572
Sehudate [---] 409
Selice Romani [---] 510, 514
Selkup [sel] 382
Sempan [xse] 391, 409
Sentani [set] 359, 501
Serbian [srp] 87, 88, 89, 91, 109, 110, 144, 256, 257, 281, 338, 339, 341–349, 497
Serbo-Croatian [hbs] 347, 507, 513
Seri [sei] 506, 513, 556
Sesake [llp] 380, 381
Seward Peninsula Inuit [---] 293
Seychellois Creole [crs] 512, 513
Shiaxa [awy] 387, 394, 409
Siane [snp] 500
Sibe Nagovisi [nco] 409
Sigliq (Inuktun) [---] 295, 299, 304
Simog Auwe [smf] 409
Sireniki (an extinct kind of Siberian Yupik) [ysr] 295
Siroi [ssd] 409
Sirva Sileibi [sbq] 368, 376, 409
Skou [skv] 409
Slavic languages [sla] 5, 7, 12, 67, 69, 79, 87, 335, 337–342, 344–350, 498, 499, 506, 507, 512
Slovak [slk] 338, 339, 341, 342, 344, 347–349
Slovenian [slv] 345–349, 497
So [teu] 510
Solomon Pijin [pis] 230, 232
Somba = Burum [bmu] 409
Sora [srb] 508
Sorbian (see Lower Sorbian)
Southern Paiute [ute] 511
Southern Yukaghir (*Kolyma Yukaghir) [yux] 572
Spanish [spa] 32, 50, 117, 250, 339, 340, 341, 346, 348, 349, 459, 465–470, 472, 476, 477, 480, 482, 483, 507, 514
Srenge Aruop [lsr] 409
Suena [sue] 373, 409
Suki [sui] 387, 409
Sumerian [sux] 158, 545–547
Swahili [swh] 183, 184, 213, 508, 513
Swedish [swe] 9–11, 116, 133, 134, 138–141, 144–146, 148, 149, 152, 166–168, 177,

178, 185, 187–191, 193–196, 198–201, 204, 205, 207, 208, 211–214, 218, 249, 250, 257, 259, 260, 262, 264, 265, 267–275, 279–281, 355, 501, 512

T

Tahitian [tht] 254, 257, 510
Taikat Arso [aos] 409
Takia [tbc] 382, 501
Tamil [tam] 103, 112, 116
Tarifiyt Berber (Rifian) [rif] 501, 513
Tarramiut (Inuktitut) [ike] 291, 292, 293, 296, 297, 298, 299, 300, 302, 304, 305, 306, 308, 309, 310, 329
Tatar [tat] 114, 512
Tause [tad] 409
Tauya [tya] 409
Tay Boi [tas] 225, 226, 232–234, 237–242, 244, 245
Tehit [kps] 409
Teiwa [twe] 392, 409
Telefol [tlf] 384, 394, 409
Terei (see also *Buin) [buo] 385, 386, 405, 572
Ternate [tft] 409
Tetun Dili (*Tetun) [tdt] 572
Thai [tha] 501, 507, 513
Thalanyji [dhl] 409
Tidore [tvo] 409
Tifal [tif] 394, 409
Tigrinya [tir] 514
Tikopia [tkp] 510
Tiwi [tiw] 376, 409
Toaripi [tqo] 566, 572
Tobelo [tlb] 386, 409
Tok Pisin [tpi] 229, 230, 232, 234, 237–240, 242, 245, 402, 505, 508, 511
Tolomako [tlm] 380, 381
Tongan [ton] 510
Totonac (see Xicotepec de Juárez Totonac)
Trio [tri] 233
Tsimané [cas] 380
Tuamotu [pmt] 510
Turkish [tur] 508, 512
Tzeltal [tzh] (see also Bachajón Tzeltal) 473, 474, 485, 501, 509, 514
Tzotzil [tzo] 511, 514

U

Ukrainian [ukr] 79, 338, 339, 341–349, 497, 507
Umbindhamu [umd] 398, 409
Umbrian [xum] 509
Umpila [ump] 409
Una =Larye, east Tanime and Bime [mtg] 409
Unami [unm] 234
Ungarinyin [ung] 409
Upper Chehalis [cjh] 572
Uradhi [urf] 398, 409
Urim [uri] 364, 409
Urningangk [urc] 409
Usan [wnu] 410
Utkulikhalingmiut (Utku) [---] 287, 291, 304, 305, 311, 327–329
Uvean (see West Uvean)

V

Vanimo [vam] 567
Venetian [vec] 28, 46, 469
Vietnamese [vie] 166, 167, 168, 225, 226, 239, 474, 501
Vulgar Latin [---] 468

W

Wadyiginy [wdj] 399, 400, 410
Waffa [waj] 410
Wajarri [wbv] 410
Wakashan languages [wak] 323, 572
Walak [wlw] 392, 393, 410
Walmajarri [wmt] 410
Walman [van] 410
Wambon Digul/Wambon Yonggom [wms] 372, 388, 395, 410
Wanggamala [wnm] 410
Wangkangurru [tiw] 410
Wano [wno] 392, 393, 410
Wappo [wao] 572
Waris Walsa [wrs] 410
Warlpiri [wbp] 10, 179, 180, 227, 410
Warrgamay [wgy] 410
Warrwa [wwr] 410
Warta Thuntai Guntai [gnt] 385, 386, 410
Waskia [wsk] 387, 410
Wayuu [guc] 380
Welsh [cym] 514, 572

Weri [wer] 385, 386, 410
Wersing [kvw] 386, 392, 410
West Greenlandic [kal] 291, 320
West Uvean [uve] 510
Western Apache [apw] 465
Western Dani [dnw] 392, 393, 410
Western Fas [fqs] 369, 373, 410
Western Lani [dnw] 392, 393, 410
Western Pantar [lev] 392
White Hmong (see also Hmong/Hmong Daw) [mww] 380, 572
Wichí Lhamtés Vejoz (*Wichí) [wlv] 572
Wik Mungkan [wim] 385, 386, 398, 410
Wik Ngathan [wig] 397, 398, 410
Wiru [wiu] 359, 410
Wuming Yongbei Zhuang [zyb] 378
Wurlaki [dji] 401
Wutung [wut] 410

X

Xicotepec de Juárez Totonac [too] 572

Y

Yakut (see Sakha)
Yali [nlk] 392, 393, 410
Yana [ynn] 508
Yanomámi [wca] 508, 572
Yavitero [yvt] 380
Yawa [yva] 358, 410
Yawuru [ywr] 410
Yay (see Bouyei)
Yele [yle] 410
Yenimu [aws] 387, 394, 410
Yeri [yev] 410
Yetfa [yet] 358
Yidiny [yii] 398, 410
Yimas [yee] 233, 367, 410
Yimas-Arafundi Pidgin [---] 232, 233
Yinhawangka [wgg] 410
Yir Yoront [yyr]/[yiy] 508, 572
Yokohamese [---] 232, 233
Yoruba [yor] 508, 571
Yukaghir (see Southern Yukaghir)
Yuki [yuk] 508
Yukuna [ycn] 513
Yupik languages [ypk] (see also Sireniki, Central Alaskan Yupik, Central Siberian Yupik, Central Yupik, Chaplino Yupik and Naukan Siberian Yupik) 286, 284, 289, 291–305, 307–310, 330

Z

Zhuang (see Wuming Yongbei Zhuang)
Zoque (see Copainalá Zoque)
Zoque [---] 514, 572
Zway [zwa] 514

Author index

A

Abaev, Vasilij I. 512
Abel, Carl 52
Ackrill, J.L. 132
Adamson, Myra 502, 510, 513
Aijmer, Karin 185
Aikhenvald, Alexandra Y. 2, 99, 136, 160, 178, 381
Aitchison, Jean 470, 474
Ajbabina, Evgenija A. 512
Al-Abed Al-Haq, Fawwaz 259, 278, 279
Aleev, Jurij G. 521
Allan, Kathryn 58
Allan, Keith 51
Allen, Jim 356
Allwood, Jens 218
Alpher, Barry 401
Altenberg, Bengt 185
Amador, Rodríguez 477
Ambadiang, Théophile 483
Amberber, Mengistu 96
Ameka, Felix K. 4, 8
Anderson, Adam W. 462
Anderson, Myrdene 461, 466
Andrew, Jane M. 133
Andronov, Aleksej V. 514
Annenkov, Nikolaj I. 497
Anscombre, Jean-Claude 46
Apresjan, Jurij D. 8, 68, 86, 88, 97–99, 119, 383
Apresjan, Valentina Ju. 326
Araya, Yoseph N. 522
Arber, Agnes 515
Aristotle 47, 132, 501, 515
Atran, Scott 495, 496, 500, 516
Augst, Gerhard 427, 432
Auwera, Johan van der 3, 107, 112, 136

B

Baayen, Harald 437, 561
Bacarreza, Donato G. 509
Bagana, Gerome 508
Bakema, Peter 133, 138, 461, 462
Baker, Colin 8
Baker, Philip 230
Bakker, Dik 159, 161, 171, 377–379
Bakker, Peter 223, 224, 229
Balandin, Aleksej N. 501
Bally, Charles 77
Barcelona, Antonio 39, 178
Barlow, Michael 28
Barsalou, Lawrence W. 203, 216, 460, 465
Basset, Yves 522
Bates, Douglas 561
Beaumont, John R. 381
Beaumont, Margaret 381
Bell, Alan 540
Benveniste, Émile 46, 349
Berglund, Britt-Marie 512
Bergs, Alexander 59
Bergström, Annika 253
Berko, Jean 432–434
Berlin, Brent 96, 460–463, 465, 466, 471, 473, 474, 494, 495, 500, 501, 513
Bertel's, A. E. 499
Berthelsen, Christian 309
Bezlaj, France 337
Biberstein-Kazimirski, Albin de 499, 506, 509
Bisetto, Antonietta 539
Black, Max 50, 404
Blagova, Emilija 506
Blank, Andreas 1, 22, 24, 26, 27, 33, 36, 37, 40, 42, 51–59, 96, 113, 336, 430, 449, 465, 470, 537, 539, 540, 551, 552
Blunsom, Phil 162
Blust, Robert A. 5, 381
Bogardus, Emory S. 336
Bogoraz, Vladimir G. 314, 316, 318–320
Bohnemeyer, Jürgen 556
Boldyrev, Boris V. 502, 513
Bonch-Osmolovskaya, Anastasia A. 4, 97, 114, 120
Booij, Geert E. 59, 224
Borgi, Anna M. 213
Borş, Anton 506
Boryś, Wiesław 337
Bowerman, Melissa 4, 8, 96, 103, 105

Bowern, Claire 356, 401, 404
Bréal, Michel 22, 24
Breedlove, Dennis E. 494, 500, 501
Bresnan, Joan 229
Briggs, Jean 287, 291, 304, 305, 310, 311, 312, 313, 327, 328, 329
Brinton, Laurel J. 27
Britsin Viktor 336
Britsyn, Viktor M. 97, 119
Brodin, Dorothy 431
Bromhead, Helen 113
Brown, Bob 410
Brown, Cecil. H. 5, 160–162, 364, 494, 495, 498–500, 504, 506, 510, 511, 514, 557
Brown, Nellie 506
Brown, Pamela 159, 161, 171, 377–379,
Brown, Peter F. 161, 162
Brown, Roger 460
Brugman, Claudia 116
Bubenik, Vit 31
Buchholz, Oda 119
Buck, Carl Darling 288, 337, 470, 504, 506, 507, 514, 557
Bulakh, Maria 494
Bulygina, Tat'iana V. 78
Burridge, Kate 51
Bustos Gisbert, Eugenio de 483
Butt, Miriam 231
Bybee, Joan L. 28, 59, 99, 101, 428, 568

C
Caballero, Rosario 138
Campbell, Lauren 406
Campbell, Lyle 31, 568
Carlin, Eithne 510
Caron, Jean 428
Cejtlin, Ral'a M. 506, 513
Černyšëv, Vasilij I. 503
Chaffin, Roger 472
Charles, Walter G. 140
Chaudenson, Robert 513
Chierchia, Gennaro 467
Church, Kenneth Ward 70, 71, 78, 79, 88, 162, 338–340, 342, 343, 348, 349, 496, 502, 506, 507, 510, 513
Cicero, Marcus Tullius 47
Ciorănescu, Aleksandru 506–508, 510

Clarke, David D. 31
Coates, William Ames 568
Coiffier, Christian 365
Coleman, Arnold D. 508
Comrie, Bernard 99, 558
Cook, Dorothy M. 508, 511, 542
Corbett, Greville G. 99
Corbin, Danielle 482
Corbin, Pierre 482
Corominas, Joan 32, 34, 41, 47, 466–468
Cortelazzo, Manlio 24, 38, 41, 46
Coseriu, Eugenio 22, 27, 32
Coteanu, Ion 506, 507, 508, 509
Coulson, Seana 120
Cox, Betty E. 502, 510, 512, 513
Cozzuol, Mario A. 521
Craig, Philip R. 249
Crawford, Judith G. 506
Croft, William 27, 39, 40, 42–44, 48, 99, 119, 135, 136, 138, 166, 340, 450, 474, 544, 569
Cruse, David Alan 39, 44, 135, 424, 458, 465, 557
Cusihuamán, Antonio 100
Cysouw, Michael 10, 138, 161, 559, 561, 571

D
Dahl, Östen 85, 99, 106, 136, 161, 557
Dal', Vladimir I. 71
Damasio, Antonio R. 203, 326, 327
Dancygier, Barbara 59
Dasher, Richard B. 1, 28, 45, 190, 219
Dauzat, Albert 337
Davidovitch, Catherine 431
Deese, James 140
Degtjarev, Gennadij A. 514
Deignan, Alice 250
Delhay, Corinne 480
Dement'ev, Georgij P. 495
DeNero, John 162
Derwing, Bruce L. 432
De Smet, Hendrik 45
Detges, Ulrich 30
Diewald, Gabriele 59
Dik, Simon C. 43
Dillmann, August 513
Dirven, René 40

Divuilu, Felix 508
Dixon, Robert M. W. 133, 139, 356, 369, 375, 381, 568
Dobrovol'skij, Vladimir N. 498
Döhler, Christian 363
Dorais, Louis-Jacques 287
Dorr, Bonnie 134
Dryer, Matthew S. 160, 557, 559, 561
Dunn, Michael 314–316, 318, 321
Durkin, Kevin 429
Durkin, Philip 24, 55
Dvořák, Boštjan 4
Dworkin, Steven N. 568
Dybo, Anna V. 113

E
Efremova, Tat'jana F. 498
Egede, Paul 307
Ekman, Paul 325
Elbert, Samuel H. 507, 512
Elistratov, Vladimir S. 81
Enfield, Nicholas J. 4, 5, 8, 11, 233
Engelenhoven, Aone van 391
Englert, Sebastián 510
Epps, Patience 5
Ernout, Alfred 46, 52
Evans, Nicholas 1, 5, 59, 95, 178, 356, 365, 375, 383
Evans, Vyvyan 50, 462
Evgen'eva, Anastasiia P. 70, 72, 73, 77, 81, 84

F
Fabricius, Otto 298
Facundes, Sidney da Silva 381
Faiss, Klaus 482
Family, Neiloufar 10, 181, 182, 184, 218, 228, 365
Fasmer, Max 118, 337, 519
Fauconnier, Giles 50, 119, 120, 450
Fedotov, Mihail R. 506
Feldman, Jerome A. 203
Feldpausch, Becky 362
Feldpausch, Thomas 362
Felger, Richard S. 506
Feyaerts, Kurt 39, 40
Field, Robin 178
Filin, Fedot P. 78, 497–499, 511, 512, 519

Fill, Alwin 432, 481, 539, 540
Fillmore, Charles J. 8, 46, 105
Firth, John Roderick 8
Fodor, Jerry A. 104
Foley, William A. 356, 365, 557
Fortescue, Michael D. 12, 285, 286, 289–292, 304, 307, 309, 311, 314, 322, 323, 328, 506, 509, 512
François, Alexander 5, 10, 133, 136–138, 157, 360, 381, 404, 557
Franklin, Karl J. 395, 404, 508
Fridman, Jurij S. 495, 519
Fried, Mirjam 59
Fuchs, Catherine 437, 515
Fung, Pascale 162

G
Gadžiev, Magomed M. 514
Gáldi, László 510, 512
Gale, William A. 162
Gal, Yarin 162
Gambill, Guy T. 270
Gamkrelidze, Tamaz V. 509
Ganenkov, Dmitrij S. 494
Gao, Hong 10, 182, 183, 184
Gauger, Hans-Martin 426, 428
Gauthier, Isabel 462
Gecova, Ol'ga G. 498
Geeraerts, Dirk 11, 15, 22, 33, 39, 40, 42, 43, 48, 50, 58, 97, 133, 134, 138, 251, 254, 258, 264, 461, 462, 537–540
Geiger, Walter E. 479
Georges, Heinrich 51
Georges, Karl Ernst 51
Georg, Stefan 318
Gevaert, Caroline 58
Gévaudan, Paul 22, 55, 59, 113, 464, 539, 540, 551
Gibassier, Pierre 462, 465
Gibbs, Raymond 4, 162–164
Gibson, James J. 213
Giger, Martha 543
Gildea, Daniel 162
Gilliéron, J. 568
Givón, Talmy 535
Gladkova, Anna N 96
Glare, Peter Geoffrey William 466, 469

Glenberg, Arthur M. 213
Glynn, Dylan 138
Goddard, Cliff 8, 96, 97, 105, 106, 113, 121
Goosse, André 483
Goossens, Louis 50
Gorenflo, L. J. 356
Gougenheim, Georges 462
Grady, Joseph 115, 120, 250, 369
Gralow, Frances L. 508
Grant, Anthony, P. 229
Greenberg, Joseph H. 336
Green, Ian 462
Green, Melanie 50
Grevisse Maurice 483
Grice, H. Paul 28
Gries, Stefan 3
Grondelaers, Stefan 11, 133, 138, 254, 258, 461, 462
Gruntov, Ilya 494
Grzegorczykowa, Renata 336
Guljaev, Evgenij S. 509
Gura, Aleksandr V. 497, 498
Guyot, Lucien 462, 465

H
Hadrovics, László. 510
Hale, Kenneth 369
Hall, Harold. A. 82
Hallwachs, Winifred 522
Hammarström, Harald 158, 159, 170, 171, 357–359, 404
Hardy, Heather K. 509
Harkins, Jean 326
Harnisch, Rüdiger 481
Harvey, Mark 404
Haspelmath, Martin 49, 99, 102, 107, 112, 119, 160, 166, 377, 501, 508–514, 557, 560, 570
Hays, Terence E. 501
Hayward Richard J. 5
Hazbulatov, Bekhan A. 514
Head, M. J. 265, 266, 267, 356, 572
Heine, Bernd 5, 118, 224, 225, 229–231, 244, 245, 510
Hendery, Rachel 10, 12, 160, 224, 355
Hennig, Willi 517
Hirst, Graeme 134

Hjelmslev, Louis 32
Hock, Hans Heinrich 31
Hoffmann, Joachim 471
Hofmann, Johann Baptist 471
Holenstein, Elmar 38
Holman, Eric W. 299
Holmer, Nils M 397
Holm, Gustav 296
Holm, John 229
Holtsberg, Anders 140
Hook, Peter 10, 177, 181, 185
Horn, Laurence 136, 571
Horton, Marjorie S. 470
Huber, Juliette 391
Hudson, Joyce 311
Humboldt, Alexander von 521
Hunn, Eugene S. 509
Hwa, Rebecca 165

I
Iacobini, Claudio 425
Ibarretxe-Antuñano, Iraide 3
Idström, Anna 3
Inenlikej, Petr I. 316
Isono, Maho 133, 134, 139, 144, 145
Ivanov, Vjačeslav V. 87, 509

J
Jacobs, Melville 229
Jacobson, Steven A. 286, 287, 302, 310, 506, 512
Jakobson, Roman 38, 48
Jakovleva. Ekaterina S. 73, 518
Janzen Daniel H. 522
Jeffrey, Charles 516
Johnson, David M. 250
Johnson, Frederick 183, 184
Johnson-Laird, Philip N. 324, 325, 470
Johnson, Mark 11, 39, 42, 48, 49, 50, 81, 115, 119, 120, 250, 252, 262, 336
Johnson, Samuel V. 229
Jones, Caroline 405
Jones, Henry S. 506, 512
Jones, Linda 410
Jones, Rhys 356
Jones, Steven 132 –136, 139, 140, 142–144, 146, 147, 149, 150, 356

Joseph, Brian D. 31, 571
Juilland, Alphonse 431
Justeson, John S. 140
Juvonen, Päivi 11, 15, 223, 229, 235, 253, 257

K
Kämpf, Uwe 471
Kane, Thomas L. 514
Kaplan, Lawrence D. 506, 512
Kari, James 323
Karlsson, Fred 570
Kaschak, Michael P. 213
Kashkin, Egor V. 97, 104, 105
Katz, Jerrold J. 104
Katz, Slava M. 140
Kaufmann, John 512
Kay, Paul 96, 160
Keesing, Roger M. 230
Keller, Rudi 27
Kemmer, Suzanne 28
Kerren, Andreas 138
Khalilov, Madzhid 558
Kholkina, Lilia S. 97, 108
Kholodovich, Alexandr A. 104
Khrakovsky, Viktor S. 104
Kibrik, Aleksandr E. 101, 314, 310
Kibrik, Andrej A. 2
Klatzky, Roberta L. 213
Klavans, Judith 162
Kleiber, Georges 44, 462
Kleij, Tom van der 134
Klepousniotou, Ekaterini 451
Kljuge, Nikita Ju. 517, 518
Kluge, Friedrich 337, 465, 494
Knox, Dilwyn 52
Koblik, Evgenij A. 495, 519
Koch, Harold 356, 359, 375
Koch, Peter 2, 4–7, 15, 21–23, 27–30, 33, 34, 39, 40, 42–46, 48, 54, 58, 59, 96, 113, 119, 136, 227, 239, 424– 426, 429, 430, 435, 444, 449, 450, 452, 457, 458, 462, 463, 476, 477, 479, 536, 555–567, 569
Köhler, Wolfgang 40
Kolosova, Valerija B. 496, 497
Kondraškin, Oleg N. 512
Konovalova, Nadežda I. 503
Konrad, Nikolaj I. 507, 509, 512

Köpcke, Klaus-Michael 480, 483
Kopecka, Aneta 4, 8, 96
Koppaleva, Julija E. 496
Koptjevskaja-Tamm, Maria 1, 2, 4–6, 11, 15, 21, 59, 95, 96, 134, 136, 137, 139, 142, 229, 249, 260, 262, 403, 429, 452, 457, 458, 541
Korigodskij, Robert N. 512
Kosnyreva, Raisa I. 512
Kostić, Nataša 144
Kövecses, Zoltan 11, 39, 40, 42, 43, 228, 239, 250–255, 257–259, 338, 449, 450
Kramarova, Svetlana G. 116
Krivoščapova, Julija A. 499, 519
Krott, Andrea 437
Krueger, John R. 552
Kruglyakova, Victoria A. 97
Krupa, Viktor 569
Kunkel, Günther 479
Kupriyanov, Aleksej V. 516
Kurebito, Tokusu 320
Kuruč, Rimma D. 511, 512
Kustova, Galina I. 116
Kuteva, Tania 5, 118, 224, 225, 230, 231, 244, 245
Kuznetsova, Julia L. 116
Kyuseva, Maria V. 97, 115

L
Laca, Brenda 475, 482
Lajus, Dmitrij L. 495
Lajus, Julija A. 495
Lakoff, George 11, 39, 42, 43, 48–50, 81, 115, 116, 119, 120, 250, 252, 253, 262, 264, 326, 328, 336, 369, 447, 496, 504
Lander, Jurij A. 116
Lane, Edward W. 499
Langacker, Ronald W. 3, 27, 45, 228, 236, 466, 473
Lang, Adrianne 364
Langner, Aleksandr N. 508
Laptuhin, Viktor V. 508
Larina, Tat'iana V. 72
Laycock, Donald C. 356, 365, 369, 374, 394, 395
LeDoux, Joseph 290, 297, 325, 326
Lee, Janet 410

Lee, Jason 402
Lee, Jenny 376
Lehmann, Christian 226, 231, 535
Lehmann, Winfred P. 31, 507
Lehrer, Adrienne 104, 252, 253, 255, 541
Leisi, Ernst 467
Leonardelli, Geoffrey J. 257
Leslau, Wolf 514, 515
Leuninger, Helen 470
Levinson, Stephen C. 4, 8, 28, 96, 121
Lévi-Strauss, Claude 546
Levontina, Irina B. 80
Lewis, M. Paul 358
Liang, Hsin-Hsin 10, 177, 181
Libben, Gary 571
Liberis, Anatas 512, 514
Li, Charles N. 474
Lichtenberk, Frank 1, 364
Liddell, Henry G. 506, 512
Lienhard, Ruth 542, 543
Liljegren, Henrik 2, 5, 158, 231, 403
Linnaeus, Carolus 516
Lipka, Leonhard 59
List, Johann-Mattis 6, 160, 172, 377–379, 381, 382
Ljubarskij, Georgij Ju. 520–522
Lloyd, Geoffrey E.R. 132
Lobanova, Anna 134
Löbner, Sebastian 462
Lockwood, Hunter 261
Lopatina, Ljudmila E. 503, 504
Lopatin, Vladimir V. 503, 504
Loughnane, Robyn 395
Lüder, Elsa 42
Luque Durán, Juan de Dios 59
Luraghi, Silvia 31
Lyons, John 466
Lytkin, Vasilij I. 509

M

Maalej, Zouheir A. 3, 11, 257
MacDonell, Arthur A. 507, 512, 513
Machek, Václav 337
Maddalon, Marta 468, 469
Maddieson, Ian 560, 562, 564
Maffi, Luisa 160
Majid, Asifa 4, 8, 96, 103, 105, 108

Maisak, Timur A. 4, 96, 97, 103, 117, 336, 494
Malkiel, Yakov 568
Manning, Christopher D. 166
Manning, Jocelyn 429
Marchand, Hans 428
Markey, Thomas 262
Markman, Ellen M. 470
Marková, Věra 142
Martinet, André 570
Marzo, Daniela 13, 15, 21, 244, 423, 425, 426, 429–431, 433, 435, 437, 438, 447, 450–452, 536, 555–567
Matisoff, James A. 2, 5, 570
Matsuki, Kaiko 254, 257
Mayerthaler, Willi 450
May, Jean 82, 84, 358
Mayr, Ernst W. 520
McGregor, William B. 177
McLanahan, Alexander G. 470
McNabb, Steven 287, 313
McNeill, John 494, 518
Meillet, Alfred 46, 52
Melamed, I. Dan 162
Mel'čuk, Igor A. 98, 104
Menéndez Pidal, Ramón 483
Merkulova, Inna A. 497
Merkulova, Valentina A. 497
Mermer, Coskun 162, 164
Michotte, Albert 204
Miestamo, Matti 570, 571
Mihalic, Frank 402
Mihatsch, Wiltrud 4, 13, 457–459, 461–468, 471, 473, 476, 481, 482, 484
Miller, George A. 140, 458, 470
Miller, Scott E. 522
Mithun, Marianne 244, 560
Mixco, Mauricio J. 559
Moliner, Maria 37, 468, 469, 471, 472, 479, 483
Moll, T. A. 314, 317–319
Monastyrjew, Wladimir 552
Montler, Timothy 509
Morev, Lev N. 501, 507, 513
Mortimer, Graham 356
Moser, Mary B. 506, 513
Mouchet, Jean 542, 543
Muehleisen, Victoria 133, 134, 139, 144, 145

Mühlhäusler, Peter 229
Munro, Pamela 506, 511, 571
Muravyova, Irina A. 316
Murphy, Gregory L. 460, 463
Murphy, M. Lynne 133 –135, 139, 144, 145, 147, 149
Murray, Andrew S. 356
Myreeva, Anna N. 513

N

Nagayama,Yukari 320
Narasimhan, Bhuvana 4, 8, 96
Nerlich, Brigitte 22, 31
Nettle, Daniel 570
Neu, Antonia 113
Neumann, Uwe 22
Newman, John. 1, 4, 95, 96, 214
Ney, Hermann 162
Ngai, Grace 165
Nichols, Johanna 5, 402
Nikunlassi, Ahti 253, 257
Nolly, Émile 225
Nordhoff, Sebastian 357
Novgorodov, Innokentij 544
Nummenmaa, Lauri 257
Nunberg, Geoffrey 43, 82, 83, 84, 224
Nuyts, Jan 3, 136
Nyrop, Kristoffer 22, 483

O

Oakley, Todd 120
Oatley, Keith 324, 325
Obata, Kazuko 359
Och, Franz Josef 162
O'Connell, James F. 355
Ogden, Charles K. 132
O'Grady, Geoffrey N. 369
O'Meara, Carolyn 556
Ošanin, Il'ja M. 502, 507, 513
Osgood, Charles E. 132, 133
Osmond, Meredith 377, 379
Östling, Robert 9, 10, 13, 157, 165, 166, 168, 224, 378, 404
Ožegov, Sergej I. 504

P

Paducheva, Elena V. 116
Pagliuca, William 101
Pakendorf, Brigitte 544
Panina, Anna S. 97, 117
Panther, Klaus-Uwe 39, 40, 42, 147 336, 533, 534, 535
Paolo, Zolli 24, 38, 41, 46
Paradis, Carita 9, 100, 131, 133–136, 138–144, 149
Pardeshi, Prashant 10, 177, 181
Parkvall, Mikael 223–225, 230, 231
Pasamonik, Carolina 323
Pascual, José A. 32, 34, 41, 47, 466–468
Paul, Hermann 22, 100, 307, 404, 482, 496
Pavlinov, Igor' 520–522
Pavlova, Elizaveta K. 97, 115
Pawley, Andrew 356, 358, 359, 377, 379
Peck, Edmund J. 296, 298
Peirce, Charles Sanders 194, 536
Peirsman, Yves 42, 43, 134, 537
Pen'kovskij, Aleksandr B. 80
Perfetti, Charles A. 429
Perkins, Revere D. 101, 540
Perrin, Loïc-Michel 259, 278, 279
Petersen, Jonathan 286, 298, 299, 301, 303
Petersen, Robert 309
Pfister, Max 51
Pharies, David 476, 479
Pierrot, Alain 46
Piirainen, Elisabeth 3
Plag, Ingo 428
Plomley, Norman JB 369
Plungian, Vladimir A. 95, 97, 99, 103, 107, 112, 115, 118
Podlipentseva, Anna A. 100
Polikanov, Dmitrij V. 508, 513
Potter, Liz 250
Pötters, Wilhelm 480, 482
Prangova, Mimi 138
Priestley, Carol 362
Prokofieva, Irina A. 101
Pryor, Matthew 83
Puddu, Mario 479
Pukui, Mart K. 507, 512
Pulvermüller, Friedemann 203
Pustejovsky, James 178, 213

R

Radden, Günter 39, 40, 42, 43, 51, 228, 239, 336, 449, 450, 533–535
Radlinski, I. 318
Rainer, Franz 476, 482, 483
Rakhilina, Ekaterina V. 4, 7–9, 86, 95–97, 101–103, 114, 115, 117, 118, 120, 134, 139, 142, 262, 336
Ramirez, Henri 381
Rasulić, Katarina 250, 253, 256, 257, 281
Raven, Peter H. 494, 500, 501
Rayfield, Donald 565, 568
Rechenbach, Charles W. 508, 513
Rettig, Wolfgang 425, 451
Rey, Alain 25, 28, 32, 34, 37, 38, 41, 47, 54, 465–469, 471, 472, 482, 483
Rey-Debove, Josette 468, 469, 471, 472
Reznikova, Tatiana I. 4, 7–9, 95, 97, 114, 120
Rhodes, Richard A. 262
Richards, Meredith M. 132, 133
Ride, William D.L. 494
Riemer, Nicholas (Nick) 3, 10, 15, 21, 39, 51, 179, 180, 184, 187, 190, 194, 196, 200, 216, 227, 228, 236, 237, 239
Riessler, Michael 560
Riggs, Stephen R. 507, 512
Riley, Darcey 162
Roberts, John 404
Robertson, David 229, 235
Roberts, Richard G. 356
Roberts, Sarah 229
Robinson, Charles H. 508, 513
Robinson, Justyna A. 58
Roché, Michel 476, 479, 480, 483
Rohdenburg, Günter 473
Romaine, Suzanne 505, 508, 511
Rosch Heider, Eleanor 32, 457–462, 465, 471, 504
Rosenman, Abram I. 98
Ross, Malcolm D. 356, 377, 379, 567
Rothstein, Susan 467
Roudet, Léonce 22, 38, 48
Rube, Verena 424, 426, 431, 435, 438, 451
Rubin, Edgar 40
Rufener, John 426
Ruhl, Charles 24
Ruiz de Mendoza Ibáñez, Francisco José 42
Rule, Murray W. 361
Rumsey, Alan 364
Russo, Maxim 13, 493, 494

S

Sahlgren, Magnus 138
Sakhno, Sergey 344
Sampson, Geoffrey 570
Sánchez de Lorenzo-Cáceres, José Manuel 472, 473, 477, 482
San Roque, Lila 10, 12, 224, 355, 361, 395
Saussure, Ferdinand de 32, 426, 428, 556
Savel'eva, V. N. 511
Scalise, Sergio 539
Ščerbakov, Antti 512
Schapper, Antoinette 10, 12, 224, 355, 364, 391
Scheidegger, Jean 426
Schmid, Hans-Jörg 27, 40, 428, 429, 461, 462, 475
Schmiedel, Ute 522
Schneider, Lucien 291, 311
Schreuder, Rob 437
Schultze-Berndt, Eva Friederike 10, 180, 181
Seche, Luiza 506, 507, 508, 509
Seche, Mircea 506, 507, 508, 509
Seebold, Elmar 481
Seibert, Paul 470, 472, 483
Seiler, Hansjakob 556
Seiler, Walter 406, 409
Senft, Gunter 96
Seto, Ken-ichi 42
Sevortjan, Ervand V. 512
Sharifian, Farzad 3, 11, 257
Shaw, James H. 426
Shemanaeva, Olga Ju. 97, 119
Sherzer, Joel 564
Shindo, Mika 250, 253, 255, 257, 258, 267, 280
Shi, Yuzhi 568
Shmelev, Aleksei D. 7, 9, 67, 78, 79
Sihler, Andrew L. 31
Silverstein, Michael 229
Simpson, John J. 468–470, 473, 479, 482
Sinclair, John 504
Sinnemäki, Kaius 570
Skok, Petar 337, 349

Slaughter, Mary M. 501
Sleptsov, Petr Alekseevic 552
Smirnitskaya, Anna A. 116
Smith, M. A. 5, 356
Smith-Stark, Thomas 5
Soanes, Catherine 504
Söderwall, Knut F. 191
Sorokoletov, Fedot P. 497–499, 511, 512, 519
Speelman, Dirk 58
Spenader, Jennifer 134
Sperber, Dan 28
Spooner, Nigel A. 356
Spreyer, Kathrin 165
Staden, Miriam van 4, 8
Stebbins, Tonya 571
Steinberg, Reinhild 4, 59, 429, 430, 459, 481
Stempel, Wolf-Dieter 476, 479, 482
Stevenson, Angus 504
Storch, Anne 178
Street, Chester S. 366, 571
Stubbs, Michael 224
Suci, George J. 132
Sutton, Pete 375
Švedova, Natalija Ju. 503, 504
Sweetser, Eve 1, 59, 178
Sylestine, Cora 509

T
Täckström, Oscar 165
Tadmor, Uri 501, 508–514, 557
Tagabileva, Maria G. 97, 108
Taksami, Čuner M. 511
Talibov, Bukar V. 514
Talmy, Leonard 336, 458
Tanaka, James W. 462
Tannenbaum, Percy H. 132
Tatevosov, Sergej G. 107, 112
Taylor, John R. 8, 32, 40, 51
Taylor, Marjorie 462
Tedford, Richard H. 518
Tenishev, Edhyam R. 465, 470
Tersis, Nicole 344
Teusink, Mariel 502, 510, 513
Theopheastus 517
Thomason, Sarah G. 229, 550
Thompson, F. Christian 494
Thompson, Laurence C. 474

Thompson, Sandra A. 474
Thornburg, Linda L. 39, 40, 42, 147
Thorne, Alan 356
Tiktin, Hariton 42
Titarenko, Mihail L. 502, 517
Tolstaya, Svetlana M. 109
Tolstoj, Nikita I. 497, 513
Toporov; Vladimir N. 87
Toutanova, Kristina 165, 166
Tranel, Daniel 203
Traugott, Elizabeth Closs 1, 27, 28, 45, 46, 59, 190, 219
Traversa, Vincenzo 431
Tribushinina, Elena 142
Trubačev, Oleg N. 336, 345, 498, 499
Tupper, Ian 366
Turner, Mark 50, 120, 450
Tzoukermann, Evelyne 162

U
Umbreit, Birgit 13, 244, 423, 425, 427, 431, 435, 438, 447, 450, 451
Ungerer, Friedrich 40, 383, 462, 475
Urban, Matthias 2, 5, 14, 160, 377–379, 383, 500, 501, 505–510, 555, 556, 560, 562, 567, 568, 570, 572
Ušakov, Dmitrij N. 503, 504
Usteri, Alfred 521

V
Vahros, Igor' 512
Vanhove, Martine 2, 4, 5, 6, 59, 96, 136, 178, 429, 452, 457, 458
Varela, Soledad 483
Vasilevič, Glafira M. 502, 513
Večerka, Radoslav 506
Vejdemo, Susanne 11, 249, 261
Verner, Geinrih K. 502
Verstraete, Jean-Christophe 45
Viberg, Åke 2, 10, 11, 95, 96, 138, 177, 178, 185, 187–190, 199, 214, 217, 218, 224, 227
Victorri, Bernard 437
Villeneuve, Christophe de 473
Volker, Craig A. 505, 508, 511
Volodin, Aleksander P. 318, 319
von Witt, Caitlin 522

W

Waddy, Julie A. 510, 513
Wälchli, Bernhard 10, 138, 161, 474
Walde, Alois 46, 52, 337, 469
Walsh, Michael J. 359
Waltereit, Richard 30, 430
Walters, Joseph C. W. 509
Wanner, Leo 98
Warming, Eugen 521
Wartburg, Walther von 468, 469, 474
Waszakowa, Krystyna 336
Watkins, Laurel J. 566
Weijer, Joost van de 133, 142
Weiner, Edmund 468–470, 473, 479, 482
Weinrich, Harald 49
Werner, Heinrich 566
Werth, Paul 24
Weshki-ayaad, Charlie Lippert 261, 270
Wester, Ruth 394
Wicentowski, Richard 166
Wichmann, Søren 159, 161, 171, 230, 377–379
Wierzbicka, Anna 8, 11, 71, 80, 96, 105, 113, 121, 326, 337, 504
Wiesemann, Ursula Gojtéj 513
Wilbur, Joshua 560
Wiley, E. O. 517
Wilhelm, Raymund 28
Wilkins, David P. 1, 5, 24, 25, 96, 121, 178, 364, 369
Willems, Dominique 383
Williams, John N. 429, 568
Williamson, John P. 507, 512
Willners, Caroline 133–135, 139–144
Wilson, Darryl 409
Wilson, Deirdre 28
Wilson, Lael 409
Winter-Froemel, Esme 22, 27, 28, 42, 56, 58
Wisniewski, Edward J. 463
Witkowski, Stanley R. 364, 514
Wohlgemuth, Jan 230
Wolfart, H. Christoph 323
Wu, Dekai 144, 162
Wurm, Stephen A. 359
Wu, Shuqiong 144, 162

X

Xia, Xuanyin 162

Y

Yarapea, Apoi Mason 395
Yarowsky, David 165, 166
Yavorska, Galina 5, 12, 335, 336
Ye, Zhengdao 121, 502
Yu, Ning 3, 11, 254, 256, 257

Z

Zalizniak, Anna A. 1, 6, 13, 75, 80, 113, 118, 119, 286, 493, 494
Zaragoza Larios, Carlos 480
Zholkovsky, Alexandr K. 98
Zhong, Chen-Bo 257
Zinov'ev, Boris I. 512
Zipf, George K. 437
Zubin, David A. 480, 483
Žukova, Alevtina N. 314, 320
Zúñiga, Fernando 10
Žuravlev, Anatolij F. 498

www.ingramcontent.com/pod-product-compliance
Lightning Source LLC
Chambersburg PA
CBHW070744020526
44116CB00032B/1920